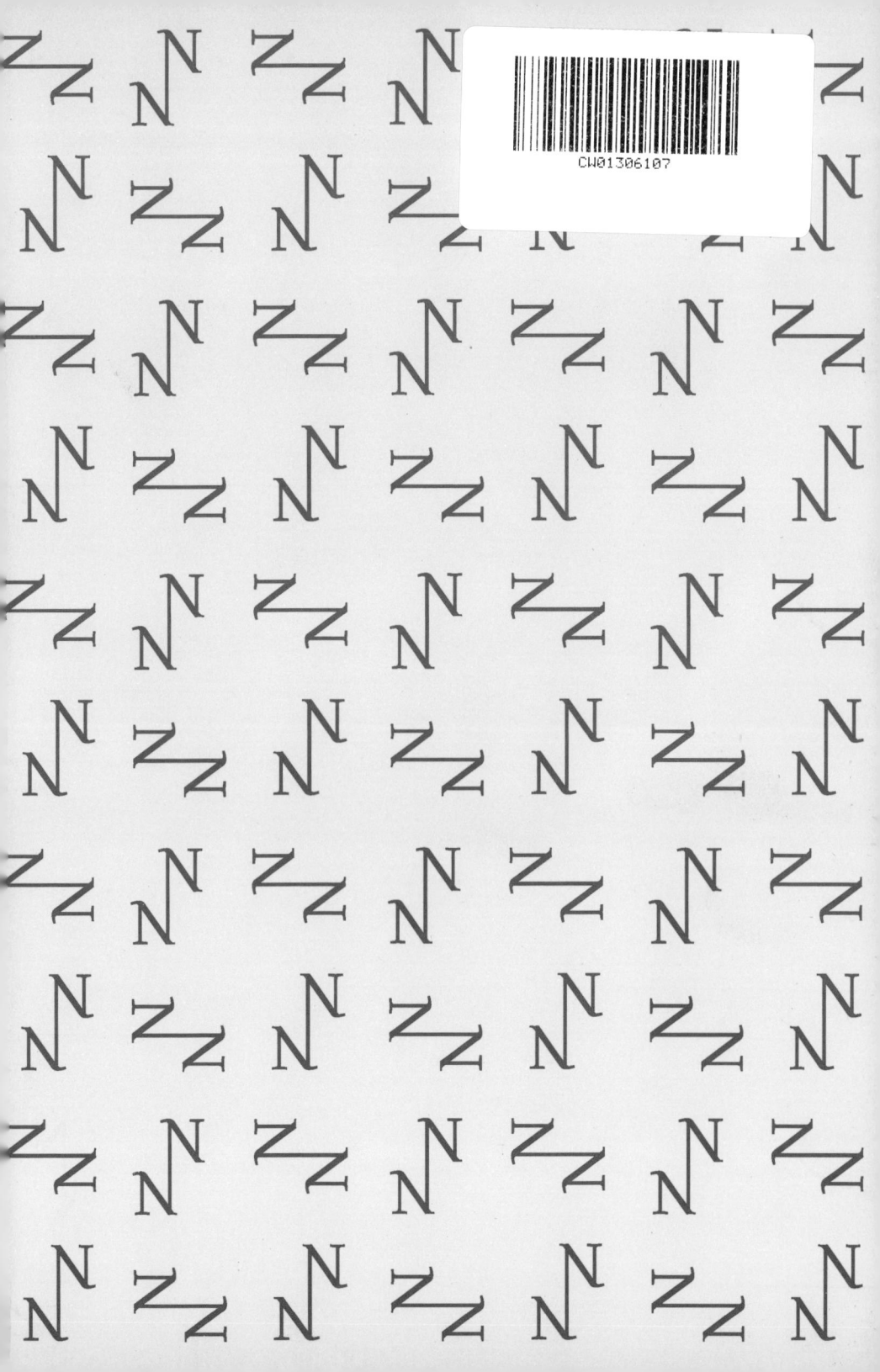

# THE NEW NATURALIST LIBRARY

A SURVEY OF BRITISH NATURAL HISTORY

## GROUSE

EDITORS
SARAH A. CORBET, ScD
Prof. RICHARD WEST, ScD, FRS, FGS
DAVID STREETER, MBE, FIBiol
JIM FLEGG, OBE, FIHort
Prof. JONATHAN SILVERTOWN

\*

The aim of this series is to interest the general reader in the wildlife of Britain by recapturing the enquiring spirit of the old naturalists. The editors believe that the natural pride of the British public in the native flora and fauna, to which must be added concern for their conservation, is best fostered by maintaining a high standard of accuracy combined with clarity of exposition in presenting the results of modern scientific research.

THE NEW NATURALIST LIBRARY

# GROUSE

The Natural History
of British and Irish Species

ADAM WATSON
AND
ROBERT MOSS

Collins

This edition published in 2008 by Collins,
an imprint of HarperCollins Publishers

HarperCollins Publishers
77–85 Fulham Palace Road
London W6 8JB
www.collins.co.uk

First published 2008

© Adam Watson and Robert Moss, 2008

All rights reserved.
No part of this publication may be
reproduced, stored in a retrieval system or
transmitted in any form or by any means,
electronic, mechanical, photocopying,
recording or otherwise, without the
prior written permission of
the copyright owner.

A CIP catalogue record for this book is
available from the British Library.

Set in FF Nexus
Edited and designed
by D & N Publishing
Lambourn Woodlands,
Hungerford, Berkshire

Printed in Hong Kong by Printing Express

Hardback
ISBN 978-0-00-715097-7

Paperback
ISBN 978-0-00-715098-4

# Contents

Editors' Preface  vi
Authors' Foreword  viii
Acknowledgements  ix
Introduction  x

1  Grouse Worldwide  1
2  Grouse Names  13
3  Red Grouse and Willow Ptarmigan  21
4  Ptarmigan  67
5  Black Grouse  101
6  Capercaillie  133
7  Behaviour  173
8  Snow-roosts  197
9  Territory in *Lagopus lagopus* and Ptarmigan  211
10  Plumage  235
11  Habitat  259
12  Nutrition  289
13  Enemies  317
14  Population Fluctuations  347
15  Management and Conservation  380

Endnotes  415
Bibliography  472
Index  517

# Editors' Preface

SURPRISINGLY THIS is the first New Naturalist volume to focus on a family or group of related families of birds since Eric Simms' *Larks, Pipits and Wagtails* published back in 1992 as No. 78. That 16-year, 28-volume drought is broken by this fascinating volume, *Grouse* by Adam Watson and Robert Moss.

World-wide, there are fewer than 20 grouse species, of which four occur in Britain and Ireland. Considering their relatively remote and certainly diverse habitats ranging from deep forests, through open moorland, to Scotland's highest peaks, the family is comparatively well known to all who enjoy wild places. In addition, in plumage all save the cocks of capercaille and black grouse are supremely well camouflaged, as befits relatively large, generally terrestrial and ground-nesting birds. For much of the year they are also secretive birds, the exceptions once again being the displaying cock capercaille and lekking cock black grouse.

Perhaps this combination of remote habitats, secretive habits and camouflage gives a special cachet to any sightings of the grouse family. There is no forgetting the first encounters – be it of a strutting cock capercaille deep in a pine forest, of experiencing the sight (and sounds) of a black grouse lek on a frosty dawn, of a ptarmigan in mountain-top snow, or the heart-stopping moment when a red grouse explodes from the moorland heather beneath the walker's feet. Beyond that, in *Grouse* the authors unveil a wealth of information on the day-to-day biology and ecology of all four species, set against a global background.

Two of the four British species, black grouse and capercaille, are in worrying decline and are the subject of intensive conservation research. Another, the ptarmigan, may be an early casualty of global climatic change as the weather changes in its extreme mountain-top habitat. The last, the red grouse, as a game bird is subject in varying degrees to commercial management by man. Problems including predators, pests, disease and starvation often accompany managed animal populations and the red grouse is no exception. As valued (and valuable) quarry species for shooters, occasional controversy is only to be expected because of their commercial worth.

So despite the handful of species within the group, the variety of life styles is such that there is much to discuss for the authors, who are both international authorities on the grouse family. Their friendly familiarity with and respect for their birds shine through the text, together with their obviously deeply consuming interest and encyclopaedic knowledge, and delight in their topic. Their serendipitous meeting so early in their careers and the subsequent long-lasting collaboration have produced for New Naturalist readers a volume of exceptional scholarship and quality.

# Authors' Foreword

How we two combined to study grouse was a matter of chance. When aged 13, AW saw his first ptarmigan on a lone climb to Derry Cairngorm in 1943 and began to record numbers, and in the winter of 1951/2 studied them there for an honours degree at Aberdeen University. With a Carnegie Arctic Scholarship at McGill University he studied museum specimens, willow ptarmigan in Newfoundland and rock ptarmigan in Baffin Island. Returning to Aberdeen, he renewed work on Derry Cairngorm for a PhD. In 1957 he moved to Glen Esk and in 1961 to Banchory for research on red grouse, and he continued work on ptarmigan. He has studied black grouse, capercaillie and Irish red grouse, and accompanied ecologists on their fieldwork in Iceland, Norway and Alaska.

At New Year 1963, we each attended a conference in the Edward Grey Institute of Field Ornithology at Oxford. RM, who had graduated in honours biochemistry at University College London, gave a talk on fulmars of the Norwegian island of Jan Mayen, which he had visited on a student expedition. He showed keen interest in chemical aspects of the work on red grouse, and in spring 1963 came north for a study of the nutrition of red grouse for a PhD. In Scotland he has continued work on red grouse, and also on ptarmigan, black grouse and capercaillie. Abroad, he studied Icelandic ptarmigan, and rock, willow and white-tailed ptarmigan during a year based at the University of Alaska in Fairbanks. More recently, he has accompanied Russian biologists in their fieldwork on capercaillie.

While writing this book, we shared a room as Emeritus Fellows of the Centre for Ecology and Hydrology at Banchory. As ever, we like arguing about grouse and studying them.

Adam Watson, Clachnaben, Crathes, and
Robert Moss, Station House, Crathes, December 2006

# Acknowledgements

PAST TEAM MEMBERS and students deserve our deep gratitude, as do colleagues who taught and stimulated us through discussions and publications. We thank many deerstalkers, farmers, foresters, gamekeepers, landowners and ski-staff for their cooperation and hospitality. Kjetil Bevanger, Alexei Blagovidov, Vladimir Borchtchevski, Larry Ellison, Susan Hannon, Leif Kastdalen, John Lee, Michèle Loneux, Doug Macmillan, Yann Magnani, Christian Marti, Kathy Martin, Chris Mellenchip, Emmanuel Ménoni, Bob Montgomerie, François Mougeot, Ólafur Nielsen, Claude Novoa, Hans Pedersen, Stuart Piertney, Roald Potapov, Bob Robel, Luca Rotelli, Colin Shedden, Andrei Sivkov, Adam Smith, Christopher Smout, Anneke Stolte, Ilse Storch, David Strang Steel, Des Thompson, Richard Tipping, Luc Wauters and Sarah Woodin helped with publications or unpublished data during the writing of the book. Specialist advice was given on base richness of bedrock by Doug Fettes, soils by Rodney Heslop, Gaelic grouse names by James Grant, and Welsh names by Elwyn Hughes and Annis and Cedric Milner. Dave Pullan created the line-drawings and Keith Morton produced a map. We are also grateful to the many colleagues who provided photographs.

# Introduction

A BOOK ON BRITISH GROUSE is timely, because recent research has clarified old problems and controversies.[1] We offer some insights developed over two working lifetimes.

The four British grouse species occupy huge world ranges and have been studied in many countries, with millions of words written about them. We do not attempt to review this vast literature, but quote from it to give a worldwide perspective on the grouse of a small though varied corner of the globe.

Government policies can affect grouse, so politicians and others should have factual information. Grouse and their habitats are of much interest to hunters and game-dog enthusiasts, and to the many others involved in outdoor recreation. Grouse are also of great value in their own right as a beautiful part of nature. Let us care for them.

## NAMES

Most authors writing in English now use the name willow ptarmigan for what was often willow grouse, and rock ptarmigan for ptarmigan. The name red grouse is so well known that it would be confusing to call it willow ptarmigan.[2] We use willow ptarmigan for races other than red grouse, and *Lagopus lagopus* for red grouse and willow ptarmigan together. For brevity we write ptarmigan when a section is clearly on rock ptarmigan. We use the old names blackcock and greyhen, and blackgame for both sexes of black grouse.

Distribution maps are readily available elsewhere (*see* Bibliography), and so we do not give them. Table 1 lists the main study areas mentioned in the text.

**TABLE 1.** The main study areas mentioned in the text.

|  | PLACE | LATITUDE, LONGITUDE | REGION |
|---|---|---|---|
| Red grouse | The Cairnwell | 56°53'N, 3°25'W | Upper Deeside, Scotland |
|  | Corndavon | 57°04'N, 3°16'W | Upper Deeside, Scotland |
|  | Forvie | 57°20'N, 1°58'W | Coast north of Aberdeen, Scotland |
|  | Glas-choille | 57°12'N, 3°10'W | Upper Deeside, Scotland |
|  | Glen Esk | 56°56'N, 2°50'W | Invermark, Angus, Scotland |
|  | Glen Tanar | 57°02'N, 3°00'W | Mid Deeside, Scotland |
|  | Glenamoy | 54°12'N, 9°45'W | County Mayo, Ireland |
|  | Kerloch moor | 57°00'N, 2°30'W | Lower Deeside, Scotland |
|  | Misty Law Muir | 55°49'N, 4°42'W | Renfrewshire, Scotland |
|  | Priestlaw Muir | 55°51'N, 2°35'W | Lammermuirs, Scotland |
|  | Rickarton moor | 57°01'N, 2°16'W | Southwest of Aberdeen, Scotland |
|  | Spyhill moor | 57°00'N, 2°28'W | Lower Deeside, Scotland |
| Willow ptarmigan | Anderson River | 70°N, 129°W | Northwest Territories, Canada |
|  | Avalon Peninsula | 47°20'N, 53°25'W | East Newfoundland, Canada |
|  | Bolshezemelskaia | 68°N, 55°E | East of Pechora, Russia |
|  | Brunette Island | 47°N, 56°W | Off south Newfoundland, Canada |
|  | Chilkat Pass | 59°50'N, 136°20'W | British Columbia, Canada |
|  | Churchill | 58°24'N, 94°24'W | La Pérouse Bay, Manitoba, Canada |
|  | Dovrefjell | 62°17'N, 9°39'E | Central Norway |
|  | Karlsøy | 70°00'N, 19°55'E | Near Tromsø, Norway |
|  | Kolyma | 69°N, 160°E | Northeast Siberia, Russia |
|  | Lövhögen | 62°N, 13°E | West of Sundsvall, Sweden |
|  | Naurzumskiy Zapovednik | 52°N, 64°E | North Kazakhstan |
|  | Timansk | 68°N, 50°E | West of Pechora, Russia |
|  | Tranøy | 69°09'N, 17°25'E | Island off Senja, Norway |
|  | Yamal | 70°N, 70°E | Northwest Siberia, Russia |
| Rock ptarmigan | Aletschgebiet | 46°N, 08°E | Swiss Alps, Switzerland |
|  | Amchitka | 52°N, 179°E | Aleutian Islands, Alaska, USA |
|  | Bathurst Island | 76°N, 99°W | Nunavut, Canada |

*(continued overleaf)*

TABLE 1. *(continued)*

|  | PLACE | LATITUDE, LONGITUDE | REGION |
|---|---|---|---|
| Rock ptarmigan | Cairn Gorm | 57°08'N, 3°40'W | North Cairngorms, Scotland |
|  | The Cairnwell and Meall Odhar | 56°53'N, 3°24'W | Upper Deeside, Scotland |
|  | Derry Cairngorm | 57°04'N, 3°40'W | South Cairngorms, Scotland |
|  | Colville River | 70°26'N, 150°40'W | Arctic Alaska, USA |
|  | Eagle Creek | 65°N, 145°W | Steese Highway, Alaska, USA |
|  | Hrisey | 66°00'N, 18°24'W | Island in north Iceland |
|  | Húsavík | 66°10'N, 17°45'W | Northeast Iceland |
|  | Lochnagar | 56°58'N, 3°13'W | Upper Deeside, Scotland |
|  | Monte Sobretta | 46°24'N, 10°26'E | Lombardy Alps, Italy |
|  | Ny-Ålesund | 79°N, 12°E | Spitsbergen, Svalbard, Norway |
|  | Sarcpa Lake | 69°33'N, 83°19'W | Northwest Territories, Canada |
|  | Ungava | 62°N, 74°W | Deception Bay, Quebec, Canada |
|  | Windy Lake | 68°05'N, 106°40'W | Northwest Territories, Canada |
| Black grouse | Forest of Birse | 57°00'N, 2°44'W | Lower Deeside, Scotland |
|  | Glen Dye | 56°58'N, 2°36'W | Upper Deeside, Scotland |
| Capercaillie | Abernethy | 57°14'N, 3°40'W | Speyside, Scotland |
|  | Glen Tanar | 57°02'N, 2°54'W | Mid Deeside, Scotland |
|  | Kinveachy | 57°16'N, 3°52'W | Speyside, Scotland |
|  | Lake Ilmen | 58°N, 32°E | Near Novgorod, Russia |
|  | Pechora-Ilich | 62°N, 57°E | Komi, Russia |
|  | Pinega | 64°N, 44°E | East of Archangel, Russia |
|  | Varaldskogen | 60°10'N, 12°30'E | East of Oslo, Norway |
| Red and black grouse | Strathmore | 55°N, 2°W | Upper Teesdale, County Durham, England |
| Willow and rock ptarmigan | Porcupine Creek | 65°N, 145°W | Steese Highway, Alaska, USA |
| All four species | Laplandskiy Zapovednik | 68°N, 32°E | Southwest of Murmansk, Russia |

CHAPTER 1

# Grouse Worldwide

## ORIGIN OF SPECIES

GROUSE ARE LARGE BIRDS adapted to cold. Creatures of the northern hemisphere, they live in Arctic, boreal and temperate regions, and spend the winter in northern or mountainous habitats without migrating south as many other birds do.[1] Their toes are bordered by small scales or feathers, which, like snowshoes, allow them to walk on snow.[2] A high metabolic rate and the habit of roosting in snow-holes help them to keep warm.[3] They subsist on low-quality but abundant foods such as woody shoots, catkins, buds, twigs, bark and conifer needles.

Molecular evidence shows that the ancestor of all grouse diverged from turkeys[4] in the Miocene (Table 2) and had given rise to all modern genera (Table 3) by about a million years ago.[6] In biogeographical terms, this is a recent and rapid response to climate change. Grouse evolved and diversified during a period[7] of global cooling, when new habitats such as boreal forest and tundra replaced more tropical vegetation in northern regions. This opened a new niche for large birds that could survive on coarse foods through long, cold winters.

The circumpolar distribution of grouse raises the intriguing question of whether the first grouse evolved in the Old World (Palaearctic) or the New World (Nearctic).[8] The continents of Eurasia and North America are geographically close, separated today by just 80km of shallow sea. Periodically, as the earth's orbit takes it further from the sun and an ice age begins, water freezes into continent-sized glaciers, sea levels drop, the lost land of Beringia emerges from the waves, and Alaska and Siberia merge into one (*see* Fig. 1). This facilitates movement of species between the northwestern Nearctic and the northeastern Palaearctic.

TABLE 2. A brief history of grouse.[5]

| 6 MILLION YEARS AGO | 3 MILLION YEARS AGO | ABOUT 3–2 MILLION YEARS AGO | 2–1 MILLION YEARS AGO | TODAY |
|---|---|---|---|---|
| Ancestor of all grouse diverges from turkeys in Nearctic | Ancestral *Bonasa* and ancestor of all other grouse diverge in Nearctic | Ancestral *Bonasa* spreads into Palaearctic and diverges into Nearctic and Palaearctic lineages | *Bonasa* species evolve separately in Nearctic and Palaearctic | *Bonasa umbellus*[N] *Bonasa bonasia*[P] *Bonasa sewerzowi*[P] |
|  |  | Ancestral ptarmigan (*Lagopus*) spreads north and into Palaearctic | The three ptarmigan (*Lagopus*) species diverge | *Lagopus leucurus*[N] *Lagopus lagopus*[NP] *Lagopus mutus*[NP] |
|  |  | Ancestor of forest and prairie grouse spreads to Palaearctic, where forest grouse evolve and diverge into ancestral *Tetrao/Lyrurus*, which spreads west, and ancestral *Falcipennis*, which spreads east and diverges into Nearctic and Palaearctic lineages | Palaearctic forest grouse diverges into *Tetrao* and *Lyrurus* | *Falcipennis canadensis*[N] *Falcipennis falcipennis*[P] *Tetrao urogallus*[P] *Tetrao parvirostris*[P] *Lyrurus tetrix*[P] *Lyrurus mlokosiewiczi*[P] |

TABLE 2. A brief history of grouse.[5] (continued)

| 6 MILLION YEARS AGO | 3 MILLION YEARS AGO | ABOUT 3–2 MILLION YEARS AGO | 2–1 MILLION YEARS AGO | TODAY |
|---|---|---|---|---|
| | | Ancestor of forest and prairie grouse spreads south in Nearctic, where prairie grouse evolve | Prairie grouse (*Centrocercus*, *Dendragapus*, *Tympanuchus*) diversify in Nearctic | *Centrocercus urophasianus*[N] *Centrocercus minimus*[N] *Dendragapus obscurus*[N] *Dendragapus fuliginosus*[N] *Tympanuchus cupido*[N] *Tympanuchus pallidicinctus*[N] *Tympanuchus phasianellus*[N] |

[N] Nearctic distribution.
[P] Palaearctic distribution.

4 · GROUSE

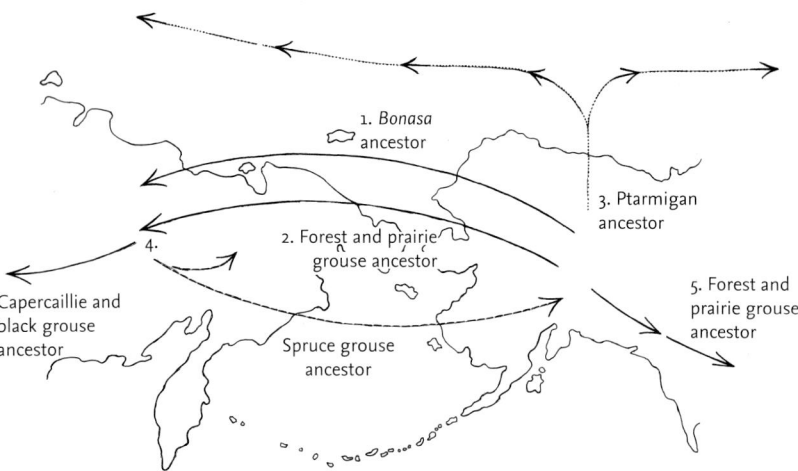

FIG 1. Map of Beringia, indicating today's sea-levels and showing the putative dispersal of ancestral grouse lineages. Arrows show how grouse, having evolved from turkeys in the northwest Nearctic (east), might have colonised the Palaearctic (west): (1) ancestor of all grouse spreads to Palaearctic, giving rise to today's woodland grouse (*Bonasa*); (2) ancestor of forest (*Falcipennis*, *Tetrao* and *Lyrurus*) and prairie (*Tympanuchus*, *Centrocercus* and *Dendragapus*) grouse evolves in Nearctic and colonises Palaearctic; (3) meanwhile, ancestral ptarmigan evolves in Nearctic, heads north and moves around the pole; (4) in the Palaearctic, ancestor of forest grouse begets two lineages – one stays in the Palaearctic, becoming capercaillie (*Tetrao*) and black grouse (*Lyrurus*), the other spreads across Beringia and gives rise to spruce grouse (*Falcipennis*); (5) ancestor of forest and prairie grouse begets prairie grouse. (Drawn by Dave Pullan)

Current opinion favours a northwestern Nearctic origin for grouse, which today are represented by 18–21 species, the number depending upon the authority.[9] In Britain we have four: red grouse (*Lagopus lagopus scoticus*), rock ptarmigan (*Lagopus mutus*), black grouse (*Lyrurus tetrix*) and capercaillie (*Tetrao urogallus*). A likely picture is that the ancestor of all grouse colonised the Palaearctic from the Nearctic via Beringia, giving rise to 'woodland' grouse of the genus *Bonasa*, today represented by ruffed grouse in North America, hazel grouse across Eurasia, and Chinese grouse isolated in the mountains of central China. Other modern grouse fall into three groups of related species: the 'ptarmigan' (*Lagopus*), the 'forest grouse' (*Falcipennis*, *Tetrao* and *Lyrurus*) and the 'prairie grouse' (*Tympanuchus*, *Centrocercus* and *Dendragapus*), the latter represented only in the Nearctic (Table 2).[10]

GROUSE WORLDWIDE · 5

**FIG 2.** Cock red grouse in spring, standing alert with combs erect among dead grey sticks of burnt heather. (Chris Knights)

**FIG 3.** Hen red grouse in late summer. She has paler, more barred plumage and smaller, pinker combs than the cock. (David A. Gowans)

**FIG 4.** Pair of red grouse, with the cock on the left showing bigger combs and darker plumage than the slightly smaller hen on the right. (Desmond Dugan)

**FIG 5.** Pair of ptarmigan in the Cairngorms during spring, part way between winter and summer plumage. The strutting cock displays his red comb and black feather necklace to the crouching hen, who retains more winter plumage than the cock. They are near the edge of small snow patches, which provide camouflage for the part-white birds. (Derek McGinn)

**FIG 6.** Capercaillie displaying to his retinue of hens. The orange breast distinguishes hen capercaillie from greyhens. Cock and hens both display white shoulder spots; these are shown by all four species of British grouse during courtship and aggressive display, but their precise function remains unclear. (Desmond Dugan)

GROUSE WORLDWIDE · 7

FIG 7. Blackcock displaying to greyhen at a lek. (Chris Knights)

**TABLE 3.** Grouse species today.

| RELATED GROUP | SCIENTIFIC NAME | COMMON NAME |
| --- | --- | --- |
| Woodland grouse | *Bonasa umbellus* [N] | Ruffed grouse |
|  | *Bonasa bonasia* [P] | Hazel grouse |
|  | *Bonasa sewerzowi* [P] | Chinese grouse |
| Ptarmigan | *Lagopus leucurus* [N] | White-tailed ptarmigan |
|  | *Lagopus lagopus* [NP] | Willow ptarmigan or red grouse |
|  | *Lagopus mutus* [NP] | Rock ptarmigan or ptarmigan |
| Forest grouse | *Falcipennis canadensis* [N] | Spruce grouse |
|  | *Falcipennis falcipennis* [P] | Siberian grouse |
|  | *Tetrao urogallus* [P] | Capercaillie |
|  | *Tetrao parvirostris* [P] | Black-billed capercaillie |
|  | *Lyrurus tetrix* [P] | Black grouse |
|  | *Lyrurus mlokosiewiczi* [P] | Caucasian black grouse |
| Prairie grouse | *Centrocercus urophasianus* [N] | Sage grouse |
|  | *Centrocercus minimus* [N] | Gunnison sage grouse |
|  | *Dendragapus obscurus* [N] | Dusky grouse (blue grouse) |
|  | *Dendragapus fuliginosus* [N] | Sooty grouse (blue grouse) |
|  | *Tympanuchus cupido* [N] | Greater prairie-chicken |
|  | *Tympanuchus pallidicinctus* [N] | Lesser prairie-chicken |
|  | *Tympanuchus phasianellus* [N] | Sharp-tailed grouse |

[N] Nearctic distribution.
[P] Palaearctic distribution.

The current distribution of species has been explained by suggesting that the Palaearctic was colonised from the Nearctic on at least three occasions, initially by the ancestor of all grouse, and then separately by two of its Nearctic descendants, first the ancestral species that gave rise to ancestral forest and prairie grouse, and second the ancestral ptarmigan.[11] The ancestral forest grouse evolved further in the Palaearctic and begat ancestral *Falcipennis* and ancestral *Tetrao/Lyrurus*. Ancestral *Falcipennis* spread eastwards through Beringia, and then diverged into the Siberian grouse and the North American spruce grouse, a process possibly initiated when central Beringia was submerged between ice ages and sea separated Siberia from North America. Ancestral *Tetrao/Lyrurus* spread westwards, evolving into two species of capercaillie and two of black grouse. Meanwhile, the prairie grouse developed separately in North America, occupying habitats similar to those used by pheasants and partridges in the Old World.

Although grouse evolved during a period of overall global cooling, the climate oscillated between warmer and colder periods. As habitats became more widespread, species presumably expanded their ranges. When habitats contracted, small populations became isolated. Hence species probably evolved in two main ways. First, during colder periods, glaciers would have separated a widespread ancestral species into eastern and western populations. These would then have evolved into sister species that subsequently expanded their ranges during warmer periods and began to compete with each other. Capercaillie and black grouse are a likely example.

Second, during warmer periods, small populations of an ancestral species would have become isolated in the south as the species' range shifted northwards. The white-tailed ptarmigan in North America, the Caucasian black grouse and the Chinese grouse are obvious examples of new species that evolved after populations became isolated in mountain fastnesses. The white-tailed ptarmigan subsequently expanded its range in North America and now competes with rock ptarmigan and willow ptarmigan. By contrast, the Caucasian black grouse and the Chinese grouse remain isolated.

Today, isolated southern populations have similar potential for evolving into separate species through geographical isolation. Thus the red grouse is evidently diverging from its ancestor, the willow ptarmigan. The main ice-sheet of the last glaciation, when Britain was still connected to the rest of Europe, melted about 11,500 years ago and the North Sea then came into existence. It is presumably since then that the red grouse developed its distinct characteristics, adapting to heather moorland and losing the ptarmigan habit of turning white in winter. British rock ptarmigan and black grouse have presumably been separated from their parent stocks for just as long, but their habitats have not put such selective pressures upon them. British capercaillie, however, probably became extinct in the 18th century and we owe our present stock to reintroductions.[12] Fossil remains show that hazel grouse occurred in Britain at the end of the last glaciation.[13] We know of no evidence of hazel grouse in Britain after the North Sea arose, but it seems likely that they were here.

## HABITAT

Many species of grouse are widely distributed, different populations often depending on different plant species. Such apparent complexity is much simplified when we classify habitats in terms of their structure and broad plant classes, rather than individual plant species. For example, capercaillie winter in evergreen forests, which can comprise species of pine, spruce, fir or even holly.[14] In such terms, each grouse species has quite narrow requirements for particular habitats.

As a group, grouse use many habitats. The three *Bonasa* are birds of mixed deciduous-coniferous forests, using mainly deciduous trees for food and conifers for cover.[15] The hazel grouse inhabits regenerating forest and has quite specific requirements for forest structure, but this can be fulfilled by different tree species and management regimes.[16] The birds need dense deciduous or coniferous cover from ground level up to about 2m in height, closely interspersed with their deciduous food trees.[17] In addition, they seem particularly vulnerable to habitat fragmentation. Silvicultural practices have made potential hazel grouse habitat rare in Britain, but it might be possible to accommodate reintroduced birds in our extensive conifer plantations by providing, for example, pollarded deciduous copses along stream banks.

After the *Bonasa* bloodline had separated from the common ancestor of all other grouse (Table 2), the three other main groups of grouse – ptarmigan, forest grouse and prairie grouse – diverged from one another. In the north, the ancestral ptarmigan gave rise to the three modern ptarmigan species, birds of tundra and Arctic-Alpine habitats, including subalpine scrub. The willow ptarmigan also occupies the edges of bogs and clearings in boreal forest, and the use of heather moorland by red grouse can be seen as an extension of this habit. Where willow and rock ptarmigan occur together, the rock ptarmigan uses drier and more open habitats, often higher up, as in Scotland. Rock ptarmigan are so called because they use rocks or boulders for cover, sidling up to them at the approach of a bird of prey, and hence are usually found on rocky ground. Where all three ptarmigan species occur together, the white-tailed ptarmigan breeds at the highest elevations.

The forest grouse make more use of coniferous trees than *Bonasa*, for food as well as for cover. Spruce grouse and capercaillie feed on pine or spruce needles for much of the year, taking ground vegetation such as blaeberry (synonym bilberry) or other *Vaccinium* species in spring and summer. Both species usually prefer pine as winter food but also eat spruce or other conifers. The Siberian grouse, however, seems to prefer spruce as its winter diet. The range of the capercaillie corresponds largely to that of its main winter food, Scots pine. Similarly, the range of the black-billed capercaillie corresponds largely to that of its different winter staple, Dahurian larch. Black grouse are primarily birds of forest edges and early stages of forest succession, usually avoiding dense forest. They also occur in a wide range of structurally similar habitats such as moors, heaths and rough agricultural fields. Their main winter foods are dwarf shrubs such as heather and blaeberry, but when these are covered in snow they take to trees such as birch and pine. Caucasian black grouse are birds of the tree-line, where montane forests merge into subalpine meadows.

The prairie grouse apparently diversified in the southern Nearctic. Four species (*Tympanuchus* and *Centrocercus*) live year-round in open habitats that are dominated by grasses and shrubs. The blue grouse *Dendragapus obscurus* occupies a wide range of breeding habitats, from sea-level to above 3,000m in altitude, and from open old-growth forest to shrubby grasslands. Even so, the key component seems to be a mixture of herbs, grasses and shrubs.[18] Although the blue grouse's breeding habitat is relatively open, most populations winter in denser coniferous forest.

## STATUS

In Britain, capercaillie are on the verge of a second extinction and black grouse are in steep decline. In both cases this is thought to be due to habitat degradation compounded by climate change.[19] The range of ptarmigan has been much reduced by browsing domestic stock animals, which have degraded to inhospitable grassland many hills that were once clothed in the dwarf shrubs upon which birds of the grouse family rely. Red grouse depend largely upon heather moorland, which in Scotland declined in extent by almost a quarter between the 1940s and 1980s.

Fortunately, the plight of capercaillie and black grouse has been recognised and steps are being taken to improve their habitat. Within its present range, the ptarmigan population seems to be sustaining itself with no further decline. And, though diminished, heather moors and stocks of red grouse, maintained for sport shooting, are probably greater than they would be without management.

Worldwide, the 18 recognised species of grouse are represented by about 130 subspecies. The conversion of natural habitats to agricultural land has led to big contractions in their ranges, especially in temperate lands such as Britain. Species that have large ranges, including remote boreal or Arctic habitats, are under no immediate threat of extinction. Those in most danger depend largely upon habitats threatened by agriculture or have distributions that are restricted for biogeographical reasons. Thus, grouse of North American prairie (*Tympanuchus* spp.) and sagebrush country (*Centrocercus* spp.), having lost much ground to cropland and rangeland, probably depend upon management of the remnant habitat for their survival. Warnings include the fate of the heath hen *Tympanuchus cupido cupido*, a distinctive subspecies of the greater prairie-chicken that became extinct in 1932, and the current plight of Attwater's prairie-chicken *Tympanuchus cupido attwateri*, which may soon be gone. Three species with small distributions – the

Caucasian black grouse, the Chinese grouse and the Siberian grouse – are considered vulnerable. Perhaps the newly recognised Gunnison sage grouse is in most danger, for it has a restricted distribution on degraded rangeland.[20]

## WORLDWIDE AND LOCAL PERSPECTIVES

The view that all life on earth is interconnected is becoming more concrete as scientists unravel the complex interplay between the physical and living processes that mould the biosphere. Like a page from prehistory, the biogeography of grouse continues to reflect the evolution of the planet. In subsequent chapters, we shall see how trends and fluctuations in grouse numbers throughout the twentieth century reflected climatic fluctuations and human activities. Climate and mankind are, of course, interrelated. The present plight of capercaillie and black grouse in Britain, for example, is attributable partly to changes in climate, which in turn is influenced by agriculture, deforestation and industry.

Fluctuations in grouse numbers, however, are not mere passive reflections of external forces. Healthy grouse populations rear more than enough young to sustain their numbers. This generates competition for living space between extended families, and that conflict generates unstable fluctuations in numbers, reminiscent of tribal struggles in humans.[21] Less fancifully, it explains the long mystery of population cycles that has fascinated ecologists since their science began.

Apologists for development often argue that the loss of endangered populations is just part of evolution, and that we should accept the inevitable with good grace. Our growing concern for other species, however, is also part of evolution. The gifts that they give us, including a rich enjoyment of natural diversity and insights into our own nature, should be there for our children too.

## SUMMARY

Grouse diverged from turkeys in the New World during the Miocene. They occupied boreal forest and tundra, habitats created by global cooling. Modern genera and species evolved from populations that became geographically isolated as their habitats contracted during subsequent climatic oscillations. As habitats expanded again, some species came to overlap, while others remain isolated in restricted ranges. Isolated species, and those that depend largely upon habitats threatened by agriculture, are the most endangered.

CHAPTER 2

# Grouse Names

GROUSE NAMES ARE NUMEROUS, reflecting the birds' historical importance as game, but the variety of names has lessened with the decline of languages and dialects. Below, we sample something of this richness in English, Scots, Gaelic, Irish and Welsh.

## GROUSE

The English word *grouse* is both singular and plural. Of uncertain origin, it has been known since the early 1500s, when it was spelled *grows*. The Latin *grus*, leading to the Old French *grue* and meaning 'crane' has been suggested as its source,[1] as has the French *greoche, greiche, griais*, meaning 'spotted bird'. The colloquial *grouse*, meaning 'to complain', probably comes from the Old French *groucier*, 'to grumble'. The verb *grucer* was in frequent use in Anglo-French from the second half of the twelfth century onwards, and from it developed the noun *gruz*, meaning 'grumbling'.[2] Hence *grouse* might mean 'grumbler', which is an apt description of the red grouse's guttural tones.

Most species have the word *grouse* as part of their English name. Ptarmigan and capercaillie do not, but other names for them do, as in white grouse and wood grouse. Where English names are used in America and, increasingly, in Continental Europe where English names are used, *ptarmigan* covers all *Lagopus* species, including willow ptarmigan (often willow grouse in Europe) and rock ptarmigan (ptarmigan in Britain). This is probably because English-speaking colonists in America called any bird that turned white in winter a ptarmigan – as did Scottish zoologist MacGillivray in 1837.[3]

Several authors list grouse names in many languages, and note that some are onomatopoeic, resembling the birds' calls.[4] This does not seem to apply to the derivation of British or Irish names, except for ptarmigan, although we fancy that the word *grouse*, uttered gutturally, resembles the growling threat call of a cock red grouse (krau, krau, krau).

RED GROUSE

Most people in Britain and Ireland call this species simply *grouse*. Grouse-moor, grouse-butt and other terms are indicative of this usage. Table 4 gives names for red grouse in the languages of Britain and Ireland. In the *Scottish National Dictionary* (SND),[6] *muirhen* is also used figuratively to mean 'girl', and *muir-pout* or *grouse-pout* (pronounced 'poot') are defined as 'poult red grouse' or, figuratively, 'girl'.[7] Old names for red grouse in Scots were *reid foul* (pronounced 'reed fool', and meaning 'red fowl'), *red game*, and *heather-cock* or *heather-hen*.[8] Another pair of names for red grouse in Scots and in the dialect of north England was *gorcock* and *gorhen*, now obsolescent though still appearing in Scots poetry. The meaning is uncertain, but *gor* might mean 'gore', depicting the bird's reddish plumage.

PTARMIGAN

The English word *ptarmigan* came from the Scots *tarmagan*. Other English names for the species are white grouse,[9] rock grouse, snow grouse, arctic grouse, barren-ground bird and, in Newfoundland, *rocker*. The name *rock ptarmigan*, which originated in North America and is now widely used, makes good sense because the bird is usually found amongst rocks, where it is suitably camouflaged. To French Canadians, it is *lagopède des rochers*, meaning 'ptarmigan of the rocks'.

The Scots form, *tarmagan*, came from the Gaelic masculine noun *tàrmachan*, with stress on tar.[10] The evidence indicates that both this word and its Irish equivalent came from an Irish and, later, Gaelic word, meaning 'noisy one' or 'rumbling one', doubtless referring to the bird's calls. The spelling *ptarmigan* was established in English when Thomas Pennant borrowed it from a Scottish book published in 1684, where *ptarmigan* was written inaptly as if from the Greek *pteron*, as in *pterodactyl*, meaning 'wing' or 'feather' (SND). The inappropriate 'p' became universal from the early 1800s.

FIG 8. Rock ptarmigan, cock and rock together. (Derek McGinn)

## BLACK GROUSE

If the word *grouse* means 'grumbler', as suggested above, it seems appropriate for the red grouse, with its guttural calls, but not for the black grouse. Presumably this original meaning for grouse was lost before the modern usage of the name black grouse was established. Since red grouse were, and are, commoner and more widespread than black grouse, people would have used the general name *grouse* for red grouse, as they still do today (*see* above). An old name for the black grouse in English, as given in the 1971 *Oxford English Dictionary* (OED), was *heath-bird*, with *heath-cock* and *heath-hen* used for the sexes. These terms were used in Scotland, too, along with the collective *heathfowl*.[11] Today, we also have names that describe the plumage – *blackcock* and *greyhen* – as well as the collective term *blackgame*.

FIG 9. The 'great cock of the wood'. (Chris Knights)

## CAPERCAILLIE

This name is from the Scots *capercailzie*. It came from the Gaelic *capall* (often *capull* in older dictionaries), literally 'mare' or, in some parts of the Highlands, 'horse' or 'colt', and *coille*, meaning 'wood' – making *capall-coille*, or 'horse of (the) wood'. 'Horse' is often used as a prefix to indicate 'large' or 'coarse', as in horse-chestnut, horse mushroom and horseradish. Thus, Dwelly (1971) in Gaelic lists *capull-coille*, or 'great cock of the wood', with *capar-coille* as a variant. Another Gaelic dictionary has *capall-coille*, meaning 'capercailzie' or 'wood grouse',[12] and an Irish one cites *capall coille*.[13] A similar noun is *capull-abhainn*, meaning 'river-horse' and referring to hippopotamus. These instances and the OED all point to the use of the word 'horse' in the sense of 'great' or 'big' rather than as the animal. Similarly, one meaning of the Irish *capall* is 'large or coarse species', as in *cnó capaill* (horse-chestnut) and *péist chapaill* (large caterpillar).

The SND quotes a 1760 reference to capercaillie as *Caper Keily* (Cock of the Wood), one in 1775 as *Caperkylie* (also 'Cock of the wood'), and one in 1835 as the 'king of game' or the 'great cock-of-the-wood', *capperkailzie*. Ian Pennie cited authors in 1676–8 who wrote of capercaillie in Ireland, including the Irish-speaking province of Connacht, where in English they called it cock-of-the-wood or cock-of-the-mountain.[14]

Alteration to the spelling *capar-coille* eased pronunciation.[15] Euphonic change is frequent in Gaelic, in Scots pronunciations of Gaelic names (e.g. Banff is pronounced 'bamf') and in English (e.g. in brought, where the 'gh' was formerly pronounced 'ch' as in 'Bach'). In his classic essay on the Gaelic of east Perthshire, Charles Robertson wrote: 'Lunnain, muinichill, and capall-coille are with us Lumainn, muilichir, and capar-coille.'[16] This shows how *capall-coille* became *capar-coille*.

The 'z' in *capercailzie* came from the Middle English and old Scots letter *yogh*, written '3' and, pronounced like the 'y' in the English word 'yonder' (SND; OED). Printers used a 'z' instead because they did not have a '3'. Likewise, 'lz' in English derives from the Middle English 'ly' according to Brown, and the Gaelic *coille* is pronounced 'kilye', with stress on *kil* and an indeterminate final 'e' as in the German '*bitte*', hence the Scots 'y' sound. Some people sound the 'z', aping the spelling incorrectly by pronouncing it as a zed, just as some pronounce Menzies with a zed. Others pronounce it as 'capercailyee', 'caperceilyee' ('ei' as in 'height') and 'capercailzee' (with 'z' as in 'zebra'), and as 'caiper' with the same three endings, as well as 'caipercaillie'.[17]

To conclude, the name capercaillie originated from *capall-coille*, meaning 'big wood-bird', 'big wood-cock' or more poetically, 'great cock of the wood'.

TABLE 4. Grouse names in the languages of Britain and Ireland.

| | SEXES | RED GROUSE | PTARMIGAN | BLACK GROUSE | CAPERCAILLIE |
|---|---|---|---|---|---|
| English (OED) | Both | Moorfowl, moorgame | Ptarmigan | Black grouse, blackgame, heath-bird | Capercaillie |
| | Cock | — | — | Blackcock, heath-cock | — |
| | Hen | — | — | Greyhen, heath-hen | — |
| Scots (SND) | Both | Muirfowl, muirfool, muir bird | Tarmagan# | Blackgame | Capercailzie* |
| | Cock | Muircock, gorcock | — | Black cock | — |
| | Hen | Muirhen, muiran, gorhen | — | Gray-hen, gray-fowl | — |
| Gaelic (Dwelly, 1971; Calder, 1972) | Both | Eun-fraoich (heather-bird), eun-ruadh (red-bird) | Tarmachan** | — | Capall-coille, capar-coille (big cock of (the) wood) |
| | Cock | Coileach-fraoich (heather-cock), coileach-ruadh (red-cock) | — | Coileach-dubh (black-cock) | — |
| | Hen | Cearc-fhraoich (heather-hen) | — | Cearc liath (grey-hen) | — |

*(continued overleaf)*

TABLE 4. Grouse names in the languages of Britain and Ireland. *(continued)*

| | SEXES | RED GROUSE | PTARMIGAN | BLACK GROUSE | CAPERCAILLIE |
|---|---|---|---|---|---|
| Irish (Ó Dónaill, 1977) | Both | — | Tarmanach | — | Coileach feá^ (cock of [the] wood) |
| | Cock | Coileach-fraoigh (heather-cock) | — | Coileach dubh (black-cock) | — |
| | Hen | Cearc-fhraoigh (heather-hen) | — | Liathchearc (grey-hen) | — |
| Welsh (Griffiths & Jones, 1995)[5] | Both | Grugiar (heather-hen), grugiar goch (red heather-hen) | Iar wen y mynydd (white hen of the mountain) | Grugiar ddu (black heather-hen) | Ceiliog y coed (cock of the wood) |
| | Cock | Ceiliog grugiar goch (cock red heather-hen) | Ceiliog gwyn y mynydd (white cock of the mountain) | Ceiliog grugiar ddu (cock black heather-hen) | Ceiliog mawr (big cock), paun y coed (peacock of the wood) |
| | Hen | — | — | — | Peunes y coed (peahen of the wood) |

# Variants include ptarmachan, tarmachan, tarmachin, tarmack, tarmagant, tarmagen, tarmigan, termagan, termagant, termigan, termigant and tormican.

* Variants include Capperkailzie, Caper Coille, Caper Keily and Caperkellie, 'the male being sometimes also called the Great Cock of the Woods, or Mountain Cock... Also simply caper... Probably a corruption of capal-coille, the great cock of the wood, from capull, a horse (for horse as used to indicate largeness, cf. horse-radish) (SND).

** Variants include tàrmachan breac na beinne (spotted ptarmigan of the hill), eun bàn an t-sneachda (white bird of the snow), gealag-bheinne (hill white-one), and sneachdag, sneachdair and sneachdan (snow-one). Gordon (1915) has tarmachan creagach (rocky ptarmigan).

^ Nicolaisen (1962), but Ó Dónaill (1977) gives this and coileach-coille as 'woodcock'.

## OTHER TERMS

Two terms from Scots and northern English now appear in international literature on grouse, though not in some English dictionaries. One is the verb and noun *beck*, meaning 'a bird's call' (especially that of a red grouse), along with the adjective and participle *becking*. The second is *clocker*, meaning 'dropping' and referring to the large lump of hoarded faeces voided by incubating hen grouse or poultry. To *clock* formerly meant 'to cluck like a broody hen' and hence 'to brood', the latter being the usual meaning nowadays. In Scots, *on the clock* is 'the state of being broody', the adjective being *clocking*, while a *clocker* is 'a broody hen'.

In English, *lek* is both 'a display-ground' and 'the behaviour that takes place at a display-ground'. In Norwegian and Swedish, the noun *lek* means 'play', from the Old Norse *leika*, 'to play'. The Old English *lacan* was 'to frolic' or 'to fight', and the Old Scots *laik* meant 'sport' or 'play' (OED; SND). North English dialect has *lake* and *play-laking* for 'sport' or 'play', and the Scots *laik* is 'plaything' or 'marble'. The north English and Scots pronunciations were like the English 'lake', though with a shorter vowel, not as in the current English *lek*, where the 'e' is pronounced as in 'hen'. Ingemar Hjorth wrote that the Swedish word *lek* referred to the behaviour, not the place, so he used *arena* for the place instead.[18]

## SUMMARY

The English word *grouse* possibly originated in the French *griais*, meaning 'spotted bird', or, more likely, in the Anglo-French *groucier*, meaning 'to grumble' – hence 'grumbling bird'. The English *ptarmigan* came from the Scots *tarmagan*, which in turn came from the Gaelic *tarmachan*. The Gaelic form probably originated in *torm*, meaning 'noise' – hence 'noisy one'. The unvoiced 'p' resulted from fancy that the word was Greek, as in *pterodactyl*. The English *capercaillie* came from the Scots *capercailzie*, which in turn came from the Gaelic *capall-coille*, literally 'wood-horse'. Here, 'horse' was used in the sense of 'big', as in horse-chestnut, and the name was translated into English as 'the great cock of the wood'. Gaels in east Perthshire pronounced the word *capar-coille* – hence the 'r' in the Scots and English *capercaillie*.

CHAPTER 3

# Red Grouse and Willow Ptarmigan

RENOWNED FOR CENTURIES as a gamebird, the red grouse has an economic value that has led to much research, so it is one of the best known of animals. Ornithologists formerly regarded it as the sole bird species unique to Britain and Ireland, but for decades it has been considered a race of the circumpolar willow ptarmigan.[1] In his book on grouse, Otto Höhn regarded it as halfway to a species,[2] and species rank has again been proposed.[3] In this chapter we discuss how red grouse and willow ptarmigan make use of vegetation as food and cover, and summarise their movements, fluctuations in numbers, survival and breeding success.

In its behaviour, the red grouse closely resembles the willow ptarmigan, but that bird has a white dress in winter and white wings at all seasons. After the last ice age, during a period when the climate of Britain and Ireland was warming, red grouse evolved a coloured plumage throughout the year, suiting the background of dark, usually snow-free moorland.

An unusual attraction of Britain and Ireland is heather moorland – millions of hectares of it. Here, the red grouse makes its home. The moors are impressive in all seasons, but especially so in August and September, when whole hillsides turn purple with millions of heather flowers. In the dark silence of early morning, the first grouse-cock crow at daybreak rings out the bird's challenge as he proclaims his moorland territory. Then 'the answer comes quick from the north, and within a couple of minutes the whole dark moorland re-echoes with wild music – an unrehearsed orchestra of Nature. What a concert!'[4]

'Grouse-moor' is moorland where grouse-shooting is the main land use. 'Heather moorland', where heather predominates, includes grouse-moor and also land where grouse are seldom or never shot. Both are valuable for other

FIG 10. Heather in bloom: food and cover for red grouse. (Stuart Rae)

FIG 11. Cock willow ptarmigan amongst willow in Alaska, showing spring plumage with a chestnut head and neck, and with a white face remaining from the winter. (Robert Moss)

wildlife, landscape and tourism. Heather and red grouse are virtually Scottish emblems, although some deplore them as romantic clichés.

The willow ptarmigan is a beautiful bird found in northern countries amid splendid scenery.[5] Hunters seek it out in autumn, a time of spectacular colour as frost turns leaves yellow or crimson. Many biologists have studied willow ptarmigan, and this chapter touches on their work, although it is mainly about red grouse. When mentioning both birds together, we use *Lagopus lagopus*, the scientific name for the species.

## THE BIRDS

### Dimensions and plumage

Slightly smaller than a pheasant, the red grouse is about as long as a wood-pigeon but with a heavier body, and cocks are 5 per cent longer than hens.[6] The dark brownish-black bill is stout, easily snapping off woody twigs as food. Adult cock red grouse weigh 600–690g, their lean point in March coinciding with vigorous territorial activity and courtship. Cocks outweigh hens in every month save March through May, when hens surpass them to reach some 670g in April, having fattened before laying eggs. In June and July, the hens, now thin after incubation, average 560g and cocks 660g.

Birds differ in size in different regions. Although red grouse have shorter bills and tails than willow ptarmigan in north Norway,[7] they are heavier, and the heaviest ones weighed by us were caught on windy, fairly snow-free moors near the east coast of Scotland. Birds weigh less and have shorter wings in interior Alaska than near its windy coast. The smallest Russian birds live in the subalpine belt of the southern Siberian mountains, larger ones live in the taiga, yet larger ones are found on tundra, and the largest of all occur in southerly Kazakhstan, where winters are cold and windy with little snow.[8] We infer from this that small races live in regions where deep, undrifted snow prevails in winter, affording good insulation for roosting. Rock ptarmigan also weigh less in such regions than on windy and often milder coasts.

A reddish-brown colour pervades the plumage of red grouse throughout the year and of willow ptarmigan in summer. Birds in west Scotland, Wales and Ireland are lighter coloured than those further east, their yellowish plumage suiting the paler background of the grassier moorland found in such regions. Willow ptarmigan in Kazakhstan are also slightly yellowish in summer, blending in with the background of dry forest-steppe.

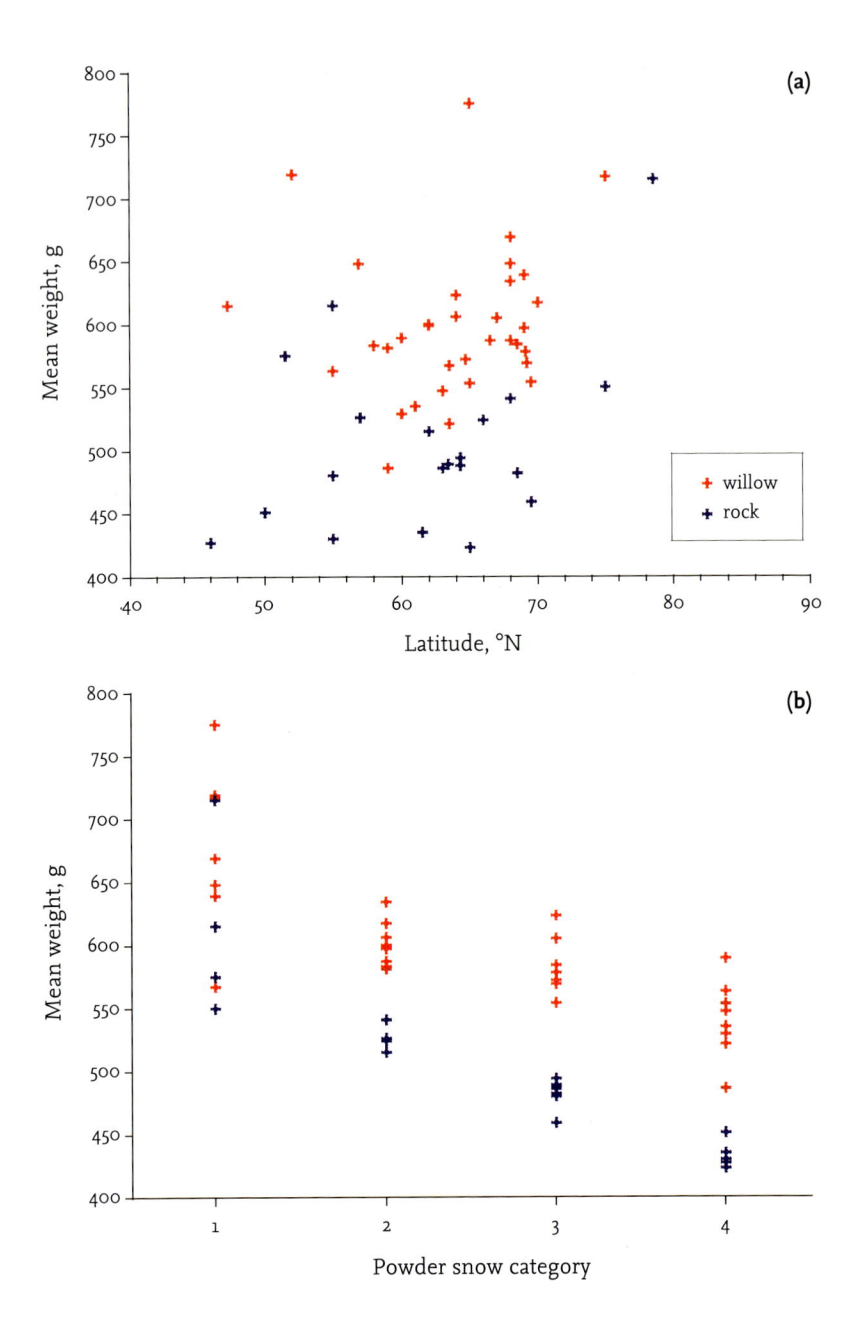

**FIG 12.** Mean winter body-weight in grams of *Lagopus lagopus* and rock ptarmigan in relation to (a) latitude and (b) categories of deep undrifted snow in winter, from scarce (1) to widespread (4).[9, 10] Mean weight includes crop contents. In most cases we calculated it by adding together mean weights for young cocks, old cocks, young hens and old hens, and dividing the total by four, but in some cases a mean was published without specifying how it was obtained, or in one case a mean of all sex and age categories was given irrespective of their proportions in the sample.

**Notes**

1. The observation that northern animals of the same species tend to be larger is known as Bergmann's rule. Northern climes are colder, and bigger animals have an advantage here in staying warm because of their smaller ratio of surface area (through which heat is lost) to body mass (in which heat is generated).

2. Willow and rock ptarmigan show this tendency only very weakly. Furthermore, willow ptarmigan are bigger than rock ptarmigan, although the latter generally live in conditions of greater wind-chill, and rock ptarmigan are bigger than white-tailed ptarmigan, which live in greater wind-chill than the other two species in the same region. This is associated with the observation (Robert Moss) that white-tailed ptarmigan spend more time under the snow than rock ptarmigan in the same area, and that rock ptarmigan spend more time under the snow than willow ptarmigan. We think that the insulation provided by snow-roosting allows ptarmigan to be smaller. Deep, undrifted powder snow provides better insulation than wind-packed snow, because it contains much more air (*see* Chapter 8). Hence, ptarmigan should be smaller where deep, undrifted powder snow is more widespread and consistently available. Being smaller would allow them to use shallower snow and so extend the area available to them. Another advantage of small size is that less food is needed. An advantage in itself, this might also result in less time being required for foraging, thereby allowing more time under the snow and thus less heat loss.

3. Data on latitude were taken from atlases and larger-scale maps. In most cases the exact location was known, but in a very few cases (such as north Greenland and Yakutia) it covered a band of latitude, in which case we took a mid-point. We used four categories as scores for the prevalence of deep, undrifted powder snow during the winter period in the various regions. This rested mainly upon published accounts by meteorologists, explorers and ecologists studying *Lagopus*, along with published photographs, and partly on personal experience of snow conditions by colleagues and ourselves.

4. Statistical analysis showed that variations in ptarmigan weight were explained better by the category of powder snow than by latitude. Because the ratio of the birds' surface area to weight is about 2:3, we used weight raised to the power of 2/3 as the variable to be explained. Most of the variation in this aspect of weight was explained by analysis of covariance ($R^2 = 0.81$). Explanatory variables were species (two categories, willow or rock ptarmigan), latitude (continuous) and snow category (continuous). Weight tended to increase with increasing latitude, but the effect was not significant ($F_{1,49} = 1.02$, $P = 0.32$).

**FIG 12. Notes** (*continued*)

Weight declined with increasing powder snow ($F_{1,49}$ = 102.5, $P$ < 0.0001). Note that weights of rock and willow ptarmigan were similar in places where powder snow occurred rarely (category 1), but that the difference between the species increased in regions with more powder snow (categories 2–4). This suggests that differences in body-weight between the two species are due largely to differences in the way they use snow, such that rock ptarmigan in regions with deep powder spend more time under snow than willow ptarmigan. Thus, the analysis showed that the difference in weight between the two species was not significant ($F_{1,49}$ = 1.76, $P$ = 0.19), whereas the interaction between snow category and species' weight was significant ($F_{1,49}$ = 4.28, $P$ = 0.0439).

5. One effect of snow on weight was that birds in regions with category 1 powder snow were 124g heavier than birds with category 4 powder snow. The SED (standard error of difference) between the mean weights of the two sets of birds was only 18g. Such a small SED relative to the large difference in mean weight signifies that the observed difference in weight was reliable.

**FIG 13.** Eggs in nests. Left to right, top to bottom: red grouse, ptarmigan, greyhen, capercaillie. (François Mougeot, Stuart Rae, Desmond Dugan, Desmond Dugan)

### Eggs and chicks

The oval eggs of *Lagopus lagopus*, slightly larger than those of a wood-pigeon, are off-white with a tinge of pale brick red when newly laid, and are marked by many brownish-red blotches. As incubation proceeds, the blotches turn dark brown and the eggs shine with a strong gloss. Hatching takes about a day.

Down covers day-old chicks to their toenails, its colour varying from largely black with little yellow or brown, to predominantly yellow and chestnut. Brood mates have a similar colour, which also resembles the down colour of their parents as chicks, so the colour is inherited.[11]

A day after hatching, chicks leave the nest. They peck vigorously at insects or heather, and run to hide under vegetation if frightened. In Scotland, most chicks hatch in late May and appear full grown at 12 weeks, although old grouse still outweigh them in August and September.[12] Chicks on Russian tundra put on weight much faster than this, and faster also than birds in forest-steppe. Chicks of Irish bogs are very slow-growing, and they also moult their chick primaries later than chicks at Kerloch in Deeside, Scotland.[13] When eggs from an Irish bog were hatched in captivity and the young given a high-protein diet, their body-weight and chick primaries grew no faster. The reason for this is that fast growth is tied in with brief summers,[14] and Irish summers are long, allowing leisurely growth before a very late onset of winter.[15]

FIG 14. Red grouse chicks, about two weeks old. (Robert Moss)

**FIG 15.** Downy chick shortly after leaving the nest, about three days old. (Desmond Dugan)

## CAMOUFLAGE

Walk across a moor and you may be startled as a red grouse suddenly rises near you with whirring wings. It flies strongly with rapid beats that alternate with glides. Adept at using wind to increase speed, a red grouse moves at the same contour rather than up or down, and often swerves or tilts quickly, a habit that makes it hard to shoot.

Red grouse are well camouflaged on snow-free ground, often staying motionless when danger threatens, and are easily overlooked by man, raptor and fox. Because the birds skulk, standard methods for assessing their numbers in national surveys – such as walking across an area or standing in one spot – greatly underestimate them.

A stark exception comes on deep snow, when the contrast makes red grouse look black and strikingly conspicuous even a kilometre away. In such conditions they gather in packs up to hundreds strong, relying on safety in numbers, and on continuous snow they are so wild that they take wing when a person comes in view even 2km away. As patches of snow-free ground appear, however, they go there and become hard to see. At their tamest on sunny spring days, pairs sometimes allow one to approach to 10m.

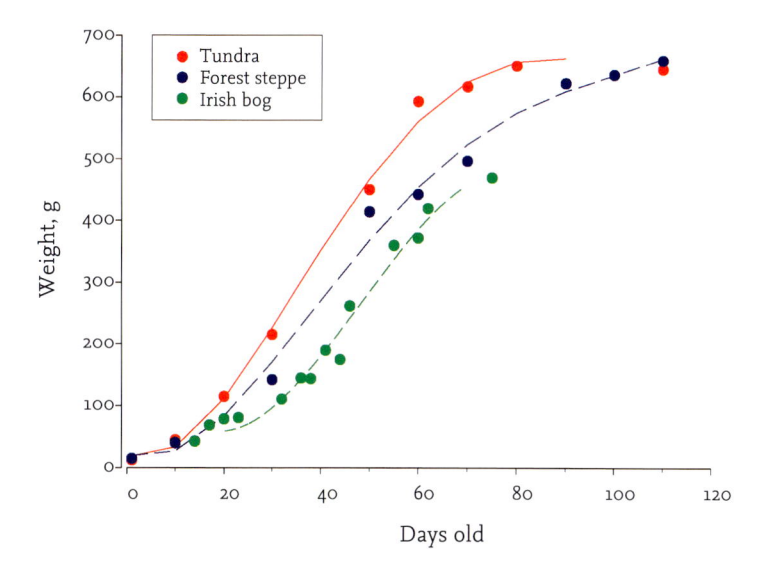

**FIG 16.** Growth in grams of young *Lagopus lagopus* (cocks and hens combined) on Arctic Russian tundra, west Siberian forest-steppe and Irish bog.[16]

### Notes

1. Fast growth of birds on tundra has been attributed to continuous daylight and abundant food, allowing feeding round the clock.[17] However, faster growth also goes along with briefer summers,[18] and tundra chicks must grow quickly in the short Arctic summer before winter's early onset. Irish chicks on Glenamoy bog grew even more slowly in their long summers, but data are incomplete and it is not clear when their growth levels out. Such big differences among three areas are presumably genetic adaptations, although nurture can affect growth rate, e.g. wild chicks grow more slowly than well-fed captives from the same stock, on Tranøy, Norway, and in Scotland.[19] The difference is, however, much smaller than the differences in the above graphs.
2. When eggs on Glenamoy bog were hatched in captivity and the chicks given a high-protein diet, their weight increased no faster. Also, wild chicks on bog where fertiliser and drains had boosted the heather's growth and nutrient content put on weight no faster than chicks on unimproved bog. We infer that slow growth may be adapted to the long, mild Irish summer and autumn, not to the infertile bog habitat.[20]
3. Chicks have extremely variable growth rates. We are therefore cautious about attributing differences among studies entirely to geographical differences, especially where data are just snapshots at one age, because differences may be partly due to differences between years, or even between broods.[21] Obviously this caveat applies to the above graphs.

FIG 17. Cock red grouse taking flight. (David A. Gowans)

FIG 18. Pack of grouse flying over snow. (Adam Watson)

Red grouse are wilder than other races of *Lagopus lagopus*, except for heavily hunted birds in Newfoundland, which formerly were tame and tended to run from a man rather than fly.[22] In Alaska, willow ptarmigan are still tame away from roads,[23] and white-tailed ptarmigan are also confiding if seldom molested, although shooting soon makes them wild.[24]

Hen willow ptarmigan seek to maximise the effectiveness of their camouflage. During spring thaws, those in white plumage tend to stand on snow, whereas hens that are partly dark stand at the snow edge, and hens in dark plumage stay away from snow.[25] Similarly, when snow lies patchily on Scottish moorland, single or paired red grouse tend to rest on dark heather, where they are hard to see.[26]

## SYSTEMATICS[27]

After regarding red grouse as the species *Lagopus scoticus* and the paler birds of Ireland and the Outer Hebrides as the subspecies *Lagopus scoticus hibernicus*, taxonomists later recognised both as *Lagopus lagopus scoticus*, one of many races of the willow ptarmigan. The paler birds also typify west Scotland and Wales, part of a gradual change from west to east in tune with the changing colour of the vegetation.

Willow ptarmigan on fairly snow-free islands off west Norway become only partly white in winter,[28] and races in Kazakhstan[29] and Newfoundland have some coloured feathers in their winter plumage. Another intermediate case is red grouse in northeast Scotland, for in winter they have many white feathers in this snowiest part of their range.

Captive hybrids have been bred from red grouse and Scottish ptarmigan, and from Norwegian willow and rock ptarmigan,[30] and wild hybrids occur.[31] In Canada, male rock ptarmigan mix with packs of willow ptarmigan before hen rock ptarmigan arrive, and a cock has been seen to sing beside a hen willow ptarmigan.[32] Such events might lead to inter-specific pairings.[33]

## WORLD DISTRIBUTION OF *LAGOPUS LAGOPUS*

Willow ptarmigan have the widest world distribution of any grouse, with a vast breeding range across Eurasia and America, from sea-level in the Arctic to high altitudes on southern mountains (Table 5). They inhabit Siberia's Altay massif south to 45°40'N and Newfoundland south to 46°37'N, and they extend northwards to 76°N in Canada's Bathurst and Melville islands, and to 76°46'N in the New Siberian Islands (Novosibirskiye Ostrova).

TABLE 5. Examples of altitudes typically frequented by breeding *Lagopus lagopus*. In general they tend to be at lower altitudes further north. However, at similar latitude they are at lower altitudes in regions with windier summers (Scotland versus Chilkat Pass; west and especially northwest Scotland versus northeast Scotland; Sgribhis Bheinn versus the more eastern Ben Loyal; and Kamchatka versus East Sayan. At windy Avalon they are lower than in several regions much further north).

| Country | Latitude (°N) | Place | Altitude (m) | Reference |
|---|---|---|---|---|
| Norway | 70 | Syltefjorden | 0–100 | Watson, unpublished |
|  | 69 | Galggojavvre | 0–600 | Watson, 1957a |
|  | 68 | Lofoten | 0–600 | Watson, 1957a |
| Canada | 60 | Chilkat Pass | 850–1,830 | Hannon et al., 1998 |
| Scotland, northwest | 58 | Sgribhis Bheinn | 0–240 | Watson, 1961, 1963a, 1965b, unpublished |
|  |  | Ben Loyal | 0–460 | Watson, 1961, 1963a, 1965b, unpublished |
| Scotland, west | 57 | Wester Ross | 0–600 | Watson, 1961, 1963a, 1965b, unpublished |
|  |  | Argyll | 0–620 | Watson, 1961, 1963a, 1965b, unpublished |
| Scotland, northeast |  | Cairngorms | 0–760 | Watson, 1961, 1963a, 1965b, unpublished |
| Russia | 55 | Kamchatka | 0–900 | Potapov, 1985* |
|  | c.50 | East Sayan | 1,900–2,650 | Potapov, 1985* |
| Canada | 47 | Avalon | 0–300 | Watson, unpublished |

* He gives original references for Russian sites.

In summer, they are found in the southeastern corner of Novaya Zemlya, and on the islands of Vaygach, Kolguyev and Sakhalin.[34] They breed on much of the Siberian mainland, including Kamchatka, and southwards to northern Manchuria and western Mongolia, and in Sinkiang's north corner and Tuva. During their breeding season in Kazakhstan, mean temperatures reach 23°C in July – equivalent to those found in Portugal in the same month. Birds live across most of north European Russia, and west into the Baltic States and most of Fennoscandia.

Willow ptarmigan inhabit the Aleutian Islands west to Unimak, and from Alaska across the north Canadian mainland and southern Arctic islands to the north shore of the Gulf of St Lawrence. In winter they move down to Lac Saint-

Jean behind Quebec City, into southern parts of Ontario and of Canada's prairie provinces, and occasionally as far south as northern USA states such as Minnesota.

Unlike rock ptarmigan, willow ptarmigan have not colonised Svalbard, Iceland, Greenland or the more remote Aleutians, or isolated southern massifs such as the Alps. Although they abound on the vast tundra of south and west Baffin Island, they have not been found in the more fragmented and isolated eastern valleys, despite good scrub habitat there. However, a formidable barrier of lofty mountains and ice-caps separates these valleys from the western tundra,[35] thereby signifying the willow ptarmigan's lesser mobility and flight power.

## DISTRIBUTION OF RED GROUSE

Red grouse are resident on moorland over much of England, Ireland, Scotland and Wales, from the coast to the upper limit of this vegetation type. In Scotland, that limit varies from 240m on Sgribhis Bheinn in the northwest to 820m on Lochnagar in the southeast, with intermediates at 600m in the west Highlands and 760m in the Cairngorms.

Birds introduced to moorland in Belgium near the German border increased after 1920 in both countries, but after 1950 became scarce after habitat loss, and the last cock was heard in April 1974.[36] Grouse were introduced to Exmoor in 1915–16, and they remain there and on Dartmoor.[37] Two introductions to the Faeroes failed.[38]

## WORLD AND NATIONAL NUMBERS

Estimates of *Lagopus lagopus* numbers[39] vary greatly because few counts have been carried out, but they suggest a world population of 12 million in spring. Countries reported to hold most are Russia with 6.8 million, followed by Canada, the USA (Alaska) and Norway with over a million each, Sweden has 400,000 birds, the UK 250,000 and Finland 180,000. An estimate for Scotland in 2003 was 130,000 pairs on an estimated 1.2 million ha of heather moorland.[40]

Ireland has 1.2 million ha of bog,[41] and many hills with more heather and higher grouse densities than are found on bog land. One estimate of its red grouse population was between 1,000 and 5,000 pairs.[42] On this, government minister Liam Hyland commented 'Grouse, by nature, are secretive birds, spending most of their lives hidden in heather. For this reason … their numbers here may be under-recorded.'[43]

## HABITAT

Many publications describe and illustrate willow ptarmigan habitats abroad.[44] Everywhere, birds make use of vegetation that is tall enough to conceal them from predators. Hens nest in freely drained heath[45] or scrub, whereas broods frequent wet flushes or moist meadows.[46]

### Red grouse

Most red grouse live on freely drained moorland and, less frequently, on wet heath. The former habitat resulted from deforestation by prehistoric man to create pasture or cultivated fields, since when a continuation of burning and grazing has prevented most of it from reverting to forest (*see* Chapter 11). Wet heath resulted mainly from a wetter climate, which led to peat growth and with it deforestation, and it too has been burned and grazed since.

Red grouse abound where their main food of short heather grows in a mixture with fairly tall heather as cover. Some of the highest densities have 'consistently been on moors with both dry heather ground and blanket bog, where heather shares dominance with cotton-grass'.[47] Cotton-grass shoots are nutritious in spring, while blanket bog supports abundant insects that are food for chicks. Even where blanket bog has eroded into peat hags, and bare peat covers much of the ground (Fig. 19), birds can be abundant.[48]

**FIG 19.** Peat hags amongst heather. (Robert Moss)

Where food abounds without cover, as on short heather after a very wide fire, only unmated cocks take territories and even they avoid the middle of the burned area. While eating short heather, birds tend to keep within a few metres of tall heather,[49] to which they run if a predator approaches. However, they avoid tall dense heather, which impedes movement and offers little accessible food.

Some birds occupy open patches in woodland. Their numbers increase in the early years after planting on moorland[50] if foresters have not eliminated the heath understorey, and among trees regenerating after felling or wind-throw, but they vanish before the canopy closes over.

### Willow ptarmigan

After rock ptarmigan, willow ptarmigan are the most northerly grouse, breeding on flat or gently sloping land with tall heath or scrub, and in open woods of birch or conifer. In dense forest they use open patches on bogs and riverbanks, and areas cleared after lightning fires or felling until the regenerating trees close up. On mountains they inhabit a belt above forest but below the terrain used by rock ptarmigan.

In the willow ptarmigan's range across the Canadian high Arctic, most ground is bare with very small amounts of food (Table 6), and the birds are consequently sparse. A so-called 'polar desert' prevails, where the summer rainfall is low, and there is little soil moisture and scanty organic matter and soil nutrients.[52]

FIG 20. Willow ptarmigan habitat, Dovrefjell, Norway: birch and willow scrub. (Adam Watson)

TABLE 6. (a) Standing crop and (b) annual plant production (both in kg per ha), and (c) range in spring numbers per km² of cock *Lagopus lagopus* and rock ptarmigan (upper row in high Arctic and Arctic refers to Canada and lower row to Eurasia).[51] Plant data were collected from Russia (Alexandrova, 1970), Scottish Alpine areas (Summers, 1978) and Kerloch (Miller & Watson, 1978); Russian plants were air-dried and Scottish samples oven-dried.

|  | (A) STANDING CROP |  | (B) ANNUAL PLANT PRODUCTION |  |  |  | (C) BIRD DENSITY |  |
|---|---|---|---|---|---|---|---|---|
|  | DWARF SHRUBS | PLANT TOTAL | DWARF SHRUBS | DWARF BIRCH | DWARF WILLOW | PLANT TOTAL | LAGOPUS LAGOPUS | ROCK PTARMIGAN |
| High-Arctic polar desert | 0 | 40 | 0 | 0 | 0 | — | 0.1–0.4, 0.5–2.5 | 0.1–0.4, 3–4 |
| Arctic tundra | 160 | 490 | 0 | 0 | 0 | 270 | 1.6–3.1, 3.3–14.2 | 0.0–3.0, 4.4–6.5 |
| Subarctic tundra | 360 | 3,160 | 36 | 228 | 216 | 870 | 0.5–85 | 0.3–34[#] |
| Alpine Beinn a' Bhuird* | 3,200–10,000 | — | 750–3,000 | 0 | 0 | — | Not present | 14–67[#] |
| Heather, Kerloch moor** | 4,200–22,000 | — | 1,700–2,700 | 0 | 0 | — | 5–179[#] | Not present |
| Mountains in Siberia, Alps, Pyrenees, Japan^ | — | — | — | — | — | — | 1.3–5.0 | 0.5–14 |
| Belarus boreal forest | — | — | — | — | — | — | 0.5–2.5 | Not present |
| Kazakh forest-steppe | — | — | — | — | — | — | 0.2–0.4[†] | Not present |

**Notes for Table 6**

In the Canadian high Arctic, a *Salix arctica* barren had an annual plant production of 3kg per ha (Bliss, 1970). Other studies showed 8kg per ha on barrens (the main habitat), 26kg per ha on a 'cushion' community, and 410kg per ha on snow flushes (Bliss *et al.*, 1984). Vascular plants on Alpine tundra at Eagle Creek had a dry-matter standing crop of 2,950kg per ha and annual production of 700kg per ha (Bliss, 1970). Subarctic dwarf birch-crowberry heath on Kola Peninsula had a standing crop of 4,700kg per ha, blaeberry heath 5,300kg per ha, and heather-lichen-heath 4,900kg per ha.

# The highest densities of red grouse and Scottish ptarmigan were on fertile soils. There is also some evidence of this for Icelandic rock ptarmigan. Heidmörk, with cock densities of only 0.3–0.6, is on a lava field with sparse food plants; in contrast, Hrisey, with a density of 7–34, has continuous heath with some hay meadows (Gardarsson, 1988) that must have fertile soil, near cultivated fields with rich topsoil (Watson, unpublished).

* All plants here are combined, and comprise mostly dwarf shrubs, 750kg per ha exposed heather and 3,000kg per ha bryophyte-rich mixed heath. Lichen-rich blaeberry-crowberry vegetation produced an annual plant production of 2,000–2,100kg per ha.

** 1,700kg per ha of standing crop was 'building' heather (the growth phases are pioneer, building, mature and degenerate) and 2,700kg per ha mature heather. Both together on high moors produced 1,600–2,300kg per ha (Moss, 1969), and near the coast 3,600–4,400kg per ha (Barclay-Estrup, 1970).

^ There is less heath here than on Scottish Alpine, subarctic and low Arctic areas, as judged from studies in Japan, the Pyrenees, and the French, Swiss and Italian Alps (Soichiro *et al.*, 1969; Boudarel, 1988; Desmet, 1988b; Bossert, 1995; Favaron *et al.*, 2006), and from photographs in Soichiro *et al.*, 1969, and in Bossert, 1995.

†Typical density. Maximum 3–4 pairs per km$^2$ (Potapov, 1985).

FIG 21. Porcupine Creek, Alaska. Willow ptarmigan mostly inhabit the tall willow scrub and rock ptarmigan mostly the short subalpine scrub, with some overlap. (Robert Moss)

Like Britain, islands off west Norway have heather moorland where sheep grazing and burning over the centuries have destroyed trees. Here, willow ptarmigan eat mainly heather, but in recent years the moorland has been reverting to scrub and woodland as pastoral farming has declined.[53] In Kazakh forest-steppe, birds rear their chicks in groves of short birch trees or scrub of birch, willow or meadow-sweet, usually nesting among tall grass or meadow-sweet stems.[54]

## DIET

### Winter

At this time of year herbs die back or are covered by snow, so instead the birds must subsist on woody shrubs or trees. Willow ptarmigan take twigs or buds of willow or birch, while red grouse feed on the leafy shoots of heather or the leafless stalk tips of blaeberry. Red grouse sometimes perch on trees to eat buds and shoots, especially in deep snow, although fire and overgrazing have almost eliminated willow and birch scrub on British and Irish moors, resulting in a poorer diet for the birds.

When we see vast areas of heather shoots and flowers in summer, it is hard to imagine red grouse ever running short of food. However, sheep, cattle or red deer can greatly reduce the vegetation over winter, in the worst cases trimming it so short that it cannot offer safe cover from predators. Birds must depart or die.

Even without grazing, green heather can turn brown through desiccation within a few days if shoots lose moisture in cold weather and then cannot replace it because the soil water has frozen.[55] Browning also occurs when the soil is not frozen, albeit more slowly, when dry, cold winds blow in late winter and spring – worst affected are the tender shoots of heather plants in their first year. Blaeberry and other heath species suffer less, so a moor with a virtual monoculture of heather offers much food in most years but carries with it a risk of famine.

### Spring

Red grouse eat mainly heather, but in spring they supplement it with plants that begin to grow earlier, such as chickweed or sheep's sorrel, and then blaeberry. All British grouse species eat shoots of cotton-grass where available, as these have a much higher content of the essential nutrients, protein and phosphorus than heather or other heath species. It is easy to tell when birds have eaten it from the telltale dark glumes[56] in their droppings.

The hare's-tail cotton-grass (often known locally as 'draw-moss' or 'moss-crop') abounds on thick peat. One of the earliest moorland plants to grow, it has

FIG 22. Cock red grouse in a sea of heather. (Robert Moss)

flower shoots that appear in late March during mild springs. By the time chicks hatch, the flower head has turned into fruits hidden in a fibrous cottony structure of beauty but bearing no nutritive value. The sparser but widespread common cotton-grass thrives in very wet patches. Its first shoots appear in May, or later on high moors and in the Alpine zone.

Cotton-grasses do not grow on freely drained moorland, so red grouse with territories in such areas must eat mostly heather in spring, which makes for a poor diet. This was the case on most parts of our study areas in Glen Esk and Kerloch.

Willow ptarmigan in Timansk (Russia), Alaska and British Columbia in spring, feed mainly on willow buds, twigs and catkins[57] all nutritious and abundant. On Newfoundland's Avalon Peninsula, where willow is scarce, almost all the spring diet comprises twigs, buds, leaves and berries of blueberry species.

**Summer and autumn**
Besides taking much heather and some blaeberry, red grouse in summer eat the leaves and flowers of herbs, moss capsules, flowers of bell heather or cross-leaved heath, and seeds of grass, sedge, rush and heath wood-rush. From a day old, chicks feed largely on newly growing heather shoots, which are quite tender in early summer. Moss capsules come next in favour, especially the *Polytrichum* species

that grow profusely on wet acidic moorland. Rich in protein and phosphorus, they are almost as nutritious as insects. Invertebrates are the third commonest food, and chicks in their first two weeks eat many of them, until becoming mostly vegetarian after three weeks.[58] In the first weeks they frequent flushes, where insects abound and the tall grasses, sedges, rushes and bog myrtle afford good cover. Later they use drier ground, feeding on heather, blaeberry, herbs and seeds. When poults are almost as big as their mothers in early August, some broods visit fields, eating grass seeds, clover and weeds while almost out of sight in thick cover.

In Timansk, Russia, willow ptarmigan chicks eat many insects until they are 20 days old, after which they turn to a more vegetarian diet.[59] Adult birds in North America eat mainly willow and horsetail with some dwarf birch, plus various other plants, and chicks feed predominantly on moss capsules, seeds of sedge and rush, flowers and insects.[60] The wet areas they frequent are presumably a rich source of insects, as in Britain.

During autumn, red grouse eat mainly heather shoots and flowers, often taking both at each peck, and smaller amounts of other items as in summer. They are fond of berries. Adult willow ptarmigan feed mostly on willow, but also take twigs of blueberry species and berries.

## METABOLISM

### Winter

Like poultry, grouse have a large crop that acts as a food store. By dusk it is full, bulging when seen sideways on, and holding nearly 120g.[61] Its contents last through the night, so that birds are effectively fed throughout the 24 hours, and continuous digestion creates permanent heat.[62] Death from food shortage during periods of snowfall seems very rare, and we have not come across it. Birds have little or no fat,[63] but conserve heat by resting and roosting in snow.

In northeast Siberia, the coldest part of the northern hemisphere in winter, willow twigs contain much protein and energy early in the season. However, because birds eat the best twigs first, those remaining in late winter are less valuable. Before it is consumed, the cold food in a bird's crop must be warmed to body temperature: twigs taken in January are at −40°C or even −50°C, and must be raised to +42°C.[64] The birds are selective at breakfast, taking small nutritious twigs in leisurely fashion, whereas at the evening meal they eat hurriedly and less selectively, especially in extreme frost, when they swallow 120 twigs per minute. Over the winter they lose weight as food quality declines, until the newly growing willow shoots in spring provide a high-quality source once again.

### Incubating hens

When she senses distant danger, an incubating hen becomes alert with raised head. As the threat comes near, she changes to a motionless sphinx-like posture, with head tucked in and eyes unblinking, making her easy to overlook. When a human approaches with a dog at heel, a hen willow ptarmigan that is not incubating increases her heart and breathing rates, whereas a hen in the later days of incubation cuts the rates greatly, in extreme cases down to only three to five breaths per minute (Table 7). This makes it harder for a fox to detect her, because she smells less and makes less noise or movement. On the point of fleeing, she changes from this motionless posture to rapid movement of head and eyes, and may burst out in sudden flight or distraction display.

**TABLE 7.** Number of heartbeats and breaths per minute in hens. First value is for Norwegian willow ptarmigan, value after comma is for Svalbard rock ptarmigan, and values in parentheses are very low rates recorded for short periods in willow ptarmigan.[65]

| ACTIVITY OF HEN | HEARTBEATS | BREATHS |
| --- | --- | --- |
| Resting, including incubating | 140, 155 | 23, 25 |
| Not incubating, seeing a man with dog at heel | 255 | 31 |
| Early incubation, seeing a man with dog at heel | 140 | 13 |
| Late incubation, seeing a man with dog at heel | 100 (10–20) | 10 (3–5) |
| Leaving the nest to feed | 224, 205 | 25–28, 28 |
| On return to incubate cool eggs | 534, 442 | 35, 35 |
| With day-old chicks, approached by a man | 450–600 | 32–40 |

**Notes**

When a man flushed an incubating hen (willow ptarmigan and Svalbard rock ptarmigan) from her nest, the heart rate soared immediately to >500. When a fulmar flew over a Svalbard hen's nest, her heart rate fell suddenly to 6, and an incubating Swiss hen's steady heart rate halved suddenly when a walker came to within 10m, and then was irregular before halving again.

When a feeding hen returns to incubate eggs that have cooled to 5°C, her breathing rate increases and her heartbeat soars to over 500 per minute within 5–10 seconds of settling on the eggs, boosting the flow of blood to the brood-patch and warming her eggs quickly. It takes 40–80 minutes before these rates return to the normal resting rate of an incubating hen (a heartbeat of 140), and they rise again briefly after she turns her eggs. On rainy or cold days when her eggs cool sooner, she leaves for fewer feeding bouts, and so loses weight more quickly, which weakens her and reduces the later survival of her chicks.[66]

Incubating hens have very little scent. Peter Hudson reported that dogs easily find incubating hen red grouse that have many threadworms, because they smell more.[67] However, incubating hens with many worms seem to survive depredation by foxes better,[68] probably because they are in poorer condition and flush more readily as a fox approaches, whereas hens in good condition with few worms are more likely to take a risk by sitting tight.

**Chicks**

Downy chicks need frequent brooding. A day-old willow ptarmigan eventually becomes hypothermic even at an ambient temperature of 30°C.[69] Hatchlings, however, respond to cold by increasing their metabolic rate,[70] such that by seven to ten days they can be active for long periods at 10–15°C without daytime brooding.[71] They produce heat by bursts of shivering in the breast muscles, or by walking.[72] However, it is not until they are older than 14 days that these responses can prevent some hypothermia at normal summer temperatures. By about five weeks, wild chicks can survive without brooding.

When captive eight-day chicks have continuous food and heat, a drop in food quality can none the less reduce growth and survival.[73] Chicks always try to fill their crops completely, and food intake is related to body-weight irrespective of their age. On cold days the small chicks cannot fully compensate for greater heat loss by eating more, and high-quality food is crucial for their growth and survival.

Captive chicks experience neither rain nor wind-chill, whereas those outdoors occasionally face a life or death struggle with the elements. Heavy rain or snow can kill chicks that are even two to three weeks old.[74] Kjell Erikstad found that cold and rain shorten the time that chicks spend feeding away from their mother's warmth, and also reduce the availability of the insects they need for growth and survival.

MOVEMENTS

**Long-distance seasonal movements or migration**

Some spectacular movements of *Lagopus lagopus* have been seen, such as 10,000 willow ptarmigan flying north through a pass in Alaska's Brooks Range one early morning in April.[75] The following explanation probably applies also to rock ptarmigan, because salient features in both species are similar, but more is known about *Lagopus lagopus*.

Northern regions have snow every winter, but much of the food in forest and scrub remains uncovered, so birds there are resident. Snow usually covers the shorter vegetation on hills or tundra, and here most birds move away, either flying uphill to ridges where drifting uncovers plants, or to valleys with scrub or trees.[76] How far they move depends on how far the nearest suitable wintering grounds are from the summer range. In British Columbia's Chilkat Pass and in most parts of Alaska, birds travel 20–50km, whereas many from tundra regions north of the Brooks Range fly south for 160km to woodland, and birds in Manitoba have been seen 800km south of the breeding range. From islands and mainland tundra in Arctic Russia, birds move up to 250km south and many cross 75km of sea, although some stay on the tundra if snow has not covered all plants.[77]

Birds in the Brooks Range move from late September, with a peak number departing in mid-October; at Chilkat Pass all have departed by mid-December; and in Russia they move between October and January. In all regions, cocks move later in autumn and for a shorter distance, and hens leave earlier and travel further. During spring, conversely, cocks head for the summer grounds earlier than hens, and arrive there sooner. In short, large-scale annual movement in far northern regions is frequent enough to be called migration, but its timing is irregular, depending on snowfall.

Movements are more noticeable when more birds participate, either because population density is high or because snow covers most food. When irregular, such movements are often referred to as irruptions. When more birds move away from areas with higher densities, this is known as density-dependent movement.[78] Whether high density can induce mass movement has not been studied in willow ptarmigan, but this seems likely from observations of rock ptarmigan in Greenland (see Chapter 4).

A recurring feature in writings on red grouse is 'grouse migration'. This involves the sudden appearance or disappearance of many birds, sometimes in snow-free periods and hence ruling out movement caused by sparse food. An example of such an appearance occurred at Glen Esk in 1959, when numbers almost doubled on the high study area in October and stayed dense until January.[79] An example of a disappearance involved many pairs leaving their territories in springs of high population density at Kerloch during the 1970s.[80] The evidence suggests that 'grouse migration' comprises irruptive movements that occur at high or declining densities during population fluctuations.[81]

**Short movements to food**
Red grouse easily scratch through shallow snow to uncover plants, but feeding becomes unprofitable when deep snow covers most vegetation. If snow blankets

**FIG 23.** Red grouse feeding on oat stooks in Glen Esk about 1960. (Adam Watson)

low moorland, birds often fly uphill to ridges where winds have blown it off the heather, but if yet lower moorland nearby has less or no snow they will fly there. Occasionally, packs of birds have been seen flying towards land with less snow, and many such records have been collated.[82] During the snowy winter of 1950/1, grouse deserted the upper glens of the Cairngorms for several months, gathering some 10km away on lower glens and near open woodland where less snow lay.[83] Movements in snow can occur between late October and April, but in most winters the snow is incomplete and birds remain in residence.

In late summer and autumn, willow ptarmigan often move to high ground where late-growing plants offer a nutritious bite.[84] In Scotland, many red grouse fly from high moorland to Alpine land in July–August, occasionally being seen at altitudes of up to 1,010m in September[85] and, infrequently, even at 1,040m in September–November on ground devoid of heather. Birds on lower moorland usually stay there, but sometimes they move up to 2km to abundant berries. Red grouse, blackgame and capercaillie formerly ate oats in fields and stack-yards, flying 1–2km to do so, but this stopped after farmers began using combine harvesters.

### Natal dispersal, philopatry, emigration and immigration

Natal dispersal is the movement of young birds from where they hatch to where they first breed. In all British grouse species it begins each autumn, when broods break up and youngsters separate from their mothers and from one another, and it gives youngsters a chance to move to less crowded land. Hens move further than cocks,[86] thereby reducing the adverse effects of inbreeding. Not all youngsters disperse far, and some – especially cocks – breed near where they hatched. This tendency, which is the opposite of natal dispersal, is known as philopatry.

Breeding dispersal is the movement of old birds between the places where they breed in one year and the next. In red grouse and Scottish ptarmigan, old birds tend to return in a later year to the same ground where they bred previously.[87] Being familiar with their old domains may help them breed successfully.

### Natal dispersal

In a study where gamekeepers on many moors ringed young red grouse, 739 were shot in their first shooting season, within a few weeks of being ringed.[88] Although grouse can be driven up to 5km for shooting,[89] only two birds had gone beyond that distance, during a period when most young are still with their parents. Of the 290 recovered in later seasons, however, 9 per cent had moved beyond 5km, one of them from Deeside to Drumochter, 42km west as the crow flies. In short, most movement occurred after the youngsters' first shooting season.

In most grouse species, two main periods of natal dispersal have been reported, in autumn and spring (*see* Chapter 14). Young red grouse and Scottish ptarmigan, however, have already taken territories by spring. Despite this, some desert their territories and move just before nesting, probably to breed elsewhere.[90] This movement is density dependent, occurring most commonly in years of high population density. In red grouse at Kerloch, it occurred mostly at densities above approximately a pair per hectare.[91] Such movement may include old red grouse (breeding dispersal), but evidence is very scanty.[92]

### Philopatry in red grouse

At Kerloch, where we marked hundreds of territorial birds and chicks, many young cocks in their first autumn took territories on or beside the territory of their father, uncle or brother, while most young hens settled further away. Related young and old territorial cock neighbours were less aggressive to one another than to strangers. As a result, clusters of closely related cocks formed, most noticeably during the years of a cyclic population increase. In years of peak and decline, young cocks tended to take territories further from their fathers, as aggression increased and numbers fell.[93] Studies since then, at Glas-choille and elsewhere, have increased understanding of philopatry, aided by new techniques of measuring relatedness that use DNA from feathers (*see* Chapter 14).

### Emigration and immigration

Natal dispersal and philopatry involve individuals, but their movements have consequences for whole populations, namely losses from emigration and gains from immigration. At Kerloch, summer emigration of red grouse with chicks was more frequent than spring emigration, and occurred especially during a big cyclic decline in numbers. Families usually left the study area once the chicks could fly well at three to four weeks, but in the mid-1970s, years of a very steep cyclic decline, pairs walked away southwards with day-old chicks. Adults returned in autumn without young, presumably having reared them elsewhere. A case of immigration occurred at Kerloch in the summer of 1971, years before the above decline, onto an area where we had boosted the amount and nutritive value of heather by applying fertiliser. Birds with chicks arrived from elsewhere and then stayed until their young were fully grown.[94]

To conclude, autumn dispersal of young is a normal event, but other movements also occur, notably at high densities and during cyclic declines in numbers.

## AVERAGE POPULATION DENSITIES

### Red grouse

Just as heather becomes scarcer in areas of wetter climate in Britain or Ireland, so too do red grouse.[95] In eastern Scotland and northern England, average densities in spring are tenfold or more higher than those in west Scotland and Ireland.

Muirburn, or the controlled burning of heathland and moorland, is commonly practised in Britain and Ireland with the aim of increasing grouse densities, and it works. That narrow fires lead to a rise in average grouse density has long been known.[96] Average densities and bags are related to the extent of heather, to the percentage of young heather after muirburn, and to the pattern of muirburn (higher densities follow narrow fires). In an experiment at Kerloch, a patchwork of narrow burnt strips increased the number of territorial grouse almost twofold three years later,[97] and similar treatment on a heather-dominated hill at Glenamoy boosted grouse numbers threefold.[98] When we repeated this on the Isle of Mull, the number of territorial cocks rose threefold on ground open to many sheep, and sevenfold where a fence excluded sheep.[99]

Average grouse density is also affected by bedrock, through its influence on soil fertility, provided that the rock is not overlain by thick peat or glacial deposits derived from different rock. An early finding in northeast Scotland, where most study areas were freely drained and had little or no thick peat, was that average densities over base-rich rock exceeded those over acidic granite.[100] Heather over base-rich rock had a higher content of the vital elements nitrogen and phosphorus than that over granite, and David Welch found more herb species, some of them indicators of fertile soil.

FIG 24. Moorland on Strathdon with heather-burning patchwork, conifer plantations, three self-sown Scots pines and arable fields. (Robert Moss)

In a later study where bedrock was graded on many English and Scottish moors, it made only a minor contribution to explaining average bags.[101] Thick peat covered large extents of the studied moors, however, thus negating a strong influence from bedrock. Another confusing factor is that cotton-grass shoots boost the birds' nutrition in spring, irrespective of bedrock. On freely drained moors in east Scotland and England, this rich food source does not occur on most territories, but it does abound on thick peat.

*Average bag sizes in England and Scotland*
English bags of red grouse tend to be bigger than Scottish ones, and counts confirm this. 'English moors tend to support more grouse per unit area than Scottish ones; limestone and other base-rich rocks occur widely and support more nutrient-rich food-plants. ... Many produce large bags of grouse from a sward management regime that would yield few grouse from the average Scottish moor over poorer rocks.'[102]

Other reasons also help to explain the superior English performance. Archaeologists know of widespread prehistoric cultivation of moorland,[103] and early agriculture boosted soil fertility for centuries, perhaps irreversibly (*see* Chapter 11).[104] Most English moorland has gentle slopes that are conducive to cultivation, which in the Middle Ages took place in the Pennines, Yorkshire Dales, North York Moors, Dartmoor, Exmoor and north Wales.[105] This would have improved soils beyond the capability of those derived naturally from the often poor local bedrock. Subsequently, peat would have swamped much of the improved soils on rainy western moorland, as in Mayo and Jura (*see* Chapter 11), but on less rainy eastern moors most ground remained freely drained, and improved soil fertility due to cultivation would have continued.

In addition, because summer temperatures decline northwards, most English moors are warmer than those in northeast Scotland, for example 1–2°C warmer in July. These warmer temperatures allowed cultivation of English moorland to higher altitudes than in more northerly areas, again contributing to the current greater fertility of much English moorland.

Although base-rich rocks underlie most English moorland, a large area lies above hard acidic millstone grit, which weathers into poor soils and yet supports some of the most productive grouse-moors. This may be because cotton-grass abounds on the peat that blankets much of this moorland, affording good food for grouse in spring. Also, precipitation and fog have transported pollutants from urban factories located near the north England moors, depositing compounds of nitrogen and phosphorus there.[106] This fertilising of heather could well have maintained abundant grouse even over poor bedrock.

Following on from this, we wonder whether recent grouse declines may be partly attributed to a reduction in old-style heavy industry. Nitrogenous compounds created through the combustion of fossil fuels and intensive production of livestock are still deposited on moorland, but the deposition of phosphorus compounds has fallen in conjunction with the decline in heavy industry. This may partly explain the smaller grouse bags shot in recent decades on some north England moors.[107]

A survey of red grouse on many English and Scottish moors revealed that the average bag increased with June air temperature and with estimates of heather production, and to a lesser extent with the presence of small burnt patches, a varied age of heather and the base richness of bedrock.[108] English moors have warmer summers than Scottish moors at the same altitude, and summers with warm Junes boost heather production. Hence one would expect big bags more often on English moors for this reason.

The same survey showed that there is a higher density of keepers (more per unit area) in England than in Scotland, and that a high density of keepers went along with bigger bags. Presumably this was due to the beneficial effects of keepers, rather than that more keepers were employed on areas that support bigger bags for other reasons.

### Willow ptarmigan

In the high Arctic, each estimate of density (see Table 6) covers only one or a few years, but estimates from different years, areas and observers are all low, so it is reasonable to conclude that average densities must be low. Densities in high-Arctic and Arctic Canada are particularly low, and are exceeded by densities in the same zones in Eurasia. This goes for rock ptarmigan in these two zones also, so we include data on them in the table for comparison.

Densities of willow ptarmigan are higher on Arctic tundra and subarctic terrain than in the high Arctic, but low in boreal woods and very low in Kazakhstan forest-steppe. Typical densities of 5–10 pairs per km² occur in Sweden and Norway.[109] Densities are low in the Swedish Highlands,[110] and most birds in southern Finland and the Baltic states live on forest bogs at densities lower than on treeless tundra. Densities on tundra and forest cannot be compared directly, however, because essentially the entire tundra is available as a habitat for the birds, but in forest only the edges of bogs or water bodies are occupied. Measurements of territory size would overcome this snag, but these data are not available in forest.

There is a low average density on the Avalon Peninsula in Newfoundland, and successively higher densities at Canada's Anderson River and Norway's Dovrefjell.[111] At British Columbia's Chilkat Pass, minimum and maximum figures indicate that the average density must be yet greater.

Burning of subalpine heath to increase willow ptarmigan densities, in emulation of muirburn for red grouse (see p.46), has been carried out at altitudes above 1,000m in south Norway. After fires were burned on 15 per cent of land in two areas, counts of territorial cock willow ptarmigan rose higher than on untouched areas, and remained so for a decade.[112] However, it was noted that little recovery of vegetation occurred after burning of lichen-dominated ground, and 'fires may cause semi-permanent damage if set in sensitive areas'. Burning cannot be recommended on subalpine heath, because of the risks of destroying the thin topsoil and seriously delaying vegetation recovery.

*On offshore islands*

Willow ptarmigan occur at higher densities on the small islands of Tranøy, Norway, and Brunette, Newfoundland, than on the nearby mainland, and on the Icelandic island of Hrisey the same has been found to be true for rock ptarmigan.[113] Because there are no foxes on Brunette or Tranøy, no stoats on Tranøy in most years, and on Hrisey no mammalian predators and very little egg-robbing by crows or ravens, the high bird densities might be attributed to the unusually few predators.

Other issues confuse the story, however. Cattle and then sheep damaged Tranøy's vegetation, and five successive years of the highest grouse densities followed the end of dairy farming as the vegetation recovered. More scrub grew on Brunette Island than on the mainland, where much of it had been destroyed by fires. Hrisey's vegetation was changing rapidly during the study, growing taller after sheep stocks had fallen, and to us the heath seemed less grazed than on the mainland. Hence in each case the predators and habitat were confounded. It seems likely that habitat quality on the islands exceeded that on nearby mainland, though deteriorating on Tranøy latterly. Also, owing to an island's relative isolation, movement between it and the mainland may be more constrained, which might increase island densities.[114]

The islands in these studies illustrate another snag, namely that biologists often choose areas with high population densities because this gives large samples for analysis. If islands are unusual, their results cannot be applied to the mainland, especially if the nearby mainland has no study area (as with Tranøy and Hrisey). We conclude that there might be an 'island effect' that causes high population densities, but if so the reasons are not clear.

### The effect of food abundance and habitat fragmentation

We attribute the very low densities of high-Arctic willow and rock ptarmigan to the scarcity of food plants and their low annual production (*see* Table 6), combined with a lack of tall vegetation as cover. Greater densities of birds in Eurasia compared with the equivalent zone in Canada fit this explanation. Likewise, higher population densities in the subarctic and yet higher densities on British moorland go hand in hand with a greater abundance of food plants. Vegetation on a very few areas has the opposite effect, as it grows too tall and dense for easy feeding, which thus accounts for low bird densities in forest. In Kazakhstan, we think that a lack of bogs and scarce food plants for chicks in the forest-steppe here are additional reasons for low densities.

Some particularly high densities of red grouse have been recorded (Table 8). At Kerloch, where an application of ammonium nitrate fertiliser increased the heather's growth and nutrient content, birds reached the highest density of pairs so far recorded. Apart from this artificial case, the greatest known density of pairs was on uppermost moorland at the Cairnwell. Because of the windy subalpine climate there, vegetation stays more or less unchanged without burning, forming a fine-grained patchwork of short heath for feeding and slightly taller heath for cover. Also, the soils are relatively fertile and so heath plants are nutritious.

**TABLE 8.** Some high and low spring densities (number per km$^2$) of red grouse.

| PLACE | COCKS | HENS | REFERENCE |
| --- | --- | --- | --- |
| Kerloch, Garrol Hill# | 206 | 94 | Watson et al., 1984a[115] |
|  | 156 | 175 | Watson et al., 1984a[115] |
| The Cairnwell | 179 | 129 | Watson, unpublished[116] |
| Meall Odhar Beag | 154 | 138 | Watson, unpublished |
| Balmoral, Allt na Giubhsaich | 123 | 101 | Watson, 1956[117] |
| Pitcarmick, Dounie# | 103 | 86 | Watson et al., 1977 |
| Glas-choille | 100 | — | MacColl et al., 2000 |
| Cairn Gorm, Speyside | 9.5 | 6.7 | Watson, 1979[118] |
| Ralia, Speyside | 3.2 | — | Hudson, 1992 |
| Forvie, trough in 1960 and 1961 | 2.8 | 2.2 | Jenkins et al., 1967 |
| Derry Cairngorm | 3–13 | 2–11 | Watson et al., 2000[119] |
| Glenamoy, Ireland | 1.9 | 1.6 | Watson & O'Hare, 1979a[120] |
| Isle of Mull, west Scotland | 1 | 1 | Watson et al., 1987 |
| Strath Shinary, Sutherland | 0 | 0 | [121] |

**Notes**

Brown & Watson (1964) gave other low densities of adults and full-grown young (e.g. on moorland valleys), including 2.3 near Tyndrum in Argyll and 1.3 in northwest Sutherland.

# Areas with fertiliser applied to heather.

FIG 25. Short, windswept heather on unburnt subalpine moorland at the Cairnwell, by the ski area car park. A few sheep grazed the area in late summer but had little effect on heather height. The dogs are pointing at a brood during a count of adults and chicks, used for measuring breeding success. (Adam Watson)

Fragmented habitat supports low average densities of red grouse. The same is true of American ruffed grouse, whose habitat was broken up by farmers into isolated or poorly connected patches.[122] Red grouse on isolated patches or promontories occur at lower density than those in the midst of uninterrupted moorland (see Chapter 9).

**Year-to-year fluctuations in density**
On any one area, the number of birds changes from year to year. These fluctuations can be studied from bags or counts. Bag records often cover many years, but they exaggerate the size of fluctuations and usually confuse adult density with breeding success. Bags fluctuate on some areas in fairly regular cycles, whereas on others they do not. In a study of bags on 289 moors, 63 per cent showed evidence of cycles, with an average period of about eight years.[123] The period rose from south to north, from about seven to about nine years.

It should not, however, be concluded from this that cycles or cycle periods are fixed characteristics of a given part of the country. On Deeside in Aberdeenshire, studies on individual estates reveal a more varied picture. Counts show a ten-year cycle on acidic upper moorland in the Cairngorms,[124] but erratic fluctuations on base-rich upper moorland at the Cairnwell. Further east there has been an eight-year cycle in bags at Invercauld,[125] no cycle in bags at Glen Tanar, and a seven- to eight-year cycle in counts and bags at Kerloch.[126] Bags can show different periods even on one moor, as at Rickarton, with a six-year period in the late 1800s and a ten-year one after 1945.[127]

In addition, long-term records sometimes show runs of clear cycles, interspersed with less regular fluctuations. Sometimes, cycles on an area stop altogether. The Finnish six-year cycle of hazel and black grouse and capercaillie in 1964–83 was so regular that a paper describing it carried the title 'The clockwork of Finnish tetraonid population dynamics',[128] yet it ceased soon after publication. Cycles also occasionally change in period length. During the first half of the 1900s, Finnish tetraonids (including willow ptarmigan) showed three- to four-year fluctuations, much shorter than the later six-year 'clockwork'.[129]

Willow ptarmigan show three- to four-year cycles in Norway and Sweden, best recorded by Svein Myrberget on Tranøy.[130] These are often associated with three- to four-year cycles of voles and lemmings.[131] In the alternative prey hypothesis (see Chapter 14), predators switch to eggs and chicks when their main rodent prey becomes scarce, so willow ptarmigan rear fewer young and a decline in their overall spring numbers follows.

Tranøy, however, supported no predators that specialised on rodents, save for stoats, which did take many eggs of willow ptarmigan in a few years, though they were absent in most. One out of six measured troughs in breeding success occurred a year before rodents crashed, which is not what would be expected from the alternative prey hypothesis. Also, two declines followed summers with low egg losses and an absence of stoats. At Lövhögen, Sweden, only three out of five measured troughs in breeding success coincided with rodent crashes, and one rodent crash coincided with a peak in the birds' breeding success. Hence losses as a result of prey switching were not necessary for poor breeding or subsequent declines.

Furthermore, winter loss of young was found to be the most important factor determining year-to-year change in spring numbers.[132] This was also the case in six other studies of *Lagopus lagopus* and rock ptarmigan that provide enough information to reach such conclusions. A lower percentage of young recruited to the breeding population was a main determinant of population decline.[133]

A wider geographical perspective is instructive here. Finnish voles and lemmings also show cycles at about three to four years, while Finnish hazel and black grouse and capercaillie do not, so the idea of prey switching falls down here. Willow ptarmigan on Newfoundland's Avalon Peninsula, at the Anderson River in Northwest Territories and at Chilkat Pass in British Columbia have fluctuations of 8–11 years, and at Kolyma in Siberia the population peaks about once per decade,[134] even though voles occur at all four areas and lemmings are also found at Anderson River and Kolyma. The three- to four-year cycles of Norwegian birds therefore seem unusual.

To conclude, a switch in prey by predators from rodents to eggs and chicks may be sufficient to cause some cyclic declines in Scandinavian willow ptarmigan, but not all. It may perhaps be sufficient to 'entrain' the fluctuations (influence their timing, as distinct from actually causing declines – *see* Chapter 14), but this has apparently not been studied. Switching cannot explain cycle periods other than those lasting three to four years.

The amplitude of a population fluctuation can be calculated by dividing the highest density by the lowest. Amplitudes from autumn counts (which include young) usually exceed those from spring counts. Big spring amplitudes for a single fluctuation were about 14-fold on Brunette Island for willow ptarmigan and at Forvie for red grouse. However, amplitudes of less than twofold occur, e.g. only 1.6 at Corndavon, and we regarded a fivefold fluctuation at Kerloch as large.[135]

Even within one moor, the timing of fluctuations can vary on different parts. On Kerloch, changes in the density of red grouse between 1962 and 1978 began on high ground next to continuous moorland and furthest from farmland and woodland, and then spread downhill until the lowest ground showed a similar decline.[136] This 'travelling wave' moved downhill at 2–3km per year, and we presume that it involved a change in grouse behaviour in response to high density. This is the only documented case of a travelling wave in British grouse species, but similar waves have been found in field voles at Kielder and in Canadian snowshoe hares. Probably they are often overlooked.

### Long-term declines

British bags of red grouse show a long-term decline in most regions,[137] and Irish bags show an even bigger decline.[138] Bags in the Outer Hebrides dropped after 1916, and fell to almost to zero after 1940.[139] In western Ireland, relatively big bags before 1914 fell after 1918, shooters bagged few birds in the early 1930s, and sport shooting almost collapsed after 1945.[140] Long-term declines further east in Scotland and England began later, with a big fall in the 1940s.[141] The changes from west to east bring to mind the possibility of a large-scale travelling wave in grouse density.

Very deep declines of red grouse in Britain and Ireland in the 1940s occurred also in Scottish bags of ptarmigan, blackgame and capercaillie.[142] Ptarmigan numbers in the Cairngorms dropped very low in the mid-1940s, as did numbers of red grouse on high moorland there.[143] Finnish bags of willow ptarmigan, blackgame and capercaillie also fell to unusually deep troughs in the 1940s, and in northern European Russia there were widespread declines in these species and in rock ptarmigan around 1939, and very low troughs in the early 1940s.[144] Therefore, management peculiar to Britain or Ireland cannot explain the size of declines or the depth of troughs over such a huge area, and a wider factor such as climate must have been involved.

In the decade after 1945, bags of red grouse did recover on some British moors, and numbers of red grouse and ptarmigan rose in the Cairngorms. Bags of Finnish blackgame and capercaillie recovered partly, though not until the 1960s, and then declined after the 1970s. This pattern resembled the particularly high numbers of red grouse and ptarmigan in northeast Scotland around 1970 followed by big declines in the mid- and late 1970s. However, bags of red grouse in many parts of Ireland and Britain failed to recover to former heights, despite partial recovery in the 1960s and 1970s. Hence big declines and deep lows were general occurrences but recoveries were not.

Failures to recover might be attributed to habitat becoming less suitable or fragmented, or to more predators, but this is not the whole story. Any attempt to explain population declines in the 1970s by confining attention to local management in Britain or Ireland would be insufficient. To illustrate a wider approach, consider bags of red grouse in northwest Scotland and willow ptarmigan in southeast Norway (Fig. 26). In 1900–85, bags of each rose and fell remarkably closely, both declining from an initial high density.[145] Scottish and Norwegian birds are subject to different climate, food, habitat, disease, parasites, predators and management. Hence the similar long-term downward trend may involve a global factor such as climatic change or pollution, affecting both countries. Therefore, wider changes can override local ones such as keeper numbers or other land management factors. It does not follow that management is unimportant – far from it – but wider issues provide us with a better understanding.

On some moors that formerly provided big bags, fewer keepers have undoubtedly resulted in poorer muirburn, less killing of foxes and crows, insufficient control of browsing, fewer grouse and smaller bags.[146] Even where keeper numbers and standards of management have not fallen, however, bags have fallen on many moors. Pessimistic attitudes and insufficient shooting effort are often to blame (*see* Chapter 15).

In contrast to the overall pattern, long-term declines did not occur on a few Scottish and English moors. If widespread climatic change caused general decline, as suggested above, management of such moors must have improved. This involves good muirburn, effective control of grazing and of foxes and crows, and reliable counts of grouse, along with rational policies for shooting. On a few moors where there had been long-term declines, such new management led to increased bags in the late 1980s and early 1990s.[147]

FIG 26. Bags of willow ptarmigan shot in southeast Norway and of red grouse in northwest Scotland in 1900–85. The data points are five-year centred averages, from 'Rypa' estate in Norway (61.5°N, 10.5°E) from Hjeljord & Kiær (1991), and means from areas 1, 2 and 3 from Hudson (1992).

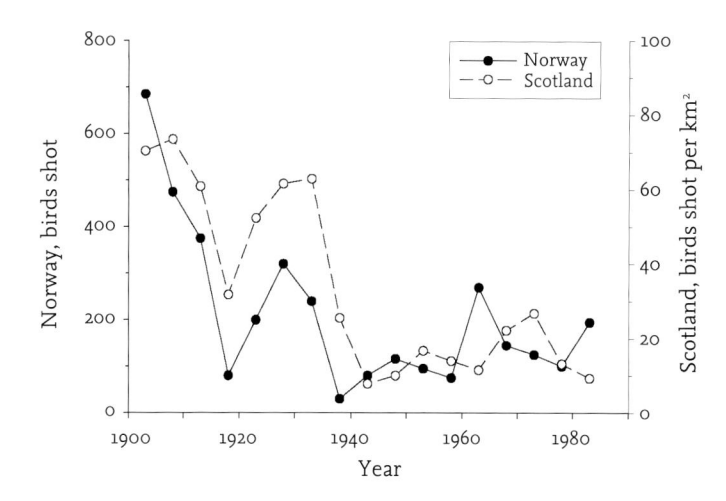

## SURVIVAL

Most estimates of annual survival rates in *Lagopus lagopus* rely on finding which adults that have been marked on a study area return to it the following year. Because this assumes that adults do not move to settle outside the area under study, such estimates of survival are minima, more properly termed 'return rates'. Adult survival rates and return rates are the same if breeding dispersal is negligible, but differ if it is not.[148] Survival can also be calculated from counts of unmarked birds, but these estimates can be biased if the overwinter survival of yearlings differs from that of old birds.[149] Survival often varies widely on a given area from year to year; Table 9 gives averaged values.

TABLE 9. Mean annual return-rate of marked adult *Lagopus lagopus*.

| PLACE | SHOOTING | COCKS | HENS | BOTH COMBINED | REFERENCE |
|---|---|---|---|---|---|
| Glen Esk | Heavy | — | — | 33 | Jenkins et al., 1963 |
| Scotland | Heavy | — | — | 35 | Jenkins et al., 1967 |
| England | Heavy | — | — | 34 | Hudson, 1986a |
| Kerloch | Almost none | 43 | 24 | 33 | Moss & Watson, 1991 |
| Churchill | Light | 57 | 39 | 48 | Martin, 1991 |
| Chilkat Pass | Light | 42 | 46 | 44 | Mossop, 1988 |
|  | Light | 53 | 44 | 48 | Hannon et al., 2003[150] |
| Tranøy | Fairly heavy | — | — | 50 | Steen & Erikstad, 1996 |

Adult willow ptarmigan in North America and Scandinavia seem to survive better than red grouse. It follows that, given similar breeding success, willow ptarmigan in their first winter must survive worse than red grouse in theirs. Perhaps experience confers more advantage in the land of willow ptarmigan than on British grouse-moors.

Cock *Lagopus lagopus* generally survive better than hens. This tallies with many counts showing more cocks than hens in spring, and with the generalisation that cocks survive better than hens in most grouse species.[151] Measured survival does not decline with age. Also, the average survival of red grouse – adult cocks and hens combined – appears to be the same (33–35 per cent), irrespective of shooting.

Because survival in *Lagopus lagopus* does not appear to decline with age, it does not follow that birds are potentially immortal. Rather, most birds die before they reach their physiological age limit. An indication of this limit is given by the longest-lived individuals. A hen red grouse that had been tagged as an adult on an English moor in spring 1980 produced a brood in each of the next five summers until she was shot in November 1984 when at least five years old.[152] A red grouse was recorded alive in its eighth year in a national ringing scheme, and two cocks at Kerloch lived into their seventh year and a third cock into his eighth.[153] At Glas-choille, an eight-year-old cock that had hatched in 1994 was still territorial in spring 2003. A willow ptarmigan in its ninth year occurred in Norway, and a nine-year-old cock willow ptarmigan and an eight-year-old hen were recorded at Chilkat Pass, British Columbia.[154]

### NUMBER OF HENS PAIRED WITH COCKS

Most territorial cock *Lagopus lagopus* pair with a hen each, a few have two hens, and a few remain unmated. In Canada and Scandinavia, where abundant willow offers nutritious food, most cocks are mated. On British and Irish moors, however, where burning and overgrazing destroy almost all willow, many unmated cocks occur, especially over poor soils. Spring counts of willow ptarmigan on British Columbia's Chilkat Pass, Newfoundland's Avalon Peninsula and the Norwegian island of Tranøy show only a small excess of cocks, far less than in most years on infertile Scottish moors.[155] In years of peak density and decline on infertile soils over granite in Scotland, up to half the territorial cock red grouse are unmated, and occasionally more.[156] On fertile moorland soils, however, or where cotton-grass affords a rich spring diet, we see a higher percentage of mated cocks.

A big excess of territorial hen red grouse has been found only in experiments. One case followed the removal of all territorial cocks in autumn,[157] and another a boost by fertiliser to the heather's production and nutrient content. When Susan Hannon removed territorial cock willow ptarmigan in spring at Chilkat Pass, she also found more hens than cocks subsequently.[158]

We conclude that the sex ratio of territorial red grouse in spring is usually fairly even, but that a large male excess tends to occur on poor soils, especially in years when densities are high or declining. A hen excess can occur after cocks are removed, and after fertiliser has boosted nutrition.

## DATE OF EGG-LAYING

Lengthening days stimulate gonad development, but the day length required for hens to lay varies with local climate.[159] Willow ptarmigan at 69°N in Arctic Canada or Arctic mainland European Russia lay their first eggs in early June, under continuous daylight. On the colder, snowier Kolguyev Island, also at 69°N, they do not lay until late June, and in the even snowier Canadian high Arctic they do not lay until the end of June or even into July. Hens at 69°N in north Norway lay three to four weeks earlier than hens at the same latitude in far snowier Arctic Canada.

At 57°N, red grouse on coastal moors near Aberdeen begin laying in early or mid-April, three weeks before hens at 70°N in north Norway. In Glen Esk, inland from Aberdeen at an altitude of 200–300m, they lay at the end of April, while on nearby hills 300m higher they lay a week later.

When captive Scottish hens from 57°N and Norwegian hens from 70°N were given artificially longer days by electric light, Scottish hens laid their first eggs when the photoperiod reached 15 hours, Norwegian hens did not lay until it reached 19 hours, and hybrids were intermediate at 17 hours.[160] Hence inherent factors determined their responses. In conclusion, different populations use increasing day length in such a way that their response fits the average local climate.

On any one area, hens lay earlier in mild springs than in cold ones, in tune with the earlier growth of food plants.[161] Some individuals also lay earlier than others nearby, e.g. heavy hens lay early on the Norwegian island of Tranøy and at Chilkat Pass, British Columbia.[162] In red grouse at Kerloch, the spread was approximately three weeks in any one year, and about 80 per cent of clutches hatched within two weeks around the median date.[163] Individual hens that were early in one year tended to be early in the next, suggesting that some are inherently early.

## NESTS AND INCUBATION

Hens nest in their first summer and normally every hen nests.[164] A hen that seems not to be nesting may have deserted her nest or lost it to a predator. We know of only two individuals that we think did not nest, both of which were in poor condition and carrying many worms.[165]

The hen chooses the nest site, which in red grouse is usually in vegetation that is taller than average for the area and typically beside an open patch where she can easily escape.[166] Some choose differently, such as willow ptarmigan beside driftwood logs on Pacific beaches adjacent to forest.[167] One hen at Kerloch made

FIG 27. Hen red grouse on nest, well hidden and camouflaged in tall heather. (Adam Watson)

an extraordinary, easily seen nest on a deep, wide patch of oat straw that had been left as cattle food.[168] At Kerloch and Spyhill, where few foxes occurred during our studies, several hens nested on recently burnt patches or in tufts of partly burnt heather, but we saw no such open and easily seen nest at the fox-ridden Rickarton.

When leaving the nest after laying, a hen usually covers her eggs with plant litter, which hides them and reduces their cooling in frost, although incubating hens generally leave eggs uncovered when leaving.[169] Eggs can fail to hatch if they freeze before incubation starts,[170] but frosts down to −3.5°C did not prevent subsequent hatching in Arctic Russia.[171] Incubated eggs do not freeze when hens leave to feed, because warm eggs in an insulated, sheltered nest cool slowly.

During snowfalls before incubation, occasionally a Scottish hen cannot find her nest and lays an egg on the snow,[172] and later it can be seen lying on the ground. Heavy snowfalls during incubation can have worse effects, forcing some Swedish and Scottish hens to desert their nests.[173]

Hens incubate their eggs for about three weeks.[174] In northern Russia, Finland and Norway, they spend about 95 per cent of the 24 hours of each day incubating, with three to four trips per day off the nest, averaging about 20 minutes each. In comparison, red grouse at Kerloch were off the nest two to three times per day.[175] Disturbed hens that leave the nest quickly may knock a few eggs out for a distance of 10–20cm, but will retrieve them on return. Even when Russian ornithologists rolled four to seven eggs for 5–20cm out and lightly covered them with grass, all eggs were back in the nest later.[176] After a hen has left her nest, she voids a 'clocker' (broody) dropping about 30–50cm long and 30cm across, usually some distance away. As in incubating fowls, clocker droppings are the result of storing faeces in the large intestine. Hen grouse do not void in their nests, except during prolonged hatching or in very bad weather when they delay departure with their chicks.

In an average 7 per cent of nests at Glen Esk, eggs were lost to predators, this figure rising to 11 per cent at Kerloch, and to 31 per cent at Glenamoy.[177] More crows and foxes occurred at Kerloch than at Glen Esk, and yet more at Glenamoy. In two Norwegian studies, 15 and 17 per cent of nests failed because of egg predators, and in the first study predators also took 5 per cent of incubating hens.[178]

CLUTCH SIZE

Like poultry, captive *Lagopus lagopus* continue to lay many eggs beyond the normal clutch size if they are removed daily. It has been suggested that hen bantams observe the clutch and thereby determine the number of eggs still to be laid, and that this might also apply to wild grouse.[179] However, when we removed some eggs from nests of wild red grouse, the hens did not lay extra eggs beyond the typical clutch size, even though they saw a smaller number of eggs than usual.[180] They finally incubated two to four eggs when the mean clutch-size was seven to eight, and willow ptarmigan act similarly.[181]

Clutch size shows no clear relation with latitude in North America[182] or Eurasia (Table 10). Within Britain, the mean in different studies varies from 7.4 eggs at Glen Esk to 9.4 on Strathmore. We think that this is related to the nutrition of laying hens, clutches being bigger on peatland where many cotton-grass shoots are available or where freely drained fertile soils support nutritious food plants. Strathmore consists chiefly of blanket bog with much cotton-grass, and lies on millstone grit with some outcrops of limestone. Cotton-grass was uncommon at Glen Esk, and abundant sheep, along with mountain hares and red deer, ate most of the first shoots.[183]

The average clutch size of *Lagopus lagopus* differs from year to year on a given area, and is bigger in years when hens lay early.[184] Also, heavy hens lay larger clutches.[185] The link is that early plant growth offers prime feeding, whereas later growth becomes fibrous, with less protein, phosphorus and energy. Thus, the early melting of snow and consequent good nutrition influence the weight and clutch size of hens in Arctic Russia.[186] The effect of spring food on clutch size works via the condition of laying hens. For example,

TABLE 10. Clutch size of Lagopus lagopus at different latitudes in Eurasia.

| COUNTRY | PLACE | LATITUDE (°N) | MEAN CLUTCH | ANNUAL MEANS | REFERENCE |
|---|---|---|---|---|---|
| Russia | Low Kolyma | 69 | 10.1 | 8.1–11.4 | Andreev, 1988a |
| Norway | Tranøy | 69 | 10.1 | 8.0–12.2 | Myrberget, 1988 |
| Russia | Yamal | 68 | 8.2 | — | Dunaeva & Kucheruk, 1941 |
| | Timansk | 68 | 11.3 | — | Mikheev, 1948 |
| | Laplandskiy | 68 | 8.0 | — | Semenov-Tyan-Shanskiy, 1960 |
| | Bolshezemelskaia | 67 | 7.9 | 6.1–10.9 | Voronin, 1991 |
| Norway | Dovrefjell | 62 | 10.0 | 8.8–10.5 | Erikstad et al., 1985 |
| Scotland | Glen Esk, high | 57 | 6.6 | 5.3–7.3 | Jenkins et al., 1963 |
| | Glen Esk, low | 57 | 7.4 | 6.1–8.1 | Jenkins et al., 1963 |
| | Kerloch | 57 | 7.5 | 6.4–8.1 | Jenkins et al., 1967 |
| | Rickarton | 57 | 8.4 | 7.7–9.5 | Moss et al., 1996 |
| | Speyside | 57 | 8.8 | — | Adam Smith, pers. comm., 2006 |
| England | Strathmore | 55 | 9.4 | — | Newborn & Foster, 2002 |
| Ireland | Glenamoy | 54 | 6.7 | 6.2–7.3 | Lance, 1972 |
| Kazakhstan | Naurzumskiy | 52 | 11.1 | — | Ulianin, 1939 |

hens at Glen Esk laid on average 6.1 eggs in 1959, a year when 14 per cent of adults died in poor condition and contained many threadworms, after heather suffered severe browning. The average clutch size rose to 8.1 in 1960, when only 2 per cent of adults died in poor condition and contained few worms, after hardly any browning.

Individual hen red grouse that lay early on a given area and within a given year tend to lay bigger clutches than late layers.[187] On the Norwegian island of Tranøy, early laying willow ptarmigan tended to outweigh late-laying ones.[188] Also, hens weighing less than 475g laid on average 7.5 eggs, compared with 10.7 eggs by hens weighing over 625g.[189]

A hen that loses her first clutch often lays a repeat, this having three to four fewer eggs. Hens that have lost chicks do not usually re-lay, but there is fairly good evidence of a hen red grouse re-laying after losing her first brood when the chicks were about a week old.[190] Occasionally, hen red grouse and willow ptarmigan renest twice or, rarely, thrice.[191] Renesting results in a late brood, which in Scotland is often a month behind. Aged only six to seven weeks at the start of the shooting season on 12 August, these grouse 'cheepers' call loudly when flushed, and they seldom reach the butts in a drive. On the Norwegian island of Karlsøy, where willow ptarmigan lost 27 per cent of their first clutches, renesting compensated in the short run for 45 per cent of lost eggs, and chicks survived up to four weeks as well from renesting as from first nests.[192] In Canada, however, a smaller percentage of birds raised from renesting returned in the following year. Also, youngsters from renest broods cope less well with the coarse winter diet.[193]

## BREEDING SUCCESS

Breeding success is the number of chicks reared per adult or per hen, including hens with no chicks. It comprises the number of young reared per successful hen (called brood size), multiplied by the proportion of hens that rear chicks. At Glen Esk, for instance, 83–95 per cent of hens raised young in three years of good breeding, but almost half failed in two years of poor breeding.[194]

Table 11 shows some examples of breeding success. Clutch size, hatching success and nest loss all affect breeding success, with nest robbing by predators particularly severe in some years.[195] In studies of red grouse and Scottish ptarmigan, however, chick loss had far more influence in most years, occurring mainly in the first few days after hatching. The viability of hatchlings determines their survival in the first week – even in captivity, where they have continuous food, water, heat and shelter. Their viability depends on egg quality, which in turn depends on the hen's condition and diet. In Sweden, Rolf Brittas found that mild springs led to early plant growth with nutritious food, which boosted the fat reserves of hen willow ptarmigan and led to good survival of chicks.[196]

**TABLE 11.** Number of young *Lagopus lagopus* reared per adult, and mean number of young reared per brood, approximately in order from north to south.

| COUNTRY | PLACE | YOUNG PER ADULT | YOUNG PER HEN | BROOD SIZE | REFERENCE |
|---|---|---|---|---|---|
| Norway | Karlsøy | — | 7.8 | 8.5 | Parker, 1984, 1985 |
|  | Tranøy | 1.4 | 2.8 | — | Myrberget, 1984b |
| Russia | Timansk | — | c. 7 | — | Dementiev & Gladkov, 1952 |
|  | Low Kolyma | 2.8 | — | 7.1 | Andreev, 1988a |
| Canada | Anderson River | — | — | 6.7 | Hannon & Barry, 1986 |
| Sweden | Highlands | — | 2.5 | 3.7 | Smith & Willebrand, 1999 |
| Norway | Dovrefjell | — | 2.6# | — | Pedersen, 1984 |
| Canada | Chilkat Pass | — | — | 4.9# | Hannon & Smith, 1984 |
| Scotland | Glen Esk, low | 1.5 | 3.2 | 4.4 | Jenkins et al., 1963 |
|  | Glen Esk, high | 1.5 | 3.2 | 4.2 | Jenkins et al., 1963 |
|  | Kerloch | 1.2 | — | — | Jenkins et al., 1967 |
|  | The Cairnwell | 1.8 | — | — | Watson, 1979 |
|  | Priestlaw | — | 6.4 | — | Phillips, 1994, 1999 |
|  | Misty Law | — | 6.1 | — | Phillips, 1994, 1999 |
| England | Strathmore | 1.6 | 3.5 | — | Newborn & Foster, 2002 |
| Ireland | Glenamoy | 0.8 | 1.7 | 2.9 | Watson & O'Hare, 1979a |
| Canada | Avalon | — | 6.6 | — | Bergerud, 1970a |

**Notes**

Some data are not strictly comparable because in a few cases counts were carried out long before young were reared – as early as two to four weeks on Norwegian areas, the Anderson River and the Chilkat Pass. Only on British and Irish areas were young counted when fully grown.

# Mean of all broods in three years, not mean of annual means as in other rows.

The quality of food for laying hens on British and Irish moorland has declined in the last few centuries, because sheep, cattle and red deer, along with muirburn, have almost eliminated willow and birch scrub, and the animals also feed heavily on other nutritious food such as cotton-grass shoots. For example, grouse breed poorly at Glenamoy, where heather on thick peat has a low content of phosphorus. In spring, freshly growing cotton-grass shoots abound and grouse eat them avidly, but intense competition from sheep and cattle leaves them very little.[197] If moorland is not overgrazed, however, very good breeding has been recorded where freely drained soils are fertile and wet peaty ground supports cotton-grass, e.g. Priestlaw and Misty Law.[198]

In red grouse and willow ptarmigan, predators, parasites and disease can reduce breeding success (see 'Enemies', below, and Chapter 13). Conversely, strong parental care, plenty of high-quality chick food and good weather can increase it.[199] In a study of willow ptarmigan at Tranøy, Norway, and Lövhögen, Sweden, eggs robbed by predators accounted for much of the year-to-year variation in breeding success, while weather before hatching explained less of it (warm weather was positively related to breeding success, and rainfall was negatively related to it). Weather after hatching seemed less important.

When Howard Parker removed crows, ravens and magpies from half of the Norwegian island of Karlsøy, willow ptarmigan bred no better and their densities in the next spring were no higher than on the half without removals.[200] This occurred because stoats took a bigger percentage of nests on the half where he had done the removals, thus compensating for the absence of avian predators.

Average breeding success is often not associated with the average population density of breeding birds. In northeast Scotland, for example, high densities of red grouse often go along with poor or average breeding success, especially on infertile soils. On some peaty Scottish moorland, however, low densities often go along with big broods. Average population density is related to the amount of food and cover on an area, whereas breeding success depends largely on the quality of food for hens in spring and subsequently for their chicks. The two do not necessarily go together. The best average breeding success recorded has been from birds at low density but with high-quality food in spring, examples including red grouse at Priestlaw and Misty Law, and willow ptarmigan at Timansk, Karlsøy and Avalon (see Table 11).

ENEMIES

In Britain, man has created grouse-moors from forest, thereby benefiting red grouse. Man is also an enemy of grouse through hunting them, killing birds on

**FIG 28.** Red grouse dead on wire. (Adam Watson)

wires,[201] by vehicles and in snares, destroying their habitat, polluting the environment and changing the climate. In North America and Eurasia, willow ptarmigan suffer from a wide array of predators, e.g. about 20 species take American adults or chicks.[202] Fewer predator species live in Britain and Ireland than on Continental Europe, partly because man has extirpated the brown bear, wolf, lynx, sea eagle and goshawk, and exterminated red kites, polecats and pine martens on most land. On grouse-moors, gamekeepers kill most extant predators, and so some species are usually absent as breeders, such as golden eagles and hen harriers.

Unnaturally, many foxes and crows have become the main predators in Britain and Ireland, after man extirpated bigger predators that kill or compete with them (*see* Chapter 13). Man also created extra food for them, in the form of carcasses from overstocked sheep and red deer, waste food in rubbish dumps and tourist scraps, invertebrates on fields, road-kills, and animals killed by wires.

Foxes, wildcats, stoats and pine martens kill adult grouse, and along with weasels, crows, ravens and gulls they also take eggs and chicks. Hen harriers kill adults and chicks, as do golden and sea eagles, peregrines, sparrowhawks, goshawks and buzzards. Short-eared owls occasionally kill chicks, and we have known a hedgehog to raid a nest to eat a few eggs. The set of predators and prey that we now have is so human-influenced that their interactions are unpredictable and perhaps unprecedented.

Several parasite species live on and in *Lagopus lagopus*, and in some years threadworms kill many adult red grouse and result in poor breeding by others (*see* Chapter 13). The tick-borne louping-ill virus can cause catastrophic mortality of adults and chicks. Though still localised, it has spread since 1980 to more moors and to higher altitude, and threatens grouse shooting. It has unleashed controversies over high densities of deer as tick hosts, and the large-scale culling of mountain hares as carriers of the virus.

## THE FUTURE

Most willow ptarmigan live on such remote land that their outlook should be bright in the near future, though man-induced pollution and climate change may alter this. Birds in the south of the range, however, have declined through the loss, deterioration and fragmentation of habitat by farming and forestry. In addition, red grouse have decreased owing to poor burning, and to overgrazing by red deer. Their abundance in years to come will depend largely on the future of heather moorland and whether it is maintained as grouse-moor or put to other use.

## SUMMARY

The willow ptarmigan has the biggest range of any grouse, covering a vast area of tundra, scrub, open woodland and moorland. Numbers tend to fluctuate in cycles, whose period varies from three or four to about ten years. Red grouse, a subspecies of willow ptarmigan, are resident on moorland and do not turn white in winter. They reach high density on moors with a patchwork of short heather as food, beside tall heather as cover. Burning can produce this mosaic, but on the highest moorland a suitable mosaic occurs naturally because the windy climate keeps vegetation fairly short. Densities of willow ptarmigan are very low in the high Arctic and Kazakhstan, where food plants are sparse. Birds lay large clutches of eggs and rear large broods on land with nutritious food for laying hens. The best breeding so far recorded involved birds at low density with access to food of high quality.

CHAPTER 4

# Ptarmigan

THE PTARMIGAN IS THE world's most polar bird, living over vast areas at or near sea-level in the Arctic. Rocks and ptarmigan usually go together, and North Americans call the bird rock ptarmigan, a usage that has spread. A Scottish writer in the early 1700s noted, 'that fine bird called the Mountain Partridge, or by the commonalty Tarmachan … makes its protection in the chinks and hollow places of thick stones from the insults of the eagles'.[1] Here we describe its habits and report its distribution, habitat and adaptations to cold. We summarise many studies on the populations, nests and breeding success of this grouse species.

Ptarmigan nest on northernmost Canada, Greenland, Svalbard and Russia. In winter they remain in all but the most northerly parts, and live year-round in Svalbard despite midwinter darkness at noon. Birds wintering in the Arctic live in regions with mean January air temperatures down to −35°C. Willow ptarmigan in subarctic Siberia winter at even lower mean January air temperatures of −45°C, but this is in sheltered valleys with far less wind-chill than on the windswept reaches frequented by rock ptarmigan. The latter also thrive on southern mountains such as the Alps. Our high Scottish hills are home to large numbers of the species, the only birds resident at all seasons in this wildest part of Britain.

The high Scottish hills also attract many human visitors, but even expert mountaineers must take care here when navigating in a whiteout or scaling steep snow or ice, and in a snowstorm must take shelter or risk hypothermia and death. To study Scottish ptarmigan in winter and spring, one must be a mountaineer and skier, but nobody can remotely match the ptarmigan's intimate knowledge of its home terrain, or its hardiness and superb ability to thrive in this extreme environment.

Also to be admired is the ptarmigan's plumage.[2] Soft feathers reach to its toenails and cover its nostrils, so it loses little heat on cold days. The plumage alters from spring to summer and from summer to autumn, the richly variegated grey, brown, white and black blending with rocks and plants to conceal the bird. Its white winter dress contrasts with its dark eyes and black bill and tail-quills, the last appearing only in flight. When a snow-white cock and hen pair on a sunny spring morning, one hears them answering each other from far away. His rattling croaks and her weird coos echo across the snowy slopes. Amid gleaming silvery light on the snow and patches of brilliant green plants freed from winter's grip, these birds are the first spring voice of the heights of Scotland.

## THE BIRD

### Dimensions

The Scottish ptarmigan is the smallest of British grouse, slightly shorter than a wood-pigeon, with cocks about 5 per cent longer than hens.[3] Scottish cocks have an average wing length of 198mm, while Svalbard cocks – the largest race – have an average of 230mm.

Scottish cocks weigh 500–550g, and are heaviest in March and lightest in April–June. Cocks exceed hens in weight in every month except in spring. At this time, hens fatten and increase their breast muscles in preparation for breeding, while cocks are busy with territorial activity and lose weight. Hens in May attain 625g, easily surpassing the cocks' 500g. By June, however, cocks still weigh 500g but hens are down to 470g, signifying the toll of incubating for three weeks with only brief trips to feed.

Rock ptarmigan are about 10 per cent smaller than *Lagopus lagopus* in the same region, and they have narrower wings, a slighter build and a more dove-like silhouette. Even so, the bigger races weigh more than small races of willow ptarmigan in other regions. For instance, rock ptarmigan of Alaska's Amchitka Island outweigh the willow ptarmigan of central Alaska.[4]

The ptarmigan's wings and tail are long relative to its body size, enabling it to fly fast when chased by raptors and making it the fastest of British grouse. The birds also make split-second turns into rocks, which is a useful habit as raptors avoid flying quickly beside rocks for fear of injury. Ptarmigan sail adeptly on turbulent currents. Seton Gordon considered them superior in flight power to red grouse, for 'they can wing their way up a steep hill face at a surprising speed',[5] and are 'remarkably strong fliers, possibly the strongest of all grouse'.[6]

When flushed, ptarmigan seldom fly far up or down a steep slope, but traverse round at similar altitude, often to return shortly after. However, they readily shoot up or down cliffs to escape a chasing eagle, a demanding tactic that may be aided by their large hearts.

Birds in interior Alaska are small, weighing only about 425g in winter,[7] and the smallest Siberian birds also live in the interior of that region.[8] Small birds typify regions with very cold winters and deep undrifted snow, where they keep warm by burrowing (see Fig. 12). On oceanic Amchitka Island, where frequent gales blow the ephemeral snow, birds in winter weigh about 575g.[9] The heaviest ptarmigan live on windy Svalbard. These birds avoid the risk of migrating over the Arctic Ocean to Norway, and instead remain resident through the midwinter darkness[10] and survive by laying down fat reserves in autumn (see 'Metabolism', p.86).

The rock ptarmigan has the largest heart of the grouse family as a percentage of its body weight; the willow ptarmigan's is smaller and the white-tailed ptarmigan's smaller still, even though the latter live at higher elevations.[11] Perhaps the rock ptarmigan's large heart evolved because the birds are such strong fliers. This would have helped them colonise distant islands such as Iceland or Japan, which have no *Lagopus lagopus*.

### Plumage

The only British bird to grow a white winter dress, the ptarmigan has three plumages, each attained by a partial moult of the old and growth of the new. In all seasons, it has white wings. Viewed from the front, during the moult from winter to summer, cocks show a broken dark frontal necklace in display to hens or other cocks (see Fig. 5). Scottish cocks in full summer plumage have greyish backs, their dark heads, necks and breasts contrasting with a few white feathers remaining from the winter. A gorgeous pale golden yellow is the hen's summer dress, her feathers heavily marked by bars of black and white, a varied pattern that provides superb camouflage when she sits on her nest or chicks. Both cock and hen in autumn are silvery grey and are more alike, the hen slightly paler and with more of a salt and pepper appearance (see Chapter 10).

Within the white winter dress, many Scottish birds show a few dark feathers on the back and head. Cocks also have a wide black bar running from the hind end of the black bill past the dark eye, whereas hens lack this or show rudimentary black spots.[12]

### Eggs and chicks

Oval in shape, the ptarmigan's eggs (see Fig. 13) resemble those of red grouse except that they are smaller, with a paler ground colour and markings that are

**FIG 29.** Scottish ptarmigan in winter plumage. (Top) The cock's throat swells and vibrates as he calls threateningly (known as 'ground beck'; *see* Chapter 7). (Bottom) The hen is giving the same call in her higher pitch. (Derek McGinn)

FIG 30. Autumn ptarmigan, Scotland. (Adam Watson, AW's eponymous father)

FIG 31. Scottish ptarmigan cock moulting from winter to summer plumage, with the frontal necklace beginning to develop. (Derek McGinn)

**FIG 32.** Scottish ptarmigan cocks in summer plumage, with combs raised (top) and giving ground beck (bottom). (Derek McGinn)

FIG 33. Scottish hen ptarmigan in summer plumage. (Derek McGinn)

FIG 34. Scottish juvenile hen ptarmigan in autumn. (Derek McGinn)

less reddish. Though they are paler than their surroundings, the eggs have a contrasting dark and light pattern that camouflages them well, making them difficult for even experienced observers to spot. As in the other three British grouse, hatching takes about a day.

Day-old chicks can climb steep rocks and run over boulders better than *Lagopus lagopus* of the same age. When suddenly disturbed on steep ground, they escape by rolling like balls down vegetation and rocks without harm, and quickly pop down holes among boulders until the hen calls them out after danger has passed. Day-old chicks can easily swim if they fall into water, and older chicks swim strongly.[13]

Soft down covers day-old chicks to their toenails. They grow quickly,[14] reaching full size slightly more rapidly than *Lagopus lagopus*. Scottish poults at ten weeks are hard to tell from adults in the field, although they have a more pointed tail and traces of down on the belly, and occasionally give thin cheeping calls when out of sight of their mother. By 12 weeks they look as big as adults, but can still be told in the field by the narrower bands of pale pigment on their flank feathers. The presence of a partly dark, wide-barred inner secondary or upper covert signifies a young bird, and sometimes it falls off as the bird takes wing. Poults attain adult weight by the end of October.[15] In his book of paintings, Keith Brockie illustrates a fine series of ptarmigan, from a day old to fully grown.[16]

## CAMOUFLAGE

Ptarmigan stay motionless so effectively that hikers often pass birds without seeing them sitting a few metres from their boots. In autumn they can be shot easily on some warm days, though they are wilder than red grouse in late-autumn gales or rain. They are at their wildest when in white or partly white dress on snow-free ground, when they are conspicuous even at 1km. In such conditions they spend much time resting beside rocks or at remnant snowdrifts, which they frequent 'throughout the day, venturing off only a short distance to feed'.[17]

Ptarmigan are easily overlooked, however, when many small patches of snow lie on dark ground, irrespective of whether the birds are white or dark. Because of the strong contrast between the light and dark, the human eye cannot easily discern such detail as an individual bird, and doubtless this goes for predators too. Ptarmigan are confiding in such conditions, and are hard to see even when they move while feeding. When in dark plumage they avoid pale backgrounds, especially nesting hens. Hence they seek places where their colour at that time is cryptic,[18] as do all *Lagopus* species.[19]

FIG 35. Ptarmigan chicks hatching. One is late. (Stuart Rae)

FIG 36. The same nest after hatching – the late chick died. (Stuart Rae)

## SYSTEMATICS

The rock ptarmigan (*Lagopus mutus*) is closely related to *Lagopus lagopus*, the willow ptarmigan (including the red grouse). Over 20 subspecies or races have been described, mostly from isolated southern islands and mountains. Races have been grouped according to autumn plumage: grey in mainland Europe and Scotland, and brown from the Urals east across America to Greenland, Iceland and Svalbard.[20] The summer plumage also shows some variation between races. Cocks in the European continent and Scotland have grey backs with some black on the breast, neck and head, but on Canada's high-Arctic islands and Greenland they are more sandy.[21] The darkest race in the world lives on Attu in the Aleutian Islands, where cocks have an almost black summer plumage. In contrast, on Bering Island towards Japan they are much paler, and in Japan itself they are darker than on Bering Island, resembling Scottish cocks.

Birds with a continuous range over vast areas show little variation even though they live thousands of kilometres apart. One race lives from the Urals east to Canada's Mackenzie River and south to the eastern Aleutians. A second occupies north Greenland and the northernmost Canadian islands, and a third the rest of Canada's Arctic islands and the mainland from the Mackenzie River south to central British Columbia and east to Labrador.

Ptarmigan that are geographically isolated in the Aleutians can differ in plumage colour between one island and another, and a recent study using DNA revealed greater genetic variation between the Aleutian races than within continental Alaska or Siberia.[22] Three races in the central Aleutian Islands have a similar pale summer dress, tending towards buff, while dark races occur on islands to the east and west.

## WORLD DISTRIBUTION

Ptarmigan breed down to sea-level in the Arctic and up to an altitude of 3,000m on some southern mountains. The species' circumpolar distribution encompasses rocky tundra, with isolated offshoots south to 35°N in Japan, and to Bulgaria.[23] A claim that they occur at a latitude of 39° in the Pamirs of Tadjikistan[24] has, however, been challenged.[25]

Ptarmigan inhabit Greenland, Iceland, Norway, Sweden, Finland, much of northern Russia from Kola and the Urals east to the Bering Strait and south to Kamchatka, and the Commander and northern Kurile islands. They occupy mountains around Lake Baikal, and the massifs of Sayan, Altay and Tarbagatay that straddle south Siberia, Mongolia, Sinkiang and Kazakhstan.

Excluding tiny islets, they breed on the nearest land to the North Pole, on the tips of Ellesmere Island and Greenland. One was shot in 1876 on Ellesmere at 82°46'N, and footprints were seen in 1882 on an island at 83°24'N on Greenland's northern tip.[26] Ptarmigan inhabit Franz Josef Land,[27] but they have not been recorded on Novaya Zemlya, Severnaya Zemlya or Novosibirskye Ostrova. The large race *hyperboreus* lives on Svalbard, Bear Island and Franz Josef Land.

In America, ptarmigan range from the Aleutians and mainland Alaska through northern British Columbia to Labrador, across the Canadian Arctic islands, and southwards along the Coast Mountains north of Vancouver and on hills in Newfoundland. Greenland birds spread quickly after being released on the Faeroes in 1890 and Scottish red grouse were introduced there about six years later. A few birds of unknown species, including a nesting hen, remained on a northern island in the 1960s.[28] Apparently they have now gone, probably as a result of overgrazing by sheep.[29]

## DISTRIBUTION IN BRITAIN

Authors in the late 1700s mentioned ptarmigan in the Lake District, and a specimen taken on Skiddaw appeared in a local museum, but by the 1820s none was seen by men who knew the hills well.[30] Ptarmigan were shot on the Southern Uplands in the late 1600s, reported in the 1700s, and shot in winter around 1822–3,[31] and in 1826 one was seen on the Merrick hill.[32] An introduction to the Southern Uplands in the mid-1970s apparently failed, as did one in Donegal, Ireland, in the late 1800s.[33]

Ptarmigan bred on Hoy in Orkney up to 1831.[34] They lived on the Outer Hebrides into the 1900s,[35] and were still on Harris in the early 1960s.[36] In the 1800s they occurred on Skye, Rum, Mull, Jura and Arran, and a pair produced young on Scarba in 1959.[37] They bred on Arran in 1977 and subsequently, and in the 1980s were on Skye, Rum, Mull and Jura.[38] In the 1990s and first years of the twenty-first century they have been seen on Arran in most years, including breeding birds, and on Mull in several years.[39]

On the Scottish mainland they breed from Ben Lomond northwards to Sutherland and Caithness, and east to Mt Keen.[40] On the isolated Ben Rinnes of Moray and Mt Battock near Aberdeen they have reared broods in some recent years, though in others no birds were seen.[41] In the late 1800s, they inhabited hills at Cabrach and Glen Livet,[42] but since 1950 only an occasional unmated cock has been seen there in summer.

In winter there are occasional records on low eastern hills where no bird has been seen in summer.[43] One was on a 378m hill in late April 1947, and in November 1953 a cock was seen on a few acres of heather along a coastal clifftop south of Aberdeen.[44]

The ptarmigan's range in Britain has contracted over the centuries as overgrazing by sheep has left little heath as food and cover on the high hills of England, Wales, Ireland, the Southern Uplands, the Inner and Outer Hebrides, Orkney and many hills of the Highlands. Increases in numbers of red deer have exacerbated this on most Alpine land in Scotland and England, and in much of Ireland too. Hills south of the Highlands could hold ptarmigan again if overgrazing were ended and heath restored.

## NATIONAL AND REGIONAL NUMBERS

Because so few counts of ptarmigan have been carried out, different estimates vary greatly.[45] One estimate for North America that allowed for fluctuations was 2.1–8.4 million adults in June, and 3.7–24.3 million birds in September.[46] A recent publication lists the largest population estimates as over a million breeding birds each in Canada and Alaska, 700,000 in Russia, 100,000–500,000 in Iceland, 150,000 in Sweden and over 100,000 in Greenland.[47]

An often repeated estimate for ptarmigan numbers in Scotland is at least 10,000 pairs in spring.[48] More accurate estimates for the Cairngorms massif alone, based on counts, ranged from 1,300 birds in a spring of low numbers to 5,000 in a peak spring and 15,000 in a peak autumn.[49] Since then, a 1.6-fold higher peak came in 1971 on the Derry Cairngorm study area, so earlier estimates have been exceeded.

## HABITAT

### Habitat and physical cover

Alpine vegetation is usually too short to conceal a bird as big as a ptarmigan, even when it crouches. Instead, it uses rocks as cover. Adults are adept at walking, jumping and fluttering among big boulders, and a group under watch can soon vanish by moving largely out of sight behind rocks.

In the breeding season, Scottish ptarmigan spend most of the daytime within 3m of the nearest rocks.[50] By hiding among rocks, they reduce the risk of attack from predators, as do white-tailed ptarmigan.[51] Although cover can take the form of one boulder or a few, it often comprises boulder lobes, scree, edges of boulder fields, rock outcrops or cliffs, and sometimes ridges or hillocks. Hens with downy chicks avoid large interlocking boulders where food is scarce and chicks could fall down deep holes. Once fully grown, however, ptarmigan often fly to such boulders to rest and preen in safety.

Densities of ptarmigan in Scotland are high on fine-grained mosaics of abundant food and boulders. Expanses of food plants without boulders usually support no territorial birds, the sole exception being when smaller features provide cover that allows a few to breed on ground without boulders, such as earth hummocks caused by freeze-thaw action.

### Climatic effects on habitat

Across Eurasia and Arctic America, the upper altitude for plants that are eaten by ptarmigan sets the upper altitude to which they feed and breed. On many American mountains, however, the smaller, closely related white-tailed ptarmigan occupies the zone uphill. This keeps the rock ptarmigan's upper limit there to a lower altitude than it would otherwise be. On steep slopes, the birds' lower limit can be an abrupt line, where short vegetation with many rocks changes downhill to taller vegetation with few or no rocks. Below this line, *Lagopus lagopus* take over.

FIG 37. Scottish ptarmigan hen with foraging chicks. They are in vegetation beside small surface boulders that provide cover but do not have any dangerously deep holes. (Stuart Rae)

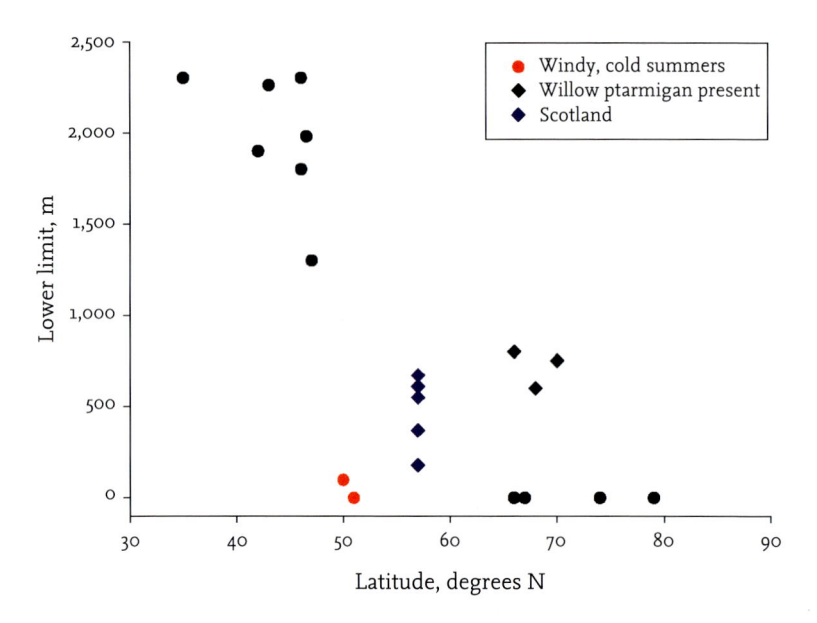

**FIG 38.** Lowest altitude (m) frequented by breeding rock ptarmigan. It rises towards the south, coinciding with the lowest altitude of prostrate vegetation. Red circles represent the Kuriles and Amchitka Island, two areas with exceptionally cold windy summers for their low latitude, and hence prostrate vegetation at low altitude. Blue diamonds represent five Scottish areas, illustrating how increasing windiness causes the lowest limit for prostrate vegetation to be closer to sea-level. Two of the black diamonds are the Norwegian islands of Lyngen and Lofoten, areas with lowest limits of prostrate vegetation that are unusually far up the mountains, in association with fairly mild summers for such high latitudes, owing to the Gulf Stream. They and central Alaska are the only areas on this graph that have willow ptarmigan, which push up the lowest altitudinal limits of ptarmigan (as in Scotland with red grouse), though this is not obvious from these data.[55]

The prostrate Alpine vegetation used by ptarmigan signifies cool summers, and it occurs at lower altitudes as one goes north. Its lower limit can differ at a similar latitude, however, where summers are colder or windier than is usual for that latitude.

### Summer habitat in Scotland

Much high ground in Scotland has few or no food plants used by ptarmigan because of the presence of boulder fields, bare soil or grassland.[52] For these reasons and the plants' slow growth, bird densities are generally below those of red grouse on moorland. Prostrate heather or mountain azalea with few boulders typifies poor habitat, while blaeberry-rich vegetation with colluvial topsoil and more boulders is good habitat.

Ptarmigan and red grouse overlap in altitude – for example, by 300m in the Cairngorms – but they seldom overlap in habitat. Red grouse nest in tall heather with few or no boulders, while ptarmigan prefer a more varied short heath with many boulders.[53] On ground occupied by ptarmigan, a patch of fairly tall heather may hold an isolated pair of red grouse or, more often, an unmated cock. On lower slopes occupied by red grouse, one may similarly find a ptarmigan pair or cock on an isolated patch of blaeberry with rocks.

Where coastal land is exposed to winds from a cool sea, Alpine vegetation extends to a lower altitude than in the more continental interior, in a gradient from inland eastern Scotland towards the northwest coast.[54] The lower limit of ptarmigan with nests or downy chicks coincides with this, being highest on the relatively continental Lochnagar and lowest on the most oceanic hills of northwest Sutherland (Fig. 38).

Upper recorded limits for Scottish breeding birds lie just short of the highest summits in a given region, and rarely exceed 1,250m, except occasionally in late summer when families with fully grown young sometimes move uphill to eat plants on the loftiest tops. Maximum densities occur below 1,100m, where food plants are more abundant and productive than higher up.[56] Scottish birds breed on suitable habitat whatever the altitude or aspect.[57] Territories and nests are on short, freely drained heath, whereas hens with chicks prefer wet soils on flushes and snow-patch hollows. They have a more catholic choice once the young are bigger, when they also exploit berries and plants at high altitude.

**Summer habitat outside Scotland**
Although rock ptarmigan breed on low ground in the Arctic, they are absent from large tracts of flat wet tundra at or near sea-level, as on some parts of mainland Russia adjacent to the Arctic Ocean,[58] around the Mackenzie and Yukon deltas, and along the Foxe Basin coast of Baffin Island.[59] These areas support willow ptarmigan instead. On relatively flat land broken by rocky outcrops, such as southwest Baffin Island and the Ungava Peninsula, the two species breed very near one another, with rock ptarmigan on stony or rocky slopes and ridges, and willow ptarmigan nearby on flat wet tundra only a few metres lower.[60]

In some countries such as Greenland and Iceland, which have no willow ptarmigan, rock ptarmigan breed in birch-willow scrub,[61] as well as in rocky habitats with short vegetation. In Iceland, much low ground supports tall heath with occasional scrub. Hrisey, an island with the highest recorded ptarmigan density in Iceland, is dominated by thick crowberry and heather[62] with hardly any boulders, and hens nest in this heath vegetation (Fig. 39). In fact, this is a typical habitat for willow ptarmigan, and at a distance it resembles a British moor. Japan, most of the Aleutians, the Alps and the Pyrenees are also without *Lagopus lagopus*, and here rock ptarmigan frequently use tall vegetation.[63] So, when relieved from competition with willow ptarmigan, rock ptarmigan use habitats that would otherwise be the preserve of willow ptarmigan.

### Habitat in autumn and winter

In Alaska, rock ptarmigan in autumn keep to higher, more open ground than willow ptarmigan, which favour lower slopes and valley bottoms with tall willow thickets.[64] In winter, however, when deep snow covers most ground vegetation, both often occupy the same habitat, though they take almost completely different diets (*see* below). Again in British Columbia, Norway and Scotland, rock ptarmigan in winter tend to stick to higher, rockier ground than *Lagopus lagopus*. But on stormy days with deep snow in Scotland, both species sometimes haunt the same ground in separate packs, well below the lowest places used by rock ptarmigan in summer.[65] Even so, most ptarmigan are found higher up, in more exposed conditions than most red grouse.

**FIG 39.** Pair of rock ptarmigan on moor-like habitat on Hrisey, Iceland. (Adam Watson)

FIG 40. Ptarmigan flock on the Cairnwell in snow. Three birds are feeding, one is preening and seven are resting in the middle of the day. (Stuart Rae)

DIET

**Winter**

Unlike the ptarmigan's varied autumn diet, which includes energy-rich berries and seeds, its winter fare comprises buds, leaves and stalks of woody shrubs, with little protein and much fibre.[66] The birds are selective, however, taking food that contains more protein and phosphorus, and less fibre, than that generally available.[67]

The winter diet in Scotland comprises mostly leaves and shoots of crowberry and, to a lesser extent, heather and the green stalk tips of blaeberry, with smaller amounts of least willow and cowberry.[68] When deep snow and storms force ptarmigan down to upper moorland, heather becomes their main food.

The birds eat many twigs and buds of willow and also some birch in Greenland and Iceland, two countries without willow ptarmigan.[69] Amchitka in the Aleutians also has only rock ptarmigan, but willow and birch are scarce here. Crowberry dominates the vegetation, and it and horsetail form the rock ptarmigan's main food source.[70]

Where both rock and willow ptarmigan occur in the same area, willow ptarmigan eat mostly willow scrub if available, whereas rock ptarmigan feed much on birch. Hence rock ptarmigan worldwide eat much birch, though taking much willow scrub in regions that lack willow ptarmigan. In Scotland, overgrazing by sheep and deer has almost eliminated such scrub. Hence the winter diet of ptarmigan here is probably poorer than before 1800, when fewer deer and sheep grazed our high hills.

Paul Gelting found that Greenland birds take some horsetail stems and reproductive capsules, both of which are quite rich in protein.[71] Although they feed mostly on buds and shoots of polar willow, the birds will also eat many leaves of mountain avens, and buds and stems of purple saxifrage. All three of these plant species are quite nutritious, and are widespread in the Arctic on exposed ground where winds blow most snow away. During midwinter noon in Greenland, ptarmigan eat larger pieces of polar willow, well illustrated in Gelting's photographs, thus filling their crops quickly. Gelting counted 9,100 items inside the average crop in early and mid-January.

**Spring, summer and autumn**
In spring, Scottish adults continue to feed on crowberry (Fig. 41), blaeberry and heather, but enrich their diet with early growing plants such as cotton-grass shoots and new leaves of chickweed or mouse-ear. Their diet on fertile hills includes more blaeberry and herbs than on infertile hills, reflecting the greater abundance of these richer foods.[72] In spring on Hrisey in Iceland, the earliest plant growth occurs in agricultural fields beside houses, and foraging ptarmigan flocks concentrate in such locations (Fig. 42).

In summer, adult ptarmigan eat a variety of herb leaves, flowers and moss capsules, as well as shoots of crowberry, blaeberry and least willow. Chicks eat plants on their first day out of the nest, but also many insects in their first two weeks. In the subarctic and Arctic they favour the bulbils and spikes of Alpine bistort, which contain 20–22 per cent protein,[73] roughly equivalent to the level found in commercial feed crumbs for poultry chicks. This plant abounds on moist soils in hollows, and though it is mostly covered in snow in winter it becomes available at the thaw. Though Alpine bistort is far scarcer on British and Irish Alpine land and moorland, it grows locally on rich moist soils such as on the Cairnwell, where sheep have been seen eating it.[74] Overgrazing has doubtless contributed to its scarcity in Britain.

The autumn diet of ptarmigan in Scotland comprises many berries, seeds of grass, sedge, rush and wood-rush, and shoots and leaves of least willow, as well as the flowers and shoots of heath species. In the Arctic, autumn snowfalls seal off much vegetation and frost preserves the berries. During the spring thaw, the berries are a palatable, surprisingly abundant food, rich in energy for bird and

FIG 41. Crowberry, the main food of Scottish ptarmigan, with a setter dog pointing at a nesting hen. (Adam Watson)

FIG 42. Flock of Icelandic rock ptarmigan foraging in a hayfield on Hrisey in spring. (Adam Watson)

human alike, and rock and willow ptarmigan eat them. Such preservation occurs too rarely in Scotland to be valuable in spring. Seldom does late-autumn snow lie long, so birds and other herbivores consume almost all berries before winter. Occasionally, ptarmigan eat some crowberries in spring, which being less palatable than blaeberries are more likely to survive the winter.

## METABOLISM

### Winter

For rock, willow and white-tailed ptarmigan, food is readily available in winter, and they can store a meal in their crop and digest it at leisure overnight. Rock ptarmigan spend much time resting in sheltered places, often in sunshine. Studies of white-tailed ptarmigan reveal similar behaviour and a low expenditure of energy.[75] In central Alaska, where winter daytime temperatures commonly sink below −20°C, rock ptarmigan spend much of the day under snow, white-tailed more so and willow ptarmigan less so.[76]

Of special interest is the Svalbard ptarmigan. Other rock ptarmigan at about 80°N in Greenland and Ellesmere Island migrate south for the darkest time of the year, without a sea crossing or with only a short one. Svalbard ptarmigan, however, would have to fly 1,000km south to reach Norway, a risky journey. Instead, they remain resident on the island, and have evolved impressive adaptations to cope with the risks of wintering so far north.[77] The Gulf Stream passes the west side of Svalbard, keeping the sea open and the climate milder than is usual for such a high latitude. Rain can fall in winter and subsequently freezes, sealing off food. To cope with such icy periods, birds fatten in autumn, a time of plentiful nutritious food. Cocks at this time weigh up to 1.2kg and fat comprises up to 35 per cent of their body-weight. Captive birds achieve these proportions despite eating less,[78] and presumably conserve energy by spending more time resting. Wild birds are almost fat-free by February, when the first daylight appears again.

### Summer

When an incubating hen ptarmigan returns to her cool eggs after a feeding trip, she increases her heart rate and rapidly pumps blood to her incubation patch.[79] Even so, cold wind, fog, rain or snow showers often prevail in early summer, so it may be wondered how the tiny chicks survive. Chicks of Alaskan rock ptarmigan that are only five days old can maintain normal body temperature for 20 minutes at an ambient temperature of 10°C, whereas Norwegian willow ptarmigan cannot achieve this until they reach ten days.[80] Alaskan chicks need to forage for only six minutes per hour, and week-old young can produce about three times as much heat, presumably by shivering, as do willow ptarmigan of the same age.

Despite their smaller size, the downy rock ptarmigan chicks are better adapted to cold than their willow ptarmigan brethren. The same applies throughout their life. They are thus better able to cope with more snow, rain, fog, cold and wind, and less shelter, than can be tolerated by willow ptarmigan. Nevertheless, even slight worsening of weather in the Swiss Alps reduces the feeding periods of downy chicks.[81] Prolonged heavy snow or rain during daytime, especially in strong winds, can cause heavy losses, such as in Iceland during a July snowstorm even though chicks were a month old.[82] Very few downy chicks survive heavy snowfalls on the Cairngorms, and more than half the young died during heavy rain in 1990 even at much lower altitudes on the Cairnwell.[83]

Ptarmigan can be too hot on warm summer days, however, and either seek shade from rocks or sit in water or snow. In hot sunshine, they and *Lagopus lagopus* pant rapidly with bills open, to lose heat quickly.

## MOVEMENTS

**Seasonal movements or migration**

In southerly countries where ptarmigan are winter residents, such as Scotland, birds often stay on the same hill throughout the year. In northernmost Canada, Alaska, Greenland and mainland Russia, however, many move south in autumn and north in spring, some flying along the coast or over the sea.[84] On the north coast of Baffin Island, they arrive in early October from Bylot Island, 'in many cases so tired by the flight that they alight on the beach almost exhausted'.[85] Some occur 'regularly in winter as far north as Thule' in Greenland,[86] and in Baffin Island. None the less, many move south in both islands, and thousands from Baffin Island arrive in autumn on the coasts of the Ungava Peninsula and Labrador, and in spring in Labrador as they fly north again.[87] Ptarmigan can be intrepid explorers, as exemplified by fresh tracks found in June at 1,600m on the expansive Penny Icecap of Baffin Island.[88]

Seasonal movements of up to 500km have been reported in northern Russia and more than 1,000km in America,[89] and a bird ringed on Disko Island in Greenland during July was recovered the following February more than 1,000km to the south.[90] The east Greenland race has 'repeatedly been taken in winter at sea and in Iceland', as proved by the gizzards of birds shot in volcanic Iceland containing grit from the non-volcanic rock of Greenland.[91] Large-scale movements in Greenland coincide with peak numbers, and so may involve density-dependent emigration (*see* Chapters 3 and 14).

The timing of autumn movement in America is irregular, associated with seasonal snowfall. Canadian rock ptarmigan are far less migratory than willow ptarmigan, tending to concentrate in the southern part of the breeding range.[92] Each species occurs in winter further south than its southern breeding limit, but willow ptarmigan go much further beyond this than do rock ptarmigan.[93]

Many male rock ptarmigan in Iceland and Alaska remain in northern parts, whereas hens move to more southerly regions.[94] Presumably it is beneficial for old cocks to stay near their former territories, so that they can occupy them quickly in spring. They return to their breeding grounds on the Icelandic island of Hrisey and at Windy Lake in Canada's Northwest Territories two to three weeks before hens,[95] and earlier than hens in Greenland, Alaska and the Swiss Alps.[96] In Svalbard and Canada, old territorial cocks returning to the breeding grounds after being away for the winter appear in their former locations.[97] In contrast, although returning hens do come to the same general area, they often choose different territories and cocks.

Youngsters disperse in autumn when broods break up. In the far north, some move far – in Iceland, for example, up to nearly 300km from where they were ringed as chicks.[98] Such movement of young presumably involves seasonal migrations of the kind observed in many old birds there, plus natal dispersal of young to breed in places away from where they hatched.

**Short movements to food in summer and autumn**

Ptarmigan often move locally to food. During summer in Greenland, hens with chicks visit moist hollows, often near small snow patches. These sites have less bare ground than usual, because continual irrigation prevents them from drying out. As a result, they support abundant willow, herbs and Alpine bistort, all of which are good chick foods. Several ptarmigan families in Greenland were seen to concentrate at former human settlements,[99] where faeces, urine and food waste from people and dogs had enriched the soil.[100]

After hatching, Scottish hens walk with their broods to flushes that support abundant invertebrates, a rich food for chicks. Later, when the chicks are partly feathered and eating mostly plants, many families visit snow patches. There, plants newly freed from the snow and in the first flush of growth are more nutritious than those of the same species that grew earlier in the summer on less snowy ground.

Many Scottish adults and well-grown young move uphill to higher, more barren ground in late July and August, where they feed much on plentiful least willow, and others move to eat berries at places with good crops. In the Swiss Alps they also go uphill in late summer, as high as 3,000m. The cocks go first and hens with broods move later, the birds returning to the breeding grounds when snow deepens at high altitude.[101] Many birds in Iceland leave the lowland breeding grounds in late summer and move into mountains above 600m.[102]

### Short movements to food in winter

In the Cairngorms, Seton Gordon watched ptarmigan moving downhill on wing and foot at the onset of a severe snowstorm and gale, and shortly afterwards they came back up again into a relatively sheltered corrie when conditions on the lower slopes had become even worse.[103] In stormy weather, packs of birds often fly to sheltered places for feeding,[104] and a big movement was witnessed in Norway during a blizzard.[105]

Many ptarmigan move downhill during early winter in deep snow in the Pyrenees, going down to scrub or birchwood.[106] Scottish birds avoid the loftiest exposed land, although they will stay even as high as 1,100m if the ground remains largely snow-free. When hard-packed snow, hoar frost and rime cover the highest ground, however, packs concentrate on Alpine land below 900m. If snow or ice covers plants there, too, the birds fly to areas of high moorland where some heather projects above the snow. There they often overlap with red grouse, although most grouse in such conditions move yet lower.

On the other hand, when deep snow blankets almost all higher moorland and lower Alpine land in the Cairngorms, ptarmigan move uphill on days without gales. There they eat heath plants on exposed ridges where wind has blown most of the snow away. In east Greenland, too, they move to exposed places where plants are snow-free.

The sexes sometimes separate by altitude, cocks in the Cairngorms staying on their territories on largely snow-covered ground more often than hens.[107] In Iceland, adults in winter flocks tend to dominate juveniles, and wintering juveniles often stay in separate groups from adults, eating different vegetation.[108]

## AVERAGE POPULATION DENSITIES

The average density of rock ptarmigan tends to be high where their preferred food plants are abundant, as in Scotland, in combination with physical cover from rocks.[109] In contrast, the Canadian high Arctic has low densities of ptarmigan and very little vegetation at all, let alone ptarmigan foods, and plant production is also very low (see Table 6).

**FIG 43.** Lower-altitude ptarmigan habitat on rich soil with boulder cover and abundant food plants (Cairnwell). (Stuart Rae)

**FIG 44.** Higher-altitude ptarmigan habitat on poorer soil with boulder cover but sparse food plants (Ben Macdui). The big difference between this example and Figure 43 arises from the combination of two factors: altitude and bedrock. (Stuart Rae)

In Scotland, food plants are less abundant at higher altitudes owing to the more severe climate and hence poorer soils. In addition, average rock ptarmigan densities on different hills at the same altitude are associated with different underlying bedrock and associated soil fertility. When the effects of altitude and soil fertility are combined, they can affect average densities greatly (Figs 43 & 44). Thus, the average density of cocks and hens on base-rich rocks at the lower-altitude Cairnwell and Meall Odhar has been 48 cocks and 45 hens per km$^2$, whereas on acidic granite at the higher-altitude Derry Cairngorm it has been only 18 cocks and 16 hens per km$^2$.[110]

**Year-to-year fluctuations in density**

Ptarmigan numbers vary greatly in different years (Table 12) and some long series of counts show evidence of cycles.[111] The number of shot ptarmigan exported from Iceland over many decades fluctuated in a ten-year cycle, and bags in three provinces of the Italian Alps and in a Swiss canton showed weak cycles.[112] Bags are less reliable than counts, however, and the Italian and Swiss bags were too short term to draw firm conclusions about cyclicity. Counts in Alaska and Canada suggest that ten-year cycles are likely,[113] but the evidence is insufficient to be sure. In one documented case on the Cairngorms, a ten-year cycle was correlated with a cycle in June air temperature.[114] At the base-rich Cairnwell and Meall Odhar 20km to the south, however, the more erratic fluctuations in numbers were associated with a different and more erratic weather feature: spring snow-lie (*see* Chapter 14).

At Alaska's Eagle Creek and in Scotland, the only areas where population studies of both sexes have lasted beyond a few years, the recruitment of young to the spring population is the demographic factor that accounts best for the change in adult numbers since the previous spring.[115] The recruitment rate rises as the population increases from a trough, but falls off rapidly towards the peak and remains low during the decline. In Scotland and Svalbard, cocks have been found to limit their spring numbers through territorial behaviour (*see* Chapter 9).[116] This may involve aggressive behaviour that limits the recruitment of young, as in red grouse, but has not been studied.

## SURVIVAL

Some information on survival of rock ptarmigan has come from marking adults on an area in one summer and noting those that return the following summer.[117] Such 'return rates' are often used as a surrogate for survival. Data from several countries, including Scotland, centre around 47–8 per cent (Table 13).

**TABLE 12.** Some peak and trough numbers per km$^2$ during spring (cocks, hens) in studies of rock ptarmigan that lasted long enough to justify references to 'peak' and 'trough'. Table 6 includes the data below, in greatly summarised form.

|  | STUDY AREA | PEAK | TROUGH | REFERENCE |
|---|---|---|---|---|
| Alaska | Eagle Creek | 4.4, 4.0 | 0.7, 0.7 | Weeden, 1963, 1965a |
| Iceland | Hrisey | 34, — | 7, — | Gardarsson, 1988 |
|  | Húsavík | 22, — | 5, — | Nielsen, 1999 |
| Scotland | Derry Cairngorm | 36, 27 | 4, 4 | Graphs in Watson et al., 1998 |
|  | The Cairnwell and Meall Odhar# | 67, 65 | 5, 5 | Graphs in Watson et al., 1998 |
|  | Carn a' Gheoidh | 21, 19 | 7, 4 | Graphs in Watson et al., 1998 |
|  | Beinn a' Bhuird | 14, 12 | 2, 0 | Graphs in Watson et al., 2000 |
|  | Lochnagar | 67, 52 | 9, 6 | Watson, unpublished |
| Swiss Alps | Aletschgebiet | 14, 11 | 10, 2 | Bossert, 1995 |

**Notes**

Counts in successive years have been carried out at Svalbard, Sarcpa Lake and Windy Lake (references in Table 13), Japan (Soichiro et al., 1969), Russia (reviewed by Potapov, 1985), Ungava (Olpinski, 1986) and Lombardy (Scherini et al., 2003), but data cover too few years to show peaks or troughs reliably.

# The peak at the Cairnwell was 75, 65 (Watson, unpublished).

**TABLE 13.** Percentage of adult rock ptarmigan marked in one summer that returned to a delimited study area in the next summer (return rate).

|  | COCKS | HENS | REFERENCE |
|---|---|---|---|
| Svalbard | 48 | 47 | Unander & Steen, 1985 |
| Sarcpa Lake | 48 | — | Holder & Montgomerie, 1993b |
| Windy Lake | 48 | 8# | Cotter, 1999 |
| The Cairnwell | — | 48 | Moss & Watson, 2001 |

**Notes**

Bergerud (1988) gave a 44 per cent annual survival for hens at Eagle Creek, using data in Weeden & Theberge (1972), and 54 per cent for hens on Hrisey, using data in Gardarsson (1971). These values were estimated from counts, and so are not return rates.

# This is such a low value that emigration to ground outside the study area is likely.

The converse of survival is mortality, and the converse of return rate is loss from the study area. Such loss consists of mortality plus net movement out of the area, possibly to breed elsewhere. There are few reliable data on survival or mortality, so it is safer to refer to return rate or loss.

Summer losses[118] at Alaska's Eagle Creek and Scotland's Derry Cairngorm were low, at around 10–15 per cent, and at the Cairnwell they were slightly higher.[119] This probably overestimated summer mortality in Scotland, because temporary movement out of the relatively small study areas caused a high proportion of summer 'loss', especially at the smallest study area, at the Cairnwell. Summer losses of marked birds at Canada's Windy Lake averaged about 20 per cent for each sex, nearly all taken by falcons.[120] On Hrisey, Iceland, more cocks than hens were lost in early summer, when gyrfalcons killed conspicuous white cocks on prominent lookouts.[121] A study of prey taken to gyrfalcon nests near Húsavík, Iceland, confirmed the excess of cocks taken in April–June, but in July the falcons brought more hens than cocks, resulting in similar losses of both sexes over the season as a whole.[122]

Losses in winter (actually measured from late July through to May) exceeded those in summer at all areas where it was estimated.[123] At Derry Cairngorm and the Cairnwell, winter losses in both sexes averaged 30–44 per cent of adults and first-year birds combined, tending to be greater after summers with good breeding.

There is little evidence on longevity, because few studies with marked birds have lasted long, and birds may move outside study areas and yet still be alive. However, there are Canadian records of two cocks living at least four and five years, and two hens living five and seven years.[124] An annual survival rate of 50 per cent would leave 6 per cent of adults alive at five years of age.

## NUMBER OF HENS PAIRED WITH COCKS

Most cocks pair with a hen each and some pair with two, while others are unmated. One cock had three hens for the summer on Victoria Island, Canada, and at Sarcpa Lake a few cocks had three each and one had four.[125] In Scotland, two hens occasionally breed with a cock, but incidences of mating with more than two have not been recorded.

Territorial cocks outnumbered hens in years of population decline on Derry Cairngorm, but in years of increase the ratio was about one cock per hen.[126] On average, the male excess here exceeded that at the Cairnwell, where 1.5 cocks per hen was the highest figure, compared with 2.0 on Derry Cairngorm. The base-rich Cairnwell has food plants that contain higher levels of protein and phosphorus than those at Derry Cairngorm. As in red grouse, large excesses of cocks are often associated with poor food quality, especially during cyclic declines.

At Derry Cairngorm, 'Though there were enough hens in February/early March to pair with all the cocks that had territories then, half of the cocks finally remained unmated'.[127] Many hens vanished suddenly in spring, such as 21 within five days in early March 1952, and 22 within ten days in March 1954, but none was found dead then, so it was concluded that they moved out. Perhaps they went to hills with lower or increasing densities.

A preponderance of territorial cocks during the nesting season has been recorded in several countries.[128] At Hrisey in Iceland, however, the sex ratio in early spring was about 1:1, but gyrfalcons then killed far more cocks than hens, resulting in many unpaired semi-promiscuous hens.[129] In a two-year study on the Ungava Peninsula, Quebec, the ratio before pair formation was again near 1:1, but although many territorial cocks later had one or more hens, many remained unpaired.[130] Similarly, in a short study at Sarcpa Lake some cocks had one or more hens, while others remained unpaired.[131] Heterogeneous habitat occurred at both areas, including poorer ground perhaps suitable for unmated cocks but not for breeding hens. At Ungava the territories of unpaired cocks were so small (see Table 21) that they may have been inadequate for hens.

### Reasons for differences in the sex ratio

Because gyrfalcons took more cocks than hens on Hrisey in spring, it was claimed that the excess of breeding cocks in Scotland and other southern countries might result from their 'unbalanced' predator situation, with no gyrfalcons killing the cock ptarmigan.[132] In two summers at Windy Lake, however, 48 territorial cocks were paired with 49 hens, and ten more territorial cocks remained unmated, despite one of the highest known nesting densities of gyrfalcons in the world, and falcons took cocks and hens equally.[133] Also, as explained above, the sex ratio in early spring was balanced (1:1) on Derry Cairngorm. In years when the area had a large excess of cocks in the nesting season, this unbalanced ratio occurred because more hens than cocks had left. Hence the claim that 'unbalanced' sex ratios are caused by predators taking more hens than cocks seems unlikely.[134]

The greater frequency of unmated cocks in Scotland is associated with poorer diet. Overgrazing sheep and deer have almost eliminated scrub of willow and birch, and continue to remove Alpine bistort and most cotton-grass shoots. This is exacerbated by the low content of protein and phosphorus in food plants on infertile soils. Thus the average percentage of unmated cocks on the infertile granite of Derry Cairngorm exceeds that on the base-rich rocks at the Cairnwell and Meall Odhar. The unmated cocks' small territories may be inadequate to support breeding hens, which leave, perhaps in search of better food or less crowded areas with a lower population density.

### DATE OF EGG-LAYING

Longer days induce egg development, but the response by local populations to the same day length varies with climate. For example, hens in north Canada lay in June, several weeks later than in the much less snowy Iceland at the same latitude. Many high-Arctic hens do not lay until late June[135] and some not until early July.

Another enlightening comparison is that between Amchitka, in the Aleutian islands, and Scotland. Amchitka lies as far south as London, but here the hens' increase in weight before egg-laying comes weeks later than in the Cairngorms, peaking in June when they lay eggs.[136] Cocks on Amchitka establish territories in early May, months later than birds in the Cairngorms. Their testes reach peak size in early June, and the hens' ovarian follicles reach peak size in late June. Hatching on Amchitka also comes one to three weeks later than at Eagle Creek in central Alaska, 1,600km further north.[137] Though oceanic Amchitka has mild winters, summer comes late and breeding follows suit.

Within a given region, hens fine-tune their response to climatic conditions by laying eggs earlier in springs that are warmer than usual. In such springs, fresh growth by plants supplies the rich food that hens need for producing eggs of high quality. In the Cairngorms, the earliest hen at low altitude in a mild, snow-free spring lays her first egg at the end of April, and the latest hen at high altitude in a snowy year does not lay until the end of June. At a given altitude, the date of laying varies from year to year in relation to May temperature, with early eggs in warm Mays, when plants grow early. The date of hatching is related to the date when blaeberry begins to grow, thus linking hatching date to diet and weather.[138]

In the Swiss Alps, some paired hens did not seem to breed in a summer with ten days of snowfall in late June.[139] Since hens usually nest in mid-June, they may perhaps have nested and then deserted. Heavy snowfalls cause many Scottish hens to desert, and this can be readily overlooked unless several visits are made during and immediately after the snowfall.

In a given year or area, some hens lay earlier than others at the same altitude or aspect. On Svalbard and the Cairnwell, heavy hens lay earlier than light hens,[140] presumably because they are in better condition at the point of lay. We think it likely that high-quality hens pair with cocks that have big territories offering good food, and good food in turn helps induce early laying.

## NESTS, EGG-LAYING AND INCUBATION

Rock ptarmigan hens nest in their first year of life. Although less is known about them than *Lagopus lagopus*, the evidence indicates that all hens nest each year. They choose the nest site, and make a shallow scrape in the ground or vegetation, lining it with plant litter and the odd loose feather.

By far the commonest nest site for a Scottish hen is short vegetation beside a boulder (Fig. 45), where the upper half of her body rises above the vegetation but the boulder provides cover, a cryptic background, and shelter. There she relies on her camouflaged plumage to avoid being seen by predators. Only exceptionally does she nest in tall vegetation, though one hen on Derry Cairngorm was overhung by a small patch of heather 25cm tall.[141] Another unusual nest there lay under an overhanging rock shelf that kept rain off the hen and eggs, and mostly hid them from the view of predators.[142]

On average, a Scottish hen lays one egg about every 1.5 days.[143] After laying, she usually covers her eggs with plant litter before leaving the nest, thus hiding them from predators and insulating them from frost, falling snow and cold rain. Even partly covered eggs are remarkably difficult to see, and the litter may also reduce scent from the eggs.

FIG 45. Ptarmigan hen on a nest in short vegetation beside a boulder – a typical Scottish site. The blaeberry shoots around the nest are just beginning to grow. (Stuart Rae)

## CLUTCH SIZE

### Average clutch sizes in different areas

Ptarmigan in Scotland lay smaller clutches than red grouse in the same region – roughly an egg fewer. Clutch size varies greatly between different countries, although the difference is not related to latitude – for example, clutches on Svalbard differ little from those in Scotland (Table 14).

TABLE 14. Mean clutch size, number of chicks per hen and brood size (number per hen with a brood) of rock ptarmigan, in order from north to south. Chicks[#] were eight days old at Ungava, ten days at Windy Lake, three to four weeks at Hrisey, four to eight weeks at Svalbard and fully grown elsewhere.

|  | PLACE | CLUTCH | YOUNG/HEN | BROOD SIZE | REFERENCE |
|---|---|---|---|---|---|
| Svalbard | Ny-Ålesund | 7.5 | 4.3 | 6.1 | Steen & Unander, 1985 |
| Canada | Victoria Island | — | — | 7.2 | Parmelee et al., 1967 |
|  | Sarcpa Lake | 8.8 | — | — | Holder & Montgomerie, 1993a |
|  | Windy Lake | 8.6 | 3.8 | 7.0 | Cotter et al., 1992; Cotter, 1999 |
| Iceland | Hrisey | 11.0 | — | 7.9[#] | Gardarsson, 1988 |
| Alaska | Eagle Creek | 7.1 | 4.0[*] | 5.4 | Weeden, 1965a |
| Canada | Ungava | — | 6.0 | — | Olpinski, 1986 |
| Scotland | Derry Cairngorm | 6.4 | 1.0 | 2.0 | Watson et al., 1998 |
|  | The Cairnwell and Meall Odhar | 6.5 | 1.6 | 3.2 | Watson et al., 1998 |
| Italy | Monte Sobretta | 7.2 | 1.7 | 4.6 | Scherini et al., 2003 |

**Notes**

Because breeding success varies during population fluctuations, only the Icelandic, Alaskan and Scottish studies lasted long enough to show reliable averages. Alaska and the Italian Alps are poorer for nutritious plants than Hrisey.

[#] Studies of chicks aged up to eight weeks lacked later observations. At Hrisey, gyrfalcons killed chicks from late July, when they were about four weeks old. Near Húsavík, almost a quarter of chicks in mid-July were killed by the end of August (Nielsen, 2003). If one allows for this, breeding success at Hrisey estimated as full-grown chicks would still be very good, but differences from Alaska, Scotland and Italy would be less than above.

[*] After Weeden & Theberge (1972), using the same years as Weeden (1965a).

Ptarmigan in Arctic Canada eat nutritious willow and lay big clutches, whereas Scottish birds depend mainly on heath species of poorer feeding value and lay small clutches. In the weeks before hens lay in Scotland and other countries, they supplement their main diet with newly growing herbs, which are far more nutritious than heath species. In Scotland they have to compete for this relatively scarce food with the large mouths of many hungry red deer and often sheep also. In conclusion, the average clutch size depends more upon food quality than latitude.

**Clutch sizes of individuals**
A hen's condition influences her clutch size in a given year. In studies at Svalbard and the Cairnwell, heavy hens laid larger clutches than light hens.[144] Probably the amount and nutritional value of food on the cock's territory influences her weight and condition before she lays.

On a given area, the average clutch size varies from year to year. For example, hens on Derry Cairngorm laid larger clutches after mild springs with early plant growth.[145] They also laid larger clutches in years of rising population than during population declines. On Hrisey, the average clutch size was related inversely to adult density, so that hens at low density produced large clutches. The Hrisey study did not last long enough to check reliably whether clutch size varies with the phase of the fluctuation as at Derry Cairngorm.

Among hens that lose their first clutch to predators or to desertion in snowstorms, some lay a repeat clutch with three to four fewer eggs, resulting in a later set of young. In Scotland these late broods contain young that are about five to six weeks old at the end of July – approximately half-grown when the young from successful early broods appear almost as big as their mothers.

## BREEDING SUCCESS

This is the number of young reared per hen. It equals brood size (the number of young reared per brood) in years when no hens fail. In most years, however, it is less, because some hens rear no young. Many hens fail in some years: at Derry Cairngorm mostly due to entire broods dying, on Svalbard to hens deserting nests in snowfalls, and at Cairn Gorm to crows robbing nests.[146] In extreme cases at Derry Cairngorm, all hens reared young in two years, and none in two other years.[147]

Breeding success varies amongst Scottish areas, and amongst countries. The study area with poorest breeding is Derry Cairngorm, slightly better on more fertile soils at the Cairnwell and Meall Odhar, and successively better in Lombardy, Eagle Creek, Svalbard, northern Canada and Hrisey (*see* Table 14).

Most deaths of Scottish chicks occur in their first week, and breeding success depends mainly on chick loss. The hatchlings' viability partly determines their mortality. Viability depends on egg quality, which in turn is influenced by the diet of laying hens, especially the amount of nutritious new plant growth available to them.[148] The quality of the hens' diet on the relatively fertile Cairnwell and Meall Odhar exceeds that on Derry Cairngorm, and chick survival usually reflects this.

Chick survival is also influenced by the amount and quality of their food, by predators and by weather. Sheep and red deer in Scotland have eliminated almost all willow scrub, and remove other nutritious foods such as Alpine bistort and cotton-grass shoots. This reduces food quality for hens and chicks, and explains poorer breeding here than in countries further north.

In Iceland, for example, hens have a good diet in spring[149] and summer. Chicks on Hrisey eat Alpine bistort, a plant so nutritious that they do not need insects to boost their intake of protein, and in most years they survive well. Subsequently, families flock to forage on old hayfields, where agriculture would have improved soils and resulted in the growth of nutritious plants.

On any one area, some hens do better than others. In studies at Svalbard and the Cairnwell, heavy hens reared bigger broods than light hens, and likewise early-laying hens reared bigger broods than late-laying hens.[150] Svalbard hens that hatched their eggs outweighed hens that deserted their nests or lost them to predators. First-year Svalbard hens increased their weight later than older hens, laid smaller clutches and reared smaller broods. In short, the hens' condition affects their later breeding success.

## ENEMIES

Northern native people kill many rock ptarmigan for food, but vast areas of the bird's range are uninhabited by humans. Large numbers have been shot by sport-hunters in Russia and Iceland, with fewer taken in other countries, including Scotland. In many southern countries, man has eliminated some predators such as wolves and wolverines. This, along with the human-induced rise in the number of carcasses of sheep and deer, and increased food refuse, has led to an increase of foxes in Britain. Arctic foxes that were unwisely introduced to several Aleutian islands have extirpated ptarmigan there.[151]

Foxes, now the main predator on Scottish ptarmigan, take adults, eggs and chicks, as do stoats and weasels, although to a far lesser extent. Next to the fox, golden eagles kill many adults and chicks, and some adults fall prey to peregrines. Hen harriers and short-eared owls occur too rarely and briefly to be of any importance, and in several years a snowy owl on Cairn Gorm plateau has fed largely on ptarmigan adults and chicks.[152] Near the very few gulleries at high lochs, common gulls take some eggs and chicks locally.

Data on the numbers of ptarmigan taken by different predators have been published from Scotland and elsewhere.[153] During a study on Derry Cairngorm, for example, foxes and golden eagles killed 62 adults, and only two others were found dead without signs of injury and in poor condition. Crows, though normally resident far below Alpine land, were attracted by food scraps at a busy tourist development on Cairn Gorm, and took ptarmigan eggs and chicks.[154] Following these losses, combined with deaths on ski-lift wires, no ptarmigan summered on the most heavily developed part of the area for many years.

Compared with red grouse, relatively few parasites live on and in Scottish ptarmigan, but they include the threadworms that kill some red grouse. In most ptarmigan these are absent or occur in small numbers, and so are not sufficient to cause ptarmigan declines.[155] In Scotland, ticks have not been recorded on ptarmigan or on ptarmigan ground. This may alter with climate change.

## THE FUTURE

Threats to ptarmigan include more wires, disturbance by people and dogs near roads, extra crows induced by human activities, habitat loss from ski development, and pollution and climate change. Overgrazing by sheep and deer has reduced heath and extirpated ptarmigan on otherwise suitable rocky hills in Scotland, England, Wales and Ireland. An end to sheep subsidies and to deer overpopulation could bring ptarmigan back.

## SUMMARY

Ptarmigan have a circumpolar Arctic distribution with southern extensions on islands and mountains. Their three plumages bestow good camouflage. Scottish birds reach high density on ground that has much food alongside boulders that provide cover. Scottish densities include the highest so far recorded, associated with abundant food, but the food is of low quality and results in generally poor breeding. Differences in the quality of the hens' food from one year to another influence breeding success. Birds in Arctic Canada occur at very low density, associated with sparse food plants, but the food is of high quality, so they lay large clutches and breed well.

CHAPTER 5

# Black Grouse

BLACK GROUSE COME and go as landscapes change. They seem adaptable because they live in a broad range of habitats, yet are vulnerable as these disappear with shifting countryside fashions. In forest-steppe or boreal forest, black grouse are birds of the forest edge and the early stages of forest succession that follow wind-throw, fire or logging. In Britain and other countries greatly affected by humans, they have adapted to habitats with a similar structure – that is, transitional between forest and open country. Such habitats often comprise novel plant species introduced by agriculture or afforestation. Successional habitats naturally change with time, and so the birds shift from place to place as ground that was once suitable becomes less welcoming.

Black grouse were widespread throughout Britain at the beginning of the twentieth century, but since then have declined in both range and number. The reasons usually given for this include habitat change and increased predation. Climate change has probably also played a role.

## THE BIRD

The adult blackcock, a bird weighing some 1,200–1,300g, is mostly black or black-brown with a metallic blue sheen and a distinctive tail. This feature is often described as lyre-shaped because the feathers on each side of it curve symmetrically outwards like the horns of an antelope (see Fig. 7).[1] His black breast, throat, crown, nape and back have a blue sheen, while his forehead, ear-coverts and chin are more blue-green. A bar of white crosses the wing. His undertail-coverts, axillaries and underwing-coverts are pure white, and the lower belly feathers are also tipped white. Above his eye is a comb of vermilion red. The beak is black and the iris dark brown. The feet are scaly grey-brown, with the toes fringed on either side by a row of overlapping horny scales that grip tree branches and also work as snow-shoes. In July through September the cock goes into partial 'eclipse', when black feathers on the head and some on the upper back are replaced by chestnut or brownish-buff feathers barred with black, these sometimes marked or edged white. These dull feathers are kept for about a month until the summer moult of primaries and tail feathers is complete.

The adult greyhen, weighing some 900–1,000g, is generally rufous-buff, more or less heavily barred with black, although some birds are more grey than rufous. The barring is broader on her upperparts. The scapulars and uppertail-coverts are tipped white to grey, as are the feathers of her underparts, except for the throat and upper breast. Her forked tail and pale wing bar – discreet emulations of the cock's bolder plumage – distinguish her from hen capercaillie, as do her white axillaries, faster wingbeats and more acrobatic flight.

The downy chicks differ from capercaillie in having a chestnut crown, sometimes mottled black or surrounded by a black line (Fig. 46). A dusky median stripe runs from the crown through the yellow-buff nape to the middle of the back, where it broadens and becomes chestnut. Otherwise, the upperparts are rufous-brown, marked yellow and black, and the underparts yellow-buff.

FIG 46. Black grouse chick in Scotland, two days old. (Desmond Dugan)

The juvenile (the stage between downy chick and immature) resembles an adult hen but is smaller. When they are about the size of a partridge and half-grown at six weeks, males begin to show black feathers through the brown. In his first year, a young cock resembles an adult but is less glossy. His head, neck, wing-coverts, scapulars and secondaries are marked with rufous, contributing to a duller appearance. The first-year hen resembles the adult, but is distinguishable in the hand by her more sharply pointed outer primaries (primaries 9 and 10),[2] whose tips have more extensive buff vermiculations.

## THE LEK

Black grouse are stylish exponents of the promiscuous lek mating system.[3] At first light, blackcocks gather to display in their smart black and white plumage, like gentlemen in evening dress at an old-fashioned ball (Figs 47 & 48). Their dance floor, however, is in the open – a sward of short grass or heather, a rushy field, an open bog, a woodland clearing, a glade or a forest margin. They avoid uniformly tall vegetation, although some leks are in tussocky vegetation, where the birds tread paths winding among clumps of rushes or bushy trees kept topiary short by browsing roe deer. Most lekking groups have a single lekking

**FIG 47.** Blackcocks at a lek in Abernethy. (Desmond Dugan)

FIG 48. Blackcocks displaying to a greyhen on a lek at Abernethy. Pine-birch woodland opens onto moorland at the forest edge here, and the River Spey lies below. (Chris Knights)

place within their tribal territory, which they use day after day. Some groups have two or three different leks – they move from one to another on different mornings, or on the same morning if disturbed.

In Britain, leks of five to ten cocks are common, but some number more than 30 and elsewhere up to 200 cocks have been recorded. A cock has two main displays: rookooing (or bubbling) and a crowing hiss. He rookoos in territorial defence and courtship. Rookooing, a musical, resonant bubbling, is a sustained repetition of the phrase 'rroo-OO-rroo-rroo' (stress in capitals). From a distance, a half-heard rookoo resembles the call of a wood-pigeon. The far-carrying resonance, which makes the sound hard to locate, is imparted by inflating special oesophageal pouches. The cock crouches and leans forward with a swollen neck, cocks his black tail feathers and arches them fan-wise, the curved outer-tail feathers almost touching the ground and the rump feathers ruffled in a contrasting white half-puffball. Singing on the spot, he turns the while to face different directions.

The crowing hiss is both a self-advertisement and a threat. With body and neck upstretched, a cock hisses harshly with wide-open beak. In more intense display, sudden wingbeats reveal striking white axillaries. During yet more intense display, the wingbeats become a fluttering jump, forming a sequence: crowing-hiss, crouch, jump. A few wing strokes take the bird perhaps 50cm off the ground, and he turns in mid-air to land facing a different direction. Flutter jumping can develop into flutter flight: the cock flies a few metres off the ground, hissing the while, and, after a curving flight, lands within his own territory. Flutter jumps and flutter flights are infectious, triggered in particular by hens' wingbeats.

Confrontations between owners of neighbouring territories involve ritual displays, reinforced by occasional fights. Two rookooing neighbours face each other, scrape their feet threateningly and feint pecks. One hisses and jumps forward, pecking towards the head of his opponent; he in turn jumps backwards, flaps his wings for balance, and exchanges pecks with the aggressor. One cock manages to grasp the other and wild combat ensues – thrashing wings, kicking feet, and tufts of feathers plucked from head or neck. Deaths are rare, but bald patches and tufts of feathers left on the lek can be seen in late spring.

Adult cocks assemble in the dark before walking or flying to the lek, hissing as they arrive in early twilight. Each cock stalks towards his territory, tail cocked, head held high and neck thick with raised feathers – a threatening posture that is maintained until he reaches the security of his own patch of ground. Lek territories

FIG 49. Finnish blackcock fighting in snow over a frozen lake. (Chris Knights)

FIG 50. Blackcock fighting on land. (Chris Knights)

are quite small – typically about 100m², although they are bigger on open flat terrain and smaller where tall vegetation such as rush clumps restricts visual contact. They can broadly be classified as 'central' or 'peripheral', with central males mating most of the hens in spring (late April and early May). On small leks, a single master cock often performs most of the copulations. There has been much debate as to whether hens prefer central territories or the owners of these territories.

Cocks use landmarks to fix their territorial boundaries. Leks on frozen lakes in northern countries, however, have few landmarks, so territories here are not fixed and the cocks that win most fights mate most hens.[4] A hen courted by a good fighter sometimes approaches a less dominant cock, who gives way or suffers a beating. Thus hens on ice test rival cocks before accepting the service of the better bird.

On dry land, fixed territories complicate the hens' choice because each cock is dominant on his own territory. On the whole, hens prefer bigger cocks with longer tails, which attend the lek more often, display more vigorously, live longer and have a relatively large central territory. The siting of a cock's territory – central

**FIG 51.** Three central cocks and a peripheral one. (Desmond Dugan)

or peripheral – reflects his mating successes in this and previous years.[5] A hen often mates with the same cock as in the previous year, if he has survived.[6] Hens also copy each other – after mating one hen, a cock is more likely to be chosen by others.[7]

Successful cocks keep their place within the lek from year to year but, as some die or retire from the lek, vacancies arise and other cocks move towards the lek centre. This makes sense, because cocks adjacent to successful cocks seem able to mate with some hens just by being close to a master.[8] Each year, new territories are formed around the current centre of coition, not that of the previous year.

There is much competition for central territories, which are therefore smaller than peripheral ones and form a dense cluster of displaying cocks. Larger leks have bigger central clusters that attract more hens, so that cocks in bigger clusters on larger leks mate more hens.[9] Bigger leks remain big over the years because more young cocks join them.[10] Although young cocks do not get a territory and rarely mate, their presence increases the mating success of adult cocks. It seems that lek size as well as cock quality attracts hens to larger leks.

Many of the cocks at a black grouse[11] or capercaillie[12] lek are related, forming an extended family, or set of families, reminiscent of kin clusters in red grouse (see Chapter 14). Related cocks gain evolutionary benefit when one of them begets offspring. The lek, therefore, is not only an arena where individuals and families compete, but also a tribal unit. Such clannishness, however, can cause inbreeding. Inbred cocks have a poorer chance of getting a territory on a lek and, if they do so, it is less likely to be central.[13] As in other grouse species, young hens disperse further than young cocks before settling to breed (see 'Movements' below), which reduces inbreeding.

Hens mostly mate but once, remating only if the act is interrupted by a rival cock.[14] Like cocks, hens vary in quality.[15] Hens in better condition visit more cock territories before choosing to mate with better cocks, and hens that mate with better cocks lay bigger clutches. Hens on leks often squabble, but there is no evidence that subordinate hens get poorer cocks – they just wait their turn.

Most cocks spend much of the year in groups. Winter groups are labile and include both sexes, although one usually predominates. In spring, a lekking group of cocks separates from the winter group, feeding and roosting together within a kilometre of the lek. Some lekking groups display from September to May, ceasing only in bad weather and during moult in June to August. Non-lekking cocks (youngsters, adults that have not earned a territory and old gentlemen retired from the fray) range more widely but sometimes visit a lek. Some cocks display alone, away from any lek, and such soloists can successfully attract hens. In spring, a single cock can sometimes be seen pursuing a hen in flight well away from any lek, although the outcome of such informal courtships is unknown.

Not all black grouse populations lek conventionally. Some display on 'exploded' leks where displaying neighbours are separated by several hundred metres. In Wales, soloists are common.[16] In the Bavarian Alps, disturbance from skiers, snowboarders and walkers has led black grouse to abandon traditional lek sites, and now the cocks display solitarily, dispersed over wide areas at temporary display sites.[17]

The evolution of leks is a topic of unconsummated speculation. Two recent discoveries give clues about their function. First, cocks at a black grouse or capercaillie lek are often related because recruits are sons of fathers already on the lek, a process called philopatric recruitment. Individuals therefore gain their status within a tribal system. Second, the non-lekking territorial red grouse tend to cluster in related groups, also because of philopatric recruitment. Hence black grouse or capercaillie in a lek (or red grouse in a kin cluster) facilitate the recruitment of their joint offspring into the tribe. Perhaps this is a general pattern: maybe all breeding cock grouse live in genetically structured tribes. If so, this implies that social systems may well have evolved through kin selection and that explanations couched solely in terms of individual selection are incomplete. There is no generally accepted explanation, however, of how some species became territorial with spacious territories that occupy all suitable habitat, whilst others developed lekking or intermediate social systems.

## SYSTEMATICS

There are seven or eight recognised subspecies of black grouse, of which only *Tetrao tetrao britannicus* is geographically isolated. This presumably happened about 7,000 years ago, when Britain became separated from Europe. The Caucasian black grouse *T. mlokosiewiczi* is a glacial relic that evolved into a distinct species. The two species once had their own genus, *Lyrurus*, and some modern authorities argue that this should be reinstated.[18]

## DISTRIBUTION AND NATIONAL NUMBERS

Plentiful in forest-steppe, where open bog grades into boreal forest, and in the early successional stages of boreal forest in northern Eurasia, black grouse occur continuously from Scandinavia to southeast Siberia (about 140°E). None the less, they declined during the twentieth century, especially from the 1970s. Declines were deepest in western and central Europe (the western and southern parts of the range), where many lowland populations disappeared and there were large contractions of range. Remaining lowland populations are mostly small (< 200) and isolated. The strongest population in this region, a glacial relic, is now in the Alps up to about 2,500m. Loss and degradation of habitat have been blamed for declines in Europe and Britain, but climate change has probably also played a part.

Widespread on heaths and moorland throughout Britain at the beginning of the twentieth century, black grouse have since declined in both range and number. In 1924, Francis Jourdain[19] described a diminishing species that had become extinct in Nottinghamshire, Leicestershire and Kent, but possibly survived in Worcestershire. In Wiltshire, Sussex and Surrey, occasional stragglers were to be found, but it was extinct as a breeding species. Scarce in Dorset and Hampshire, black grouse were also much reduced in Devon and Somerset, and almost extinct in Cornwall. The species was scarce in Wales, but still existed around Brecon and Montgomery, and in some of the border counties such as Herefordshire and Shropshire. On Cannock Chase (Staffordshire) it was still common, and a few bred in north Staffordshire and north Derbyshire, and thence along the Pennines to the Scottish border, ranging into all the northern counties of England. In Scotland, it occurred throughout the mainland and in many of the Inner Hebrides, but not in the Outer Hebrides or the northern islands. Today, the bulk of the remaining population occurs in Scotland, where the birds are still widely distributed, although some remain in north England, especially the north Pennines, and there are a few in Wales.

Worldwide, the breeding population of black grouse numbers several million.[20] In Britain, a countrywide survey concluded that there were some 6,000–7,000 displaying cocks in 1995–6, equivalent to perhaps 20,000–30,000 breeding birds.[21] Numbers continued to decline during the late 1990s, and in 2005 another survey revealed about 5,000 displaying cocks.[22] Game-bag records show a decline of about 90 per cent in the number of birds shot between the start of the twentieth century and the 1980s.

Declines are not inevitable, however. Numbers increased in Sweden and Slovenia during the 1990s.[23] In Scotland, where numbers continue to decline overall, especially in Argyll and the Southern Uplands, those in Highland, Grampian and Tayside seem stable. This may reflect regional differences in land use. In Wales and northern England, heroic and apparently successful attempts are being made to reverse the decline in black grouse through careful habitat management.[24]

## HABITAT AND DIET

### Habitat

Black grouse live in habitats that are transitional between woodland and open grassland or moorland, mostly in boreal, subarctic and Alpine climes. Their main natural habitats are forest-steppe (Fig. 52), margins between open bog and woodland (Fig. 53), early successional stages in boreal forest following wind-throw or lightning fire, and tree-line habitats on mountainous ground. In cultivated landscapes, they choose habitats of a similar structure to those in the wild, readily using the alien plant species that come with agriculture or afforestation.

Trees are usually an essential component of black grouse habitat, but the canopy should not be so closed that it shades out food plants such as herbs, heather, blaeberry or dwarf rhododendron.[25] In Britain, however, broods may be found on open moorland up to a kilometre from trees. Suitable structure is provided by scrub or scattered copses of small pine, spruce, larch or birch that border rough grassland, moorland or bog, as well as glades, clearings and patches of burned or wind-thrown woodland with natural regeneration. Much

FIG 52. Black grouse habitat in Kazakhstan: forest-steppe. (François Mougeot)

FIG 53. Black grouse habitat in Finland: forest edge and open bog. (Dave Pullan)

FIG 54. Good forest-edge habitat for black grouse at Abernethy. (Desmond Dugan)

of the ground vegetation is about knee-height, but it provides variation in height and also density, open enough to allow the birds to walk through it and to dry out after rain. In summer, moulting cocks use thick cover such as rushes, juniper or bracken.

In central Europe, traditional agricultural practices sustained woodland grouse until well into the twentieth century. Domestic animals grazed the forest, opening up glades, and farmers removed plant litter for animal bedding. This created open canopies and poor soils, thereby favouring ericaceous shrubs such as heather and blaeberry, and consequently black grouse and capercaillie.[26] Prehistoric forests may also have been kept open by deer, aurochs (wild cattle), tarpan (wild horse), bison, beaver and wild boar. In Britain and Ireland, however, milder winters allowed farmers to keep higher densities of stock at all seasons. These destroyed or reduced tree cover on the more fertile soils and were less favourable to woodland grouse. On infertile soils, some pinewood persisted, but much was transformed to heath.

In Britain, black grouse were formerly widespread on scrubby lowland heaths, moorland edge and rough agricultural ground. Within living memory, they and red grouse, together with capercaillie in Scotland, were a common sight on autumn oat stubble, stooks and stacks around hill farms (see Fig. 23). They also frequented weedy turnip fields. As bogs were drained, broods came increasingly to depend upon flushes, rough grassland and hayfields for the invertebrates needed for early chick growth. Most black grouse in Britain now occur on heathery moorland up to an altitude of about 500m, where they often do well following afforestation (see below).

Clear-fells mimic storm damage and black grouse sometimes do well after industrial logging. Their increase in the 1990s in Sweden, for example, followed clear-felling. They showed no general increase, however, with the onset of industrial clear-felling west of the Urals in the late twentieth century, although perhaps this was prevented by something else. European grouse populations mostly declined during this period, even where habitat remained intact, which hints at some adverse climatic factor affecting more than one species (see Chapter 14).

Promises that black grouse would flourish in our novel British plantations as these were felled, replanted and restructured during the late twentieth century were not fulfilled. The reasons for this are still being discussed, but an obvious aspect is that heather and blaeberry – staple foods of black grouse for much of the year – do not usually reappear in abundance after Sitka spruce has been clear-felled. In part, this is probably because Sitka spruce often suffers from 'heather check' when planted on heather moorland. The trained response of British foresters to heather check has been to kill the heather with herbicides, so allowing spruce to resume growth. Also, planting of Sitka spruce is often carried out very soon after felling, thereby allowing heather and blaeberry little time to recover before canopy closure recurs. Furthermore, Sitka spruce and other aliens shade out heath plants, much more so than Scots pine. Any other adverse effects of these plantations are unknown, as the ecosystems created by British foresters are unique and so no traditional store of knowledge has yet built up.

### Diet

Black grouse eat a wider range of foods than other British grouse, their diet varying with the season and habitat. For much of the year, their staple diet is typically dwarf shrubs such as heather and blaeberry, until in deepening winter snow they take to juniper and then to trees. They prefer birch catkins, then buds and eventually twigs, but where birch is scarce they readily eat Scots pine. Other winter tree foods include alder, willow, hazel, spruce and beech.

In England, a small nonconformist population of black grouse survives in the now largely treeless northern Pennines. It is not clear whether this relict of a woodland past could survive long periods of deep snow. Their prospects would probably be improved by copses of birch or Scots pine. As it is, they use mostly heather moorland and bogs in autumn and winter, and grassland in summer. Breeding hens and moulting cocks are found especially in rushy grassland, where

**FIG 55.** Blackcocks in a birch tree in winter. (Chris Knights)

they eat herbs, grasses, rushes and sedges.[27] Some birds in southwestern Scotland and the Borders use similar habitats.

In spring, blackcocks and, in particular, greyhens supplement their diet with various newly growing plants, such as herb leaves, flowers, green catkins of willow and birch, larch buds and leaves, and especially cotton-grass shoots. In summer, the young chicks need many invertebrates during their first three to four weeks. They find them in wet ground – bogs, herb-rich grassy flushes, rushy flushes, heather moorland, open woodland, rough grassland including hayfields, rushy fields, abandoned hill farms and crofts, and grassy moorland. Plant foods of adults and chicks in summer reflect their habitat: on grassland they include leaves, flowers, fruits and seeds of herbs, sedges, rushes and grasses; and on heather moorland they comprise more heather and blaeberry. In late summer and autumn, the birds take berries, including blaeberry, crowberry, rowan and hawthorn.

### Habitat improvement

Current methods for black grouse habitat improvement rely more on anecdote and subjective experience than rigorous scientific demonstration.[28] A good starting point is that many plantations on British moorland are unnaturally hard-edged, with no transitional zone between closed-canopy plantation and open ground (Fig. 56). Commonly, trees grow densely up to a boundary fence. Outside the fence, heavy grazing by sheep or deer often keeps the vegetation much shorter than the knee-height preferred by black grouse. Christmas-tree plantations, however, are often used by black grouse. These have a permanently open canopy that can sustain dwarf shrubs, and so provides a long-lasting transitional zone.

The creation of a transitional zone along plantation edges (*see* Fig. 58) can lead to increases in numbers of black grouse. Thinning the edge trees by up to 90 per cent lets enough light through the canopy and onto the ground for heather and

FIG 56. Sitka spruce in northeast Scotland, planted on a grouse moor where there were once red and black grouse. Such hard-edged woodlands are not favoured by black grouse. (Robert Moss)

FIG 57. Sitka spruce and 'improved' pasture in North Wales, forest edge that is unsuitable for black grouse. This was once a heather moor. (Robert Moss)

blaeberry to grow. Practitioners consider that thinning should reach at least 50m, or preferably 200m, into the plantation. The straight edges should be scalloped, thereby providing alcoves where birds can hide from raptors. Tangled wind-throw at plantation edges also affords useful cover, especially for chicks. Another positive step is to reduce sheep or deer numbers on adjacent moorland or rough grassland, and then take down the boundary fence, so reducing grazing sufficiently to allow vegetation outside the plantation to grow to knee-height. Such measures should result in more black grouse, but the initial increase will be short-lived unless the ground vegetation is kept in a state of patchy growth. This can be done by rotational grazing, burning or swiping, such that some patches are always in a state of rapid growth (see below).

The number of grazing animals should, if practicable, be alternately reduced and increased, so that the ground vegetation is grazed short and then allowed to grow on a rotation of about six years. Some ground, however, should be managed on a longer rotation to provide the knee-high vegetation cover preferred by black grouse. Rotational burning or swiping of heathery vegetation should have similar effects. If afforestation is the main land use, plantations should be left with 30 per

**FIG 58.** This black grouse habitat at Penaran in North Wales was solid Sitka spruce nine years before the picture was taken. (Robert Moss)

cent or more of open heathery space to be grazed or swiped rotationally. Also, planting should be staggered so that blocks of trees less than ten years old are always available.

Removing fences once plantation trees are tall enough to tolerate sheep or deer is common practice and is useful in preventing deaths from birds flying into fences. However, it is of little value if grazing animals destroy heather or blaeberry cover inside the plantation. If it is not practicable to reduce sheep or deer numbers outside a plantation, it may be better to thin the trees and leave the fence in place, marking it to reduce collisions.

Centuries of concerted effort have gone into draining Britain, so that wet and boggy habitats are now unnaturally scarce. In more natural situations, black grouse and capercaillie broods make much use of bogs, as they harbour many of the insects upon which young chicks depend. In Britain, young broods of all four grouse species are often found on or near wet ground – this is especially obvious in dry summers. The blocking of woodland and moorland drains to re-create bogs should therefore benefit woodland grouse, and trees should not be planted on wet flushes.

### Afforestation and grazing: general background

To judge from bag records,[29] black grouse were quite plentiful in Britain from the mid-1950s to the late 1970s. All four British grouse did well during the late 1960s and early 1970s, but black grouse were abundant for longer, probably because they also benefited from afforestation.

Large but short-lived increases in black grouse numbers are often observed following afforestation of heather moorland or moorland edge.[30] Between 1950 and 1980, large upland tracts were planted with Sitka spruce or lodgepole pine at about 2,000 trees per ha, with perhaps 5–10 per cent of unplanted open space. Recent plantations tend to have more open space, 30 per cent being not unusual. In the 1990s the planting of native Scots pine at 1,100 trees per ha became more common, especially in Perthshire and further north in Scotland.

As a plantation canopy spreads and intercepts more light, heather and blaeberry turn brown and die (Fig. 59). After the canopy has closed, typically at 10–15 years in dense plantings, heather and blaeberry survive only in open spaces that have been left unplanted or where trees have been checked or have died.

Canopy closure and associated loss of dwarf shrubs can explain declines of black grouse in moorland plantations,[31] but not initial increases. Afforestation of moorland with Sitka spruce or lodgepole pine usually involves fencing, ploughing and fertilising, as well as planting trees. The planting of native pine is generally preceded by fencing but not usually by ploughing or fertilising, though the soil is quite often cultivated or 'scarified' with a deep tine, and the trees are planted on large upturned sods called mounds.[32] There is also some evidence

**FIG 59.** Canopy closure and ground vegetation: in the foreground are heather and blaeberry; in the mid-ground heather is dying to leave blaeberry; near the trees is stunted blaeberry; and under the closed lodgepole pine canopy no green plants grow. (Robert Moss)

that forest fires and swiping of moorland vegetation are followed by short-lived increases in black grouse, much as is seen after afforestation.[33]

All these management procedures affect ground vegetation. After fire or swiping, ground vegetation grows back and regains height. The fencing typical of moorland afforestation excludes sheep or deer, and again the ground vegetation grows in height.

**Afforestation and grazing: case histories**
In 1991–3, David Baines assessed the effect of grazing[34] upon black grouse in northern England and southern Scotland by comparing 20 moors with different sheep densities.[35] The birds' breeding density and breeding success were higher on moors where sheep densities were lower. The plant species composing the vegetation did not differ between moors with more or less grazing, but the vegetation was shorter on the more heavily grazed moors and these supported fewer insects, which might have affected breeding success. Interestingly, the presence of a gamekeeper on a moor went along with three times fewer carrion crows, but not with better breeding of black grouse.

From this it seemed that reducing the density of grazers should increase black grouse on heavily grazed moors. This prospect was assessed by comparing black grouse on ten pairs of sites in northern England.[36] Ten 'treatment' sites encompassed areas where grazing had been reduced on moorland edges, often through government incentives to reduce sheep numbers, between 1991 and 1995. These were contrasted with ten 'reference' sites with no grazing reduction. Black grouse were counted during 1996–2000. On only two of the treatment sites did the number of displaying cocks increase markedly, and on two sites it declined relative to the reference sites. On the face of it, this was a disappointing result. But it gave a clue: the numbers of displaying cocks had tended to increase initially after grazing reductions and then to decline, much as is seen after afforestation.

Observations by RSPB staff at Abernethy pinewood nicely illustrate the consequences of grazing reduction.[37] The wood comprises largely mature Scots pines with an open canopy, and ground vegetation dominated by heather with some blaeberry. After the RSPB bought the estate in 1988, they reduced grazing with the main aim of allowing more trees to regenerate, by removing sheep in 1991 and then culling red deer more heavily. The progress of the increased cull was assessed by counting deer twice a year, in March and October, over about 20km² of woodland and 70km² of open ground, from Forest Lodge in the middle of the pinewood up to the summit of Cairn Gorm. Black grouse and capercaillie were counted at the same time.[38] Black grouse increased and then declined, just

120 · GROUSE

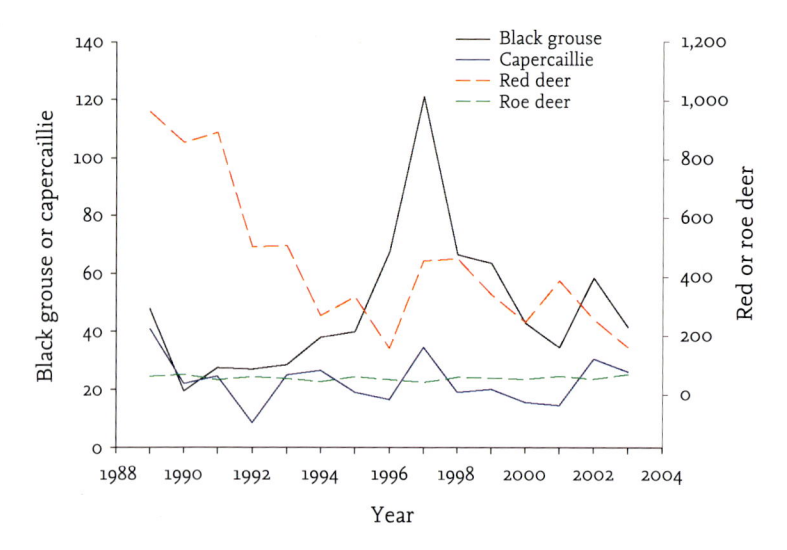

**FIG 60.** Numbers of black grouse, capercaillie, red deer and roe deer seen during deer counts at Abernethy pinewood (means of March and October counts). A decline in red deer was followed by a transient increase in black grouse but not capercaillie.

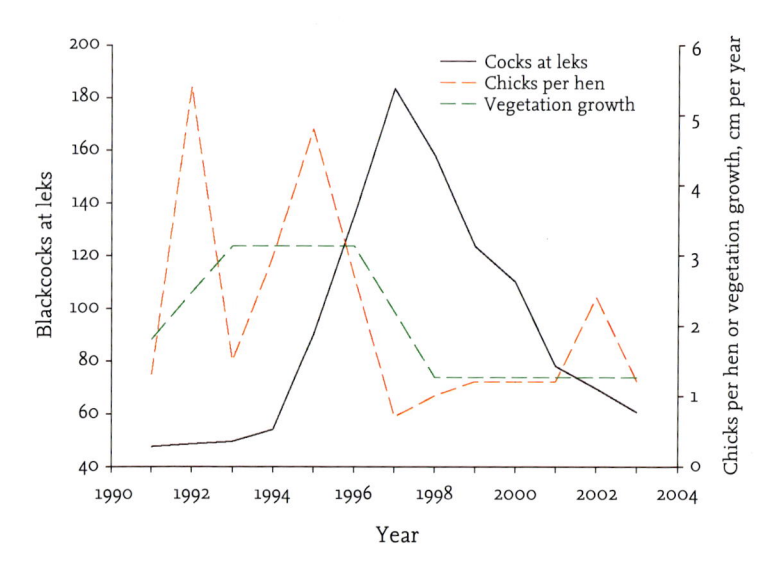

**FIG 61.** Number of blackcocks displaying at leks in Abernethy pinewood each spring, breeding success in the previous summer and vegetation growth since the previous year.

like the boom and bust after plantations are established, but capercaillie showed no obvious trend (Fig. 60).

The pinewood at Abernethy was mature, and so canopy closure was negligible, as was the associated loss of dwarf shrubs.[39] Although parts of the wood were planted, any ploughing or fertilising had been done so long ago that they could not have contributed to the changes in black grouse numbers.[40]

Fluctuations in the number of displaying blackcocks followed much the same pattern as black grouse seen during deer counts, rising until 1997 and then declining (Fig. 61).[41] Staff also estimated breeding success in the reserve by using dogs to help count greyhens and chicks in late July. Increases in lek counts up to 1996 were broadly associated with good breeding success in the previous summer, and the subsequent decline after 1997 was associated with poorer breeding. The best breeding success (5.4 chicks per hen[42] in 1992), however, was followed by only a tiny increase in displaying cocks.

Fewer deer and no sheep led to the ground vegetation growing taller.[43] The heights of the 'field layer' (mostly heather) and of the underlying moss both increased (Table 15). The deeper moss was presumably not a consequence of reduced grazing, but rather of less trampling by sharp ungulate hooves.

**TABLE 15.** Height and structural variation (coefficient of variation) of ground vegetation following reductions of sheep and deer at Abernethy pinewood (45 quadrats).[44]

| | HEIGHT OF GROUND VEGETATION (CM) | | | | | |
|---|---|---|---|---|---|---|
| YEAR | FIELD LAYER | | MOSS | | DIFFERENCE# | |
| | HEIGHT | VARIATION | HEIGHT | VARIATION | HEIGHT | VARIATION |
| 1989 | 28.2 | 34.7 | 2.3 | 31.2 | 25.9 | 37.1 |
| 1992 | 33.9 | 34.9 | 6.6 | 120.3 | 27.3 | 53.9 |
| 1997 | 49.8 | 28.2 | 12.1 | 39.4 | 37.8 | 33.0 |
| 2003 | 56.2 | 23.5 | 14.3 | 35.5 | 41.9 | 28.3 |

| | ANNUAL GROWTH OF GROUND VEGETATION (CM) | | | | | |
|---|---|---|---|---|---|---|
| YEARS | FIELD LAYER | | MOSS | | DIFFERENCE# | |
| | RATE | VARIATION | RATE | VARIATION | RATE | VARIATION |
| 1989–92 | 1.81 | 136.9 | 1.44 | 194.1 | 0.37 | 981.1 |
| 1992–7 | 3.13 | 71.4 | 1.03 | 189.0 | 2.11 | 132.7 |
| 1997–2003 | 1.26 | 150.5 | 0.36 | 184.0 | 0.90 | 186.2 |

# Difference = height of field layer – moss height

Vegetation height might be important in itself or as an indicator of something else that influences black grouse. This might be physical cover for the birds, vegetation structure, food-plant quality or invertebrate abundance. Certainly, there must be vegetation tall enough to provide sufficient cover. In this case, because birds walk on top of thick moss, the difference in height between the top of the moss layer and that of the field layer might be a more accurate reflection of cover than the height of the field layer alone. Also, vegetation can become too tall and dense to allow chicks to forage readily and to dry out after rain. In short, reduced grazing set in train a complex set of changes, each of which might have influenced black grouse.

Dwarf shrubs grew fastest in 1992–7 (see Table 15), broadly coincident with the period of good breeding success and increasing numbers. Variety in the height of the moss layer was greatest in 1992, as the vegetation in some quadrats recovered faster than others from previous trampling. Clearly, great changes in the vegetation occurred up to 1997 and continued, albeit more slowly, up to 2003.

Although annual changes in the number of cocks at leks were correlated with breeding success in the previous year (Fig. 62), they were found to be more closely associated with the rate of growth in the height of the field layer. This suggests that the boom in black grouse at Abernethy was due as much to birds choosing to settle in the pinewood as to more youngsters being reared there. These possibilities are not exclusive: a good reason for birds to settle on fast-growing swards might be that such swards sustain better breeding success.

The decline after 1997 was associated with the sward becoming taller and denser, and reverting to slower growth (see Fig. 61). The same changes had no apparent effect upon capercaillie abundance (see Fig. 60), but black grouse are adapted to earlier stages of forest succession than capercaillie. Perhaps the contrasting responses of the two species to grazing reduction are an aspect of this difference. The details remain mysterious and worth further study.

Faster-growing swards are typically more varied and provide better opportunities for chicks to forage and to dry out after rain. In addition, fast-growing plants might be more nutritious[47] or support a more useful range of edible invertebrates than short, heavily grazed swards or tall mature ones. Whatever the mechanisms, grazing reduction promises to be useful for managing black grouse.

## MOVEMENTS

Black grouse are more mobile than other British grouse in that their distribution can change rapidly in response to transient changes in habitat. This involves

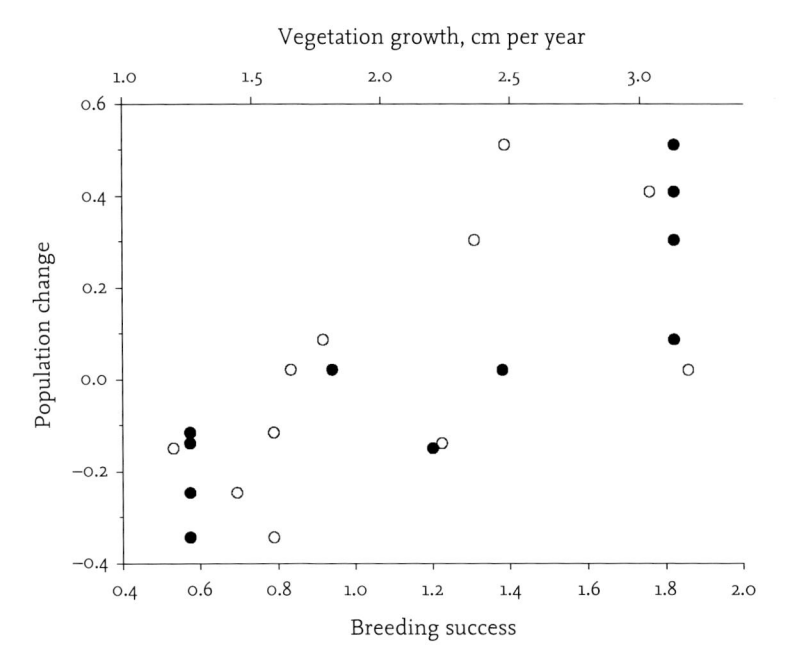

FIG 62. Annual population change (proportionate increase or decrease from one year to the next) in the number of blackcocks displaying at Abernethy leks was correlated with breeding success ($\log_e$[chicks per hen + 1], open symbols) and with vegetation growth rate (closed symbols).[45] Statistical analysis showed the association with vegetation growth to be the stronger of the two.[46]

young birds dispersing from their hatching place to settle and breed elsewhere (natal dispersal). Youngsters probably settle on attractive new habitat but avoid ground that is becoming unsuitable. Old birds may remain in deteriorating habitat but must eventually die, and if no youngsters settle the ground it will become deserted – so giving the impression of population movement. To what extent birds that have already bred in one place will move to another (breeding dispersal) is not clear.

In tracts of fairly stable habitat, black grouse are usually described as mainly resident or even sedentary.[48] In continuous habitat, leks are typically spaced at intervals of 1.5–2km and the home range of a lekking group of adult blackcocks can be as little as 1–2km². Adult greyhens are less sedentary, and may have separate summer and winter ranges, but generally they spend most of their time within an area of 5km² or less. In snowy conditions, flocks may wander more widely. In the taiga zone, eruptive movements of hundreds of kilometres have occasionally been reported, apparently when birds are at high density. Such movements have not been recorded in Britain, but evoke reports of 'migration' in red grouse.

As in other grouse species, black grouse in their first year of life show two main seasons of movement: autumn (late September to early November) and the following spring (mid-April to early May). Eight young hens in the north Pennines, for example, nested on average 9km from their place of capture.[49] Young cocks were more sedentary. None of 12 young cocks was found more than 1km from its tagging place in its first spring. Instructively, however, two during the winter were found 8km and 11km respectively from their place of catching, indicating that they had explored before settling near their rearing place.

## POPULATION FLUCTUATIONS

The decline of black grouse in Britain during the twentieth century seems to have had two main components: changes in climate and changes in habitat. Bag records show all four grouse species fluctuating broadly together until the Second World War, when there was a big decline. Before then, variations in their abundance were associated with fluctuations in the North Atlantic Oscillation (NAO), a crude measure of weather conditions (see Chapter 14). This applied to all four species in their different habitats, and is strong if indirect evidence that changes in their numbers were due in part to changes in weather. Bags after the Second World War have not been analysed in the same way, but weather probably continued to play a role, notably in the joint abundance of all four species in the late 1960s and early 1970s.

Declines in black grouse before the Second World War were not, however, uniform throughout the country, as might be expected if they were due solely to large-scale variations in weather. Bag records from two large estates illustrate this nicely (Fig. 63). After 1900, bags at Buccleuch estate in southwest Scotland rose to peak at about 1915 and then declined erratically until the Second World War. At Atholl estate in east-central Scotland, bags showed no obvious trend until they declined along with those of Buccleuch in the mid-1930s. The two sets of bags also showed differences in their short-term fluctuations. The Buccleuch records included many short fluctuations that lasted about six years from trough through peak to trough again, but this regularity was not apparent at Atholl. Interestingly, six years corresponds to the time taken for reduced grazing to take effect (see above). This fits the idea that the short fluctuations at Buccleuch reflected episodes when ground vegetation was recovering from heavy grazing or perhaps fire. We suggest that the steeper decline at Buccleuch was associated with a faster

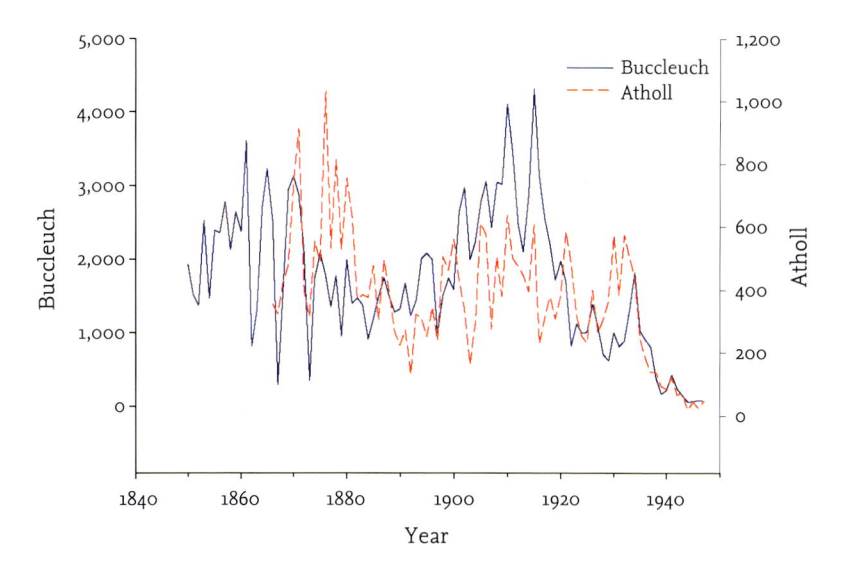

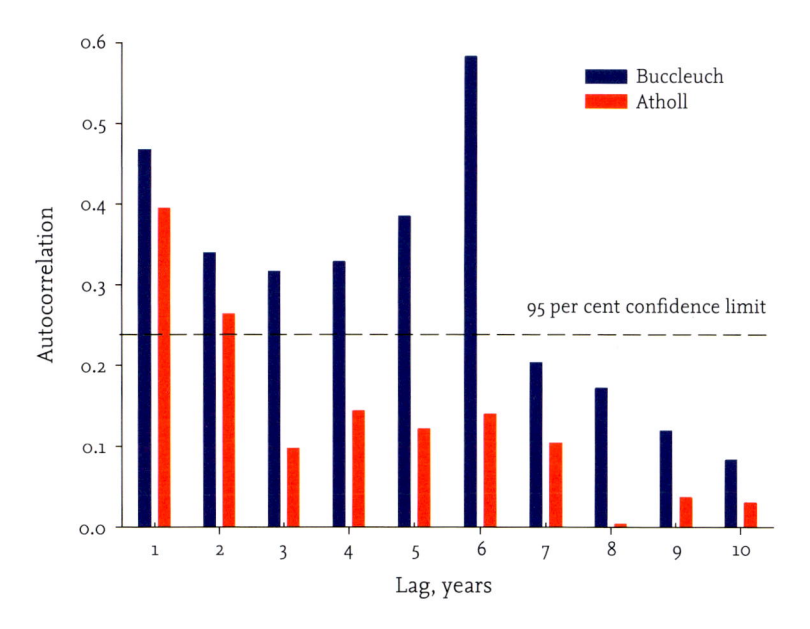

FIG 63. Black grouse at Buccleuch and Atholl estates. Upper: total bags. Lower: autocorrelation coefficients of bags. The Buccleuch bags showed significant autocorrelations at up to six years, reflecting a process that lasted six years but was not apparent at Atholl.[50]

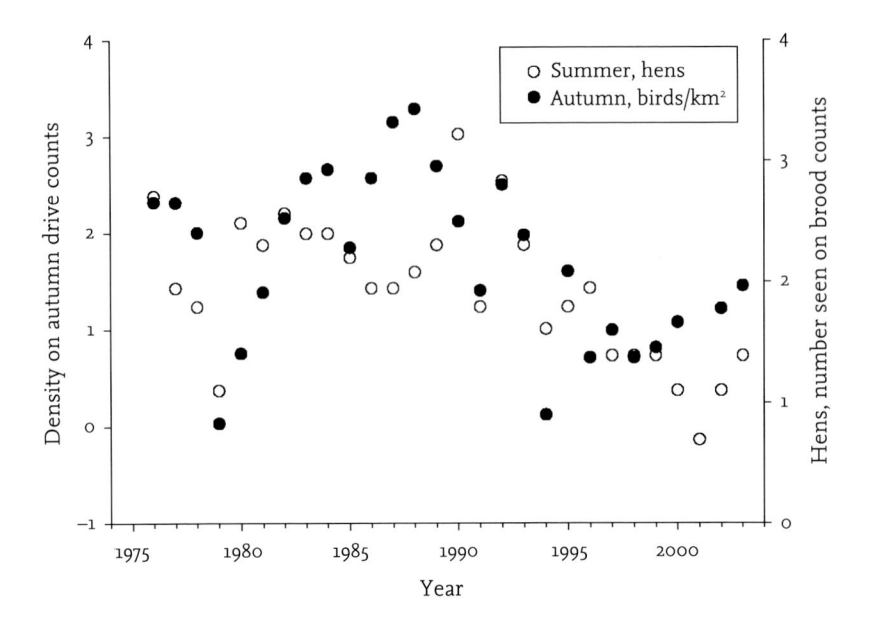

FIG 64. Density of black grouse seen in Glen Tanar old pinewood during autumn drive counts (cocks and hens, young and old, in an area of 4–7km$^2$), and the number of greyhens seen during brood counts in July (area 2.7km$^2$).[54]

deterioration in habitat, including loss of heather and scrub due to heavy grazing by large stocks of sheep. Such loss was widespread through much of upland Britain during this period.

Another factor broadly coincident with the decline of black grouse on sporting estates in the early twentieth century was an increase of pheasants released for put-and-take shooting. This alien, like black grouse, is a bird of woodland edge, and so the two compete directly. Also, captive-reared pheasants carry diseases and parasites that can affect black grouse.

The continuing decline of British black grouse in the late twentieth century is usually attributed to habitat loss and deterioration. In their 2003 website, for example, the Game Conservancy Trust gave 'four main reasons: being killed by predators; the loss of insects important in the diet of black grouse chicks; being killed by flying into deer fences; and the loss of pre-thicket forestry as blocks of conifer woodland mature'.[51]

Reviewing the literature, David Baines suggested that declines across Europe have been associated with the number of young reared per hen 'decreasing by

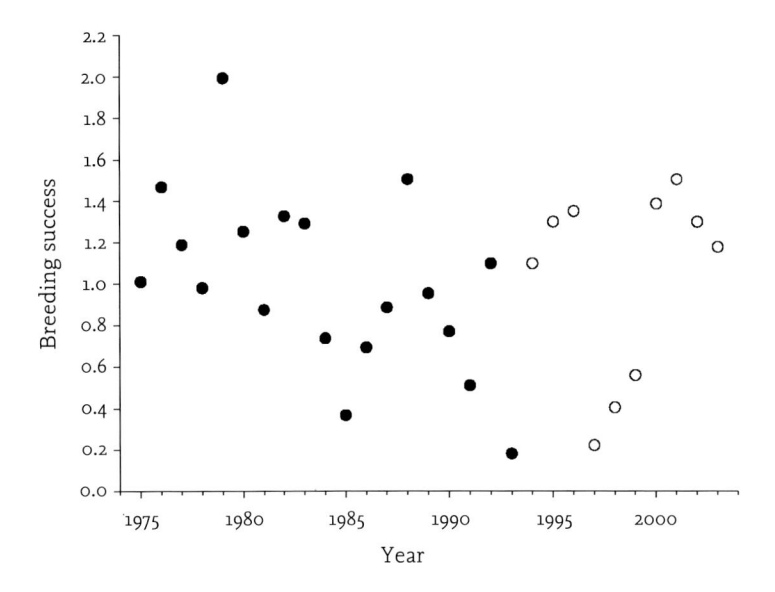

**FIG 65.** Breeding success (log$_e$[chicks per hen + 1] in July) at Glen Tanar. Success fell between 1975 and 1993 (closed symbols) but showed no further decline – and may even have increased – thereafter (open symbols).

approximately 60 per cent between 1950 and 1990'.[52] Another review proposed that the three most likely causes of poorer breeding were: habitat changes, which reduce availability of invertebrates for chicks; predation; and wet, cool weather in June.[53]

RM's counts from the old pinewood of Glen Tanar in Deeside show a decline in black grouse during the 1990s (Fig. 64). Breeding success, however, began to decline earlier, from some two to three chicks per hen in the late 1970s, to about 1.3 chicks per hen in the early 1990s (Fig. 65).[55] Subsequently, there was no further decline in breeding success and there may even have been some recovery during recent years. Perhaps breeding success in the late 1970s and early 1980s, although falling, remained sufficient to sustain numbers. By the late 1980s and early 1990s, however, it may have been insufficient to do so.

Annual variations in breeding success at Glen Tanar in 1975–2003 showed no obvious relationship with weather records.[56] During the study, however, there were striking, if anecdotal, changes in insect abundance. In the 1970s, for example, house-flies were so abundant during our counts of broods in July that on most days they circled our heads, dogs and humans alike, in their thousands

FIG 66. Dog with flies, as seen one July during the 1970s at Glen Tanar. (Robert Moss)

(Fig. 66). RM once clapped his hands and crushed 24 flies, so outperforming the tailor of legend ('seven at one blow') more than three-fold.[57] By the turn of the century, however, there were rarely more than ten flies per head. Midges and especially mosquitoes also seemed to decline in abundance in July. Any connection between the abundance of flies, midges and mosquitoes and the breeding success of woodland grouse is uncertain. If, however, the insects eaten by chicks also declined, this might have contributed to the chicks' poorer survival.

## CLUTCH SIZE AND BREEDING

The greyhen's nest is a shallow scrape in the ground, some 15–20cm in diameter and 4–6cm deep. It is lined with vegetation such as heather, grass or moss from the surroundings, and is usually sheltered by tall vegetation or low scrub, much taller and denser than that favoured by red grouse. Her eggs are buff with light spots of ochre or red-brown, and typically number 5 to 11, although sometimes there are as few as four or as many as 15 (*see* Fig. 12). They are laid at intervals of one-and-a-half to two days, and hatch after about 24 days of incubation by the hen alone. While the hen is incubating, she leaves the nest to feed two to three times a day. If her eggs are lost to a predator, she may scrape a new nest and lay again, but with fewer eggs than in her first nest.

Black grouse are the last of the British grouse to hatch. In east Scotland the mean date of hatching is mid-June, but in the north of England it is a week or more later. It has been suggested that peak hatching of moorland black grouse in Scotland coincides with the peak availability of their chief insect food – moth caterpillars on bog myrtle – whereas in north England it coincides with the later peak of sawfly larvae, their main insect food in this grassier habitat.[58] In the old pinewood of Glen Tanar, however, there is little bog myrtle and moth caterpillars reach peak numbers in early June, when capercaillie hatch.[59] By mid-June, caterpillar numbers decline as they pupate. Even so, broods of black grouse that hatched in Glen Tanar in mid-June and were counted in late July contained as many chicks as those on nearby moorland.[60]

Greyhens breed in their first year, but studies of radio-tagged hens show youngsters to be generally smaller and lighter, laying smaller and fewer eggs than older hens.[61] The proportion of clutches hatched seemed to be similar, but young hens reared much smaller broods than older birds. This may be partly because they were inexperienced and vulnerable to predators. Interpreting results from radio-tagged hens, however, is complicated by the observation that they rear fewer chicks than unmarked hens.[62]

## SURVIVAL AND REPRODUCTION

Black grouse have a potential lifespan of nine years or more, but, like most wild animals, usually die well before reaching old age. About half the adults usually die each year, and so an adult of any age can expect to live a further two years. In different studies, the average annual survival of adults has varied from about 40 per cent to 70 per cent per year. Table 16 indicates how many chicks must be reared each year to support a population of black grouse. If, for example, half the breeding adults in a closed[63] and constant population die between breeding seasons in successive years, then the number of young recruits required to replace them is equal to half the number of breeding adults. If there are equal numbers of each sex, then each hen must rear one recruit.

TABLE 16. The average number of chicks that must be reared per hen to maintain numbers in closed black grouse populations, given various survival rates for adults and first-year birds.#

| ANNUAL SURVIVAL, ADULTS | RECRUITMENT,* YOUNG PER ADULT | FIRST-WINTER SURVIVAL | CHICKS REARED PER HEN (CPH) | BREEDING SUCCESS, $\log_e$ (CPH +1) |
|---|---|---|---|---|
| 0.8 | 0.2 | 0.7 | 0.57 | 0.45 |
| 0.8 | 0.2 | 0.5 | 0.80 | 0.59 |
| 0.8 | 0.2 | 0.3 | 1.33 | 0.85 |
| 0.7 | 0.3 | 0.7 | 0.86 | 0.62 |
| 0.7 | 0.3 | 0.5 | 1.2 | 0.79 |
| 0.7 | 0.3 | 0.3 | 2.0 | 1.10 |
| 0.6 | 0.4 | 0.7 | 1.14 | 0.76 |
| 0.6 | 0.4 | 0.5 | 1.60 | 0.96 |
| 0.6 | 0.4 | 0.3 | 2.67 | 1.30 |
| 0.5 | 0.5 | 0.7 | 1.43 | 0.89 |
| 0.5 | 0.5 | 0.5 | 2.00 | 1.10 |
| 0.5 | 0.5 | 0.3 | 3.33 | 1.47 |
| 0.4 | 0.6 | 0.7 | 1.71 | 1.00 |
| 0.4 | 0.6 | 0.5 | 2.40 | 1.22 |
| 0.4 | 0.6 | 0.3 | 4.00 | 1.61 |

# For adults, survival is annual. For first-year birds, survival is over their first winter from the time of brood counts (late July–early August) to the next year's breeding season. This is because hens breed in their first spring and so are recruited into the breeding population at that time.
* Recruits in spring t+1, per adult in spring t.

Not all reared chicks, however, survive to become recruits. Indeed, the survival of youngsters from their first autumn until the next spring is typically less than the all-year survival of adults. Hence the number of chicks that a hen must rear to maintain a constant population depends partly upon the proportion of reared young that survives.

In northeast Scotland, the only available estimate of annual adult survival is 0.51 for radio-tagged hens in the early 1980s.[64] If we assume a first-winter survival of 0.40, this suggests that on average each hen would need to rear 2.5 chicks per year to maintain a constant population. Between 1975 and the 1990s, the number of chicks reared per hen in Glen Tanar (see Fig. 65) fell from an average (2–3 chicks per hen) that seems to have been sufficient to sustain numbers, down to a level (1.3 chicks per hen) that was not sufficient. Similarly, the decline in black grouse at Abernethy after 1997 went along with an average breeding success of about 1.3 chicks per hen. Referring to Table 16, we can see that this would have been sufficient to sustain numbers only if adult survival had been about 0.7.

Such high survival can be achieved. At the turn of the twenty-first century in the north Pennines, for example, the annual survival rate of radio-tagged adults was about 0.7 and that of first-year birds about 0.5.[65] Breeding success was about 1.2 chicks per hen, just enough to keep the population constant.[66]

The immediate cause of adult deaths is often predation by weasels, stoats, foxes or raptors. It can be argued that a population with low breeding success, as in the north Pennines for example, survives only because predators are scarce owing to culling by keepers, thereby allowing full-grown black grouse to live longer. In a population with high breeding success, however, adults must compete with more youngsters and so are more likely to lose social status and physical condition, and hence to become more vulnerable to predators. Thus, long adult lives could be an indirect result of poor breeding success and reduced competition for space, food and cover.

## THE FUTURE

As part of the UK Biodiversity Action Plan (a government commitment to the 1992 Rio Summit), an action plan for black grouse was launched in 1998. Local projects began in Wales, the north Pennines, Argyll and Bute, and Dumfries and Galloway. Declines in the endangered local populations in Wales and the north Pennines have, for the moment at least, been reversed by better management of dwarf shrubs and increased killing of crows, foxes, weasels and stoats. In much of Britain, the bird's future will depend partly upon management, and partly upon such imponderables as climate change and the widespread impact of herbicides and other pollutants upon insect life.

## SUMMARY

Black grouse are classic and much-studied exponents of the lek system of reproduction. Recent studies of black grouse, capercaillie and red grouse are leading to a deeper understanding of the role of individuals and of extended families in social systems and population dynamics. However, the question of why species such as black grouse display at leks whereas others such as red grouse are territorial remains unanswered. Black grouse are birds of transitional habitats where forest edge grades into moorland, grassland or bog. In much of their world range they remain plentiful, but in southern parts, including Britain, they are in steep decline. This is attributed partly to loss of habitat and partly to reduced breeding success, which in turn may be associated with climate change. In Britain, land use during the nineteenth century and earlier maintained heathland, moorland and woodland habitats to which black grouse readily adapted. The increasingly intensive agriculture of the twentieth century, especially the overgrazing of moorland and scrub, led to loss of such habitat and the birds went with it. Measures that can reverse this trend are described.

CHAPTER 6

# Capercaillie

APERCAILLIE, SOULS OF the forest, are the largest grouse in the world and have the greatest difference in size between the sexes (*see* Fig. 6). Their large size demands extensive tracts of good habitat, and a thriving population of capercaillie is therefore thought to indicate a healthy forest ecosystem.[1]

The history of capercaillie in Britain and Ireland reflects the history of man's almost complete destruction of native forest. By the eighteenth century, Scotland retained the largest remnants of native forest, home to the last surviving native capercaillie. Even here, however, centuries of felling, burning and overgrazing had left the landscape mostly treeless. The few capercaillie in the scattered remnant woods were hunted for food and sport, until the last recorded birds were shot in 1785.

In the eighteenth and nineteenth centuries, new woods were planted. Attempts to reintroduce capercaillie met with success in the 1830s. In the new woods, predators were killed by game-preservers and the bird abounded, to the pleasure of sportsmen and naturalists alike.

However, mankind is fickle. Much old timber was sacrificed during the two world wars, and so the Forestry Commission (FC) was set up following the First World War with a remit to plant more trees. Capercaillie and black grouse became regarded as pests because they ate the needles and buds of planted conifers.[2] Foresters and gamekeepers crushed eggs and chicks underfoot, and the adult birds were shot to reduce numbers. In some gamebooks, capercaillie bag records are found not alongside game such as red grouse, but in the section devoted to vermin.

In the 1960s, tax laws changed and caused more sporting estates to sell shooting that was previously the preserve of proprietors and friends. Guests from Europe and America, who paid to shoot red deer and red grouse, were astonished that capercaillie, black grouse, roe deer and mountain hares were treated as vermin, and asked to shoot them. The capercaillie was reinstated as a fine gamebird in the eyes of the shooting fraternity, and in the 1970s a day's capercaillie shooting cost as much as a day at the grouse.[3]

By 1990, capercaillie were in obvious decline. Most estates enacted a voluntary ban on shooting but the decline continued. The Scottish Office, at the behest of the then Secretary of State Lord James Douglas-Hamilton, initiated a programme of scientific research. The reasons for the decline were comprehended, and recommendations made for reversing it. Fulfilling these recommendations now requires a concerted effort by woodland managers.

FIG 67. Cock capercaillie, showing his massive beak and throat feathers raised beard-like in display. The cutting edge of the upper mandible is marked greenish with pine resin. (Stuart Rae)

## THE BIRD

Capercaillie are large, broad-winged birds with rounded tails. The sexes differ greatly. The huge adult cock, blackish at a distance, weighs about 4kg, and measures some 90cm from beak to tail and about 120cm across his spread wings. His massive skull and hooked, horn-white beak are heavier than is needed for feeding, doubling up as a weapon. He is unmistakable on the ground and in flight. At a shoot in Speyside in the 1970s, a German veteran of the Second World War appreciatively described a group of high-flying driven cocks as 'like a group of bombers'.

FIG 68. Capercaillie cock displaying. (Stuart Rae)

FIG 69. Capercaillie cock in flight. (Robert Moss)

FIG 70. Hens at lek. (Desmond Dugan)

The adult hen, brownish at a distance, approaches 2kg in weight and measures some 60cm from beak to tail, with a wingspan of about 90cm. She is twice the weight of a greyhen, but the two can be confused. In the field, note that the tail of a hen capercaillie is rounded, whereas that of a greyhen is slightly forked in a restrained version of the blackcock lyre. The capercaillie has neither the greyhen's whitish axillary feathers, nor her pale wing bars, but the capercaillie's breast does have a distinctive patch of orange-buff.[4] In addition, the lighter and more agile greyhen rises more steeply from the ground and turns more sharply in flight.

Young hens, although slighter than adults, are practically indistinguishable from the latter in the field by three months of age. Young cocks have similar colouring to adults, but they enter their first winter part-grown, a kilogram or so lighter, with shorter tails, narrower tail feathers, relatively slender beaks and narrow heads. Cocks in their second year are indistinguishable from adults in the field, but their skulls attain full fighting width only in their third year.

Juveniles resemble dull hens. As their first feathers grow through the down, males and females begin to differ in the colouring of mantle, crown and earcoverts – distinguishable in the hand by a month of age. Females' feathers are brownish, barred on the mantle and crown, while males' are greyish and more streaked. In the field, cocks look distinctly greyer by about six weeks, and black feathers start to show when the birds are some eight weeks old. The grey-black male juveniles are normally larger than the brown females, but in years with small broods the males are typically fewer and occasionally smaller than their sisters, reflecting conditions that are too harsh for normal growth.

## ASPECTS OF BEHAVIOUR

**Mating system**

Capercaillie are polygamous, the cocks displaying together at traditional sites called leks (*see* Fig. 6). Hens attend a lek, mate with a cock and then scatter to individual nesting places, rearing their young alone. The mating system is midway between that of classical lekking species such as black grouse, which are territorial on the lek but not off it, and the dispersed territoriality of other forest grouse such as the ruffed grouse, the cocks of which display on separate territories.

An established capercaillie cock usually displays on the same small stance each spring morning. A small lek typically comprises a group of stances a few tens of metres apart, centring on a dominant cock that attracts most hens. Less attractive cocks attempt to seduce hens away from the master, especially when he is mating or seeing off another cock. Sometimes his stance is usurped by a challenger. During a single spring at one Speyside lek, three successive individual cocks took the dominant role on the same stance.[5] After morning display, cocks move up to a kilometre from the lek centre, remaining on their own piece of ground.[6]

The number of cocks displaying at a lek is typically between three and 20, but can be 70 or more, and solitary displaying cocks are common. The largest recorded lek in Scotland had over 40 cocks in 1990, but by the late 1990s it was reduced to

FIG 71. Cock's-eye view of the hens in his harem. (Chris Knights and Terry Andrewartha)

less than 20. In virgin boreal forest in northern Russia during the late twentieth century, the average number of cocks recorded at leks in the Ilexa Basin was 24, and in the Pinega nature reserve eight.[7]

Cocks usually gain a permanent stance in their third or fourth year. Those in their second year, and some in their third, typically have larger home ranges[8] further from the lek centre, although a second-year cock was dominant at a small Scottish lek.[9] Young cocks visit several leks, often in bands, where they display tentatively on branches, only to retreat when threatened by older cocks. Near Aboyne in Deeside, on a traditional lek largely destroyed by clear-felling, a single recognisable old cock displayed for 11 years. In some years he was joined by a second cock, but in 2004 he disappeared, replaced by a first-year cock.[10] So, in desperate conditions, young cocks can stand in for adults.[11]

### At a lek

Four o'clock on a fine April morning, deep in the forest it is still dark, the small birds silent at their roosts. Through the quiet air comes a resonant click, as a capercaillie cock stirs on his thick pine branch. There follow more slow clicks, then a drum-roll of clicks, a pop like a cork being drawn from a bottle, and a noise like a knife being whetted. The last sound is the rushing of air as the capercaillie cock roars his challenge to others. But we cannot hear much of the roaring, as it is below our limit of hearing.[12]

The cock jumps to the ground and continues his song, parading among the tree trunks, head raised, tail spread vertically and wings held stiffly down, scraping the ground and rustling the vegetation as he passes. It is still too dark to see him. The song repeats faster and faster, and suddenly stops, replaced by gruff, threatening belch-calls as another cock approaches. The belch-threats are no bluff. The cocks front up a short distance apart (Fig. 72), belch-call, ritually bow, and aim occasional pecks at each other. If one does not give way, they close and fight in earnest, stabbing and pecking, often tearing feathers from each other's heads (see Fig. 139). They strike with one or both wings, using the carpal joint like a boxer's fist. After a minute or two, both are exhausted, and they take a rest between rounds, only to start again. An indecisive fight is concluded by the contestants walking slowly backwards, belching and bowing, neither turning tail. After a decisive fight, the victor pursues the loser, often out of sight.

Grey light creeps in. Cocks strut and sing. At the sound of hens' wings, the cock sings harder and faster, and displays his flutter-jumps. Beginning another song, he runs forward a few steps, jumps noisily into the air with rapidly beating wings, glides briefly with tail spread, and flutters back to the ground a few metres away (Figs 73 & 74).

CAPERCAILLIE · 139

FIG 72. Cocks fronting up to each other. (Kevin Cuthbert)

FIG 73. Two views of cocks in mid flutter-jump. (William Cuthbert)

FIG 74. Cock landing at the end of a flutter-jump. (Kevin Cuthbert)

FIG 75. Hens watch a cock displaying at a lek in Abernethy. (Desmond Dugan)

FIG 76. Hen on a branch at a lek in Abernethy. (Desmond Dugan)

Sun strikes through the canopy and lights hens perched on thick branches (Figs 75 & 76). They watch the cocks, and mutter and cackle in deep voices. They have been here on several mornings. Today, one hen makes her choice. She flies down to a cock, stops in his path, flattens herself to the ground, spreads her wings and lies quivering in front of her chosen mate. He circles her in full display, sings repeatedly, and then struts on, apparently ignoring her solicitations. She gets up, shakes herself, trots after him and again prostrates herself. The other hens take wing. One after another they fly down to the favoured cock and make a harem. He continues to display, and they continue to follow and solicit him, fighting amongst themselves, jostling for position and sometimes also displaying like cocks (Fig. 77).

A single dominant cock has up to a dozen hen followers. He mates perhaps one or two an hour (*see* Fig. 78), the morning display often ending with some hens unmated. Fighting, displaying and mating might be tiring, but that hardly seems sufficient reason for his strange, indifferent behaviour. A blackcock, after all, expeditiously mates any hen that offers herself. Perhaps a retinue of capercaillie hens attracts other hens, which reckon that such an attractive cock is likely to have good genes.

FIG 77. Hen displaying like a cock. (Chris Knights)

FIG 78. Cock servicing hen. (Chris Knights)

FIG 79. Capercaillie hen preening after copulation. After mating, a hen stands up, shakes her feathers and then preens herself. (Desmond Dugan)

In fine weather, cocks can be seen displaying sporadically at any season except midsummer, when they are in heavy moult. Such displays are often from a tree, not necessarily at a lek. In Scotland, regular lek displays typically begin in the first half of April and end quite suddenly in late April or early May. Hens attend from mid-April to early May, hen numbers peaking on about 20–25 April. Some hens renest after losing their first clutch, and they must get mated again after the main lekking season is over.

Most leks are deep in the wood, typically in a slightly more open patch with sparser trees, although exceptions occur. On a lek in a Perthshire plantation, for example, birds continued to display in the open after the block of trees around the lek had been clear-felled (see Fig. 80).

Perhaps one cock in a thousand loses his fear of humanity and boldly attacks people, as well as deer, sheep and vehicles.[13] An irate cock can inflict much damage. His peck breaks skin through a thick tweed jacket and a blow from his wings leaves a painful bruise. If you are attacked, stand on one leg and place the sole of your boot against his chest. He pushes against the boot in a trial of strength, but stops the pecking and buffeting. You can then hop an inelegant retreat. During

FIG 80. Capercaillie cock displaying in the open at a Perthshire lek, now defunct. This lek was originally in a clearing in a block of Sitka spruce. The trees were felled after spruce had regenerated on part of the clearing, as seen in this 1990 picture. The birds continued to display on the original clearing, and also around it on forest roads (shown) and in the clear-felled area. The lek disappeared some years after the clear-felled area was replanted, even though the original clearing was left unplanted. (Robert Moss)

the lekking season, many cocks show pink patches of bare skin on the head, where feathers have been torn out during fights (see Fig. 139). It is unusual for cocks to be killed during a fight, but many expire, wounded and apparently exhausted, in May after the lek.

### Distraction display

Hens with chicks usually show distraction display when flushed by a human or other predator. A good display, as in other grouse, involves running in front of the dupe with body and tail held low, one or both wings dragging as if injured. This is rare in Scotland. Here, a flushed hen typically rises from tall heather close to the intruder, her tail spread and rounded. She dips low over the heather as if finding it difficult to fly, keeps low for 10–20m, then rises and flies directly away and out of sight. This effectively lures dogs and presumably other predators away from her chicks. She circles back and lands unseen in a nearby tree, where she waits until the intruder has gone.[14]

## Lek counts

Counts of cocks at leks are the easiest way to monitor population trends. In Britain, the statutory authorities arbitrarily consider a local population of any bird species to be of national importance if it contains more than 1 per cent of the national population. Hence the proportion of cocks that attend leks is of practical importance for designating Special Protection Areas (SPAs).[15] The number of cocks at a lek normally peaks during a few days in late April. In a typical survey, one or two counts are done between late March and early May. These very probably miss some young cocks, sub-adults on the periphery, and adults not at the lek that morning.

Youngsters and sub-adults typically comprise about half the total cock population.[16] On rainy mornings, some adult cocks display near their roost site and do not trouble to attend the lek. In addition, some habitually display alone in all weathers, at stances removed from any lek. Hens and cocks are presumably equal in number, and so we have a rule of thumb: the total breeding population is about four times the number of cocks seen during lek surveys.[17]

The contribution of each lek to a population can be assessed from the frequency distribution of counts (Fig. 81). From this, the proportion of the known lekking population that occurs in leks of each size is readily calculated (*see* Fig. 82). For practical purposes, it is reasonable to assume that this distribution resembles that of

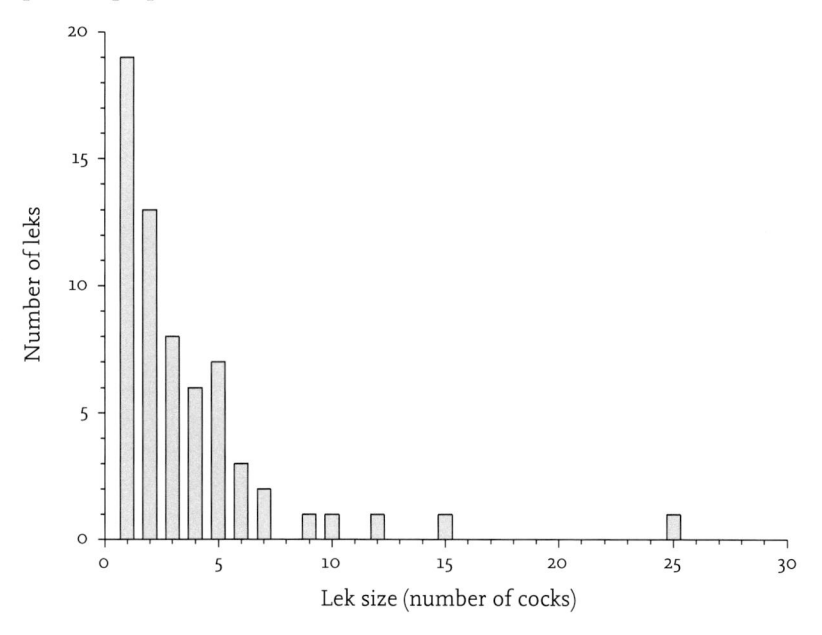

FIG 81. Counts of cocks at all known leks in Scotland, 2004.

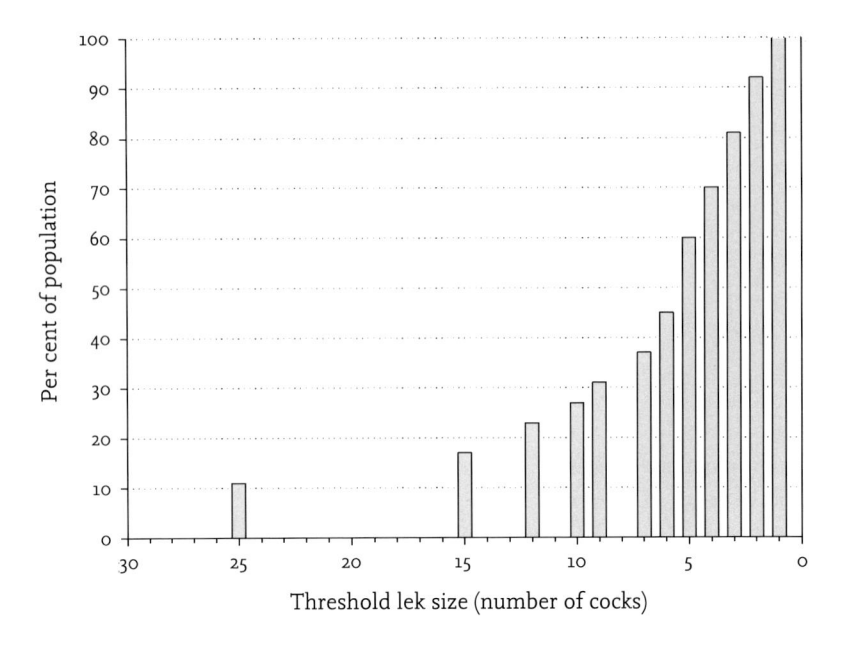

FIG 82. Percentage, of the total number of cocks counted in Scotland, that was at leks of the 'threshold size' or above. For example, leks with five or more cocks contained 60 per cent of the population.

the total population.[18] Thus, if all leks of five or more cocks were in SPAs, these should contain 60 per cent of the Scottish breeding population.

## SYSTEMATICS

Up to 12 subspecies of capercaillie are traditionally recognised from size and coloration,[19] but genetic evidence suggests that these require revision and simplification.[20] The nominate (first described) subspecies *Tetrao urogallus urogallus* breeds in Scandinavia. Birds from the Cantabrian mountains in Spain *T. u. cantabricus*, the Pyrenees *T. u. aquitanicus* and the Balkans *T. u. rudolfi* are smaller than other subspecies and may have a different evolutionary history. Genetic evidence suggests two distinct lineages from birds that survived in different glacial refugia: a western '*aquitanus*' lineage from Iberia and the Balkans, and an eastern '*urogallus*' one from South Asia or Beringia.[21] The reintroduced Scottish stock are probably mongrels from at least two different subspecies.

## DISTRIBUTION AND NUMBERS

The worldwide breeding population of capercaillie is perhaps 2–3 million birds,[22] half or more of them in the Russian Federation. They still occupy much of their original range, continuous throughout the boreal forest from Scandinavia to eastern Siberia. Breeding densities are now about two birds per km$^2$,[23] rarely reaching above six per km$^2$,[24] comparable with present densities in occupied Scottish woods. Densities in boreal forest west of the Ural mountains, however, declined with the onset of industrial clear-felling, and densities in Scotland are now much lower than in the 1970s.

In central and western Europe, the southwest part of the capercaillie's range, the species' montane coniferous habitat has a naturally patchy distribution.[25] This is now much reduced and fragmented by agriculture and development. Many local extinctions have occurred across temperate Europe since the 1950s, and here most surviving populations are small and isolated.

The wholesale destruction of old pine forests was the primary cause of the extinction of capercaillie in Britain and Ireland. In England, they became extinct by about 1670, and in Ireland by 1770. The last record of native Scottish capercaillie was from Balmoral in 1785, when two cocks were shot on the occasion of a marriage rejoicing.[26]

After several failed attempts, capercaillie were successfully reintroduced to Scotland from Sweden in 1837–8. Their subsequent spread from Taymouth was assisted by translocations and fresh imports from Sweden, Austria, Norway and Finland, and possibly also Denmark and Russia.[27] They reached their maximum spread by the outbreak of the First World War, when they were breeding from Golspie in Sutherland in the north to Stirling in the southwest, and from the Cowal Peninsula, Argyllshire, in the west to Buchan, Aberdeenshire, in the east. During the First World War, much mature timber was felled and this restricted their potential range. To our knowledge, the most recent releases in Scotland were in the late 1980s and early 1990s, involving birds reared in captivity from mixed local and Norwegian stock, the latter from imported eggs. The contributions of various bloodlines to the present gene pool are uncertain, and current work on DNA from feathers is clarifying this question.

By 1880, shooting bags were providing a rough index of abundance.[28] The record for a day's shooting was 69 birds at Dunkeld, Perthshire, in 1910.[29] During the twentieth century, bag records and counts show that capercaillie in Scotland fluctuated in broad synchrony with the other three grouse species and with the North Atlantic Oscillation (*see* Chapter 14). This suggests that the abundance of all four species was similarly influenced by weather. The most recent period of joint abundance – the 1960s and early 1970s – was associated with a long run (1962–70) of above-average June temperatures.[30] There are said to have been about 20,000 capercaillie in Scotland in the mid-1970s.[31] Surveys from winter line transects showed roughly 2,200 birds in 1992–4, about 1,100 in 1998–9 and 2,000 in 2003–4.[32] The decline apparently stopped between 1999 and 2003.

Capercaillie do best in a continental climate. Several authors note how their distribution shifts along with climate, numbers declining as continental weather gives way to more oceanic conditions, and reviving as the reverse occurs. In Scotland, capercaillie now breed mostly in the more continental east, north of the industrial belt, but, when more abundant, they bred as far as Argyll in the west and the Tweed Valley in the south.[33]

## HABITAT

The capercaillie is primarily a bird of boreal climax forests.[34] It usually lives in old-growth coniferous forest, open enough to support ground vegetation that is rich in dwarf shrubs,[35] and intermingled with bogs and patches of the natural tree regeneration that follows fire, snow-break or wind-throw. Forest structure is more important than tree species or age, and the bird can prosper in a range of forest types, including suitably managed plantations (Figs 83–86). Blaeberry is a preferred summer food and capercaillie thrive best where it abounds.

In temperate regions, capercaillie usually occur in conifer-dominated habitats, including tall, dense forests of spruce or fir, and mixed forests with an understorey of birch or aspen. At the southern extremity of the Ural range, some birds move into broadleaved forests in summer and some remain in them year-round.[36] Capercaillie also live year-round in the broadleaved forests of the Cantabrian mountains in Spain.

Forestry practices strongly influence habitat structure and hence capercaillie. Dense conifer forests are more suitable when opened up by snow-break or wind-throw, whereupon the broken or thrown trees provide good cover. In Scotland, open Caledonian forest was once thought to be the best capercaillie habitat. Norway spruce, however, has a thicker canopy and provides better cover than Scots pine, so capercaillie often feed in pine but roost in spruce. Thus, an open pinewood with copses of spruce provides better habitat than pure, open Caledonian pinewood. The biggest lek and the highest breeding density recorded in Scotland, however, are from a Scots pinewood planted largely in the 1950s.

FIGS 83–86. Some capercaillie habitats in Scotland.

FIG 83. Caledonian forest with blaeberry, the birds' main summer food, and a fallen tree as cover. (Desmond Dugan)

FIG 84. Juniper in Caledonian forest gives good cover, especially for moulting cocks. (Desmond Dugan)

FIG 85. Recently thinned Scots pine plantation at Inshriach in 2006. Hens had just started to breed here, although it lacks good ground cover. (Robert Moss)

FIG 86. Forest bog at Inshriach, used by capercaillie broods. (Robert Moss)

In winter, capercaillie typically use fairly open forest, with hens and sub-adult cocks less than three years old found in denser stands than older cocks.[37] This might be because hens are smaller and can fly more easily through denser trees. The same does not apply to sub-adult cocks, which may instead favour denser stands to avoid older cocks.[38]

Leks are often on slopes or raised sites in open forest, although many exceptions occur. In Scandinavia, tree densities at leks are typically 400–1,000 trees per ha, but in Caledonian pinewood the trees have wider crowns and many leks occur at lower tree densities. An open arena with moderate tree densities and short ground vegetation allows cocks to display themselves to advantage, to see one another and to spot approaching predators. In unmanaged boreal forest, such habitat is generally found on poorer soils. In plantations, tree densities depend largely upon silviculture, and foresters can maintain suitable lek habitat by appropriate thinning. Grazing greatly influences the height of ground vegetation (Fig. 87). If a lek site is being overwhelmed by tall heather, it can be cut, or feed blocks can be used to attract deer, which will then browse and shorten the heather.

The structure of ground vegetation is as important to capercaillie as tree structure. Broadly speaking, chicks thrive better where there is more blaeberry.

FIG 87. Fenceline at Ballochbuie in the 1980s. Before the deer fence was erected in 1970, both sides were equally heavily grazed. (Adam Watson)

However, a brood will do best if the chicks have, within easy reach, food, water, cover from predators and places to dry out after rain.[39] 'Easy reach' means a few tens of metres. In boreal forest, broods use bogs, where their insect food is abundant. In Scotland, where forest bogs are now rare because of draining by foresters, good habitat for chicks comprises a varied mixture of tall and short vegetation, including blaeberry. Close by should be good cover such as juniper bushes, piles of brash, tree thickets or wind-throw, and low branches onto which chicks can flutter when disturbed. Steep slopes help chicks take to the air when escaping predators.[40] Broods of well-grown chicks use moorland and clear-felled areas with good food and cover, and will feed on berries more than 500m from continuous woodland.

Overbrowsing by deer or domestic stock can shorten ground vegetation until it provides little cover and few insects for chicks.[41] Conversely, underbrowsing can allow heather to grow tall and dense, to the virtual exclusion of blaeberry. Lack of blaeberry, and the difficulty of walking through rank heather, make such habitat less suitable for capercaillie chicks. A moderate level of browsing that provides a varied mixture of short and tall vegetation should benefit the birds.[42] Deer, aurochs, tarpan, bison, beaver and wild boar probably provided this in prehistoric European forests.

In western Europe, thousands of capercaillie are killed each year by flying into fences and overhead wires.[43] In Scottish woods, deer fences are a danger, and during the 1990s they were one of the main causes of capercaillie mortality.[44] After this was discovered, a number of fences were removed or marked,[45] although many remain.

Capercaillie are big birds that require large areas of forest. It takes about 15km$^2$ of pristine boreal forest to support each lek.[46] This area, however, includes large open bogs, water bodies and other unsuitable ground. In Varaldskogen, an exploited boreal forest in southeast Norway, there is about one lek per 7km$^2$.[47] The distance between a lek and its nearest neighbour is typically 2–2.5km, so that in continuous suitable habitat each lek would in theory require about 5km$^2$ of forest to support it.

A single lek cannot support a viable capercaillie population. It would become extinct through mishaps, or enfeebled by inbreeding. In Scotland, the distance moved by young hens from where they were radio-tagged as poults to their first nest averaged 12km.[48] For capercaillie, therefore, Scottish woods are small and fragmented, and habitat management should be on the scale of entire watersheds.

Most lowland forest in temperate Europe is unfit for capercaillie, owing to altered habitat structure, human disturbance and, possibly, increased predators. Remnant populations are largely restricted to the upper slopes of montane forests. Scottish capercaillie are unusual in not being thus restricted, but are

FIG 88. Capercaillie cock decapitated by flying into a deer fence. He bent two wires. The orange plastic was an early attempt to prevent such accidents, but it seems that the cock tried to fly under it as if under a branch. Marking should make the entire fence look like an obstacle to flight. (Kenny Kortland)

FIG 89. Capercaillie hen on nest. (Desmond Dugan)

increasingly threatened by disturbance and development in their main stronghold, Speyside. Ironically, much of this is due to the desire of people to live in or near the Cairngorms National Park. The priority placed by the park board on rural development is an ominous trend that poses yet another threat to capercaillie.

**The forest industry**

The biggest threats facing capercaillie worldwide are habitat destruction and deterioration, through exploitation and climate change. In Scotland, following centuries of wholesale forest destruction, large areas of new woodland were planted from the eighteenth to the twentieth centuries. In a search for large volumes of fast-growing timber, the British forest industry in the second half of the twentieth century increasingly planted lodgepole pine and Sitka spruce.[49]

These two alien species are grown at high densities that shade out blaeberry at canopy closure, and so provide inferior habitat for woodland grouse (see Fig. 59). When planted on moorland, Sitka seedlings often suffer from competition with heather and stop growing before the canopy closes – known as 'heather check'. Patches of checked Sitka, especially on wet ground, can provide good habitat for capercaillie broods. But the forester's response to heather check has been to spray the heather and associated blaeberry with herbicide, so allowing the trees to grow but destroying much potential habitat for woodland grouse. An older way of growing trees on heather moorland was to plant Scots pine mixed with larch, a practice still widely carried out in the 1950s. Properly thinned, such mature plantations provided excellent capercaillie habitat. This valuable practice is now out of favour, however, and, after felling, most such plantations were replanted with Sitka spruce.

Most capercaillie in Scotland live in woods dominated by Scots pine and therefore most conservation efforts are properly directed at pinewood.[50] Sitka spruce plantations, however, can support capercaillie if appropriately managed.[51] British plantations of Sitka spruce form a new ecosystem, and wildlife is still adapting to them. As plantations reach maturity, they are felled, providing opportunities for restructuring. This could include planting and thinning trees at wider spacing, thereby allowing light through the canopy and encouraging the growth of dwarf shrubs. Such growth would benefit many species, including capercaillie.[52]

A moderate level of browsing probably provides optimum chick habitat (see above) and some silviculture may also benefit chick survival. Hens in woods with green brash left lying from silvicultural operations in previous years reared more chicks than usual.[53] Perhaps more light from newly opened canopies stimulates plant growth, or perhaps decaying brash provides more insects as chick food. Just how silviculture affects breeding success is unsolved and worth further study.

DIET

**Winter**
In winter, capercaillie live in trees and eat mostly conifer needles, although on mild, snow-free days they sometimes take ground vegetation.[54] In boreal or mountain forest, cocks often roost during the day under the cover of low, sweeping branches of Norway spruce, but in Scotland they usually roost in the canopy. When there is snow that is powdery and deep enough, however, they will roost in snow-holes for much of the day and all night.

Over much of the capercaillie's range, Scots pine is the birds' winter staple. Indeed, the worldwide distributions of capercaillie and Scots pine roughly coincide. Where Scots or Arolla pine are absent, the birds feed on other conifers. Norway spruce is the dominant tree in parts of their range but, as in Scotland, is not usually eaten in quantity.[55]

Capercaillie in Scotland readily feed on introduced conifers such as Douglas fir, larch and Sitka spruce. In plantations, capercaillie ate Sitka spruce and pine roughly in proportion to their abundance.[56] Hens took more spruce than cocks, possibly reflecting their choice of denser trees rather than a dietary preference. In plantations with very little pine, the adults' main food for most of the year comprised Sitka spruce. Larch was favoured in spring and autumn, but, being deciduous, was not eaten in winter.[57]

**Spring**
Spring is a crucial time for laying hens, which must supplement their staple diet with nutritious, newly growing plant material if they are to lay the good-quality eggs that give rise to viable chicks. Hens of several grouse species are known to eat more spring growth than cocks. Studies of capercaillie in various countries have emphasised the importance of newly growing shoots of cotton-grass. In boreal forest, the main items in a typical spring diet[58] might comprise Scots pine, blaeberry, cotton-grass shoots, berries that have overwintered under snow and, on richer soils, the flowers and leaf buds of larch.[59] In temperate forests, beech buds are eaten in spring.

In Scotland, the spring diet of capercaillie hens has been little studied but there is evidence that they use cotton-grass.[60] Red and black grouse also visit cotton-grass bogs in spring, where their droppings contain ample evidence that it forms much of their diet.

Our woods have been drained to the extent that bogs with cotton-grass are now scarce. Hence many capercaillie probably have to do with less of this valuable food than they would like, to the detriment of their eggs and chicks. Management for capercaillie includes the reinstatement of bogs, where cotton-grass can grow and where invertebrates – a valuable food for chicks – can flourish.

In Scotland, capercaillie and black grouse often feed in larch trees, especially in spring, when it can form a substantial proportion of their diet.[61] Larch flowers and swollen leaf buds appear quite early in spring and probably provide a useful dietary supplement to laying hens. Its nutritive value has not been studied, however, and it is not known whether it provides as valuable a food as cotton-grass.

**Summer**

In summer, adult capercaillie in Scots pinewood continue to eat pine needles, but in May they turn more to pollen cones and spend much time on the ground, where they take dwarf shrubs, especially heather and the stems, leaves and berries of blaeberry.[62] Heather is, however, a plant of oceanic climes and so is scarce or absent in much of the birds' worldwide range. Instead, they supplement blaeberry with a variety of leaves and shoots of other dwarf shrubs, berries, ferns, seeds of rush and sedge, horsetails, herbs, and capsules of *Polytrichum* moss.[63]

In a plantation in Perthshire, dominated by Sitka spruce and with scarce blaeberry, adult cocks spent much of their summer on open ground where mature Sitka spruce had been clear-felled and replanted with new seedlings.[64] The wet gley soils here supported dense vegetation that provided the cover required by moulting cocks. These ate mostly needles from young Sitka spruce and seeds from the fruiting heads of sedges. Even in pinewood with abundant blaeberry and heather, seeds from sedges on wet patches of open ground are eaten by hens and chicks in late summer.[65]

While moulting cocks lurk in thick cover, hens and chicks are in more open habitat. For chicks, blaeberry is a key food. It also supports many invertebrates, which form much of the chicks' diet in their first month, before they change to a largely vegetable diet. Studies of the diet of young chicks are few, but all concur that caterpillars of moths or sawflies usually provide the main bulk of their invertebrate food, and that blaeberry is the main plant eaten.[66]

In addition to dwarf shrubs, the summer diet of adults and chicks in Scotland can include needles of larch and Sitka spruce, bracken and other ferns, seeds of sedges and rushes, and various unidentified herbs.[67]

**Autumn**
In autumn, capercaillie spend more time in trees, taking a diet largely transitional between that of summer and winter. Hens in boreal forest slowly increase the proportion of conifer needles in their diet from late summer onwards, but cocks switch to conifers only with the first permanent snow cover in late autumn. Aspen leaves seem to be an autumn speciality, and in oak forests acorns can be a main food source. In Scotland, birds are often seen in larch, and cocks switch to conifers without the stimulus of snow cover.[68] Capercaillie ate oats on stubble fields, stooks and stacks up to the 1970s and were also fond of forage rape.[69]


METABOLISM: THE PENALTIES OF SIZE

Capercaillie chicks grow fast on a poor diet. Hens are almost fully grown after three months, but cocks do not reach adult weight until the following summer, and their skulls are not fully developed until the spring after that. Despite these thrifty adaptations, cock chicks must grow faster than hens, and so require more and better food. Thus, when foraging is difficult and few chicks are reared, more hens than cocks survive (*see* Chapter 12).

Smaller males would survive better than larger ones, and so there must be natural selection for small size. However, this must evidently be offset by strong selection for large males. An obvious advantage of size is that larger cocks win fights at leks and so attract hens. Hence sexual selection for large cocks seems to make capercaillie less well adapted to their physical environment.[70]

The difficulties encountered by growing capercaillie chicks affect their survival. Broods of ptarmigan, red grouse and black grouse suffer most mortality in their first two weeks. Afterwards, if not killed by enemies or extreme weather, they usually survive well. But capercaillie broods, even in benign conditions, continue to lose chicks for several more weeks. In Glen Tanar, the survival of broods after about a month of age was related to their condition, and this in turn was related to the number of days with rain shortly after hatching in early June.[71] Capercaillie seem less able than slower-growing grouse species to overcome early handicaps.

Such difficulties in turn appear to limit the distribution of capercaillie.[72] The smaller black grouse grow more slowly and can better withstand wet summers. Consequently, they occur in much of rainy western Scotland, whereas capercaillie are confined largely to the drier east.

## MOULT

Adults undergo a complete post-breeding moult. In cocks this starts with the innermost primaries in May, after their main display, and they continue to moult heavily from June to August. At this time they are reluctant to fly, and seek thick cover.

Hens moult slightly later than cocks, especially hens with young, which delay moulting their main tail feathers until late July or early August. Whether tails are still complete or have missing feathers, plus the presence or absence of distraction display, is therefore useful in telling whether hens have chicks.

Birds sometimes retain their outer two primaries, not moulting them, from one year to the next. Such feathers are worn and faded, noticeably different from freshly grown feathers. This can be used to tell the age of a bird in the hand. A bird of adult weight with retained first-year primaries, for instance, is in its second year.

Capercaillie use fright-moult to distract predators, shedding feathers while narrowly escaping from a fox, for example, which is left with a mouthful of tail feathers. In spring, when hens are heavy with eggs, a pile of shed female tail feathers is a regular sight in capercaillie woods. And if they are not killed upon impact when flying into fences, birds sometimes fright-moult, each leaving a pile of feathers from body and tail.

## LONGEVITY AND SURVIVAL

Adult cock capercaillie generally outlive hens, so compensating for their poorer survival as chicks. A few cocks, including two in Scotland, lived to at least ten years in the wild,[73] but to our knowledge no hens have reached this age. Annual survival in Scotland during the 1990s was 81 per cent for adult cocks and 63 per cent for adult hens, or 72 per cent overall, comparable with other studies worldwide.[74] This implies that the average adult, of any age, can expect another two to three years of life. The survival of birds in their first year was poorer – 50 per cent – because many dispersing young flew into fences.

Despite their large size, birds of the grouse family are comparatively short-lived. The 72 per cent annual survival rate of capercaillie is the highest of all the grouse and is similar to that of white-tailed ptarmigan, a very small species. Hence, against the usual rule that bigger species survive longer, grouse species show no relationship between body size and longevity.

# BREEDING

**Nest and eggs**

In Scotland, hens mate in late April or early May, begin laying within a few days, complete a clutch in just over a week (*see* Fig. 13), and start incubation with the last or penultimate egg. Incubation lasts about 26 days and hatching is usually in early June, the period from mating to hatching being about six weeks.

The nest, a shallow scrape in the ground, is sparsely lined with vegetation taken from the surroundings. Sites vary, some sheltered by tall heather in open forest, some on bare ground under closed-canopy Sitka spruce. They are usually

FIG 90. Hen capercaillie turning her eggs. (Chris Knights)

FIG 91. Unusual capercaillie nest at Craig Leek, Invercauld. The nest is on a ledge near the top of the rock (arrowed). (Ernest Cowieson)

hidden from avian predators by overhead cover, often on slightly sloping or raised sites, an escape route oriented so that the hen can leave readily if disturbed.

Some hens lay eggs in their first spring, some wait until their second spring, and a few delay until their third spring, a decision presumably influenced by body condition. Eggs are yellowish white with a few brown spots, average 57 × 42mm in size, weigh about 50g and look much like those of a chicken. The number of eggs in a clutch varies from 4 to 16, more usually numbering between five and nine, averaging about seven.

Hens that lose their first clutch while laying or early in incubation sometimes renest. In Norway, about a third of the hens that lost their first clutch to predators renested, and hens in better condition were more likely to renest.[75]

**Chicks and their viability**
Mother and downy chicks leave the nest about a day after hatching. The chicks are sensitive to cold and require brooding to at least three weeks. Their survival depends at first upon their innate vigour, which stems from the quality of the eggs from which they hatched, itself influenced by their mother's diet and condition when laying.[76]

Capercaillie chicks grow fast and, more than other grouse, rely on invertebrates to supplement their early diet. They favour caterpillars of geometrid moths, such as the winter moth and July highflyer, which are large and easy to catch. The sole Scottish study on chick diet, carried out in 1991–6, showed that broods survived better when they ate more and larger caterpillars.[77] However, chick survival was poor even in years of caterpillar abundance and benign summer weather, so something else obviously depressed survival. Chick viability was a likely candidate.

Spring changed in Scotland during the last quarter of the twentieth century. In the 1970s, winter was typically cold, and mid-April was a period of sudden warming and fast growth of plants. In the 1980s and 1990s, however, winters became milder and the April warming more prolonged (see Fig. 92). Plant growth began earlier but was more erratic, with stops and starts spread over a longer period. Capercaillie bred well in years of sudden April warming and poorly in years with prolonged springs (see Fig. 93). The likely connection is that abrupt spring growth provides hens with a nutritious diet, thereby allowing them to lay good-quality eggs that hatch into viable chicks. Slow, erratic spring growth is probably less nutritious, so making for poor-quality eggs and weakly chicks.

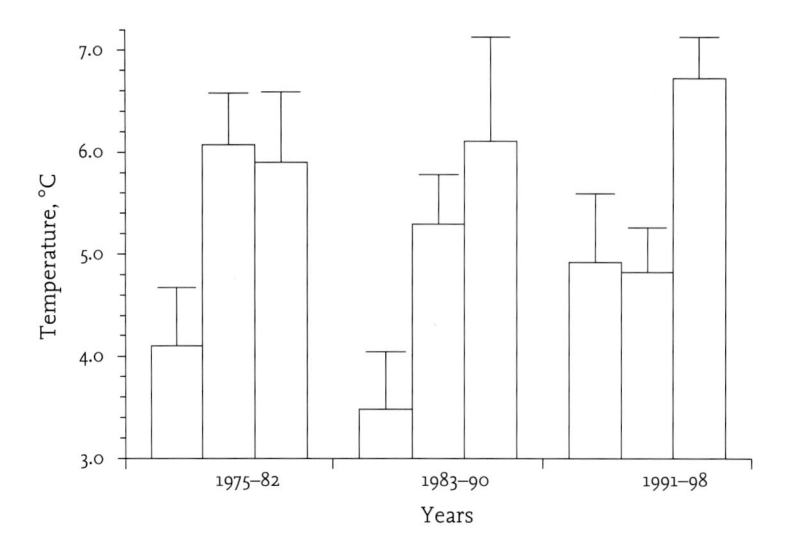

FIG 92. April warming became more prolonged between and 1975 and 1998. The three columns in each period (1975–82, 1983–90, 1991–8) show the mean air temperature in the first, middle and last ten days of April respectively (the bar is the standard error of the mean) at Glen Tanar. In 1975–82, a cool early April was followed by a warm mid-April. In 1991–8, by contrast, early and mid-April were about equally mild. The index of April warming used in Figure 93 reflects this change. It is $([T_2 - T_1] - [T_3 - T_2]/2)$, where $T_1$ is the mean temperature in the first ten days of April, $T_2$ is the mean temperature in the middle ten days, and $T_3$ is the mean temperature in the last ten days.

## MOVEMENTS

Capercaillie are broadly resident, but adults often move between winter and summer home ranges. Natal dispersal, a different kind of movement, occurs once in a lifetime when youngsters leave their rearing place and seek somewhere to live. Some birds settle and breed close to where they were reared, while others roam before settling far from home.

Woodland grouse, including capercaillie and black grouse in the Old World,[78] and ruffed, blue and spruce grouse in the New World,[79] have two main periods of directional movement: autumn and spring. This applies to seasonal movements between summer and winter home ranges, and also to natal dispersal. Distances quoted for such movements are as the crow flies and do not necessarily reflect distances travelled, especially the meanderings of natal dispersal.

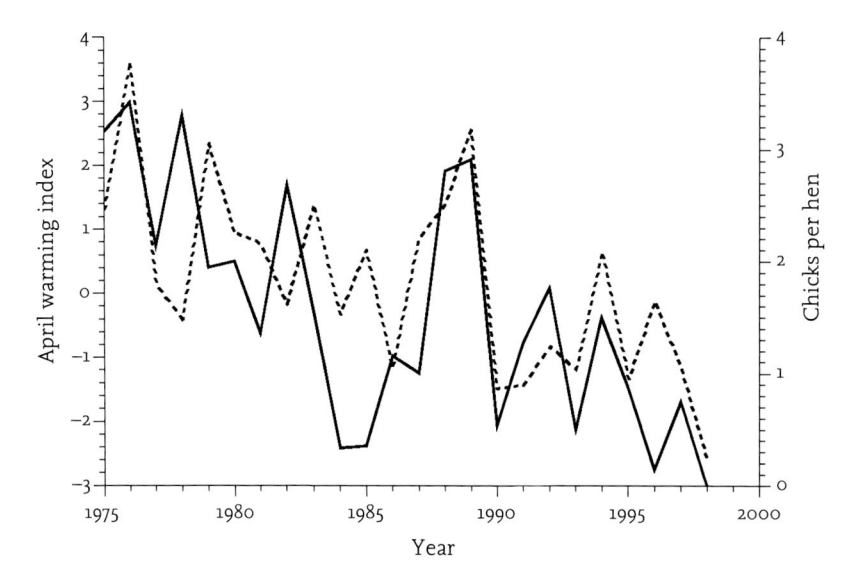

FIG 93. Between 1975 and 1998, capercaillie produced fewer chicks (solid line) as the index of April warming (dashed line) declined. The index was high when April warming came late and abruptly, and low when warming began early but was erratic and prolonged. Plant growth presumably tracked temperature.

**Seasonal movements**

Once they have settled after natal dispersal, adult capercaillie return to the same summer and winter home ranges each year. The distance between summer and winter ranges of individual birds probably depends upon the habitat's grain[80] and structure. At one extreme, seasonal movements of 30–40km between separate coniferous and deciduous forests in the south Urals are distinct and regular enough to be called migration.[81] In Norway, the Bavarian Alps and the Pechora-Illych reserve in Russia, radio-tagged individuals wintered on average only 1–2km from their summer range. Some moved hardly at all, their summer and winter ranges overlapping, while others moved up to 8km (Pyrenees), up to 9km (Bavarian Alps) or more than 10km (Norway).[82] Annual home ranges of radio-tagged adults are typically several square kilometres.

The winter home range of an adult cock often includes his lek. In spring, cocks spend more time on and near the lek, rarely moving more than 1km from its centre. Some adult hens, having wintered in a small area, roam widely in spring and visit several leks before returning to nest in their summer range.

An adult hen caught on a lek in Abernethy pinewood nested in Strathavon,[83] 18km to the east. At Varaldskogen in Norway, radio-tagged adult hens usually visited only one established lek in spring, but in Bavaria several hens visited more than one lek. Hens may visit more leks if these are small.[84]

Distances moved by broods after hatching probably depend upon habitat and food supply. Few studies have described the home-range sizes of broods, but in the Bavarian Alps six broods used home ranges of 75–350ha,[85] whereas in Scotland another six broods used only 10–60ha.[86] The 10ha range was in a wood with ample blaeberry and abundant caterpillars.

### Natal dispersal

Much information on dispersal comes from young birds ringed in summer and shot in autumn. Young can roam widely before settling to breed, some then settling far from their place of origin but others returning close to it. Thus, a hen radio-tagged in Glen Tanar travelled 20km west to Coilacriech in her first autumn and then returned to Glen Tanar to breed 4km from where she was first marked. Information from shot birds must therefore be interpreted with care.

Capercaillie hens, as in other grouse species, disperse further than cocks. Most radio-tagged capercaillie cocks settled near their chick ranges.[87] In Scotland, natal dispersal distances of 15 radio-tagged young hens averaged 12km, varying from 1km to 30km.[88] Some hens moved in autumn, some in spring, and some in autumn and again in spring.

When capercaillie expanded their Scottish range after they were reintroduced in 1837–8, it was often noted that hens appeared in new areas before cocks, consistent with hens dispersing further than cocks. In the absence of capercaillie cocks, hybrids of capercaillie and black grouse frequently appeared (Fig. 94).[89]

Natal dispersal in autumn, after broods break up, is to be expected as youngsters seek somewhere less crowded to live. It is less obvious why there should be another, spring peak in natal dispersal. In the Pyrenees, aggression was observed among hens in spring, as they defended territories encompassing scarce brood habitat.[90] Perhaps such aggression stimulates young hens to disperse. Spring dispersal of hens in boreal forest might result from competition for scarce supplies of cotton-grass shoots,[91] a high-quality food.

### Irruptions

Capercaillie, like some other grouse species, occasionally gather in large flocks and travel long distances. Such movements have been widely noted in anecdote by hunters and naturalists, but, being infrequent, are hard to study. They seem to be irruptive in character, though sometimes termed migration. Eight birds from

FIG 94. Blackcocks at a Finnish lek, with black grouse-capercaillie hybrid. (Dave Pullan)

Finland and Sweden, recovered more than 1,000km south of where they were ringed,[92] may be examples of such movement.

Lauri Siivonen[93] showed that black grouse, capercaillie and hazel grouse in Finland fluctuated together in three- to four-year cycles of abundance between 1929 and 1949. He collated records of mass movements of black grouse and capercaillie, which occurred during autumn in years of peak breeding density. During the 1940s, however, average densities were low and no mass movements were recorded.

Evidence from other grouse species shows that cyclic population declines are associated with greater dispersal of young (see Chapter 14). Hence more dispersal among capercaillie may occur during cyclic declines. If the population decline follows a high peak, dispersing birds may gather into large flocks that travel far. If so, such flocks should comprise mostly young birds, but we have no evidence to back this up.

There is little chance of capercaillie irruptions in Scotland in the near future. Numbers of birds are low and there is no evidence of population cycles. Cycles generally require large areas of homogeneous habit and Scottish woods are fragmented. In a fragmented landscape, population regulation is likely to be by density-dependent dispersal out of source areas of good habitat into sink areas of poor habitat, where mortality is high and breeding poor.[94]

## FRAGMENTATION, METAPOPULATIONS AND CONSERVATION

It is difficult to study the effects of fragmentation upon capercaillie in Scottish woods, because no wood is large enough to serve as an unfragmented control. We therefore look to experience elsewhere.

### Fragmentation

Industrial logging in boreal forest causes habitat loss and deterioration, and demands more roads, which make poaching easy. This is probably one reason why capercaillie are sparser in regions of industrial logging than in virgin forest.[95] Another explanation for declines that follow logging is habitat fragmentation.

Fragmented forest supports lower densities of capercaillie than continuous mature forest. An explanation for this, popular in Fennoscandia, is that the exploited ground supports higher densities of generalist predators that hunt into the remaining patches of mature forest. In southern Fennoscandia, where agriculture has fragmented the forest, predators such as red foxes and pine martens are more abundant than in the north,[96] and woodland grouse breed more poorly.

Fragmentation may not lead to more predators and poorer breeding where logging, as opposed to agriculture, fragments the virgin forest. In this case, density-dependent dispersal may drain birds from virgin patches into the surrounding logged areas. The alarming evidence is that a virgin patch of habitat measuring several hundred square kilometres may be insufficient to maintain capercaillie densities when surrounded by degraded, logged habitat.[97]

The outcomes of fragmentation are likely to vary with the type of ground between the remaining patches of good habitat. If it is grassy, it is likely to support more small rodents, which in turn support more predators. If the newly logged ground does not support more rodents or other prey, there should not be more predators. Density-dependent dispersal might, none the less, cause declines in numbers of birds in remaining patches of mature forest. Both processes probably occur in Scotland.

### Metapopulations and conservation

In fragmented landscapes, the quality of secondary habitat is crucial. If emigrants from patches of better habitat survive poorly in secondary habitat, the better habitat can be drained of birds and suffer a decline in density. If emigrants survive well, albeit at lower density, they can form a reserve that returns to the better habitat when living space becomes available.[98]

Birds also move between patches of good habitat. In the Bavarian Alps, capercaillie live in patches of mountain forest separated by open farmland valleys below the tree-line, and by Alpine pastures, other Alpine vegetation, and rocky ground above it. As in much of Europe, Bavarian capercaillie declined during the twentieth century. Birds were more likely to decline or disappear from peripheral patches of forest than from patches at the core of the range. Genetic evidence implied that there was limited dispersal between capercaillie in patches as little as 10km apart.[99] Researchers therefore recommended a network of suitable woods separated by not more than 5–10km.

In Scotland, it is unlikely that capercaillie in any single block of continuous woodland can sustain themselves in the long term. But birds move between blocks, forming a network, or 'metapopulation'. A metapopulation comprises several subpopulations, each in its own patch of woodland and none able to survive on its own. Birds in some patches become extinct in unfavourable years, but these patches are then colonised by birds from other areas when conditions become more favourable. The chances of a patch losing its capercaillie increase with increasing isolation, decreasing size and decreasing habitat quality.[100]

In Scotland, six areas hold most of the remaining capercaillie (Easter Ross, Moray, Speyside, Deeside and Donside, Perthshire and Loch Lomond). As in the Bavarian Alps, birds in each area are genetically distinct.[101] We can therefore think of six local populations forming the national metapopulation. Each local population has a different environment, which reduces the chances of all six becoming extinct simultaneously. If one becomes extinct, it can be colonised from another.

Current conservation therefore involves safeguarding each local population. Dispersal between them should increase the chances of the national population surviving local catastrophes and also of maintaining its genetic variety. In the longer term, dispersal between local populations is being increased by connecting them with a network of suitable woods.[102]

POPULATION TRENDS

**Extinction of Scottish capercaillie**
Capercaillie were on sale in Perth market in 1746[103] and the last birds known in Scotland were shot in 1785, which suggests that hunting gave our race its death blow. By the mid-eighteenth century, however, their forest habitat was at a low ebb after centuries of felling, burning and cattle-browsing.[104] Their decline also coincided with the Little Ice Age, a climatic event of the sixteenth to eighteenth centuries that involved cold, wet summers, in which capercaillie do not thrive.[105]

**Declines of capercaillie in the twentieth century**

It is often remarked that declines of capercaillie in Scotland during the twentieth century followed the felling of mature plantations and Caledonian pinewoods during the two world wars. In the case of the Second World War, this mirrors the more widespread observation that densities in the boreal forest west of the Ural mountains declined with the onset of industrial clear-felling.[106] Habitat loss, however, cannot explain the big decline that occurred in Scotland during the 1980s and 1990s.

Populations grow or shrink according to the balance between reproduction and death. A population can increase if birds rear more young than are needed to replace adult deaths, and it declines if young are in short supply. In the 1990s, hen capercaillie in Scottish woods reared on average about 0.9 chicks each year, whereas 1.1 should have maintained a constant population.[107] In 16 studies throughout Europe, including Russia, median[108] breeding success was 1.6 chicks per hen per year. A stable population in Glen Tanar averaged 1.8 chicks per hen during 1975–83,[109] more than enough to sustain the population, to allow it to expand its range, and to allow a crop to be taken by shooters. All this confirms that low breeding success was the primary cause of the birds' continued decline during the last quarter of the twentieth century.

In principle, the decline could have been halted by lessening adult mortality, so reducing the number of chicks needed to replace adult deaths. A voluntary ban on shooting began in the early 1990s, but it did not prevent further decline. Studies then revealed that the two main causes of adult death were predation and, unexpectedly, collisions with forest fences.

Calculations showed that capercaillie might not have declined had there been no deaths from flying into fences (Fig. 95).[110] With fences as they were in the 1990s, hens each needed to rear 1.1 chicks per year to replace adult deaths. Without deaths on fences, they needed to rear only 0.6 – less than the 0.9 observed. Hence current management aims to increase adult survival by marking fences to reduce kills,[111] or, preferably, removing them altogether from core capercaillie areas.[112]

Fences at woods are usually erected to prevent red deer eating newly planted trees. Planting and associated costs such as fencing have long been funded by grants from the FC, but there was not money to take fences down once the trees had grown tall enough to be safe from red deer. Decaying fences accumulated for over half a century, many serving no purpose but killing woodland grouse. This has now changed, and grant-funded fence removal or marking began on a large scale in 2000.[113]

Public monies, largely from a European Union LIFE programme that ended in 2006, have also being used to subsidise the legal killing of crows and foxes, and

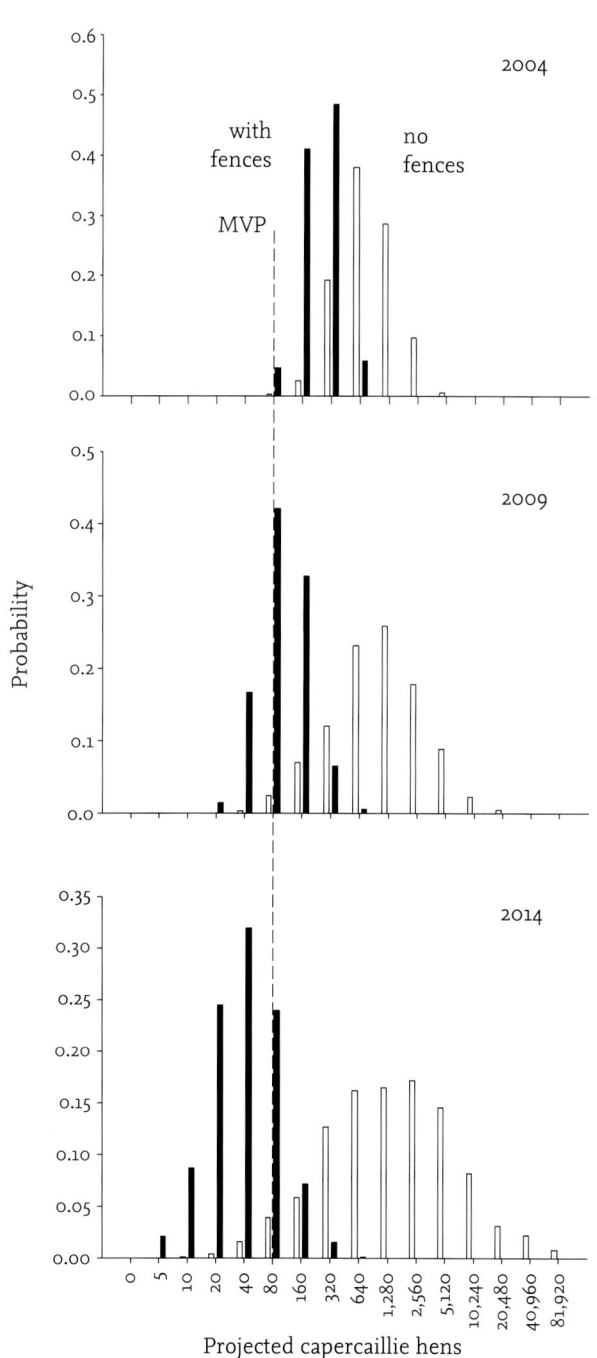

FIG 95. Probability distributions for the number of hens in Scotland, with (black columns) and without (white columns) deaths on fences, projected from 1999. MVP is the minimum viable population, below which recovery is unlikely.

to increase the quality and quantity of brood habitat. Such measures should help the capercaillie's survival.

*Snares*
Killing of foxes by gamekeepers is legal and accepted. In the mid-1990s, advised by irresponsible consultants, many estates instructed keepers to spend less time on traditional methods of fox killing. These included killing cubs and vixens at dens, ambushing foxes by lying out with a rifle, shooting at night with spotlights, and using packs of hounds to drive foxes out of woods towards a line of guns. Instead, keepers were told to use many more snares, as sold by the consultants. Snaring certainly kills foxes efficiently, but it is unselective and is banned in most civilised countries.[114]

Snares kill non-target species such as deer, hares, wildcats, badgers, otters and capercaillie.[115] Cock capercaillie are caught more often than hens, with about five cocks killed for each hen. The subsequences of the use of snares are shown

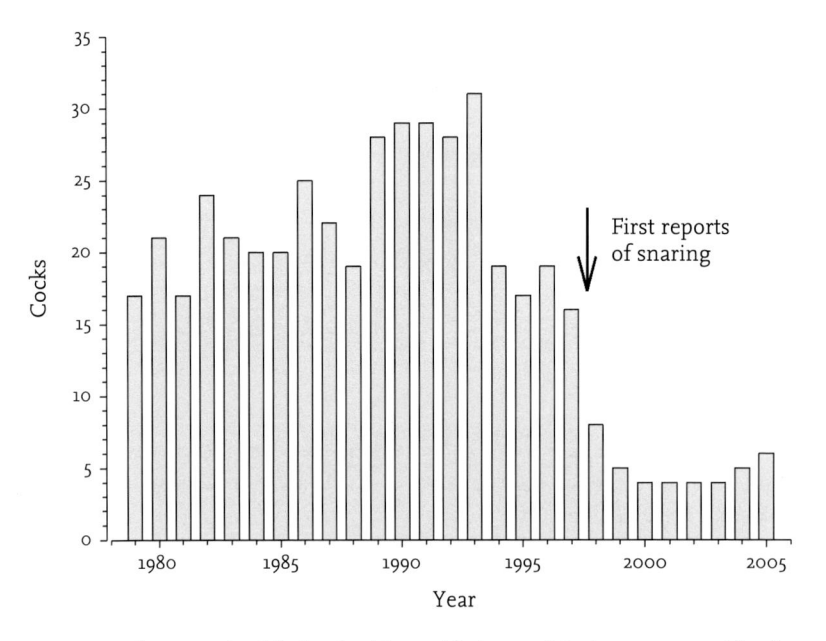

FIG 96. Cocks counted at leks in Glen Tanar old pinewood during 1979–2005. The first reports of snaring here were in 1997. Reports of reckless snaring stopped in 2000 but cock numbers had not recovered by 2004, associated with poor breeding success in the glen after 1997.

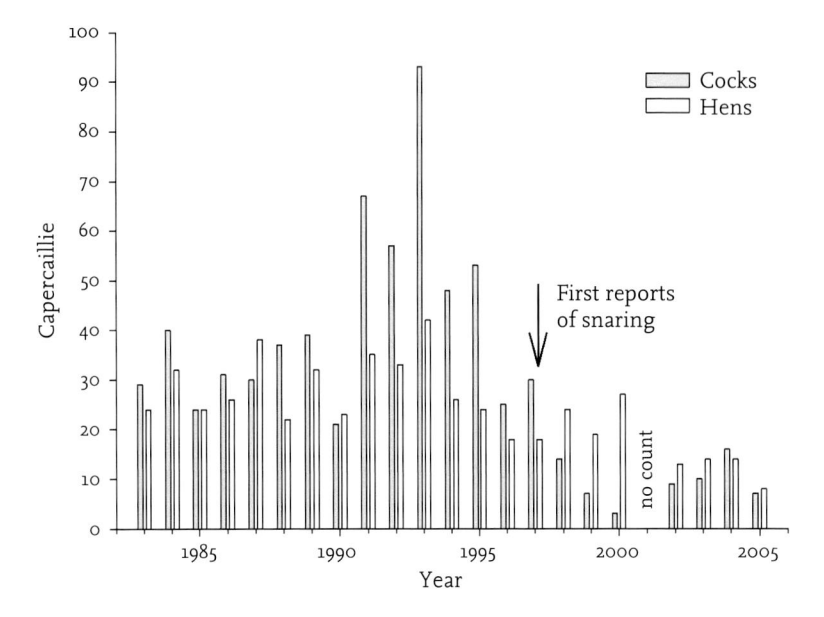

FIG 97. Autumn drive counts at Glen Tanar in 1983–2005.[116] Until 1997 more cocks than hens were seen, but then the ratio plummeted before showing some recovery after reports of reckless snaring (which started in 1997, arrow) ceased in 2000.

in Figures 96 and 97. After snaring was first reported, the number of cocks seen at leks plummeted. Whereas beforehand there were more cocks than hens during autumn drive counts, hens subsequently outnumbered cocks.

## THE FUTURE

If the trends observed during the 1990s had continued, capercaillie would have been effectively extinct in Scotland by about 2015. The decline, however, seems to have halted. This was due partly to improved breeding success in 2000–3 (about one chick per hen), associated with better weather. Changes in management, including marking and removing fences, and also increased predator control, probably contributed too. These changes were funded largely by the Scottish Executive, the European Union, the FC and Scottish Natural Heritage. The capercaillie's future in Scotland will continue to depend upon the weather, and upon continued sympathetic management of woodlands by public and private landowners alike.

## SUMMARY

The capercaillie is the largest grouse in the world, probably because hens mate with the largest cocks, which win the most fights. It lives in coniferous forest, the adults eating mostly pine, fir or spruce needles, and the chicks depending largely upon blaeberry and associated insects. The bird's very size makes great demands upon its environment, the chicks requiring more insects and the adults more space than other grouse. Consequently, it is seen as a touchstone of forest health. Its past numbers have fluctuated, together with those of other grouse, in line with variations in weather. It probably became extinct in Britain and Ireland in the eighteenth century, when woods were at a low ebb, and was reintroduced to Scotland in the 1830s. It then spread widely, but declined in the last quarter of the twentieth century. This decline was probably due to more erratic and prolonged springs affecting the diet and condition of laying hens, so reducing their breeding success. Without the efforts now being made to improve the bird's habitat and stem the decline in population, the capercaillie might well have become extinct again in Scotland by about 2015.

CHAPTER 7

# Behaviour

GROUSE HAVE EVOLVED SPECTACULAR displays and ornaments that enhance them, such as the blackcock's lyre-shaped tail and the ptarmigan's red erectile combs. Many authors have described grouse displays and calls in detail,[1] so here we confine ourselves to outlining their main features. Chapters 5 and 6 cover displays of blackgame and capercaillie, and in this chapter we note those of *Lagopus lagopus* and rock ptarmigan, drawing attention to their similarities. Much more attention has been paid to the spectacular displays of grouse than to any other aspect of their behaviour. It is at least as interesting, however, to see how they conduct themselves in the day-to-day business of coaxing a living from harsh environments.

This chapter emphasises such maintenance behaviour, the activities of making a living and daily survival. We note how birds of each British grouse species communicate with their fellows by calls and postures, including those of aggressive and sexual behaviour. We also summarise how these birds eat, drink, fly and care for their plumage. Where they choose to rest and roost is vital for their survival, and we discuss their reactions to enemies, including forming packs where they are safer from predators. Lastly, we describe their parental care, which differs greatly among the four species.

## SOCIAL SYSTEMS OF BRITISH GROUSE

British grouse have two types of social system, these depending on the species. Cock and hen *Lagopus lagopus* and ptarmigan form pairs on large territories that are defended until chicks hatch. In contrast, blackcock and male capercaillie display at small territories on communal leks, and once serviced there, hens leave for their nesting haunts, where they incubate eggs and rear young without the help of guarding cocks.

There are, however, similarities between the territorial and lekking species. All four species often pack in winter. In spring, when red grouse hold well-spaced territories, occasionally two or three cocks (rarely up to five) contest where their territories meet at a corner, and the displays there resemble a lek.[2] Cock red grouse also sometimes threaten one another like this when meeting off their territories. In a flock of male Alaskan rock ptarmigan loafing on the snow and feeding during their leisurely spring migration, RM saw some cocks defending small territories for a few minutes when hens appeared, again like a temporary lek. Hence red grouse and rock ptarmigan sometimes show lek-like behaviour.

Conversely, blackcock and cock capercaillie sometimes display off leks in a more spaced pattern, and blackcock can have an 'exploded' lek (see Chapter 5). Such instances bring to mind the social system of American woodland grouse, which is intermediate between the extremes of lekking (*Tetrao*) and monogamous territorial (*Lagopus*) behaviour. Cock ruffed and blue grouse defend display-sites on dispersed territories, but they do not form permanent pairs with hens. The drumming logs of ruffed grouse are often clumped along the edges of thick forest, and yearling cock blue grouse tend to clump around the territories of adult cocks.[3]

## GROUSE CALLS AND ASSOCIATED POSTURES

Most grouse calls involve aggressive or sexual behaviour, while some signify contact (such as a hen calling her chicks) or warn of approaching predators. They include an extraordinary variety of sounds. Producing the calls requires an elaborate anatomical apparatus, including special throat pouches that help project sound.[4]

Many calls of *Lagopus lagopus* and rock ptarmigan have similar phrasing,[5] but the latter sound different because of their low croaking pitch. Hens call in a higher pitch than cocks, as do immature cock red grouse when they start crowing at eight to ten weeks, before their voices break. Of Norwegian willow ptarmigan, it has been said: 'According to musicians the hen calls with a high flute-like soprano, while the cock has a somewhat hoarse and metallic alto or mezzosoprano.'[6] Hen rock ptarmigan give higher-pitched calls than hen *Lagopus lagopus*, sounding like cooing doves or squealing puppies.

The same call can vary somewhat between countries – for example, Norwegian cock willow ptarmigan sound harsher than red grouse.[7] The songs of adjacent cocks also sound different to a good musical ear. At Glenamoy, P. J. O'Hare could tell unerringly which cock, invisible in the dawn twilight, gave each song.

Some publications illustrate calls by sound spectrographs that show timing and frequency,[8] but most readers find this obscure. Calls have usually been described with words, although these are unstandardised and seldom indicate stressed syllables. The International Phonetic Association (IPA) has devised a set of symbols to indicate pronunciation, stress and tone in human speech.[9] These cannot represent musical calls, however, far less the weird pops, clicks and shuffling calls of blackcock or capercaillie. None the less, IPA symbols are better at describing the calls than unstandardised words, where possible – Table 17 shows some examples.

**TABLE 17.** Some calls in *Lagopus lagopus* and rock ptarmigan, expressed phonetically.[10]

|                  | LAGOPUS LAGOPUS            | ROCK PTARMIGAN        |
|------------------|----------------------------|-----------------------|
| Alighting song   | 'aː‚ka‚ka‚ka‚ka‚ka...... ko'wa‚ko'wa | 'aː‚ka‚kaː.......ka‚ka‚ka |
| Flushing song    | as above                   | 'ar‚a·‚ka‚kaː         |
| Ground song      | kɔ‚kɔ‚kɔ‚kɔ‚krr            | ko'waːk               |
| Attack           | ko'wa ko'wa ko'wa          | kwa kwa kwa           |
| Attack intention | ko'weː‚ko‚ko               | ko'wa·‚o              |
| Threat           | krau krau krau             | *cock* krrr, *hen* ki'a |
| Escape           | kɔ kɔ kɔ                   | kʌ kʌ kʌ              |
| Sexual chase     | kɔk kɔk kɔk                | ko'wa ko'wa ko'wa     |

KEY TO PHONETIC SYMBOLS
(after the International Phonetic Association)

| a fat  | ʌ sun                              |
|--------|------------------------------------|
| e day  | u do                               |
| i see  | ' main stress on next syllable     |
| o bone | ‚ secondary stress on next syllable |
| ɔ pot  | · half-long vowel                  |
|        | ː long vowel                       |

**Note**
In a paper by Johnsen *et al.* (1991) on Norwegian willow ptarmigan, AW helped by using IPA phonetics for some calls.

Calls that warn against predators are very alike in *Lagopus lagopus* and rock ptarmigan, while those of sexual display are less so, despite similar phrasing. In contrast, song in flight, flushing song and ground song are very different in the two species, perhaps because they have an advertising function for hens – an unattached hen often flies to a cock that has given one of these calls.[11]

Postures that accompany the main calls are so alike in *Lagopus lagopus* and rock ptarmigan[12] that we describe them together here, but because blackgame and capercaillie show big differences we note these in chapters 5 and 6. None the less, there are similarities amongst all four species. Common to all is flight intention, with crouching legs and bobbing body, sleek feathers and invisible combs. Common, too, is the cock's frontal aggressive approach to another cock, as he puffs his body feathers, droops his wings, struts, fans his tail and expands his comb, while at each shoulder he displays a large white spot. Common again is how he alters this frontal aggression to less aggressive courtship, with sideways dancing or bowing as he approaches a hen, drooping the wing next to her and twisting his fanned tail towards her.

**During aggressive interactions**
In his song flight or aerial beck, a cock *Lagopus lagopus* or rock ptarmigan rises steeply, sails momentarily, and then descends on rapidly beating wings with fanned tail and outstretched head. On alighting, he calls while jerking his tail up and down, with body feathers puffed out and wings drooped. The hen gives shriller becks, rises less high in flight, and seldom calls after alighting. A cock often makes a directional beck towards a neighbour, and this generally induces the neighbour to beck. On a windless day, a thunderclap or avalanche can induce cock Scottish ptarmigan to beck.

In calm air, aerial becks of cock *Lagopus lagopus* or rock ptarmigan can be heard 2km away, and singing blackcock at 1km. Singing capercaillie are much harder to hear, perhaps because part of the sound they produce is below the threshold of human hearing. To our ears, the exact location of a distant rock ptarmigan is harder to judge than in red grouse, and blackcock are yet greater ventriloquists. The clicks of a singing capercaillie, however, are easy to locate.

Less intensive than aerial becking is the ground beck of *Lagopus lagopus* or rock ptarmigan. A bird delivers it while standing with its throat puffed and vibrating (Fig. 98). The rock ptarmigan's version is most machine-like: a snoring, ticking croak that lasts for several seconds and resembles the sound of a turning fishing reel. It is often heard when two cocks parade at a boundary, and sometimes in disputes between foraging cocks when Scottish birds are in packs.

FIG 98. Cock red grouse with an inflated throat during a ground call. (David A. Gowans)

Some calls involve attack, or the less aggressive attack intention, or the even less aggressive threat. In attack, a bird stretches its head forwards with inflated neck, while running with beak open, wings drooped and tail fanned as it chases a retreating bird, which it may grasp with its bill and beat with its wings. In attack intention, it does not run, but crouches with neck feathers less erect. In threat, it stands with upright head and neck.

These postures can lead to a fight, when the two birds jump in the air and spar on the ground while striking with wings, feet and bills (see Fig. 99). Usually they do not lose feathers and seldom fight longer than a few seconds, most encounters being ritual displays where one bird soon feels submissive and withdraws. Occasionally, however, serious fighting erupts, lasting up to about two minutes, when birds may lose feathers. According to one account, when Scottish ptarmigan 'cocks fight on steep ground they often roll over and over, frequently up to 20 metres and rarely up to 50 metres, down steep hillsides and rocks'.[13]

In escape intention, a bird crouches as if ready to fly, sleeking the feathers on its head, neck and breast, showing no comb, bobbing its tail and body, and holding its wings slightly outwards and downwards. A cock often raises his crown

**FIG 99.** Cock ptarmigan sparring. (Derek McGinn)

feathers, which makes him look more hen-like and tends to reduce the attacker's aggressiveness.

Aggressive postures mostly involve cocks of the same species, but occasionally two species fight or threaten. In the few cases recorded, willow ptarmigan usually dominated rock ptarmigan, and red grouse dominated blackgame, but outcomes with red grouse and Scottish ptarmigan were fairly evenly balanced.[14]

### Social contact and warning of predators

In the posture of social contact, a hen solicits for a cock or a parent calls to lost chicks. The bird stands high with raised neck and head, looking around and calling until the cock or lost chick appears.

A bird warns of a fox or raptor with a distinct call for each, while standing with erect body, neck and head. This alerts others, which turn to look at the calling bird, learn the predator's location, and call in turn. On the appearance of a fox, red grouse and ptarmigan produce a wave of sound that follows the fox as it crosses an area.

**During sexual behaviour**

Sexual behaviour is similar in *Lagopus lagopus* and rock ptarmigan. Several calls accompany it, the loudest being a sharp single repeated call by cock and hen while he chases her on the ground or in flight. During the chase, he dives at her, trying to move her to his territory.

In winter, Scottish red grouse show sexual behaviour more often than ptarmigan, but it occurs among ptarmigan in every month of a mild winter. When birds are in packs on snow-covered ground, however, neither species shows it, except briefly on fine spring days.

A hen *Lagopus lagopus* or rock ptarmigan that is seeking a cock flies from one territory to another, courted by each cock in turn. When she leaves, he often pursues in an aerial chase and a nearby cock may join. On each territory, she decides whether to stay or leave. The cock bows, struts and waltzes around her with drooped wings and open beak, while dragging his primaries through heath or crusty snow with a rasping sound. He drums his feet in a rapid stamping, making a sound that is audible to human ears within 4m. Above his head rise his brilliant red combs, with sunlight shining through them. In another display he sits and rapidly wags his head from side to side, presenting his two combs to the hen in a rapid whirl of crimson.

In both species a hen ready for coition with a cock spreads her wings slightly. As he walks onto her back, she lifts her tail and twists it sideways as he makes

FIG 100. Marks of a courting rock ptarmigan cock in snow, showing footprints and wing marks. (Adam Watson)

contact for several seconds. He then jumps off and shows further courtship while she shakes her feathers vigorously.[15] Captive hen willow ptarmigan lay fertile eggs for about eight days after separation from a cock,[16] so just one successful copulation may suffice to fertilise a whole clutch.

### INDIVIDUAL DISTANCE

Birds usually keep well apart, even when in packs. This 'individual distance' increases with body size, and among British grouse is smallest in ptarmigan and greatest in capercaillie. Most paintings of adult grouse show them almost touching, which is perhaps artistic licence. An exception is Keith Brockie's realistic painting of two ptarmigan in snow.[17]

An observer can readily discern individual distance in feeding birds. Adult red grouse usually keep about 60cm apart, maintaining this by brief threat or attack.[18] Frequently a bird displaces another from food or from coming too close, by making brief threats or calls. When red grouse or Scottish ptarmigan roost in packs, individuals are seldom closer than 30cm and usually more than 50cm apart (Fig. 101).[19] Staying apart while sleeping should reduce risks from predators because, if a predator attacks, it is less likely to find more than one bird.

As in poultry, adults of all four species relax their individual distance while bathing in sunshine, dust or snow, when nearby birds come so close that a few almost touch. Also, capercaillie hens in a harem competing for the cock's attentions may touch while jostling for position. Another obvious exception is that hens brood their chicks, which red grouse and Scottish ptarmigan do until the poults are six weeks old. Thereafter, feeding poults may almost touch the hen, and the whole family roosts close together, often touching, until the chicks are fully grown.

### EATING AND DRINKING

Feeding grouse walk across the ground or snow from plant to plant, biting shoots with a sideways action that is also used when they feed in bushes or trees. Rock ptarmigan remove twigs 'with the tip of the bill and a quick sideways turn of the head. This lightning-like movement bends the twig at a sharp angle against the cutting edge of the bill and breaks it off with an audible snap.'[20] Although red grouse and Scottish ptarmigan sometimes stretch up to reach grass seeds and often eat plants shorter than themselves, red grouse prefer to eat heather that is 20–35cm high,[21] where they do not have to bend down or stretch up. They usually

BEHAVIOUR · 181

FIG 101. Roost hollows of red grouse in snow, no closer than 30cm apart. (Adam Watson)

FIG 102. Ptarmigan hen with well-grown chicks. (Stuart Rae)

**FIG 103.** Tracks left by red grouse foraging bush by bush. (Adam Watson)

avoid plants taller than 35cm – in other words, that are above the 30cm height of a standing bird's head.

At all seasons, birds in the open do most of their feeding near cover. Rock ptarmigan do so within a few metres of boulders,[22] while the other species feed near tall vegetation. Blackgame and capercaillie feeding on the woodland floor also keep close to cover, which includes live and dead standing trees, stumps, wind-thrown trees, juniper bushes, and branches on felled plots.

**Feeding in snow**

Grouse often scratch through light snow to expose food, typically down to 6cm, although in Britain they rarely dig to feed. In Scotland we have not known of a grouse digging more than 10cm for food, although depths of up to 30cm have been recorded in Icelandic ptarmigan.[23] When deep snow covers all plants, red grouse and Scottish ptarmigan fly to exposed ridges, where they eat shoots projecting above drifted snow, and red grouse sometimes feed in bushes or trees. Scottish ptarmigan rarely descend to woodland, although one was seen eating buds on a gnarled birch on the morning after a storm.[24]

Norwegian rock ptarmigan 'often follow the reindeer in the winter and dive into the holes made by these animals, thus obtaining a few berries'.[25] In the Arctic, they feed where foraging caribou, reindeer or musk ox have scraped snow off plants, and Scottish red grouse and ptarmigan often eat heather that has been exposed by red deer.[26]

**Monthly and daily routines**
At Spyhill, John Savory counted the pecks of red grouse that were feeding mostly on heather. His lowest monthly figure was in November, when hens on average pecked 10,300 times per day, and from February they increased the rate each month to a peak of 30,500 in May before incubation.[27] Cocks also pecked least in November, with 11,500 per day, but their peak was 19,900 in March, a month of much territorial activity.

On snow-free winter days in Scotland, adults of all four species eat for a minor part of the day. They usually have a feeding peak shortly after rising in the morning, but eat most intensively and hurriedly in late afternoon, resulting in a lower quality of food, as they stuff their crops before the long night. Apart from brief breaks to drink and defecate, incubating hens feed almost continuously during the short periods off their eggs, again taking food of low quality.

**Selective eating**
Feeding can be leisurely, however, resulting in the selective choice of high-quality foods, such as when gravid hens eat for much of the day in the few weeks before and during the period when they lay eggs. In spring, all four species obtain nutritious food by eating plants that start growing early, such as cotton-grass shoots, and blackgame and capercaillie later take the red flowers of larch. Hence birds take a greater variety of foods in spring and summer, with fewer heath plants than in winter, and more herbs, flowers, moss capsules, grass seeds and invertebrates.

In late summer, Scottish ptarmigan often move to hollows that were inaccessible at nesting time because of deep snow. The same happens in east Greenland, where rock ptarmigan eat freshly growing Alpine bistort on snow-patch hollows.[28] From late July to October in Scotland, birds of all four species sometimes move to feed on berries and bog sedges, frequently at higher altitudes. Capercaillie that venture into the open to do this usually remain on slopes, where they can easily take wing into nearby woodland if disturbed. For capercaillie, higher altitude is often just a steep slope above a wood, but for blackgame it can be up to 1.5km away and 300m higher in altitude, exceptionally even into ptarmigan habitat.[29]

**Grit and water**
Birds of all four species frequently swallow rock granules, preferring quartz when available. Most of the grit stays in the gizzard, a stomach with a tough, leathery, corrugated lining that moves in strong contractions, powered by thick, hard muscles. The contractions combine with the grit to pulverise food coming down from the crop. All four species – and especially hens in spring – frequent roadsides and tracks to get grit. In deep snow, red grouse often, and rock ptarmigan occasionally, go to Scottish roads to eat grit that has been spread to give cars a good

FIG 104. Hen red grouse eating grit. (David A. Gowans)

grip. In Alaska and Canada, where deep snow can lie for months, spruce grouse frequent roadsides in September–October, swallowing large amounts of grit before the first snowfalls.[30] Poultry and captives of all British grouse eat and excrete grit daily if they get it ad lib, but can retain it for weeks if there are no fresh supplies.

Although their food contains much water (for example, there is 50 per cent moisture in heather), birds of all four species drink daily at pools or streams, and pairs of red grouse in spring fly up to 1km from their territories to do so. Birds also take raindrops and dew off plants. In the 1930s, keepers put out dew-pans on dry eastern moors so that grouse did not have to travel far for water. Red grouse and Scottish ptarmigan often swallow hoar frost or snow, but in prolonged extensive snow they usually fly or walk to the few places with open water at springs, and drink copiously there rather than taking snow. To drink water is much easier than swallowing snow, and it costs far less in terms of heat loss.[31]

PLUMAGE CARE AND FLIGHT

Birds of all four British grouse species spend much time each day on plumage care. A bird preens with its bill, anointing it with oil from the preen gland at the base of the tail and then transferring the oil to the feathers (see Fig. 106). Plumage care also includes bathing in sunshine, water, snow or dust.[32] A bird bathing in sun, snow or dust lies on one side, stretching the other wing and leg, fluffing its plumage so that bare skin and the inner parts of its feathers are exposed, and

FIG 105. Hen red grouse drinking. (Desmond Dugan)

**FIG 106.** Preening red grouse. (David A. Gowans)

**FIG 107.** Red grouse hens bathing. (David A. Gowans)

often closing its eyes. At times, it kicks its feet and moves its wings and body to cast water, dust or snow onto the plumage, working this deeply into the feathers. A grouse flushed while dust-bathing leaves a rocket-like trail of dust as it takes off. Often a bird gets so covered in dust that its plumage matches the ground around it. After preening or bathing, it usually sheds the water, dust or snow by shaking its feathers vigorously. Birds about to dust-bathe select bare, loose, dry soil for bathing, often on paths or tracks. Willow ptarmigan on an island off Newfoundland liked to dust in anthills.[33] Blackgame and capercaillie are fond of the south sides of big old 'granny' pines on slopes, where ground that has been dried by the roots creates ideal dust-bathing conditions.

Flight in all four species involves several rapid beats followed by a brief sailing glide. If you are within 50m of a flying bird in calm conditions, you will hear a soft whistle as it beats its wings and a hum as it glides. Most flights are short, but birds can easily fly from one hill or wood to another. Red grouse will fly up to 5km from an eagle, and rock ptarmigan have flown from Greenland to Iceland.

## RESTING

In all four British species, a bird rests while sitting or standing with head drawn in and body feathers slightly puffed out. It often closes its eyes momentarily, and sometimes tucks its head under one wing like a domestic fowl. In daytime, grouse rest most frequently around noon and in the early afternoon, as do diurnal birds generally.

During daytime in winter, red and black grouse and capercaillie often rest on snow underneath low branches of pines or spruces. There they usually sit on the snow without scratching a bowl, and the foliage overhead reduces heat loss by radiation. Such trees have been eliminated on most moors, but on moorland in mid- and lower Deeside, where scattered trees have colonised, red and black grouse often use densely foliaged stunted Scots pines and Norway spruces. Dense coniferous or deciduous cover up to 2m above ground level is critical for hazel grouse in Eurasia,[34] and in Britain it affords useful shelter for woodland grouse. Many mature British plantations that would otherwise be a good habitat for woodland grouse are now too open because foresters have reduced cover by thinning uniformly, removing wind-thrown trees and 'brashing' (lopping off lower branches).

Rock ptarmigan often rest on the leeward side of boulders or snowdrifts, where they sit basking in sunshine. Sometimes they rest on or beside dark rocks or vegetated banks that are warm from sunshine. Red and black grouse and capercaillie also sunbathe on banks, and hen capercaillie often venture out of woodland to do so.

## ROOSTING

All grouse species roost like poultry, staying silent and scarcely moving. On a bright night at full moon, especially when hoar frost or a dusting of snow adds extra light, cock red grouse will occasionally crow in calm weather. However, they do this far less often than cock pheasants in the same area.

When grouse are scarce, you can walk far without seeing birds, but their marks reveal their presence, such as fresh dung where they have spent the night. The greenish-grey winter droppings of capercaillie are harder to spot, for they resemble the colour of the understorey feather mosses and blaeberry. When a woodland grouse roosts on the ground, its droppings form a discrete pile, but when it has slept high in a tree they are more scattered and broken by the time they reach the ground. All four species roost in snow if it is deep enough (see Chapter 8).

**Red grouse and ptarmigan**
Whether Scottish red grouse and ptarmigan roost as singletons or pairs rather than in flocks in late autumn and winter varies with snow conditions, weather, and nearness to the coming spring. When deep snow lies, they mostly roost in flocks, especially on stormy nights, but also in snow-free conditions on nights with gales and heavy rain. Hence, in midwinter, on sheltered moorland the red grouse mostly roost alone or in pairs and small groups, whereas on the high Cairngorms there is usually snow and strong wind, so ptarmigan here roost mainly in packs even when it is mild. On lower moors, a few dominant cock red grouse roost alone on their territories even when snow covers most ground, especially on calm nights after they have been on their territories all day, a habit that probably increases their sense of ownership. Even cock ptarmigan can be found roosting alone in such conditions, especially when snow is just a dusting or a shallow covering. The frequency of roosting singletons or pairs increases towards the spring, whatever the snow conditions or weather, in correspondence with the frequency of territorial behaviour during the day.

At Spyhill, roosting red grouse at all seasons spent the night in short heather that was one to seven years old, using taller heather or recently burnt ground far less.[35] Even when they do use tall heather, red grouse often choose tiny gaps and roost with their backs open to the sky. Sometimes they roost on the top of tall degenerate heather that has bent sideways to form a flat surface, the birds supported by it, centimetres off the ground. So, on frosty mornings, 'Nearly every bird is white with hoarfrost all over its back, upper tail and crown but not over its breast and throat, which shows that it roosted with uncovered back.'[36] Unlike the silvery-white spangles of hoar frost on plants or stones, that on the birds is a fine powdery dusting, giving them a pale ghostly hue even an hour after they rise in the morning. Although a bird under tall heather would reduce its heat loss, it would make an easier catch for a fox. Grouse are so well adapted to cold that in temperate conditions they do not need to make heat conservation their paramount concern. In contrast, an inexperienced person in ordinary clothing would die sitting in heather overnight during a frost.

Red grouse often choose to roost in wet areas with surface water where they would hear the splash of an approaching fox – such as at Glenamoy, on short vegetation surrounded by water. When hens have broods, they use small patches of short vegetation or bare gravel or peat, surrounded by taller vegetation. The same goes for ptarmigan, except that boulders tend to be beside their roost sites rather than taller vegetation. Brood hens of both species like to use human paths, where small patches of bare ground with nearby cobbles or vegetation afford shelter and cover.

**Blackgame and capercaillie**
In winter at Glen Dye, Bob Robel found that radio-tagged blackcocks usually roosted in tall heather or scrub.[37] On rainy nights they often used trees, and when deep snow lay on the nearby moor they roosted amongst tall heather on the floor of mature coniferous woodland. On dry mild nights they slept on the moor, usually in groups of three to ten, each group scattered over an area of 0.5–2ha. In all seasons at Kerloch, black grouse (including hens with broods) roosted amongst tall heather where much of it had fallen over, leaving openings.[38]

Capercaillie roost mostly in trees, although moulting adults and hens with small chicks use tall heather or other rank vegetation, and older chicks use branches once they can fly up to them. An adult in a tree prefers dense cover such as Norway spruce, and stands on a thick branch fairly near the trunk or sits with its breast lying on the branch.[39] In the Scottish winter, capercaillie often roost singly or in small groups.

## PACKING

A grouse flock is traditionally called a pack, which can be anything from a small group to thousands of birds.[40] Although grouse of all four British species are often solitary, and red grouse and Scottish ptarmigan often occur in pairs, unmated cock *Lagopus lagopus* and rock ptarmigan gather together even in midsummer, as do hen capercaillie that have no chicks. The biggest packs occur at high population densities in deep snow (*see* Fig. 18), and in Scottish ptarmigan when birds are mostly white and poorly camouflaged on days with mainly snow-free ground. Packs of up to about 5,000 willow ptarmigan have been seen during winter in America, and up to 1,000 red grouse in snow.[41] The largest ptarmigan pack recorded in Scotland numbered 450 on a November day, when they flushed with a loud noise of wings and fluttered like snowflakes across a dark, almost snow-free corrie.[42]

In winter, blackgame packs in Russia sometimes numbered 200–500 at a time during the early 1900s, with up to 1,000 in birches, but more recently up to 200–300.[43] The sexes tend to separate in Scotland and Finland, with packs mainly of cocks or of hens. Adult cock and hen capercaillie are often solitary in winter, but they and young cocks also form groups of usually less than ten, or larger packs when population densities are high or in cold winters. Some winter packs comprise mainly young and old hens, others mainly young cocks.

A pack of birds, all maintaining individual distance, affords each bird some room to select food, while more eyes and ears readily detect predators. Being safer, big packs often feed at greater distance from cover – red grouse occasionally feed on short heather so far from cover that birds do not take territories on it.

## REACTIONS TO ENEMIES

A red or black grouse or Scottish ptarmigan flushes well ahead of a golden eagle flying near the ground, but stands on watch with head turned upwards if the eagle is high up.[44] By contrast, it crouches motionless when a flying peregrine appears near the ground. These differences fit the facts that eagles usually kill on the ground or just above it as grouse take off, whereas peregrines kill flying birds.

Eagles do occasionally kill grouse in full flight by stooping at speed from a greater height, but they are seldom successful in this. In two incidents on the Cairngorms, a flying ptarmigan being chased by a golden eagle flew towards people, escaping from the predator because the eagle flew away on seeing the people. On both occasions the ptarmigan partly closed its wings, 'dropped in a near-vertical twisting dive to within a few metres of the ground, and then ran to crouch among boulders only ten metres from me and my companions'.[45] An early author wrote that a covey of red grouse being chased by a sparrowhawk came into a shooter's butt during shooting.[46]

## PARENTAL CARE

Hens care for eggs and for chicks until these finally become independent and leave the brood. After mating with hens, blackcock and cock capercaillie take no part in parental care. In contrast, male rock ptarmigan guard nesting hens at least until late in incubation and often afterwards, while cock *Lagopus lagopus* stay with hens and chicks until the young reach independence.

The hens sit tight during incubation, slinking silently off the nest when leaving to feed and on their return. Occasionally a hen stays too long, however, and is killed by a fox or eagle. John Phillips found a hen red grouse that had died on her nest as fire swept the moor, and under her featherless black, singed carcass lay a pathetic sight: a heap of day-old chicks dead but untouched by flame.[47] In June 1999, two hen Scottish ptarmigan were found dead on their nests after a snowstorm late in the incubation period (Fig. 108).[48]

When a human or dog disturbs a nest or chicks, grouse show distraction displays, which often succeed in their goal of causing the intruder to overlook the nest or chicks. In the least vigorous displays, the bird flies heavily near the ground. In the most vigorous, it flaps in front of the potential predator, calling loudly and attempting to divert it away from the nest or brood.

Distraction display has been studied much in *Lagopus lagopus*[49] and, to a lesser extent, rock ptarmigan. Both sexes of these two species participate in the behaviour.[50]

FIG 108. Incubating hen ptarmigan amongst snow. (Stuart Rae)

FIG 109. Hen ptarmigan distracting the photographer. (Stuart Rae)

A hen ptarmigan usually shows stronger display than a hen red grouse, and can lead a man more than 400m before flying to her chicks. A hen or cock of either species will occasionally attack a man or predator coming near a nest or chicks. One male rock ptarmigan in Arctic Canada, 'uttering his belch-like challenge, flew violently and repeatedly against Ian McLaren's tent on the night of 8 June'.[51] We think his sleepless night resulted from pitching his tent too near a nest.

Greyhens and hen capercaillie usually show less intense though not less frequent distraction display from nests or chicks than *Lagopus lagopus* or rock ptarmigan. Occasionally, however, they flutter along the ground in injury flight or heavy flight, and frequently fly slowly near the ground, effectively distracting a dog or human.

Biologists use dogs to find chicks so that these can be counted or caught for marking. When a grouse shows distraction display, even trained dogs usually lie down, refusing to seek chicks, and Vidar Marcström noticed that only a small minority of dogs will search for chicks while a hen is displaying.[52] Our experience tallies with his, although a dog intensively conditioned by daily work with eggs and chicks can be trained to ignore a displaying hen. Whether a fox ignores her might also vary with experience. A fox was watched as it flushed a greyhen and later a hen capercaillie, and although both hens showed strong distraction display, the fox ignored this to seek the chicks, and caught and ate two from each brood.[53]

Hens brood chicks until they are well feathered. In torrential rain or hail, they shelter chicks even seven weeks old by standing over them with spread wings,[54] and *Lagopus lagopus* then have an advantage because cock and hen share several chicks each. During intense downpours, red grouse often lead chicks to the verge of tracks or tarmac roads, where they dry out after the rain, a habit shared with lapwing, oystercatcher and golden plover.

## GATHERING SCATTERED YOUNG

After a disturbed brood a few weeks old scatters in flight, parents of *Lagopus lagopus* or rock ptarmigan fly to follow the young and give contact calls, whereupon some chicks fly to the parents, and parents then fly to other scattered chicks that are calling. In red grouse, 'cock and hen often separate to follow different chicks, and then gather the remainder from distances of up to 500m by calling'.[55] The time to regroup varies with the number of chicks and how widely they scatter, but many broods up to six or seven weeks old will regroup within half an hour and almost all within an hour.[56] Families with well-grown chicks usually fly together when disturbed, but any that flush later are likely to be followed by a parent.

Greyhens and capercaillie hens collect scattered broods in much the same way. On being flushed, they typically fly off, grunting alarm to their chicks, which hide by burrowing under tall vegetation. A hen then circles round to perch in a tree, watching until the danger has passed, and usually gathers her chicks within a couple of hours.

Beaters on a shooting drive disturb red grouse severely. Families usually stay together in flight, but many are shot before the survivors land beyond the butts. Usually they have half an hour's respite while people collect shot birds and then leave for a second drive. During this time, and even before completion of the first drive, surviving parents fly to their original location and give contact calls. The surviving young fly in ones or twos to each original location, and after about an hour the families have regrouped.[57]

### Combining of broods

In all four species, two or more broods sometimes flush from the same spot, especially at rich food sources. Two or three families of red grouse are occasionally so close in their first two weeks that they flush within a few metres, and we know of instances where a chick disturbed in such a situation was repeatedly in the 'wrong' brood subsequently. Fully grown broods of red grouse come together more often, but tend to flush as separate units when disturbed, although they may amalgamate once they are well on the wing. Such amalgamations occur mostly in years of high density and good breeding.[58]

This also applies to rock ptarmigan, for example at Eagle Creek in Alaska, where broods sometimes amalgamate at high density.[59] Hrisey in Iceland supports an unusually high density of these birds, and hens and broods at about two weeks old form groups of two to four families, which gather into packs as the chicks grow.[60] During years of high density and good breeding in Scotland, occasionally several hen ptarmigan with broods of different age form a loose group, along with cocks and broodless hens.[61] In such a group, most broods are already well grown when they combine.

Amalgamations of broods are sometimes called crèches, but the usual implication of a crèche, whether avian or human, is that there are shared parental duties or some evidence of cooperative care by non-parents. This may involve a real parent that skips parenting for some of the time, but this has not been studied in grouse. In red grouse and Scottish ptarmigan, adults in such a group give warning of predators, but each respective brood hen accompanies her own brood.[62]

**Behaviour common to *Lagopus lagopus* and rock ptarmigan**
Parental behaviour has been observed and studied more in these two species than in greyhens and capercaillie, and we now outline it in more depth.

When a hen is laying or incubating or has chicks, the cock's alarm calls warn her of approaching predators. In the weeks before hens lay eggs and until the end of the incubation period, a cock red grouse or Scottish ptarmigan with a hen often attempts to divert a man or dog away from her.[63] He leads the intruder away in a widening circle, and returns to her after successfully foiling the average dog or person. When no danger threatens, he spends much time being vigilant beside her, staying alert while she feeds.[64] In a Canadian study, male rock ptarmigan became less vigilant once their hens started to incubate.[65]

**Behaviour specific to *Lagopus lagopus***
The *Lagopus lagopus* cock shows more care than the male of any other grouse species. He guards his hen against predators for a few weeks before she lays eggs and until the eggs hatch, and guards her and the chicks until the young appear fully grown, or sometimes even later. Frequently, he shows distraction display when his hen is disturbed from the nest, more so when she has small chicks, and sometimes when the chicks are older. Occasionally his display surpasses hers. He often shares parental duties, caring for part of the brood while they are feeding, collecting chicks after flushing, and brooding them. If his hen is killed, he will rear the brood. However, some British and Irish cocks leave their hens and young

– at Glen Esk, for example, this happened more often in years when birds were in poor condition.

Only the hen incubates, though Hugh Allen watched extraordinary behaviour with captive pairs of willow ptarmigan in Norway, where two cocks drove hens off their nests, incubated and turned the eggs, and developed brood patches.[66] One captive cock red grouse sat on eggs, and a second cock often sat beside the incubating hen with his head resting on her, and brooded her eggs when she was off feeding.[67] These observations may imply that this species retains the capacity for a cock to incubate eggs if the hen dies. Wild cocks often rear chicks after their hens die. In one case at Kerloch, a stoat killed a hen while she brooded day-old chicks, whereupon her cock took over and reared some of them.

When a man or dog approaches a brooding hen, she remains motionless and then bursts out in distraction display, often calling and beating her wings as if injured. She attempts to lead one away, and frequently diverts attention enough for a person, dog or fox to miss her eggs or chicks.[68] One Kerloch hen regularly showed such strong display, even when a neighbouring hen's brood was being disturbed, that trained dogs became confused and sometimes failed to find any chicks, and perhaps this might confuse foxes too.[69] Such staunch behaviour occurs only if a hen is in good condition. Hen red grouse flush more readily than this in years when they have heavy threadworm burdens, often doing so without any distraction display. This happened at Glen Esk in 1958 and 1959, when many hens were in poor condition and some emaciated ones died. We also noticed hens flushing more readily at Rickarton in 1986.[70]

At Glen Esk, a greater percentage of parents showed distraction display during years when birds bred well than when they bred poorly.[71] In an English study, hens that showed more frequent display also raised bigger broods,[72] and Norwegian willow ptarmigan that displayed had bigger broods than those not displaying.[73] When Norwegian hens with downy chicks were implanted with prolactin, the hormone that makes pregnant mammals produce milk and fowls go broody, they showed more display than other hens, and flushed at closer range.[74]

Susan Hannon, Kathy Martin and students studied parental care in Canadian willow ptarmigan.[75] Hens that shared a bigamous cock were more likely to lose nests than monogamous hens, and cocks that had become widowers reared smaller broods than widows or pairs. After some paired cocks were removed in an experiment, the remaining complete pairs raised bigger broods than hens that had been widowed at hatch.[76] A Norwegian study showed that single hens suffered heavier mortality during incubation and in the two weeks after hatching.[77] In short, cocks defend hens from predators and help them to rear families, resulting in bigger broods and fewer hens dying.

For an experiment at Churchill, Canada, mated cocks were removed at the onset of incubation, whereupon unmated cocks joined the widows and defended chicks that they had apparently not fathered.[78] However, because more than half of the first nests failed and most of these failed widows then laid a replacement clutch, the formerly unmated cocks that had joined them became real fathers in the end.

**Behaviour specific to rock ptarmigan**
Cocks spend less time with their broods than *Lagopus lagopus* do. The least faithful are in the far north, such as Arctic Canada, where cocks usually leave their hens and territories shortly before the eggs hatch. On Hrisey in Iceland, cocks very seldom accompany hens with chicks, and only exceptionally show distraction display. Faithfulness in the far north can vary, however. Although no Svalbard cocks stayed with their families in one year, all stayed in a second year,[79] a few at Eagle Creek in Alaska stayed, and cocks on Prince Patrick Island in Canada were seen defending hens with broods.[80] Greenland cocks often return to the families when chicks are two-thirds grown and can fly strongly.[81] By then the cocks, no longer starkly white, are cryptic in their dark autumn plumage, and so would not draw the attention of predators to the broods.

Scottish cocks are more faithful. A few show distraction display to a predator in the last week of incubation and more often when hens have small chicks. Sometimes they stay with the family until chicks are fully grown.

SUMMARY

Cock red grouse and rock ptarmigan sometimes show lek-like behaviour at places on or off their territories, and conversely blackcock and cock capercaillie sometimes display in a more spaced manner than on their leks. The calls of *Lagopus lagopus* and rock ptarmigan have similar phrasing, but sound different because rock ptarmigan croak. Postures that accompany aggressive and sexual behaviour are similar in both *Lagopus* species. In all four species, birds maintain individual distance from one another. Although most attention has been paid to displays, the birds spend most time resting, preening and eating. During autumn and winter, they tend to pack, with larger packs forming when birds are at high density or in snow. Cock *Lagopus lagopus* usually stay with their families until chicks are fully grown or later, while blackcock and cock capercaillie do not care for hens, eggs or young. Rock ptarmigan guard hens before and during incubation, but Arctic cocks usually leave just after hatching, whereas Scottish cocks often show later care, sometimes until young are fully grown.

CHAPTER 8

# Snow-roosts

HUMANS EVOLVED in the tropics and retain the characteristics of tropical mammals. Our vulnerability to cold can be reduced by clothing, shelter and experience, but people still die of hypothermia in their homes during winter and some out on the hills even in summer. How grouse use snow to keep warm is interesting, and has lessons for humans.

Caribou and musk ox are so big that they lose relatively little heat from their bodies and do not need to burrow under snow for insulation, unlike many smaller animals.[1] In Scotland, mountain hares make snow-burrows, and in severe frost abroad so do redpolls, goldcrests, tits and many other small birds.[2] All grouse species rest and roost in snow.[3] Bishop Pontoppidan of Bergen wrote in 1755 that willow ptarmigan 'seek covering and warmth by burying themselves in the snow',[4] and Thomas Pennant in 1771 that Scottish rock ptarmigan in winter are 'the colour of the snow, in which they bury themselves in heaps, as a protection from the rigorous air'.[5] The smallest willow and rock ptarmigan live in interior regions such as Alaska and Siberia, where undrifted, deep, soft snow prevails in calm, cold winters, and we infer from this that the excellent insulation provided by such snow allows the birds to be smaller (*see* Chapters 3 and 4).[6]

## RESTING ON OR IN SNOW

When red grouse or Scottish ptarmigan rest in strong wind-chill for a few minutes, they raise their feathers to form a canopy that encloses much air, tuck in their heads, and crouch, facing the wind like balls, with minimal surface area. For longer spells of daytime resting in snow, especially around midday, they take shelter by digging

198 · GROUSE

FIG 110. Red grouse in a snow-bowl. (David A. Gowans)

bowls (Fig. 110) or sometimes by burrowing sideways to sit at the entrance.[7] Red grouse occasionally use closed burrows during the daytime (see below), and blackgame and capercaillie also dig bowls and both open and closed burrows.[8] Seton Gordon watched in daytime as Scottish ptarmigan moved to hollows made by his footsteps in crusted snow, and a bird sat in each hollow, dozing or pecking snow until 'herded out' by others.[9]

## HOW GROUSE MAKE AND LEAVE SNOW-ROOSTS

Birds of all four British grouse species make surface hollows by scratching with their feet and shovelling with their bills. To burrow in powder snow they often fly in,[10] either into a steep drift or down into horizontal snow, and quickly bury themselves without leaving marks on the surface. Frequently they walk to the site and then dig burrows, and those in a group start digging simultaneously.[11] Each bird kicks snow backwards to plug the entrance, and using feet and body it tunnels forwards, finally sitting in a chamber with a snow-roof above it. Finnish blackgame sometimes burrow in a sinuous or strongly curved line, or in a complete loop, perhaps to fool predators.[12]

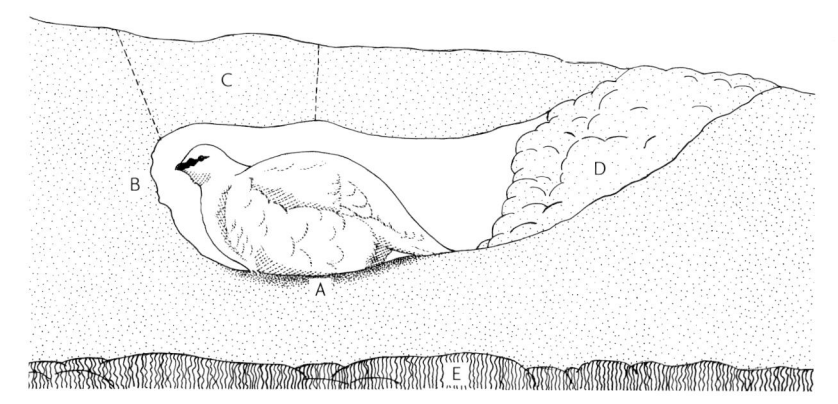

FIG 111. Ptarmigan in a snow-burrow. After flying into the snow, it burrows forwards, kicking back excavated snow to fill the entrance, and then sits in an air chamber. In the morning, it stands up to push its head through the roof, climbs through this hole, and walks or flies away. The roof is about 8cm thick and the chamber 16cm high. Key: (A) floor of compressed snow; (B) marks where bird has touched or pecked snow; (C) route of exit hole broken through at dawn; (D) loose snow kicked back to seal the entrance hole and tunnel; (E) ground below snow. (Drawn by Dave Pullan)

In the morning, birds often fly straight out through the roofs of burrows, leaving wing marks on the snow. More usually, a grouse in a burrow stands up, pushing its head through the roof. After a brief look, it climbs up through the roof, leaving the roofing snow as broken plates that lie at the edge of the exit hole or nearby (see Fig. 101). It then voids one or two caecal droppings on snow outside the hole, and walks or sometimes flies to feed. When hundreds of red grouse have roosted in burrows and walk to the nearest heather for breakfast, their tracks and droppings litter the formerly immaculate snow (see Figs 101 & 102).

Individuals use a new bowl or burrow each night, though in hard, icy snow the same bowl is occasionally used for two or even three nights by a Scottish ptarmigan, with dung piling up. Such hard snow is far less frequent on moorland, and red grouse in such conditions move downhill to roost in heather, or uphill to find softer snow.

When disturbed during daytime from burrows in powder snow, Alaskan rock ptarmigan, willow ptarmigan and white-tailed ptarmigan often fly a short distance (often just 20–30m), then dive headlong into the snow and disappear immediately.[13] Staff at Scottish ski centres often see the same behaviour when their piste-grooming machines disturb red grouse from burrows at night, and occasionally in daytime during heavy snowfall.[14]

FIG 112. After a cold night, a pack of grouse have walked from their closed snow-burrows. (Adam Watson)

## TYPES OF SNOW IN RELATION TO ROOSTING

The Inuit and Sámi have 40 separate words for different kinds of snow, but here we note only the commonest kinds. Most snow comprises hexagonal crystals whose points stick to each other in a snowflake. After a heavy fall of fluffy flakes during a calm night on moorland, snow covers all heather like a vast umbrella. The moor appears deserted in the morning, but red and black grouse are under the snow and emerge later, usually in the afternoon.[15] When such a fall blankets pines and understorey vegetation, capercaillie also vanish, and are probably under the snow.[16]

Within a few hours of snow reaching the ground, the points of its crystals start to vanish into water vapour by sublimation. This leaves the crystals as fine grains, which later begin to bond with one another. In cold, calm air, the bonding creates loose, fragile powder snow.

Wind breaks off so many crystal points during a gale-borne snowfall that you see no snowflakes in a storm. Fallen snow blows along the surface or high up into the air in writhing snow plumes, and so is continually redistributed, while sublimation removes more points and entire crystals. When this tighter powder gathers in a hollow, its consistency resembles that of flour. If you inadvertently drop a car key or ski binding into 60cm of it you may lose it. It was in such conditions that the worst tragedy in British mountaineering history occurred: the Feith Buidhe Disaster, in which six schoolchildren died in November 1971 on Cairn Gorm owing to unwise leadership. When caught outdoors in a winter storm, the Sámi formerly slept comfortably in the powder, with just their noses peeping out.[17]

Wind transforms powder snow by blowing it into a myriad of tiny grains, and continual wind then packs these grains so hard that a man or caribou can walk on the surface. Such a snow covering is typical in Inuit country, Svalbard, the Russian tundra and Scotland's high hills. Ptarmigan can dig bowls in it, but usually choose softer, more recent drifts, whose chalky whiteness contrasts with the greyish older snow.

Thaws or rain are frequent in Scotland, and subsequent frost makes the wet snow so icy that one cannot walk safely even on flat ground without crampons. A bird cannot dig into this, but finds softer snow by flying to a different altitude.[18] Further change comes with a big thaw, which turns all snow into loose ice granules called 'spring snow', easy to dig into but too wet for a comfortable burrow.

## SNOW AS INSULATION

Soft snow provides good insulation because it consists mostly of air, as you can see by standing on it, when your boots plunge almost to the ground. Just 2.5cm of rain is equivalent to well over 30cm of fresh snow, and water has a density 20 times that of cold, newly fallen snow.

By roosting in or under snow, a bird reduces its heat loss by warming the air around it, and it also suffers no wind-chill. George West found that willow ptarmigan in winter have a 'lower thermo-neutral' temperature (the temperature below which a resting bird in air will lose heat) of −6.3°C, compared with 7.7°C in summer.[19] Birds in winter fill their crops quickly and can spend up to about 95 per cent of the 24 hours of each day under snow. Down there, they are often well within their thermo-neutral zone, surrounded by air that is warmer than −6.3°C. West calculated that they could exist at an ambient temperature of −93°C, if they had ready access to willow or other nutritious winter food and deep powder snow for roosting.

## ADVANTAGES OF SNOW-ROOSTS

On a clear night, a grouse without vegetation or snow above its body loses far more heat than one would expect from air temperature alone, because extra heat radiates to the cloud-free sky.[20] For example, in an air temperature of −40°C, a bird in the open on a starlit night may lose heat at the same rate as a bird in the open on a cloudy night or under trees, in an air temperature of −56°C. This applies equally to a person at night in the open, bringing with it grave risks of hypothermia. Roosting under snow prevents this heat loss, and vegetation overhead reduces it.

When ruffed grouse in Missouri roost in cedars, this cuts the heat lost from their bodies via radiation to the night sky by 60 per cent.[21] Missouri birds prefer to burrow under snow, but when they cannot find enough they favour cedars, which are trees of dense foliage. Being under snow reduces their metabolic rate by 33 per cent compared with roosting in the open, while roosts in cedars cut it by 19 per cent and roosts in deciduous trees by only 6 per cent. We think that other benefits of dense coniferous foliage would be interception of rain, snow and falling frost crystals, and shelter from wind. Also, on a calm, frosty night a bird in a tree would be in warmer air than on the ground, because of the temperature inversion that is created as cold, dense air sinks.

At Chilkat Pass, British Columbia, where packs of wintering willow ptarmigan stay under snow all night and for most of the day, Dave Mossop watched what happened when a fox stalked one of the invisible birds, presumably by scent.[22] All the stalks that he watched were unsuccessful, because a different bird that happened to be nearer to the fox than the bird being stalked would flush and raise the entire pack. After many years of study in Minnesota, Gordon Gullion wrote that ruffed grouse under snow are 'virtually immune to predation, for neither raptor nor mammalian predators have much success finding birds in these burrows'.[23] One reason for this is the noisiness of snow.[24] The slightest crackling or squeaking of snow caused by a dog walking on it or by a man on ski or foot alerts red grouse or Scottish ptarmigan underneath, and they fly out.[25]

The value of snow is manifest when birds cannot use it. Blackgame suffer heavier mortality when snow is absent, or too hard to dig into, or too shallow.[26] When severe frost prevails in Minnesota on successive nights without snow or with shallow snow, ruffed grouse become thin, suffer more losses to predators, and breed poorly next summer.[27]

Because of a warming climate, deep snow is now less frequent and icy crusts are commoner. Suitable snow for burrows has become scarcer in Scottish woodland, where we have not seen capercaillie snow-holes since 1984. Paradoxically, capercaillie may not find it easier to keep warm in the increasingly mild Scottish winters, because wet windy weather could be worse for them retaining heat, just as it is for people without waterproof clothing. This has yet to be studied.

## TOPOGRAPHY AT SNOW-ROOSTS

Although most studies of snow-roosts in grouse have involved flat or gently sloping snow, *Lagopus lagopus*, rock ptarmigan and white-tailed ptarmigan often choose short, steep snow banks or banked drifts. Temperatures under and in snow vary with topography.[28] At an air temperature of −45°C in Siberia, the soil surface under 25cm of snow had a temperature of −30°C below coniferous trees, while the surface of bare gravel in a floodplain under the same depth of snow was a warmer −15°C. This is because gravel ridges contain much air, a good insulator, whereas moist or wet soils contain much ice, a poor insulator. A bird making a snow-burrow above gravel would therefore reduce heat loss better than a bird choosing to burrow under conifers.

In blizzards, Scottish ptarmigan often fly uphill at dusk, to roost among boulders on exposed summits where most snow blows past. On these ridges a human can barely stand and sometimes must crawl, yet the birds settle down to roost without fuss, scattering so that each has a hollow in snow on the leeward side of a boulder.[29] This is the favourite site for ptarmigan in the Cairngorms and also in northeast Greenland; the drift behind the boulder is often not much bigger than the bird itself.[30] There it sits facing the wind, with the top of its head 2–3cm below the snow surface, its bill making marks at the top of the snow-wall in front, and its tail touching the snow behind. The positions of these marks and of faeces show that the bird keeps a roughly similar seat all night. If the wind changes direction during the night, however, the direction of spindrift moves gradually round and the bird with it, as revealed by the more widely scattered positions of the marks and faeces next morning.[31]

Ptarmigan sometimes choose to roost on cliff ledges or cliff-top cornices, where they are safe from foxes or stoats. In one case, about 120 birds dug bowls in hard snow on a 40–50-degree gradient below an overhanging snow cornice above 200m-high cliffs.[32] Smooth ice glazed the awesome precipices, which plunged to sunless depths far below. The birds chose well.

## SNOW DEPTH FOR BOWLS AND BURROWS

In Scotland, red grouse and ptarmigan usually dig open bowls, making them deeper in hard frost, and in severe frost burrowing underneath snow.[33] In hard snow that can bear a human's weight, they dig bowls 2–3cm deep; in spring snow or slightly frozen snow they dig bowls 5–7cm deep, or occasionally up to 20cm deep; and in powder snow they dig bowls 20–30cm deep. On calm nights they occasionally burrow straight down for 20cm in powder snow and then sideways, or sideways for 20–50cm into a vertical drift. Red grouse often burrow sideways for 50cm and occasionally for up to 1m.[34]

Finnish blackgame usually need soft snow that is 27cm deep for burrowing, but can penetrate quite hard crusts within the snow-pack.[35] Snow as shallow as 23–25cm can suffice in early winter, when the birds burrow down to the ground and hence lose less heat because the ground is warmer than the snow and air above it. Even a snow depth of 21cm can be enough, although the birds then have to accept a thinner roof. In very deep snow they usually burrow only 33cm down, and have a roof less than 10cm thick.

Cock capercaillie require at least 50cm of snow to burrow and hens 40cm, although their burrows are not usually deeper than 20cm below the surface.[36] Indeed, blackgame and capercaillie avoid making burrows more than 40cm below the surface, even in snow of far greater depth. Perhaps this is because a bird in a deeper burrow would be more vulnerable to predators (see 'Disadvantages of Snow-roosts' below).

## OPEN BOWLS OR CLOSED BURROWS

In snowy conditions, red grouse and Scottish ptarmigan choose where to spend the night at dusk. Although suitable snow often occurs near their feeding sites, sometimes it is too loose or hard to dig a bowl or burrow, or a storm may have arisen with heavy drifting. In such situations they fly off to find better conditions. In stormy weather, Scottish ptarmigan usually fly uphill to exposed summits, while red grouse search out less exposed drifts. Willow ptarmigan roost in burrows under snow only at air temperatures below –10°C,[37] and burrows of red grouse in northeast Scotland are typical on calm, frosty nights.

Scottish ptarmigan dig open bowls much more frequently than burrows. Windy nights are the norm on high Scottish hills, as they are in the terrain of rock ptarmigan in Greenland and north Alaska.[38] If a bird were to burrow inside

SNOW-ROOSTS · 205

FIG 113. Entrance to (on the left, under ski stick – the hole around the stick is made by the basket) and exit from (right) a closed red grouse snow-burrow. The burrow's ceiling has collapsed, showing the line of the entrance corridor. Other marks in the snow are footprints made by birds in the morning. (Adam Watson)

FIG 114. Two open snow-bowls used by ptarmigan on the Cairnwell. The holes are in a small drift of powder lying on the icy grey snow seen in the foreground. The marks on the drift show where a bird tried several times to climb its steep side before succeeding. (Stuart Rae)

a deep drift at a sheltered site, it would run a serious risk of being entombed by metres of drifted snow during a blizzard, whereas a bird in an open bowl at an exposed site is completely safeguarded from this hazard. By contrast, in central Alaska, where deep powder snow and calm air are typical, rock ptarmigan usually burrow.

On summer nights, when snow is too loose and wet for a burrow, Scottish ptarmigan often dig snow-bowls, even using tiny remnant snow patches on warm August nights. In such cases, reducing heat loss seems irrelevant, so perhaps the birds are attempting to reduce the risk from predators or just trying to keep cool.

On nights when air temperatures are above 0°C, blackgame roost in trees.[39] At air temperatures below −3°C, they usually make closed snow-burrows, although they must use trees if the snow is too hard to penetrate. They dig open bowls about 11–19cm deep in soft snow that is too shallow for burrows, and in crusty or granular snow that would be unsuitable for a closed burrow. Occasionally they roost in burrows even at air temperatures above −3°C, which raises the idea that they may be attempting to reduce predation rather than heat loss.[40]

## CONDITIONS IN A SNOW-BURROW

Finnish blackgame make snow-burrows that consist of a chamber 16–31cm high (usually 18–24cm), with a snow-roof 1–20cm thick (usually less than 10cm).[41] Because still air provides good insulation, with a heat conductivity only a fifth that of snow, a spacious chamber avoids loss of heat through conduction because the bird's body does not touch the sides. Air temperature has been measured inside a greyhen's roost chamber at 5mm above her back (Table 18), and reached 12°C for most of the night.

All four British grouse species in burrows at typical depths fairly near the surface can readily detect an approaching person on foot, on skis or on a machine, perhaps by vibration through the snow. Arto Marjakangas inferred that a bird burrowing more deeply would not hear approaching predators, because a tape recorder buried at a depth of 20cm in the snow detected hardly any audible sound from an alarm clock on the surface.[42]

In northeast Siberia, Alexander Andreev used tame willow ptarmigan for his studies on winter adaptation.[43] He wrote, 'It took at least two nights to acquaint the laboratory-raised ptarmigan with snow and train them to use snow as

TABLE 18. Examples of temperatures (°C) outside and inside snow-burrows of grouse.

| SPECIES | OUTSIDE THE BURROW# | IN THE ROOST CHAMBER | REFERENCE |
|---|---|---|---|
| Black grouse | — | 12* | Marjakangas, 1986 |
| Capercaillie | −20 | 0 | Marjakangas et al., 1984 |
| Ruffed grouse | −35 | −12 to −3 | Gullion, 1970 |
| Hazel grouse | −40 to −45 | −1 to −6** | Andreev, 1978, 1980 |

# Temperature taken 15cm above the snow surface in the case of ruffed grouse, in others not specified.
* Reached 2°C after 60 minutes and 12°C in 90 minutes. The temperature of undisturbed snow at the level of the burrow was −4°C.
** After six hours.

protection from frost. To do this, I first prepared hand-made snow burrows with an open roof and tunnel. After placing the birds inside the burrow, the tunnel and roof were gradually closed with pieces of packed snow.' Later the birds made their own burrows. The downward flow of heat through the floor of a roost chamber exceeds that going through the roof 1.6-fold, but the willow ptarmigan's densely feathered snowshoes prevent its body heat from melting the snow on the floor.[44] Such melting would reduce insulation by removing air pockets and also by increasing conduction of heat via the melt-water.

Andreev also used tame birds to study how hazel grouse, a very small species, cope with cold.[45] After exposure to cold for 30 minutes inside a cage on undisturbed snow, a cock buried himself. The temperature in his roost chamber varied from −15°C up to 0.3°C, depending little on the outside air temperature. How the cock buried himself had far more influence, including factors such as the tunnel's length, bends in the tunnel, and especially whether he left an opening between the chamber and the entry tunnel, or closed it with a plug of snow. If he made a tight plug, the temperature in the chamber could approach 0°C even in very severe frost, whereas it fell to −7°C or −9°C if he left an opening. At outside air temperatures of −40°C to −45°C, the chamber's temperature (see Table 19) came close to 0°C occasionally. When the outside temperature rose above −35°C, the cock avoided becoming overheated by making an opening in the roof with his bill, whereupon the chamber temperature fell quickly from −5°C to −16°C.

TABLE 19. Percentage of the 24 hours of a day spent by grouse in snow-burrows during winter.

|  | REGION | PER CENT | REFERENCE |
| --- | --- | --- | --- |
| Willow ptarmigan | Chilkat Pass, British Columbia | 93 | Mossop, 1988 |
| Black grouse | Finland | 94[#] | Marjakangas, 1986 |
| Capercaillie | Kola Peninsula, Russia | up to 80 | Semenov-Tyan-Shanskiy, 1960 |
| Hazel grouse | Siberia | up to 92 | Andreev, 1980 |

**Notes**
For capercaillie the figure covers the dark part of midwinter, for hazel grouse from November to March.
In Leningrad and Novgorod regions, at air temperatures of −20°C down to −38°C, willow ptarmigan, black grouse, capercaillie and hazel grouse spent 22–23 hours in burrows and fed for one to two hours in nearby trees (Potapov, 1974). Potapov's Table 2 shows willow ptarmigan, rock ptarmigan, blackcock, cock capercaillie and hazel grouse spending 17, 20, 22, 19 and 21 hours respectively in burrows at an outside air temperature of −20°C, the temperature inside ranging from −10°C to −6°C. The time spent outside varies with air temperature, with about two hours spent outside in very cold air (from −50°C to −40°C), but four hours out at −20°C, and six to ten hours out at from −10°C to −5°C.
[#] Blackcocks eating entirely oats at a feeding station, feeding once daily in the morning.


## PROPORTION OF THE DAY SPENT IN SNOW-ROOSTS

At midwinter in colder parts of their range, grouse species spend most of the 24 hours of each day under the snow (*see* Table 19), emerging only to feed or if disturbed. At Chilkat Pass, British Columbia, where diurnal raptors kill many willow ptarmigan, birds spend the daylight hours out of sight under snow, emerging for intense feeding during twilight at dawn and dusk.[46] They do not eat in early afternoon, the warmest time of day, perhaps to reduce the risk of being killed. East Greenland lies so far north that the sun is below the horizon in December and January, resulting in far shorter day length than at Chilkat Pass, and rock ptarmigan in December feed hurriedly during the two hours of faint light around noon.[47]

## DISADVANTAGES OF SNOW-ROOSTS

After a bird goes to roost in a snow-hole when the outside air temperature is below $-3°C$, warmer air sometimes arrives during the night and melts the snow surface. If a frost then ensues before morning, a crust of ice forms on the surface, potentially trapping birds. The gravest risk would be when heavy rain falls and a sharp frost follows, creating a thick, hard, icy crust that may be impenetrable. Cases have been reported of blackgame unable to get out of their snow-burrows, notably in Finland in 1983, when skiers at one place released 40 birds, many of them exhausted and bleeding after trying to struggle through a hard crust that had formed overnight.[48] Arthur Bent related an account of willow ptarmigan in Newfoundland frequently being imprisoned in snow and later found dead in spring.[49]

Another hazard is related to predators. When a fox approaches, capercaillie tend to stay in their burrows until the last possible moment and then burst forth,[50] so when ice slows them, they can be easy prey.[51] Out of 278 winter deaths of rock ptarmigan that Bob Weeden found at Eagle Creek, predators killed most of them, although eight had died in a small snow slide and he judged that two had probably been trapped in snow-roosts during storms.[52] We have not seen such cases in Scotland.

## EFFICIENCY OF GROUSE VERSUS HUMANS IN MAKING A SNOW-SHELTER

An experienced Inuit with a snow knife takes about an hour to build an igloo, the time varying with the snow conditions and the size of the igloo, and two will finish the job sooner.[53] An experienced Scottish party with snow shovels takes one-and-a-half to three hours to make a comfortable snow-hole.[54]

In contrast, *Lagopus lagopus* and rock ptarmigan make bowls or burrows within 10–30 seconds, depending on the hardness of the snow. Birds of *Lagopus* species often dive headlong into loose powder, taking less than a second to vanish. When they burrow into more cohesive snow they seal the entrance with excavated snow in two to three seconds.

## SUMMARY

Grouse use snow as insulation against the cold when resting and roosting, by digging bowls where they sit with their backs open to the sky, or by burrowing underneath the surface and sealing the entrance by kicking back excavated snow. Red grouse make bowls on nights of light frost, and burrows in hard frost. Rock ptarmigan in windy climates such as Scotland, Greenland and north Alaska usually dig open bowls in wind-packed snow behind rocks, whereas in central Alaska they burrow in the undrifted soft snow that prevails there.

CHAPTER 9

# Territory in Lagopus lagopus and Ptarmigan

B RITISH GROUSE SHOW TWO kinds of territorial behaviour. Blackcock and cock capercaillie defend small territories at communal leks, whereas cock *Lagopus lagopus* and ptarmigan defend spacious territories that divide up practically all the suitable habitat. The most obvious function of cock territorial behaviour is to attract hens for mating and to rear offspring.

This chapter describes territorial behaviour and how territory boundaries are established in *Lagopus lagopus* and ptarmigan. The average size of territories taken by birds in different places varies from area to area, and within areas the average size changes from year to year. We explain how male aggression affects territory size, and consider how food, cover and territorial behaviour limit grouse numbers.

If you watch *Lagopus lagopus* or rock ptarmigan on their territories you will see cocks advertising themselves and disputing with neighbouring cocks. On moorland with abundant red grouse, the cackling of many cocks makes a continual background sound, and is interspersed with the high-pitched yelping of hens, a noisy grouse society. On the Cairngorms in late winter, ptarmigan show a burst of territorial behaviour on the first calm sunny morning after a big thaw. The snow-white cocks rise and fall in their song flights with curved beating wings, shining against a deep blue sky.

Red grouse show territorial behaviour at all seasons except during late summer, when they are in heavy moult, and likewise Scottish ptarmigan. As in birds generally, they sing most frequently in the gloaming. At any population density, the first song comes on average more than an hour before sunrise. When both species are at low density, they usually show territorial activity, including calling, only at the dawn or dusk chorus, in light too dim for anyone to see them from afar.[1] An exception is in the Arctic, where birds have such a short time between arriving in packs and breeding that they show territorial behaviour in broad daylight, even at very low density.

Territorial behaviour has been studied more fully in *Lagopus lagopus* and rock ptarmigan than in most animals. Territorial behaviour limits spring numbers, and after years of debate it is now firmly established that variations in territorial behaviour cause variations in numbers of birds (see Chapters 3, 4 and 14).

## TERRITORY IN *LAGOPUS LAGOPUS* AND ROCK PTARMIGAN

A territory is that exclusive area where a cock dominates other cocks and the hen paired with him dominates other hens.[2] It supplies the bulk of their food in spring and until their chicks hatch. Cocks divide up the ground and defend their plots by calling, attacking intruders, and meeting neighbours at mutual boundaries. Hens become territorial by pairing with such cocks.[3] The cocks decide how big their territories will be each year, and their average territory size determines how many territories there will be per unit area – in other words, the population density. The main sex that determines spring density is the male,[4] while hens decide with whom they will pair.

Hens show aggression to other hens that come near the cock or enter his territory. Although they call less often than cocks, their high-pitched notes of aggression towards other hens are sometimes frequent during bursts of territorial activity at dawn, and occasionally in daytime.[5]

### How territories are maintained

Both *Lagopus lagopus* and rock ptarmigan maintain territories by showing aggressiveness in three broad ways. The first, most frequent, method is advertisement, where a bird stands or calls on a prominent spot such as a hillock, or makes flights with aerial songs called becks. Often a singing cock lands near the edge of his territory, whereupon his neighbours respond and a wave of calling by several cocks can follow. For most of the day there may be no calling, but each territorial cock spends much time standing erect and alert, on the lookout.

A second way to maintain territory is to threaten or attack others of the same sex, including ejection of strangers. A third way involves those actions that determine the precise positions of territorial boundaries, such as ritual border encounters between neighbouring territorial cocks.

Hens show the first two ways of maintaining territory but seldom the third, because their territorial behaviour emphasises exclusive pair bonds with cocks rather than geographical locations. In an exception to this at Chilkat Pass, British Columbia, Susan Hannon found that each monogamous hen willow ptarmigan defended the cock's territory against other hens, and in the case of bigamous cocks each of the hens defended her own smaller sub-territory against the other bigamous hen, including boundary disputes.[6] In red grouse this has not been observed, though each bigamous hen frequents her own favoured part of the territory, a part where she later nests. This part is not exclusive, for both hens are often with the cock, showing no animosity towards one another. None the less, the same individual hen red grouse consistently dominates the other hen when the two do interact, sometimes chases it, and accompanies the cock more often.

Territorial behaviour in hen rock ptarmigan is less common than in hen *Lagopus lagopus*, and was not seen on the Ungava Peninsula and at Sarcpa Lake in Canada.[7] However, it was seen further north in Arctic Canada at Bathurst Island.[8] Scottish hens show it in autumn, winter and spring, especially when first pairing with cocks and in bursts of territorial or sexual behaviour during late spring.[9]

At high population densities in spring, birds of both species defend territories strongly throughout the day, and quickly expel intruders. At low densities, however, red grouse, willow ptarmigan at Dovrefjell in Norway and Scottish ptarmigan restrict territorial behaviour to dawn and dusk, and in daytime allow others to come onto ground that they defended at dawn.[10]

*Encounters*

The commonest encounter involves two neighbouring cocks 'walking in line' about 50–60cm apart as they parade together along their common boundary. They face the same direction, and both show postures and calls of threat, attack intention and escape intention (*see* Chapter 7).[11] Occasionally this leads to an attack, which often results in one cock driving the other away, or a fight that makes one of them flee. Usually, the attacker wins, but occasionally the tables are turned and the attacker loses. Both cocks almost always retain their original territories and boundaries, but the disputes continually test their vigour.

One process at work here is that cocks compete for territories. High population density and consequent strong competition for territory tend to induce higher rates of song flights and territorial disputes per bird. There is then seldom silence in daytime, whereas birds at low density give spontaneous calls that are almost entirely restricted to dawn and dusk.

In any region or at any population density, cocks attack and fight frequently when first establishing territories, because those that manage to possess a domain

**FIG 115.** Two red grouse cocks displaying at their territorial boundary. (David A. Gowans)

**FIG 116.** Tracks in snow where two cock red grouse displayed at their territorial boundary for 20 minutes. (Adam Watson)

thereby gain in dominance and in their ability to attract hens. Cock willow ptarmigan at Chilkat Pass spent more time defending territories and fighting against newly established neighbours than against familiar ones.[12] If cocks of either species have little time to establish territories before the onset of nesting, as in the Arctic, territorial behaviour can induce many fights even at low density. On Bathurst Island in the Canadian high Arctic, for instance, neighbouring male rock ptarmigan were usually a mile (1.6km) apart, so the average territory covered a square mile (2.6km$^2$).[13] Despite this low density, they flew to meet one another in encounters that often turned into violent fights. One or both cocks lost feathers, with up to dozens pulled out in a single encounter and occasionally a piece of comb torn out. So, attacks and fights are frequent and intense even at low density in regions where birds have little time to establish territories between their arrival in wintry conditions and settling down to breed soon after.

If they have much time, however, as in Scotland, where territories are established in autumn, most encounters eventually tend to become ritualised posturing, which none the less tests the neighbours' bottle on a daily basis. The familiarity of unchanging neighbours breeds relative tolerance, and many encounters between the cocks are brief.

In contrast, a stranger cock is immediately attacked by the territory owner, and sometimes two neighbouring owners lay aside their differences by combining forces to attack the stranger, no matter whose territory he has invaded. In one instance in Alaskan willow ptarmigan, cock A allowed neighbouring cock B to continue chasing intruding cock C on A's territory, until the intruder fled.[14] At Sarcpa Lake, encounters of rock ptarmigan were longer and more intense when a non-territorial bachelor challenged a paired territorial cock than when paired neighbouring cocks met.[15]

During late spring, a territorial cock red grouse or Scottish ptarmigan will occasionally chase a non-territorial male stranger over several territories without stopping, even though the chased bird flees, and likewise with Alaskan willow ptarmigan.[16] Such attacks can force the subordinate birds to fly to unoccupied ground, where they are sometimes found dead later, with wounds and congealed blood on their napes and heads.

The intensity of encounters does not depend simply on cocks, however. Each hen decides which cock she will join, and this sometimes provokes serious disputes among cocks. Often she flies out of her territory, whereupon her cock gives chase, sometimes joined by neighbouring cocks. Sometimes she returns to her former territory, but frequently she lands on a different one, along with the chasing cock beside her. If so, he is then immediately attacked by the owner of the territory upon which he trespasses. The hen also provokes disputes by walking into a neighbour's territory, with similar results. By these means she tests the vigour of different cocks as a prelude to deciding which will be her mate. Also, disputes induced by a hen can sometimes result in territorial boundaries being changed.[17]

### Territory maps and boundaries

Several studies have used mapping to measure the area of individual *Lagopus lagopus* and rock ptarmigan territories (Tables 20 and 21).[18] In red grouse, territory maps were used to assess the positions of territorial boundaries in relation to landmarks and patches of vegetation, including heather classified according to age.[19] Boundaries were not strongly influenced by the extent or position of vegetation patches. Physical features such as fences, walls or tracks had a big influence, however, a point noticed anecdotally before,[20] but now confirmed by statistical analysis.

TABLE 20. Range in annual mean territory size (ha) and extremes in individual territory sizes of red grouse (Kerloch) and rock ptarmigan (other areas).

| PLACE | YEARS | RANGE IN ANNUAL MEANS | EXTREMES IN TERRITORY SIZE | REFERENCE |
| --- | --- | --- | --- | --- |
| Kerloch, Scotland# | 15 | 0.6–4.3 | 0.1–7.0 | Palmer & Bacon, 2000 |
| Hrisey, Iceland | 3 | 2.7–17.7 | 1.3–25.1 | Gardarsson, 1988 |
| Ungava Peninsula, Canada | 2 | 5.0–7.2 | — | Olpinski, 1986 |
| Sarcpa Lake, Canada* | 4 | 20.8–26.6 | 18–70, mean 26.6 | Brodsky, 1986; Holder, 1990 |
| The Cairnwell, Scotland** | 3 | 2.5–3.4 | — | Rae, 1994 |

\# Mapping by AW and Raymond Parr.
\* Mated cocks. Over a period of four years, unmated cocks had an overall mean territory size of 108ha, with extremes of 62–142ha (Holder & Montgomerie, 1993a).
\*\* Medians.

Boundaries often run along landmarks. Both *Lagopus lagopus* and rock ptarmigan use ridges or hillocks, and red grouse also use fences and the ground below electricity wires, where each pole is a landmark. Some territories are roughly circular, a few are triangular with a long extension at the most acute angle, more are approximately square or rectangular, and many are polygonal (*see* Fig. 176).[21]

TABLE 21. Annual mean territory size (ha) of cock *Lagopus lagopus* and rock ptarmigan in relation to number of mates. In the longer studies at Glen Esk and Dovrefjell, the range of annual means is given.

| PLACE | YEARS | UNMATED | MONOGAMOUS | BIGAMOUS | REFERENCE |
|---|---|---|---|---|---|
| Lower Glen Esk, Scotland | 5 | 0.8–2.2 | 1.7–4.3 | 1.9–4.7 | Watson & Miller, 1971 |
| Dovrefjell, Norway | 5 | 2.1–5.9 | 4.4–8.9[#] | — | Pedersen, 1984 |
| Chilkat Pass, Canada[*] | 3 | 1.5 | 2.2 | 4.1 | Hannon, 1983 |
| Svalbard | 2 | 16.6 | 21.5[#] | — | Unander & Steen, 1985 |
| Ungava Peninsula, Canada | 2 | 2.4 | 4.0 | 8.6[**] | Olpinski, 1986 |

[#] Mated, combining bigamous and monogamous.

[*] Means based on combining all individual territory sizes over a three-year period. For Svalbard and Ungava, the two annual means are added and the total divided by two.

[**] Two or more hens per cock.

### Methods of mapping territories

Depending on the aims of study, four methods of territory mapping have been carried out, using large-scale maps. These showed vegetation based on vertical aerial photographs and ground checks, and other features added by observers, such as boulders, electricity poles and isolated trees.[22] On uniform sections of Glen Esk and Kerloch with few landmarks, we inserted posts at regular intervals to help plot locations accurately.

The first method entails the time-consuming mapping of boundaries in daylight, by plotting the boundary parades of adjacent cocks. This is necessary if accurate data on territory size are needed to compare with data on the number of hens or the amount of food. It is feasible, however, only when spacing remains stable on successive days. With red grouse in eastern Scotland, where densities tend to be high, this method works from August until May. However, as territory boundaries are unstable in most autumns, in practice the method was used at Glen Esk and Kerloch mostly after November, with greatest effort in January–April. Early mornings before sunrise were best and forenoons good, but work was most productive during afternoons of fine weather in late winter and spring. This method has also been effective when used with willow and rock ptarmigan in spring.[23]

Compared with early work at Glen Esk and Kerloch, predators have been more abundant in studies at Rickarton and Glas-choille, and cocks have shown less daylight territorial activity and particularly fewer boundary parades in daytime. It seems that cocks feel less confident and indulge in fewer prolonged conspicuous daytime encounters when diurnal predators are common. This led to a second mapping method, in which each cock's daytime advertising display sites were plotted in addition to boundary disputes, because insufficient disputes were seen to allow the mapping of precise defended boundaries.[24] None the less, drawing a line around each cock's outermost observed points created a polygon. The polygons showed which cocks had bigger territories than others, though not their exact boundaries or sizes.

The third method involves listening for calls at dawn or dusk, and works with birds at any density. It is especially useful at low density, when observers seldom see birds but can hear territorial calls and so can detect their locations.[25] It has been used for observations on red grouse at Glenamoy and Mull, red grouse and rock ptarmigan at Cairn Gorm, red grouse in years of low density at Kerloch and Rickarton, and willow ptarmigan at Dovrefjell.[26] By making repeated observations on successive dawns or dusks, an observer can map territories almost as precisely as in the second method. A lone observer cannot cover all cocks on an area of say 50ha accurately in a given dawn, as can be done in daytime with birds at high density, but extra observers who note times and directions can achieve this, through a triangulation.[27] Territorial hen red grouse can also be heard at dawn and dusk, at distances of up to 400m and sometimes even 1km.

The fourth method is to plot each cock and hen while one moves across a study area. This was often done with red grouse at Glen Esk and Kerloch from a vehicle used as a mobile hide, and with Scottish ptarmigan by observers on foot. It involves making observations of territorial and sexual displays, individual differences in plumage, tag colours and numbers, and coloured rings. For red grouse it was called a car census, and for ptarmigan a territory census.[28] When repeated on several days, it provides accurate counts and shows which territories are bigger than others, though data are cruder than in the first three methods. In addition, immediately after making observations we often searched small sections with pointing dogs. This resolved any uncertainties, by flushing the birds.

Pioneering work on the territorial behaviour of red grouse at Glen Esk in 1958–61 and 1961–78 at Kerloch involved detailed mapping of exact boundaries by the first method. The most precise mapping requires intensive near-daily effort by observers living close to the study areas, to make the most of fine weather. Good visibility is needed over the whole ground, from numerous viewpoints accessible to a vehicle.[29]

This method can reveal an approximate spacing pattern within a few days. When birds are at high density, territorial cocks meet so often that the observer may be lucky enough to discover the main spacing on a 20ha area within an hour. On a Glen Esk area with excellent viewpoints, for example, about 300m of parades were observed amongst seven territorial cocks in 35 minutes on a fine afternoon in February 1961, including along most of one cock's boundary.[30] However, accurate mapping of territorial boundaries on a larger area of, say, 1km$^2$ is feasible only when boundaries remain stable for at least several weeks.

Boundaries occasionally stay unchanged for many months. In an extreme case on a 7ha section at Glen Esk, the number, identity, territory size and boundaries of six territorial old cocks in August 1960 remained materially unchanged until May 1961. At Glen Esk, Kerloch and Rickarton, minor changes in the complement of territorial cocks occurred over winter when an occasional territorial cock left or died, to be replaced by a previously non-territorial cock. Observers could keep track of this by daily work, concentrating on the small area involved in each change.[31] This was not possible in the more recent study at Glas-choille, however, because too many changes occurred when territorial cocks were killed by predators or left the area, to be replaced by other cocks. Indeed, some territorial cocks that left the study area returned a year or more later, indicating a more labile territorial system than in the earlier work at Glen Esk, Kerloch and Rickarton.[32]

### Annual reorganisation of territory in red grouse

This account is based on detailed studies of red grouse when spacing remained stable. It is at one end of a spectrum, the Arctic spring with willow and rock ptarmigan establishing territories shortly before the breeding season being the other end, and red grouse at Glas-choille somewhere in between. Red grouse give a useful insight into the establishment of territories because cocks establish them in autumn, months before the breeding season. This allows us to study territory establishment separately from territorial behaviour during the breeding season.

At Glen Esk and Kerloch, territorial cock and hen red grouse generally survived well over winter. At Glas-choille, however, a more labile situation prevailed, as described above. None the less, despite greater turnover there, the number of territorial birds each spring was close to that in the previous autumn.

Old cock and hen red grouse return to their spring territories in late July and August, and maintain these by territorial behaviour at dawn and dusk, and occasionally during the daytime. Then in September and October there comes a radical annual reorganisation of territory ownership and size, as young cocks take new territories and many old territorial birds lose their territories. At Glen Esk and Kerloch, this usually happened over a short period, sometimes within a few days, coinciding with an increase in aggressive calls and attacks, and often a decline in numbers.[33] Such a great change precluded accurate boundary mapping because details changed too much from day to day or even hour to hour. However, birds showed relatively stable boundaries in good snow-free weather later in the autumn, after the contest was over, thereby allowing effective mapping.

A temporary reorganisation of territories has been observed in a few springs, when heavy snow covers high moorland or Scottish Alpine land, but melts on nearby lower slopes.[34] The snow forces territorial red grouse or ptarmigan to move downhill. Although territorial residents can easily eject a few immigrants, many intruders will squeeze residents into small territories and eventually some intruders take small territories themselves. As soon as vegetation appears high up, however, the intruders return there, while those on the lower slopes resume the same territories and numbers as before. A single count during the temporary reorganisation can therefore be wildly misleading.

## DAYTIME TERRITORIAL BEHAVIOUR

All territorial cocks and some hens call at dawn and dusk, but often not in daytime. Differences between areas are striking, with daytime silence on some, and noisy calling continuing on and off throughout the day on others nearby.

## In Britain and Ireland

At high population densities, cock red grouse and Scottish ptarmigan spend much time in daylight on prominent hillocks or ridges, sitting or standing alert and occasionally giving ground calls or flying to give a beck. Each cock has several perches, which are often conspicuous because the extra dung deposited here favours the growth of herbs, moss and grass rather than heath (Fig. 117). Some ptarmigan have perches on cliffs, such as the 200m-high crag of Lochnagar, spectacular sites that mountaineers can reach only by severe rock- or ice-climbing.

When at low density, however, red grouse and Scottish ptarmigan have not been found to use such perches at any time of day. They confine territorial calling to twilight at dawn and dusk,[35] as do willow ptarmigan at low density on Dovrefjell in Norway.[36]

When flushed by a human, a territorial cock of either species usually becks as it takes wing and again when landing, whatever the density. Seton Gordon noticed that ptarmigan on Mull were extremely silent, however, with not a single call even from cocks that he disturbed on their territories.[37] Ptarmigan density there is very low, associated with scarce heath that results from heavy rainfall and also overgrazing by sheep and deer. It has been claimed that the daytime silence of

FIG 117. A ptarmigan lookout on the Cairnwell in late winter, enriched by droppings so that sedges and moss grow instead of the surrounding heath. (Adam Watson)

grouse in the Outer Hebrides characterises *Lagopus scoticus hibernicus*,[38] but in fact it typifies red grouse and Scottish ptarmigan at low density anywhere.

Cock red grouse and Scottish ptarmigan call at dawn and dusk during all months, except when in packs on deep snow. At Glenamoy in spring, mated cock red grouse called at dawn more often than unmated ones.[39] The duration of the dawn period of calling was correlated with density. It lasted only 20 minutes at densities of about one cock per km$^2$, but 100 minutes at about eight cocks per km$^2$, when cocks continued so long after dawn that observers for the first time could see the last callers. The amount of calling also varied with population density, with just one or two becks per cock at low density.

When eggs from nests of wild hen red grouse at Glenamoy were taken for rearing in a nearby aviary, however, cocks in separate cages only a few metres apart called continually in broad daylight, while perched on high branches. Likewise, cocks raised from eggs laid by wild hens at Kerloch and Rickarton gave continual noisy calls when kept at close quarters in aviaries, as did cock willow ptarmigan from Dovrefjell eggs when in an aviary. When kept in aviaries at far higher densities than in the wild, birds from the same population therefore showed far more territorial behaviour throughout daytime than birds in the densest wild population.

In conclusion, British and Irish cocks at high density crow loudly in daytime and use prominent perches. Diurnal predators pose less risk to birds at high density, when there are many eyes on watch and many voices to warn of their approach.

**In the Arctic and Amchitka**

There is more to the intensity of display than density alone, however. Even at the very low density of a pair per square mile (2.6km$^2$) on Bathurst Island in the Canadian high Arctic, male rock ptarmigan spent much time in late May and June on hummocks, from which they flew to meet one another in aggressive encounters. And despite a low density on Svalbard, territorial cocks behaved likewise, each with at least two to four favoured perches.[40]

Arctic birds have only a few weeks between their arrival and subsequent nesting, and we think that this explains their frequent territorial behaviour in broad daylight, despite very low densities. An interesting case is Amchitka Island in the Aleutians, which at 51°N is much further south than Scotland, let alone the Arctic. The sole count there that we know of was in 1969, showing only 2.5–7.5 pairs per km$^2$.[41] Cocks took territories early in May, far later than in Scotland and at about the same date as in Iceland. Despite the low density, they showed vigorous territorial activity in daytime. Hence daytime activity can occur without

FIG 118. Ptarmigan cock (left) with hen, making himself obvious in a low-density population (less than one pair per km$^2$) in May near Reykjavik, Iceland. Purple saxifrage is in flower, right foreground. (Adam Watson)

high density in situations where the establishment of territories comes so late that little time remains before birds must start nesting.

## TERRITORIES ON POOR OR PERIPHERAL GROUND

Some ground supports few or no territories (and mainly unmated cocks at that), because food or cover is sparse. Examples of such ground with red grouse include peat or gravel with little vegetation, wide rushy flushes, heather that is dominated by grass or bracken, and heather kept short by wind-scour, browsing or frequent burning.

Ground with poor food or cover tends to be vacant at low densities of birds, even though it may hold territorial pairs or unmated cocks at high density. At Kerloch, small areas that had little food or cover owing to overgrazing by cattle and sheep remained unoccupied in springs of low density. On Derry Cairngorm, cock ptarmigan took territories on exposed wind-scoured heather only in years of high numbers.[42] In both species, the vegetation on unoccupied areas appeared no worse than in years of high density when it was unoccupied. Hence poor habitat may be sufficient for an unmated cock or pair at high density, but not at low density.

On good habitat, peripheral ground often supports breeding pairs successfully at high density, yet may be unoccupied at low density. Breeding willow ptarmigan on the Norwegian island of Tranøy showed this, at low density avoiding isolated areas where they had few neighbours.[43] A similar example on grouse-moor was White Hill at Rickarton, a fairly isolated triangle with farmland on two sides and holding red grouse only in years of high density, despite abundant heather and cover.[44] Scottish ptarmigan also show this frequently.[45] We infer that birds avoid taking territories where there are few or no others nearby, a likely reason being that a bird on a solitary territory would have no neighbours to give early warning of predators.

There are other sites that red grouse tend to avoid. One is the toe of a slope with a conifer plantation at the bottom, and another the steep slopes of a gully or glacial melt-water channel with rocks on its sides. Avoidance of predators may again be involved.

## TERRITORIAL BEHAVIOUR AT DIFFERENT SEASONS

**Autumn**

In northeast Scotland, young and old cock red grouse and ptarmigan begin to show daytime territorial behaviour usually in late September or October.[46] Male rock ptarmigan in the Swiss Alps defend territories in autumn,[47] and willow ptarmigan have long been known to show autumn territorial behaviour on Newfoundland's Avalon Peninsula as early as September, and at Nueltin Lake west of Hudson Bay.[48] At Chilkat Pass, British Columbia, all adult cocks and about half the adult hens returned to former territories in late October or November during the first snowfall, and left about mid-December when deepening snow reduced food and cover.[49]

It used to be thought that Norwegian willow ptarmigan do not show territorial behaviour in autumn,[50] but Hans Pedersen and others found a resurgence of autumn territorial calling by cocks at Dovrefjell in Norway.[51] Because cocks confine this to twilight, observers who visit in daytime would overlook it. It may often be overlooked elsewhere for this reason.

**Winter**

On subarctic and Arctic lands, willow and rock ptarmigan experience a long snowy winter and show no territorial behaviour at that time. Patches of food that might be defended are often soon buried by snowfall or drifting. Instead, the birds roam in packs for months, postponing territorial behaviour until the spring thaw.[52] This applies also to rock ptarmigan in the Swiss Alps, a region with heavier snowfall and consistently longer snow-lie than the Scottish hills. In some regions, populations have wintering grounds that are distinct enough from their summering grounds for the movement between them to be called migration (*see* Chapter 3).

During winter, most Scottish red grouse and rock ptarmigan stay in packs throughout the 24 hours on days when there are strong winds, heavy rain or snowfall, or deep snow cover. Because fewer gales and snowfalls occur on moorland, red grouse have more opportunity to show territorial behaviour than ptarmigan. During mild winters with little snow and much calm weather, however, both species show territorial and pairing behaviour during every month, usually in the morning but occasionally on and off through the day until mid-afternoon.[53]

**Early spring**

When the main thaw comes to snowy regions in spring, cocks of both species arrive back from their wintering grounds, or if they are resident in winter (as in Scotland), they disperse out of the flocks. Cocks then take territories on tiny patches of snow-free ground, provided that some food plants are exposed. Scottish ptarmigan do this even at 99 per cent snow cover, and maintain it as long as the food plants on the territories remain snow-free. When fresh snowfalls cover the plants, however, as commonly happens with both species in Scotland and further north, birds abandon their territories and usually form packs until the next thaw.[54]

In the snow-free conditions that often prevail on low Scottish moors, red grouse after midwinter increase the frequency and intensity of their territorial behaviour, at dawn, dusk and in the morning. More notably, they frequently increase them throughout the morning, and often throughout the daytime. The onset of this change usually comes in late January or February, but can be as late as March or even towards the end of April on high moorland in severe winters. In Scottish ptarmigan, the main burst of all-day territorial behaviour usually comes in late February or early March, although it started as early as the beginning of January in the very mild year of 1964, and not until the end of April in 1951, when deep snow covered almost all ground.

At Porcupine Creek in Alaska, the more dominant cock willow ptarmigan established territories in the creek bed, where tall willow scrub offered abundant food.[55] The hill slopes lacked tall vegetation, so the less dominant cocks had to wait until some snow-free patches appeared there before they could establish territories. Meanwhile, rock ptarmigan stayed in packs that broke up later, with new territories and pairs forming on the slopes as fresh higher ground became snow-free, and the territories of three marked cocks moved uphill as the snow melted. Hence territories were defended, even though they were not fixed in location during the early stages.[56]

**Late spring and summer**
In the few weeks before laying and during incubation, cock and hen feed in the territory, and usually she nests in it. Occasionally a hen red grouse nests just outside, in which case her cock extends his territory to include an extra small slice around the nest. After the eggs hatch, most hens with chicks leave the territory in the first few days (sometimes on the first day), usually accompanied by the cock in *Lagopus lagopus*, though less so in rock ptarmigan.[57] We infer from this that staying on the territory is not necessary for rearing chicks, and that birds often incur an advantage by leaving it.

Hence it is not surprising that vigorous territorial behaviour in daylight almost ceases during the weeks when the broods are being reared. The most that happens is that some cock *Lagopus lagopus* and Scottish ptarmigan briefly return to their territories to crow at dawn and, to a lesser extent, at dusk.[58] If a hen red grouse or Scottish ptarmigan loses her clutch, however, the cock resumes territorial behaviour and courtship on his old territory in daylight, and a second nest often follows.

By late July and early August the broods have been reared, and territorial activity increases markedly. Cock red grouse usually return to their old territories to call in twilight at dawn and dusk, and afterwards the mated cocks then rejoin their hens and young. In several cases in Scotland and Ireland, cocks called at dawn on their former territories, but counts with dogs shortly afterwards revealed no birds.[59] Subsequent dawn visits revealed that hens and fully grown broods were on higher ground outside the study area, and that the cocks deserted them briefly to call on their old territories before returning to their families before daylight. Immediately before they returned, the hens gave contact calls, doubtless informing the cocks of their locations. The cocks then gave the last becks of the morning when landing beside the hens.

## SHIFTS OF TERRITORY FROM SPRING TO SPRING

Intensive studies with large numbers of colour-tabbed red grouse at Glen Esk and Kerloch showed that individual territory sizes often altered between one spring and the next, roughly corresponding with a change in population density.

None the less, where a cock had a territory two or more years running, his territory in later years usually included some ground that he had occupied in the previous year. At Kerloch, for example, out of hundreds of cocks that had territories in the previous year, only two shifted to a different part of the study area.[60] Hens were more footloose.[61]

Cock willow ptarmigan at Chilkat Pass, British Columbia, showed more shifting from one spring to another (known as breeding dispersal) than cock red grouse at Glen Esk, Kerloch or Rickarton. For instance, 9 per cent of cocks (mainly unmated) shifted territories at Chilkat between one spring and the next.[62] The three Scottish moors are at low altitude and typically get mild winters, so birds were on their territories during the day in every winter month, often for most of the winter in mild seasons. By contrast, birds at Chilkat Pass did not show territorial behaviour in the depths of the months-long winter, and many wintered outside the study area. It seems that a long period of territorial behaviour between autumn and spring allows birds to maintain their territorial boundaries more precisely.

This may not be quite the whole story, however. Red grouse at Glas-choille took territories in autumn and maintained them during winter as at Glen Esk, Kerloch and Rickarton. Nevertheless, the territorial system was more flexible, involving more turnover of territorial owners. During studies carried out between 1992 and 2003, about half the old cocks on the 53ha core study area were immigrants.[63] Within that core, many cocks shifted their territories hundreds of metres (many territory radii) from one spring to the next. It might be argued that, because Glas-choille stood at a higher altitude and hence had snowier winters than the three lower moors, red grouse there behaved more like the willow ptarmigan at Chilkat Pass.

Most old hens paired with the same cocks in successive autumns if these had kept their territories, but paired with nearby cocks if their cocks from the earlier year had lost territories or died.[64]

TERRITORY SIZE

**Average size differences between areas and years**
Studies that have continued for some years show that the average territory size differs from one area to another. This broadly reflects counts of grouse numbers on the same areas, so the higher the average density, the smaller the average territory. Territories on study areas have been mapped in Scottish red grouse, willow ptarmigan at Chilkat Pass in British Columbia and Dovrefjell in Norway,

and rock ptarmigan in Iceland, Svalbard, Arctic Canada and Scotland (see Tables 20 and 21).[65] Because the population fluctuation at Chilkat Pass lasted for more years than the number of years of territory mapping, any inference must be tentative. However, it seems that average territories of willow ptarmigan were larger at Dovrefjell than at Chilkat Pass and the Scottish moors, and that rock ptarmigan at Svalbard had larger territories than birds at Hrisey, Ungava and the Cairnwell.

It has often been suggested that changes in food supply from one year to the next cause fluctuations in the average territory size of birds generally.[66] Thus, in red grouse the abundance and nutritive value of heather might affect aggressive behaviour and territory size. Certainly, extreme impacts such as severe winter browning of heather are followed by changes in territory size. However, these changes usually occur many months later at the next annual reorganisation of territories, when other factors have also changed, including fewer young birds competing for territory, after a summer of poor breeding that was consequent upon the poorer winter-browned food.[67]

Experiments throw some light on this. An application of ammonium nitrate fertiliser at Kerloch boosted the growth and nitrogen content of heather, which in turn resulted in smaller territories during the increase phase of a population cycle, but another application during the subsequent decline failed to prevent cocks taking successively larger territories.[68] The evidence is that short-term alterations in food cannot explain all year-to-year changes in average territory size, and hence are not necessary for such changes (see Chapter 14).[69]

**Territory size in a given year and area**

In a given year, territory sizes of individual cocks on an area vary considerably (see Table 21). There are three influences here: (1) territories are larger on patches with less food or poor-quality food, or with less physical cover provided by vegetation height; (2) territories on patches with hillocks are smaller than those on more open ground nearby; and (3) some cocks are more aggressive, take larger territories and attract more hens than other territorial cocks on the same area, even though influences (1) and (2) are broadly similar.

Issue (1) can be regarded as analogous to the observation that the abundance of food and cover vary between widely separate moors. The sole difference is that in this case the variation can be highly localised within areas as small as 25–50ha. On such areas at Glen Esk and Kerloch, cock red grouse on poorer patches such as grassy bogs had large territories close to, and in some cases adjacent to, cocks on better patches where heather predominated and territories were smaller.

At Kerloch, Art Lance found that the cocks' territory size in a given year was not related to the area or proportion of young heather on the territory.[70] Instead,

FIG 119. Flat moorland supports lower densities of red grouse than hillocks because cocks take larger territories where they can readily see each other. These pictures show adjacent stretches of ground at Glen Esk. (Adam Watson)

territory size was related negatively to an index of the nitrogen content per hectare in the heather shoots. One component of his index, the abundance of green shoots (as measured by their percentage cover of the ground), was important only on territories with sparse heather. Otherwise, the average content of nitrogen was more important – in other words, the richer the content of nitrogen, the smaller the territory. This shows that cocks adjusted their territory size on sparse heather according to food quantity, and on abundant heather according to food quality.

Let us turn to issue (2). At Glen Esk, where territories did not differ significantly in the productiveness of their green heather shoots per hectare,[71] cocks took larger territories on flat ground than among hillocks.[72] Because neighbouring cocks can see each other more readily on flat ground, we infer that this would be stressful, and so they compensate for this by taking larger territories so as to be further apart. This did not happen in years of very high density, however, when cocks crowded onto flat ground as well as hillocky ground. On crowded flat ground, a cock could see all his neighbours if all cocks merely raised their heads. We think that this would be particularly stressful to cocks restricted to territories on flat ground with little seclusion, and would be likely to lead to population decline.

Issue (3) involves some cocks taking larger territories than others on the same type of ground. During studies in Scotland and the Arctic, more aggressive male rock ptarmigans took larger territories than less aggressive cocks.[73] In Scotland, studies with much larger numbers of marked red grouse showed that the more aggressive cocks occupied larger territories. Cocks implanted with testosterone at Kerloch became more aggressive and took bigger territories at the expense of their neighbours, and an experiment at Glen Tanar confirmed this on a much larger scale, at the level of the population and not just the individual bird.[74]

To conclude, average territory size varies from year to year. Within years, cock red grouse take bigger territories where heather is sparser or has poorer nutritive value. On ground of similar heather abundance and nutritive value, more aggressive cocks take bigger territories.

**Territory size, number of hens and breeding success**
Average territory size varies much between years, with no evidence that the annual variations are generally related to food quality. Hence the variations discussed in this section are not of absolute territory size but of relative territory size within years. If relative territory size affects breeding success but absolute territory size does not,[75] then relative territory size may well reflect pair quality.

In both *Lagopus lagopus* and rock ptarmigan, cocks with two hens have bigger territories than monogamous cocks on the same area, and unmated cocks have yet smaller ones (see Table 21). This was the case in Scottish red grouse at Glen Esk and Kerloch, willow ptarmigan at Dovrefjell and Chilkat Pass,[76] and rock ptarmigan at Ungava and Svalbard.[77]

Having noted that aggressive cocks take big territories and pair with more hens, we turn to what characterises such cocks. On Svalbard, male rock ptarmigan that arrived early on the breeding grounds took bigger territories and subsequently paired with more hens than cocks that arrived late. Likewise, in a study of rock ptarmigan for one breeding season at Colville River in Arctic Alaska, more hens paired with cocks that arrived early.[78]

In the Alaskan study, moreover, cocks that had big combs attracted more hens, and a cock had more hens if his territory held many willow twigs, the main food.[79] Since a hen favours a territory with a good cock and with much food, and a good cock usually takes a territory with much food, it is impossible to tell from such cases whether she prefers the home, the owner or both. After a study of vegetation on the territories of willow ptarmigan at Dovrefjell, for instance, it was suggested that the owner was more important, but this was dubious.[80]

Some element of male quality does seem to be involved, however. At Dovrefjell, mated cocks outweighed unmated ones. Bigamous cocks at Chilkat Pass tended to be older than monogamous ones, and old male rock ptarmigan at Ungava took larger territories than young cocks. During later work at Chilkat, the 'condition' of individual willow ptarmigan was estimated by weighing them and then adjusting for their body size as indicated by wing length. Hens in good condition settled no earlier on territories and chose territories no bigger than average, but they were more likely to pair monogamously than hens in poorer condition, which frequently paired bigamously.[81] In another study at Chilkat, cocks and hens were shot on their territories, and birds that replaced them were then shot.[82] The combs and body-weights of the replacement hens were no smaller than those of the residents, but replacement cocks were in poorer condition than resident cocks.

Broadly uniform heather swards on study areas at Glen Esk and Kerloch were found to have a similar amount and age of green heather per unit area. On such ground, mated cocks had larger territories than those that remained unmated, and hence had a larger amount of green heather.[83] At Kerloch we tried to find what controlled the hen's choice in a spring when territorial cocks outnumbered hens two to one, by measuring the quality of food at sites where we had seen hens feeding.[84] On a section with poor food due to overgrazing by sheep and cattle, hens took longer to decide which territory to choose for nesting. As usual, mated cocks had bigger territories than unmated cocks. Although territories with richer feeding sites tended to be smaller, the hens favoured large territories, so 'some factor other than food quality, but related to territory size, must have affected the hens' choice'. Other studies had shown that aggressive cocks take large territories and pair with more hens, so a hen's choice of cock and territory may depend on his aggressiveness or on an associated factor such as his courtship, attentiveness or comb size.

When three territorial cocks were implanted with testosterone in late winter, they expanded their territories, sang more frequently, paired with more hens, and chased hens more often.[85] One of the three had been mated before the experiment, but from two weeks after the implant he was paired with an extra hen that had previously been with a neighbouring cock. By two weeks he had expanded his territory and sang more. Hence the extra hen might have been attracted by his increased territory, or by his greater territorial and sexual activity, including his comb size, or by both.

In experiments at Glenamoy and Kerloch, applications of fertilisers boosted the heather's growth and nitrogen content.[86] This resulted in territories with more hens per cock than on unfertilised control areas, and one experiment at Kerloch led to the unusual situation of more hens than cocks on the territories. This might suggest that territory quality influences female choice. Cocks may still be involved, however, because better cocks take better territories. Also, a hen's decision whether to leave or stay with a courting cock depends on his relative vigour. In short, a hen choosing a good cock is also going to have a good territory.

Another aspect of territory size is whether it influences breeding success. At Glen Esk and Kerloch, hens whose territories held larger amounts of green heather reared more young, although not significantly so, which indicates that breeding success depended little upon the quantity of potential food.[87] A drawback of this study, however, was that it did not include chemical analysis of the heather, to distinguish quality from quantity. A later study at Kerloch did include such measurements. It revealed that hens on territories where heather had a higher content of nitrogen reared more young.[88] Our experiments with fertilisers also showed that hens on enriched heather reared more young than those on control areas.

## DOES TERRITORIAL BEHAVIOUR LIMIT SPRING NUMBERS?

Much has been written about this subject in birds generally.[89] Some authors have proposed that territorial behaviour does limit numbers, others that it merely determines which of the individuals that survive until spring get the best territories, after their number has already been reduced by food shortage over winter.[90]

Studies of marked red grouse at Glen Esk and Kerloch showed that territorial behaviour in autumn limits numbers the following spring.[91] After some of the cocks on an area at Glen Tanar were implanted with testosterone in spring, they enlarged their territories at the expense of neighbours, some of whom left, so territorial behaviour limited numbers and caused a local population decline.[92] At Glas-choille, territorial behaviour in autumn again limited spring numbers.[93]

During two decades, Peter Hudson and colleagues often claimed that behaviour does not limit numbers of red grouse, though their arguments were fallacious.[94] More recently, a large-scale experiment led by François Mougeot on two English and two Scottish moors has shown that increased aggressive behaviour, caused by implanting old cocks with testosterone in autumn, limited numbers in the following two springs and led to population declines.[95] Since Hudson is one of the authors, evidently he no longer maintains his earlier claims.

On marginal areas with poor habitat, net immigration may be needed to maintain numbers, and limitation of spring numbers by territorial behaviour in autumn may be less frequent. Red grouse were studied at one such poor area, Glenamoy. Here it was found that territorial behaviour in autumn limited spring numbers in two years out of five.[96] In the other three it did not, because territorial birds suffered heavy winter losses that were not fully replaced, so the number of territorial birds in autumn exceeded that in the following spring.

Three experiments with willow ptarmigan elucidated this problem. After territorial cocks and hens at Chilkat Pass in British Columbia were removed in spring, others that had not held territories on the study area took replacement territories; the same also occurred at Dovrefjell in Norway.[97] Hence territorial behaviour limited numbers on both areas. At Porcupine Creek, Alaska, a small proportion of the male spring population was non-territorial,[98] which suggests that limitation by territorial behaviour may occur more widely.

In rock ptarmigan, two studies provide evidence. Territorial cocks and hens that were shot in a corrie of Derry Cairngorm during spring were replaced, and despite many territorial birds being shot on half the study area, the two halves held similar numbers in late April.[99] On Svalbard, about half the territorial cocks and hens that had been shot in spring were replaced.[100] Territorial behaviour limited numbers in both studies.

## SUMMARY

Cock *Lagopus lagopus* and rock ptarmigan defend territories against other cocks, and hens pair with cocks on the territories and dominate intruding hens. A territory provides food and cover for the pair until their chicks hatch. Its average size over the years varies between different areas, being smaller where food and cover abound. The average territory size on an area fluctuates between years, and annual changes in food or cover are not necessary for these fluctuations. None the less, on a given area in any one year, the size of individual territories is negatively related to the food and cover on them. In addition, aggressive cocks take large territories and pair with more hens, while unmated cocks have small territories. Autumn territorial behaviour in red grouse often limits density in the following spring. In willow ptarmigan in Canada and Norway, and in rock ptarmigan in Scotland and Svalbard, spring territorial behaviour can limit spring numbers.

CHAPTER 10

# Plumage

To thrive in the cold, grouse have evolved a dense plumage, and in this chapter we discuss the insulation provided by it. Because grouse are often abundant, they attract many predators, but they reduce the risk of attack through camouflage and strong flight, both of which are provided by their versatile plumage. Like stoats, ptarmigan turn white in winter, a phenomenon that has long interested naturalists, and they are also unusual among birds in having three seasonal plumages and corresponding moults. We discuss plumage and moult in willow ptarmigan and rock ptarmigan, which turn white in winter, and in red grouse, black grouse and capercaillie, which do not. All four species show changes in colour as individual feathers grow, in relation to changes in hormones. Finally, we describe the bills, claws and striking red combs of the four species, and mention recent research showing that the combs reflect ultraviolet light, which is unseen by man but visible to grouse.

## THE NEED FOR MOULT

Feathers suffer wear and tear, both of which reduce insulation, waterproofing and flight ability. Each year, grouse grow new feathers of glossy bloom. In late summer and early autumn, adults undergo the main moult of the year, starting with the innermost primary, and including the primary and secondary wing-quills and main tail-quills, along with most feathers on the body.[1] This poses risks as the birds cannot fly well until new flight-quills have grown, but they accomplish the change in the warmth of late summer, when plumage insulation is least important and good food is readily available. Feather growth requires protein, which is frequently in short supply in habitats on poor soils. If you hold a moulted main wing- or tail-quill up to the light, you can sometimes see crosswise fault bars, mute evidence of checks in growth when a bird was short of protein or otherwise stressed nutritionally.

Birds with chicks must be able to fly well, and so they delay their moult. In red grouse and Scottish ptarmigan, unmated cocks moult first, next the failed hens, then paired cocks with young, and lastly hens with young. Mated male rock ptarmigan usually abandon their families sooner than mated cock *Lagopus lagopus*, and also moult earlier. Blackcock, cock capercaillie and unmated cock red grouse shed so many feathers in a short period that they skulk in tall vegetation, unwilling to fly and sometimes tail-less.

In addition to the main annual moult, rock and willow ptarmigan renew most body feathers to form a white winter plumage, and shed it to grow coloured spring feathers. Red grouse are in a class by themselves, as they are in almost perpetual moult on some part of the body, a slow process that should reduce nutritional stress.

There has been an attempt to classify avian moult and plumage objectively.[2] However, it is not easy to apply this to the complex generations of feathers in *Lagopus*, especially the protracted moults of southern races.[3]


## PLUMAGE IN YOUNGSTERS

Young red grouse soon escape danger by fluttering at a week, flying 4–5m at ten days, and covering 100m by three weeks – or further with a tail breeze. Rock ptarmigan fly sooner, and at three weeks can scatter up to 400m when disturbed.[4]

Fluffy down covers day-old chicks. Wing-quills show more prominently in day-old capercaillie than blackgame, and in blackgame more than *Lagopus lagopus* or rock ptarmigan. These differences tally with incubation periods, as capercaillie embryos are longest in the egg, blackgame intermediate and the others shortest. Down covers the legs of all day-old grouse chicks, and the toes of *Lagopus lagopus* and rock ptarmigan. Newly hatched red grouse have shorter down and more bare skin on their toes and legs than willow or rock ptarmigan,[5] a subtle adaptation to mild conditions.

The age of red grouse can be judged by their plumage development from a day old until they appear fully grown at 12 weeks.[6] Rock ptarmigan grow slightly faster, and at ten weeks are hard to tell in flight from adults. Fully grown young grouse have pointed tips to their outermost two primaries, which they keep until the following summer. Older birds have rounded tips. Also, if the tip of the second outermost primary has more speckling than the tip of the third, the bird is young. This applies to willow, rock and white-tailed ptarmigan (dark speckling on white feathers), and to red grouse, blackgame and capercaillie (pale brown or creamy speckling on dark feathers).[7]

When blackgame or capercaillie reach six weeks, cocks can be told from hens by their larger size and, more reliably, by the first patches of black feathers. At three months, young cocks still have narrower tails than old birds. Young hens at three months are less bulky than old hens, but this is hard to judge unless a nearby adult hen affords easy comparison.

In autumn and early winter, youngsters have a 'bursa of Fabricius', a blind pouch inside the cloaca, obvious on dissection as an opaque creamy-coloured sac up to 1cm across, which helps develop their immune system. In old birds the sac is much smaller.

## PLUMAGE OF BLACK GROUSE AND CAPERCAILLIE

Black grouse undergo their main annual moult from June to October or November, sometimes starting in May and ending in December. Greyhens with young start and finish later than hens without young, and later than blackcock. In June–July, blackcock moult some feathers on the head and neck, and grow new shorter, rounder feathers there with white or rufous edges or bars, and without aftershafts.[8] These rather resemble greyhen feathers, and may indicate a low level of testosterone. Blackcock retain these feathers for a month, before shedding them during the complete autumn moult, when they replace them with characteristic dark blue glossy feathers that last until the following June.

Capercaillie also have one complete annual moult, cocks starting in May after their displays at the lek are over, and hens from late May to early July after chicks hatch. Both adult cocks and hens shed their body feathers from July until September or October. Like greyhens, capercaillie hens with young start and finish moulting later than broodless hens. Like blackcock, capercaillie males shed some feathers on their heads and necks in May–June, and grow new short feathers there with a brown colour or narrow grey bars, which are more like hen feathers. Capercaillie cocks shed these summer feathers in July during the main body-moult, replacing them with glossy dark feathers that last until the following May–June.

## MOULTS IN *LAGOPUS* SPECIES THAT TURN WHITE

Rock, willow and white-tailed ptarmigan have three annual moults and subsequent plumages, including a white winter dress for camouflage, which occasionally has a rosy flush in live birds.[9] The timing of the moults varies with climate.[10] Summer dress in Norway begins to appear a month earlier than in colder, snowier Canada at the same latitude. The rate of moult and plumage growth also varies with climate, being fast in Arctic regions where summers are short, and slow in southern regions with long summers, such as Scotland.

## PLUMAGE OF WILLOW PTARMIGAN

One annual moult in willow ptarmigan would suffice for plumage maintenance, but three are required for camouflage. Camouflage in spring and summer, however, does not require the physiological expense of a full moult (unseen white winter feathers can be retained in spring and summer). Also, especially further north, seasons are short and the requirement for camouflage can conflict with the need for cocks to display and for hens to retain the ability to fly well while rearing chicks. These conflicting pressures can lead to incomplete spring or autumn moults, and to differences between the sexes in the timing of moult (earlier in cocks than hens in spring, so that they can display, and later in hens than cocks in autumn, so that they can rear chicks).

Cocks show spring plumage before hens, growing a reddish nuptial plumage like a hood on the head, neck and breast while hens are still mostly white (*see* Fig. 11).[11] On Hitra and nearby islands off west Norway, cocks sprout the first of these feathers by late February, on the more snowy south Norwegian mainland during mid-March, and in the yet more snowy interior the feathers appear a fortnight later.[12] Subsequently, some hen-like feathers appear on the cocks' heads, necks and breasts. Although these have been regarded as signifying a fourth moult,[13] they involve only some of the feather follicles on the head, neck and breast,[14] so in fact there may be only three moults.

Hens in spring and early summer finally catch up with cocks, and then surpass them by growing a more complete summer plumage, with less winter white retained on the underparts and no white on the back. Their summer feathers are heavily barred black and buff, with some creamy or yellow spots, and are much paler and more barred than male feathers. The cocks' summer plumage is less dark than the spring dress, with some pale narrow barring. Cocks in southern races grow a fairly complete summer plumage, but high-Arctic cocks keep the chestnut hood and white back of the spring dress until about mid-July.

The sexes are much more alike in autumn than in summer. Autumn feathering has a richer brown hue, often blackish brown in cocks, and hens show darker upperparts than in summer, with finer barring and more vermiculations. Most hens start their autumn moult later than cocks and develop a less complete autumn dress, retaining more of the barred summer feathers.

Winter plumage is white, except for a black tail that is out of sight until the bird takes flight. High-Arctic birds already show many white feathers on their upperparts in late August and some are mostly white at the start of September,[15] whereas in south Norway they moult later, the first white feathers appearing on the back at the end of September, leading to a white plumage by early November. Young birds become white later than old, and young from renest broods moult much later.[16]

On Hitra, where snow lies ephemerally and the mean temperature of the coldest month remains above freezing, birds delay winter moult until October, dark feathers still cover much of the back in January, and the white wing-quills carry much dark pigment.[17] Snow in Newfoundland and Kazakhstan lies much longer than on Hitra, but in winter here the birds usually have some coloured feathers on the head and neck, and rarely on the back. In most Kazakh birds the central pair of greater upper tail-coverts is also coloured in winter,[18] as in red grouse and, occasionally, Scottish rock ptarmigan. Although Kazakh winters are short, ending in March, midwinter temperatures drop to −45°C.[19] The winters are also very windy, the shallow snow blowing about, to uncover a variegated landscape with patches of snow-free ground and withered grass. Winters in oceanic Newfoundland are far less cold than in continental Kazakhstan, but frequent thaws combined with a windy climate often create a speckled landscape with dark patches. In both places, a few coloured feathers afford camouflage in a variegated landscape with patches of darker, snow-free ground.

## PLUMAGE OF ROCK PTARMIGAN

### Seasonal plumages

In summer plumage, Scottish ptarmigan cocks are mainly grey, and hens golden brown although some have much grey. Cock feathers are finely barred with many fawn vermiculations, whereas hen feathers carry wide bars of black on a buff or orange ground colour, peppered with some white. The lower breast and legs remain mostly white, especially in cocks.

Autumn feathers on the belly and wing are white, but grey on the rest of the body, with fine vermiculations and a salt-and-pepper appearance. Scottish birds are a very pale race, silvery grey in colour. This camouflages them at a season when they spend much time resting among boulders that are grey from the colour of rock lichens growing on them. The hens' feathers have slightly wider bars than those of cocks, far narrower than the wide bars of summer.

The winter plumage is white, save for black tail feathers and a black stripe from the cock's bill to behind his eye. Hens occasionally have a few black dots around the eye, and rarely a black patch, though this is far smaller than in cocks.[20]

### Dark feathers in winter plumage

In countries with mild, relatively snow-free winters, a few dark feathers occur in the rock ptarmigan's white plumage. Two documented examples are in the Cairngorms and on Amchitka Island in the Aleutians,[21] where birds do not attain the fullest winter plumage until January or February. Even then, many have a few dark feathers on the back, neck and head, some retained from the autumn plumage and some growing in winter, the latter often with dark or black bases and white tips.

Amchitka hens have more dark feathers than cocks. This corresponds with cocks wintering on the snowier upland (highest point 373m) and hens on the lowland, where snow-lie is usually patchy and more coloured feathers afford better camouflage.[22] Birds studied on the Cairngorms had fewer dark feathers during cold, snowy winters than in mild ones with little snow. This applied also to captive birds that had been reared from eggs laid by wild Scottish hens. They were kept in outdoor cages on lowland Deeside, which gets far less snow and warmer winters than the hills where the birds' wild parents lived.[23] The captives also grew many more dark feathers in winter than their wild counterparts. It was not clear, however, whether these variations were due to differences in snow or in temperature.

### Timing of summer plumage

Already in late February, male rock ptarmigan in the Cairngorms begin to grow the first dark spring feathers underneath their white dress. They show them externally in March, and are ahead of hens until mid-April (see Fig. 5), when the hens overtake them to form a more complete summer plumage.[24] The timing of the onset of spring moult changes little between years, but subsequent rates of moulting and plumage growth do vary. Birds darken later on Derry Cairngorm than on the lower, less snowy Cairnwell, and on a given hill they stay white later in a cold, snowy spring than in a mild one.

Amchitka cocks are also ahead of hens in March and until mid-April, when the hens pass them, and photographs of pairs in the Alps and on Attu in the Aleutians also show cocks ahead of hens in spring.[25] Cocks in such areas eventually have a dark summer plumage that is almost as complete as in hens.

On the Cairngorms in spring, territorial cocks with hens have more summer plumage than territorial unmated cocks, the latter have more than non-territorial cocks, and mated hens have more than unattached hens.[26] Also, mated cocks occupy larger territories than unmated ones, and are more aggressive and vociferous.[27] Hence aggressive birds get larger territories and grow summer plumage earlier, presumably because of higher hormone levels.

In the far more snowy subarctic and Arctic regions, a very different order of moult prevails after wintering birds return to their breeding grounds and take territories. Cocks are far behind hens in developing coloured plumage. Still white in early June, high-Arctic cocks appear conspicuous on snow-free ground, while hens soon grow a dark plumage that camouflages them when sitting on eggs or tending chicks. In late May, high-Arctic hens start to show coloured feathers, and they have a camouflaged summer dress by the time that they start incubating, when about half the snow cover has gone.[28] Cocks start to grow coloured feathers on the head at about the same time as hens, but this becomes so suppressed that they remain almost white in early summer after all snow has vanished, and are visible to the naked eye at a distance of 2km.

**White Arctic and subarctic cocks in early summer**
Naturalists have wondered why male rock ptarmigan in Arctic and subarctic lands keep their white winter plumage until after the snow has vanished, so becoming extremely conspicuous (*see* Figs 39 & 118), while the hens don a cryptic dark summer dress. The white cocks may well be more vulnerable to predators, and it has even been suggested that they thereby divert predators from the hens.[29]

Ornithologists have long reported that the immaculate white plumage of the rock ptarmigan becomes dirty in midsummer.[30] Bob Montgomerie found that Arctic cocks intentionally soil their plumage as soon as their hens begin laying eggs, and the amount of soiling peaks by the time that incubation starts, making cocks six times less conspicuous to observers.[31] In contrast, two cocks of medium dirtiness became immaculate again within 24 hours of their hens' clutches being lost to predators. Hence the unsoiled white plumage may confer an advantage to cocks in sexual display. Scottish cocks are also white during their most intense period of sexual display, usually in February or early March.

Keeping a white male dress for display may involve what biologists call the 'handicap principle', where an individual carries a character that is a handicap (for example, is conspicuous to predators), and yet this is selected during evolution because it shows to a female that the carrier would make a good father for her offspring. One might put it: look at me, I avoid predators despite my handicap.

The question still arises why Scottish cocks in late March and April develop a partially dark plumage. This is less conspicuous than white plumage, even though it appears striking in sexual display to hens. The answer may lie partly in the fact that the spring display period in Scotland lasts much longer than that in the Arctic. Also, the period of snow-lie in Scotland is much shorter than in the Arctic. Retaining a white plumage throughout the long Scottish spring might simply be too dangerous to be worth the risk. Hence only the initial sexual display involves a white dress. By the time that the cocks begin to develop their partially dark plumage, most have already bonded with a hen and the dark plumage may suffice to maintain this pair bond, although some hens still change their partners. By late March–April, there may be less need for handicap-type displays and these might be more dangerous.

There is some evidence that white Arctic cocks incur heavier predation than hens. On Hrisey in Iceland, gyrfalcons killed a higher percentage of cocks than hens during the egg-laying and incubation periods.[32] At Windy Lake in Canada, however, an area with one of the highest known densities of gyrfalcons in the world, they and other predators took cocks and hens equally during the incubation period and also in each month of the breeding season.[33] Furthermore, the prey taken to gyrfalcon nests at Windy Lake comprised similar proportions of each sex in May–June and July–August.[34] Also, those who studied rock ptarmigan during the breeding season in other Arctic or subarctic habitats at Eagle Creek, Bathurst Island and Ungava did not mention heavier losses of cocks to predators, or found no losses to predators (Svalbard).[35]

Hence, heavy predation on cocks may not be typical of Arctic or subarctic habitats, and Hrisey may be an exception. In spring there, ptarmigan are found on dark-coloured heath with hardly any boulders, so the white cocks look starkly more conspicuous than cocks on nearby mountains with many boulders. Hrisey means 'scrub island', but the scrub that once existed and that would have provided better cover has long vanished owing to overgrazing by sheep. Also, ptarmigan density on the island is exceptionally high for Iceland, making it a magnet for falcons. None the less, the habitat affords such good conditions for breeding hens that it is a magnet for cocks, too, despite their heavy losses. It seems that sheep may therefore ultimately be responsible for the hen-skewed sex ratio there.[36] It would be enlightening to know whether ptarmigan in areas with better cover from boulders on the mountains only a few kilometres away, on either side of Hrisey, also show this skew, and whether cocks suffer heavier losses to predators than hens, but this has not been studied.

Although high-Arctic cocks are whiter in summer than those on subarctic Hrisey, they occur at such low density that it may be less profitable for predators to hunt them. Hence the unusually high ptarmigan density on Hrisey may contribute to the difference in the sex ratio of preyed birds between it and Windy Lake.

### Timing of autumn and winter plumages

Arctic rock ptarmigan do not have time to develop complete autumn and summer plumages in the same way as Scottish birds. High-Arctic cocks grow coloured summer feathers on their necks and backs in late June, but only briefly and partially before starting to develop a coloured autumn plumage. Their autumn dress is less complete than in Scotland and Amchitka, and includes a few dirty white feathers from the previous winter. High-Arctic hens with chicks do grow a summer plumage, but they have little autumn plumage before starting to develop a new white dress for the rapidly coming winter. As a result, their autumn dress is as suppressed as the cocks' summer dress. Hence both sexes in the Arctic largely sacrifice one plumage, the cocks dropping most of the summer plumage and the hens most of the autumn plumage.

High-Arctic cocks and hens are already growing white feathers in August, leading to immaculate whiteness by late September or early October. An adult cock in Baffin Island was sprouting winter feathers on 1 August,[37] and birds at Thule in north Greenland on 5 August.[38] By contrast, cocks in Scotland and on Amchitka in the Aleutians grow a complete autumn plumage, although Scottish hens with broods begin one or two weeks later than broodless hens and also cocks, and in the end attain a slightly less complete dress. Scottish and Amchitka cocks show the first white feathers on the back and nape in October, and hens grow winter plumage sooner than cocks. Young birds whiten later than old ones in the same year.[39]

## PLUMAGE OF RED GROUSE[40]

Because red grouse are in almost continuous moult throughout the year, seasonal changes in plumage are gradual. They do not develop the white winter dress of rock and willow ptarmigan, and so there are only two moults and plumages.

### Seasonal differences

Cocks begin their autumn moult in June, grow a set of new primaries and tail feathers by the end of August, and continue a slow moult of body feathers until midwinter. From August onwards, both sexes sprout darker body feathers than in early summer, with less barring, although hens remain paler than cocks. Sprouting feathers in hens become increasingly barred, until by late November or December the hens differ greatly from the cocks, being much paler and more barred.

By midwinter, most cocks are largely dark red, dark brown or blackish brown, with feathers that have few or no bars but fine vermiculations, whereas hens have a brown plumage with many feathers carrying conspicuous golden bars and spots. After December, cocks almost stop moulting for a month or two, but hens continue, albeit more slowly, growing feathers that become more barred with each month.

From March, cocks start to grow hen-like feathers, barred with light buff or yellow on the head and neck, but this proceeds very slowly and the new feathers do not appear in large numbers until May.[41] During June, the whole head and neck may have these feathers, and the back a few. Hence the spring moult is only partial, gradually becoming heavier in June–July and merging with the autumn moult.

Hens, by contrast, show a fairly heavy body-moult in March–April, and grow feathers that are banded with wide yellow and blackish-brown bars. This slows down when they start to incubate, by which time the barred plumage provides good camouflage. Their body-moult then rises to a peak in July, when the new feathers resemble those growing on cocks quite closely, a characteristic associated with shrinking of the ovaries and testes to their smallest size for the year. Some hens that have lost nests or young, and that have not relaid eggs, can grow autumn plumage almost as early as cocks, whereas those with late broods still retain a few old primaries in October. Hens in poor condition with many worms delay moulting even more.[42]

**Seasonal differences relative to willow and rock ptarmigan**

Some differences in moult timing between red grouse and willow and rock ptarmigan can be ascribed to behaviour. The equivalent of the spring moult and plumage of willow and rock ptarmigan takes place in red grouse during autumn. In all three, the timing coincides with a big resurgence of territorial behaviour. The equivalent of the heavily barred plumage of hen willow and rock ptarmigan in late April–early June occurs among red grouse in March–April. In all three, this plumage occurs when hens lay down material for eggs, lay eggs, and start to incubate them.

### Variation among individuals

Good illustrations of the main varieties of red grouse plumage have been published.[43] Cocks in winter vary, some being reddish chestnut, dun-brown or blackish. Blackish males usually have some reddish feathers or white spots or both, and birds with mixed plumage are commonest.

Most cocks and hens have some white feathers or white-tipped feathers on their heads, flanks and wings. The whiter cocks have white bellies, legs and lower breasts, heavily white-spotted upper breasts, wings and tail, and large white patches on heads, necks and backs. Such cocks are characteristic of northeast Scotland, the UK's coldest, snowiest region in winter, but examples have occurred in most of the range.

A completely white bird occurs rarely.[44] Several keepers in different regions told us they had once seen a white grouse during their lifetimes on the moors, and said it was so conspicuous that they could see it on heather a mile (1.6km) away. Occasionally a pale 'leucistic' grouse appears.[45]

### Variation between regions

One reason for the paler, more yellowish appearance of grouse in Ireland and the Outer Hebrides is that, in all seasons, the sprouting feathers of birds there are paler than on birds in eastern Britain. Another reason, involving plumage in winter and spring, is that grouse in the far west shed more old feathers and sprout more new feathers in winter than eastern birds, and winter-grown feathers in any region are more yellowish than autumn-grown ones, because they carry more yellow or creamy pigment on the bars and speckles.[46] Hence, for instance, west Irish grouse in winter develop a more yellowish winter plumage. In late spring, however, grouse in Ireland and northeast Scotland show less difference. By then, the latter have caught up to some extent, by shedding more old feathers in spring than Irish birds, and correspondingly they sprout more new ones with some yellow pigment, albeit later.

Many birds from Wales and west Scotland are also pale in winter, such as on Mull, other islands in the Inner Hebrides and on the west mainland coast. This camouflages them against the pale western moorland, which is dominated by grass, sedge and rush, in contrast to the dark heathery moors of east Scotland and England.

These differences in plumage colour constitute what taxonomists call a cline, changing gradually from dark in the east to pale in the west. Occasionally, a pale individual occurs on low moorland in east Scotland, and a dark one in the west. However, out of hundreds of birds seen by us in Mayo in Ireland and in west Scotland, not one was blackish. Also, none had much white on the upperparts or on the underparts, apart from the legs and feet.

## CHANGE WITHIN PIGMENTED FEATHERS OF *LAGOPUS*

Finn Salomonsen found that the colour and pattern of pigment on individual feathers alters even as they grow, with the tip (which grew earliest) differing from the middle of the feather, and this in turn differing from the latest-growing part at the base. He suggested that this change (for example, in spring from an unbarred dark grey tip to a heavily barred hen-like base with some orange pigment) coincides with gonad development. Such changes are widespread in red grouse and Scottish ptarmigan at every season, and also occur in other races of willow and rock ptarmigan, and in white-tailed ptarmigan.[47]

Ray Hewson monitored changes in the individual feathers of captive-reared Scottish rock ptarmigan kept in an unheated building.[48] Each feather growing in winter reflected a brief cold snap by developing a whiter part during the cold period. The cause of such fine-tuning may be hormonal changes while the feather is growing, in response to a drop in temperature or a snowfall. This partial whitening occurred in association with lower temperature, which in natural conditions would often be associated with snow. This does not rule out the possibility that birds respond to snow itself, and even birds inside a building with no snow might have been responding to snow they could see outside the windows. Nor does it exclude the obvious point that whiteness is an adaptation to snow, not cold.[49]

## PHYSIOLOGY OF PLUMAGE AND MOULT IN *LAGOPUS*

### Day-length, local climate and moult

In commercial egg farms, poultry that are given longer day-length with electric lighting lay eggs in midwinter; conversely, they stop laying in summer if they are given a shorter day than they would experience outside. When Per Høst gave extra duration of light to captive willow ptarmigan in winter, cocks developed the spring nuptial plumage and hens the dark summer plumage, while both came into breeding condition and one hen laid eggs.[50] Having brought a cock into spring nuptial plumage in February, he then gave it a short seven-hour day-length, whereupon it moulted and grew a white winter plumage without first developing a dark autumn one. When he gave both sexes a much shorter day-length during the summer months, they developed a brief dark autumn plumage, before prematurely moulting it and growing the white winter dress.

*Lagopus lagopus* and rock ptarmigan use the local light cycle as a trigger to start moulting and then to start growing a new summer or winter plumage.

However, the point at which declining light triggers the moulting and subsequent growth of winter plumage varies between regions with different climate. Hence birds turn white earlier in cold, snowy northern Canada than at the same latitude in milder Iceland. Also, birds in Scotland and doubtless elsewhere have evolved fine-tuning, turning white faster in cold, snowy autumns than in mild ones with little snow.

**Hormonal influences**
In one study, cock and hen willow ptarmigan grew their summer plumage at the usual time, despite their gonads having been removed in winter, a result that apparently ruled out any influence from gonad hormones. Later research, however, showed that castrated cocks do not develop the spring plumage of dark chestnut on the head and neck, so this does depend on testosterone.[51]

Arctic male rock ptarmigan have almost no distinct spring plumage, unlike southern races and willow ptarmigan. They retain almost all of their winter plumage for territorial and sexual display in spring, and remain almost white until midsummer, when they begin to grow a partial brown plumage. After testosterone was injected into a territorial cock in Arctic Canada on 23 June, he remained almost white while the upperparts of other cocks became completely brown.[52] Hence the development of dark plumage was blocked by a high level of testosterone.

When small patches of feathers were plucked from captive willow ptarmigan during winter, new white feathers grew on the bare patches. However, after the birds had been injected with pituitary hormones, dark feathers grew instead. It was concluded from this that the white plumage requires no hormonal stimulus,[53] that testosterone and pituitary hormones are necessary for the growth of the cocks' dark spring plumage, and that declines of both hormones induce more hen-like summer feathers on cocks (*see* Table 22). Because cocks of all British grouse grow such feathers in early summer, this explanation may apply to all four species.

After a low point in late summer, the combs of red grouse enlarge in autumn. This coincides with the onset of vigorous territorial and sexual display, and with a reddish-bronze plumage on the cocks' heads, necks and breasts, resembling that of willow ptarmigan in spring. They keep this plumage through winter and spring, and then grow feathers with pale hen-like bars in a summer plumage from April until June, when the comb has stopped increasing and has declined slightly. Red grouse have adapted to mild British winters by extending their spring territorial behaviour and associated plumage back into the autumn.

Scottish cock ptarmigan begin to grow dark spring feathers on the head and neck in late February–early March, when their testes are increasing in size and

TABLE 22. Seasonal plumages of grouse in relation to hormonal state.[54]

| | COCK SPRING DISPLAY PLUMAGE | HEN SPRING PLUMAGE | COCK SUMMER PLUMAGE | HEN SUMMER PLUMAGE | COCK AND HEN AUTUMN PLUMAGE | COCK AND HEN WINTER PLUMAGE |
|---|---|---|---|---|---|---|
| Willow ptarmigan | Reddish hood from March[#] | None separate from summer plumage | Feathers on rest of upperparts become more barred[*] | Heavily yellow-barred dark feathers from April | Feathers on upperparts and flanks become less barred, some white on flanks | White[**] |
| Red grouse | Reddish hood in autumn, the rest of the body without hen-like bars, all kept until spring | As above | As above for some feathers on hood and rest of upperparts and flanks | As above from March | They grow the spring plumage | None separate from autumn plumage |
| Rock ptarmigan | Some dark feathers on hood from March onwards[#] | As above | As above | As above from March | Grey or brown, feathers on upperparts and flanks less barred, some white on flanks | White[**] |
| Black grouse | Feathers without hen-like bars grow in autumn, and are kept until spring | None separate from autumn plumage | As above for some feathers on hood | None separate from autumn plumage | None apart from spring display plumage grown in autumn (see under 'Cock spring display plumage', left) | None separate from autumn |

**TABLE 22.** (*continued*)

|  | COCK SPRING DISPLAY PLUMAGE | HEN SPRING PLUMAGE | COCK SUMMER PLUMAGE | HEN SUMMER PLUMAGE | COCK AND HEN AUTUMN PLUMAGE | COCK AND HEN WINTER PLUMAGE |
|---|---|---|---|---|---|---|
| Capercaillie | As above | As above | As above for some feathers on hood | As above | As above | As above |
| Hormonal state^ | Rising luteinising hormone (LH) and testosterone | Rising LH and probably follicle-stimulating hormone (FSH) | Less LH and testosterone | Rising LH | Photo-refractory;† less LH and gonadal hormones | None known |

# Starts later in northern populations.

\* Hannon & Wingfield (1990) confirmed that less testosterone and LH in cocks in late May induce moult and then growth of new feathers.

\*\* The apparent lack of a hormonal cause for the white winter plumage of willow ptarmigan and rock ptarmigan is in line with Tickell's (2003) suggestion that feathers in all bird species are white by default.

^ All dark plumages also involve melanophore-stimulating hormone (MSH).

† Long spring days stimulate gonads to enlarge and produce gonad hormones, ova and sperm. In summer, gonads come out of breeding condition despite the long days and so are called 'photo-refractory'. This coincides with the end of breeding and the annual moult of wing and tail.

their combs are rising very rapidly to full size,[55] and before hens show their first summer feathers. In April, the cocks' growth of spring feathers slows down while their testes increase greatly, and hens then overtake them in the extent of their summer dress. By this stage the cocks are growing hen-like barred feathers, unlike the black unbarred feathers that typify their partial spring plumage. We regard this male spring plumage, with dark feathers on the head and neck, as the equivalent of the hooded spring plumage on the head, neck and breast of cock willow ptarmigan.

### Variation in relation to climate

In Iceland and Alaska, thawed snow-free patches of ground where territorial behaviour and pairing can take place do not occur before late April or early May. Compared with Scotland, far less time remains before hens start incubation, and the cock's combs and testes increase more synchronously. It might be argued that male rock ptarmigan do not have enough time to grow a partial spring plumage with many dark feathers as in Scotland, but cock willow ptarmigan in the high Arctic are equally short of time and yet do grow a partial spring plumage.

High-Arctic male rock ptarmigan are even later than birds in Iceland, for they do not take territories before the end of May. Although they show a few summer feathers on the crown, they remain mostly white while the hens lay eggs and incubate. Only when their combs and testes decline in June do they shed many white feathers and grow a partial summer dress other than on the crown.

Common to willow and rock ptarmigan in all areas is that territorial behaviour and associated pair formation begin when both sexes are mostly white. This coincides with a big increase in comb sizes, and varies from late February during an average winter in Scotland, to late May in the high Arctic. Later, cocks of both species (except for Arctic male rock ptarmigan) develop a partially dark spring plumage that looks spectacular during courtship display. Hence, although the first stages of pairing in Scotland begin early, hens are willing to shift partners at any time before laying. As we suggested above, maintaining the pair bond is a likely reason for cocks growing a display dress with many dark feathers. It might be too risky to do this earlier in the season, when there is often a complete snow cover. More thawed ground in their habitat could also explain why Arctic willow ptarmigan develop hoods, whereas Arctic rock ptarmigan do not develop a spring plumage.

### Insulation properties of *Lagopus* plumage

The winter plumage of rock ptarmigan contains more feathers than in summer or autumn,[56] with extra follicles coming into development in preparation for cold

FIG 120. After-shaft on autumn ptarmigan flank feather. (Robert Moss)

weather. Winter feathers are longer and have denser, thicker bases, and the downy lower part of each extends further towards the tip than in summer or autumn plumage. In addition, the after-shafts of sprouting winter feathers in rock ptarmigan are longer and usually more downy.[57] It seems likely that this also occurs in other grouse species.

In Norwegian and Svalbard rock ptarmigan, the combined weight of skin and feathers does not differ between winter and summer,[58] yet captive Norwegian rock ptarmigan and Alaskan willow ptarmigan have a lower metabolic rate in winter than in summer.[59] The summer plumage is thinner and looser, however, and hens have more bare skin and blood vessels on their incubation patches.[60] Hence the weight of the skin and feathers may not be a good measure of insulating capacity.

Although the insulation of different seasonal plumages has not been measured, winter dress is doubtless superior. Some of this may be provided by the barbules[61] in the white feathers of willow and rock ptarmigan, which contain tiny air-filled cavities.[62] These should reduce conduction and convection of body heat. Also, the barbules should retain heat inside each air cavity by a greenhouse effect, receiving incoming radiation from the sun but reducing outgoing radiation from the body.

In willow ptarmigan and other grouse species in Siberia, winter feathers are denser than in summer because their barbs and barbules are longer and also more numerous per given length of feather.[63] The dense feathers can be raised to form an umbrella-like outer canopy, which can be puffed out or retracted to enclose more or less air for insulation.

The plumage of rock ptarmigan is better insulated than in tropical birds, but conducts heat more rapidly than in larger Arctic birds such as snowy owls.[64] Despite having large, naked, webbed feet, Arctic glaucous gulls can walk on snow at −50°C without harm, and can tolerate very low temperatures in their legs and feet for hours, keeping their feet just above freezing. It seems likely that rock ptarmigan have similar mechanisms for reducing blood flow to the extremities without incurring the risks of frostbite, for only in hard frost do they raise their metabolic rate to keep warm in winter. Tropical mammals, such as humans, respond to cold through ruinously costly shivering and increased blood flow to the extremities, whereas large Arctic mammals such as Arctic wolves or huskies do not increase their metabolic rate even in extreme cold. Intermediate between these extremes, the relatively small rock ptarmigan would be encumbered by heavy plumage like that of a snowy owl, and survives extreme cold by roosting in snow (see Chapter 8).

## REFLECTANCE OF WHITE PLUMAGE IN *LAGOPUS*

Fresh snow has a reflectance of 80 per cent, like that of white feathers with solid barbules, such as in gulls. The air cavities in white *Lagopus* barbules increase the feathers' reflectance by 5 per cent above that of the airless white barbules of seagulls. This makes a white grouse slightly more conspicuous against fresh snow, and should reduce camouflage slightly, a possible cost to set against any benefit from reducing heat loss. A potential advantage of the higher reflectance might be that birds may find it easier to maintain social contact or to display more effectively if they stand out slightly against the snow. White ptarmigan in sunlight do seem to shine more brightly than snow. Stu MacDonald wrote, 'To appreciate what a splendid creature the Rock Ptarmigan is, one must see it in life in its Arctic environment. The winter plumage, so flat and chalky white in museum skins, is vivid in the living bird.'[65] Thus, the birds' barbule structure may affect their appearance.

## LAGOPUS SNOWSHOES

The willow ptarmigan's snowshoe takes a track pressure of only 12–14g per $cm^2$, the lowest in the grouse family.[66] This must cut energy loss from sinking into soft snow, as well as allowing the bird to walk around more easily while feeding. Wading in deep snow soon saps the energy of even the fittest mountaineers and can be fatal unless they have skis or snowshoes. The feathers on the legs and feet of willow ptarmigan are longer and denser than in other ptarmigan, and curl round to the sole, reducing heat loss from the toes and making the feet good snow shovels as well as effective snowshoes.

Red grouse have less luxuriant snowshoes than willow ptarmigan.[67] Likewise, the winter snowshoes of Scottish rock ptarmigan have less dense and shorter feathers than those of Arctic rock ptarmigan. Rock ptarmigan have narrower snowshoes than willow ptarmigan, befitting the generally wind-packed snow of their range, as opposed to the softer snow of willow-ptarmigan country. When both species were tested on soft snow, their depth of penetration showed no material difference, however, presumably because the willow ptarmigan's heavier weight counteracts the floating effect of its snowshoes.[68]

In their adaptation to travelling on snow, rock ptarmigan could be said to resemble the Inuit, whose Arctic country in winter usually has drifted snow that affords easy walking and also speed for the Inuit sledge, with its narrow runners. In contrast, willow ptarmigan could be said to resemble the subarctic and boreal North American Indian, whose country has deep, soft snow that makes travel almost impossible without the Indians' superb snowshoes and their toboggan, with its flat, smooth bottom and upward-curving front.[69]

## BILLS, CLAWS AND TOE SCALES

Bills and claws suffer wear and tear, and all four species shed the old coatings once a year. Of red grouse it has been stated:

> Old grouse shed their toe nails in July–September and young do not, so an old nail in the process of becoming detached is also a sure sign of an old bird. A transverse ridge or scar across the top of the new nail, showing where the old one was formerly attached, may last for a few weeks, indicating an old bird. Young grouse have long smooth sharp claws, but old birds show faint transverse corrugations on their new claws, which tend to be thicker and blunter.[70]

FIG 121. Cock ptarmigan strolling up icy snow. (Derek McGinn)

New claws are hard and strong, with sharp points and edges that afford a good grip on wet rocks, hard snow and icy patches. During sudden squalls, rock ptarmigan grip the snow with their claws, crouch low with heads down facing the wind, and duck lower during violent gusts. In gales, AW has seen standing and crouching men blown over, but not a resting red grouse or Scottish ptarmigan. Also, friction from the claws and the transverse ridges of rough skin on the underside of the toes allows ptarmigan to climb steep, hard snow, ice or rock faster than the most skilled mountaineers.

Blackgame and capercaillie lack feathers on their toes, but they do have a row of hard elongated scales called pectinations along each side of the toe, like short teeth. These help them grip wet or icy branches. Birds shed them in early summer and grow new ones by early autumn. Both species in colder regions of Russia have longer pectinations, and white-tailed ptarmigan have very small ones, even though their toes are feathered as in rock ptarmigan and *Lagopus lagopus*.[71]

## COMBS

A fowl has a red comb along its crown and red skin below each eye, extended in cockerels and turkeys to drooping wattles. In severe cold, these bare patches of skin would lose much heat and risk frostbite. Overcoming this, grouse have evolved an erectile comb above each eye, which they can quickly make flaccid and hide under the feathers (Fig. 122).[72] As in fowls, the upper rim of the grouse's comb has serrated projections like the teeth of a human comb. The projections are more numerous but smaller than in a fowl's comb, and can be extended vertically upwards, in cocks with the teeth above the bird's crown almost like small red horns. Cocks have larger, thicker and darker red combs than hens, with taller teeth and bigger papillae.[73] Combs of rock ptarmigan and *Lagopus lagopus* have a relatively flat surface, whereas those of blackgame and capercaillie have papillae with a coarser grain than in *Lagopus*, resembling tiny frilly projections.

For most of the time, birds of all four species keep their combs down, raising them only in sexual or aggressive display. Richly supplied with blood vessels, the

FIG 122. Ptarmigan hen on a nest with its comb completely hidden by feathers. (Stuart Rae)

**FIG 123.** Cock red grouse with combs erect. (David A. Gowans)

combs can almost instantaneously engorge with blood, dilate in thickness, stiffen to full extent and darken in colour.[74] An erect comb in both hen and cock grouse signals aggressive, territorial and sexual behaviour. In cocks it is a secondary sexual character, its size dependent on testosterone.

The combs in all four species reach maximum size in both sexes during spring. In red grouse they are already large in late autumn and early winter, and remain so throughout midwinter. They usually begin to increase again in late winter, well in advance of the testes reaching their full size in April.[75] Scottish ptarmigan enlarge their combs rapidly in late February–early March, again long before the testis and ovary reach full size in May at the time when most hens start incubation.[76]

In Canada, Stu MacDonald noticed that combs of male rock ptarmigan become less fleshy, small and pale by the time their hens are incubating, and that the upper portion of each projection 'shrivels and seems to be sloughed off'.[77] Although the combs of Scottish cock ptarmigan and red grouse begin to decline when hens start incubation, they regress far less than the rapid decline of their testes, and remain quite large through the summer and autumn. In winter, red grouse and Scottish ptarmigan have much bigger combs and gonads than their Arctic counterparts, and they also show vigorous territorial and sexual display in winter, unlike Arctic cocks. In line with this, the blood of red grouse in winter contains more luteinising hormone (which stimulates the testis to produce testosterone and the ovary to produce oestrogen) than that of Norwegian willow ptarmigan.[78]

Comb sizes in cock red grouse are related to the birds' aggressiveness and dominance, and implants of testosterone increase all three aspects of maleness.[79] Three studies, one of willow ptarmigan in British Columbia and two of rock ptarmigan in Arctic Canada and Alaska, showed that cocks with small combs paired with fewer hens than cocks with large combs.[80]

The erect combs of *Lagopus lagopus* and rock ptarmigan glow red in sunlight.[81] François Mougeot and colleagues have found that the combs of all four British grouse species also reflect ultraviolet light of a frequency invisible to humans but probably visible to grouse.[82] Although the combs of cock red grouse are redder than those of hens, the hens' combs show a more intense ultraviolet coloration than those of cocks. Comb colour, both red and ultraviolet, is probably a signal during aggressive and sexual encounters.

Comb size and redness in cock red grouse vary with body condition, such that vigorous cocks have large red combs. The colour of grouse combs comes from carotenoids, a group of yellow, orange and red plant pigments. Recent research has revealed that comb redness in cock red grouse is related to the level of carotenoids in their blood plasma and to the level of testosterone. In addition, comb redness and plasma carotenoids decline when birds carry many threadworms in their guts. The redness and the size of the comb may therefore act as a combined signal to hens that a cock is vigorous and in good body condition, likely to make a good father for her offspring. The reflectance of ultraviolet light by combs may be an extra signal, for in both sexes the ultraviolet declines as threadworm burdens increase.

## SUMMARY

Adults renew their main flight-quills in late summer. Birds that have bred successfully moult later than birds without young. Willow and rock ptarmigan have three main moults, red grouse two, and black grouse and capercaillie one. Willow and rock ptarmigan occurring in southern regions where there is some snow-free ground in winter show some dark feathers in their winter plumage. The summer feathers of hen *Lagopus lagopus* and rock ptarmigan have wide bars of dark and yellow, while those of cocks have narrower bars. Blackcock and male capercaillie grow some hen-like feathers after their lek displays end.

Changing day-length triggers the start of winter and spring moults in willow and rock ptarmigan, but local climate determines when the moult starts and the rate of change thereafter. Scottish ptarmigan can fine-tune this by altering the rate of change, according to whether the season is milder and less snowy than usual. In willow ptarmigan, increases in gonadal and pituitary hormones induce the growth of coloured spring plumage, and declines in them induce the growth of hen-like barred feathers on cocks in summer. White feathers contain air-filled cavities that should enhance insulation. Above each eye, grouse have an erectile comb of red skin that also reflects ultraviolet light, unseen by humans but visible to grouse.

CHAPTER 11

# Habitat

HABITAT IS THE RANGE of environments in which a species occurs.[1] To understand current habitats, it helps to consider how they evolved over time. Past habitats of British grouse developed as a result of geological processes, climate, landforms, soils and human impact. In this chapter we discuss how these factors affect today's habitats and grouse abundance. We emphasise Britain and Ireland, but the principles apply elsewhere. Habitats of grouse abroad are mentioned in Chapters 3–6, and many publications describe and illustrate them.[2]

British and Irish grouse live in an unusual variety of landscape for such a small part of the world.[3] Red grouse have their home on moorland, a semi-natural habitat that is mostly human-induced, while ptarmigan live on high Scottish hills, southern extensions of the subarctic wilderness. Black grouse thrive on low moorland with rushy bogs or scrub, and in open birchwood or pinewood. The capercaillie is the 'Great Cock of the Wood', the crown of Scotland's magnificent old Caledonian pinewood.

## GEOLOGICAL PROCESSES

### Bedrock

Over 1,000 million years ago, Scotland and the northern half of Ireland lay on the southeast margin of a continental plate that geologists call Laurentia.[4] To the southeast lay two separate continental plates, Baltica and Avalonia, the latter including England.[5] All three later collided to fuse, involving intense mountain-building that began over 400 million years ago. The roots of these mountains comprised coarse-grained igneous granite, formed by uprising, cooling and hardening of molten rock deep in the earth. The mountains became the Caledonian range, stretching from eastern USA and Canada through Greenland to Scandinavia, Svalbard and Scotland.[6] Later, Europe and America separated by continental drift. Millions of years of erosion removed rock many kilometres thick, and most of our granite hills today are the worn remains of these huge mountains, formerly of Himalayan proportions.

The sedimentary rocks found across Britain and Ireland were derived from sediments settling in water, such as sandstone from soil sediments and limestone from animal skeletons. During the formation of the Caledonian mountains, intense heat or pressure metamorphosed some of the sedimentary rocks into harder schist. Where surface rocks fractured, molten rock (lava) spurted from volcanoes, and as it flowed down it cooled quickly to form fine-grained igneous rock.[7]

Grouse land in Britain and Ireland overlies a great variety of bedrock, such as hard quartzite or granite beside soft limestone, or cliffs with white quartzite above brown sandstone (Table 23). This leads to unusually varied landscape, soil, flora and fauna.

**TABLE 23.** The main and subsidiary bedrock on British and Irish grouse land.

| REGION | MAIN | SUBSIDIARY |
| --- | --- | --- |
| Highlands | Micaceous sandstones, siliceous and feldspathic sandstones, granite, quartzite | Mica-schist, dark or graphitic schist, limestone, basalt, hornblende-schist, diorite, gabbro |
| Southern Uplands | Shale, greywacke | Granite, andesite, basalt, limestone |
| Northern England | Limestone, millstone grit | Andesite and other volcanic rocks in the Lake District, granite on Dartmoor, siliceous sandstone on Exmoor |
| Wales | Shale | Slate |
| Northern Ireland | Basalt and other volcanic rock, mica-schist | Granite in the Mourne Mountains |
| Republic of Ireland | Limestone | Granite in Wicklow, mica-schist, siliceous sandstone |

**Effects on grouse**

Geological processes left most ground in Britain and Ireland as lowland plains or valleys, productive for grouse. With the advent of humans in a temperate climate, however, these lowlands became ideal for cultivation, so that suitable habitats for grouse became unsuitable fields and settlements. Since then, grouse have used the remaining land, rejected for cultivation because it was too steep, too rocky, too wet or at high altitude.

Bedrock affects soil chemistry, which in turn affects the chemical composition of food plants. Heather and blaeberry over base-rich bedrock have a higher content of the vital elements nitrogen and phosphorus than over acidic granite, and red grouse, ptarmigan and mountain hares are more abundant there.[8]

Most acidic rocks are hard and coarse-grained, contain much silica, and weather into poor soils. Base-rich rocks are softer and finer-grained, with a higher content of basic substances such as lime, potash and magnesia. Coarse-grained rocks weather into loose barren soils, whereas fine-grained rocks break down into cohesive fertile soils. As a result, a hill over base-rich bedrock tends to have less bare ground than a hill of the same altitude over acidic bedrock, and often the type of vegetation growing there differs strikingly. Assessing bedrock can therefore be a guide to habitat quality (Table 24).[9]

TABLE 24. Assessing the richness of bedrock for soil fertility and vegetation.

| | |
|---|---|
| RICH | Black or graphitic schists; carbonate-bearing forms of sandstone, shale and igneous rocks; chlorite and calc-schists; limestone; marble |
| INTERMEDIATE | Andesite; basalt; diorite; dolerite; gabbro; green beds; hornblende-schist;# mica-schist; shale; slate |
| POOR | Granite; quartzite; greywacke; micaceous and siliceous sandstones and metasandstones; quartzofeldspathic gneiss; serpentinite and other ultrabasic rocks* |

# This covers 'epidiorite', a term now disused by geologists.
* These are so basic as to be toxic, with poor soils and mainly grassy vegetation.

**Notes**

1. The above is a general classification. At any one locality the rock may be deeply weathered or fault-shattered, with a secondary deposition of carbonate, which increases base-richness. We should also consider topography, climate, altitude, and the rock's hardness, grain size and solubility. For example, some limestone is so soluble

TABLE 24. NOTES (*continued*)
that hilltops are covered with infertile flint-gravel, because the chalk that formerly embedded the rock has been washed away along with the fertile soils, which are now confined to valleys and lower slopes. Old Red Sandstone is poor and weathers slowly. After glaciers grind it down, however, its fine grain aids the development of high-quality soils at low altitude.
2. The Moine rocks of the west and northern Highlands, and the rocks of the Grampian Group in the central Highlands are predominantly composed of poor-quality rocks. This contrasts with the Dalradian rocks of the southern and northeast Highlands, where rich and intermediate rocks are more common.
3. The table can apply also to Alpine land and woodland. Except in southern England and the highest Alpine land, a caveat is that glacial deposits may have been derived from different distant bedrock (loose rocks on the surface are useful clues to this). Also, deposits that have developed on site – such as acidic or fen peat, alluvium from streams, or wind-blown sand – can locally override the influence of underlying bedrock.

FIG 124. Effect of bedrock on vegetation in Glen Derry. The grassier part of the slope on the left has fairly rich diorite below, while the heathery area on the right overlies infertile flaggy metamorphosed sandstone. (Adam Watson)

## CLIMATE

**Before and during the last ice age**

Much of Britain once lay near the Equator, where tropical forest decomposed to form coal. During hot periods, chemical action rotted some hard rock such as granite, leading to better soils than is usual for an acidic rock. Wind, rain and streams wore down the hills to form valleys and plains.

For many millions of years, periodic glaciations were separated by warmer interglacial periods in one of which we now live. During the most recent major glaciation 18,000 years ago (Table 25), ice up to 1,500m thick covered Scotland, and was joined to Scandinavian ice that deposited Norwegian rocks on the Scottish coast. Ice covered Ireland, extending to the Bristol Channel and almost as far as Oxford and London. The sea lay 100m lower than now, and land joined England to the Continent and Britain to Ireland, until rises in sea-level overran these bridges.[10]

TABLE 25. Dates of some events that help explain habitats today.

| LINE NUMBER FOR REFERENCE | YEARS BEFORE PRESENT | EVENT |
|---|---|---|
| 1 | 18,000 | Ice-sheet covers Ireland and most of Britain except southernmost England |
| 2 | 14,500 | Much of the ice melts |
| 3 | 14,000 | Extensive juniper, then willow as far north as southern Scotland |
| 4 | 13,700 | Woolly mammoth in Scotland |
| 5 | 13,000 | Rapid warming to a climate broadly like that of recent millennia |
| 6 | 12,000–11,500 | Minor glaciation, with Arctic tundra on most land; wolverines in England |
| 7 | 11,500 | Abrupt warming; juniper expansion |
| 8 | 11,000–10,000 | Birch and hazel everywhere except bogs and high hills |
| 9 | 10,500 | Pine-birch-hazel forest into the far south of England |
| 10 | 10,000 | Pine arrives in County Donegal from a possible ice-free refugium west of Ireland |

*(continued overleaf)*

TABLE 25. *(continued)*

| LINE NUMBER FOR REFERENCE | YEARS BEFORE PRESENT | EVENT |
| --- | --- | --- |
| 11 | 9,500 | Pine up to north England and south Ireland, elm into most of Scotland |
| 12 | By 9,000 | Pine across England and Ireland, into Wester Ross; hunter-gatherers on Rum |
| 13 | 9,000–8,000 | Warmest summers; most English pine replaced by oak, or by alder on wet soil |
| 14 | 8,800 | Pine widespread in mainland Highlands except the furthest north |
| 15 | 8,000–5,700 | Greatest extent of forest; first human deforestation to create lowland pasture |
| 16 | Before 7,800 | Most pine in southwest Scotland replaced by oak and alder |
| 17 | 7,000–6,500 | Land bridge connecting England to the Continent breached by the North Sea |
| 18 | 6,000 | Cool, wet climate; peat growth; cereal farming in the main European valleys |
| 19 | 5,700–4,400 | Woodland retracts in west Scotland, but pine spreads to north coast |
| 20 | 5,000–4,000 | Peat expansion in the west (in west Glen Affric before woodland decline) |
| 21 | 5,000 | Forest clearance for pasture and cultivation begins on lowlands |
| 22 | 4,400 | Pine decline in north and west Scotland and Ireland, though not in east Scotland |
| 23 | 4,000 | Pine vanished in much of west Scotland and west Ireland |
| 24 | 4,000–3,000 | Human deforestation of much moorland for pasture and cereal cultivation |
| 25 | 3,000–700 | Cool, wetter climate ends most cultivation on what is now moorland |
| 26 | 700–500 | Warm, dry climate; expansion of cultivation on lower moorland |
| 27 | 500–200 | Cool, wet climate ends the above expansion; many high farms abandoned |

**TABLE 25.** *(continued)*

| LINE NUMBER FOR REFERENCE | YEARS BEFORE PRESENT | EVENT |
| --- | --- | --- |
| 28 | From 350 | Increase of tree plantations, on a small-scale until 200 years ago; increase in sheep farming |
| 29 | 300–250 | Least woodland |
| 30 | 240–220 | Fewest red deer |
| 31 | From 150 | Rise of sporting estates, with corresponding increase of red grouse and red deer |
| 32 | 60–20 | Subsidies to convert moorland to farmland or woodland, and to drain it |
| 33 | 60–0 | Subsidies for sheep and cattle farming; increase of red deer on moorland |

Glaciers wear down mountains and cover land under the ice with ground-up rock called till or boulder clay, which contains much silt and clay, and is compacted by the great weight of ice. At the sides and in front, glaciers push up moraines, which are less compacted and hence more freely draining. Huge rivers flowing from the melting ice wash most silt and clay out of any till or moraines in their path, producing fluvio-glacial deposits of very freely drained sand and gravel, with rounded, water-worn stones.

**A minor glaciation following the last ice age**
After much of the ice melted 14,500 years ago (*see* Table 25, line 2), woolly mammoths lived in Scotland. Then, 13,000 years ago, the climate warmed rapidly, resembling that of recent millennia. Pollen deposited in peat and in lake beds shows that grass abounded, with juniper and willow colonising, followed by birch.[11]

The climate subsequently cooled again and birch vanished, to be replaced by grass, heath with much crowberry, and sedges on wet ground. A minor glaciation ensued 12,000 years ago, as an ice-sheet centred on Rannoch Moor covered much of the west Highlands, and corrie glaciers and small ice-caps topped other hills in the Highlands, the Lake District, Snowdonia and Ireland. Lowland Britain and Ireland supported crowberry heath, including Arctic species such as least willow. Bones of collared lemmings from this period have been found at Edinburgh, extinct giant elk in Scotland,[12] wolverines in England south to Devon, and an Arctic marine fauna in the Firth of Clyde.[13]

FIG 125. Moraine freshly deposited in front of a glacier on Baffin Island, 1953. (Adam Watson)

### After the last minor glaciation

The minor glaciation ended as warmth arrived abruptly 11,500 years ago (*see* Table 25, line 7). Juniper scrub spread widely, to be replaced by birch and hazel almost everywhere but the high hills. Pine colonised most of England, although it was generally replaced later by oak, elm and lime on fertile lowland soils. On English

FIG 126. Rounded hills on Baffin Island, of a similar altitude to high British hills. A glacier with moraines is on the right, and ice-caps behind. This is what our hills would have looked like during the last glaciation about 12,000 years ago. (Adam Watson)

and Welsh uplands there grew birch, hazel and oak, with Scots pine on poorer ground. Pine covered much of Ireland to the Atlantic coast, and expanded in Galloway and most of the mainland Highlands during the period of warmest summers.

At the forest maximum 8,000 years ago, moorland dominated by crowberry occurred in a narrow belt above the uppermost woodland, and on exposed coasts, bogs, and forest clearings after lightning fires. The uppermost limit of woodland (the timberline) had moved uphill,[14] so Alpine land occupied a far smaller area than now.

At this time much more broadleaved woodland grew than pinewood. An oak-elm-lime mixture dominated southern England, oak-elm-hazel in northern England and much of Ireland and central Scotland, and birch-hazel-oak on east Scottish lowlands and west Scotland. Birch-hazel scrub grew on the north coast of Sutherland and Caithness, and in the Western and Northern Isles. Alder and willow abounded on riversides and other wet ground, and aspen with holly and, locally, yew grew on better soils. Shallow lakes were bigger and more numerous than now, and bogs covered much lowland.

Richard Tipping mapped Scotland's ancient woodlands using radiocarbon dating of pollen. This method cannot distinguish woods from scattered trees, though 'there would have been very few places from which no trees could be seen'.[15] Such maps may give a 'false impression of uniformity', but 'Small-scale climatic,

FIG 127. Ancient pine roots, embedded in thick peat, exposed by erosion that has cut a deep hag in the heather moorland. The piles of dead purple moor grass, left by a spate of rainwater, indicate continued erosion. (Stuart Rae)

geological, and topographic contrasts over short distances would have introduced an astonishing beauty, richness and diversity of woods within individual valleys.'

With the advent of a wet climate, peat spread over large tracts of Britain and Ireland, especially in the rainy west. Pine retracted from Galloway and Rannoch Moor, heather expanded and the timberlines dropped lower. By 4,000 years ago, pine had gone from many western regions but remained in the drier east.

### CLIMATE, HUMANS, DEFORESTATION, INFERTILITY AND PEATLAND

Frank Fraser Darling stated that man caused the deforestation and infertility of the Scottish Highlands from AD800.[16] In fact, most deforestation occurred BC, but the question remains how much deforestation, infertility and peatland were caused by prehistoric man and how much by changes in climate. It is generally agreed that man caused most of the deforestation in the northeast Highlands. Some scientists disagree that humans deforested the west and thus caused its infertility and peatland,[17] though others hold that humans played a part by enabling or accelerating peat formation.[18] Interactions between human and climate are sometimes ignored, yet human and climatic influences are not necessarily exclusive.

For forest to be converted to peatland, dead plant litter must remain partly decomposed. This occurs in waterlogged soils that lack sufficient oxygen for decomposition to take place, which in turn are more likely to occur in a wet climate. Because processes that encourage evaporation of water – such as grazing or cultivation – discourage the creation of peat, the rate of peat formation can depend on the balance between climate-induced and human-induced changes in water balance. Trees lose much water to the atmosphere by evaporation and transpiration, replacing it from their roots and thus drying the soil. Because deforested heath has less foliage than trees, it draws up less water, soils become wetter, and water tables may rise, which should favour peat.

As discussed above, it has been hard to separate climatic from human influences affecting the development of peatland, but here we note two studies that separated them. In west Glen Affric, an area once forested but now dominated by treeless wet heath, thick peat expanded long before forest collapse.[19] And near Hudson Bay in Canada, a region unaffected by human deforestation or agriculture, peat thickened and timberlines retreated south,[20] during periods when peat also grew and forest declined in Britain and Ireland. The evidence points to a widespread oceanic climate in the northern hemisphere, expanding peat and extirpating woodland.

To conclude, human-induced deforestation is not necessary to turn forest to peatland, but in some parts of Britain and Ireland it may be sufficient and may have exacerbated climatic impacts. When there is a fine climatic balance between waterlogged and freely drained soil, tree removal may tip it towards the former and hence the creation of peat.

## HOW GROUSE WOULD HAVE FARED DURING AND AFTER THE ICE AGE

The only large ice-free refuge in Britain and Ireland during the last main ice age 18,000 years ago lay south of the Bristol Channel and the Thames, then an Arctic tundra with willow and rock ptarmigan. Bones of willow ptarmigan have been found in Hungary, Monaco and Italy, far south of the species' present range, and those of rock ptarmigan in southeast England, the Channel Islands, central Europe and Virginia, with more willow than rock ptarmigan in southern or lowland areas.[21] After the ice melted, valleys and floodplains would have offered fertile soils and bogs for grouse. Southern England warmed, leading to the growth of scrub and then woodlands of birch and pine, suiting willow ptarmigan and then blackgame and capercaillie.

Hazel grouse probably lived in Britain after the last main ice age. They would have thrived in the woodlands, which contained birch, hazel, willow, alder and aspen, along with some pine, yew and holly. Also suitable would have been the last phase of broadleaved woodland that colonises after fire or wind-throw in pinewood, such as that found in Finland today, where there is a succession of willow ptarmigan, blackgame, hazel grouse and capercaillie, in that order.[22]

Blackgame would have favoured open woodland, scrub and moorland near trees. Their remains have been found on the north Caithness coast and on North Uist in the Outer Hebrides, dating from the Pictish period before the Norse colonisation, in places devoid of natural woodland or scrubland today.[23] Capercaillie would have abounded in pinewood, and during summer in blaeberry-rich birchwood and oakwood. The large expansions and retractions of pine and other tree species (*see* Table 25, lines 9–14, 16, 19–23) would have ensured dynamic rises and falls in the numbers and range of the five grouse species.

LANDFORMS AND SOILS

Landforms result from the interaction of geological processes with climate, and include large-scale features such as valleys, down to small ones such as hillocks and hollows. They affect grouse by providing physical cover, and by influencing soils and vegetation.

**Soil formation**
Soils are formed by the interactions of parent material, comprising weathered rock that has not moved, and deposits moved to the locality by ice, water, gravity and wind; climate; soil organisms, plants and animals, including humans; land relief, such as mountain, floodplain, altitude, slope and aspect; and time.[24] Scientists classify soils by the sequence, thickness and colour of their 'horizons', or layers, starting at the surface with litter from dead plants and working down the 'profile' (vertical section in a soil pit) to the parent material (Fig. 128).[25] Freely drained, uncultivated moorland and woodland soils in Britain and Ireland generally show several distinct horizons (*see* Fig. 129), whereas a single thick layer of peat (*see* Fig. 130) accumulates on very poorly drained ground. Drainage is influenced by gradient, topography (for example, a basin drains differently from a hilltop of the same gradient) and the nature of the soil material. It ranges from excessive (as in gravel), through free, imperfect, and poor, to very poor (as in peat).

**Key**
P living plants
L litter (dead plants) from previous growth
F fermenting litter being rotted by decomposer organisms, with some of the original plant structures obvious to the naked eye
H 'humus' layer of well-decomposed organic matter with few or no recognisable remains. (In wetter soils there is a dark, peaty O horizon below H, not shown here – see Fig. 130. It comprises organic matter that accumulates owing to little decomposition in wet anaerobic conditions)
A generally 'eluvial' (washed out; so called because material has been moved from A to B by water percolating downwards), with an upper part that is typically darker than the lower, stained by dark matter washed down from H
B generally 'illuvial' (washed in), including clay and silt washed down from A
C unconsolidated mineral material, little altered by soil-forming processes, and consisting of weathered rock particles above bedrock or deposits, the 'parent material' of the soil

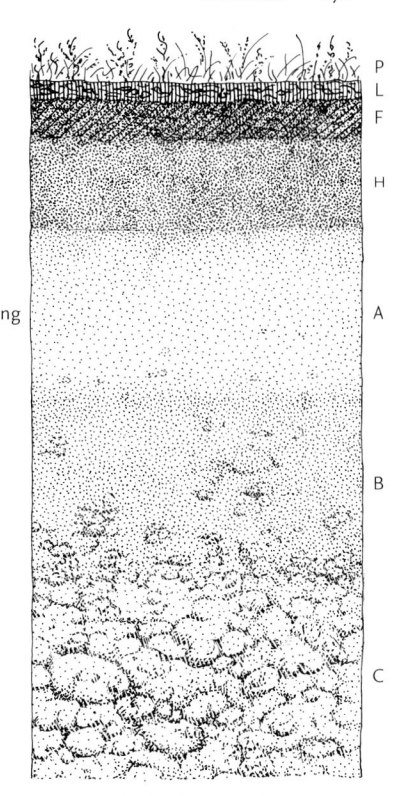

FIG 128. Different horizons, or layers, in a soil pit. In this diagrammatic podzol, horizons L–H are organic (derived from plant and animal remains), A–B are mainly mineral (derived from rock), C is all mineral, and A, B and C denote increasing depth. (Drawn by Dave Pullan)

1. Organic soil, or topsoil (F–A), lies above paler mineral soil, or 'subsoil' (B–C). Cultivation disrupts L–A and sometimes B.
2. Uncultivated podzols have very acidic surface layers that lack a crumb structure. The humus found here is often called 'mor' or 'raw humus', and is home to few or no earthworms. Horizon A has an upper dark layer with some humus, above a thicker ash-grey layer with little humus.

Removal of clay, silt and nutrients from horizon A results in a coarser, less cohesive, infertile topsoil. In the lower part of horizon A, sand grains become bleached, hence its ash-grey appearance, and iron compounds are precipitated as yellow-brown oxides within the upper layer of horizon B.

In iron humus podzols, humus from horizons H–A darkens the upper layer of horizon B, forming a Bh horizon. Iron humus and peaty podzols can have a dark reddish-brown iron pan, 1–2mm thick, below the Bh horizon. A bright yellowish-brown layer lies below the Bh horizon of iron humus podzols, and under the A horizon of other podzols.

3. Peat has thick O horizons. Organisms are scarce in acidic, wet, anaerobic, cold

conditions, so hill peat is very infertile. Peat has been defined as soil with > 30cm thickness of peaty layers, but can be many metres thick. 'Fen peat' is derived from plants such as grass above base-rich parent material, as opposed to heath above acidic parent material. It can be fertile when drained, as in the Cambridgeshire fens.

4. In brown earths the A horizon contains mineral material intimately mixed with 'mull' humus (from a Danish word for mould). This A horizon has a well-developed crumb structure and is home to many earthworms and other decomposer organisms, and organic surface layers are thin or absent because litter decomposes quickly. The A horizon is dark brown, the upper B horizon brown and the lower B horizon a paler brown, the layers grading into one another.

FIG 129.

FIG 129. The soil profile of an iron humus podzol on heather moorland. Under the heather (P) is a thin layer of litter (L) of the same brown colour as the heather stems, and obvious only at the highest point of the pit. Below this lies a thicker, darker brown, fermentation layer (F). Then comes a band of very dark grey (almost black) humus (H), containing tiny mineral grains, which are a sign of completely humified material and hence not peat. The bottom of the humus grades into a thin uppermost blackish layer of mineral soil coloured by leached humus (upper A), grading in turn into a very thick and much paler ashy grey (almost pale grey) layer of leached mineral soil with less humus (lower A). Below this is a thin, very dark brown band, slightly darkened by humic deposits in the uppermost subsoil (upper B), a thick yellowish-brown layer of leached subsoil (B), and even thicker layers of reddish-brown subsoil (lower B). The C horizon (below B) is not shown. (Gordon Miller)

The fertility of most soils depends largely on the minerals they contain, which are particles usually derived from local bedrock. A common exception occurs after ice grinds bedrock in one area and deposits it above a different rock elsewhere, whereupon the acidity and nutrients in the mineral soil reflect the deposits. Also, water flowing across underlying rock and issuing at the surface has a chemical content that reflects the bedrock.

FIG 130. Thick layer of peat (O) above glacial deposits (C). (Robert Moss)

FIG 131. Molehill on a grassy flush that has been enriched by nutrients from groundwater, set on a heathery slope. (Stuart Rae)

These influences profoundly affect vegetation. On infertile moorland, including that above thick peat, flushes are conspicuous from their abundant rushes, grasses and flowering herbs, indicating soils locally enriched by waterborne nutrients. Bog myrtle, which fixes atmospheric nitrogen, adds further fertility in many moorland flushes. At Alpine flushes, bright green moss and herbs signify fertile conditions, due to continuous irrigation by nutrient-rich water.

### Natural soil development and human modification

By 'soil development', scientists mean the changes that result in a mature soil in a steady state, with a full set of horizons. The natural processes involved in soil development are weathering, leaching, podzolisation, gleying, and peat formation (Table 26; see also Fig. 128).

TABLE 26. Processes of natural soil development in temperate regions.

| PROCESS | MECHANISM | RESULT | EXAMPLE |
| --- | --- | --- | --- |
| Weathering | Rock breaks into smaller particles | Granule size and chemical content affect fertility | Base-rich basalt leads to fertile brown earth, acidic granite to coarse, poor soil |
| Leaching | Nutrients and other materials are washed downwards, out of the surface soil (faster in coarse soil and heavy rainfall) | Poor conditions for plant growth and the decomposition of dead plants | Poor, acidic, sandy or gravelly soil, especially infertile in regions of high rainfall such as west Britain and west Ireland |
| Podzolisation# | A leaching process probably induced by the products of 'raw humus' (see Fig. 128), or involving iron and aluminium compounds transported down the profile from upper layers | Topsoil has an ash-grey layer due to bleached sand grains | Podzols on freely drained glacial deposits derived from acidic rock, common under heather or pine, and infertile |

TABLE 26. (*continued*)

| PROCESS | MECHANISM | RESULT | EXAMPLE |
| --- | --- | --- | --- |
| Gleying | Anaerobic (no oxygen) owing to waterlogging* of soil pores | Reddish-brown mottling in upper subsoil, above a layer that is blue-green, as the oxide of iron here is in a ferrous state (less oxygen is attached to the iron molecule) | Gley soils, compacted and sticky, typical of poorly drained hollows |
| Peat formation | As above | Undecomposed litter** builds up very thickly | Permanently waterlogged peat, in which plant roots do not reach mineral soil |

# Podzolisation occurs on freely drained soil derived from acidic parent material, in climates where precipitation exceeds the plants' water loss via evaporation and transpiration. Very freely drained sand or gravel leads to iron podzols, abundant in the boreal forest of Scandinavia and northern Russia, but in Britain infrequent because of the oceanic climate. There are British examples, however, such as in northeast Scotland. A bigger excess of precipitation, or poorer drainage, induces in turn iron humus podzols, peaty podzols, gleyed soils and thick peat.

* Waterlogging also occurs in peaty podzols after wet weather, where an impermeable layer (an iron pan) bars water from percolating further down. This creates a perched water table, with freely drained soil underneath the pan down to the general groundwater table at greater depth. Where the parent material (C horizon) comprises glacial till or moraine, there is often a thick cement-like induration that also bars downward percolation. In receiving sites such as hollows where water gathers, gley soils are then common.

** Litter decomposition can be fast in dry conditions but slow in wet ones, and fast with base-rich litter such as from ash trees and grass, but slow with acidic litter such as from heather or pine. Wet conditions arise from a large excess of precipitation over evapotranspiration, due to heavy precipitation or to poor drainage under low precipitation. Because wet conditions often impede downward leaching, wet mineral soils can be more fertile than podzols. On the other hand, organic matter, especially litter that is acidic, decomposes slowly in wet conditions, often favouring peat formation. Plants on thick hill peat depend for most of their nutrients on deposits in precipitation. Locally, however, groundwater flowing over bedrock or through subsoil comes to the surface, and spreads nutrients downhill in flushes that enrich both peat and plants.

Much of northern Scotland falls within the world zone of boreal coniferous forest, while most of southern England and much lowland elsewhere in Britain and Ireland lies in the next zone to the south – deciduous forest. Scientists generalise that climate largely determines these zones, though soils and vegetation may be locally influenced more by relief (as in bogs) or by parent material (as with limestone).

Some soils have poorly developed horizons because of their youth, or because some factor has prevented the stability needed for horizon development, such as soil or sediments deposited by streams (alluvium) or resulting from movement on slopes (colluvium).[26] Scientists generally agree that natural soil development is very slow – at least 1,000 years is the suggested time for a temperate soil to reach a steady state.[27] A scientist would need Methuselah's 969 years to solve this problem decisively by studying the same sites for centuries, for when undisturbed natural soils are checked over several decades they usually show no material change.

The skeletal soils occurring after glaciation tend to be more fertile than many of the soils that they develop into subsequently. Soils in the first few millennia after the last ice age would have been generally fertile, not yet impoverished by leaching. Since 7,300 years ago, however, there have been several periods of a cool, wet climate, which would have facilitated leaching. John Birks concluded that acidification since the ice age has been natural, with widespread development of infertile soils 'as a result of the acidic nature of much of the local bedrock and till, coupled with intensive leaching under a cool, moist climate'.[28] There are local exceptions, such as fertile soils on base-rich bedrock, and on alluvium, colluvium, flushes, and ground altered by humans.

Humans change many soils, often strongly modifying the effects of natural factors.[29] Cultivation for farming disrupts upper horizons, so that formerly infertile podzols come to resemble relatively fertile brown soils and have been classified thus in soil surveys.[30] Drains and modern ploughs shatter indurated layers,[31] thus lowering groundwater tables and increasing nutrient uptake, but also causing soil erosion. Artificial fertilisers and pollutants provide extra nutrients.

**Soil type and vegetation**

Although many differences in soils arise because sites differ physically, soil scientists agree that certain vegetation can affect soil type. For example, pine and heather produce acidic litter that usually decomposes slowly, whereas ash trees produce base-rich litter that decomposes rapidly. The former tend to lead to podzols, and the latter to brown earths. However, effects of vegetation are sometimes overstated, for instance the suggestion that birch encroaching on heather turns podzols into brown earth within several decades.[32] To test this, birches were planted in Yorkshire heather, but after three decades the soil 'remained a fully differentiated podzol'.[33]

Plants often favour certain soils and some species are good indicators of soil fertility. For example, podzols are more acidic than brown earth, and heather or pine predominate there, while herb-rich grass or ash trees prevail on brown earth. This happens usually because dominant plants outcompete others, not because the latter cannot grow there. Heather, blaeberry and pine can all grow on fertile natural soils and on fertile cultivated soil.

To conclude, mature podzols with well-developed horizons are less fertile than young soils from the same parent material, but brown earth and cultivated podzols are more fertile. Other things being equal, fertile soils support vegetation that tends to have more plant species, and to be more nutritious, than infertile soils nearby.

## PREHISTORIC HUMAN IMPACTS ON SOIL

Concentrations of hazelnut shells show that hunter-gatherers lived in the mild climate of the island of Rum 9,000 years ago. In South Uist, pollen of birch and hazel declined 8,000 years ago as pollen of grass and heather increased, signifying human clearance of woodland and expansion of pasture. On lake floors in lowland Scotland, increases of grass and sedge pollen coincided with the occurrence of charcoal 2,000–5,000 years ago, signifying human-induced deforestation along with fire and grazing.[34] All heather moorland lies below the current potential natural timberline. Humans have destroyed all natural timberlines in Britain and Ireland, save for fragmentary relics in the Cairngorms (see Fig. 132). Timberlines – which are the highest altitude at which natural woodland can grow – are evident in many countries with less overgrazing and burning, such as Canada.

Cultivation of cereals spread to Britain from the Continent, the first signs in Scotland appearing 5,800 years ago in the mild climate of lowland Arran and Kintyre. Large-scale impacts became evident 5,000–4,000 years ago on great tracts of lowland across Britain and Ireland, as human deforestation produced moorland pasture for farm animals or fields for cultivation. In an example 5,000 years ago, birch-hazel scrub declined on Orkney's exposed coast, as humans and farm animals turned an understorey of tall herbs and ferns into pasture within 200 years.[35] Human deforestation of upland began later but proceeded on a massive scale, along with the use of fire and introduction of farm animals, leading to the replacement of woodland by moorland.[36]

Farmers cleared most forest in Britain and Ireland, but this was not the case in northern Europe. Our gentler relief and longer growing seasons favoured

FIG 132. Relic timberline of Scots pine at Creag Fhiaclach, Glen Feshie, reaching almost half way up the slope. Juniper scrub extends above this limit. Willow and birch scrub has been extirpated by browsing. (David Duncan)

cultivation,[37] so farmland now covers 77 and 68 per cent of Britain and Ireland, respectively, but only 3 per cent of Norway. Agriculture on deforested land maintained more people (estimated at over 300 times more) than hunting in forest.[38] Furthermore, the amount of pasture available after deforestation greatly exceeds that on the shaded, drier soils under mature woodland, so it supports more farm stock. Because of our mild winters, stock can stay outdoors and need less supplementary feed from summer crops.[39] Hence, stock density in Britain and Ireland exceeds that in countries with cold winters, and effects on grouse habitats are more severe.

**Cultivation on what is now moorland or woodland**
Cultivation began to affect much British and Irish upland from 5,000 years ago, continuing there until early in the first millennium BC. In Shetland and Mayo, for example, recent removal of peat for fuel revealed prehistoric field systems on mineral soil under the peat. These dated from 4,800 and 4,500–3,200 years ago, respectively, the Mayo ones starting after forest clearance and ceasing as peat developed.[40] On Jura, pollen of cultivation weeds dating back 4,000–3,000 years has been found beside settlement remains, on land that had been broadleaved woodland and is now wet heath above thick peat.[41]

On the many eastern moors and woods that remained peat-free, archaeologists readily found stone-clearance heaps (Fig. 133) and enclosures from prehistoric farming. If you visit a site marked on a map as 'field systems' or 'settlements', you will see moorland or woodland, often treasured for its supposed wildness. However, 3,000 years ago the same scene would have been a hive of industry: many people summered here, living in circular huts (see Fig. 134) roofed by poles and thatch, growing crops, and tending cattle, sheep, goats and pigs.[42]

Later, from around 3,000 years ago (see Table 25, line 25), a wetter, windy climate with cool summers lasted for centuries, ending most cultivation of moorland before the birth of Christ. In a later warm period, a smaller expansion of cultivation peaked in the 1100s. Evidence of this can be seen in the plough ridges, enclosures and settlements on much moorland such as the Lammermuirs, well above the upper limit of fields since 1850.[43] These areas were subsequently abandoned in the cold, wet centuries of the Little Ice Age up to 1750, as moorland took over again.

After cultivated fields revert to woodland, the resultant vegetation differs from that in primary forest. These differences relate to changes in soil properties brought about by agriculture, which persist for at least three centuries and are perhaps almost irreversible.[44] In northern France, deforestation to make way for fields during the Roman occupation in AD50–250 was followed by abandonment

FIG 133. Stone clearance: boulders cleared from land in Glen Esk that was used for cultivation by prehistoric farmers more than 2,000 years ago. (Adam Watson)

FIG 134. Prehistoric hut circle, measuring 9m across, on heather moorland, Deeside. The stone circle, now overgrown by heather, was once the foundation of a hut made of wooden stakes (wattles), comprising a circular wall 1.8–2m high and a roof apex reaching 6m high.[42] The abandoned grass fields at lower altitude in the background were farmed in the 1800s. (Adam Watson)

and reversion to forest, yet the altered soil fertility and vegetation persist today.[45] Similar cases in other continents are becoming more widely known.[46] Cultivation also favours soil organisms that decompose plant litter, thus reducing the likelihood that an infertile acidic peat will form.[47]

We infer from this that ancient cultivation has boosted soil fertility and the nutritive value of food plants on much modern moorland and woodland, and thus increased the abundance of red grouse, blackgame and capercaillie today and in the recent past.

## HABITATS OF RED GROUSE

### Before deforestation

The former natural vegetation on most land that is now moorland would have been forest, with some open woodland and scrub, and bogs too wet for woodland to develop. It would have reverted to forest after lightning fires or wind-throw.

To judge from the more natural conditions found in other parts of the species' range, the main habitats of *Lagopus lagopus* before deforestation in Britain and Ireland would have occurred on a belt of heath[48] between the timberline and the Alpine zone. In addition, they would have been found on exposed coasts, forest bogs, and in forest after fire or wind-throw kept the land open for several years until regenerating new tree canopies closed overhead. Today, densities of red grouse increase in plantations established on moorland[49] and in naturally regenerating woodland, until canopy closure. After deforestation, their range and abundance would have soared at the expense of woodland grouse, especially capercaillie.

### Types of moorland

Heather dominates most moorland, hence the term heather moorland. Heather moorland with much blaeberry occurs almost entirely in the zone of former forest. That forest would have had a blaeberry-rich understorey, holding a smaller proportion of heather than on most of the heather moorland that replaced it.[50] Heather with blaeberry is the main vegetation in the north Pennines and high ground in North Yorkshire.[51] In Wales, it shares dominance with a blaeberry-grass mixture that occurs more locally in Scotland and signifies less heather as a result of overgrazing.[52]

Peatland is moorland with thick peat, usually defined as at least 30cm of organic matter above the mineral soil (*see* Fig. 130). It forms the chief land type in the far north and northwest of Scotland and in northwest Ireland, as well as in substantial areas elsewhere in Britain and Ireland. One variety of peatland, called blanket bog because it blankets the landscape across slopes and flat ground, has very thick wet peat and vegetation with sparse heather. Another, called raised bog, develops as a dome on lowland basins, its heather-dominated vegetation signifying a drier climate. Peatland differs from heather moorland because it receives more water than can drain away.[53]

The main vegetation on peatland is wet heath, dominated by sedge, rush and moss. On gentle slopes where the peat is over 1m thick, deergrass and cotton-grass predominate, whereas on the wettest flat bogs the cross-leaved heath and *Sphagnum* moss take over.[54] Heather grows sparsely on peatland, with a greater abundance on slopes than on flat bog. One seldom sees blaeberry, but crowberry thrives on peaty hummocks and slopes.

Heavier rainfall accounts for the key regional difference between wet heath in the west and heather moorland in the east. Relief, however, imposes local variation, so that even in the far west we find heather moorland on steep slopes, hillocks and ridges. And in the east, despite its low rainfall, wet heath occurs on very poorly drained basins, and on gentle slopes below groundwater springs. Wet heath also covers much flat, thick peat in east Sutherland and Caithness, where it is locally called 'flow'.[55]

## How natural is moorland?

The moorland that replaced natural forest has what botanists call 'semi-natural' vegetation. Although this comprises the same species that grow under old pinewood, their relative abundance differs greatly,[56] with far more heather. Hence deforestation increases heather, and muirburn tends to favour heather even more, because plants of this group withstand fire better than some other species. Because muirburn prevents natural succession to the climax woodland,[57] heather moorland is a man-induced 'fire climax'. Where burning ceases or declines greatly, trees and scrub soon colonise. One reason for muirburn is that young heather regenerating after fire provides a more nutritious bite for farm stock. Another unnatural feature of moorland since the late 1800s has been muirburn carried out in small patches to increase numbers of red grouse. Standards of muirburn on grouse moors have declined more recently, involving bigger burnt patches or fire rotations that are too short in some places and too long in others.[58]

Almost all moorland is burned more frequently than the occasional sporadic fire caused by lightning in 'wilderness' (land affected primarily by natural forces). Also, except in rare cases where they are fenced out, farm animals or red deer occur at higher densities than large wild mammals in wilderness. Foxes and crows thrive on human-induced extra carcasses of sheep and deer, and on road-kills, feed for farm animals, and waste in rubbish dumps. Now unnaturally common, they are unnaturally serious predators.

Declines in heather-dominated land, associated with overgrazing, began before 1750 in north Wales and Galloway.[59] In 1850–1900 the declines spread in Wales, Scotland and Ireland, and they have continued ever since. Overgrazing favours grasses, sedges and rushes, because the growing point of these plants is at the very bottom of the stem and stays undamaged if an animal eats the shoot tip. In contrast, the growing point on heath, trees and scrub is at the tip, the first piece to be eaten.

A striking feature on otherwise treeless wet heath is that trees and scrub abound on islets, large boulders, cliff ledges, stream gullies and ravines – in other words, places inaccessible to sheep and deer.[60] This raises the idea that grazing may have caused treeless wet heath. However, other factors occur besides grazing. First, sites where trees grow beside wet heath suffer no muirburn. Also, tree establishment would be favoured in the inaccessible sites because soils there are freely draining, owing to rapid run-off over rock lying close to the surface or to steep slopes. Moreover, steep slopes in areas of wet heath have fertile colluvial soils, which are good for tree establishment. The nearby wet heath differs radically, because its poorly drained wet peat is hostile to tree establishment.[61] Much wet heath would probably remain as such, therefore, even if its present unnaturally high levels of burning and grazing were to cease.

**Sustainability of current use of moorland**

Some believe that moorland degrades soil fertility, and that such deterioration began first in the west. Declines in bags of red grouse during the twentieth century usually came earlier in western regions of Scotland and Ireland, and declines in the land's carrying capacity for sheep and in its 'lambing percentage' (number born per 100 ewes) also occurred there.[62] It has been claimed that burning and overgrazing exhaust soil, that nutrients are lost as sheep and cattle carcasses are exported to lowland areas,[63] and that nutrients in rain may be insufficient to replace these losses.[64]

This was studied at Moorhouse, a largely peaty grouse-moor in Cumbria, by finding whether nutrient inputs from precipitation matched outputs in streams.[65] Inputs exceeded outputs, except possibly for phosphorus, a nutrient that is usually limiting for plant and animal nutrition on peatland, so any net loss of it could be critical.[66] The estimated inputs of nutrients were probably too low, however, for they excluded the large amounts in fog, rime, and dry aerial deposition,[67] in flushes from groundwater flowing across rock and through subsoil, and in the accretion of fresh soil from rock weathering. Also, sheep-ranching on Moorhouse did not reduce soil fertility in experiments lasting 11–31 years.[68] On the other hand, muirburn on grouse-moors involves small, relatively low-temperature fires, whereas large, hot fires entail bigger losses of nutrients.[69] Hence the frequently hot, large, short-rotation fires that typify western sheep-walks would entail greater nutrient losses. The question remains open.

Declines in lambing percentage and carrying capacity for sheep might be explained by climate change, as has been suggested for grouse bags (*see* Chapters

3 and 14), especially an increasingly wet climate in the west.[70] Another explanation is vegetation change caused by overgrazing, resulting in less heather and more bracken, and on sheep-walks a spread of unpalatable grass, sedge and rush. Yet another might be a lack of gamekeepers or shepherds.

Another possibility for these declines is that soil erosion exceeds the formation of new soil. On eastern grouse-moors, where most fires are narrow and where sheep, cattle or deer occur usually at low density, we regard soil erosion as immaterial, with the important exception of peat hags. In western and northern parts of Scotland and Ireland, however, where shepherds burn wide fires every few years, sheep at high density have bared much ground and eroded the peat,[71] and during severe downpours we see run-off that is heavily charged with peat and mineral soil. An eventual decline in grouse food on such areas seems likely.

To sum up, the area of heather moor in Britain and Ireland first increased as a result of deforestation, long before the Roman invasion, and in the last few centuries has decreased owing to overgrazing and other human factors such as tree-planting and reclamation to agricultural grassland (see Table 25, lines 32–33). Whether the remaining area now supports lower densities of grouse because of human-induced declines in fertility is moot. This is less likely on grouse-moors than on heavily burnt overgrazed sheep-walks above very poor soils, where much soil can be lost by erosion.

## HABITATS OF ROCK PTARMIGAN

Internationally, the montane zone is the belt of coniferous woodland on mountains, below the subalpine zone's stunted trees and the treeless Alpine zone higher up.[72] The Alpine zone is home to Scottish ptarmigan. Here, glaciers during the last ice age gouged out corries and left ice-smoothed rock that was later shattered by intense frost to become boulder fields, and melt-water channels eroded the bedrock and boulders. These landforms affect ptarmigan abundance by providing cover, as well as habitats for blaeberry, a favoured food plant.

Alpine soils vary more than those on moorland or woodland, because of the greater variety of topography, climate and snow-lie. On fairly steep slopes, colluviation keeps soils fertile. Springs that shed groundwater have moss-dominated vegetation, which supports many insects eaten by chicks (Fig. 136), while the large expanses of freely drained soils favour the heath that comprises the adults' main food plants. Also, churning by frost prevents the development of induration in the upper soil layers, thus maintaining free drainage. Heath dominates the dry, eastern Scottish hills, but it and ptarmigan also abound in the

FIG 136. Herb-rich subalpine flush, amongst short, wind-clipped heather, Cairnwell hills. (Stuart Rae)

wet west on ground where bedrock lies near the surface, providing rapid run-off and freely drained soil.

Largely prostrate vegetation creeps along the windswept ground, and exposed places have patches of bare, scoured soil. Plants grow slowly here, and much of the annual increment dies back from the effects of wind and weather, so the vegetation stays at virtually the same height over the years. Many moorland species grow in the Alpine zone, including abundant heather on the lower half of it, but the few muirburn fires that extend up from the moorland peter out quickly because there is too little fuel and much bare ground here. Heather-dominated vegetation extends to higher altitudes on exposed ridges, and luxuriant crowberry grows among stable large boulders. Blaeberry dominates colluvial slopes with small boulders, and also hollows that hold snow until late spring. Though scarce on boulder fields and among heather, ptarmigan abound on luxuriant crowberry and, especially, on blaeberry.

Snow can fall in any month in the Alpine zone, and in cold winters there may be no thaw for months, although thaws reach the highest summits occasionally in most winter months. Because wind almost always accompanies heavy snowfalls, exposed ridges remain largely snow-free, while blown snow gathers in hollows. In snow-free periods, gales blast surface grit and pebbles through the air, ripping out vegetation. Fog often prevails, and during frost the tiny fog droplets freeze into thick, hard crystals of rime on windward surfaces. Hoar frost from frozen water vapour sometimes covers all surfaces more loosely.

In shallow hollows, deep snow lasting until June prevents frost-churning of soil, the shelter reduces abrasion of plants by wind, and irrigation by melt-water induces more plant growth in dry weather. As a result, a thick topsoil develops here, with little bare ground. Mat grass dominates the vegetation, providing easy walking for people but unfavourable for ptarmigan. It contains hardly any heath plants for food, and a ptarmigan that stands on it appears conspicuous to predators because of the uniform background.

In deeper hollows, snow lies so long that it drastically shortens the growing season, so that plants are dotted sparsely on bare gravel. Soil below long-lying snow is more fertile than usual for that parent material, owing to extra inputs of nutrients from invertebrates stranded on the snow and from wind-blown plant debris and aerial dust. Droughts do not limit plant growth here, provided that some snow remains as a source for irrigation.

Snow delays the onset of plant growth. Near the edge of melting snow patches, plants start growth long after those on snow-free ground have passed this stage and become fibrous. Like a prolonged spring season, this changing band lasts for weeks, allowing plants that are newly freed from winter's grip to start fresh, nutritious growth. Ptarmigan favour these places in mid- and late summer.

Although far more natural than moorland, the Alpine zone has been damaged by sheep and deer, resulting in less heath and more grass on many hills, especially the base-rich ones.[73] Only high Scottish hills over infertile acidic rock, which are hence less attractive to sheep and deer, still have near-natural Alpine vegetation.

## HABITATS OF BLACK GROUSE

The more natural conditions found in Scandinavia and Russia offer clues as to the original habitats of British blackgame. These would have been forest-steppe (probably the best habitat according to the literature), scrub regenerating after fire or wind-throw, open bogs that are too wet for trees, and scrub above the timberline and on exposed coasts. Blackgame favour the broadleaved scrub that regenerates first after fires in boreal forest. Willow ptarmigan in Sweden colonise ground soon after fires or clear-cutting, whereas black grouse come later, at the stage when scrub or young copses have grown.

Blackgame do well in ancient native pinewood with glades of open ground that are maintained by grazing sheep, deer, cattle or horses. Birds are found in such areas at all seasons, though in autumn they often leave to eat berries on nearby moorland, and in spring to crop the shoots of cotton-grass. Their numbers increase in coniferous woods planted on moorland,[74] gradually declining as the tree canopy closes, although foresters in recent decades have reduced or eliminated the essential heath understorey and so discouraged blackgame.

In a few valleys, blackgame live mainly on moorland, although they visit nearby pines, birches and other trees to feed, especially in deep snow. They favour edges between moorland and farmland, especially where copses or scrub provide buds, catkins, leaves and berries as food. Much of the freely drained lower moorland beside modern fields carries the remains of field systems from prehistoric cultivation, which would have improved soils and the nutritive value of today's vegetation. Nearby peat-bogs hold cotton-grass, whose shoots afford good food
in spring. Grazed fields provide good sites for leks, as well as early growing weeds for a nutritious bite in spring.

Greyhens select dense, mature heather or rushes for nest sites, far taller than vegetation used by nesting red grouse and very well hidden from above. Overgrazing by sheep, cattle or deer, or too much burning or scrub removal, eliminates this valuable cover.[75] Hens with small chicks strongly favour groundwater flushes with tall rushes or grass, along with some short herbs. Here, the continuous flow of nutrient-rich water prevents development of the soil to a podzol, instead inducing a fertile young soil with abundant invertebrates for chicks.

## HABITATS OF CAPERCAILLIE

Capercaillie would have occupied a large area when pinewood reached its maximum extent (*see* Table 25, line 15). Scots pine with some birch formerly covered much of Ireland and Scotland, especially in the west and centre, and in Scotland eastwards to lower Deeside. It also dominated parts of England and Wales that have infertile, freely drained soils. By the 1700s, almost all pinewood had gone in England, Wales and Ireland, and loggers clear-felled most of Scotland's remnants. Prolific natural regeneration of 'young firs' (Scots pines) usually followed in Scotland, because deer were absent or scarce, and landowners planted many pines. These came too late for capercaillie, however, which need trees several decades old.

Pinewood with much blaeberry is the best habitat for this species (see Chapter 6). Several types of pinewood vegetation have been recognised in Norway and Britain, but the British classification is somewhat oversimplified.[76] A fresh attempt, with grouse habitats and soils in mind, would be useful.

Most soils under ancient pinewood in Scotland are unsuitable for farm crops because of very freely drained glacial deposits, steep slopes, flushes, thick peat, boulders or surface bedrock. Two of the biggest such woods, Abernethy and Rothiemurchus, lie on outwash sands and gravels from the great Spey glacier.[77] Although it has been asserted that the survival of Rothiemurchus wood testifies to its care by past generations,[78] in reality it is an accident of the last ice age, which left infertile soils unsuitable for cultivation.

## SUMMARY

The ways in which habitats have developed through geological processes, climate and human impact help to explain habitats today. Bedrock can have profound effects on natural soils, vegetation and grouse abundance. After the last ice age, warming led to the growth of Arctic vegetation and then to forest with scrub, before humans arrived. We discuss how grouse fared then, when rich habitats covered entire countries. Later, a wet climate caused deforestation and peat expansion in west Britain and Ireland, favouring red grouse at the expense of woodland grouse. Prehistoric farmers deforested most of the lowland, confining grouse to poor soils with moors or woods. Human deforestation on eastern upland created moorland pasture on poorly drained soil, and allowed cultivation of much freely drained soil. Most of the cultivated moorland was abandoned as the climate deteriorated, and became pasture. We infer that increased soil fertility from ancient cultivation still boosts the nutritive value of plants on much moorland and woodland today, and thus the local abundance of red grouse, blackgame and capercaillie. Freely drained moorland reverts to forest if humans stop burning and reduce overgrazing. Only acidic infertile Alpine land is nearly natural. Sheep have reduced heath on many base-rich hills, probably extirpating ptarmigan from south Scotland, England, Wales and Ireland.

CHAPTER 12

# Nutrition

BIRDS OF THE GROUSE family thrive for much of the year on abundant but coarse staple foods, which are fibrous and low in protein. This chapter explains how they cope by way of digestive and behavioural adaptations, but none the less depend upon seasonal foods of better quality. Weather and climate interact with nutrition to influence breeding success and numbers.

## COARSE DIET

Heather is a poor food. Domestic sheep and cattle lose weight on a diet of heather, needing grass to supplement it. Red grouse, on the other hand, thrive mostly on heather year-round, processing it with a lighter and apparently simpler digestive apparatus than the ponderous four-stomached ruminant gut. A 650g red grouse

FIG 137. Grouse feeding on a sward of heather. (David A. Gowans)

FIG 138. Grouse-eye view of heather shoots with flowers. (Robert Moss)

FIG 139. Capercaillie cock taking a snack of needles from a fallen pine branch after a morning at the lek. (Kevin Cuthbert)

eats about 130g of heather a day,[1] which would scale up to about 3.6kg or roughly 12 litres of heather shoots for a 65kg human being.[2] In winter, birds of the grouse family typically subsist on coarse, abundant plant foods that are low in nutrients, especially protein, phosphorus and sodium, and high in indigestible stuffs such as fibre, tannins and resins. The ground-dwelling red grouse and rock ptarmigan eat largely dwarf shrubs, heather being the staple food of red grouse, and heather, blaeberry and crowberry that of ptarmigan. The classic winter food of the arboreal capercaillie is Scots pine needles, but in Scotland they also eat much Sitka spruce where it is prevalent.[3] Black grouse have the most varied diet of the four British grouse, the majority feeding mainly on blaeberry and heather in winter. When snow covers the ground they take readily to trees, where they eat birch catkins, buds and twigs, or, where birch is scarce, Scots pine needles.

## THE MECHANICS OF DIGESTION

The grouse gut is structured like that of the familiar farmyard fowl, though proportioned differently. Both these gallinaceous birds have a food-storage organ, the crop, and both produce two distinct kinds of droppings. The grouse, however, is better at digesting coarse foods.

FIG 140. Red grouse flapping its wings after voiding a dropping. (David A. Gowans)

FIG. 141. Red grouse roost heap: shiny, viscous, chocolate-coloured caecal droppings lying on fibrous, cylindrical intestinal droppings with white caps of urine. (François Mougeot)

The main divisions of the gut (Fig. 142) include the oesophagus, the crop, the first stomach (proventriculus), the second stomach (gizzard or ventriculus), the long small intestine and caeca,[4] and the short colon.[5] The colon exits at the cloaca, which also receives urine from the kidneys via the ureters. Undigested food is stored in the crop, a capacious, elastic, expansible thin-walled sac, which is an outpocketing of the oesophagus and lies at the base of the neck. In daytime, the crop contains little food, but just before going to roost at night a grouse fills its crop almost to bursting, emptying it gradually while asleep.

Directly, or via the crop, food particles pass through the glandular proventriculus and into the gizzard, a large muscular organ lined with leathery ridges and filled with particles of grit (see Fig. 146) that act as teeth, grinding coarse food to a pulp. The pulp is eased through the small intestine by peristaltic contractions until, partly digested, it reaches the colon. At the start of the colon are side entrances to the two caeca (see Fig. 147), tubular blind guts of roughly the same diameter as the small intestine and colon. Their narrow neck-like entrances act as valves, regulating the flow of partly digested food into the main body of the caeca.[6]

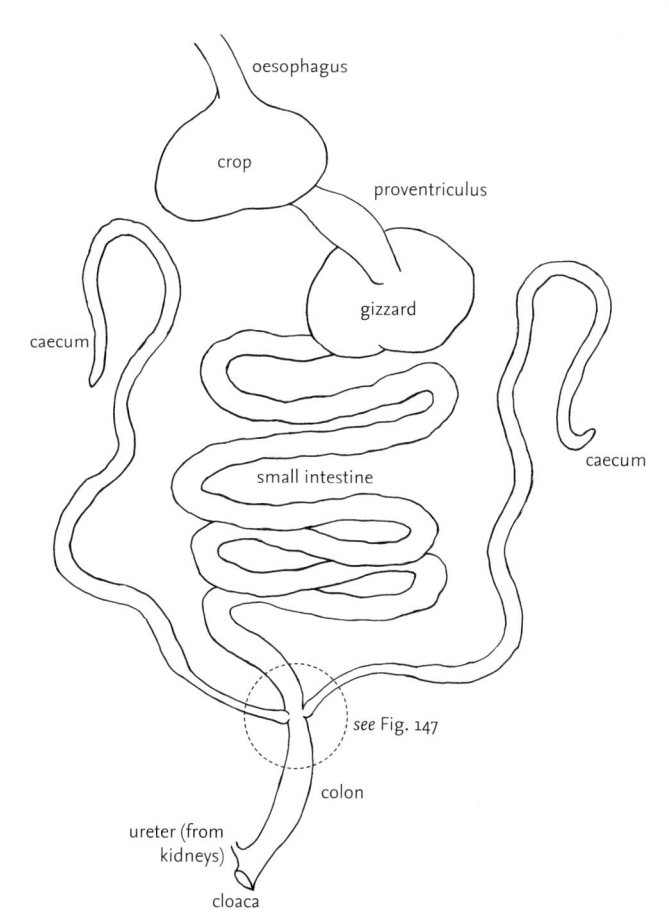

FIG 142.
The grouse gut. (Drawn by Dave Pullan)

FIG 143.
Hen ptarmigan eating sedge fruit, Svalbard. (Stuart Rae)

**FIG 144.** Ptarmigan chick eating heather shoot. (Stuart Rae)

The force behind this flow comes from reverse peristaltic contractions of the muscular colon, which push part of the urine backwards from the cloaca and into the caeca. The reverse flow of urine helps to wash fluid and small particles from the contents of the colon into the caeca, where they ferment. Larger, more fibrous particles are prevented from entering the caeca by the valve-like entrances.[7]

The more fibrous fraction of the partly digested food pulp bypasses the caeca, and goes direct from the small intestine through the colon to the cloaca, to be excreted as firm, fibrous, cylindrical droppings, often tipped with white caps of urine. Such intestinal droppings are voided frequently through day and night, and roost heaps of these show where a bird has spent the night. A nesting hen, however, avoids soiling her nest by storing intestinal droppings in her colon and excreting them two to five times a day as outsized clocker droppings while feeding away from the nest.

NUTRITION · 295

**FIG 145.** Heather particles from the crop of a wild red grouse, framed by heather shoots browsed more or less heavily by captive birds. (Robert Moss)

**FIG 146.** Grit from the gizzard of a red grouse (top right) and a blackcock (bottom), compared with commercial grit from Cornwall (top left) sold for spreading on grouse moors. (John Phillips.)

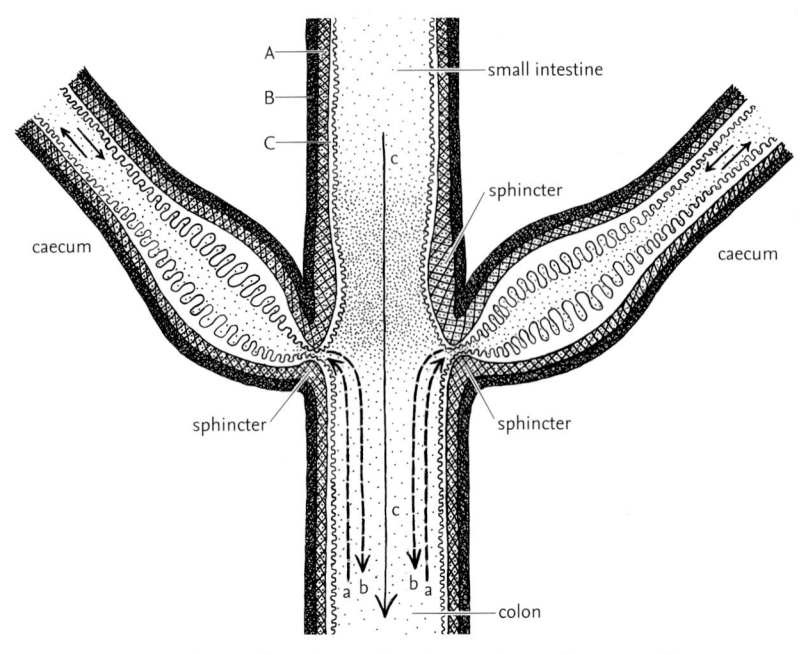

FIG 147. Diagram showing how digesta flows into and out of the caeca. The arrows indicate (a) the reverse flow of urine from the cloaca through the colon into the caeca, when the intestinal sphincter is closed and the caecal ones are open; (b) emptying of the caeca, mostly at dawn, to produce caecal droppings; and (c) normal flow of digesta with open intestinal and closed caecal sphincters, giving rise to intestinal droppings. (Drawn by Dave Pullan)

**Key**
A, transverse muscle in gut wall
B, longitudinal muscle
C, gut lining with finger-like villi.

The main emptying of the caeca occurs once a day. Shortly after a bird wakes in the morning, it voids the six to eight soft, shapeless, semi-liquid caecal droppings that are typically found on, or close to, roost heaps. Caecal droppings, which are residues of the fermentation process that takes place in the caeca, are typically brownish yellow when first voided, but rapidly turn a darker brown as the surface weathers. Contrary to old keepers' tales, the caecal droppings of red grouse are not grouse diarrhoea, nor do they signify an outbreak of grouse disease.

FIG 148. Red grouse clocker dropping lying next to normal intestinal droppings and mountain hare droppings. (George Reid)

CAECAL FUNCTION

Small particles of fibre are fermented in the caeca. Plant fibre comprises cellulose that is more or less encrusted with lignin.[8] Cellulose from the thin walls of living plant cells, unadulterated with lignin, is ground to fragments in the gizzard, and small particles of it are easily fermented by microbes in the caeca.[9] In contrast, the structural cellulose of thick cell walls, especially if lignified, resists grinding in the gizzard. This includes, for example, the woody cores and outermost parts of bark from twigs, structural parts of stems and leaves, seed husks and berry seeds. Such stuff constitutes much of the fibre that passes undigested through the colon without entering the caeca.

None the less, some particles of lignified cellulose (lignocellulose) from such sources do enter the caeca. Lignin is usually found to be quite indigestible in mammals and birds, and, bound to cellulose, protects the latter from fermentation. But 'lignin' is a loosely characterised chemical entity, some fractions of which are more digestible than others. Wild red grouse that are eating heather excrete only about half as much lignin as they eat, apparently digesting an unusually large proportion.[10] Perhaps heather lignin differs chemically from the grass lignins usually studied, and may be more readily digested.

In chemical terms, lignin is easier to oxidise than to reduce. Lignin digestion requires oxygen,[11] which is generally in short supply in the reducing environment of the gut. Perhaps oxygen, dissolved in refluxing urine while it passes through the cloaca, is transported to the caeca.[12] If so, this could help to explain efficient digestion of lignin in grouse caeca. The possibility has not, however, been investigated.

The backwards flow of urine from the cloaca does more than wash small particles into the caeca, for it helps to retain water and to recycle scarce nutrients such as protein, phosphorus and sodium. The nitrogen compounds from refluxed urine are used by caecal microbes to make protein, and probably, as in ruminants, microbial protein is eventually broken down to its constituent amino acids and then absorbed by the birds.[13] Also, ammonium nitrogen from the urine is absorbed from the caeca and probably used to synthesise non-essential amino acids and protein.[14]

Many textbooks make the general claim that birds excrete uric acid as the main end-product of protein metabolism. When eating coarse foods that are low in protein, however, grouse excrete digested protein-nitrogen mostly as ammonium salts and rather little as uric acid.[15] Uric acid must be maintained in colloidal form in the urine to avoid crystallisation and consequent tissue damage.[16] The colloidal spheres contain protein, which would seem wasteful when this is in short supply. So instead of excreting uric acid, grouse apparently economise on protein by excreting ammonium salts instead.

## GUT SIZE AND FOOD DIGESTION

Birds on a coarse, natural diet have to eat large amounts. Also, the proportion of a coarse food that is digested depends upon the length of time it spends in the gut. Hence a bird's ability to subsist on coarse foods increases with the size of its gut. But birds must fly, which dictates that guts must be as small and as light as possible. Grouse achieve this by rapidly processing the more fibrous fraction of their food, while retaining, for leisurely fermentation in the caeca, the most nutritious part of the material that remains after digestion in the small intestine.

Gut size adapts to the coarseness of the diet.[17] Grouse eating highly digestible foods have relatively small gizzards and short, narrow guts. On somewhat coarser diets they digest enough food by eating more and by increasing the size of their gizzards. On yet coarser diets, the bulk of food they can process is restricted by the capacity of the gut.[18] As foods get coarser, the intestines and, especially, the caeca increase capacity and the microbes in the caeca change, thereby facilitating the fermentation of cellulose and the extraction of energy through the production of volatile fatty acids.[19] Grouse eat bulkier foods in winter than in summer, and their guts are then longer and more massive. The caeca are typically 20 per cent longer and weigh twice as much in winter as in summer.

Interestingly, annual changes in gut size can occur without the stimulus of a bulky winter diet. The guts of captive red grouse, fed ad lib on highly nutritious pellets, enlarged between summer and winter.[20] Rock ptarmigan begin to eat the winter buds of shrubs before the first lasting snowfall.[21] These kinds of evidence suggest that grouse have a seasonal cycle in gut length, a cycle that anticipates enforced seasonal changes in diet.

In captivity, grouse fed on grain-based diets have very short guts. The intestines and caeca of a stock of captive red grouse shortened generation by generation as the stock became further removed from its wild origins.[22] After two to three years in captivity, the length of the small intestines of these captive birds stabilised at about 70 per cent of that found in wild birds. The length of the caeca fell to about 50 per cent and was still decreasing after four years, when the experiment ended.

In the wild, the long guts of red grouse are presumably maintained by natural selection, and the wild population has enough genetic or epigenetic[23] variation to allow guts to shrink rapidly when the selective pressures imposed by their coarse diet of heather are removed.[24] No doubt other costly adaptations to coarse diets are similarly labile. If a population of grouse had been captive for as long as domestic fowl, it is likely that many of their adaptations to natural foods would have diminished or disappeared altogether.[25]

We can think of the guts of gallinaceous birds such as grouse as existing in two modes.[26] In low-fibre mode, the intake of food is small and is not limited by its sheer bulk, the intestines and caeca are short and do not vary in size with intake, and surgical removal of the caeca has little effect on the birds' ability to digest their food. In high-fibre mode, the bulk of coarse diets limits the birds' intake and, therefore, the intestines and caeca enlarge with the increasing intake, and the caeca are probably essential, although this has not been tested by surgical removal. Almost all physiological studies of caecal function in gallinaceous birds (mostly on domestic fowl but a few in captive grouse) have been carried out in low-fibre mode. The results of such studies cannot safely be extrapolated to birds in high-fibre mode.

A bird can better digest coarser foods if it has more capacious guts and associated adaptations. Hence the proportion of a food that is digested – its 'digestibility'[27] – is as much a property of the bird as of the food itself. A natural winter food such as heather is typically 40–50 per cent digestible in wild red grouse with long guts, but only 20–30 per cent in captive birds with the short guts that come from a relatively concentrated artificial diet.[28]

The digestibility of natural foods varies widely with season. New-grown shoots of summer heather, for example, are about 80 per cent digestible to captive red grouse. Tables of the digestibility of staple agricultural foods are widely used to calculate the digestibility and metabolisable energy content of compounded diets produced in pellet form for domestic animals. For wild animals eating natural foods, however, an attempt to produce similar digestibility tables would be a will-o'-the-wisp.

Natural variations in gut size can be used to make inferences about natural variations in diet. In Alaska, individual rock ptarmigan eating more berries – a preferred and readily digested food rich in soluble carbohydrate (sugars and starch) – had shorter caeca than other birds in the same flock.[29] Such evidence suggests that individual differences in diet persist long enough to influence caecal length. Evidence from several grouse species, including rock ptarmigan, shows that the more dominant sex and age classes have shorter intestines and caeca, indicating that they use their status to get preferred foods.[30] This may be relevant to observations that grouse of different sexes or ages sometimes use different habitats in winter.

## BEYOND DIGESTIBILITY – PLANT TOXINS

Birds raised in captivity on digestible grain-based diets lose weight when given natural fodder without a period of adaptation. For coarse winter foods, it is tempting to attribute this simply to the ill-adapted captives' poor digestive abilities. Captive red grouse, however, lose weight even when fed highly digestible summer heather or blaeberry. The paradoxical evidence suggests that the new growth of their main natural food is toxic to red grouse.

Captive red grouse given fresh, newly grown shoots of either heather or blaeberry digested 70–80 per cent of each.[31] Surprisingly, they lost weight rapidly, despite eating large amounts. The problem of weight loss was circumvented by giving the birds diets composed partly of either heather or blaeberry, and partly of standard maintenance pellets, which were 52 per cent digestible when given alone. The digestibilities of diets with small proportions of natural foods exceeded 52 per cent (Fig. 149), as expected. But, paradoxically, as the proportions of natural foods increased, so the mixed diets became less digestible, until, in some cases, they were less well digested than pellets alone. The birds lost little or

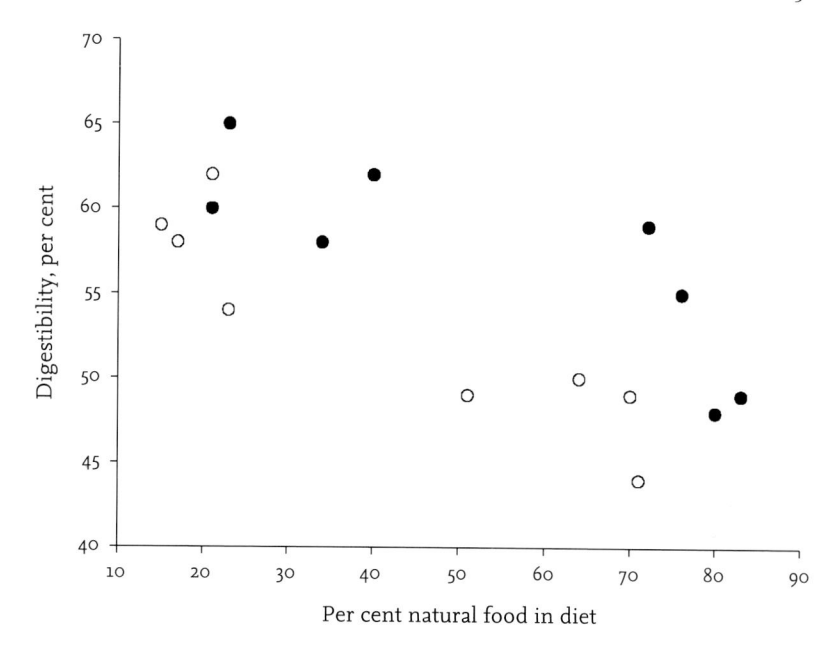

FIG 149. Digestion by captive red grouse of diets with various proportions of natural summer foods (heather ● and blaeberry ○) and artificial maintenance pellets. Paradoxically, the digestibility (percentage of dry matter) decreased as the proportions of natural foods increased, even though the digestibility of natural foods (80 per cent in heather and 74 per cent in blaeberry) exceeded that of maintenance pellets (52 per cent).[32]

no weight during these trials, and so the maintenance pellets had counteracted the toxic effect of new growth, while the new growth inhibited digestion of the mixed diets.

The captive birds compensated for the lower digestibility of heather-rich diets by eating more of them (see Fig. 150). They hardly did so, however, with the equivalent blaeberry-rich ones. This suggests that they were better adapted to heather than to blaeberry, and is consistent with wild red grouse eating much more heather than blaeberry, even where the latter abounds.

These results, evidently the tip of an uncharted metabolic iceberg, indicate that the chemical defences of plants against grouse involve digestion-inhibiting toxins. Wild birds are adapted to nullify plant defences, but captives seem to lose some of these abilities. Adaptations lost so readily are evidently facultative, and probably physiologically costly.[33] Also, the chemical defences of different plant species differ from each other. Hence the adaptations of different grouse species

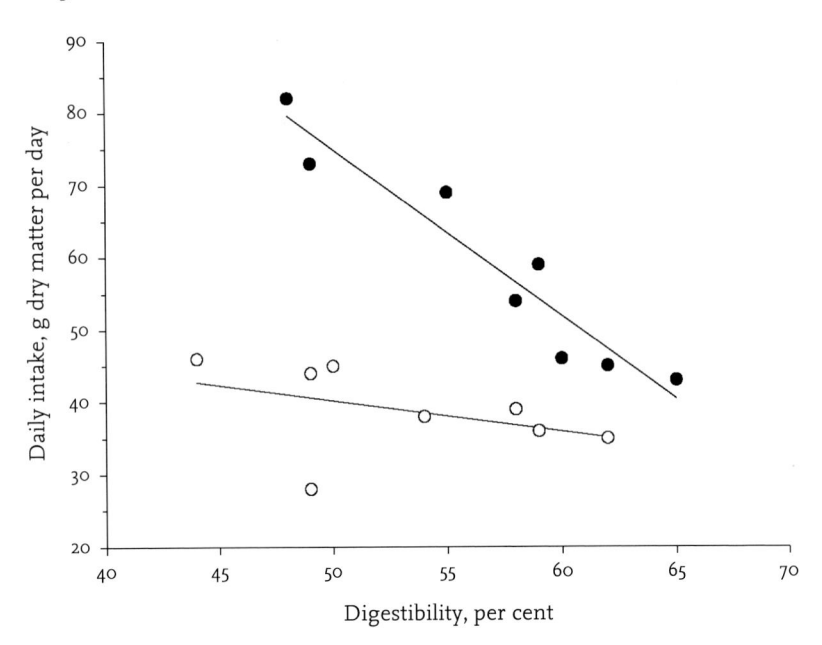

**FIG 150.** Daily intake by captive red grouse of diets with various proportions of natural summer foods (heather ● and blaeberry ○) in relation to their digestibility. They ate more food as its digestibility declined, obviously so with the heather diets but barely for the blaeberry ones.

should also differ from each other, which in principle helps to explain their different food preferences. This topic is largely unexplored.

## PLANT DEFENCES AND PROTEIN ECONOMIES

There is a vast scientific literature on plant defences against herbivores, and on how herbivores overcome these defences at physiological costs to themselves, often couched in terms of an evolutionary arms race. The topic has been little studied in grouse, but a winter diet of dwarf shrubs or conifer needles seems to make it difficult for the birds to get enough protein for their needs.

Polyphenols are the most widespread plant defence against herbivores. These include lignins, which inhibit digestion of the cellulose in plant cell walls (*see* 'Caecal Function', above), and tannins, which inhibit digestion of protein. Together, these polyphenols make up about a third of the dry weight of heather shoots in winter. During the course of digestion, red grouse absorb toxic phenolic molecules and detoxify their main breakdown product, benzoic acid, by conjugation with the amino acids ornithine and glycine, secreting the resultant conjugates into their urine.[34]

Conifer needles rely for defence partly on coarse fibre, but also on terpenes and other resinous compounds. The end result is comparable with red grouse eating heather, for blue grouse eating conifer needles in North America excrete the same amino acid conjugates.[35] The nitrogen costs of detoxification to red grouse on a diet of heather and to blue grouse eating conifer needles seem similar, accounting for up to a quarter of the nitrogen in their food.

Protein nitrogen is in short supply in winter fodder and a quarter seems a large metabolic cost. Ornithine and glycine, however, are non-essential amino acids, which can probably be synthesised from urine nitrogen that is refluxed into the caeca and absorbed by the birds as ammonium ions. If so, detoxification of the harmful products created from the digestion of polyphenols and resins might use recycled, non-essential nitrogen, and so be less costly than it seems.

## FOOD SELECTION

Metabolic adaptations are one way of coping with coarse or toxic foods. Another method adopted by grouse is selecting what they eat, the strength of selection varying with a bird's physiological state, the season and the time of day.[36] Selection can be seen as a hierarchical process. At the basic level, a grouse chooses to eat certain plant species – for example, capercaillie prefer Scots pine to Norway spruce. Within the chosen species, it prefers particular individual plants, and thus arboreal grouse typically use certain individual trees heavily, but others of the same species little or not at all. And within the chosen plant, a bird prefers particular structures – for instance, a black grouse in a birch tree prefers catkins to twigs. If eating twigs or shoots, a bird decides whether to peck small, delicate morsels from the tips or to take bigger, coarser portions.

Birds pack their crops with food before going to roost at night. They are pressed for time and hence less selective than earlier in the day. Thus, red grouse get better food during the day by feeding more slowly and taking smaller particles of heather than at dusk.[37] Similarly, during relatively mild days in the Arctic winter, willow ptarmigan in northeast Asia feed slowly as they walk through shrub willows or dwarf birches.[38] In the evenings or during periods of extreme frost, they browse in the crowns of bigger willow species, thereby getting coarser particles at a faster rate.

At least three other factors determine which plant species a bird decides to eat.[39] First, part for part, some species are more nutritious than others, having more nutrients, being more easily digested or being less toxic. Willow, for example, is generally more digestible, contains more protein and phosphorus, and is less heavily defended than birch. Again, berries are a much-favoured food because they contain high levels of soluble carbohydrate. But not all berries are equal. Blaeberries soon disappear from Scottish hillsides in autumn, but some crowberries remain uneaten until spring. This is because blaeberries are more digestible and contain more protein, phosphorus and soluble carbohydrate than crowberries. It is easy to identify with the birds' choice in this case, for to us blaeberries are sweeter and juicier than crowberries.

A second factor is that grouse species that live together tend to develop different dietary preferences. In Iceland, the rock ptarmigan is the sole naturally occurring vertebrate herbivore, and in winter it prefers willow to birch. In interior Alaska, the willow ptarmigan (the same species as red grouse) also prefers willow to birch, but in winter the rock ptarmigan eats much more birch than willow. Presumably the rock ptarmigan has adapted to birch in Alaska owing to competition from the bigger willow ptarmigan, which has won the better diet.

FIG 151. Blaeberries in autumn, after most leaves have fallen. (Robert Moss)

In Fennoscandia, willow ptarmigan again prefer willow to birch, but willow is less abundant here and so the birds eat mostly birch.[40] In Britain, scrub willow and birch have largely disappeared from moor and hill, and so red grouse must get by mostly on heather, while ptarmigan subsist largely on heather, blaeberry and crowberry.

A third factor determining a bird's dietary preferences is its adaptations. In Alaska, the rock ptarmigan has adapted to a winter diet of birch, and prefers birch to willow even when there are no willow ptarmigan nearby.[41] In autumn, however, rock ptarmigan occupy higher ground than willow ptarmigan and, secure from competition, eat willow and birch in proportion to their availability.

Grouse make much finer distinctions than crude categories such as 'willow' and 'birch' convey. The many species of willow and birch vary in size from dwarf shrubs to trees, and, within each species, the different parts of the plant vary in nutritive value. Birds generally take catkins of birch, for example, in preference to the less nutritious buds and twigs. They prefer blaeberries and crowberries to leaves and shoots of the same plants. When eating heather, they take the tips of shoots in preference to the less digestible, woodier parts.

Wild red grouse eat heather shoot tips that are more digestible, and richer in protein and phosphorus, than other tips of the same size picked nearby by humans attempting unsuccessfully to emulate the birds. Faced with a sward of heather, red grouse tend to feed on richer patches and, within patches, choose the more nutritious shoots, being more selective when feeding on poorer patches. They can identify patches of heather that have been experimentally fertilised to increase their protein content, and prefer these to unfertilised areas. Even in captivity, caged red grouse can distinguish bundles of fertilised from unfertilised heather, but eat more from the fertilised bundles only when breeding, growing or in poor condition.[42]

## FOOD ABUNDANCE

The staple foods of grouse are usually abundant and the birds eat a tiny proportion of them. One can hardly imagine red grouse devouring a noticeable proportion of the heather on a grouse-moor, for example, or capercaillie depleting a pinewood of its needles.

But the quality of different food items varies, the birds are selective feeders, and preferred foods can be in short supply. In the extremely cold winters of northeast Asia, for example, willow ptarmigan face a progressive depletion of their willow food during the winter, partly because mountain hares and moose

**FIG 152.** Willow (*Salix pulchra*) in Porcupine Creek, interior Alaska, during spring 1970. In April (top), when willow ptarmigan arrived on their snow-covered breeding grounds, these catkins were a favoured food. By the first few days of May (bottom), the birds had eaten all the available catkins, the only ones left being at the ends of long twigs out of reach. (Robert Moss)

use the same willow thickets. In one study,[43] birds in autumn ate fine willow twigs some 0.8–1.5mm in diameter. During winter, the twigs eaten became thicker and heavier. Finally, the remaining twigs were too thick for the willow ptarmigan to cut and so the birds turned to willow bark. This in itself is fairly nutritious, but eating it is laborious and, to avoid losing too much heat, birds had to return to their snow-holes before they had eaten enough. Consequently, they often lost weight, until the snow melted and better foods became available. Indeed, it seemed that a shortage of good-quality winter food could affect their condition in spring and so influence their breeding success in summer.

Crucial high-quality spring foods can also be in short supply, due perhaps to late growth or because a scarce food is overexploited. The newly growing shoots of cotton-grass, for example, are favoured by several species of grouse. In the basin of the Ilexa River near Archangel in Russia, they are eaten by capercaillie and also by small rodents, hares, moose, reindeer, bears, wolverines, cranes and other birds, and even pine martens. A shortage of cotton-grass shoots, it is argued,[44] could affect the quality of the capercaillie's diet and depress their breeding success. In Britain, sheep or deer also compete with red and black grouse, ptarmigan and capercaillie for cotton-grass shoots, perhaps with similar consequences.

FIG 153. Cotton-grass flowers. (Desmond Dugan)

If the best food is in short supply, an increase in grouse density might cause a decrease in diet quality. On Rickarton moor, for example, the proportion of digestible protein in the diet of breeding red grouse was lower in years of higher grouse density.[45] This might have been due to a shortage of cotton-grass shoots or of the most nutritious heather shoots.

Weather can also reduce the amount of food available to grouse. Winter snow often covers dwarf shrubs. This has little effect on capercaillie, which in winter eat mostly conifer needles, or on black grouse, which can use birch or pine trees. Red grouse and ptarmigan dig through loose snow, or more often move to windswept ridges where food plants protrude above the snow. Icy conditions, however, due to freezing rain or to the melting and refreezing of snow, can prevent birds from foraging. Such conditions are common on Svalbard, where rock ptarmigan carry unusual amounts of winter fat, so insuring themselves against starvation in icy periods. Occasionally, ice can prevent even arboreal grouse from feeding. In one example, freezing rain encapsulated the twigs of aspen, the main winter food of ruffed grouse, and many birds died.[46]

Heather thrives best in relatively mild, oceanic climates and is vulnerable to 'browning' in late winter and early spring. Browning occurs in weather that is normal in continental climates but less frequent in oceanic Britain, during which the ground freezes, the sun shines and humidity drops. Unless covered by a protective blanket of snow, heather plants faced with such conditions lose water from their leaves faster than they can replace it through their roots, and as a result their leaves turn brown and so become unappetising to grouse. Some heather damaged in this way recovers and some dies. Either way, the amount of food available to breeding grouse can be much reduced. For example, about three-quarters of the heather was damaged in this way at Rickarton moor in March 1985, and breeding success that summer was only 1.2 chicks per hen, the poorest observed during a ten-year study.[47] Much of the heather that survived this event undamaged was protected under patches of snow.

In the spring and early summer of 2003, much heather in northeast Scotland was damaged or killed by unusually dry conditions. At the same time, the largest outbreak of heather beetle in living memory was ravaging heather moors. This plague of pests began in the west of Scotland in 1997,[48] reached Speyside in 2003 and was still active in 2004. The outbreak caused much worry among landowners, but there is no reliable account of how much it influenced grouse numbers.

Browsing by domestic stock is a less natural form of damage to food plants. Such browsing of heather over winter can be so heavy that a good autumn stock of red grouse almost disappears by spring. Much heather may remain on the ground, but is too short to provide the birds with cover from predators. Food without cover is of little use to grouse and so, though present, becomes unavailable.

In brief, the staple foods of most grouse populations seem to be in large excess of the birds' requirements. High-quality foods that provide crucial supplements to the diet can, however, be in short supply. Also, occasional catastrophes can make much of the staple food unavailable. Such events might not occur in a short study lasting only a few years, thereby leading to incomplete conclusions about the importance of food abundance to grouse populations.

## NUTRITIONAL BOTTLENECK – SPRING HENS

In British conditions, the nutrient requirements of grouse are most critical twice a year: in spring, when hens lay eggs; and in summer, when the young chicks are growing fast. Hens put on weight before breeding, but reserves alone are insufficient for a clutch of eggs. Most of the energy and protein required for a clutch must come from the food eaten during the week or two of laying.

As the staple food plants begin to grow in spring, they become more digestible and richer in nutrients. Red grouse hens, however, begin to lay so early in the year that the shoots of their main heather food have barely started to swell at the tips. Hen and cock feed close together, she taking smaller pecks than him and so getting a higher proportion of new growth.[49] But this apparently is not enough, and hens seek other, earlier-growing foods.

Grouse generally supplement their spring diet with leaves of early growing herbs and other digestible, nutrient-rich plants. Ptarmigan on Scottish hilltops, for example, take spring leaves of common mouse-ear, heath bedstraw and sheep's sorrel. On lower land, red grouse, black grouse and capercaillie are attracted to boggy ground where they find new shoots of cotton-grass, while black grouse and capercaillie are seen in larch trees eating buds and flowers.

Spring growth can be erratic, starting with warm weather and checked by cold. During a check, the nutrient content of growing shoot tips can fall. Even when new growth looks unchanged, it may be less nutritious. It is therefore too simple to think that early springs provide good nutrition and late springs poor. A prolonged spring that starts early but is then checked can leave hens in poor condition. In one study, for example, breeding success in ptarmigan was related not to the date of first growth, but to the number of days of unchecked growth before the hens started laying.[50]

On the heather-dominated, dry, infertile, granitic grouse-moors of northeast Scotland, however, early growing herbs and cotton-grass are scarce and red

FIG 154. Greyhen in spring larch. (Desmond Dugan)

grouse resort to picking out the growing shoot tips of cross-leaved heath and bell heather.[51] This seems to be solely because these two plants begin to grow earlier than heather, for they contain less protein, phosphorus and soluble carbohydrates than heather, and at other seasons the birds largely ignore them. A greater proportion of the energy and nutrients in such new growth is presumably available to the birds than in the slower-growing heather. New growth also contains a hormone-like factor that stimulates egg-laying.[52]

The importance of newly growing plant material to the spring nutrition of red grouse and ptarmigan is well documented. They select such food out of proportion to its availability, and tend to rear more young when the spring flush is early, such that laying hens have had access to unchecked new growth for longer. Less work has been done on capercaillie and black grouse, but similar generalisations probably apply to them too.

A well-fed hen lays good-quality eggs, and these in turn hatch into vigorous chicks that survive well. This was discovered when clutches of red grouse and ptarmigan eggs were taken from the wild, and the chicks hatched and reared in standard conditions in captivity. Almost all chick mortality occurred in the first

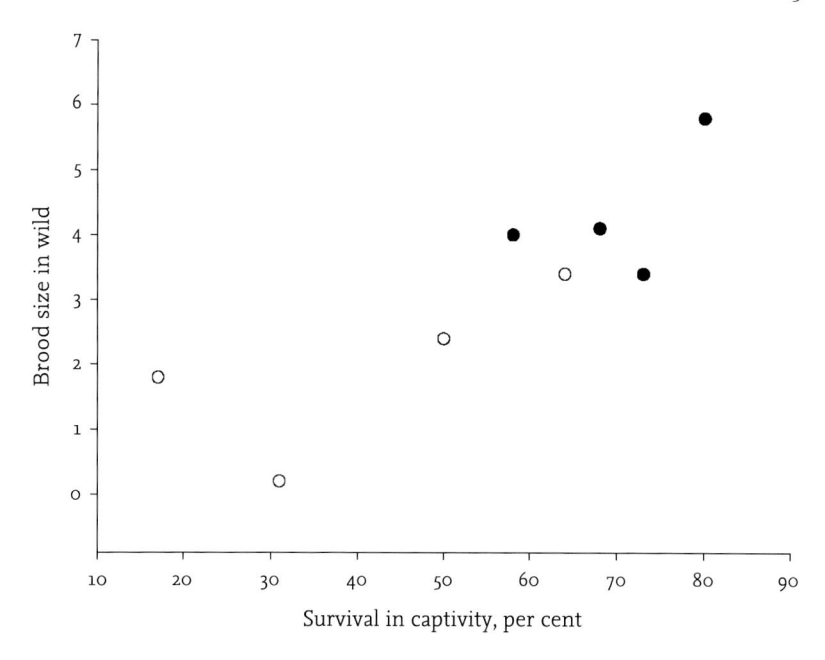

FIG 155. Brood size of wild rock ptarmigan in Scotland and the proportion reared in captivity from eggs taken in 1968–71 from a hill with base-rich soil (●, Cairnwell hills) and one with acidic soil (○, Derry Cairngorm).[53]

two weeks. Chicks hatching from the poorest clutches sometimes died within a few hours of hatching, well before the yolk sac was exhausted. The proportion that died varied markedly between years and study areas. The example given here (Fig. 155) is from ptarmigan. Breeding success in the wild populations, from which the eggs were taken, was also measured. Survival in captivity and in the wild varied together, and so it was inferred that both were determined by a common antecedent cause, namely egg quality.

The viability of ptarmigan chicks from the Cairnwell hills exceeded that of chicks from the Cairngorms. The Cairnwell soils, derived mainly from relatively base-rich schists and other base-rich rocks, were more fertile than the granitic Cairngorms soils, and the Cairnwell birds had a richer diet. It seems that the effect of bedrock upon soil fertility was reflected in the quality of the laying hens' diet, and that this in turn influenced the chicks' viability and the number of chicks reared per brood.

On the infertile granite, egg quality tended to be better in years when springs were early and the laying hens had longer access to unchecked new growth of their main foods, heather, blaeberry and crowberry. However, on the richer schists this relationship was not clear, possibly because the boost to nutrition provided by spring growth was less critical to hens already on a relatively rich diet. Of course, early growth of the birds' staple food plants might simply have indicated early springs, and other newly growing plants were probably an important part of their diet.

Well-fed hens lay better-quality eggs partly because they are in good condition. In Sweden, the diet of willow ptarmigan was found to be dominated by blaeberry, bog whortleberry and new shoots of cotton-grass.[54] The hens were in better condition and reared more young after earlier springs, when they had been eating more cotton-grass shoots, and the diet was consequently more digestible as well as richer in protein and phosphorus. The hens' condition in spring was also related to their condition in late winter, suggesting that winter circumstances might influence breeding success too.

Hens in good condition may also lay more eggs, but average clutch size varies little from year to year, and the main determinants of annual variations in breeding success are nest losses and chick mortality. A hen in poor condition is more likely to desert her nest,[55] but most nest losses are usually attributed to predation. Interestingly, a few studies and many anecdotes suggest that a hen's condition influences the chances of her nest being taken by a predator. Perhaps a hen in good condition sites it with greater care, is more thorough about covering her eggs with vegetation when leaving the nest after laying, sits tighter and so is less likely to reveal the nest to a passing fox, or is more wary of disclosing her nest to watching crows when leaving to feed.

As in many other birds, individual hens that begin to lay earlier in the year also lay larger clutches. This is something of a gamble. In good years, more eggs should result in more chicks. But in years when spring comes late, an early bird's diet can be insufficient to support good-quality eggs. In such years, red grouse chicks hatched from large early clutches can be unviable and die soon after hatching.[56]

### NUTRITIONAL BOTTLENECK – SUMMER CHICKS

Grouse chicks grow rapidly for about 12 weeks on a largely vegetable diet. Although summer plant foods are more varied and nutritious than winter ones, the chicks need a supplement of invertebrates for their first few weeks to provide them with protein and other nutrients. The chicks of bigger species have to grow faster and may need a larger supplement, although the evidence is confusing. For example, red grouse chicks can get by on a diet containing as little as 5 per cent of insect food,[57] typically the flightless crane-fly *Molophilus ater* and the larvae and nymphs of the spittle bug *Philaenus spumarius*. The diet of very young chicks of the same species (willow ptarmigan) in a study in northern Norway, however, comprised some 60 per cent insects, mostly caterpillars, bugs, aphids and flies.[58] None the less, capercaillie chicks seem to eat more invertebrates for longer than any other grouse species,[59] consistent with the idea that bigger and hence faster-growing species need more invertebrates.

It seems inevitable that year-to-year variations in the availability of invertebrates must affect chick survival. Good evidence to this effect is surprisingly scarce. Studies on red grouse and willow ptarmigan have shown that chicks grow faster when they have a greater proportion of invertebrates in their diet,[60] and that the slowest-growing broods survive poorly.[61] But no study has shown that the broods on a given area survive better in years when they eat a greater proportion of invertebrates.

Part of the answer to this puzzle is probably that the quality of plant food fluctuates from year to year, such that the chicks' need for invertebrates also varies. In addition, chicks may simply eat less food overall in years of poor survival, with no change in the proportion of animal food taken. Finally, invertebrates must vary in their value to growing chicks – a big juicy caterpillar is evidently more nutritious than a small dry beetle.

On the island of Tranøy in Norway, the summer of 1974 was warm and dry, but 1975 was cold and wet. In 1975, the chicks of willow ptarmigan spent less time foraging and avoided wet areas with dense vegetation. Sweep-netting for invertebrates on the ground revealed few differences between the years, and in each year the chicks' crops contained the same proportion of insects. In 1974, however, the chicks ate half as much food again as in 1975, and fed selectively on caterpillars (80 per cent of their insect food), which occurred in wet areas with dense vegetation. In 1975 they ate mainly smaller insects such as aphids and flies. From each brood, an average of four chicks survived in the summer of 1974, but only half a chick in 1975.[62]

In a Scottish study,[63] the breeding success of capercaillie was related more strongly to the size of the caterpillars available than to their abundance on the ground. In general, it seems that chick survival can be related to the qualities of the invertebrates available, that the most nutritious invertebrates can occur in particular habitats, and that accessibility of invertebrates in these habitats can be influenced by weather.

Over the years, we have watched and handled many ptarmigan, red grouse, black grouse and capercaillie chicks, leaving us with an anecdotal but definite impression. The smaller species are more vigorous, the larger more lethargic. On the ground, ptarmigan run about and forage more quickly than red grouse, which in turn are more active than black grouse, and these are more active than capercaillie. In the hand, all chicks have quiescent periods punctuated by bouts of struggling. Chicks of ptarmigan and red grouse tend to struggle most often and most vigorously, the other species less so, in order of size. At the same age, ptarmigan and red grouse chicks fly most strongly when flushed, capercaillie most weakly. Within a species, male capercaillie chicks have to reach twice the weight of females and so grow much faster. After their difference in size and plumage has become obvious, at about six weeks of age, males fly less readily than females and are more easily exhausted.

In short, chicks of the bigger species and the bigger sex grow faster, probably need more invertebrates in their early weeks, and seem to be less active. They may also have less energy for activities such as foraging and escaping from predators. It is as if chicks that devote more energy to growth have less for other activities.

These differences between species translate into broad differences in breeding success. Clutch size differs little between the four British grouse species,[64] but red grouse usually rear more chicks per brood than greyhens, and greyhens more than capercaillie. Scottish ptarmigan do not fit this pattern, but most of them live on poor soils and experience catastrophic weather, such as summer snowstorms, more often than the other three species.

Males, being bigger, must grow faster than females, and so, if chick survival is inversely related to growth rate, we expect a difference between sexes within species. Indeed, female black grouse and capercaillie chicks survive better than males. In clement years with good breeding success, roughly equal numbers of male and female chicks are reared. But, when times are hard and breeding success is poor, more females than males survive. Furthermore, the difference in survival is greater for capercaillie, in which the difference in size between sexes is greater.[65] Hence survival seems inversely related to growth rate, especially in hard times. The bigger, more lethargic chicks must find more food, especially invertebrates, to support their faster growth.

## NUTRITIONAL BOTTLENECKS – DOUBLE BIND

We have discussed how nutrition can affect breeding success, indirectly through the condition of laying hens in spring, and directly through the chicks' diet. In each case, available food is at its best for a short period. In spring, this is just as the hens' food plants begin to grow (*see* Chapter 6), and in summer it is when the invertebrates eaten by chicks are most abundant. Chicks thrive if they come from good-quality eggs and hatch when invertebrates are at their peak.

The number of days between the onset of egg-laying and chick hatching is more or less fixed. But the length of time between the onset of plant growth and peak invertebrate abundance is much more variable. Spring in Britain has advanced in recent decades and birds generally have been breeding earlier. If grouse lay earlier, the chicks might hatch too early to benefit from the peak of invertebrate abundance.[66] For capercaillie, there is evidence from the 1990s that moth larvae, their favoured insect food, pupated and became unavailable while the chicks were still relying on insects as a dietary supplement.[67] There is, however, no good evidence that this represented a change from earlier years, or that it reduced breeding success.

## NUTRITION AND DISTURBANCE

Disturbance is a topic of increasing importance in grouse conservation. Despite lack of firm evidence, it therefore seems useful to speculate about likely effects of disturbance upon grouse breeding success and survival. In the wild, grouse chicks generally grow more slowly than in captivity and, in some studies of wild grouse, growth rate has varied in relation to invertebrate abundance. It seems likely that continued disturbance will affect the chicks' ability to forage, especially for invertebrates, and that this might slow their growth to a point where it imperils survival.[68] This seems particularly likely in faster-growing chicks of bigger species, notably capercaillie, for these are intrinsically more sluggish and depend more heavily upon invertebrates.

The grouse family probably evolved in response to global cooling and occupied the newly created niche for a large bird that could subsist on coarse foods through long winters (*see* Chapter 1). Days are short in winter and the time available for foraging correspondingly limited. Grouse minimise the amount of food they must gather and digest by resting for much of the day, often in snowholes.[69] Disturbed birds must eat more food to compensate for the energy used in flight and, with increasing disturbance, there must come a point where they simply cannot get and digest enough food to maintain the fire of life. If so, the amount of disturbance they can tolerate without succumbing to slow starvation may well be limited. Such an effect is likely to be more critical in bigger birds, especially the capercaillie, which are more cumbersome and expend more effort when taking flight.

## SUMMARY

Grouse subsist over the winter on plant foods that are abundant, but coarse, fibrous and low in protein. Their adaptations include well-developed caeca, in which they digest fibre and conserve protein by recycling urine. They are also selective about what they eat, choosing a good-quality diet from the food available. Food shortages in winter, due to browsing by larger herbivores or to catastrophic weather, can reduce the birds' survival and breeding success. Even so, effects of diet upon survival and reproduction are more commonly seen in laying hens and growing chicks. Hens supplement their spring diet with early growing nutritious vegetation. When this is not available, as in late springs, they get into poor condition and lay deficient eggs that hatch into less viable chicks. Young chicks depend upon a supplement of invertebrates for a few weeks after they hatch. If they cannot get enough, as in wet weather, they grow more slowly or die.

CHAPTER 13

# Enemies

PREDATORS, PARASITES AND DISEASES are topical issues in grouse management. British and Irish grouse face these enemies on land that has been greatly modified by humans. While we fashioned moors that benefited red grouse, we deprived our other three grouse species of much natural habitat and altered the set of enemies with which all four must now contend. Some natural enemies have been reduced or exterminated, some have increased, and new ones have been introduced.

## PREDATORS OF GROUSE

In Britain and Ireland, the natural balance between predators and prey is distorted. To understand the consequences of this, we revisit principles of predator-prey relationships and compare our situation with more natural ecosystems. Academic students of predator-prey relationships use confusing jargon but the underlying ideas are simple. We also discuss an ethical basis for the killing of predators.

### Some principles of predator-prey relationships

Predators and prey evolved together. From the shifting tricks of mutual survival emerge patterns that ecologists call rules. A good rule of thumb from island biogeography is that larger land masses support more species. Ireland now has only one grouse species while Britain has four, fewer than in Europe. Our grouse also have fewer predator species.

Two shibboleths attend academic discussions on predators and prey. First, the impact of a predator species upon the abundance of its prey depends partly upon the ratio of predator to prey. Changes in this ratio, due to the predator's reproduction, death or movement, are called the predator's 'numerical response'. Second, the impact on the prey depends also upon the proportion of that prey in the predator's diet. Changes in this proportion are termed the predator's 'functional response'.

Grouse populations can be cropped by predators, because prey populations can compensate for losses. When some grouse are killed, others live longer or rear bigger broods. If survival or reproduction fully compensates for deaths, the impact of predation upon prey numbers is negligible, and the ratio between predator and prey remains unchanged.[1] If deaths are wholly or partially additive,[2] the predator-prey ratio can increase, until the predators starve or leave the area (numerical response) or turn to other prey (functional response).

Grouse avoid predators by taking cover. In summer, a cryptically coloured rock ptarmigan hides from gyrfalcons by sidling up to a rock of its own colour and freezing next to it. A willow ptarmigan escapes a goshawk by diving under a bush, into which the hawk, clumsy-footed and fearing for its delicate wings, dares not venture. Red grouse prefer feeding on short heather but usually keep close to tall heather, where they take cover when a raptor approaches. Hill shepherds, especially in western Scotland and Ireland, often burn large tracts of heather every few years to give sheep better food, but incidentally reduce stocks of red grouse by depriving the birds of cover in tall heather. Similarly, wind-thrown trees in plantations provide cover for capercaillie and black grouse, but are commonly removed by tidy-minded foresters.

Another way of avoiding predators is shown by rock ptarmigan in the Cairngorms. They live on large, infertile tracts where prey such as rodents, hares and birds are few, and hence predators, mainly foxes and golden eagles, are scarce. Enriching such infertile ground, however, destroys its value as a refuge from predators, as illustrated by the ski development at Cairn Gorm. Here, tourists' food scraps attracted carrion crows and gulls, generalist predators alien to this habitat but common on lower ground nearby.[3]

Grouse also live on richer soils where there are more rodents and other prey that in turn support more predators (numerical response) than in the Cairngorms. In such dangerous conditions, avoidance of predators involves a third consideration. If grouse have good cover and are scarce relative to other prey, they can survive because predators concentrate on the other prey (functional response). Thus, foxes and pine martens depend largely upon small rodents, the main biomass in many grouse habitats.[4]

Predators such as hen harriers and goshawks often move far in response to variations in prey abundance. The idea that prey move to reduce their risk of being eaten is less well established. Borchtchevski,[5] however, proposed that capercaillie densities in the Ilexa River basin in northern Russia were regulated by emigration and immigration, even though predation accounted for almost all their deaths. By moving, he suggested, birds kept their densities low enough to keep residents relatively safe from predation.[6]

The conclusion that a natural balance between grouse and their predators can depend upon large tracts of uninterrupted habitat has practical consequences. More predators from richer habitats can encroach upon woodland or moors fragmented by developments. Grouse habitat worldwide is increasingly fragmented and enriched by agriculture, by planting and fertilising trees, or by tourist developments, leading to more grassy vegetation, more prey such as rodents or rabbits and, in the case of tourist developments, more food scraps. In Britain and Ireland, all this has led to a perceived need to kill predators.

The distinction between predator and prey is not clear-cut. Grouse chicks eat caterpillars and so grouse are predators of moths and sawflies. Also, smaller predators often fall prey to bigger ones. Ecologists call this 'intra-guild' predation. Thus, lynxes eat foxes, and foxes eat pine martens. Golden eagles kill foxes, pine martens, stoats, weasels, buzzards, hen harriers and crows.[7] In semi-natural ecosystems that retain their top predators, smaller predators are often scarcer than in disturbed habitats, probably because smaller predators are displaced or eaten by bigger ones.[8] Thus increases in goshawks, or declines in their preferred prey, have been associated with local extirpations of kestrels, sparrowhawks and long-eared owls.[9]

When bigger predators are removed, smaller predators often increase, a process termed 'meso-predator release'.[10] A general observation is that foxes are more abundant where lynxes and wolves have been exterminated. Without wolves and lynxes, foxes often become the dominant mammalian predator. When sarcoptic mange suppressed foxes in Fennoscandia, pine martens increased (*see* 'Pine Martens and Capercaillie', below).[11]

### Iceland – a simple semi-natural predator-prey system

In Iceland, rock ptarmigan form the main prey of gyrfalcons. In the grouse world, this is as close as it gets to a single predator species depending upon a single prey. Gyrfalcon numbers certainly depend upon ptarmigan numbers. Nielsen[12] found that the total number of gyrfalcon territories followed ptarmigan density with a three-year time lag. In mathematical models, such lags can lead to unstable, cyclic dynamics. In practice, gyrfalcons ate a greater percentage of the ptarmigan population during the decline and low phases of the ptarmigan population cycle, but the evidence did not establish that falcons caused the decline.

In the Cairngorms, ptarmigan also show ten-year cycles, but there are no gyrfalcons or other predators that specialise in eating ptarmigan. This and other evidence suggests that ptarmigan show unstable population dynamics naturally, and are not dependent upon a predator to drive them.[13] Nielsen, however, suggested that the Icelandic fluctuations are a simple predator-prey cycle. We reach two conclusions. First, even simple, well-documented predator-prey relationships are difficult to fathom without experiments. Second, rock ptarmigan in Iceland are often abundant, despite a ferocious predator that specialises in eating them.

The number and variety of predator species that kill rock and willow ptarmigan in the Arctic and on continental areas exceeds that in Iceland. In northern Canada, adults suffer predation by gyrfalcon, peregrine falcon, snowy owl, Arctic fox and red fox, and their chicks and eggs by long-tailed skua, gulls, rough-legged buzzard, raven, short-tailed weasel (stoat) and Arctic ground squirrel.[14] Again, this shows that, on large tracts of unfragmented habitat, well-adapted grouse can survive when beset by such enemies, without protection from game preservers. Conversely, introduced Arctic foxes became a severe predator in the Aleutian Islands, even exterminating ptarmigan on some islands.[15] On extensive mainland habitats, local depletions are often made good by birds moving in from elsewhere, but on small islands, or on fragments of mainland habitat isolated by agriculture or development, the population may not be rescued by immigration.

### The boreal forest – complex predator-prey relationships

In virgin boreal forest in Russia, the biomass of prey available to predators is roughly 150kg per km$^2$, with perhaps 60 per cent of this comprising rodents and 25 per cent grouse.[16] Rodent density in different regions varies broadly with the amount of grassy vegetation, and this in turn is dependent upon soil fertility. There is also annual variation because many populations of small rodent show cycles of abundance every three to five years. Grouse rear fewer young in years of rodent scarcity, probably because predators such as pine martens eat fewer rodents and more grouse in such years,[17] thereby embodying the functional response.

Predatory mammals in Russian boreal forest include brown bear, wolf, red fox, lynx, glutton (wolverine), badger, European otter, polecat, sable, pine marten, European and American mink, stoat, weasel and the introduced raccoon dog. To have an appreciable impact on grouse numbers, however, a predator must be relatively abundant and must eat grouse regularly. According to studies in the Russian Lapland and Pechora-Illych nature reserves (Table 27), only glutton, fox, pine marten and stoat fall into this category, while in the Ilexa River basin[18] only glutton and pine marten qualify. Foxes and stoats are quite rare at Ilexa, where their rodent prey are scarce over the infertile soils.

TABLE 27. Grouse (capercaillie, hazel grouse, willow ptarmigan, black grouse and rock ptarmigan combined) in the diet of mammalian predators in two Russian boreal forest nature reserves, percentage frequency of remains in scats (number of scats in sample is given in parentheses). From Semenov-Tyan-Shanskiy (1960).

|  | STOAT | | PINE MARTEN | | GLUTTON (WOLVERINE) | | RED FOX | | BROWN BEAR |
| --- | --- | --- | --- | --- | --- | --- | --- | --- | --- |
|  | SUMMER | WINTER | SUMMER | WINTER | | WINTER | SUMMER | WINTER | SUMMER |
| Lapland | 0 (137) | 5 (133) | 3 (485) | 18 (214) | | 19 (113) | 8 (358) | 21 (433) | <1 (150) |
| Pechora-Illych | — | 8 (546) | 5 (58) | 15 (577) | | 6 (810) | 14 (392) | 24 (1,031) | <1 (400) |

TABLE 28. Relative impact of predatory birds on grouse species (capercaillie, black grouse, willow ptarmigan and hazel grouse, plus rock ptarmigan in the Lapland reserve) in three Russian forest nature reserves. The figure on the left is the percentage of all records of grouse being eaten by a given species of bird of prey. The middle figure in parentheses is the average density of each predator (individuals per km²). The figure in bold on the right is an index of the impact on grouse per individual predator, calculated by dividing the left figure by the middle one.

| SPECIES | LAPLAND (68°N) BOREAL FOREST | PECHORA-ILLYCH (62°N) BOREAL FOREST | LAKE ILMEN (55°N) MIXED FOREST |
|---|---|---|---|
| Goshawk *Accipiter gentilis* | 29 (2.5) **11.6** | 37 (7.4) **5.0** | 24 (8.8) **2.7** |
| Golden eagle *Aquila chrysaëtos* | 23 (1.6) **14.4** | 17 (1.6) **10.6** | 17 (9.6) **1.8** |
| White-tailed eagle *Haliaeëtus albicilla* | 31 (4.6) **6.7** | 16 (4.3) **3.7** | 0 (16.2) **0** |
| Eagle owl *Bubo bubo* | 2 (0.3) **6.7** | 6 (2.5) **4.0** | 34 (9.4) **3.6** |
| Spotted eagle *Aquila clanga* | — | — | 21 (12.2) **1.7** |
| Buzzard *Buteo buteo* | — | 16 (31.4) **0.5** | 2 (15.0) **0.1** |
| Gyrfalcon *Falco rusticolus* | 10 (1.1) **9.1** | — | — |
| Black kite *Milvus migrans* | 0 (0.2) **0** | 6 (7.1) **0.9** | 0 (22.0) **0** |
| Rough-legged buzzard *Buteo lagopus* | 4 (9.8) **0.4** | 0 (0.2) **0** | — |
| Sparrowhawk *Accipiter nisus* | 1 (1.8) **0.6** | 1 (6.2) **0.2** | + (6.2) **t** |
| Imperial eagle *Aquila heliaca* | — | — | 2 (1.6) **1.3** |
| Honey buzzard *Pernis apivorus* | 0 (0.1) **0** | + (2.3) **t** | — |
| Hobby *Falco subbuteo* | — | 1 (4.7) **0.2** | — |
| Peregrine falcon *Falco peregrinus* | — | 0 (1.0) **0** | 0 (2.6) **0** |
| Merlin *Falco columbarius* | 0 (5.3) **0** | 0 (0.2) **0** | — |
| Kestrel *Falco tinnunculus* | 0 (1.7) **0** | 0 (1.0) **0** | — |

TABLE 28. (continued)

| SPECIES | LAPLAND (68°N) BOREAL FOREST | PECHORA-ILLYCH (62°N) BOREAL FOREST | LAKE ILMEN (55°N) MIXED FOREST |
|---|---|---|---|
| Red-footed falcon *Falco vespertinus* | — | o (0.4) | — |
| Montagu's harrier *Circus pygargus* | — | o (0.2) | — |
| Hen harrier *Circus cyaneus* | — | o (0.4) | — |
| Marsh harrier *Circus aeruginosus* | — | — | o (5.6) |
| Osprey *Pandion haliaëtus* | o (5.5) | o (4.1) | o (2.4) |
| Hawk owl *Surnia ulula* | o (8.3) | — | — |

**Note**

o means that this predator species was present but no grouse were recorded in its diet; + indicates a trace was found in its diet; — indicates the predator species was not in the original tables and so was presumably scarce or absent; and t indicates a trace impact (close to zero). Other species of raptors, not shown to eat grouse, were present but are not included here. Compiled from tables in Semenov-Tyan-Shanskiy (1960).

There are more species of predatory birds (*see* Table 28) than mammals in boreal forest. As with mammals, the abundance of each raptor varies from place to place. Of the raptors, goshawk, golden eagle, white-tailed eagle, eagle owl and gyrfalcon take most grouse. Although individual buzzards, and to a lesser extent black kites, eat grouse less frequently, they can be abundant and so kill appreciable numbers of grouse.

In the Lapland reserve, predatory mammals and birds accounted for roughly equal numbers of kills of each of the five grouse species (capercaillie, black grouse, hazel grouse, willow ptarmigan and rock ptarmigan). In the Ilexa study, the main predator of capercaillie was goshawk (75 per cent of recorded kills), followed by golden eagle (9 per cent), pine marten (6 per cent), glutton, eagle owl and white-tailed eagle (each with 3 per cent), and spotted eagle, buzzard and black kite (1 per cent combined).[19] The rarity of foxes at Ilexa explains why few capercaillie kills were attributed to mammals.

Britain and Ireland lie in the temperate zone, not the boreal one, and so might be more comparable with the Russian Lake Ilmen, in the zone of mixed forest just south of the boreal (*see* Table 28).[20] Here, individual eagles and goshawks ate fewer grouse than in the boreal forest, perhaps because of the greater variety of other prey. Overall, however, eagles and goshawks in this temperate reserve were more abundant than in the boreal forest, and so killed similar numbers of grouse.

**Britain and Ireland**

Bear, wolf, lynx, boar, white-tailed eagle, osprey, goshawk and black kite were exterminated from Britain in historical times, while polecat, pine marten, wildcat, red kite and hen harrier became confined to small enclaves. The intensive predator killing that was widely practised on the new sporting estates of the nineteenth century relaxed somewhat during the late twentieth century. This allowed ospreys to re-establish themselves, especially near fish farms, and goshawks to be restored by escapes from falconers and by unauthorised releases. Hen harriers spread unaided from their Orkney enclave; pine martens and polecats extended their ranges with the help of unsanctioned translocations; red kites from Wales were bred and released with government approval; and white-tailed eagles were re-established by importing youngsters from Norway. Wildcats also spread, but, reduced by recent snaring and swamped by interbreeding with feral domestic cats, there are probably few pure members of the species left in Britain.[21]

Crows and foxes are the main egg-robbers of British grouse, although crows are scarce in most ptarmigan habitat. Stoats and weasels are widespread egg-robbers, while the depredations of cats, pine martens, gulls and ravens are more local. All the above eat some chicks, as do the smaller raptors, hen harriers

FIG 156. Eggs below a crow's nest, mostly of red grouse. (Desmond Dugan)

especially taking many red grouse chicks. Hedgehogs occasionally take a few eggs of red grouse, although they do not usually destroy the whole clutch. Badgers and adders are also occasional predators of grouse eggs.

In Britain and Ireland, the main predator of adult grouse is the fox. In a ten-year study in east Scotland, foxes killed 38 per cent of radio-tagged red grouse hens on their nests.[22] Although scarce over infertile granite, stoats and weasels are commoner over base-rich soils with patches of nutritious grass, which are favoured by voles and rabbits. These form their main prey, but in summer a few take eggs, chicks and adult grouse. Both predator species have increased along with recent increases in numbers of moorland rabbits, so their killing of moorland grouse can be considered more serious than formerly was the case.

A fox killing an adult grouse usually takes a roosting bird at night, whereas eagles, hawks, harriers and falcons kill in daylight, and avoid hunting in poor light near dawn and dusk. In their usual way of catching adult grouse, eagles and harriers fly low and surprise a bird, pouncing to catch it on the ground or as it takes wing. We see headlong chases by eagles so often, however, that they probably do catch some grouse by this method. Peregrines perch on a lofty crag as they watch for prey, but more often soar high in the sky before stooping upon their quarry.[23] Sparrowhawks flit through woodland or across nearby moorland, perching briefly between flights, and catch their prey by surprise. Buzzards prefer to sit on a perch

FIG 157. Ptarmigan hen killed and buried by a fox. She was in summer plumage. (Adam Watson)

FIG 158. Golden eagle's nest on a branch of an old pine in a Caledonian forest. Red grouse and mountain hare are prey, seen alongside an unhatched eagle egg. (Desmond Dugan)

FIG 159. Feathers from a ptarmigan killed by a golden eagle. (Adam Watson)

FIG 160. Female hen harrier feeding a red grouse to its three young. The chicks differ in size because they hatch a day or two apart and the biggest get fed first. The largest chick here has taken more than it can easily swallow. (N. Picozzi)

**FIG 161.** Peregrine falcon mantling its red grouse prey. (Desmond Dugan)

**FIG 162.** Red grouse killed by a peregrine, which was flushed by the photographer. (Adam Watson)

and wait for prey. Goshawks hunt like sparrowhawks but also use peregrine tactics, watching from exposed perches or soaring and then stooping.

Many predators are killed by game preservers and some by conservationists, although the interests of the two groups differ. Healthy grouse populations rear more offspring than is necessary to replace natural losses, and predators and hunters crop the surplus. However, game preservers want the surplus and regard predators as competitors. On grouse-moors, for example, it is generally reckoned that an autumn minimum of some 65 red grouse per km$^2$ can sustain profitable driven shooting, though some put the figure higher. Predators can depress autumn densities below this threshold and so lose an estate a lucrative asset. Thus, eagles are scarce on many grouse-moors because of persecution by gamekeepers, who have almost eliminated the goshawk on Scottish sporting estates after its earlier increase in the 1970s. Hen harriers, buzzards and other raptors are also routinely killed by some keepers, as are pine martens and badgers.

Conservationists see predators differently. In most studies of the effects of predator killing on birds and mammals, the breeding success of the prey was found to increase with predator killing. In some studies the prey's breeding density also increased, although in some it did not.[24] Conservationists do not crop surplus birds for pleasure or economic benefit, and so see less need than game preservers to maximise the breeding success of gamebirds. They prefer a wider range of species and stress the economic benefits of wildlife tourism. Even so, the Royal Society for the Protection of Birds kills crows and foxes in Abernethy pinewood to benefit capercaillie, and Scottish Natural Heritage kills hedgehogs on North Uist to protect the nests of wading birds.

Can British uplands be managed to satisfy conservationists and game preservers alike? The Langholm experiment set out to measure the impact of raptors upon red grouse, providing facts upon which rational discussion about raptor killing could be based. The experiment entailed killing crows, foxes, stoats and weasels, but abandoning the usual, if illegal, killing of raptors.[25]

During 1992–6, hen harriers on the 48km$^2$ Langholm moor increased from two to 14 breeding females, and peregrines from three to five or six pairs. Predation, especially of grouse chicks by harriers, apparently suppressed the number of red grouse. Past bag records at Langholm had fluctuated on a six-year cycle, but bags did not peak in 1996 as expected from these records. Bags from two other moors in the same region, which had previously fluctuated together with those at Langholm, did reach high numbers in 1996. Although this evidence did not attain rigorous scientific standards, it provided a reasonable case that raptors, especially harriers, had spoiled Langholm as a good grouse-moor. Autumn density in 1992–6 averaged 66 grouse per km$^2$, barely enough for driven shooting.

Regrettably, Langholm was not a typical grouse-moor and so did not provide the intended basis for rational discussions about raptor killing on grouse-moors in general. Grazing by sheep and outbreaks of heather beetle had led to about half the heather-dominated vegetation becoming grass-dominated between 1948 and 1988. The grassier moorland supported higher densities of small rodents and meadow pipits, which in turn provided abundant food for harriers. Without sheep-induced grassy swards, Langholm might well have been able to sustain better shooting.[26]

Had the study continued, golden eagles might have returned to Langholm. Golden eagles kill hen harriers and anecdotal observations suggest that harriers tend to avoid eagle hunting grounds.[27] Golden eagles, like harriers, kill grouse and are persecuted for that reason. A golden eagle needs some 230g of food a day while a harrier needs about 80g.[28] On this basis alone, one pair of eagles is equivalent to about three pairs of harriers. Eagles, however, take much carrion, prefer mountain hares to grouse, and do not usually take small grouse chicks. Hence a pair of eagles might have much the same impact on a grouse-moor as a pair of harriers. At Langholm, by reducing harrier numbers, eagles might have allowed driven shooting to continue unabated.

Is it possible for driven grouse shooting to thrive within the law, with keepers killing foxes, crows, stoats and weasels, but not persecuting eagles, harriers and other protected species? A few successful grouse-moors have been operated largely within the law, and fewer still wholly so. Gamekeepers who tolerate raptors or suggest that raptors might be tolerated, however, have been victimised by some of their less open-minded brethren and find it difficult to speak openly.[29]

It is likely that raptors suppress grouse stocks below what is possible on a raptor-free moor. But high stocks on a raptor-free moor might lead to an increased incidence of parasitic disease, a threat that keepers sometimes try to counter by treating grouse with anthelmintic (worming) drugs coated on grit eaten by grouse. Medicated grit, however, cannot always prevent outbreaks of grouse disease. If excessive grouse densities lead to disease, irrespective of medication, the killing of raptors might lead to greater fluctuations and lower average bags. It is often suggested that, by killing the most heavily parasitised grouse, raptors keep disease at bay without the use of drugs. Furthermore, if owners of grouse-moors continue to instruct keepers to kill raptors or prevent their successful breeding, they may find that society will eventually ban their sport outright.

In British and Irish conditions, some predator control is a necessary part of conservation. Discussion would be cooler if predator control had an agreed ethical basis. Few people have ethical objections to killing pests such as rats, although many would rather leave it to somebody else. Most conservationists accept that foxes, crows, stoats and weasels can be pests. So, too, is the American mink, an introduced creature that has been blamed for the near extermination of water voles throughout most of lowland Britain. Game preservers additionally regard raptors and martens as pests, whereas conservationists regard them as a part of our natural heritage that should be there for all to enjoy. A reasonable start to any discussion would be that foxes and crows, for example, are much more abundant in Britain and Ireland than in more natural landscapes. An ethical case for culling a predator, therefore, would be made if it could be shown that the predator is unnaturally abundant and is suppressing desired creatures to unacceptably low levels.

## PINE MARTENS AND CAPERCAILLIE

Pine martens are woodland predators that eat mainly small mammals, but they also feed on the eggs, chicks and adults of birds, including woodland grouse. Some argue that martens contributed to the decline of, and threaten the future of, the endangered capercaillie in Scotland, and that their killing should be made legal. But what is the evidence for this?

FIG 163. Young pine marten with finch prey. (Stuart Rae)

During the heyday of predator killing in Britain, pine martens were reduced to a few small enclaves, the main one in the west of Scotland. During the last few decades of the twentieth century, with help from translocations, the animals regained much of their former range in the Highlands and northeast Scotland. The spread of the pine marten and decline of the capercaillie occurred at roughly the same time.

In much of their range, however, capercaillie were already in steep decline before pine martens arrived in any number. Capercaillie in the woods of Kinveachy estate in Speyside, for example, began to decline in 1979–80,[30] yet pine martens were not noted there until 1986.[31] Similarly, in mid-Deeside pine martens were not seen regularly until the 1990s,[32] by which time the capercaillie decline was well underway.

A survey compared the breeding success of capercaillie with the abundance of various predators, including pine martens, in 14 Scottish woods in the mid-1990s.[33] Capercaillie reared fewer chicks where crows, foxes and raptors (mostly buzzards and sparrowhawks) were more abundant. An index of marten abundance, however, was not related to breeding success of capercaillie. Also, the average nationwide capercaillie breeding success in 2001–3 exceeded that in the late 1990s, and capercaillie numbers increased between nationwide population estimates in the winters of 1998/9 and 2003/4. Hence capercaillie and pine martens seem able to coexist in Scotland, as they do in the rest of their joint range.[34] But keepers kill pine martens, albeit illegally, and some argue that capercaillie would have declined further had pine martens been left unchecked.

During the large absence of pine martens for much of the twentieth century, few studies of them were carried out in Scotland, and then mostly in the west, where there are now no capercaillie. Therefore we look abroad for better information on the relationship between numbers of pine marten and capercaillie.

The staple food of pine martens and many other woodland predators is typically small rodents.[35] More of the alternative foods such as berries, nuts, seeds, insects, worms, frogs, hares, squirrels, carrion and birds, including capercaillie and other grouse species, are taken when rodents are scarce. Thus, during the periodic lows of a typical three- to four-year vole cycle, martens take more of the alternative foods and woodland grouse rear fewer young.[36] Studied in the Pechora-Illych reserve in Russia (Fig. 164), scats of pine martens showed that they usually ate more grouse when small rodents were scarce; but in one year with few rodents, grouse were spared because martens ate many berries and pine nuts.

On the poor soils of the Ilexa River basin near Archangel in Russia, rodents are scarce and predators rely heavily on woodland grouse. Pine martens are the most abundant mammalian predator of grouse, killing 0.1–1.3 per cent of the population of capercaillie.[37] This is a very small fraction, but does not include

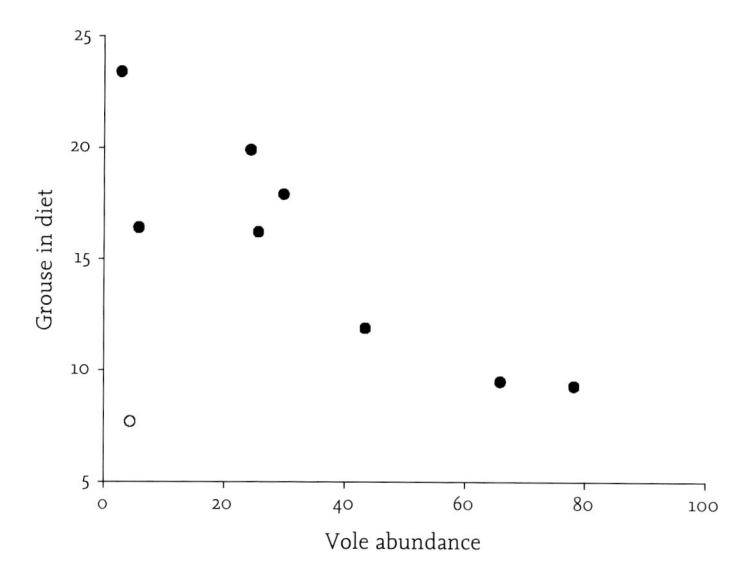

FIG 164. Grouse remains (per cent occurrence) in winter scats of pine marten in relation to an index of vole abundance in the Pechora-Illych nature reserve in 1949–58 (from Fig. 75 in Semenov-Tyan-Shanskiy, 1960). There was a clear inverse relationship except in 1958 (open symbol), the sole year when berries and pine nuts formed the biggest single category in the martens' diet. Other categories were: invertebrates, frogs, birds' eggs, grouse, other birds, small rodents and other mammals.

their depredation of eggs and chicks, so leaving open the question of how great an impact they have upon the capercaillie population.

Capercaillie have long been hunted and pine martens killed for fur in Europe. Records from three large estates in southern Bohemia during 1750–1890 provide a useful example from less industrial times.[38] Here, there was no association between the numbers of pine martens killed for fur and the numbers of capercaillie shot for sport.[39]

In Finland, as one travels from north to south, fairly continuous forest gives way to an increasingly agricultural and fertile land, where forest is more fragmented. This change in landscape is associated with decreasing breeding success of capercaillie and black grouse, increasing abundance of red foxes and pine martens, and decreasing abundance of stoats.[40] Many have concluded that foxes and martens cause the poorer breeding success of woodland grouse in south Fennoscandia. Supporting this view, experimental killing of foxes and martens on a Swedish island increased the breeding success of grouse.[41]

The island experiment, however, did not distinguish the separate impacts of fox and marten. Nor did it explain the role of stoats, which are more abundant in north Finland, where grouse breed better. Perhaps conditions in north Finland favour both grouse and stoats.

We use data from the Finnish study to check whether year-to-year variations in grouse breeding success were related to the abundance of pine martens. In the south of Finland there was no significant association. In the north, the raw data (Fig. 165) also suggested no association, but after one allows for annual variations in vole and marten abundance, breeding success was better in years with few foxes. It was also better in years with more voles, which fits the idea that predators kill fewer grouse when there are more voles to eat. However, after allowing for annual variations in vole and fox abundance, it appeared that grouse breeding success was better in years with more pine martens, the opposite of what one might expect.

That woodland grouse rear more young when there are more pine martens may seem surprising. Other evidence reveals a likely mechanism. An outbreak of sarcoptic mange among red foxes in Norway, Finland and Sweden reduced fox numbers, whereupon pine martens increased, probably because foxes kill martens or compete with them for food.[42] Small game, including capercaillie, black grouse, willow ptarmigan and mountain hares, also increased. This suggests not only that foxes depressed martens and grouse, but also that martens have less impact than foxes upon grouse abundance.[43]

A scarcity of foxes benefits both pine martens and capercaillie. Moreover, pine martens are less likely to eat capercaillie when small rodents are abundant. Hence capercaillie and pine martens should be able to coexist where there are few foxes and also many small rodents and other foods. Also, the taking of capercaillie eggs and small chicks by foxes and pine martens is probably opportunistic,[44] and so good ground cover, especially for nests and broods, could allow coexistence between woodland grouse and pine martens.

## PARASITIC WORMS

Grouse intestines are home to several species of tapeworms, roundworms and threadworms. Large tapeworms *Paroniella urogalli*[45] are flat, segmented worms, well known to anyone who flushes red grouse in late summer. As young grouse take flight, lengths of creamy-white worm spurt from their backsides to dangle grotesquely before breaking off in egg-laden segments. The large roundworm *Ascaridia compar* is often found in the small intestines of Old World grouse, but is

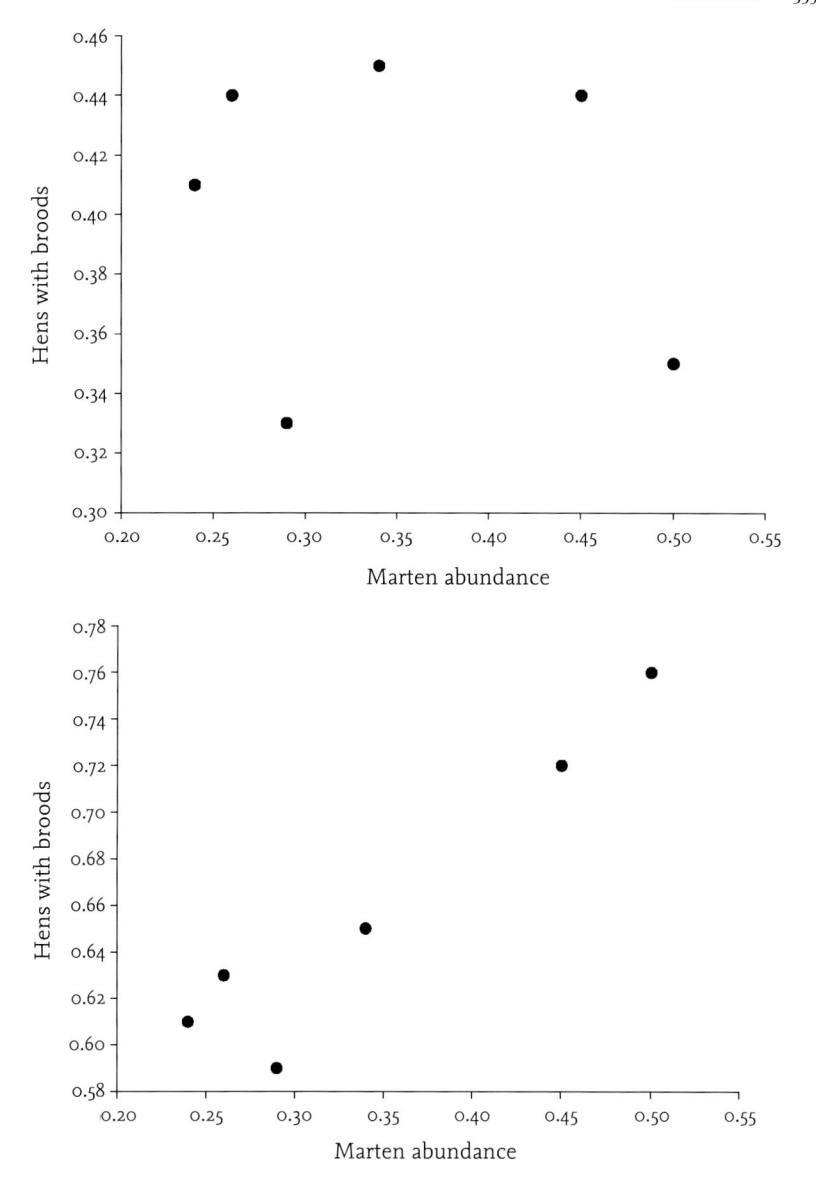

FIG 165. Capercaillie breeding success (proportion of hens with broods) in relation to marten abundance (index from tracks in snow) in part of northern Finland in 1989–94. Top: raw data. Bottom: the relationship between breeding success and marten abundance, after allowing for the effects of vole and fox abundance (this is a 'partial residual' plot).

rarely reported in grouse in Britain.[46] Caecal threadworms, intestinal threadworms *Capillaria* spp. and the diminutive tapeworm *Hymenolepis microps* are barely visible to the naked eye.[47]

In Britain, the main research has been on the caecal threadworm *Trichostrongylus tenuis*, agent of 'grouse disease' in red grouse. Otherwise, the occurrence and effects of parasitic worms in British grouse have been little studied. The tapeworms *Paroniella urogalli* and *Hymenolepis microps* are common in red grouse, and are widespread in ptarmigan and capercaillie in other European countries, and hence presumably in Britain.[48] The roundworm *Ascaridia compar*, however, seems to be found mostly in more continental climates, which may explain why it is seldom seen in Britain.

The caecal threadworm *Trichostrongylus tenuis*, conversely, seems to be confined to mild climates. It occurs in small numbers in the willow and rock ptarmigan of coastal Scandinavia, but not in more continental parts.[49] The temperate conditions of moorland Britain seem to favour this parasite. Ubiquitous in red grouse, it also occurs in Scottish ptarmigan, but heavy burdens are unusual in ptarmigan and have been reported mostly at low altitudes. It has not been reported in black grouse or capercaillie, probably because it cannot establish itself in these species.[50]

Red grouse on many moors are routinely treated with anthelmintic drugs. These can be administered by catching birds and dosing them directly through the mouth, but the easiest method is to lay out medicated grit, which birds can pick up in their own time. Such treatments are aimed primarily at *Trichostrongylus tenuis* but must also affect other parasites. Direct dosing can increase the breeding success of red grouse, and in a five-year study on a grouse-moor in county Durham,[51] where average burdens of *T. tenuis* were in the thousands, medicated grit reduced burdens and increased the average number of chicks reared from 3.5 per hen to 5.6.[52]

### Tapeworms

The tiny tapeworm *Hymenolepis microps* occurs in the duodenum of grouse and is widely distributed in Britain and Europe, although none was found in a sample of 1,065 red grouse from the Scottish Highlands.[53] During a study of willow ptarmigan on the Norwegian island of Karlsøy, the percentage of chicks infected with *H. microps* jumped from less than 10 per cent to almost 50 per cent between August and September, while the percentage of infected adults was falling.[54] This might have been because the most infected young chicks were being killed by worms, but we know of no direct evidence that *H. microps* affects breeding success in grouse.

In boreal Russia, tapeworms were not found in capercaillie and willow ptarmigan from November to January, but were present in most birds during summer.[55] In Scotland, the large tapeworm *Parionella urogalli* occurred in over 70 per cent of red grouse in summer and winter. More worms were gravid (full of eggs) in summer, however, when they were three to four times their winter weight.[56]

The large *Parionella urogalli* seems to be less pathogenic than *Hymenolepis microps*, even though the swollen gut of a bird heavily infected with *P. urogalli* bulges with worms. In Scotland, tapeworm burden was not related to the host bird's condition. In Canada, very high burdens of *Parionella* species did not appear to affect the growth of ruffed grouse.[57] In Canada again, the condition (protein and fat reserves) of willow ptarmigan did not differ between birds parasitised with *Parionella* species and those not parasitised.[58]

**Caecal threadworms**

Outbreaks of 'grouse disease' in red grouse seem more frequent in the milder conditions of north England than in north Scotland, although this may be related also to higher densities of grouse on English moors. Cobbold[59] first associated heavy burdens of caecal threadworms with disease, and Leiper[60] investigated the simple life history of the worm (*see* Fig. 166). The Committee of Inquiry on Grouse Disease[61] subsequently identified the worm in over 2,000 birds dissected during outbreaks of disease, so providing a firm basis for grouse disease being trichostrongylosis.

Adult worms reside in the birds' caeca and are remarkably long-lived, such that most die only when their host dies.[62] Eggs laid by female worms are voided in the semi-liquid caecal droppings of grouse. After a few days, or longer in colder conditions, first-stage larvae hatch and begin feeding on micro-organisms in the droppings. They grow and moult, losing their outer cuticle like a snake shedding its skin, into second-stage larvae. These develop further into third-stage larvae, which do not feed but migrate out of the caecal droppings, retaining their second-stage cuticle as protection against desiccation. These infective third-stage larvae are ready to enter a host, and move onto heather tips in the hope of being ingested by a feeding grouse.

The odds against success for a third-stage larva are enormous. An adult female worm produces about 100,000 eggs a year. Of these, on average less than ten must establish themselves in another grouse to maintain the worm population. So, when conditions for transmission are favourable, there is ample scope for rapid increases in worm burdens and consequent outbreaks of grouse disease. If the proportion of eggs that become established as adult worms (the transmission rate) is fairly constant, parasite burdens will be largely determined by the density of hosts and the worms in them. Conversely, transmission rates

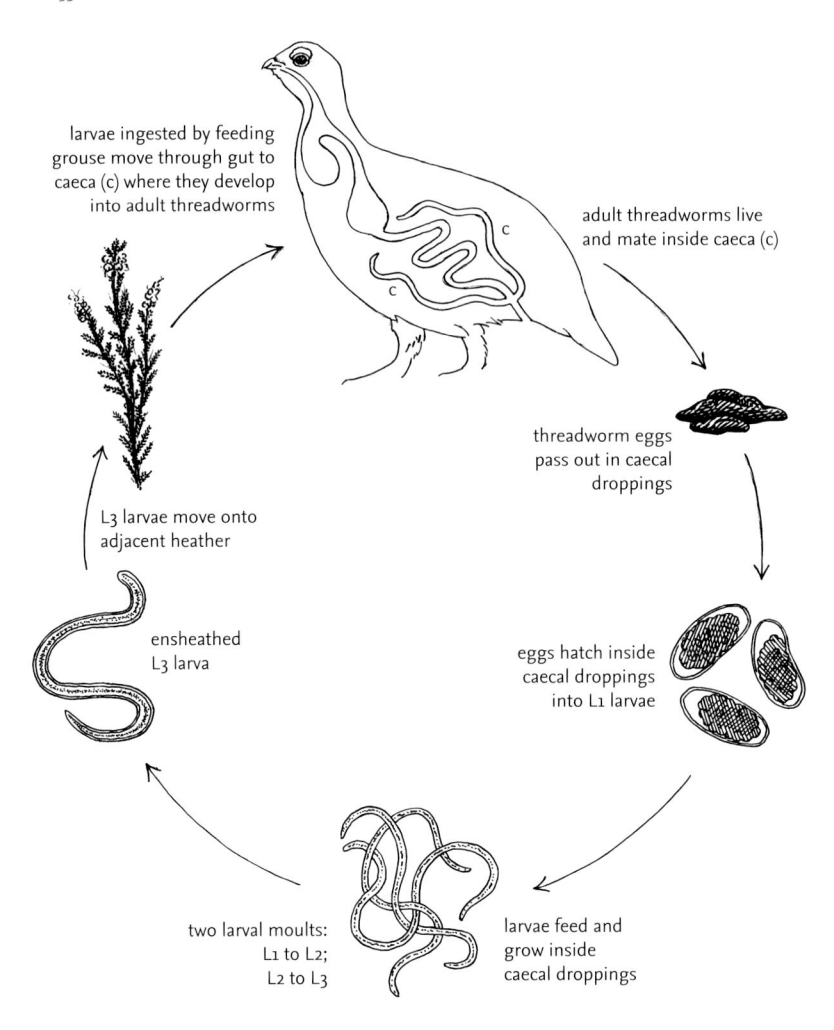

**FIG 166.** Life cycle of the caecal threadworm *Trichostrongylus tenuis*. (Drawn by Dave Pullan)

might be determined by environmental conditions that vary widely, causing worm burdens to fluctuate independently of host density. In reality, both density and environment affect worm burdens,[63] so that high grouse density and wet summer weather are each conducive to increased burdens.[64]

Following the Committee of Inquiry on Grouse Disease, the next scientific study to document grouse disease was at Glen Esk in 1957–61.[65] Emaciated hens with large worm burdens were found lying dead on their nests in 1958 and 1959, and the breeding population declined between 1958 and 1960. Despite this, surviving birds reared enough young to ensure that in autumn all the ground was occupied by territorial birds and that some were denied territories. Hence the decline was associated with pathological worm burdens, but the declining population was limited by territorial behaviour.

At the time of the Glen Esk study, interpretation was hindered by two complications. First, birds shot in autumn with large worm burdens, similar to those found in emaciated and moribund birds in spring and summer, were in good condition. Only later did it transpire that adult worms are relatively benign.[66] The main damage is done by developing larvae as they burrow into the birds' caecal walls during their two-week development period.

A few developing larvae do little damage to their host's caeca, but there is a twist. During autumn, many ingested larvae do not develop, but remain buried in the caecal walls in a state of arrested development or hibernation. A stock of arrested larvae builds up in the caeca. In spring, these develop simultaneously and, if they number in the hundreds or thousands, cause massive damage. This explains why outbreaks of grouse disease usually begin in spring, although diseased birds, emaciated and unable to fly, can be seen throughout summer. It also explains why the same burden of adult worms can appear innocuous in autumn but fatal in spring.

Caecal threadworms are long-lived and so a grouse accumulates an increasing burden of worms during its lifetime. Hence old birds often have many more worms than young ones. But, because arrested larvae that are developing in spring do most of the damage, old suffer no more than young during outbreaks of grouse disease.[67]

A second complication during the Glen Esk study was severe 'browning' of the birds' heather food in the springs of 1958 and 1959. In frosty dry conditions, green heather foliage can become so desiccated that it turns brown and dies, reducing the amount and quality of the birds' food. Because worm larvae tend to concentrate on the remaining edible green shoots (*see* Fig. 167), heather browning probably accentuates trichostrongylosis.

With hindsight, we can disentangle the complexities of the Glen Esk study. Removing parasites with anthelmintic drugs can moderate cyclic declines in the numbers of red grouse, but it does not prevent the declines (*see* 'Parasites and population cycles', below). This fits the idea that, by increasing mortality and reducing breeding success, worms and heather damage together modified the Glen Esk birds' social structure (*see* Chapter 14). This may have caused cocks to take larger territories, with the result that numbers declined more than they would have done without parasites. Hence worms, heather browning and

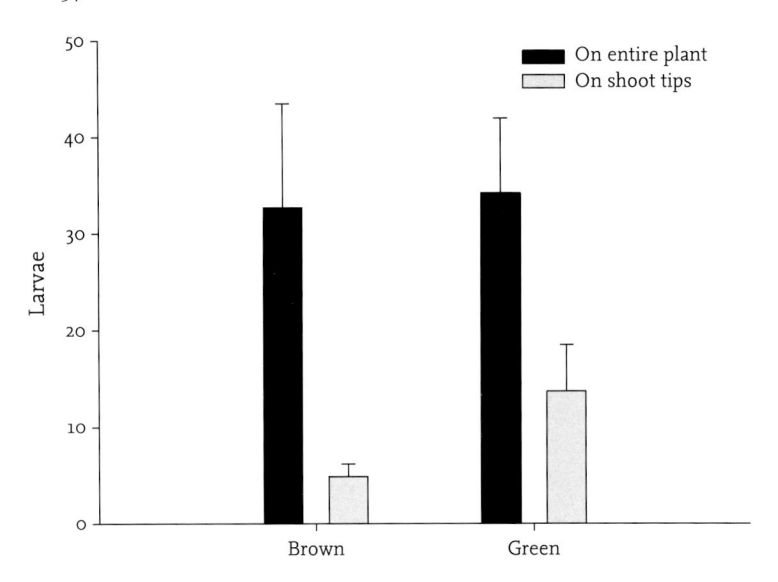

FIG 167. Caecal threadworm larvae (*Trichostrongylus tenuis*) on living (green) and dead (brown, frosted) heather plants. Out of 3,000 larvae put on the ground, similar numbers moved onto each type of plant, but about three times as many ended up on the shoot tips of green plants as on those of brown plants. (Note: the bars represent standard errors uncorrected for differences between the nine paired replicates.)[68]

territorial behaviour all probably played a role in the Glen Esk decline. More generally, cyclic declines associated with changes in the birds' social behaviour certainly occur without heather browning or trichostrongylosis. Conversely, the severest outbreaks of disease on overstocked grouse-moors probably kill so many birds that limitation of numbers by social behaviour may be temporarily suspended.

### Parasites and population cycles

If grouse disease causes population cycles, as claimed for over a century,[69] removal of parasites with anthelmintic drugs should stop the cycles. An experiment in north England aimed to test this prediction. The authors claimed that 'Treatment of the grouse population prevented population crashes, demonstrating that parasites were the cause of the cyclic fluctuations'.[70] Their own data (Fig. 168) show that this claim was overstated.[75] Although anthelmintics can improve breeding success and survival, population cycles continued despite the treatment. Better work in Scotland and England confirms this conclusion.[76] Grouse disease

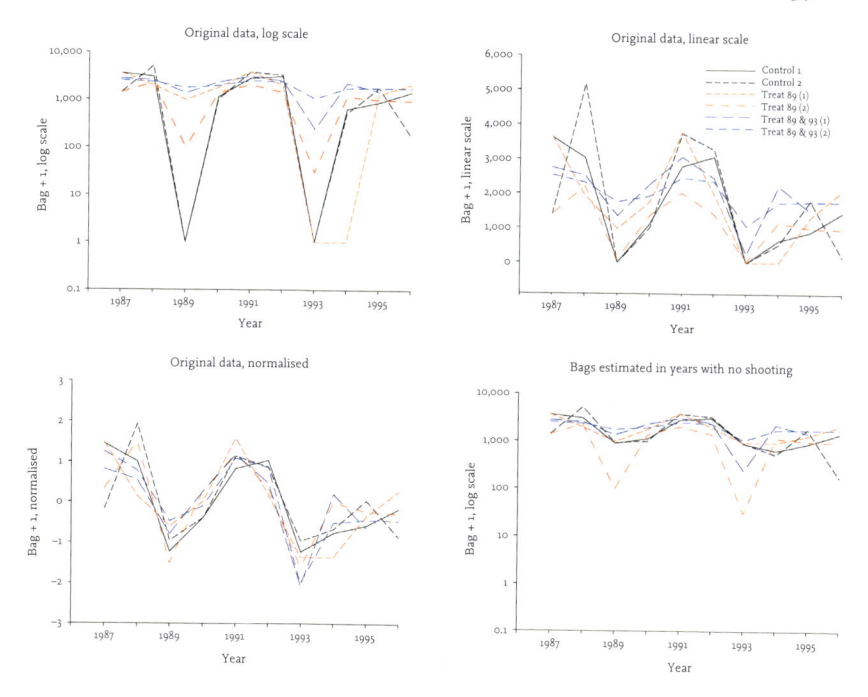

**FIG 168.** Parasite removal experiment.[71] Bags (birds shot in autumn on six different moors) as originally presented (top left). When plotted on a logarithmic scale as in the original, bags show apparent differences between treated and untreated (control) populations (red lines indicate grouse treated with anthelmintic drugs in spring 1989 only; blue lines indicate grouse treated in 1989 and 1993). Note that differences among moors depended mostly on years without shooting, when of course there was no bag (and hence no sample). When bags were plotted on a linear scale (top right), differences were less apparent and it was clear that bags on all areas had continued to show cycles, irrespective of the treatment. Normalising[72] the data (bottom left) removed differences in amplitudes among moors, and showed a similar cyclic pattern on all moors. To remove bias due to inclusion of years with no shooting as zeros, we estimated what the bags would have been if shooting had taken place in such years.[73] The result (bottom right) is on the same scale as the first plot (top left), and comparing the two reveals distortions in the first plot due to inclusion of years with no bag as zeros. Indeed (bottom right), bags from some of the treated populations declined more than those from controls.[74]

certainly causes population crashes on overstocked moors, especially after wet summer weather enhances parasite transmission, but population cycles occur even when parasites are removed.

### Parasites and behaviour

In red grouse, parasites interact with bird quality and condition to influence a bird's aggressive behaviour, and this in turn influences the birds' density. The subtle interactions now being unravelled can be understood by assuming that each bird has physiological resources that it can invest in various ways.[77] To resist parasites, for example, a bird invests in its immune system. To gain a territory and attract a hen, a cock invests in its own aggressiveness via testosterone production. More testosterone imparts less immunity against parasites, and vice versa. By sacrificing its condition, a cock can invest more into immunity and testosterone, but then has fewer reserves against hard times. A better-quality cock, however, can invest more into immunity and testosterone while remaining in good condition.

This brings us to the 'immunocompetence handicap principle'. To rear more young, a cock needs a better-quality hen. He attracts her by being more aggressive, getting a bigger territory, and signalling his quality by displaying bigger combs. These require more testosterone, a costly investment. Overcoming this handicap proves him a better-quality cock, which can provide his hen with a bigger territory and with offspring that are better able to resist parasites.[78]

## LOUPING ILL

### The disease

Louping ill, a disease of the central nervous system, can wreak havoc on red grouse. Caused by a virus transmitted by the sheep tick *Ixodes ricinus*, it is primarily a disease of sheep, but it also affects wildlife and humans.[79] Mortality in sheep is typically about 10 per cent. Many animals develop a characteristic 'louping' gait, in which the front legs move forward together, followed by the back legs.[80]

The louping-ill virus is the most westerly member of the tick-borne encephalitis group of viruses. After a one- to two-week incubation period, humans infected with tick-borne encephalitis get a fever that abates within a few days. Several days later, a second fever develops, often associated with confusion, reduced consciousness, fits or limb weakness. In humans, louping ill is the mildest form of tick-borne encephalitis, and is seldom fatal.[81] However, in red grouse about 80 per cent of birds experimentally infected with the virus died of it.[82]

### The virus

Louping-ill virus was probably brought into the Irish and British uplands by sheep. Molecular analysis shows at least three genetically distinct types, namely Irish, Welsh and British.[83] The virus seems to have first appeared less than 800 years ago in Ireland, whence a descendant spread into Wales and subsequently to the Scottish Borders. From there it dispersed throughout Scotland, northern England and Norway. The main spread apparently coincided with livestock movements over the last 300 years.

### The tick

Sheep ticks have four stages in their life history. An adult female tick lays about 2,000 eggs in the mat of moist, decomposing plant litter that forms the upper layer of many woodland and moorland soils. This protects ticks from winter frost and in summer provides moisture for their rehydration. Having overwintered in the mat, eggs hatch in spring. Newly hatched larvae are tiny (the size of a pinhead), six-legged, translucent and hard to see. Hungry, they climb the vegetation and await a host. This can be a bird or a mammal ranging in size from a small rodent to a red deer.

Successful larvae engorge themselves on blood and then drop off, burrowing again into the mat to develop into nymphs. Nymphs are much bigger than larvae (1.5–2mm long) and have eight legs. They climb again and wait for another host. On grouse, larvae and nymphs are usually found on the head, where the birds find it difficult to remove them by preening. They use their feet in clumsy efforts

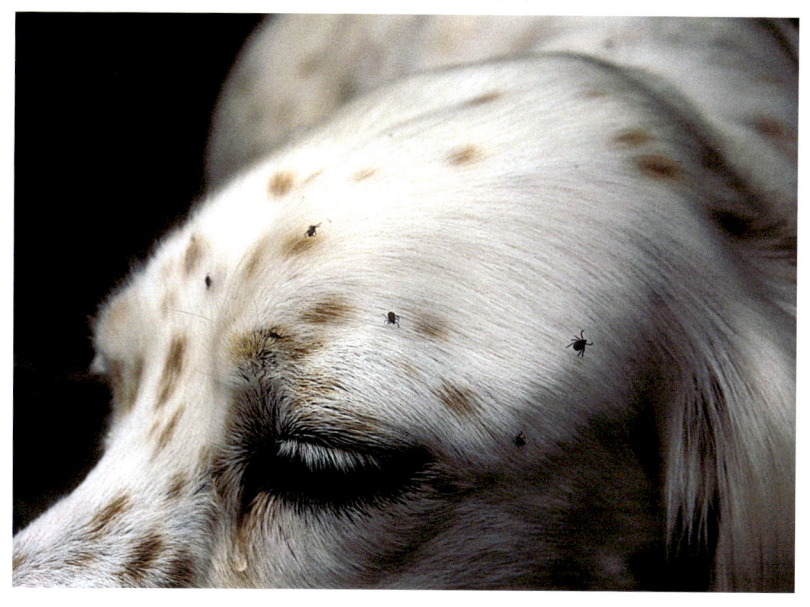

FIG 169. Sheep ticks on English setter. (Desmond Dugan)

to scratch ticks from their heads but also scrape off tender, newly growing feathers. Bald patches of pink, featherless skin show that a bird has suffered many ticks.

Distended nymphs drop again to the mat, where they develop into adults before once more climbing in quest of a host, the main ones being sheep, deer and mountain hares. Adults are the only stage in the life cycle when the sexes can be distinguished. Questing females are 3–4mm long but, once bloated, can reach 10mm. After feeding and mating with the much smaller males, they again drop to the litter where they lay their eggs. The tick life cycle can be completed in 18 months, but may take several years.

**Epidemiology**
Louping ill can spread in at least three ways. First, a tick that feeds on a host with high concentrations of virus in its blood can transmit the disease to its next host. This occurs mostly through sheep.[84] Second, the virus can pass from infected to uninfected ticks that are feeding close to each other on mountain hares,[85] but apparently not on deer or rabbits. Third, it can be spread directly from one host individual to another by droplet infection, without the intervention of a tick.[86] Droplet infection could well occur among grouse chicks being brooded by their mother, but this has not been studied. Rabbits and small rodents are thought not to play an important role in the persistence of louping ill.[87]

On hills where hares and deer are scarce, the removal or routine vaccination of sheep can eliminate louping ill from grouse stocks. This has worked in parts of northern England. But in some regions of Scotland, louping ill has remained prevalent despite the vaccination of replacement ewes for over 30 years.[88] Apparently, hares or deer are sufficient to sustain the disease and so depress grouse stocks.

Captive black grouse, capercaillie and pheasants that were experimentally infected with louping-ill virus all recovered, though some looked unwell for a few days.[89] About 20 per cent of infected red grouse recovered, but Scottish rock ptarmigan and willow ptarmigan from Norway all died with high levels of virus in their blood. These dissimilar responses to infection probably reflect each bird race's differing exposure to tick-borne encephalitis viruses during its evolution. The viruses and the ticks that transmit them occur naturally in woodland throughout the Palaearctic. Woodland birds have probably developed resistance from long association with tick-borne encephalitis viruses. But races of open ground, above or to the north of the timberline, have had less contact with the viruses and less opportunity to develop resistance.

The disastrous effects of louping ill upon red grouse follow two historical accidents. First, forest clearance allowed red grouse to occupy large tracts of artificially sustained heather moorland where the climate is mild enough for ticks to thrive. Second, sheep brought the disease onto moorland. Some healthy wild red grouse have antibody to the virus, suggesting that the bird has developed some immunity, and, with continued exposure, its resistance is likely to increase.[90]

**Management**

If hares or deer can sustain louping ill on grouse-moors, it seems rational to try the effect of removing them. Experimental reduction of hares on one moor in Speyside was followed by much reduced tick burdens on chicks of red grouse, but this had no effect upon the number of grouse available for shooting.[91] In a separate trial on another Speyside moor where louping ill was a known problem, however, increased grouse bags followed mass killing of mountain hares and deer.[92]

Since the early 1990s, the disease seems to have been affecting red grouse in some areas where it was not previously recognised. This could be due partly to milder winters allowing better tick survival, and partly to increased numbers of hosts, notably red deer. Mass killing of mountain hares with the aim of protecting grouse from louping ill is becoming widespread. The Speyside trials may have been straws in a gathering wind that is already seeing mountain hares being greatly reduced on many Scottish moors.

Until the 1970s, red deer were regarded as vermin on many grouse-moors and shot on sight. This policy was relaxed as estates attempted to increase income by having deer stalking and grouse shooting on the same ground. This might have been counterproductive if it allowed grouse to become infected with louping ill. Managers who greatly reduce mountain hares to protect their grouse stocks might consider reverting to the traditional practice of treating red deer as vermin.

## DISEASE AND CLIMATE CHANGE

Grouse evolved during a period of global cooling and so climate warming is unlikely to favour them (*see* Chapter 1). Milder and wetter weather might promote the transmission of caecal threadworms and louping-ill virus. Conversely, warmer and drier conditions might reduce transmission rates by lowering humidity and thus making worm larvae and ticks more prone to desiccation. At the moment, anecdotal evidence is that ticks are now found on dogs in every month of the year, quite unlike a few decades ago, and louping ill appears to be spreading amongst red grouse.

Further spread of ticks and louping ill to Alpine ground could be disastrous for the ill-prepared rock ptarmigan, which has no natural immunity to the virus.

This seems less likely in the Cairngorms, where there are very low densities of mammalian hosts, but more likely on relatively fertile soils such as on the Cairnwell Hills, where mountain hares, voles and red deer are abundant. Excessive numbers of red deer are a likely agent for spreading ticks and louping ill to previously unaffected moors and Alpine land (see Chapter 15).

## SUMMARY

Humans have altered habitats and extirpated large predators in Britain and Ireland, thereby allowing medium-sized predators such as foxes and crows to become unnaturally abundant. The killing of such predators for the benefit of ground-nesting birds therefore has a rational and ethical basis. Some current practices, however, are controversial or illegal.

Pine martens kill capercaillie and are often said to threaten the bird's future in Scotland. The evidence, however, is that the two species should be able to coexist in Scotland as in other countries.

The most damaging parasite of red grouse is the caecal threadworm *Trichostrongylus tenuis*. High grouse density and wet summer weather are each conducive to grouse disease, which is caused by this parasite, but threadworms are often blamed for declines that actually result from the birds' own behaviour. Disease certainly causes population crashes on overstocked moors, especially after wet summer weather enhances parasite transmission, but population cycles continue even when parasites are removed.

The virus disease louping ill, transmitted by sheep ticks, is fatal to red grouse. Since the early 1990s, the disease seems to have been affecting red grouse in some areas where it was not previously recognised. This could be due partly to milder winters allowing better tick survival, and partly to increased numbers of hosts, notably red deer.

Climate change involving milder and wetter weather might increase both grouse disease and louping ill.

CHAPTER 14

# Population Fluctuations

ANIMALS OF DIFFERENT SPECIES, including birds of the grouse family, often fluctuate in abundance together, despite living in different habitats and having different life histories. An obvious explanation, that each species is influenced by the same weather, proved difficult to demonstrate until the discovery of the North Atlantic Oscillation (NAO).[1] Paradoxically, it is often easier to show a link between animal population fluctuations and this crude index of prevailing weather than with local meteorological measurements such as rainfall or temperature. We illustrate the explanatory value of the NAO with bag records from the four species of British grouse.

Within this broad climatic framework, detailed studies give insights into the biological processes that determine the dynamics of thriving populations on the scale of a scientific study area, typically a few square kilometres. It happens that such processes vary with the structure of the landscape. Thus, the dynamics of grouse populations in large tracts of homogeneous habitat differ from those in more fragmented habitats.

The scientific study of population fluctuations is known as 'population dynamics'. This chapter is mostly about the fluctuations in grouse numbers that occur from year to year. Other chapters give more on how grouse abundance varies from place to place.

Landscape and weather set the stage upon which short-term fluctuations in grouse numbers occur. Such fluctuations are often cyclical. There is a long-standing debate about causes of population cycles in boreal herbivores such as voles, lemmings and hares, and in birds of the grouse family. Studies of grouse, especially red grouse, are now resolving this problem.

## WEATHER AND GROUSE NUMBERS

### Grouse abundance and the North Atlantic Oscillation

Bag records from all four species of British grouse (Fig. 170) tend to fluctuate together, reflecting periods of general tetraonid[2] abundance and scarcity.[3] Moran showed that bags of all four species on 'a number of Scottish estates' in east-central Scotland fluctuated together between 1866 and 1938 (Table 29), and suggested that bags of all four species were influenced by weather.[5]

TABLE 29. Cross-correlation coefficients between bags of four grouse species in east-central Scotland in 1866–1943. Bottom left, raw bags; top right, filtered bags.[4]

|  | RED GROUSE | PTARMIGAN | CAPERCAILLIE | BLACK GROUSE |
|---|---|---|---|---|
| Red grouse | — | 0.36** | 0.35** | 0.45**** |
| Ptarmigan | 0.46** | — | 0.34** | 0.15 |
| Capercaillie | 0.56** | 0.39*** | — | 0.39*** |
| Black grouse | 0.49**** | 0.07 | 0.34*** | — |

**Notes**
**$P < 0.01$, ***$P < 0.001$, ****$P < 0.0001$, based on filtered bags.
These results resemble those of Moran (1952), but are not identical because the data that we used differed somewhat from his.

To illustrate this, we compare a measure of general tetraonid abundance in east-central Scotland with the NAO (Fig. 171). The fit is imperfect, but peaks in the NAO during the early 1900s and 1920s were evidently associated with peaks in tetraonid abundance. More formally, the equation that best explains tetraonid abundance included a running mean of four NAO values, including the current value and the previous three years' values.[6]

The 1866–1943 bag records did not distinguish between young and old birds, but recent records of red grouse shot show the NAO to be related to the proportion of young in the bag.[7] Hence, for red grouse at least, some aspect of weather that is related to the NAO seems to affect breeding success, and breeding success is known to influence subsequent population densities.

This broad relationship raises several questions. For example, the NAO reflects the strength and persistence of the Azores area of high pressure, which is associated with mild weather and westerly winds in western Europe. But what are

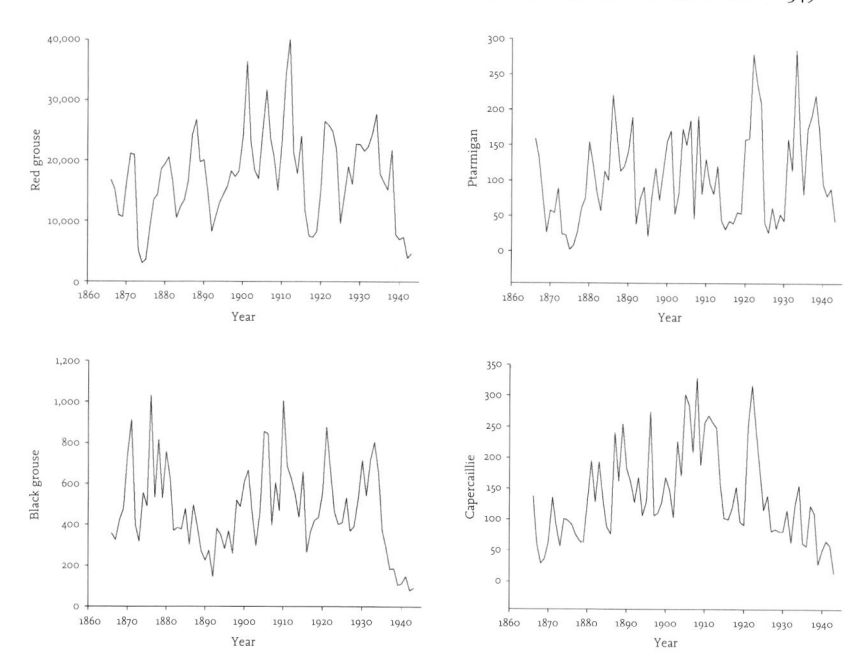

FIG 170. Annual bags of red grouse, ptarmigan, black grouse and capercaillie from east-central Scotland, 1866–1943.

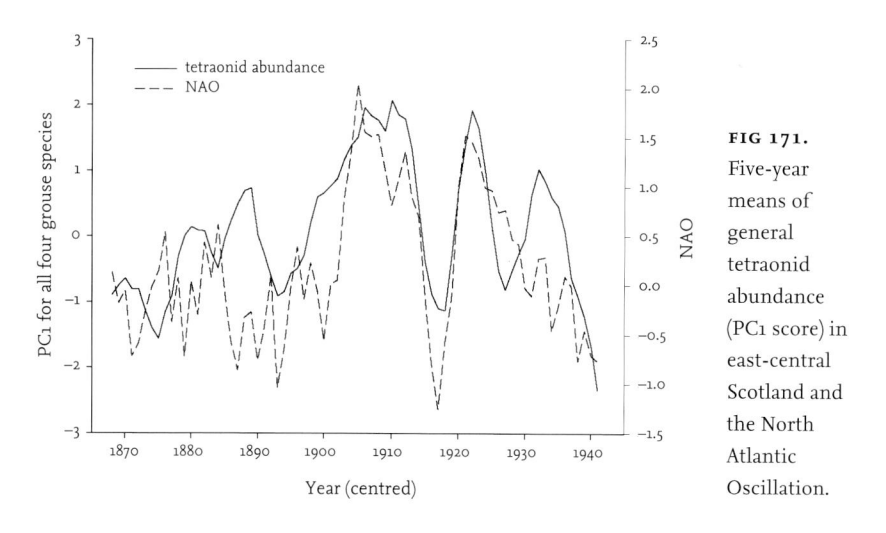

FIG 171. Five-year means of general tetraonid abundance (PC1 score) in east-central Scotland and the North Atlantic Oscillation.

the relevant local meteorological factors affecting grouse?[8] The next section tackles this question for rock ptarmigan and red grouse on the Cairngorms massif and the Cairnwell hills.

**Population cycles and weather – entrainment**

The idea of entrainment elucidates the relationship between population fluctuations and weather. Thus, grouse numbers fluctuate irrespective of weather, but weather influences the fluctuations. If weather shows a regular pattern, grouse numbers reflect this pattern, though not exactly. Also, different populations of the same species might be entrained by different aspects of weather.

Many but not all species of the grouse family are known to show regular population cycles. In species that do show cycles, not all populations are cyclic, and not all cyclic populations show the same period. The quoted period of a cyclic population fluctuation is an average value, because successive fluctuations often differ in length. For grouse species, commonly reported cycle periods include three to four years, six to seven, and about ten (also called eight to eleven) years. Longer periods may also occur but evidence for these is equivocal (Fig. 172).[9] Cycle period is not species-specific – red grouse, for example, have shown cycles of four to five years, six to seven years, seven to eight years, and ten years. Furthermore, populations of different grouse species that coexist in the same area tend to fluctuate together. Hence fluctuation pattern and cycle period seem to depend more upon local circumstances than upon species. One reason for this may be that local population fluctuations adopt the period of local weather patterns. The fluctuations do not mirror weather patterns exactly, but they do seem to be under their influence.

Red grouse and rock ptarmigan on the Cairngorms massif in Scotland have fluctuated together in ten-year cycles (see Fig. 173a). But in the nearby (20km distant) Cairnwell hills, the same species show unstable but erratic fluctuations (see Fig. 173b), similar in amplitude to the cycles in the Cairngorms but with no fixed period.[15] Within each range of hills, the two species fluctuate more or less together, but fluctuations in the two ranges are out of phase with each other (Figs 173a and 175). In this case, the role of weather can be understood only when we take soils into account. The study sites in the Cairngorms lie over granite that gives rise to generally infertile soils, supporting ptarmigan food plants of lower nutritive value, while on the more fertile Cairnwell hills with mostly base-rich bedrock the same plant species are of higher nutritive value. Interactions between weather and diet quality can explain the different dynamics on the two hill ranges.

The ten-year bird cycles on the Cairngorms massif relate closely to a ten-year cycle in June temperature. Records from the nearby village of Braemar show peak

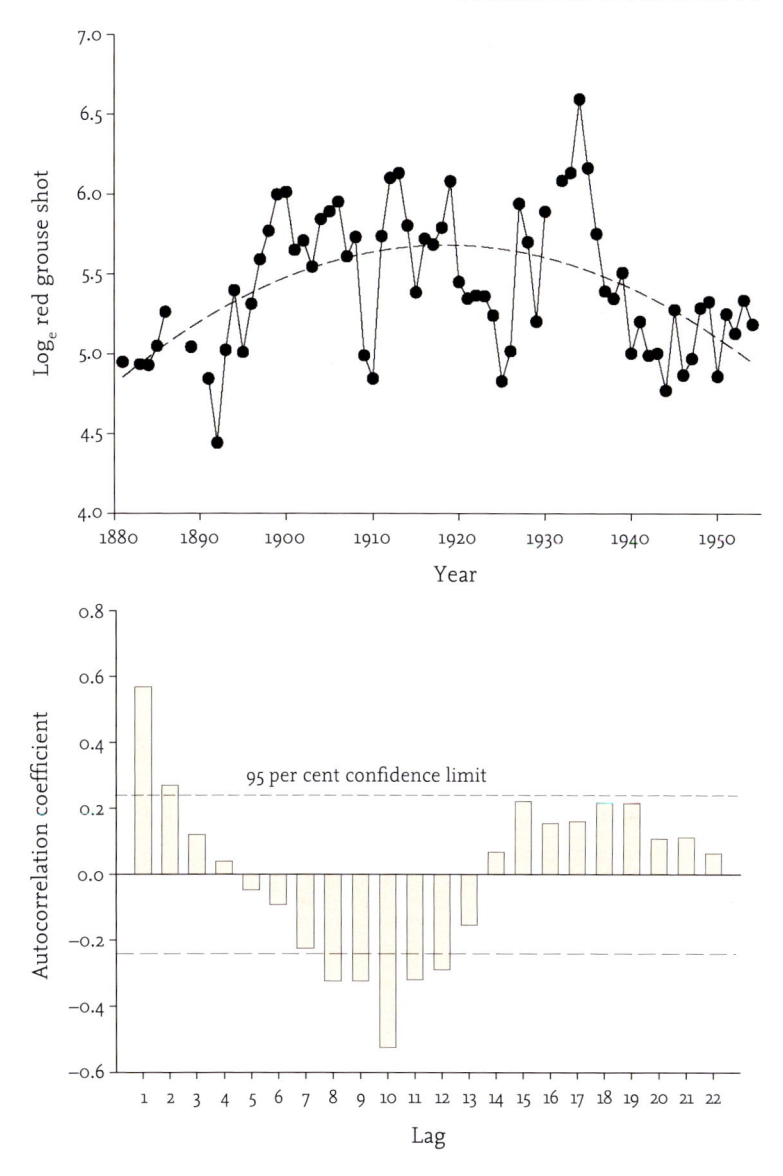

**FIG 172.** Equivocal evidence for a 20-year cycle in bags of red grouse at French Park, Ireland.[10] Top: bags (log$_e$ basis) and trend (dashed line). Gaps represent missing data. Bottom: autocorrelations.[11] The significant negative autocorrelation at a lag of ten years suggests a 20-year cycle, but the data are equivocal because they represent only three putative cycles and the 20-year autocorrelation coefficient is insignificant.[12]

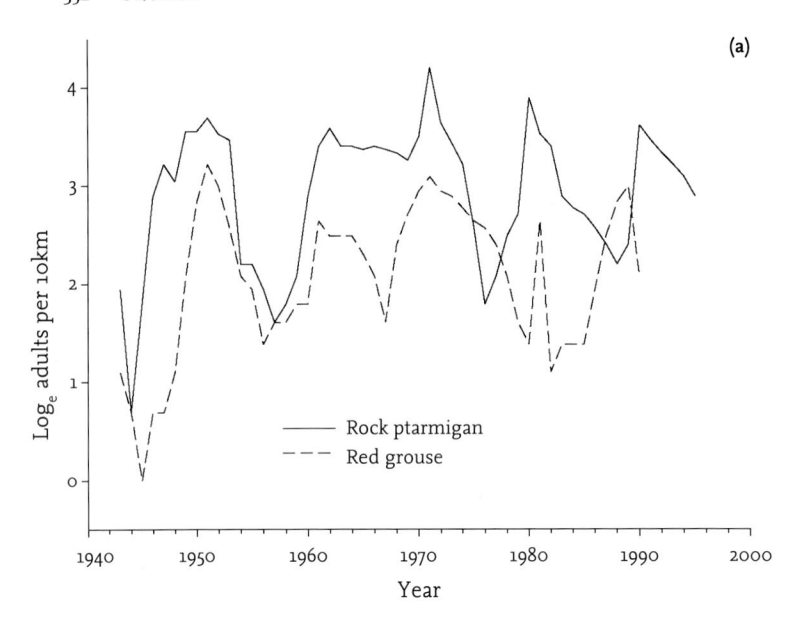

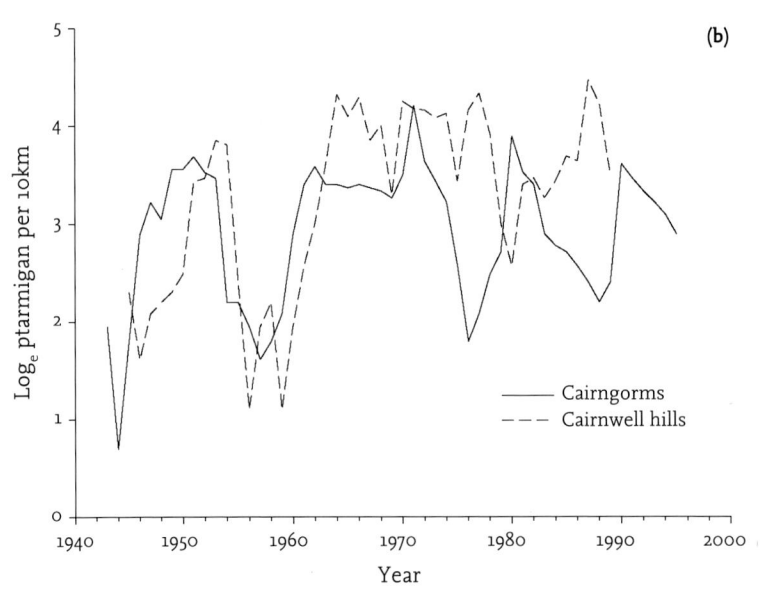

FIG 173.

OPPOSITE PAGE:

**FIG 173.** (a) Numbers of rock ptarmigan and of red grouse in the Cairngorms (recorded as adults seen per 10km of transect walks in May–September), a measure closely related to spring density (birds per km$^2$). The numbers of both species peaked more or less together once a decade, hence the two fluctuated in partial synchrony and showed ten-year cycles.[13] (b) Numbers of rock ptarmigan in the Cairngorms and the Cairnwell hills (adults per 10km of transect walks). The birds in the Cairngorms showed clear ten-year cycles, and their raised baseline in the 1960s was associated with an exceptional run of warm Junes. The Cairnwell birds fluctuated erratically and out of phase with those in the Cairngorms.[14]

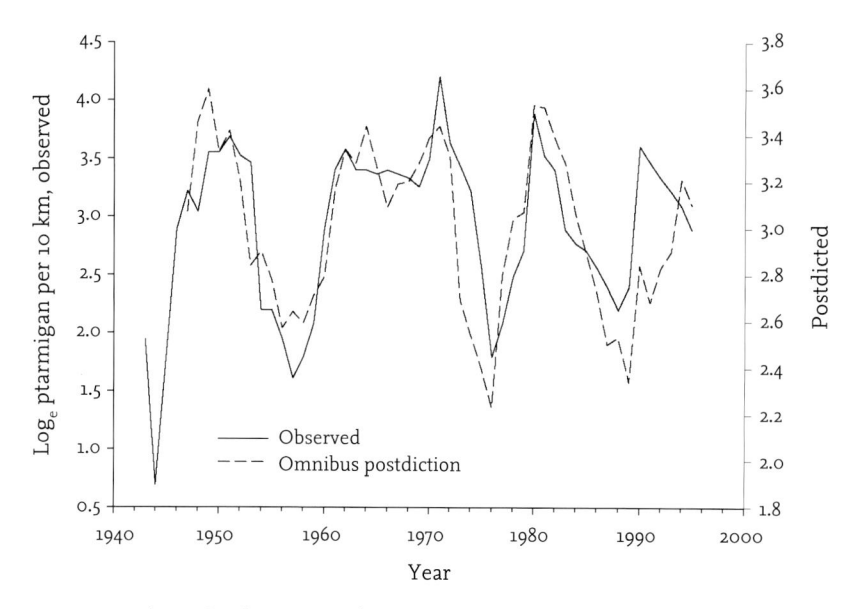

**FIG 174.** Numbers of rock ptarmigan (adults per 10km of transect walks) in the Cairngorms, as observed and as postdicted from the June mean temperature at Braemar village by an 'omnibus' model with no input from observed ptarmigan numbers after 1944.[16]

June temperatures occurring at ten-year intervals, intriguingly as isolated single-year spikes and not as high points of a smooth curve. Peaks in ptarmigan and red grouse come one to two years after the cyclic peaks in June temperature, but the bird cycles do not mimic the temperature fluctuations exactly.

A simple model, of the same type as the equation relating tetraonid abundance to the NAO (*see* endnote 6), gives a good account of ptarmigan cycles on the central Cairngorms sub-massif (Fig. 174).[17] It is essentially a running mean of June temperatures dating back four years, together with a delayed density-dependent term representing a damped cycle.[18] A plausible explanation depends on the observation that, in the infertile Cairngorms, the breeding success of ptarmigan is related to June temperature, as follows.

June temperatures spike every ten years or so, and this gives a decennial boost to reproduction, probably through better food for the chicks – more insects, or improved plant growth or plant quality. Better reproduction results in more youngsters recruited to the breeding population in the following year, and hence an increase in spring density. As in red grouse (*see* below) and irrespective of weather, high recruitment in one year begets high recruitment in the next, a form of positive feedback in population growth. Spring density peaks one to two years after the initial increase in reproduction. At peak density, the population becomes crowded and birds are more aggressive. This causes a continued decline in density due to continued aggression and reduced recruitment, associated with lower breeding success and probably increased emigration of youngsters to other sub-massifs.[19]

Whatever the biological mechanism, the ten-year cycle of ptarmigan and red grouse in the Cairngorms was clearly linked to a ten-year cycle in June temperature. This raises the question of why the nearby Cairnwell fluctuations (*see* Fig. 173b) were not entrained to June temperatures. On the more fertile Cairnwell, ptarmigan occurred at higher densities, and had better nutrition and also better reproduction that, crucially, was not related to June temperature.[20] Instead, fluctuations were related negatively to spring snow-lie and positively to temperature (Fig. 175). Neither of these shows regular cycles, nor do Cairnwell ptarmigan.

The equation describing the Cairnwell fluctuations incorporates the same damped cycle as the Cairngorms equation, but modified by different weather (snow-lie and temperature), and so results in an erratic fluctuation.[21] Although this fluctuation has a cyclic component, it would be confusing to call it cyclic, because it does not show a single dominant period. A term that covers both kinds of fluctuation is 'unstable'.

Weather cycles themselves need not be permanent features of a climate, for they seem to come and go in an unpredictable and chaotic fashion.[22] This might explain how grouse cycles come and go, and how they change their period over the years (*see* below).

## POPULATION DYNAMICS AND BEHAVIOUR

The story so far is that grouse populations show unstable dynamics, and that interaction with weather and soil fertility can result in cyclic or erratic fluctuations. However, this explanation does not include the biological mechanism that causes

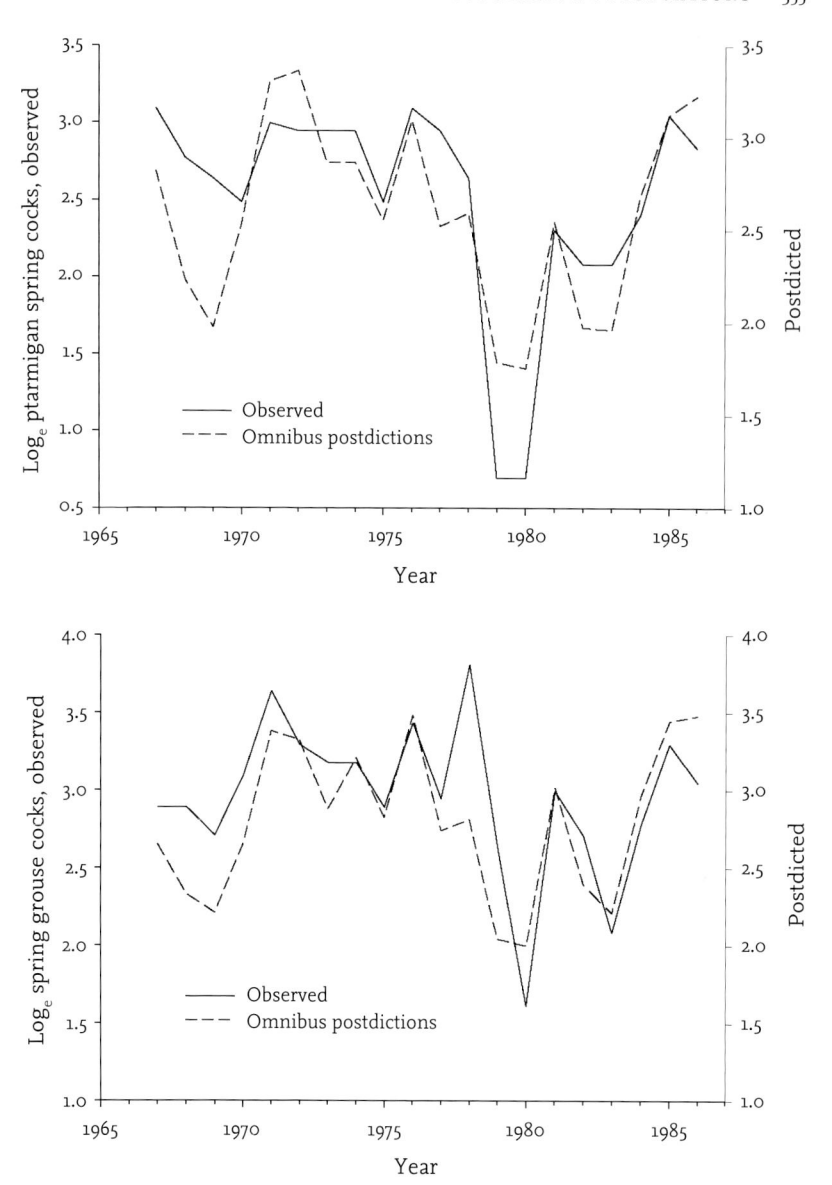

FIG 175. Numbers of rock ptarmigan (top) and red grouse (bottom) in the Cairnwell hills: number of spring cocks observed, and number postdicted from spring snow-lie and mean air temperature in early May. Postdictions are from 'omnibus' models, with no input from observed numbers after 1966.

the unstable dynamics, a topic that has long fascinated ecologists. The equations that were used successfully to 'postdict' grouse numbers (see Figs 174 & 175) do not necessarily correspond to biological mechanisms. Thus, annual variations in numbers are caused initially by something in the birds themselves. This 'something' changes in relation to weather. The equations do not specify the something, nor how weather affects it, and so they are empirical, not mechanistic.[23]

Some of the first mathematical models in ecology showed that model population cycles can result from predator-prey interactions.[24] Models also substantiate the yet earlier insight that 'overcrowding creates disease', such that population cycles might result from successive episodes of overcrowding, disease-induced decline, and subsequent recovery.[25] Another possibility is that animals at high densities deplete their food, starve into decline, and then recover from low densities when their food regains abundance.

These mechanisms, conceptually similar, each fall into the category of 'trophic interactions' or 'extrinsic processes'.[26] Fieldworkers, however, are often impressed by the time and energy that individuals of the same species spend competing with each other. Such observations led to the view that animals are able to regulate their own density below any limit set by resources or natural enemies,[27] which implies that spacing behaviour can regulate density and hence is an 'intrinsic process'.[28]

Critics assert that classical theories of population dynamics do not explain how unstable dynamics can arise from intrinsic processes. So entrenched is this view that cycles are often cited as evidence of trophic interactions. Biologists and sociologists interested in the fundamental question of how cooperation between organisms evolved, however, have refuted this criticism. Cooperation occurs when individuals benefit more from helping each other than from behaving selfishly. Models with individuals either cooperating or acting selfishly often result in unstable population fluctuations.[29] Increasing populations go along with more cooperation, whereas declines are associated with increased selfishness. This result provides a broad theoretical basis for the idea that intrinsic processes involving the behaviour of individuals can cause unstable population dynamics.[30]

Population cycles are fascinating in themselves, but are also useful in population biology, because each successive cyclic fluctuation is seemingly a repetition of the same event. This allows scientists to develop hypotheses about population regulation during one fluctuation and to test them during the next. In particular, work on red grouse has developed, refined and tested the hypothesis that spacing behaviour can cause unstable population fluctuations, of which cycles are one obvious manifestation.[31]

### Basic concepts in population dynamics

To explore population fluctuations further, we need some basic ideas. Obviously, animal numbers are limited by resources such as food and cover, other species that compete for the same resources, and natural enemies such as predators and parasites. For gamebirds we include shooters as natural enemies. Weather, in turn, influences the availability of resources and the impacts of natural enemies. These limiting factors determine the size of animal populations through effects on reproduction, death and movement. One approach to explaining fluctuations in population size is therefore to measure reproduction and mortality, the vital rates of a studied population, and to find whether variations in vital rates are explained by fluctuations in limiting factors.

Movement is also an important determinant of population size, but in practice is harder to study than reproduction or death. Population ecologists often delimit an area of ground and define the animals within it as their study population. Some animals move out of the study area and become difficult or impossible to follow, while others of unknown provenance move in. This complicates the calculation of reproduction and mortality, and so early modellers, pretending that inward and outward movement (immigration and emigration, respectively) cancel each other out, ignored movement and emphasised 'closed' populations, in which changes in population size are determined solely by the balance between reproduction and death.

This sweeping simplification led to the compelling concept of density dependence. Clearly, an animal population could not increase without limit. Presumably, some factor in the environment, such as disease or lack of food, imposed a limit through its effect on a vital rate, thereby regulating the balance between reproduction and mortality, causing the model population to decline from high densities, and allowing it to increase from low densities. Therefore, to detect the factor regulating a real population, one could take the mortality rate due to each candidate factor and plot it against population size.[32] The regulating factor should be revealed by a plot that shows the candidate mortality rate increasing with rising density.[33] A mortality factor that passes such tests is said to 'regulate' population size.

This school of thought, greatly elaborated, remains popular. Some models now go further by incorporating movement. Also, regulating factors can act with a time lag, thereby delaying their effect. Models incorporating such delayed density dependence can produce unstable population fluctuations, including cycles. Despite its present numerical complexity, this view remains essentially one of passive population dynamics, in which the size of an animal population is determined by its vital rates and perhaps movement, these being regulated solely by the population's resources and natural enemies. This nurtures a conservative view that studies of behaviour are unnecessary for an understanding of population dynamics.

If you watch birds in the field, however, a very different impression can emerge. Most red grouse, for example, live in a sea of heather, which provides them with abundant food and cover. They spend relatively little time eating or taking cover, and usually rear far more young than are needed to replace adult losses. This is, of course, why they are gamebirds – in most years the autumn population can be heavily cropped without depressing the breeding population the following spring. The size of breeding populations can certainly be limited by damage to the heather food or by the ravages of natural enemies, but these do not explain all the observed fluctuations. If the birds are marked so that they can be recognised individually and are then watched carefully, a pattern of social behaviour emerges.

Red grouse are territorial birds, each spring territory being held by a cock, which is usually paired with a hen. In summer, the territorial system relaxes, and families – pairs with their broods of young – roam unhindered by territorial boundaries. In the half-light of dawn, the father of a wandering brood wings back to his territory and briefly crows title before returning to his family.

By autumn the young are fully grown, each family returns to its home territory and the father aggressively reasserts his old territorial boundaries. The young cocks also begin to display aggression, and, using the parental territory as a base, attempt to establish their own territories nearby. Soon, families break up as each young cock tries to get his own territory, perhaps to some extent with the help of his father. Some young birds succeed, forcing old cocks to cede ground or ousting them. Some fail, and join with ousted old cocks, often in wandering bands of 'floaters'.[34]

By the end of winter, most floating cocks have died because they did not have a territory. On grouse-moors where gamekeepers kill most predators, almost all territory owners typically survive the winter to form the following year's breeding population. In more natural circumstances, some territory owners are killed by predators, allowing an equivalent number of floaters to occupy the vacated territories and so survive. Hence the number of territories in spring is more or less determined by the competition for territories in autumn.[35]

A hen gains her place in the breeding population by consorting with a territorial cock. Some hens choose a cock during the autumn contest and stay with him until spring, some move from one cock to another, and a few wander from cock to cock until they finally settle, just before laying eggs in spring. A territory is typically occupied by a pair, although occasional cocks have two hens and bachelor territorial cocks are common. Even so, cocks largely determine hen numbers. If a territorial cock dies and is not replaced, the hen soon leaves and looks for another cock. Hens that fail to pair with a cock become floaters, sharing the fate of cock floaters.

Some territorial birds emigrate to less crowded ground just before laying. Such pre-laying emigration is density dependent and, in our experience, comprises mostly young birds.[36] It is observed most frequently at very high spring densities, exceeding about 100 territories per km$^2$.

Such observations suggest that social behaviour determines population density, in this case largely the cocks' territorial behaviour during the autumn territorial contest. Some, unconvinced by such evidence, have argued that social behaviour serves merely to distribute animals after their numbers have been limited by resources or natural enemies. Only in the last few years has unequivocal evidence been provided that animals can regulate their own densities.

**Role of territorial behaviour in population dynamics of red grouse**

Red grouse territories typically occupy most of the available moorland,[37] and so spring population density is essentially the inverse of mean territory size, as determined largely during the territorial contest of the previous autumn. Aggressiveness influences territory size, and territory size probably influences aggressiveness. Thus, on a given tract in a given year, the more aggressive cocks have the larger territories. Then again, comparing different years on the same moor, cocks at higher average density, with more numerous smaller territories crowded together, show more aggressiveness.[38] This leads to complex interactions between aggressiveness and density, which are now being unravelled, partly by the experimental use of testosterone implants to increase the cocks' aggressiveness, and partly by mathematical deduction.

Aggressiveness in cock red grouse is related to the amount of testosterone in their blood, and a few milligrams of testosterone can have profound effects on population dynamics. This was first illustrated by an experiment at Glen Tanar in which testosterone was implanted into half the cocks on a study area in spring (*see* Fig. 176). The implanted cocks took larger territories and ousted many unimplanted males, thereby causing an increase in average territory size and a decline in breeding density.[39]

This experiment showed that an increase in aggressiveness can reduce population density. Other than that, however, implications for population dynamics were not clear. A year after the implants, spring territory size and density on the experimental area had reverted to that of the control, and so the

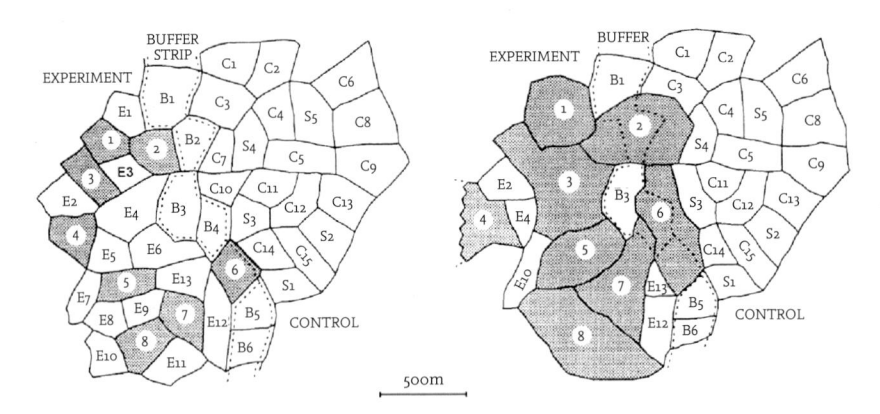

FIG 176. Effects of testosterone implants on spring territory size and numbers of red grouse at Glen Tanar in spring 1993. Shaded territories are of implanted cocks before (left) and after (right) implants. Similar results occurred in 1992, except that cocks in the opposite half of the study area were implanted.

increase in aggressiveness had no long-lasting effect on population density. Also, the implants were done in spring, not in autumn when the territorial contest that fixes population density occurs. In addition, implants of testosterone are obviously unnatural.

The next experiment rectified these drawbacks. To appreciate its ingenious design, we must understand the likely role of kinship in population cycles of red grouse. Population density is determined largely by the cocks' mean territory size in a given autumn. The general idea that population fluctuations are caused by changes in mean territory size, in turn due to changes in aggressive behaviour, is the 'territorial-behaviour hypothesis'.[40] This is now well established, but it does not explain what causes the changes in aggressiveness. The 'kinship hypothesis' is a specific version of the territorial-behaviour hypothesis that does explain the changes in aggressiveness.

Changes in population density from one spring to the next are determined partly by the mortality of established old territorial cocks, and partly by the recruitment of young cocks to the territorial population. Although the mortality of old cocks varies from year to year, it bears no consistent relation to the population cycle's 'phase' (its increase or decline). Recruitment varies more than adult mortality and is the main determinant of population change, being greater during the increase phase of cycles and less during declines. And kinship seems to influence the proportion of young cocks competing for territories that gets recruited into the territorial population.

### Kinship

That related animals behave differently towards each other than towards unrelated individuals is well documented. So, too, is 'helping', whereby young animals help their parents to rear further offspring. This can be understood in terms of kin selection: doubtless it is selectively advantageous to help with the rearing of kin. It should also be advantageous to help kin get recruited into the breeding population.

Kin are less aggressive towards each other than towards non-kin.[41] Young red grouse cocks tend to get territories close to their father's territory, thereby forming kin clusters (extended family units) of related territory owners. Such clusters build up during the increase phase of a cycle and decay during the decline.[42]

Each kin cluster is thought to influence future densities through its effects on recruitment. Comparisons within years show that a young cock that is hatched into a larger cluster has a greater chance of getting a territory.[43] Extrapolate this result to differences between years, and it follows that young cocks should recruit more successfully in contests that start on average with more or larger kin clusters, provided that the population is not already so crowded as to make further recruitment impracticable. Similarly, at equal densities, recruitment should be low in contests that start with fewer or smaller kin clusters, unless density is low enough to make recruitment easy. Observations during a recent population cycle confirmed that the proportion of cocks within kin clusters rose along with recruitment during the increase phase of the cycle, that both began to fall just before peak density, and that they continued to fall during the decline.[44]

Mathematical modelling brings observations together to show how the growth and decay of kin clusters might lead to population cycles (*see* Fig. 177).[45] Kin clusters are dynamic entities that grow through recruitment and that decay from the death of established members. Some recruitment is necessary for a cluster to maintain itself. In an increasing population, recruitment exceeds mortality by a sufficient amount to allow kin clusters to grow in size. Eventually, however, the population becomes so crowded that it cannot increase further and recruitment is inhibited.[46] Unable to sustain themselves, kin clusters break up, and so aggressiveness among neighbours increases, triggering a population decline. There are now no kin clusters to facilitate recruitment, and the population decline continues for a few years until it has reached a low density. This makes recruitment easy, whereupon kin clusters reform as density begins to increase again.[47]

The experiment that we next describe was designed with the kinship hypothesis in mind. Old cocks (those that had held territories in the previous spring) were implanted with testosterone in September–November to make them more aggressive. It was predicted from the kinship hypothesis that increased

362 · GROUSE

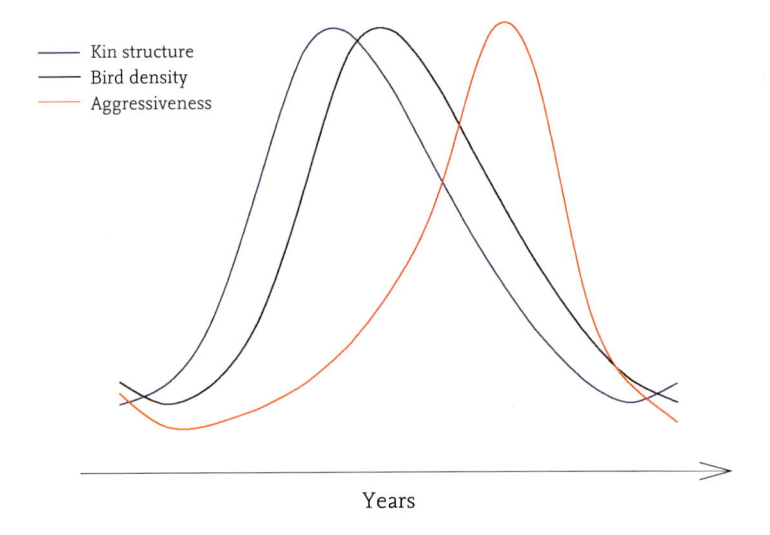

**FIG 177.** Model fluctuations in population density, kin-cluster size and aggressiveness of red grouse during a population cycle, according to mathematical formulations of the kinship hypothesis.[48]

aggression would reduce the recruitment of young cocks and hence the size of kin clusters.

It was not known whether the enlarged autumn territories would revert to their original size when the testosterone in the implants had been exhausted. If so, this might allow young cocks to be recruited, albeit later than usual, and any effect of the experiment might be as transient as in the previous experiment carried out in spring at Glen Tanar (see Fig. 176). Alternatively, if territories were fixed in the autumn, the enlarged territories should remain, resulting in reduced densities and smaller kin clusters the following spring. According to the kinship hypothesis, these smaller kin clusters should cause reduced recruitment in the autumn a year after the implants. In consequence, the size of kin clusters and density should remain lower on the experimental areas for at least two springs after the autumn of implantation. The boldness of these predictions meant that this was a risky experiment, in the best sense of the word.[49]

**Manipulating recruitment**

The experiment was carried out twice,[50] once in northern England and once in northeast Scotland, where the kinship hypothesis originated. In each country, the experiment used two separate moors simultaneously.

Implants of testosterone changed the outcome of autumn territorial contests. On 1km$^2$ experimental areas of moorland, most of the old cocks were implanted with testosterone. During the territorial contests, implanted old cocks gained bigger territories, which entailed lower densities and prevented most of the young cocks that had been reared that summer from establishing territories on the study area. The testosterone in the implants was exhausted after three months, but the density of the experimental populations remained depressed throughout the winter, and onwards into the following spring and summer (Fig. 178). Meanwhile, on nearby control areas, the normal course of events developed: many young cocks gained territories and densities remained higher than on the experimental areas.

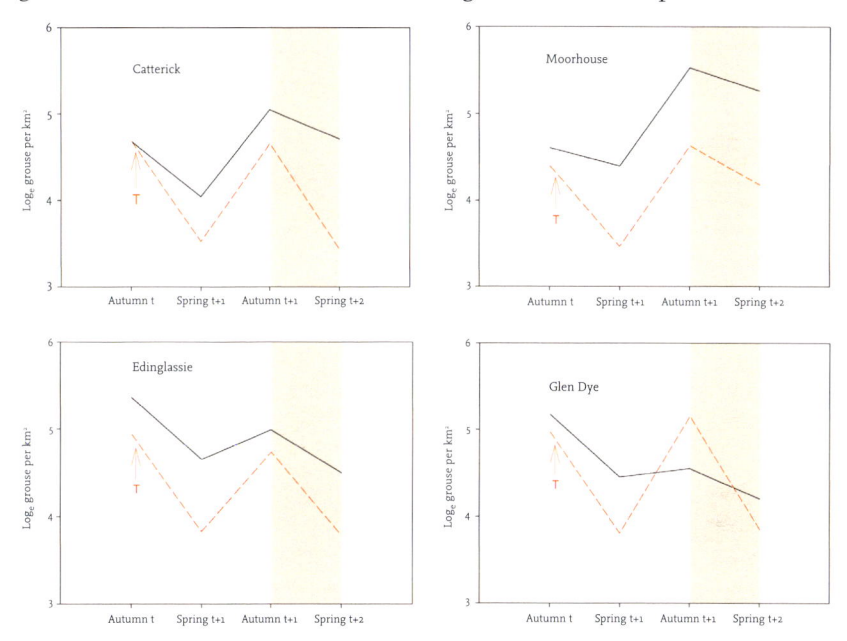

FIG 178. Effects of testosterone implants (T, arrow) on the density of red grouse (cocks and hens) on four 1km$^2$ study areas in England (Catterick and Moorhouse) and in Scotland (Edinglassie and Glen Dye) during autumn and spring. Control areas, black solid lines; implants, red dashed lines. The increases between spring t+1 (April) and autumn t+1 (late July–early August) are due to young being reared. In each case, the implanted population declined faster than the control (overwinter losses were greater, as shown by steeper slopes between autumn and spring), not only in the first winter after implants, but also in the following winter (between autumn t+1 and spring t+2, highlighted grey), when no birds were implanted. Hence, well after they were exhausted, the testosterone implants continued to affect all four populations.[51]

This confirmed that breeding density was reduced by more aggressive territorial behaviour in the previous autumn. Furthermore, it showed that the reduced density of territory owners, established during the autumn contest and held long after the cause of the reduction (a transitory, artificial pulse of testosterone) had vanished.

Indeed, the effects of testosterone upon density did not stop at the breeding season immediately after the implantation, but carried through until the following breeding season a year later. Despite no further implants, grouse density and the recruitment of young cocks remained significantly lower on the experimental than on the control areas for at least two consecutive breeding seasons. Furthermore, grouse density again declined more on the treated areas than on the controls.

As expected from the kinship hypothesis, the declines in density caused by testosterone implants were associated with a reduction in kin clusters of territorial cocks. Parasites could not explain these results, for the declines were not associated with increased burdens of the parasitic caecal threadworm *Trichostrongylus tenuis*.

**Implications of the experiment**

This experiment provided clear evidence that red grouse have the ability to regulate their own density below any limits set by resources or natural enemies, in line with the territorial-behaviour hypothesis.[52] The outcome of a territorial contest can be influenced by the previous contest. In effect, the recruitment of young cocks in one contest is influenced by the birds' 'memory' of the previous contest. The kinship hypothesis suggests that this memory is held in the form of kin clusters, but one can deduce the effect of the memory without knowing in what form it is held.

Based solely upon the results of this experiment and other known facts about the birds' life history, mathematical deduction shows how territorial behaviour, interacting with present density and a memory of past density, can moderate recruitment and so lead to unstable dynamics.[53] Together with vital rates, the mathematical form of the two-way interaction between recruitment and density determines whether dynamics are stable or unstable.[54]

The main result of the modelling is that unstable dynamics should occur if changes in aggressiveness at least match changes in density. In the real world, two forms of aggressiveness were measured during a 14-year (1964–77) study of two population cycles on Kerloch moor, during which population density fluctuated fivefold.[55] Meanwhile, the rate at which cocks gave territorial songs fluctuated sixfold among years, and the rate at which they had territorial boundary disputes with each other fluctuated more than 20-fold. Hence proportional changes in density were more than matched by proportional changes in two measures of aggressiveness. It seems that the theoretical requirements for unstable dynamics to be caused by territorial aggressiveness are realistic.

In general, resources and enemies affect animal numbers by influencing vital rates and hence population dynamics. But the experimental and theoretical evidence from red grouse shows that we should not expect all fluctuations in density to relate *directly* to factors such as food, cover, disease or predation. According to the kinship hypothesis, for example, unstable dynamics can be the result of competition for land amongst extended families. But vital rates should affect the size of these families. Hence resources and enemies might well influence animal numbers *indirectly*, through their effects upon competition among families. The idea that resources and enemies can influence population dynamics indirectly, through their effects upon social structure, brings fruitful insight to the dry, deficient mantra that animal populations are regulated by density-dependent vital rates.

### Breeding success during cycles

If breeding success is so poor that insufficient young are reared to replace adult losses, then, without immigrants, a population must decline. During population cycles in birds of the grouse family, breeding success is usually lower during the decline phase than during the increase. Such observations tempt some to conclude that reduced breeding success causes declines. An alternative view is that cyclic declines engender poorer breeding.

The main documented demographic cause of population cycles in seven studies – rock ptarmigan in Alaska, Iceland and Scotland, willow ptarmigan in Norway and Newfoundland, and two of red grouse in Britain – was variation in the recruitment of young birds into the breeding population.[56] Recruitment occurred in two stages. First, during cyclic declines the birds' breeding success was lower – in other words, fewer young were reared to independence per adult. Second, a smaller proportion of these independent young survived the winter and recruited into the breeding population. However, mean breeding success differed greatly among populations within species, such that cyclic increases in some populations occurred with lower breeding success than during cyclic declines in other populations (*see* Table 30). It follows that variations in breeding density were not driven by the same variations in breeding success in all populations of the same species. Further, there was no inverse relation between mean breeding success and average adult survival. Hence populations with better mean breeding success had greater overwinter losses of independent young. An equivalent statement is that, in populations with better breeding success, smaller proportions of the reared young recruited into the breeding population.

TABLE 30. Mean breeding success (young reared per adult) during the increase and decline phases of population cycles, with average annual survival rates of adult hens.[57]

|  |  |  | BREEDING SUCCESS (RANGE) | | |
|---|---|---|---|---|---|
| BIRD | REGION | YEARS | INCREASE | DECLINE | HEN SURVIVAL |
| Rock ptarmigan | Alaska | 1960–5 | 2.5 (2.2–2.9) | 1.5 (1.4–1.6) | 0.44 |
|  | Iceland | 1964–9 | 3.9 (3.2–4.3) | 2.2 (1.4–2.6) | 0.54 |
|  | Cairngorms, Scotland | 1946–57 | 1.7 (0.7–2.3) | 0.3 (0.1–0.4) | 0.48 |
| Willow ptarmigan | Newfoundland | 1956–65 | 3.2 (2.7–3.3) | 2.1 (1.8–2.3) | 0.30 |
| Red grouse | Forvie, Scotland | 1961–70 | 1.8 (1.4–2.1) | 0.6 (0.3–0.8) | 0.24 |
|  | Rickarton, Scotland | 1979–87 | 2.2 (1.3–3.0) | 1.2 (0.7–1.8) | 0.24 |

The above evidence shows that variations in winter losses of independent young rock ptarmigan and *Lagopus lagopus* were the key determinant of recruitment, and, in studies of red grouse, many such losses were due ultimately to territorial behaviour. In the other cases just mentioned, and perhaps in other grouse species, some form of behaviour, not necessarily territorial, may be the ultimate cause also (*see* the last paragraph of 'Causes of Grouse Population Cycles', below).

The idea that poor breeding success during cyclic declines is an effect and not a cause of decline is still largely untested. The hypothesis that population cycles and other manifestations of unstable dynamics are due to variations in recruitment, mediated by behaviour, does not require variations in breeding success to occur. From an evolutionary point of view, however, it seems reasonable that a hen should invest less in rearing young during decline years, when the stresses associated with increased aggressiveness are probably greater than in increase years and the 'fitness benefits' per egg laid are smaller.[58]

## THE ROLE OF MOVEMENT AND LANDSCAPE IN POPULATION FLUCTUATIONS

### Movement

To understand how grouse populations fluctuate, we must take their spatial organisation into account. Kin clusters in red grouse are a specific example. More broadly, spatial organisation involves movement. A basic fact about movement is that, during natal dispersal, young hen red grouse move further than cocks and do not usually settle next to their natal territory. Another fact emerges from the spatial scale upon which several population experiments have been carried out. In the testosterone experiments above, for example, the 1km$^2$ experimental and control study areas were only 0.5km apart, and yet large differences in density were maintained for more than a year after the implants. This suggested a strong spatial structuring that prevented immigration and compensatory recruitment from neighbouring tracts that were much larger and had a higher density. This fits with other population studies, in which the demographic effects of experiments on areas as small as 16ha have been confined largely to these areas.[59] The evidence suggests that cocks are largely responsible for maintaining such spatial structuring.

Cocks and hens that fail to get territories during the autumn territorial contest become floaters that range widely, often in bands that provide some protection against attacks from territory owners. Old birds that have lost their territories sometimes get a new one elsewhere, but most die landless. Some floaters get territories by replacing territory owners that have been killed, for example, by predators. Others disperse and may establish territories in areas that are perhaps less crowded than their natal patch, where they are unlikely to form part of any kin cluster. There is evidence that immigrants increase aggressiveness on their new area.[60] Hence they might depress local densities or even precipitate a cyclic decline that would otherwise have been delayed until a later year. Dispersing floaters, in any case, are likely to suffer higher mortality than territorial residents. Most floaters are usually young birds. Hence the increased rate of dispersal associated with cyclic declines should be accompanied by higher mortality of young birds.

The root, or ultimate, cause of death in floating birds is their failure to join a breeding population.[61] Chased by territory owners, prevented from feeding where they will and from using cover effectively, such birds are stressed and lose condition. Thus, floaters are more vulnerable to predators than are territorial birds, so that the immediate, or proximate, cause of their death is often predation.[62] Stressed birds are also more vulnerable to parasitic or other disease. So, a study that failed to account for the birds' social status might incorrectly conclude that predation or disease was the main cause of a cyclic decline, when it was, primarily, due to the workings of the social system.

**Travelling waves**
When cycling populations of red grouse or ptarmigan are counted over several square kilometres, it becomes apparent that the fluctuations across the study area do not occur together and are only partly synchronous. Peaks and troughs seem

to follow each other over the ground like ripples across a pond; this pattern is called a travelling wave,[63] and has also been observed in cycling populations of voles and snowshoe hares. Such patterns might be due to dispersing floaters triggering successive declines in contiguous areas, but evidence is lacking.

Theoretical models suggest that population cycles and travelling waves could arise in a constant environment, through unstable dynamics alone. In reality, however, variations in natural enemies and resources certainly affect reproduction and survival. Hence, fluctuations in numbers are likely to be due to interactions between extrinsic factors that affect vital rates directly, and intrinsic factors that affect recruitment through variations in spacing behaviour and movement. We now consider one of these interactions.

**Habitat fragmentation and population cycles**

Much anecdotal evidence suggests that grouse cycles worldwide occur mostly in large tracts of fairly homogeneous habitat, and that fragmentation of such habitat by, for example, agriculture is associated with the disappearance of cycles. This has been attributed to increased dispersal out of fragmented habitat patches into population sinks, and to increased predation from generalist predators. For example, forest grouse and rodents show cycles in north Fennoscandia, but not in the more fragmented agricultural south where increased generalist predators are thought to suppress the cycles. Work on red grouse and ptarmigan in Scotland provides examples of generalist predators suppressing cycles.

The illegal killing of raptors is common practice on grouse-moors, because raptors are supposed by moorland managers to reduce stocks of red grouse available for shooting. An experiment at Langholm moor in southern Scotland aimed to test this hypothesis (see Chapter 12).[64] The killing of raptors, especially hen harriers, was stopped and their numbers increased. More harriers ate more grouse, grouse numbers declined, and the population cycle that had previously been apparent in shooting records stopped, while the cycle continued on nearby moors where the traditional, albeit illegal, killing of raptors continued.

A ski development on Cairn Gorm provides another example where generalist predators damped a population cycle (Fig. 179).[65] Though alien to this Arctic-Alpine habitat, carrion crows were attracted from the valley below by people's discarded food scraps. On the most developed area near the main car park, rock ptarmigan at first occurred at high density, but then lost nests to the influx of crows and reared abnormally few broods. They also died flying into ski-lift wires, and declined until none bred for many summers. On a nearby higher area with fewer wires, ptarmigan lost nests to frequent crows and reared abnormally few broods, but seldom died on wires. Here, adult numbers declined and then

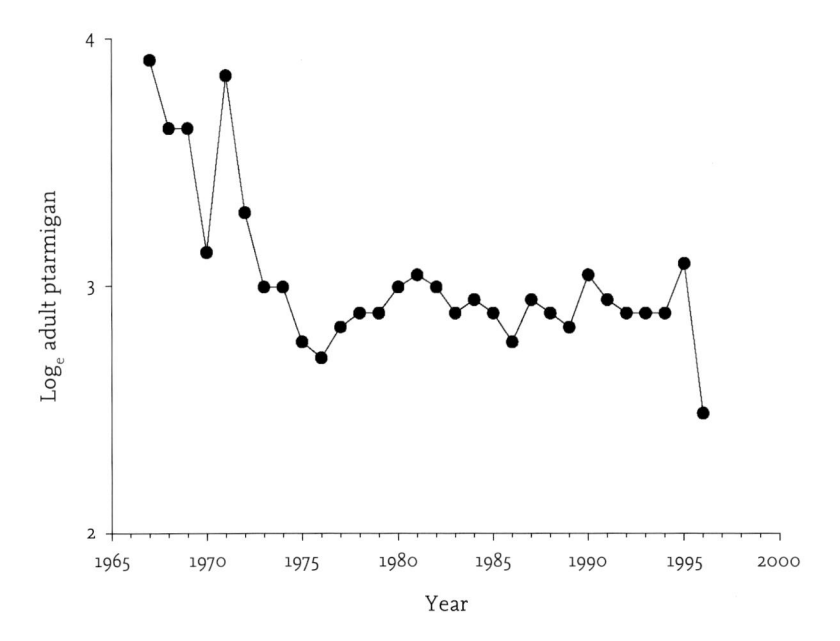

FIG 179. Non-cyclic fluctuations in rock ptarmigan (adults on 271ha) near the ski development at Cairn Gorm. Development began in 1961, after which ptarmigan numbers declined and then stabilised at a lower density, while numbers nearby (see Figs 173b & 174) continued to show cycles.[66]

became unusually steady for over two decades, with no significant cycle (Fig. 179). On a third area further from the car park, ptarmigan lost fewer nests to the less frequent crows, but bred more poorly than in the massif's centre and showed cycles of lower amplitude than there. On a fourth area yet further away, with few or no crows, ptarmigan bred equally as well as in the massif's centre and showed cycles of the same amplitude as there.

These examples help to show the role of large areas of fairly homogeneous habitat in generating population cycles. Fragmented habitat is likely to engender more losses of eggs or chicks from increased numbers of generalist predators, or more emigration of young followed by death in population 'sinks', which are typically areas of ground occupied by generalist predators and lying between habitat fragments. Because cyclic populations occur in homogeneous tracts, with lower densities of predators and longer distances to sinks, they should rear and recruit a higher proportion of young than non-cyclic populations in fragmented

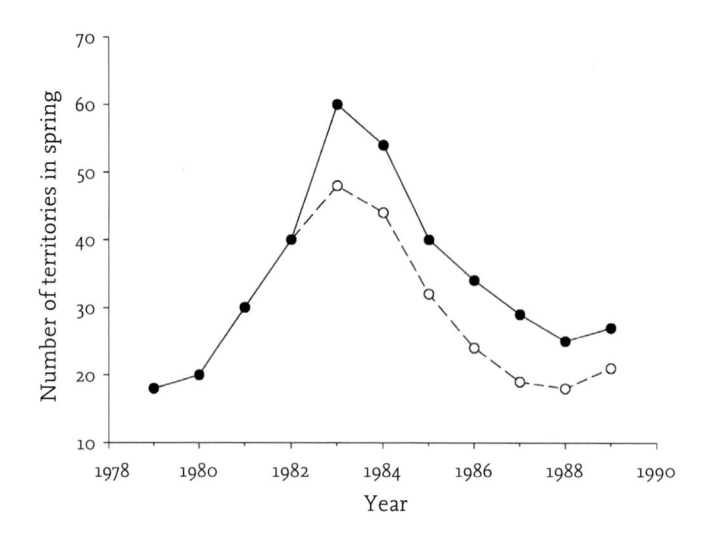

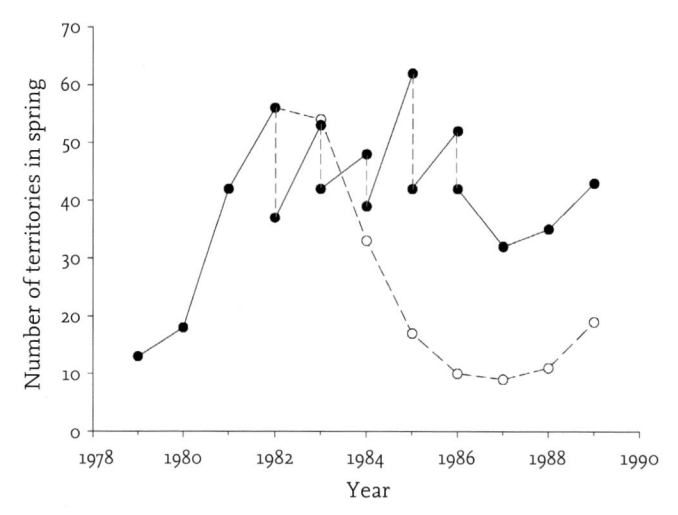

FIG 180. Number of spring territories of red grouse during an unperturbed population cycle on a 318ha control area (top), and during a cycle perturbed by removing cocks in the increase phase of the population fluctuation on a 203ha experimental area (bottom) at Rickarton moor. The vertical red dashed lines (bottom) show numbers before and after removals in spring. The black dashed lines show predictions made in spring 1982, using a model developed previously from fluctuations observed on a different study area.[68] (The brief 1986–7 decline on the experimental area followed severe damage to heather by winter weather in 1985 and increased caecal threadworm burdens in 1986.)

habitat. This should facilitate the development of greater population densities and larger kin clusters.

The next step in the argument is illustrated by an experiment with red grouse,[67] which prevented a population cycle by removing cocks in the increase phase, thereby stopping them from attaining peak density (Fig. 180). The control population peaked and then showed the predicted cyclic decline, but the experimental population showed no cyclic decline. Hence peak numbers may be necessary to initiate the process – presumably the catastrophic breakdown of kin clusters – that marks the beginning of cyclic declines.

In short, it seems that large tracts of fairly homogeneous habitat, where generalist predators are scarce and opportunities for dispersal limited, may be necessary for peak numbers. Peak numbers seem to be necessary for cyclic declines, and, consequently, large tracts engender population cycles.

## CAUSES OF GROUSE POPULATION CYCLES

Having explored the roles of weather, soil fertility, habitat continuity or fragmentation, and behaviour in population regulation, we can now assess some alternative explanations for the population cycles that occur in birds of the grouse family worldwide. The multiplicity of cycle periods within species among areas, and the similarity of cycle periods among species within areas, makes it clear that we are not dealing with a single process. Hypotheses about population cycles must explain three issues: what drives cycles (this is the 'something' described under 'Population Dynamics and Behaviour', above); intra-specific variations in cycle period; and inter-specific synchrony.

Entrainment by weather (see p.350) or other extrinsic processes can explain the second and third issues. Another explanation of inter-specific synchrony is the 'Moran effect'. This postulates that random variations in weather can bring independently cycling populations into synchrony. The main difference between the Moran effect and entrainment is that entrainment involves a weather cycle (see Figs 174 & 175), whereas the Moran effect does not. The widespread low numbers of grouse and other animals in northwest Europe in the early 1940s (see Figs 170–174) might be seen either as an example of the Moran effect or of entrainment, as might the remarkable synchrony among the six moors in Figure 168. The distinction is slight. Neither, however, explains what drives cycles.

Grouse cycles seem to be an expression of intrinsically unstable population dynamics.[69] Even in a constant environment, models of unstable dynamics can produce population cycles, chaotic fluctuations, and erratic fluctuations that are part cyclic and part seemingly random. More realistically, however, intrinsically unstable dynamics are likely to interact with local conditions, which themselves might fluctuate, to produce the observed fluctuations in grouse numbers. In modelling terms, the outcome should depend partly on vital rates and partly on the form of the interaction between density and recruitment. In turn, vital rates should depend upon local conditions.

At least three types of erratic fluctuation have been recorded. First, like weather cycles,[70] grouse cycles may come and go. In Finland, for example, forest grouse (capercaillie, black grouse and hazel grouse) showed such clear cycles during 1964–84 that a paper based on these years was entitled 'The clockwork of Finnish tetraonid population dynamics'.[71] Between 1989 and 1999, however, grouse populations in Finland were quite steady.[72] Second, cycles may change in period. Shooting bags of red grouse at Rickarton moor gave evidence of a six-year cycle in the late nineteenth century, but a ten-year one after the Second World War.[73] In Finland, Siivonen gave evidence of three- to four-year cycles in forest grouse in 1929–49, whereas the 'clockwork' cycles of 1964–84 had a six-year period.[74] Third, each fluctuation can be cyclic in the limited sense that it comprises some years of population increase followed by some of decline, but the periods of successive fluctuations can differ. Thus, the counts of ptarmigan in the Cairnwell hills show a mixture of six- and ten-year fluctuations (see Fig. 173b).

An obvious problem with generalising from British results to population cycles in grouse worldwide is that the results and models involving behaviour apply only to red grouse, in which recruitment is moderated by autumn territorial behaviour. Most species of grouse have a polygamous social system, unlike that of red grouse, in which monogamous pairs maintain exclusive breeding territories. In migratory populations in particular, it seems improbable that autumnal territorial behaviour plays a major role in moderating recruitment. Even so, one can restate the territorial behaviour hypothesis for grouse cycles in the more general form that intrinsically unstable dynamics in birds of the grouse family involve behaviour that moderates recruitment (and hence loss of non-recruits),[75] even if the social systems through which this mechanism operates, as well as the seasonal timing, differ within and among species. In this form, the hypothesis might also apply to mammals that show population cycles, such as voles, lemmings and hares, although there is little evidence.

**Cycles and predation**

The evidence that behaviour can cause unstable population dynamics in red grouse does not rule out the hypothesis, popular in the literature, that natural enemies can cause predator-prey cycles. Modelling suggests that simple two-part predator-prey cycles are most likely when the predator is a specialist. The best relevant example of a single main cyclic prey species and a largely specialist predator is rock ptarmigan in Iceland, where the birds are preyed upon by gyrfalcons. During a population cycle in Iceland,[76] increased numbers of falcons took the heaviest toll of ptarmigan during the decline and the low phase of the cycle, as required by the predator-prey hypothesis. The evidence did not show, however, that the number of ptarmigan killed was in itself sufficient to bring about the decline. Ptarmigan, already excluded from the potential breeding population by aggressive behaviour, might have been more vulnerable to falcons. Or, falcons might have amplified a behavioural decline in ptarmigan by reducing the size of groups of related cocks that would otherwise have formed kin clusters.

In Britain, there are no grouse-specialist predators, and so the predator-prey hypothesis for population cycles does not seem relevant. Also, most predators have been routinely killed on many grouse-moors for over a century, while grouse there have continued their cycles.

The alternative prey hypothesis for tetraonid population cycles suggests that generalist predators might switch from their primary, cyclic, mammalian prey to grouse when the former are scarce. This has been suggested for three- to four-year cycles in parts of Fennoscandia and ten-year cycles in North America, where small rodents and snowshoe hares are the putative primary prey, respectively. The usual version of the alternative prey hypothesis is that predators cause the cycles simply by killing grouse. If so, grouse cycles are a mere adjunct of mammal cycles, themselves unexplained. More interestingly, it is also possible that prey switching by predators might entrain unstable population fluctuations in grouse, so affecting their timing, but not causing their instability.

There are, however, differences in tetraonid cycle length between Sweden and north Finland, where the period is three to four years, and south Finland, where it was six years in 1964–84 and now seems erratic. As the period of the small-rodent cycle in both countries is typically three to four years, the southern Finnish cycles cannot be explained by the alternative prey hypothesis. Similarly, vole cycles in Britain are also three to four years in length, but cycles of red grouse and Scottish ptarmigan can be ten years. In Britain, in short, it seems that predators can suppress cycles, but it is unlikely that they are a widespread cause of them.

**Parasites and cycles**
Parasites, like predators, are natural enemies of grouse. The idea that regular fluctuations in the numbers of red grouse are a parasite-host cycle dates back well over a century. Outbreaks of fatal 'grouse disease' due to the caecal

threadworm *Trichostrongylus tenuis* were, in the nineteenth century, of unknown aetiology, but James Dalziel Dougall[77] considered that 'overcrowding creates disease' and that the 'whole mischief arose, primarily from over-stocking, and, secondarily from gamekeepers most improperly killing off the falcons', which he termed 'sanitary commissioners' because they killed the most heavily infected birds. He 'personally ascertained by enquiry amongst the more aged Highlanders that "disease" was in their early days quite unknown', and quoted the bitterly eloquent words of an old lady, who had a sheep farm in Argyllshire, that the disease was 'a curse of God Almighty on the grouse, because now-a-days the lairds let the moors to Sassenach gentlemen'. He explained that 'after widespread havoc... a period of health sets in' and that these alternations between health and disease were so regular that he had been able to predict in print the years when outbreaks would occur.

Most red grouse carry some caecal threadworms, and burdens are often in the thousands. The parasite seems to occur primarily in red grouse and in the conspecific willow ptarmigan, with rock ptarmigan as an accidental host, and to be confined largely to the more temperate parts of the birds' range. The red grouse is especially adapted to temperate conditions, being the only *Lagopus* subspecies that does not turn white in winter. Worm burdens reported in willow ptarmigan are typically lower than in red grouse. Hence proponents of the parasite-host hypothesis for other tetraonid cycles must find other parasites to explain them.

The 'overcrowding creates disease' hypothesis is easy to understand. Red grouse should increase until they are overcrowded, when caecal threadworms should proliferate, heavily infested grouse should die in large numbers and the survivors should produce few young, thereby generating a crash in numbers. Such crashes have been recorded by Dougall and by many authors subsequently.

A modern version of this hypothesis is more subtle, and postulates that parasites can cause cycles without necessarily involving mass mortality of adult birds (*see* Chapter 13). Parasite burdens should increase with increasing grouse density, until the birds' reproductive rate and perhaps the adults' survival are adversely affected. This should lead to population decline, but not necessarily to a precipitous crash involving birds dying in large numbers.

An outbreak of grouse disease occurred at Glen Esk in the late 1950s.[78] During the springs of 1958 and 1959, some territorial adults died, but survivors reared more than enough young to replace adult deaths. Territorial behaviour took place as usual in the autumn, thus excluding some old and some young birds from the next spring's breeding population. Mean territory size increased following each year of disease, and so density declined between 1958 and 1960.

Disease and territorial behaviour hence acted together, the parasites reducing the young available for recruitment, and territorial behaviour regulating their recruitment. With hindsight, the kinship hypothesis suggests how parasites might have influenced territorial behaviour. Lower breeding success in one year presumably engendered smaller kin clusters in the next, thereby causing fewer young birds to be recruited to the territorial population.

Outbreaks of grouse disease range in severity from declines associated with poorer breeding but little extra mortality, to precipitous crashes involving mass mortality associated with huge worm burdens. High grouse density and wet summer weather seem to be predisposing conditions for increased worm burdens.[79] Weather plays an important role because it affects the parasites' transmission rate. When conditions favour the transmission of parasites from bird to bird, outbreaks of disease can occur at fairly low grouse densities. These obviously involve fewer deaths, and are less often remarked than the spectacular mass mortality of artificially overcrowded grouse-moors.

Dougall's perceptive account of the fluctuations engendered by grouse disease needs some amendment in the light of a century and a half of further study. We now understand that the agent of disease is the caecal threadworm, and that weather together with grouse density are major determinants of worm burdens. Moderate outbreaks of grouse disease are likely to engender changes in territorial behaviour, which amplify the effects of the disease, inducing longer declines than would be expected from deaths due to disease alone. Severe outbreaks of disease seem to be commoner in parts of northern England, these perhaps engendered by the wet climate and the unnaturally high peak population densities associated with muirburn and the killing of Dougall's 'sanitary commissioners'. Even in the drier conditions of northeast Scotland, however, population crashes associated with mass mortality and heavy worm burdens have been reported on grouse-moors where predators were rigorously reduced.

## LANDSCAPE AND POPULATION DYNAMICS

The animal populations of entire landscapes are harder to comprehend than those of the usual smaller area used for scientific study. This more speculative section, therefore, is woven from a mixture of fact, experience and insight.

The observation that population cycles are associated with large tracts of fairly homogeneous habitat provides a link between population dynamics at the scale of a study area or a grouse-drive (a few square kilometres) and habitat on a larger scale. To understand population fluctuations on the scale of a grouse-moor or woodland estate, something must also be known about the surrounding landscape.

Lowland Britain and Ireland are now largely dominated by an agriculture that provides few toeholds for grouse. Over the centuries, man has drained wetlands, and has converted forest to heath vegetation and heath to arable crops or grass pasture. This broad succession has proceeded more slowly in the uplands, where most of our grouse now remain.

The main factors affecting past and present trends in numbers of British and Irish grouse have been fivefold: destroying forest and replacing it with scrub or moorland; destroying scrub and heather moorland, and replacing it with grassy vegetation; planting uplands with exotic conifers; exterminating some species of predators and altering the abundance of others; and weather and climate change. Many of these are covered separately in other chapters. Here we bring them together in a broad sketch of how past land management continues to affect British grouse.

**Forest destruction and fragmentation**

Below the timberline, those tracts of the British and Irish uplands that retain the dwarf shrubs so crucial for grouse are unnaturally devoid of trees, for in past centuries the uplands were deforested and kept without trees by grazing and muirburn. Black grouse, birds of forest edge, scrub and moorland, survived this historic deforestation. However, capercaillie, souls of the forest, depend upon open coniferous forest and reportedly became extinct in the eighteenth century, when tree cover reached its lowest ebb.

In Fennoscandia, fragmentation of native forest occurred more recently than in Britain, and its effects upon woodland grouse are therefore better documented. During the twentieth century, especially in southern parts of Norway, Sweden and Finland, the forest industry created patchworks of old-growth forest, broken up by clear-felled areas. One consequence of this, in Sweden for example, was that black grouse increased during the 1990s as the openings created by clear-felling provided good habitat, including open scrub and dwarf shrubs, whereas capercaillie declined as their mature forest habitat was reduced to fragments.

The effect of clear-felling upon woodland grouse, however, is much influenced by the type of ground vegetation that flourishes after logging, especially the balance between scrub, heath vegetation and grassy vegetation. Open scrub and heath vegetation support black grouse, but grassier vegetation supports more voles, which in turn sustain more predators such as foxes and crows. These hunt not only in the clear-fells but also within the old-growth fragments, so that the capercaillie remaining in woodland fragments amongst clear-fells suffer more predation than those in extensive tracts of old-growth forest.

### Destruction of scrub and heather moorland

In Britain, the destruction of mature forest and its replacement by scrub and heather moorland would at first have favoured black and red grouse at the expense of capercaillie. Then, from the eighteenth century onwards in the uplands, sheep numbers increased, and in the nineteenth century red deer, previously scarce or absent, were encouraged on Scottish sporting estates. Browsing by cattle, sheep and deer eliminated much scrub such as willow, hazel and birch, thereby removing an important source of food and cover for black grouse. Any dwarf shrubs remaining on heavily browsed ground were reduced in height, so providing less cover for birds. A century ago, black grouse were still abundant in widespread open scrubland, but declined as sheep and deer eliminated this important habitat.

The effects of browsing on upland vegetation depend partly upon soils. On richer soils, browsing by sheep and the effects of other agricultural practices favour grassy vegetation by reducing or eliminating dwarf shrubs. As a result, red grouse decline and then largely disappear, as in much of the now grassy Welsh uplands and the border country between England and Scotland. Above the timberline, prolonged browsing of heath vegetation by many sheep has eliminated much ptarmigan habitat on the hilltops of southern Scotland and northern England. On poorer soils there are fewer sheep and deer, and hence dwarf shrubs can grow and red grouse and ptarmigan are more likely to survive, though scrub is widely eliminated by browsing.

### Reforestation

Extensive reforestation with pine and larch began in the mid-eighteenth century and accelerated in the nineteenth century, so helping the reintroduced capercaillie to thrive. Twentieth-century plantings of exotic conifers such as Sitka spruce and lodgepole pine are, however, mostly so dense that insufficient light reaches the ground to sustain dwarf shrubs, making these forests of little value to woodland grouse after canopy closure. A few degraded remnants of the old Caledonian forest, now greatly treasured, support some of our densest populations of capercaillie, but the birds can also thrive in open planted pinewood with heather and blaeberry underneath.

Black and red grouse often increase where young conifers have been planted on heather moorland, but then decline as the canopy closes and shades out dwarf shrubs. It was once hoped that black grouse would also thrive in Sitka spruce clear-fells and restocked areas. Experience shows that this does not generally occur, and one reason seems obvious: the birds depend upon heather and blaeberry, which are scarce on most Sitka restocks.

**Predators**

Most of our terrestrial wildlife survives on agriculturally poor or marginal ground, where it depends largely upon the activities of humans. In particular, unless they are killed by gamekeepers on sporting estates, medium-sized predators such as the fox are unnaturally abundant and kill many ground-nesting birds such as grouse. This is partly because grassy moorland provides more vole, pipit and rabbit food for predators, but perhaps also because man has exterminated large predators that kill medium-sized predators.

Large predators, near the top of their food chain, typically occur at low densities. Medium-sized predators, however, breed more quickly, and if unchecked reach greater abundance. Hence the extermination of large predators should lead to a greater abundance of predators overall, and so more predation of ground-nesting birds.

Wolves and lynxes, for example, eat foxes, and in parts of Europe where wolves are abundant the foxes are scarce. Foxes eat pine martens. Eagles and goshawks eat many crows and also kill smaller raptors. When hen harriers became unusually abundant on Langholm moor, for example, they apparently suppressed the numbers of red grouse. The archetypal grouse-moor-owner's answer to such a problem is to instruct his keepers to kill hen harriers. Part of a more balanced approach might be to allow eagles to kill harriers, but many landowners persist in killing eagles as well as the other raptors that comprise Dougall's 'sanitary commissioners'.

**Weather and climate**

Some fluctuations in the numbers of grouse and other wildlife are so widespread that local factors, such as changes in land use or management, cannot explain them. During the twentieth century, shooting-bag records of red grouse in northwest Scotland and willow ptarmigan in southeast Norway were remarkably similar (*see* Fig. 26).[80] Large bags in the early part of the twentieth century fell to a common trough about 1918, recovered to a peak about 1930, and then declined shortly before the Second World War. After the war, numbers remained much lower than they had been before. Scottish red grouse and Norwegian willow ptarmigan have different diets, live in different habitats, suffer in the main from different diseases, and are subject to different management practices by humans.

It seems obvious that a widespread common factor such as weather or pollution affected numbers of grouse in both countries.

**Consequences of land management practices on grouse in Britain**
In the much altered British countryside, red grouse and rock ptarmigan continue to show population cycles where large tracts of unfragmented habitat remain to them. Cyclic declines in red grouse and ptarmigan are natural and should be followed by cyclic increases. This can be inconvenient for managers of grousemoors, who in principle can prevent a cyclic decline by shooting hard in the increase phase, but cyclic declines are no cause for alarm about the survival of the local population.

The habitat remaining to black grouse and capercaillie in Britain is much more patchy and fragmented. This can explain why these two species now show no evidence of population cycles. Indeed, today their habitat is so depleted that both are in danger of extinction.

## SUMMARY

All four species of British grouse tend to fluctuate in numbers together, under the influence of weather. On large tracts of continuous habitat, red grouse and rock ptarmigan show unstable dynamics, sometimes manifested as regular cycles. In other parts of their world range, capercaillie and black grouse also cycle, but not in modern Britain, where their habitat is greatly fragmented. Large tracts of homogeneous habitat engender unstable fluctuations in grouse species, but fragmented habitat does not.

Weather, food, predators, parasites and disease influence recruitment and behaviour. They therefore influence numbers directly via reproduction and mortality, and indirectly via social structure, recruitment and movement. Numbers of red grouse are regulated by territorial behaviour. This moderates recruitment, and recruitment in turn determines densities. Territorial behaviour and recruitment are influenced by social structure, particularly the size of clusters of related cocks. In turn, recruitment affects cluster size. Results from red grouse cannot be applied directly to other species that do not show autumnal territorial behaviour. Even so, we commend the insight that resources and enemies influence population dynamics indirectly through their effects upon social structure and movement, as well as acting directly upon vital rates. We suggest that these two generalisations may apply in other grouse species, and perhaps more widely in animals that show unstable population dynamics.

CHAPTER 15

# Management and Conservation

MANKIND NOW DOMINATES the earth, driving thousands of species to extinction. Although many grouse may seem safe in their remote terrain, pollution and climate change are widespread threats. However, grouse benefit from interest in conservation among hunters, walkers and others who take outdoor recreation. In this chapter we consider some important management issues, but not how to manage grouse, for that is well covered elsewhere.[1] Instead, we discuss hunting, some record British bags, and the question of whether hunting affects grouse numbers internationally. Changes in British and Irish moorland since 1945 are summarised, along with some topical issues such as heather beetle, raptors and options for moorland. We touch on the management of British woodland, and end with a summary of the impacts of ski development, pollution and climate change on grouse.

## HUNTING

We use 'hunting' in its international sense of any human killing of wild animals. Shooting seasons are described elsewhere.[2] Many people enjoy shooting as a sport, while others wish to ban it. We have shot grouse for study but not for sport. Here we take no side, but simply give facts on game management.[3]

### In the far north
To northern people, willow and rock ptarmigan were important foods, and they snared large numbers.[4] The Inuit used their feathered skins as clothes or towels, and ingested vitamin C in winter by swallowing their warm intestines.[5] Shot

ptarmigan helped explorers to live off the country, and their raw flesh saved exhausted Peter Freuchen and Inuit boy Mala after a week eating grass, roots and hare dung.[6]

Indigenous people in America and Russia traditionally shot many willow and rock ptarmigan for eating or for dog food at all seasons, so much so, in fact, that they extirpated rock ptarmigan near settlements.[7] Bob Weeden reported that Inuit and Indians in 61 Alaskan villages annually took 53,000 'ptarmigan' in years of average numbers.[8] One villager said, 'After you fellows leave, I pray the Lord will forgive me all the lies I tell you', so perhaps they killed even more than they admitted.

**TABLE 31.** Some record British grouse bags taken in a day. Bags have fallen over the last century in Britain, Ireland and abroad (*see* Chapters 3–6), sometimes precipitating bans on hunting.[9]

|  | PLACE | YEAR | DATE | METHOD | NUMBER SHOT |
|---|---|---|---|---|---|
| Red grouse | Lancashire# | 1915 | 12 August | Drive | 2,929 |
| Ptarmigan | Achnashellach* | 1866 | 25 August | Walk | 122 |
|  | Bachnagairn** | 1880s | September | Walk | 110 |
|  | Lochnagar^ | 1964 | 29 October | Drive | 90 |
|  | Beinn a' Bhuird† | 1974 | late August | Drive | 114 |
| Blackgame§ | Cannock Chase | 1860 | — | Drive | 252 |
| Capercaillie§ | Dunkeld | 1910 | 4 November | — | 69 |

# Littledale & Abbeystead moors; the season's bag was 17,078 on 7,000ha (Gladstone, 1930).
* Gordon, 1915.
** John Robertson, pers. comm. 2006. His grandfather and two stalkers shot this bag.
^ Counted by AW at the Balmoral game larder.
† Noted by gillie Graham Boyd to AW.
§ Vesey-Fitzgerald, 1946.

## In developed countries

Most authors mention numbers shot during grouse-drives, but not numbers crippled, where wounded birds fly on without being retrieved, usually to die later. During grouse-drives in Britain, very few red grouse that are shot are not bagged.[10] Hunting elsewhere is less organised, however, with losses varying up to one crippled per one in the bag.[11] Biologists in France allow for cripple losses when setting bag limits.

### Red grouse

During a drive, beaters wave white flags and shout to scare grouse into flying towards a line of distant butts, where hunters hide. The beaters start walking in a straight line, but the outer beaters walk faster so that the line closes as it nears the butts, each drive covering 80–400ha. When grouse are at lower density, hunters 'walk up' in line abreast of one another, with dogs ranging close, and at yet lower density they use pointing dogs to range widely and find birds.

In a study that used data from many grouse estates and many years, bags were said to be a 'good proxy' for grouse density in certain statistical analyses.[12] Within

FIG 181. Driven grouse over butts. (David A. Gowans)

moors or study areas, however, hunters usually kill a greater percentage of driven birds when density is high than when it is low.[13] On a Glen Esk study area, for instance, they took 48 per cent of August numbers at high density in 1957, but only 16 per cent in 1959 when density had fallen.[14] On the adjacent Millden moor, which had similar densities, different shooters bagged about 10,000 in 1957, but none in 1959 because they sought bigger bags elsewhere. Hence hunting effort varies, which is one reason why bags usually exaggerate changes in grouse numbers.[15] Effort is often not recorded. Also, bags confound breeding stocks with breeding success unless they record the proportion of young in the bag.

Some hunters used to shoot single cocks in late autumn, thinking they were aggressive old birds that expelled young cocks and could not fertilise hens.[16]

FIG 182. A day's grouse bag in the larder. (David A. Gowans)

This was dubious, because it is hard to tell young from old cocks in late autumn, and single cocks are often less aggressive than paired ones. However, it was a forerunner of present understanding that numbers can be altered by adjusting aggressiveness (*see* Chapter 14).

In field trials, dogs compete to find grouse and then await their handlers without flushing the birds. Dedicated enthusiasts pursue this sport even though they seldom or never shoot a grouse, and are a strong voice for conserving moorland, especially in Ireland. The breeding of game-dogs has benefited research on grouse. Pointers and setters help with counts, and find nests, chicks and dead birds better than any person. They have been indispensable and inspirational.

Poachers used to kill many birds, especially in Ireland, and crofters snared them on oat-sheaves and fences. A crafty Moray crofter used to hide as a train approached, and then jump out so that grouse feasting on his oats would fly to collide with the train and hence become his supper.[17] Some farmers shot birds from public roads up to the early 1970s, but, like illicit distilling, poaching died as people became more affluent.

An old kind of poaching was 'becking', where a man walked out to await the dawn.[18] When the first grouse cocks crew, he imitated a hen's nasal whining, whereupon a cock flew in and was shot.[19] In 'carting', the hunter walked beside a horse and cart, to which grouse paid little attention. Abel Chapman also used carting to study grouse behaviour in the 1880s.

### Willow and rock ptarmigan

North American hunters shoot a very small percentage of the willow ptarmigan present, except near roads.[20] Newfoundland hunters near roads shot on average 13 per cent, and later records showed 5–40 per cent taken annually, with the biggest bags in years of poor breeding and falling numbers.[21] Hundreds of thousands of hunters live from Norway east through Russia.[22] In a study with radios on both hunters and willow ptarmigan, the hunters walked on average 16km per day and shot 20 per cent of the birds on the study area, mostly near their cabin.[23] A Swedish study revealed a mean of 21 per cent shot.[24]

Rock ptarmigan are gamebirds in many countries, but are protected in a few such as China and Japan. Russian sport-hunters shoot many, while North American hunters take few because of the mostly inaccessible terrain. Iceland exported millions of rock ptarmigan in the late 1800s and early 1900s, but banned shooting in years of low numbers, including 2004–5.[25]

Scottish ptarmigan have been shot for centuries, and on the Cairnwell hills there are two lines of stone butts, built in the 1800s for hunters to shoot driven ptarmigan. Hunters now 'walk up', still shooting ptarmigan on a few estates.

### Blackgame and capercaillie

Bags of blackgame were big in southwest Scotland during the 1890s and early 1900s, but have fallen greatly, such that today hardly any are shot in Britain. In Fennoscandia they come third in bag totals after willow ptarmigan and hazel grouse, and Russian hunters take many. French hunters shoot blackcock in the Alps and Pyrenees. Here, shooting bans have been imposed in some small reserves, but these hold few blackcock if heavily shot ground lies nearby, and in any case cocks often wander outside the reserves in autumn.[26] Biologists recommend that reserves should be enlarged and shooting prohibited within 5–9km of them.

The capercaillie has long been a trophy in many countries. Hunters in central Europe traditionally shot lekking cocks, a practice still followed today, although it is now discouraged. Many driven birds were shot in Scotland during the 1960s and 1970s, but numbers have plunged and shooting has been banned because of the looming threat of extinction.

### Effects on populations: a background

After some birds die, the remaining ones face less competition and so may survive better or rear more young. On the other hand, if one cause of death becomes less frequent, another may increase. Biologists call these processes 'compensation'. If compensation is total, better survival, or better breeding, or less emigration, or more immigration makes good all losses, and so the population remains at the same density. If there is no compensation, all losses are 'additive'. Partial compensation commonly occurs. Compensatory net immigration can occur in exploited areas near reserves of unexploited animals, from which immigrants can come.

Fisheries biologists have contributed a better understanding of exploitation in animals generally. As the rate of fishing rises, it reaches a 'maximum sustainable yield', beyond which extra effort catches fewer fish and risks making fishing unprofitable or extirpating the stock.[27] Red grouse, however, are not fish.[28] They show unstable population fluctuations, often manifested as fairly regular cycles in both shot and unshot populations. The way to achieve maximum yield is to shoot hard during the increase phase of a cycle, enough to prevent birds reaching a peak and undergoing the consequent decline, but not so hard as to reduce the following year's breeding stock excessively (*see* Chapter 14).

### Effects on grouse species generally

Compensation is important because it allows the quarry to be cropped without seriously depleting the stock. In a review of the literature, Larry Ellison concluded that total compensation for shooting of adult grouse has been demonstrated only in red grouse and perhaps ruffed grouse, and only in red grouse did he find evidence for total compensation of shot juveniles.[29] In other species he found evidence of total or partial compensation, where shot and unshot areas continued to support similar densities, or where normal sex ratios continued despite no hens being shot. Birds could have immigrated to shot areas,[30] and immigration is a form of compensation. Because the small areas studied held only part of a relevant larger population, Ellison was unable to conclude that compensation occurred in the larger population. His review and similar accounts have been useful steps towards understanding compensation in grouse species, but are not sufficient to explain compensation in unstable fluctuations.

### Effects on blackgame and capercaillie

In these two species, several studies where populations were stable illustrate the utility of the classic view of compensation. Take a study of blackgame in the French Alps, where greyhens are protected. An average male bag of 37 per cent distorted the sex ratio next summer from one cock per hen to one cock per two hens.[31] Because the greatest distortion followed hunting after summers of poor breeding, biologists regarded this as a warning of little or no compensation.

In his review, Ellison pondered a rational basis for hunting grouse, given the paucity of reliable evidence. He suggested the conservative assumption that hunting is additive to other adult mortality, while juveniles show some compensation, as in a proposal for Scottish capercaillie in the 1970s.[32] That proposal rested on calculating the percentage that might be shot without reducing numbers next spring, a percentage varying with how well the hens had bred. Gus Jones reported that successive hunts in plantations during one autumn did not reduce capercaillie numbers, which even rose slightly.[33] He attributed this to immigration from a nearby wood, where loggers were cutting granny pines that the birds favoured, and 'the vulnerability of capercaillie to exploitation may be difficult to appreciate without greater understanding of movements'. Hence the concept of compensation is hard to apply when birds move. It is yet harder to apply in unstable fluctuations (*see* below).

### Effects on *Lagopus lagopus* and rock ptarmigan

The classic view of compensation is that, each year, populations tend to return towards their long-term average or equilibrium density. Unstable populations differ, however. Starting at low density, increases in numbers are followed by further increases, until they reach a peak. Then declines are followed by further declines, until they reach a trough. Hence numbers fluctuate around an average density, overshooting on the way up, and again on the way down. During a population cycle in red grouse, compensation occurs each year around the equilibrium density for that year. But the equilibrium density changes through the cycle: during the increase phase it rises, and during the decline it falls.

Several papers relevant to the effect of hunting on *Lagopus lagopus* have appeared in the last decade.[34] The most notable, involving a large experiment in Norway,[35] illustrates the difficulty of studying compensation in unstable populations. In the four-year study, hunting effort was experimentally varied on different areas. The idea was that, if compensation in overwinter mortality occurred, it would be greater where more birds were shot. This assumed that compensation would occur in relation to an equilibrium density that was fixed for each area. This seems unlikely, in which case the authors' conclusion that only partial weak compensation occurred is unreliable.

Another difficulty was that the main variation in overwinter survival occurred from one area to another, so it is crucial to know which areas were 'cores' and which 'sinks'.[36] Readers cannot assess this, because baseline data from before the experiment were not presented. The concept of compensation is meaningless on a sink, where net losses outweigh net gains.

So, what determines the annual equilibrium density in unstable populations? Such understanding is now reasonably advanced in red grouse (*see* Chapter 14). With or without hunting, spring density (or equilibrium density) in this species is determined by the number of territories taken in the previous autumn, which varies from year to year. The effects of hunting should differ between the increase phase, when hunting can prevent the peak and hence the decline (as in our Rickarton experiment; *see* Chapter 14), and the decline phase, when it is too late to prevent further falls in numbers.

## BRITISH AND IRISH MOORLAND SINCE 1945

### Subsidised activities

Since the UK Agriculture Act 1946, much heather moorland has been destroyed (Table 32). Freely drained moorland at low altitude, partly cleared of boulders for cultivation by early man, was ideal for subsidised conversion to agricultural grassland in order to support larger stocks of subsidised sheep and cattle.[37] Subsidised planting of trees destroyed much other moorland. Both uses, however, proved uneconomic.[38]

In the 1950s–70s, governments tried to maximise agricultural production, and paid grants for the digging of open drains on much British and Irish moorland, because drains increase heather and grass as forage. As a side-effect, the drains damaged flushes that were a prime habitat for chicks of red grouse, blackgame

TABLE 32. Declines in the areas of British heather moorland and native woodland, and increases in numbers of sheep and red deer.

| LAND USE | LOCATION | PERCENTAGE CHANGE | PERIOD[#] | REFERENCE |
|---|---|---|---|---|
| Heather moor | England and Wales | −27 | 1947–80 | Thompson et al., 1995 |
| | Cumbria | −65 | 1940s–70s | Sydes & Miller, 1988 |
| | Scotland | −23[*] | Late 1940s–late 1980s | Mackey et al., 1998 |
| | Dumfries & Galloway | −60 | Late 1940s–late 1980s | Mackey et al., 1998 |
| | Grampian Region | −35 | Late 1940s–late 1980s | Mackey et al., 1998 |
| | North York Moors National Park | −25 | 1950–79 | Simmons, 2003 |
| | Peak District National Park | −36 | 1913–79 | Anderson & Yalden, 1981 |
| Woodland | | | | |
| *Broadleaved* | Scotland | −23 | Late 1940s–late 1980s | Mackey et al., 1998 |
| *Mixed broadleaved and coniferous* | Scotland | −37 | Late 1940s–late 1980s | Mackey et al., 1998 |
| *Ancient pine* | Scotland | −47 | Late 1940s–late 1980s | Mackey et al., 1998 |
| | Scotland | −25 | 1957–87[**] | Bain, 1987 |
| *Other pine* | Scotland | −48 | Late 1940s–late 1980s | Mackey et al., 1998 |
| Livestock | | | | |
| *Sheep* | English and Welsh LFAs[^] | +87 | 1951–81 | Sydes & Miller, 1988 |
| | Scottish LFAs[^] | +18 | 1982–98 | Mackey et al., 2001 |
| | Southwest Wales | +298 | 1950–90 | Fuller & Gough, 1999 |
| | North Wales | +171 | 1950–90 | Fuller & Gough, 1999 |
| *Red deer* | Scotland[†] | +99 | 1963–2000 | Deer Commission for Scotland, 2001 |
| | Cairngorms/West Grampians | +44 | 1967–2000 | Deer Commission for Scotland, 2001 |

*(continued)*

**TABLE 32.** (*continued*)

| LAND USE | LOCATION | PERCENTAGE CHANGE | PERIOD[#] | REFERENCE |
|---|---|---|---|---|
| *Red deer* | East Grampians | +142 | 1966–94 | Deer Commission for Scotland, 2001 |
| | East Grampians, Strathtay[§] | +616 | 1979–99 | Deer Commission for Scotland, 2001 |

[#] Losses of moorland and woodland continued after the cited surveys ended. At the World Summit on Sustainable Development at Johannesburg in summer 2002, the UK Government and Scottish Executive tabled the UK Forest Partnership for Action, in which 'The Partnership is committed to the restoration, protection, and expansion of native woodlands in the UK'. Despite this, the Scottish Government continues to allow housing developments in Speyside native woodland, including pinewood on the Ancient Woodland Inventory.

[*] 67 per cent to new coniferous plantation and 9 per cent to 'improved' grassland.

[**] 50 per cent of that on Forestry Commission land was lost and 16 per cent of that on private land.

[^] Less favoured areas, which are upland parishes where farmers get extra subsidies.

[†] Estimates of red deer numbers are 155,000 in 1960 (Lowe, 1961) and 350,000–450,000 in 2003 (Hunt, 2003); the population was at its lowest ebb in the 1780s (Lowe, 1961; Watson, 1983). Inspection of historical literature indicates a 1780s total population far less than 1 per cent of current numbers (Watson, unpublished).

[§] All grouse-moors. Other regions include deer forests as well as grouse-moors.

and wading birds. Despite this damage being well documented,[39] estates are still making drains, now with their own money.[40]

**Muirburn**

Good muirburn for grouse and sheep creates a patchwork of young and old heather, providing nutritious food and adequate physical cover, and maximising the length of edge between young and old heather (*see* Fig. 186). This was publicised long ago,[41] and well understood by older generations of gamekeepers. Since 1945, however, most grouse-moors have been inadequately burned.[42] Some low ground has not been fired for 30 years or more, and its heather is now up to a metre high, supporting very few grouse. More often, underburning does involve some fires, but few of them, so most heather is too old.

FIG 183. The same stretch of Glen Esk moorland before (top, 1960, with cock grouse on its territory and a pile of limestone ready for spreading), and after conversion (bottom, 1994, heather has been 'improved' to grass, through government subsidy).
(Adam Watson)

FIG 184. Heather moorland ploughed for tree planting. (Stuart Rae)

FIG 185. Grouse butt, once on heather moorland, now in a Sitka spruce plantation. (Robert Moss)

FIG 186. Edge between tall, old heather and short, more recently burnt heather. Grouse feed on the short vegetation, close to the tall heather where they take cover. (Robert Moss)

The opposite, commoner extreme is overburning. Muirburn every three to four years shifts heather towards grass, sedge or rush (Table 33).[43] This typifies western moorland, where shepherds light most fires and make them wide. Although using a longer rotation, deerstalkers also make wide fires, often burning 50ha at a time, and occasionally 100ha.[44] Wide fires can cause soil erosion, and in dry conditions they become too hot, consuming topsoil and greatly delaying the recovery of heather.

TABLE 33. Management activities that affect British and Irish grouse habitats.

| LAND USE | ACTIVITY | EFFECTS |
|---|---|---|
| Grouse-moor | Draining | More heath, less cotton-grass and fewer flushes |
| | Underburning or no burning | Heather too tall and dense |
| | Ground burnt every few years | Less heath, more grass and bracken |
| | Wide fires | Poor cover, soil erosion |
| | Fencing | Kills grouse |
| | Reducing mountain hares | Reduces ticks, leads to less buffer prey |
| | High density of red deer | Less cover and heath, more grass and ticks |

*(continued)*

TABLE 33. (continued)

| LAND USE | ACTIVITY | EFFECTS |
|---|---|---|
| Farming | Liming, fertilising, seeding | Destroys heath |
| | As above, plus cultivating | As above |
| | Fencing reseeded areas | Kills grouse |
| | Draining | Damages flushes, reduces cotton-grass |
| | Many sheep or cattle on moors | Less cover and heath, more grass |
| | Many sheep or cattle in woods | As above, plus less tree regeneration |
| | Supplementary food | Concentrates above effects |
| Forestry | Burning before planting | Less heath in the short run |
| | Draining | Damages flushes, reduces cotton-grass |
| | Cultivating | Less heath, more grass and bracken |
| | Fencing | Kills grouse, cover too dense# |
| | Dense planting* | Shading kills heath |
| | Underplanting by conifers | Kills original old trees |
| | Planting larch with no pine | Kills heath, creates a grass sward |
| | Using herbicides to kill heath | Little or no heath |
| | Brashing (low branches cut) | Destroys dense live cover up to c. 2m |
| | Burning of brash | Destroys good cover |
| | Using logging machines | Less heath, more grass and bracken, compacted soil, wet ruts favour ticks |
| | Clear-fells, 'selective'** felling | As above, plus no woodland habitat for years |
| | Removing stumps | Reduces blaeberry and cowberry |
| | Removing dead trees | Less cover, fewer insects and blaeberry |
| | Felling before trees mature | Less heath, especially blaeberry |
| | Snaring | Kills grouse |

# Watson, 1993.
* Planting Scots pine for commercial timber typically uses a 1.8m spacing (Mason et al., 2004).
** A Forestry Commission euphemism; only scattered isolated trees remain.

Since 2000, a new type of overburning has appeared on many moors in northeast Scotland. Keepers correctly burn narrow fires, but then in the next few years burn new ones alongside (see Fig. 187). Entire hillsides soon lack tall heather and associated edge habitat, which is a recipe for fewer grouse than occurred before this type of burning began.[45] On a few estates, fires burn into subalpine heather, a damaging move because vegetation takes decades to recover there.

**FIG 187.** New-style overburning of heather. Fires in successive years burn into each other, leaving no edge. (Adam Watson)

### Grazing

Sheep or cattle at low density can benefit grouse by making trails that allow birds access into tall heather, and their dung introduces agricultural weeds that are good food for grouse in spring. On a part of Kerloch with few cattle, the beasts kept heather in a steady state without fire, maintaining red grouse at high density for several years. It was a delicate balance, however, and was later disrupted easily by the introduction of extra cattle.

Overgrazing, trampling and the deposition of dung by sheep, cattle or red deer can cause faster loss of heather than frequent burning. Sheep and deer numbers have increased greatly (*see* Table 32).[46] In western regions of Ireland and Scotland, many crofters rent or own their own fields, but share the moorland as rough grazing. Garrett Hardin called communal grazing 'The Tragedy of the Commons', where it pays individuals to overstock in the short run rather than tighten their belts for the long-term good of the ground and community.[47] Many crofters overstock communal land, and burn it too frequently and irresponsibly, lighting large fires that occasionally burn all night in late spring. Overgrazing along with overburning also impoverishes grazing for sheep, as well as reducing heather and cover for grouse, and causing soil erosion.

FIG 188. Overbrowsing by red deer causing grass to replace heather in Glen Clunie. (Adam Watson)

To rural inhabitants of northern Britain, a black hill is heather-moor and a white hill is grassland. This is because on a snow-free winter's day the heather appears dark, almost black, whereas the grass is pale and whitish because much of it has withered. Often the two form a striking pair on either side of a fence that separates few sheep on the black side from many on the white (*see* Fig. 189). A grey hill is intermediate. Black, grey and white can occur on freely drained or poorly drained heather moorland, and overgrazing can turn black to white in a few years.[48] Less often one sees a green hill, where overgrazing of heather on fertile soil turns it into smooth, fine-leaved, bent-fescue grassland, green in winter. It offers better food than a black, grey or white hill for sheep, cattle and red deer, and supports more of them.[49] However, red grouse and other wildlife of heather lose out with grey, white and green.

Here is an example. On a 43ha area of Kerloch, sheep and up to one to two cattle per hectare ate 53–74 per cent of the annual production of heather, which decreased in ground coverage from 80 to 5 per cent over ten years.[50] Meanwhile, red grouse declined from 15 cocks and 13 hens to zero.[51]

In another case, a farmer wintered more sheep and cattle at Glen Esk.[52] Heather usually declines when the density of unshepherded wintering ewes exceeds one per

FIG 189. Sheep are at high density on the white hill to the left of the fence, and at low density on the black hill to the right. The soil is the same on both sides. (Stuart Rae)

hectare, but in the late 1980s a 13ha section carried 12 sheep per hectare and almost one cow per hectare in winter and spring. By 1989 its heather had become prostrate, bitten, woody stems 2cm high, amongst heavily cropped grass. During the 14 springs of 1957–70, the same area, then only lightly grazed, carried 6 to 24 red grouse, one to ten blackgame and two to eight partridges. In 1989–98 it held none.

Many insects eat moorland plants without doing serious damage, but caterpillars of heather beetle can devastate heather.[53] When beetles emerge in spring from pupae in the ground, they can occur in hordes. In late April 1976 on Mull we saw millions rising from heather into a gentle breeze, their wings a myriad of shimmering spots in the sunshine. An unusually severe outbreak started in western Scotland in 1997, and by 2003–4 it had spread to the Spey-Findhorn region. The beetles like wet patches, and outbreaks have been more frequent in recent years across the west and central Highlands, following a large increase in rainfall there.[54]

Bracken now blankets much freely drained moorland at low altitude, especially in mild western regions of Britain and Ireland. Many Welsh valleys that were once heathery are now a sea of bracken, supporting no grouse. People formerly cut bracken for animal bedding, and cattle damaged it by trampling and eating it, so the shift from cattle to sheep since the 1700s would have increased it. For red and black grouse, the costs of bracken greatly outweigh any benefits.[55]

Cutting bracken for three successive summers delays its recovery for three decades,[56] and herbicide checks it temporarily, but it is remarkably persistent and produces chemicals that deter other plants. It frequently eliminates heath species and prevents their recolonisation.

Waterlogged soil discourages bracken, so drainage encourages it. In recent years it has spread in pinewood and birchwood following soil disturbance (*see* Table 33).[57] Frost kills the young fronds, but summer frosts are now fewer than they once were.

### Shooting policies, finance and taxation

Rational policies for shooting red grouse have been known for decades but are seldom applied.[58] It has long been recommended that shooting should be hard, and that it should begin early in the season.[59] This is particularly important in years of increase, so that the stock does not reach a high density that will precipitate an ensuing decline. Of course, it needs to be appreciated that hard shooting must not become overshooting.[60]

There was an example of good practice in southwest Scotland at Leadhills, where former head keeper Kenny Wilson settled on a target number of grouse to be left unshot at the end of the shooting season, counted grouse before the season, and arranged shooting hard enough to attain his target.[61] This probably

FIG 190. Bracken encroaching onto heather moorland at Kerloch. (Robert Moss)

prevented numbers from reaching a peak. Many declines are caused by some change at high density, such as more aggression or an outbreak of disease. To avoid this, birds should be prevented from reaching a peak, as in our Rickarton experiment (*see* Chapter 14).[62]

Only a few managers seem able to act upon this knowledge. Too often, pessimism leads to fewer days of shooting and lower bags, even when grouse numbers on the moor have not declined and the bag per day remains unchanged. Moreover, press reports reveal that many managers do not know their stock size before the season opens, by which time it is too late to organise much extra shooting. When grouse are more abundant than expected, it is difficult to achieve the necessary bag, because too few shooters have been booked. Present-day shooters are usually not only poorer marksmen than their forbears, but are also less flexible, needing to make arrangements months before August, and hence are unable to take advantage of an unexpectedly big crop of grouse.

Management can be influenced greatly by the kind of person who buys or rents a moor. For instance, one wealthy entrant since 2000 quadrupled the number of keepers and transformed a neglected Scottish moor to a well-burned one within three to four years. In August 2003 there came a different, ominous portent for management. After land agents took charge of the Gannochy in Angus, a well-known sporting estate and grouse-moor, they sold it as separate lots to maximise profits.[63] Management, however, is more difficult on a small beat with only a single keeper than on a large estate where several keepers can combine efforts on teamwork such as muirburn, and where there are other economies of scale.

For decades, owners of Scottish grouse-moors had to pay sporting rates to local authorities, which in effect was a tax on the average bag. This taxed turnover, not profit, and so was inequitable and counter-productive. Since the tax was lifted in 1995, the only taxes on shooting have been income taxes on annual profits. Because most owners make a loss (*see* 'Options for moorland', below), shootings generate little income tax. Nevertheless, shooting has long been one of the few rural land uses that are unsubsidised by taxpayers.[64] In effect, therefore, it is already taxed relative to subsidised uses such as farming and forestry.

There are increasing calls for land-value taxation.[65] However, this could result in increased running costs of moors, unless governments designate moors as conservation areas with a zero rating.

### Destruction of scrub and hares, and snaring

On east Scottish grouse-moors with few deer or sheep, self-sown pine, birch, rowan, willow and juniper spread widely in 1945–85,[66] but much of this has since been destroyed.[67] We know of estates that received taxpayers' money from the

MANAGEMENT AND CONSERVATION · 399

**FIG 191.** Birch and Scots pine recolonising heather moorland in Glen Gairn. (Adam Watson)

**FIG 192.** Regenerating Scots pine on heather moorland, destroyed by cutting. (Adam Watson)

Forestry Commission (FC) to plant trees on some moorland, while removing self-sown trees from other parts of the same estate. On the other hand, owners of other moors with extensive encroaching trees decided to allow natural reforestation to continue, and a few of them supplemented it by planting. In the 1990s the FC changed its policies, and for years it has given grants to moor-owners for natural tree regeneration and for new native woodland by planting.[68]

Because mountain hares carry ticks, and ticks transmit louping-ill virus, keepers on many Scottish moors since the late 1990s have killed hares with the aim of reducing ticks and louping ill in red grouse (*see* Chapter 13). Already, hares are scarce on some moors where they formerly abounded. This removes a prey that diverts predators from grouse, reduces the food of protected raptors, and conflicts with the European Union Habitats Directive.[69] It contradicts claims by the Scottish Gamekeepers' Association that keepers 'promote biodiversity', and hands new arguments to those who wish legislation to ban the shooting of grouse.

For decades, snares set by keepers and farmers to catch rabbits and hares killed a few red grouse and blackgame inadvertently. Far more snares are now set to kill foxes, but they also kill capercaillie, wildcats, roe deer and badgers, as well as domestic cats and dogs. In the 1990s the number of snares increased on grouse-moors and, especially, in nearby woodland (*see* Chapter 6).

**Raptors**

Persecution from the nineteenth century to the modern day has extirpated some raptor species from much moorland.[70] The Second World War brought a respite as eagles and harriers colonised some grouse-moors, but after 1946 they were soon eliminated. There has since been poisoning, shooting, trapping, burning of nests, robbing or breaking eggs, and disturbing birds so that eggs do not hatch.[71] Some of the best-known estates in the land have been involved.

Much of this persecution has been due to peer pressure from keepers, managers (called 'factors' in Scotland) and estate owners who are ultimately responsible. It is often a matter of faith that raptors are 'vermin', not to be tolerated. We have known a few keepers who regarded muirburn and other issues as more important and who protected raptors. They came under pressure from the orthodox majority, however, and eventually changed their ways.

Persecution eased in 1960–80 as international research emphasised habitat rather than raptors as crucial for animal abundance. Harriers and eagles bred on some moors where none nested in the 1950s. Enlightenment began to fade after 1985, however, following persistent one-sided publicity by the Game Conservancy (GC), whose Director, Richard Van Oss, wrote, 'Government may have to consider whether to allow restricted control of some protected species.'[72]

**FIG 193.** Golden eagle, killed by poison. (Stuart Rae)

And Lord Mansfield, 'if we cannot control the numbers of… hawks we are simply providing a feast for them. Society has got to make up its mind on a means of control of predators.'[73]

Peregrine expert Derek Ratcliffe wrote, 'any attempt to put the clock back on this issue would be greeted with uproar'.[74] The Heather Trust warned against alienating other countryside and conservation bodies whose membership was 'many times that of the field sports organisations'.[75] None the less, the Scottish Landowners' Federation (SLF)[76] publicly sought licensed culling of harriers.[77] After investigating the law, however, their legal adviser Duncan Thomson concluded, 'I therefore do not believe that there is any prospect of licensed killing of raptors in the foreseeable future'.[78] The SLF's Law and Parliamentary Committee approved his paper on 1 February 1996, but shortly afterwards he was not in their employ. Calls continued for harriers to be caught, for release elsewhere.[79]

Lobbying by the GC led to the Langholm project, where a landowner in south Scotland protected hen harriers and peregrines for a study of predation.[80] It became a watershed (*see* Chapter 13). Harriers increased, and took so many grouse chicks and adults that the estate cancelled all shooting. Generalising from this to British moors would be invalid, because the Langholm moor is atypical,[81] but many who disliked harriers did just this.

Later, dead rats and poultry chicks were left for the Langholm harriers to feed to their young.[82] Harriers with this supplement gave their young only 4.5 grouse chicks per harrier nest, while harriers without it gave 33.3 per nest. Even so, the number of grouse chicks lost was ten times bigger than that expected from harrier predation. Hence chick mortality was overwhelmingly due to other causes.

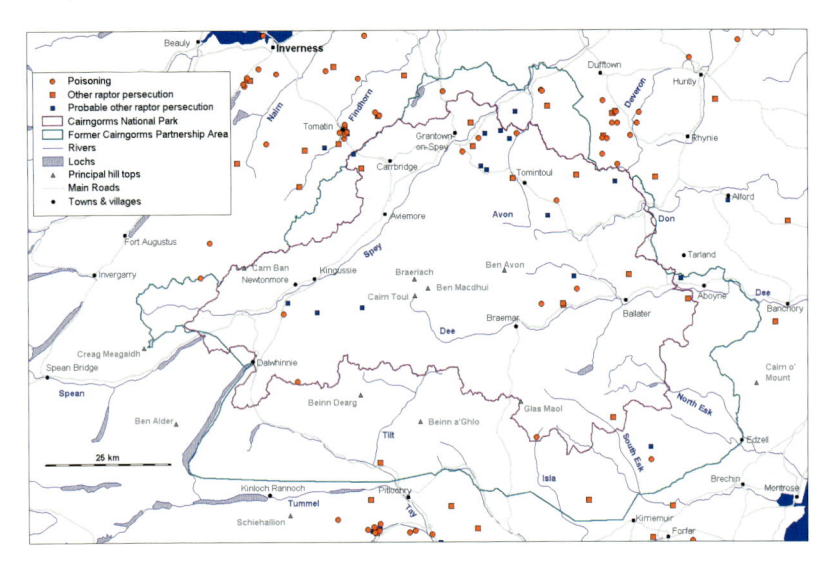

FIG 194. Incidents of poisoning and other illegal killing of raptors in the Cairngorms region in 1995–2003. (Map by Keith Morton, RSPB)

John Phillips tried a novel kind of supplementary feeding at Misty Law. He erected dovecotes, introduced feral doves in spring, supplied food, water and nest material, and opened pop-holes so that doves could come and go. Over two years, peregrines killed many doves and anecdotal observations suggested that they took fewer grouse.[83]

Meanwhile, persecution of raptors rose on Scottish grouse-moors,[84] from six known poisoning incidents per year in 1981–92 to ten per year in 1993–2000. In 2004–5, there were 33 confirmed incidents of raptor poisoning across Scotland and 36 of other persecution of birds of prey, including shooting, illegal trapping and nest destruction. There were 42 confirmed cases of poisoning in 2006, the highest rate for over 25 years. Figure 194 gives an example of persecution in the Cairngorms region during 1995–2003. The new Cairngorms National Park is no deterrent, for an adult cock golden eagle and, later, an adult hen in a different valley were found poisoned within it in the summer of 2006. The number of police wildlife officers has risen greatly, and army forces helped with surveillance of Scottish harriers in 2004. These are costs to taxpayers.

The law[85] now includes custodial sentences for the persecution of raptors, but nobody on the staff of a shooting estate has been jailed for such an offence. Some past cases with apparently firm evidence did not reach court because procurators-fiscal refused them, thus fuelling the public perception that some in the justice establishment put owners' interests above national interests. Sheriffs have often imposed small fines,[86] or let offenders off with warnings, though an Inverness sheriff in 2005 did impose a fine of £1,500 on a grouse-keeper, who appealed against the conviction. Gamekeepers have formed associations that defend their activities and lobby politicians.[87] In 2004, a lawyer for the Scottish Gamekeepers Association persuaded sheriffs to reject filmed evidence, because the landowner had not permitted the Royal Society for the Protection of Birds (RSPB) to be on the estate, and other cases have fallen because of delays occasioned by defence lawyers.[88]

Raptors have aesthetic and economic value to society. Wildlife tourism is increasing rapidly, already supporting far more jobs in some parts of the Highlands than grouse shooting, and many visitors pay to see raptors, such as sea eagles on Mull. Those who go to the Scottish hills for recreation say that they would be willing to pay an extra tax for desired changes, such as £72 each person per year for better protection of rare birds.[89]

The buzzard shows what could be enjoyed by the public if persecution ended. Though formerly killed widely, this species has returned in strength, especially on lowland, and countless people appreciate it. Sparrowhawks and peregrines have also increased on lowland, and give pleasure to many. More enjoyment would come if eagles returned to eastern moors and woods. These examples illustrate the real, though hidden, costs to the public of killing raptors.

Most conflicts can be resolved if both sides meet and compromise,[90] and there have been meetings on raptor-grouse conflicts.[91] When one side practises illegal acts, however, it is difficult to see whether the public would approve any compromise. Other suggestions to end persecution include legislation with mandatory jail sentences, removal of gun licences, game shooting permitted by a licence that could be removed,[92] and cross-compliance, such as denying state grants and exemptions of inheritance tax to owners of estates where the law on raptors has been broken. To conclude, grouse shooting could continue without the illegal persecution of raptors, but its future seems insecure if persecution continues unabated.[93]

### Options for moorland

Seven main options for using moorland are: (1) maintaining the status quo, including game shooting; (2) the farming of sheep and cattle; (3) tree planting; (4) natural reforestation; (5) industrial peat extraction; (6) conservation for moorland wildlife; and (7) walking and other informal tourism.[94]

Option 1, the status quo, emphasises game shooting. The red grouse is the only species that is primarily dependent on moorland and brings direct economic value to it.[95] On some moorland, red deer surpass grouse in value, especially in the west, where little grouse shooting occurs. However, deer at high density have seriously damaged much moorland and woodland.[96]

Moorland for game shooting also offers public benefits in terms of wildlife and landscape,[97] and some owners are now subsidised for this.[98] Public benefits from different but more natural wildlife and landscape would arise with option 4.

Most owners make a loss (Table 34), but making a profit is not the usual reason for owning a grouse-moor.[99] However, those who buy and then sell moors have made large gains since 1960, because increases in their value have greatly surpassed inflation.[100]

**TABLE 34.** Jobs (full-time equivalent, or FTE) and revenue (£ million) from named activities.

| REGION AND ACTIVITY | YEAR | FTE JOBS | REVENUE[#] | REFERENCE |
|---|---|---|---|---|
| **UK** | | | | |
| Nature conservation | 1999–2000 | 18,000 | — | Shiel et al., 2000 |
| Bird-watching | 1998 | — | 187 | Murray & Simcox, 2003 |
| Wildlife | c. 2002 | 35,000 | 4,800 | Murray & Simcox, 2003 |
| **Scotland** | | | | |
| Grouse shooting | 1989 | 978* | 6.3 | McGilvray & Perman, 1991 |
| | 1994 | 584* | 6.2 | McGilvray, 1996 |
| | 2000 | 630* | 26.7 | Fraser of Allander Institute, 2001 |
| Deer stalking | 1996 | 850 | 10.4 | Cobham Resource Consultants, 1997 |
| Mountaineering** | 1995 | 6,100 | 164 | Jones Economics Ltd et al., 1995 |
| Abernethy RSPB | 1998–9 | 80^ | 1.4 | Shiel et al., 2000 |
| Red kite, Black Isle | 2000 | Over 3 | 0.12 | Dickie et al., 2006 |
| Sea eagle, Mull | 2005 | 36–42 | 1.4–1.6 | Dickie et al., 2006 |
| Whale-watching | c. 2002 | — | 10.7 | Murray & Simcox, 2003 |
| Wildlife and landscape | 2003 | 93,000[†] | 2,200 | Scottish Natural Heritage, 2004b |
| **Wales** | | | | |
| Red kite | 1995–6 | 114 | 2.9 | Dickie et al., 2006 |
| **England** | | | | |
| Peregrine, Forest of Dean | 1999 | 18 | 0.55 | Dickie et al., 2006 |

**Notes to Table 34**
Two useful studies are not in the table. In upper Teesdale and Weardale, shooting raises £1.9 million in a good grouse year (Lovel, 2005, from the Moorland Association). A more comprehensive detailed study (Higgins et al., 2002) revealed that most of the 218 Highland sporting estates, on 1,842,000ha or 27 per cent of privately owned Scottish land, whether managed for grouse, deer or fish, required an annual five-figure sum from the owner to balance the books. Sixteen per cent always or usually made a profit, 64 per cent always or usually a loss, and 21 per cent made a profit in some years and a loss in others. Of the nine owners who allowed their finances to be published, seven on average lost £131,570 and two made profits averaging £12,124, the overall average for the nine being a loss of £99,638, and with losses ranging from £1,121 to £580,496.
# The large revenue from grouse shooting in 2000 reflected larger grouse stocks and more shooting.
* Direct jobs of full-time and part-time grouse staff, whose wages generate expenditure that maintains extra 'induced' jobs. Additional 'indirect' jobs depend on supplying goods and services bought by shooting parties and by moor-owners to sustain their grouse business. Induced and indirect expenditure form the 'multiplier effect'. Adding direct wages to the multiplier effect results in estimates of the contribution made by grouse shooting to Scotland's gross domestic product. In 1989, 1994 and 2000 this came to £10.3 million, £4.7 million and £17 million, respectively. Deficits (loss to owners) were £3.7 million, £10.7 million and £6.2 million, respectively.
** Mountaineering, hill-walking and associated activities in the Highlands and Islands region.
^ This comprised 14½ direct jobs on Abernethy and 65 indirect jobs. As a private estate it had a keeper, and in shooting seasons a gillie and staff at Forest Lodge, at most two direct FTEs, with forestry work carried out by outside contractors and shooters spending money as visitors do now.
† More than 90 per cent of this was in the private sector.

Option 2, farming sheep or cattle, is usually part of the status quo and accompanies game shooting. However, in some places it predominates, to the detriment of grouse. Generally uneconomic without subsidy, such farming can severely damage moorland. For decades, subsidies per head of ewes and cattle encouraged overstocking, with poor animal welfare in some areas and more sheep dying. In turn, the resultant carcasses induced increases of foxes, crows, ravens and gulls, which also took grouse eggs and chicks, and in the case of foxes additionally killed more adult grouse.

Option 3, tree planting, has been subsidised since 1920. In 1988, the UK government ordered a presumption against further large-scale coniferous afforestation of English moorland above 800ft (244m). Without subsidies, option 3 is uneconomic,[101] yet much moorland continues to be planted in Scotland and Ireland.

Option 4 is natural reforestation. On many freely drained east Scottish grouse-moors with few red deer, trees naturally colonised land after sheep stocks declined, leading to new woodland in some areas. Since the mid-1980s, however, much of this reforestation has been reversed by cutting and burning. On moorland with many red deer, overgrazing has long prevented tree regeneration, but pines spread widely after the FC extirpated red deer at Cairn Gorm, and large reductions of deer numbers led to birch expansion near Loch Laggan and pine at Abernethy and Glen More.[102] Natural reforestation results in attractive scenery, encourages wildlife, offers shooting, provides timber without the cost of planting, and reduces flooding. It happens widely abroad,[103] and could be more widespread on moorland and farmland in Britain and Ireland.

Option 5, industrial peat extraction, is especially extensive in Ireland, and destroys moorland. Usually unsustainable and often criticised,[104] it causes large emissions of gases that add to global warming.

Option 6 is management to produce a more varied wildlife.[105] Some British conservationists would minimise burning on blanket bog, cease it on shallow soils, increase it on young heather to raise nutrient turnover, and reduce it on old heather to boost cover for grouse or raptors, and to encourage the growth of patches of scrub or trees.[106] Such intervention would lead to fewer red grouse, smaller bags, reduced estate incomes and less moorland if owners could turn to subsidised tree planting as at present.[107]

Option 7, walking and other informal outdoor activities, including wildlife tourism, usually has to fit in willy-nilly with other options. Despite this, it currently supports the economy in much of upland Britain more than any other option (see Table 34).

## WOODLAND MANAGEMENT

This section emphasises Britain and Ireland, although it does touch on international studies of fire (for other management abroad, see Chapters 5 and 6).

### Fire
Many fires burnt old Caledonian pinewood during the period 1750–1950, and good tree regeneration often followed.[108] Since 1950, however, fires have been extinguished quickly through the use of fire-retardant chemicals, mist-sprays in knapsacks, mechanical sprayers in helicopters or towed by tractors, signposted

water sources, 'fire rendezvous' points and water tanks, and vehicle tracks that allow quick transport.

Lightning fire is natural in boreal forest[109] and removes most of the humus that builds up in pinewood podzols. This mineralisation of surface soil horizons by fire is good for regenerating pine and blaeberry;[110] whereas thick humus reduces pine regeneration, and in Scotland favours heather. Fire on Russian and US forest bogs also boosts the growth and berry production of whortleberry and cranberry.[111]

Although a natural fire in North American boreal forest can cover up to 200,000ha, most fires burn less than 4–5ha at a time. In Scottish pinewood since the late 1800s, fire often started between spring and autumn, sometimes during heatwaves, and occasionally burnt several hundred hectares at a time. However, many natural fires in Scotland are small because rain soon extinguishes them.

It has long been suggested that fire in Scots pinewood would increase tree regeneration.[112] British foresters and conservation bodies generally abhor fire,[113] though Russian and North American foresters often recognise its benefits. The RSPB is now experimenting with fire in Abernethy pinewood, as is Glen Tanar estate in Deeside. The aim is to improve habitat for capercaillie by increasing blaeberry and by achieving a more open vegetation on undergrazed sites.

**Grazing**

Some ancient pinewoods and broadleaved woods deteriorated after the early or mid-1800s because of overgrazing by red deer, sheep or cattle. They destroyed almost all young trees and juniper, reduced the height and abundance of heath, removed physical cover by eating branches, and damaged or eliminated herb-rich vegetation (*see* Table 33). Soil disturbance by severe trampling from cattle or red deer at high density encouraged bracken to spread after these animals were removed.

The opposite extreme, undergrazing, also had adverse effects. In some ancient woods, the exclusion or severe reduction of deer, sheep and cattle harms woodland grouse. Undergrazed heather grows too tall and rank, making it unfavourable for capercaillie chicks. Examples in old Caledonian pinewood can be seen at Glen Tanar and Ballochbuie, where new fences excluded red deer, and at Abernethy, where a heavy cull has greatly reduced deer density. Fences that exclude red deer can lead to severely overgrazed swards outside and totally undergrazed inside (*see* Fig. 87), as well as killing woodland grouse.

**FIG 195.** Red deer stags in the shade of a tree on a hot June day. Much of the remaining heather is cropped short and mixed with the grass that is replacing it. (Adam Watson)

**FIG 196.** Caledonian pinewood so heavily grazed by red deer that almost all heather and blaeberry have been replaced by short grass. (Stuart Rae)

### Forestry practices since 1939

Some ancient pinewood and broadleaved woodland was felled in 1939–45, but wartime felling concentrated on plantations. After 1945, much mature woodland was destroyed by clear-cutting, or damaged by underplanting with subsidised introduced conifers (Fig. 197) or by heavy selective felling (see Table 32). Outside designated conservation areas, intensive practices in the remaining ancient woods reduced the heath understorey, expanded grass and bracken and eliminated many old planted woods by clear-felling, while extra fencing killed more grouse (see Table 33).

These changes contributed to declines of blackgame and capercaillie, which have now gone from many places where they formerly abounded.[114] A tragic example occurred on Deveronside decades ago, after 1948. Intensive practices driven by the FC destroyed much pine and birch here, replacing them with alien conifers and extirpating both birds over a large area.[115]

The destruction of broadleaved woods was followed by declines or even localised extinctions of blackgame. In some cases, FC staff ring-barked all broadleaved trees after planting conifers.[116] In 1990, senior FC officers defied the FC's published policy on broadleaved woodland by grant-aiding a Deeside landowner to clear-fell birchwood and aspen wood, replacing them with Sitka spruce.[117]

FIG 197. Birch underplanted with Sitka spruce near Banchory. (Adam Watson)

Much broadleaved woodland with blaeberry and juniper survived the Second World War on steep, rough hillsides, where soils made fertile by colluvium and flushes supported nutritious herbs and insects. Where such slopes adjoined moorland or pinewood and were not overgrazed, they held blackgame and sometimes capercaillie, but planted Sitka spruce destroyed much of this valuable habitat after 1950.

On the positive side, some owners of private estates kept deer stocks low and maintained natural regeneration of ancient woodland, resisting FC pressure to plant trees. The benefits to the public can be seen today in examples such as Glen Tanar and Rothiemurchus. A few private owners maintained plantations as continuous woodland over the decades, by felling only individual trees and replacing them mainly by natural regeneration. Good examples are at Abernethy, and at Blelack on Deeside.

Since the late 1980s, the FC has changed its policies greatly. In ancient woodland on its own land it has removed introduced species, such as at Glen More. On private land, its grants and advice encourage owners to maintain or expand native woodland. Its concentration on timber production has lessened, and it now stresses a wider appreciation of woodland landscape and wildlife as public benefits. Along with private landowners, conservation bodies and biologists, the FC now tries to help capercaillie and other threatened wildlife.

**Options for woodland**

Despite welcome changes in FC policies, inconsistency remains between the continued – albeit lesser – stress on timber production, and rising emphasis on woodland for wildlife, public recreation and tourism. The last three require protection of existing ancient woods, reinstatement of natural forest, and maintenance of 'continuous tree-cover in all woods by radical changes in felling practices'.[118] Reinstatement includes respect for the pristine, centuries-old soils that are central to the evolution of complete forest ecosystems. A cautionary note should be struck about recreation, for it can seriously damage woodland soils and wildlife. Resolution of this requires zoning, a well-established practice in town planning, though one that is too often absent in rural affairs.

## SKI DEVELOPMENTS

Ski lifts have increased in number greatly in many countries. These developments destroy habitat, disturb grouse and kill birds on wires (Figs 198 & 199), while new roads or lifts give easy access for summer tourists. In central Europe, food scraps

MANAGEMENT AND CONSERVATION · 411

FIG 198. Ski-tow wires in ptarmigan habitat near the Cairnwell. (Stuart Rae)

FIG 199. Head of a ptarmigan decapitated by a ski wire near the Cairnwell. (Stuart Rae)

from tourists attract corvids[119] and foxes, which then also take grouse. A British example of a ski development is Cairn Gorm, the busiest tourist station on Scottish Alpine land. Food scraps left by visitors attracted lowland crows, which became daytime residents and then turned to eggs and chicks as a food source. Hardly any ptarmigan reared young and wires killed many adults, the result being that no birds bred on the most heavily developed section for many years.[120]

Much has been published on the effects of ski developments abroad.[121] Wires kill many grouse in the Alps and Pyrenees, and ski developments in the Alps reduced blackgame density, extirpated them locally, and caused abandonment of leks.

Several lessons can be learned from such studies. Take Cairn Gorm, for example. When the ski manager was told about the crows, he erected signs, requesting visitors not to discard food and explaining why. When nearby landowners were informed of the problem at liaison meetings, they increased their efforts to kill breeding crows on nearby low ground. This led to fewer crows on high ground, and better breeding by ptarmigan.

In central Europe, threats to grouse from both ski and summer tourists led to zoning to reduce or ban visitors from sensitive habitats.[122] This is difficult because of the massive increase in visitor numbers, as well as the development of new sports that require more land and facilities. None the less, when reasons are explained and alternatives are offered, cooperation has been good. This points the way ahead for resolving other conflicts between public recreation and grouse conservation.[123]

## POLLUTION

Nitrogenous and other compounds from urban industry have fallen in precipitation and fog onto much British and Irish moorland and Alpine land.[124] North English moors lie near Britain's main industrial towns. In the 1800s, the nitrogen content of woolly fringe-moss there was twice as high as in northwest Scotland, and in the late 1900s it was up to sixfold higher. Such increases would have enriched heather and boosted numbers of red grouse. However, continued heavy deposition of ammonia in the Netherlands eventually exterminated heather, replacing it with wavy hair-grass on dry heath and purple moor grass on wet heath.[125] A little nitrogenous pollution can benefit grouse, but a lot can be disastrous.

Sulphur compounds have increased as industrial pollutants in precipitation and fog, often called 'acid rain' because the gas sulphur dioxide combines with water to form sulphuric acid. Moorland soils in northeast Scotland became more acidic in 1960–88, and if this trend continues the production of heather and other dwarf shrubs may decline.[126] In Czechoslovakia, acidic deposition near industrial towns damaged heath and trees used by blackgame and capercaillie, and killed much blaeberry.[127] Rime and hoar frost concentrate aerial pollutants, and later work in Czechoslovakia revealed industrial pollution by heavy-metal compounds as well as acidic deposition. On days when much hoar frost lay on trees and ground vegetation, birds had to consume polluted hoar frost when feeding. Both grouse species became extinct in the area of study.[128]

Man's chemical pollution has spread widely in the form of organochlorine compounds such as DDT and polychlorinated biphenyls (PCBs). Pollution by organochlorine pesticides became widespread after 1950, but in Britain and Ireland it mainly affected lowland farms and so had little impact on grouse habitats.[129] After the explosion at Chernobyl nuclear power station in April 1986, however, heather in some western parts of Britain contained radioactive caesium for many years, as did red grouse and red deer that grazed there, and many sheep are still (2006) too radioactive to be slaughtered for human consumption.[130]

In willow ptarmigan from the remote Northwest Territories in Canada, no detectable organochlorine pesticides or PCBs were found in eggs, and only low amounts in the hens' livers and muscles.[131] At the Ungava Peninsula, however, which is closer to the country's industrial cities, the livers and muscles of birds contained appreciable amounts of cadmium, lead and selenium.[132] Scandinavian willow ptarmigan showed unnaturally high levels of zinc, cadmium and copper.[133] To conclude, most studies show lower levels of pollutants in grouse than in lowland birds, but very little is known about possible effects on survival or breeding success.

## CLIMATE CHANGE

Climates fluctuate for natural reasons, such as variation in the earth's distance from the sun. Britain's climate has warmed by 0.5°C since 1900, mostly since 1980, a rate so great and so fast that most meteorologists consider it unnatural, attributing it to human-induced increases of carbon dioxide, methane and other gases that trap solar heat in the atmosphere. They predict a warmer, wetter and windier Britain and Ireland of the future.[134]

Warming may alter ocean circulation. The Gulf Stream brings subtropical surface water from the Gulf of Mexico into the northern North Atlantic, keeping western Europe much milder than Labrador at the same latitude. More fresh water from faster melting of Arctic ice and snow now threaten its stability. If it were to collapse, the British and Scandinavian climate would be colder than it is now, at least in the short run.

**Impacts on grouse**

Climate change is here now, and it is already affecting wildlife such as black grouse and capercaillie (*see* Chapters 5 and 6). Some claims of these effects, however, rest on the invalid assumption that habitats depend solely on temperature, and ignore the evidence[135] that summers 7,500–5,000 years ago were far warmer than they are now. Examples of such claims are that warmer temperatures will squeeze the Scottish ptarmigan's favoured blaeberry and crowberry uphill, shift timberlines uphill, and threaten Caledonian pinewood with extinction.[136] Yet the boulders that suit blaeberry and crowberry would remain, and both species grow on warm Scottish lowland. Gales are now commoner[137] and climatologists predict an even greater frequency, which would shift timberlines downhill.[138] Most pinewood grows on infertile sands and gravels that would continue to favour Scots pine, and this species abounds in hot Mediterranean countries.

Although such claims about climate change are not always based on fact, grouse are adapted to cold climates and a warmer climate will not usually benefit them. The rate of change is so fast that unexpected impacts may occur. Grave threats now face humans, as well as the wildlife that shares the planet with us and depends on us.

## SUMMARY

Impacts of hunting on grouse numbers are poorly understood. In red grouse, however, the evidence indicates that heavy shooting in years of increase can prevent subsequent declines. Subsidies for farming and forestry have destroyed much British and Irish grouse habitat since 1945. Muirburn standards have fallen, and overgrazing by sheep and red deer has damaged habitats. Heather beetle, ticks and bracken are increasing threats. Raptor persecution continues, despite stiffer penalties. Options for moorland include natural reforestation, and informal recreation now raises more money than shooting. The main options for woodland are to reinstate natural forest and to maintain truly continuous tree cover. Industrial pollutants contaminate grouse and adversely affect their food plants, and climate change is a widespread threat.

# Endnotes

Where simply the author's name and date of publication are given in a note, full details of that title are to be found in the Bibliography (*see* p.472).

## INTRODUCTION

1 Lawton, 1990. This publication is a historical summary of British grouse research since 1956.
2 Sangster *et al.*, 2004. 'Willow Ptarmigan (Red Grouse)', and 'The correct scientific name of the Red Grouse is *Lagopus l. scotica*' and 'of the Rock Ptarmigan is *Lagopus muta*'. We ignore such renaming.

## CHAPTER 1

1 Although some northern breeding populations avoid deep snow by wintering hundreds of kilometres south of their breeding range, and many populations move shorter distances between summer and winter habitats.
2 Ground-dwelling species (e.g. red grouse, ptarmigan) have feathered toes, whereas arboreal species (e.g. hazel grouse, black grouse, capercaillie) have small scales or 'pectinations', whose primary function is probably to grip branches (Drovetski, 1992).
3 Their basal metabolic rate is higher than that of a generalised non-passerine bird of the same body weight (Andreev, 1988b, 1991).
4 Meleagrininae.
5 Simplified from Drovetski (2003). Other work agrees largely with this family tree but gives different estimates of the time when grouse diverged from turkeys (6 million years ago according to Drovetski, and 20 million years ago according to Pereira & Baker, 2006). This is because the 'molecular clock' used to estimate timescale is debatable. The Miocene lasted from about 23 million to about 5 million years ago, and so both estimates agree that grouse diverged from turkeys during that epoch. Like the Pliocene and Pleistocene, the late Miocene was a period of global cooling, and so the statement that grouse evolved during such a climatic period stands, irrespective of the timescale.
6 Drovetski, 2003.
7 The Pliocene and Pleistocene.
8 Together, the Nearctic and the Palaearctic comprise the Holarctic, which is more or less the northern hemisphere north of the Tropic of Cancer.

9 Until recently, 18 species were generally recognised, but the blue grouse has just reverted to two separate species, the dusky and the sooty grouse. Some authors argue that the red grouse should be restored as a species from its present status as a subspecies of willow ptarmigan, and that the southwestern and northeastern subspecies of spruce grouse should be restored to species (Gutiérrez et al., 2000; Lucchini et al., 2001; Dimcheff et al., 2002; Schroeder, 2006).
10 The 'ptarmigan' group includes the red grouse. Molecular evidence is causing some authors to revert to the old split between *Tetrao* (the two capercaillie) and *Lyrurus* (the two black grouse), a convention we use in this chapter.
11 Drovetski, 2003.
12 *See* Chapter 6.
13 Harrison, 1987.
14 The exception proves the rule. In the Cantabrian mountains of northern Spain, there are few native conifers and capercaillie winter in forests of beech, oak or holly.
15 Although some populations of ruffed grouse, like capercaillie, seem able to survive without conifers.
16 Storch, 2000a.
17 Such as birch, alder, rowan, beech, aspen, hazel and willow.
18 Zwickel, 1992.
19 *See* Chapters 5 and 6.
20 The Caucasian black grouse, the Chinese grouse and the Siberian grouse are probably 'vulnerable' according to IUCN criteria, and the Gunnison sage grouse is considered 'endangered' (Storch, 2000a). The lesser prairie-chicken is being considered for federal listing as 'threatened' or 'endangered'.
21 *See* Chapter 14.

## CHAPTER 2

1 Brown, 1993.

2 www.anglo-norman.net/articles/missinglink.xml, accessed 5 September 2006; Rothwell, 1991.
3 MacGillivray, 1837, 1855. He named all *Lagopus* as ptarmigans, Britain having brown ptarmigan or red grouse or red ptarmigan, and grey ptarmigan or common ptarmigan.
4 Hantzsch, 1914; Soper, 1928; Macpherson & McLaren, 1959; Wilson, 1976; Cramp & Simmons, 1980; Höhn, 1980; Johnsgard, 1983; Hagemeijer & Blair, 1997; Lindström et al., 1998. Several names are onomatopoeic (Holder & Montgomerie, 1993a). Chinese names for willow and rock ptarmigan include *niao*, like a hen's nasal contact call, whereas Inuit names resemble male calls, e.g. *akigikvik* for willow ptarmigan in Baffin Island and *nakatogak* for rock ptarmigan in east Greenland. Capercaillie in Russian is *glukhar*, with stress on *khar* and sounding guttural like part of the bird's song, and Sámi has *tsuukhts* (Semenov-Tyan-Shanskiy, 1960), sounding like the last swishing part of the song.
5 Cymdeithas Edward Llwyd (1994). Cymdeithas Edward Llwyd, a natural history society that works in Welsh, has attempted to standardise common names of animals, with the approval of museums and the Countryside Commission for Wales. The list has the plural of red grouse as *grugieir cochion*, ptarmigan plural as *grugieir gwynion*, blackgame plural as *grugieir duon*, and capercaillie singular as *grugiar coed* and capercaillie plural as *grugieir coed*.
6 Grant, 1941; Grant & Murison, 1956, 1965, 1974.
7 *Muir* is Scots and *moor* English, both pronounced 'moor', although *muir* is increasingly heard as 'myoor', following its spelling. Variants are the Aberdeenshire 'meer', west Angus 'mair', and central 'mair' or 'mør', with the middle vowel sound pronounced like the Danish ø.
8 MacGillivray, 1837; Longmuir, 1867; SND.
9 Gordon, 1915.
10 Spoken with an extra vowel to ease pronunciation, as 'taramachan', and meaning

'a ringing sound', like the cock's call. The accent indicates a long vowel, but in his dialect surveys James Grant (pers. comm. 2006) always heard it short. The derivative *torman* is often used in Gaelic poetry for the sound of streams running down hillsides (James Grant, pers. comm. 2006), with the onomatopoeic pronunciation 'toroman'. In Ross-shire, *tormachan an t-sléibhe* was used for ptarmigan, which adds to the likelihood that *tarmachan* derived from *tormachan*. To conclude, the evidence indicates that *tarmachan* means 'grumbler' or 'croaker' (Dwelly, 1971; Lockwood, 1976; Ó Dónaill, 1977; MacLennan, 1979; MacBain, 1982; Brown, 1993).
11 For example, heathfowl in a list that includes *muirfowl* (Rose, 1785).
12 MacEachainn, 1971.
13 Ó Dónaill, 1977.
14 Pennie, 1951.
15 James Grant (pers. comm. 2006) considers this the likely explanation of the transmutation, since 'l' often becomes 'r', e.g. *bruadal* becomes *bruadar*.
16 Robertson, 1898.
17 Robinson, 1985.
18 Hjorth, 1970.

## CHAPTER 3

1 Salomonsen, 1939.
2 Höhn, 1980.
3 Gutiérrez et al., 2000.
4 Chapman, 1924.
5 Steen, 1989.
6 Cramp & Simmons, 1980.
7 Kloster, 1928.
8 Potapov, 1985.
9 Explanation of deep, undrifted snow powder categories: (1) scarce, due to frequent wind (or many days with snow-free ground), e.g. east Greenland, Taimyr, Kazakhstan, Komander Islands, Svalbard (Glen Esk, Amchitka, Hitra); (2) uncommon, due to fairly frequent wind and open landscape (or calm conditions but very shallow snowfall), e.g. Cairngorms Alpine land, Avalon, Iceland, Seward, southwest Alaskan coast, Kodiak, Anadyr, Koryak, Finnmark (Yakutia); (3) common, despite more wind than in 4, because of heavy snowfalls or shelter from mountains and woodland or scrub, e.g. Senja, Lierne, Finnish Lapland, Leningradskaia, Altai, middle Yukon River, northwest British Columbia, west Newfoundland; (4) widespread, due to deep snowfall and fairly calm, cold air, e.g. central Alaska, upper Yukon River, interior Yukon Territory, central Urals, Switzerland, Siberia.
10 References on body-weight, snow and climate for Fig. 12. *Lagopus lagopus*: Kristoffersen, 1933; Ulianin, 1939; Myrberget et al., 1969; West et al., 1970; Pulliainen, 1976; Andreev, 1982; Thomas, 1982; Myrberget, 1984b; Mossop, 1988; Watson, unpublished, at Glen Esk. Rock ptarmigan: Lid, 1927; Grammeltvedt & Steen, 1978; Thomas & Popko, 1981; Mortensen et al., 1983, 1985; Steen & Unander, 1985; Watson, 1987b; Emison & White, 1988; Ó. Nielsen, unpublished, at Hrisey; Brenot et al., 2005, the birds were very light (mcan 417g) in the continental climate of the French Alps, and 449g in the more oceanic Pyrenees, but these were autumn weights, and so are not used in the graph. Both species: Semenov-Tyan-Shanskiy, 1960; Moss, 1974; Cramp & Simmons, 1980; Potapov, 1985, and references therein; R. Potapov, pers. comm. 2007. Snow and climate: Pruitt, 1960; Borisov, 1965; McKay et al., 1970, and references therein; Fullard, 1976; many ecological references in Chapters 2 and 3.
11 Henderson, 1977; Moss & Watson, 1987.
12 Jenkins et al., 1963.
13 Lance, 1975.
14 Potapov, 1985.
15 At Glenamoy there is virtually no winter in meteorological terms, i.e. days with a mean temperature below freezing.
16 Yurlov, 1960; Lance, 1975; Voronin, 1978.

17 Dementiev & Gladkov, 1952.
18 Potapov, 1985.
19 Myrberget, 1975, Fig. 1; Watson & Moss, unpublished.
20 Body-weight rose quite fast at Avalon (Bergerud et al., 1963), north Norway (Myrberget, 1975) and Churchill (Hannon et al., 1998), and yet slower at Kerloch. Winter comes later at the first three than on Russian tundra, and later still at Kerloch. Hudson (1986a) reported quite fast growth in north England, but did not name locations or altitudes, so climate cannot be assessed.
21 Myrberget, 1975.
22 Bent, 1932.
23 Moss, 1972a.
24 Bent, 1932.
25 Moss, 1972a; Steen et al., 1992.
26 Watson, unpublished.
27 Classification by resemblances and differences, often synonymous with taxonomy.
28 Hanson, 1935; Salomonsen, 1936, 1939.
29 Lorenz, 1904; Potapov, 1985.
30 Watson & Moss, unpublished; Steen, 1989.
31 A juvenile cock shot in 1967 on Meall Odhar had much white on its body and wings, but its size and reddish feathers seemed like a red grouse (Watson, 1967c). Also on Meall Odhar a dead juvenile found in August 1990 showed the same features (AW, unpublished). A hybrid shot on Kinveachy estate in 2005, one of a brood of three (Frank Law, pers. comm.), was identified as such from DNA evidence (Stuart Piertney, pers. comm.).
32 Parmelee et al., 1967.
33 During spring in Alaska, a hen rock ptarmigan solicited a cock willow ptarmigan that had a small patch of dark spring feathering on each side of his head. Evidently his dark patches resembled a male rock ptarmigan's black moustache enough to stimulate her inappropriate behaviour (Moss, unpublished).
34 Potapov, 1985.
35 For example, in the Cumberland Peninsula.

36 Cramp & Simmons, 1980. The first tentative introduction was in 1870, but was not very successful (Michèle Loneux, pers. comm. 2005). Other releases during 1910–20 in east Belgium along the German border led to abundant birds, but they became scarce after 1950 as habitat loss proceeded. The last Belgian record was in April 1974, of a cock heard in the Hautes-Fagnes Nature Reserve, created in 1966 at 670m altitude along the German border (Ruwet, 1988). The cock was on Fagnes de la Baraque Michel, where blackgame still occur.
37 Witherby et al., 1944; Hudson, 1993.
38 An introduction in the 1890s failed (see Chapter 4). In the 1970s, Deeside birds were released on the islands. They nested, but cats killed some hens and the birds became extinct. Overgrazing by sheep had also reduced food and cover (Watson, unpublished).
39 Myrberget, 1976; Cramp & Simmons, 1980; Steen, 1989; Hagemeijer & Blair, 1997; Stone et al., 1997; Storch, 2000a, b.
40 Adam Smith, pers. comm. 2007, based on counts by the Game Conservancy Trust.
41 Hammond, 1979.
42 Hudson, 1993.
43 In O'Dwyer, 1995. Watson et al. (1995) estimated over 10,000 pairs, extrapolated from counts.
44 For example, Bent, 1932; Höhn, 1980; Steen, 1989.
45 For a definition of 'heath', see Chapter 11.
46 For example, Kastdalen et al., 2003.
47 Ratcliffe, 1990.
48 Watson & Miller, 1976.
49 Savory, 1986; Palmer & Bacon, 2001.
50 Parr, 1992.
51 Longstaff, 1932; Soper, 1940; Manning, 1948; Dementiev & Gladkov, 1952; Harper, 1953; Jenkins, 1953; Manning et al., 1956; Höhn, 1959; Macpherson & Manning, 1959; Semenov-Tyan-Shanskiy, 1960; Manning & Macpherson, 1961; Savile, 1961; Jenkins et al., 1963, 1967; Watson, 1963c, 1965a, b, 1979,

unpublished; Savile & Oliver, 1964; Bergerud & Mercer, 1966; Parmelee *et al.*, 1967; Soichiro *et al.*, 1969; Williamson & Emison, 1969; Bergerud, 1970a; MacDonald, 1970; Géroudet, 1978; Watson & O'Hare, 1979a; Marcström & Höglund, 1980; Luder, 1981; Parker, 1981a, 1984; Alamany & de Juan Monzon, 1983; Fasel & Zbinden, 1983; Montgomerie *et al.*, 1983; Ryzhanovskiy *et al.*, 1983; Myrberget, 1984b; Pedersen, 1984; Potapov, 1985 and references therein; Unander & Steen, 1985; Hannon & Barry, 1986; Olpinski, 1986; Martin & Cooke, 1987; Boudarel, 1988; Brodsky, 1988a; Gardarsson, 1988; Mossop, 1988; Ryabitsev, 1989; Huber & Ingold, 1991; Cotter *et al.*, 1992; Holder & Montgomerie, 1993b; Holder, 1994; Bossert, 1995 and references therein; Nielsen & Pétursson, 1995; Hannon *et al.*, 1998; Watson *et al.*, 1998, 2000; Cotter, 1999; Scherini *et al.*, 2003; Smith *et al.*, 2005; G. Scherini & G. Tosi, unpublished.
52 'Polar desert' is shown by vegetation maps (Beschel, 1970; Alexandrova, 1970, 1988), and is characterised by low plant production (Alexandrova, 1970, 1988; Bliss *et al.*, 1984) and low precipitation with cold summers (MacKay *et al.*, 1970). Eurasian polar deserts have richer soils, more plant species and less bare ground than North American ones (Svoboda, 2002). The milder 'Arctic desert' (Kankaanpää, 2002) extends further south in Canada than in Eurasia. Vegetative cover and production are greater in Arctic Eurasian heath, and greater still on Scottish Alpine land and moorland (*see* Table 6). The greater vegetative cover and production in high-Arctic and Arctic Eurasia than in these zones in Canada explain the lower densities of willow and rock ptarmigan in Canada than in the equivalent zones in Eurasia.
53 Fewer sheep, along with little or no burning, have caused much coastal heathland to change to scrub and woodland.
54 Ulianin, 1939; Höhn, 1980. Photographs show loose, sandy soil, indicating dry weather conditions. There are no bogs, and birds in the southeast of the range breed in semi-desert (Roald Potapov, pers. comm. 2007).
55 Watson *et al.*, 1966.
56 Bracts at the base of each flower in the floret spike.
57 Mikheev, 1948; Hannon *et al.*, 1998.
58 Savory, 1977.
59 Dementiev & Gladkov, 1952.
60 Hannon *et al.*, 1998.
61 Irving *et al.*, 1967a.
62 Stokkan, 1992.
63 Kitshinskiy, 1975. Although on the New Siberian Islands, the most northerly land occupied by willow ptarmigan, birds deposit much fat in autumn.
64 Andreev, 1980.
65 Gabrielsen *et al.*, 1977, 1985; Gabrielsen & Steen, 1979; Gabrielsen & Unander, 1987; Steen *et al.*, 1988a; Ingold *et al.*, 1992.
66 Slagsvold, 1975. Air temperature in June during the incubation period is related to the percentage of young in the subsequent shooting bag.
67 Hudson, 1986a.
68 Moss *et al.*, 1990b.
69 Jørgensen & Blix, 1988. Ambient temperature is air temperature at bird level.
70 Aulie & Moen, 1975.
71 Boggs *et al.*, 1977; Pedersen & Steen, 1979.
72 Aulie, 1976a, b.
73 Jørgensen & Blix, 1985.
74 Höglund, 1970; Erikstad, 1979, 1985b; Erikstad & Spidsø, 1982; Erikstad & Andersen, 1983. Chick growth and survival were poorer in cold summers with few insects than in a warm summer with many insects (Erikstad, 1985b). Rain and cold reduced the feeding times of two- to five-day chicks by 60 per cent, and their crops held almost twice as much food in a warm, dry summer as in a wet, cold one. Chicks grew more slowly and survived worse in broods that moved more, presumably in search of food. In cold, wet summers, chicks aged zero to eight days in small broods grew faster than those in large broods. Chicks in large broods spent longer being brooded, with less time for eating.

75 Bent, 1932; Dementiev & Gladkov, 1952. The 'orderly action of winter flocks led Eskimos and northern Indians to regard them as organized societies and, in their mythology, to designate them as ptarmigan "people"'(Irving et al., 1967b).
76 Weeden & Ellison, 1968; Hannon et al., 1998.
77 Cramp & Simmons, 1980. Zimmerman et al. (2005) noted willow ptarmigan at sea in calm weather near the Alaskan coast on 30 August, when 125 flew over the sea and around a boat. A few 'appeared to be exhausted after landing on the vessel, exhibiting rapid breathing with open beaks', but panting also signifies birds being hot. At least ten landed on the water to rest. Other observations of birds flying at sea are given, including two bathing, and a rock ptarmigan sitting on the water.
78 A greater percentage moves at high than at low density.
79 Jenkins et al., 1963.
80 Watson et al. (1984b) called it 'spring emigration'.
81 See Chapter 14.
82 Leslie, 1911.
83 Watson, 1966.
84 Andersen, 1986; Andersen et al., 1986. A variant is that Kazakh birds that have bred in woodland move to open steppe after the first snowfall, but return to winter in woodland (Ulianin, 1939).
85 Watson, 1966, unpublished.
86 For example, Jenkins et al., 1967; Hörnell-Willebrand, 2005.
87 A case of homing involved a cock that was radio-tagged in spring 1987 on Strathnairn, released 35km away, and then refound on Strathnairn a year later (Hudson et al., 1988).
88 Jenkins et al., 1963. Also, in a Grouse Migration Enquiry in 1932–9, Scottish keepers ringed young red grouse (1938, Field, p. 1289). Out of 56 birds recovered in their first shooting season, 52 were shot on their own moors, some 'within 100yds. [90m] or 400yds. [370m] of the spot where they were ringed',

three went 1–2 miles (1.6–3.2km), and one 8 miles (13km). Out of 12 shot in later years, seven were on their own moors, four moved 1–2 miles (1.6–3.2km), and one 12 miles (19km). Four of the seven were in their second year and one each in their third, fifth and seventh years. Scandinavian willow ptarmigan after their first shooting season tend to move more (Cramp & Simmons, 1980, citing Olstad, 1953; Hörnell-Willebrand, 2005).
89 Jenkins et al., 1967.
90 Watson, 1965a; Watson et al., 1984b. A case occurred after we applied fertiliser to boost heather growth and protein content at Kerloch (Watson et al., 1984a). The area held an extremely high density of territorial grouse from autumn to spring 1971–2. Just before nesting, about 40 per cent of cocks and hens emigrated. The area would have provided good food for wintering and for hens to build reserves before nesting, but was so crowded that few chicks would be recruited. Hence, we suppose, birds went elsewhere to breed.
91 Watson et al., 1984b. In willow ptarmigan, too, two-thirds of territorial birds emigrated from Tranøy just before nesting, in 1971, a year of high density (Myrberget, 1984b, 1989a). Their age was not reported.
92 Some old willow ptarmigan at Chilkat Pass shift to different territories in a subsequent spring (Schieck & Hannon, 1989; Hannon & Martin, 1996), but willow ptarmigan there do not hold territories over winter like red grouse.
93 Lance, 1978a; Mountford et al., 1990; Watson et al., 1994; and Myrberget (1989a) in willow ptarmigan.
94 Watson et al., 1984a.
95 Watson & Miller, 1976.
96 Lovat, 1911; Moore et al., 1975.
97 Miller et al., 1970. Muirburn occurred annually for four years. Grouse density rose in the last year of burning and stayed high for two more years. To keep it high may require burning every few years.

98 Lance & Phillips, 1975.
99 Watson et al., 1987.
100 Watson, 1966, 1979; Picozzi, 1968; Moss, 1969; Watson & Hewson, 1973; Nethersole-Thompson & Watson, 1974; Moss et al., 1975.
101 Hudson, 1992.
102 Phillips & Watson, 1995.
103 Parry, 1978; Simmons, 2003.
104 This contrasts with soil damage caused by modern farming, but it involves deep ploughing in autumn or winter on enlarged fields (usually up and down slopes), compaction by machines, and autumn-sown crops with much bare ground. Prehistoric cultivation was carried out in summer, with hand tools used to work the surface soil.
105 Parry, 1978.
106 Lee et al., 1992.
107 John Lee, Des Thompson & Sarah Woodin, pers. comm. 2006.
108 Hudson (1992) used weather data to estimate heather production, because annual production on Kerloch was related positively to summer air temperature and negatively to rainfall (Miller, 1979).
109 Lindén & Pedersen, 1997.
110 Marcström & Höglund, 1980.
111 Bergerud, 1970a; Pedersen, 1984; Hannon & Barry, 1986. Densities at Avalon are 1.4 cocks per km$^2$, at Anderson River 7.7 and at Dovrefjell 15.
112 Phillips et al., 1992a.
113 Mercer & McGrath, 1963; Bergerud & Mercer, 1966; Myrberget, 1988; Gardarsson, 1988. In 1962, the 19,000ha Brunette Island, 16km from mainland Newfoundland, had an estimated 37.9 cocks per km$^2$, falling to 3 per km$^2$ in 1965. This compared with 1.5 per km$^2$, falling to 0.7 per km$^2$, on the mainland in the same years. The 137ha Tranøy had an average density of 74 adult birds per km$^2$, with a peak of 85 pairs per km$^2$. There was no study area on the nearby big island Senja, but far lower densities there were obvious to Norwegian biologists and to AW who was with them. At Hrisey there was no study area on the nearby mainland, but lower densities there were obvious to Icelandic biologists and to those of us who were with them.
114 When a fenced plot prevents voles from moving in or out, they increase to a very high density (Krebs et al., 1969). Even though an island does not prevent grouse moving in or out, it may constrain movement more than on the mainland.
115 On a 16ha area in spring 1973 (upper) and 1972 (lower).
116 Watson (1979) gave densities on two areas combined. The table gives data in spring 1978 on the 14ha Cairnwell and the adjacent 13ha Meall Odhar Beag. No fires had burned since 1950. Keepers eliminated crows in most years and killed foxes. Shooting was by occasional 'walking up'.
117 On 28 March 1954, an area over granite at 450–550m. The hen figure is from Watson, unpublished.
118 Unburned unshot upper moorland. Watson (1979) combined cocks and hens, and Watson (unpublished) has separate values. Ranges across years were 4.7–14.2 in cocks and 0–14.2 in hens.
119 Unburned unshot upper moorland. Statistical analyses (Watson et al., 2000) used the data of Watson (unpublished). The table shows ranges across years.
120 Means for 14 study areas in 1969 before experimental treatments began on some areas, density ranges being 0–4.9 for cocks and 0–3.7 for hens.
121 Counts in 1958 on 200ha of mostly grassy overgrazed moor near Kinlochbervie.
122 Watson & Moss, 1979; Bergerud & Gratson, 1988.
123 Haydon et al., 2002.
124 Watson et al., 2000.
125 Authors' analysis, unpublished.
126 Moss & Watson, 2001.
127 Moss et al., 1996.
128 Lindström et al., 1995.
129 Siivonen, 1952.
130 Myrberget, 1984b, c, 1987a, 1988, 1989b; Steen et al., 1988b.

131 See, for example, the lemming study by Framstad et al., 1993.
132 Steen & Erikstad, 1996.
133 Moss & Watson, 2001. In this review there were seven examples from *Lagopus lagopus* and *L. mutus* combined.
134 Bergerud, 1970a; Hannon & Barry, 1986; Andreev, 1988a.
135 Mercer & McGrath, 1963; Weeden, 1963; Bergerud & Mercer, 1966; Jenkins et al., 1967; Watson, 1979; Watson et al., 1984b; Myrberget, 1984b. Semenov-Tyan-Shanskiy (1960) recorded August numbers from close to 0 and up to 20 per km$^2$ in Laplandskiy, and 3–135 seen per 100 hours in September–December.
136 Moss et al., 2000a.
137 Hudson, 1992.
138 Watson et al., 1995.
139 Mackenzie, 1952.
140 O'Hare, 1973.
141 Barnes, 1987; Hudson, 1992.
142 Mackenzie, 1952.
143 Watson et al., 1989.
144 Siivonen, 1948, 1952; Semenov-Tyan-Shanskiy, 1960.
145 Moss & Watson, 2001.
146 Phillips & Watson, 1995.
147 Straker-Smith & Phillips, 1994; Phillips & Watson, 1995.
148 Estimates of survival from radio-tagged birds are more accurate, but are usually imprecise owing to small samples. Also, radios may affect survival. Studies in red grouse and willow ptarmigan found no impact of radios on survival, but their statistical power to detect such an effect was low. A few studies in other species suggest an impact, e.g. predators at Windy Lake killed a higher percentage of radio-tagged male rock ptarmigan (Cotter, 1991). The type of harness may affect survival, but in Cotter's case it made no difference whether he used necklaces or back harnesses.
149 Bergerud, 1970a, 1988; Johnsgard, 1983; Bergerud & Mossop, 1984. Apparent 'survival' from one spring to the next can be calculated by dividing the number of 'old adults' (in their second or later springs) on an area in the current spring by the number of old plus 'young adults' (in their first spring) present in the previous spring. This and similar methods, however, take no account of movement. The method that confounds adult survival with that of newly reared youngsters uses the number present in spring divided by the total number (adults and young) present in the previous autumn.
150 They used radios to follow birds from spring to autumn, and rings to find return rates after winter. Raptors killed many birds, including cocks establishing territories, hens before laying and during incubation and in the early brood period, and both sexes in the late-brood and moult periods. Autumn hunters shot 1.4–3.0 times more cocks than hens.
151 Moss & Watson, 2001.
152 Hudson, 1986a.
153 Watson & Miller, 1976; Watson, unpublished.
154 Myrberget, 1976; Hannon et al., 1998.
155 Weeden, 1963; Bergerud, 1970a; Myrberget, 1984b; Hannon et al., 1998, 2003. For example, 1.2 cocks per hen at Chilkat Pass, Avalon and Churchill.
156 Jenkins et al., 1963, 1967; Watson et al., 1984b. In addition, on Yamal, 30 per cent of territorial cocks were unmated after a fourfold increase in density over four years (Ryabitsev, 1989).
157 Watson & Jenkins, 1968.
158 Hannon, 1983. Several cock willow ptarmigan had three hens each and one had four.
159 Manniche, 1910; Soper, 1928; Bent, 1932; Mikheev, 1939, 1948; Salomonsen, 1939, 1950; Dunaeva & Kucheruk, 1941; Macpherson & Manning, 1959; Semenov-Tyan-Shanskiy, 1960; Jenkins et al., 1963; Watson, 1965a; MacDonald, 1970; Cramp & Simmons, 1980; Johnsgard, 1983; Montgomerie et al., 1983; Potapov, 1985; Steen & Unander, 1985; Potapov & Flint, 1987;

Holder & Montgomerie, 1993a; Hannon et al., 1998; Cotter, 1999.
160 Sharp & Moss, 1981.
161 Jenkins et al. (1963, 1967) recorded differences in average hatch dates. They drew no conclusion about weather, but hatching came early after mild springs in 1957 and 1961, and late after the cold snowy springs of 1958 and 1962. Laying dates of willow ptarmigan at Churchill are correlated with dates of snow melt (Martin & Wiebe, 2004).
162 Myrberget, 1987b; Hannon et al., 1998.
163 Moss et al., 1981. The median is the mid-point when observations are arranged in order of size, commonly used where there is a skew, as is usual with laying dates. The order in which individual hens began laying was related to that in the next year. This also applied to their clutch size, weights of eggs and newly hatched chicks, and chick survival.
164 For example, Dunaeva & Kucheruk, 1941; Jenkins et al., 1963; Bergerud, 1970a. At Kolyma, a low percentage of young in late summer was attributed to 'unmated or non-breeding' birds (Andreev, 1988a). In Scotland, low percentages of young usually result from deaths of downy chicks. This is easily overlooked unless visits are made almost daily.
165 Watson & Moss, unpublished. One at Glen Esk in 1959, when many hens died, and one at Rickarton.
166 Jenkins et al., 1963; Campbell et al., 2002.
167 Bent, 1932.
168 Watson, 1977b.
169 Watson & Jenkins, 1964.
170 Semenov-Tyan-Shanskiy, 1960.
171 Dementiev & Gladkov, 1952.
172 Gordon, 1925.
173 Höglund, 1970; Watson, unpublished.
174 In red grouse (Jenkins et al., 1963; Watson & Moss, unpublished) and willow ptarmigan (Westerskov, 1956; Bergerud, 1970a), although the incubation period is 19 days on Timansk (Dementiev & Gladkov, 1952) and 18 days in Kazakhstan (Ulianin, 1939).

175 Semenov-Tyan-Shanskiy, 1960; Pulliainen, 1978; Erikstad & Spidsø, 1982; Lance, 1983.
176 Dementiev & Gladkov, 1952.
177 Jenkins et al., 1963, 1967; Watson & O'Hare, 1979a.
178 Myrberget, 1985; Munkebye et al., 2003.
179 Steen & Parker, 1981.
180 Moss & Watson, 1982.
181 Sandercock, 1993.
182 Mercer, 1968; Hannon et al., 1998.
183 The possibility that clutch size has increased with time cannot be ruled out, because data at Glen Esk were from 1957–61, at Kerloch from 1962–5, at Rickarton from the 1980s, and at Strathmore and Speyside from the 1990s.
184 Jenkins et al., 1963; Bergerud, 1970a; Erikstad et al., 1985; Myrberget, 1986a.
185 Myrberget, 1986b.
186 Voronin, 1991.
187 Moss et al., 1981.
188 Myrberget, 1987b.
189 Myrberget, 1986b.
190 Kirby & Smith, 2005.
191 Martin, 1984.
192 Parker, 1981a, 1984, 1985.
193 Martin & Hannon, 1987. In early autumn, young willow ptarmigan from renest broods were poorer at eating and at processing coarse winter food of twigs than earlier young (Stokkan & Steen, 1980).
194 Jenkins et al., 1963.
195 Jenkins et al. (1967) recorded a mean of 13 per cent of nests robbed (the range in different years was 6–30 per cent) for red grouse at Kerloch, and Myrberget (1988) recorded 28 per cent of nests robbed (a range of 9–86 per cent in different years) for willow ptarmigan at Tranøy. In British grouse, the proportion of eggs that hatch (excluding robbed and deserted nests) tends to be high, e.g. averaging 90 per cent or more in red grouse and Scottish ptarmigan. It can vary between years, e.g. at Glen Esk from 70 per cent in a poor year to 95 per cent in a good year when hens laid big clutches (Jenkins et al., 1963). None the

less, this was of little import for breeding success, compared with chick losses (Watson, 1971).
196 Brittas, 1988. He studied breeding indirectly by noting the percentage of young shot in autumn.
197 Watson & O'Hare, 1980. Glenamoy bogland held an average density per km² of five grouse in spring and about 100 blackface ewes. In terms of biomass per km², this comes to 3kg of grouse and 4,500kg of sheep, not including the lower density but far larger size of Aberdeen Angus cattle.
198 Phillips, 1994, 1999. A 350ha area at Priestlaw held low spring numbers in nine years, varying from nine pairs to 36 cocks and 39 hens, but they bred well (in different years, 4–10 young were reared per hen). Birds at Misty Law bred almost as well (3.6–9.6 young per hen) over 14 years, but in the five years before a full-time keeper was appointed they averaged only 0.7–2.1 young per hen. Raptors were protected at Misty Law throughout.
199 Jenkins et al., 1963; Marcström & Höglund, 1980; Steen et al., 1988b.
200 Parker, 1984.
201 Bevanger (1995) estimated that the 95,000km of high-voltage electricity wires in Norway kill 50,000 willow ptarmigan annually.
202 Hannon et al., 1998. On Bolshezemelskaya, unusually heavy losses of adults and especially first-year birds occurred in 1971–5, when lemmings were scarce and predators turned to willow ptarmigan (R. N. Voronin, 1976, *Ékologiya* 5, 95–8, cited by Cramp & Simmons, 1980).

## CHAPTER 4

1 Mitchell, 1906. The anonymous Scottish account was from 1721–44, probably the early 1720s.
2 Pennie, 1957; Watson, 1965b, c, 1972; Höhn, 1980; Steen, 1989; and photographs therein.
3 Cramp & Simmons, 1980.
4 Moss, 1974; Elison, 1980; Emison & White 1988.
5 Gordon, 1915.
6 MacDonald, 1970.
7 Moss, 1974.
8 Potapov, 1985, pers. comm. 2005. Russian birds are smallest in the subalpine belt of Tarbagatay, Altay, Sayan, Hahgay and Transbaikal.
9 Elison, 1980; Emison & White, 1988. Holder & Montgomerie (1993a) reported large birds in 'extreme northern and Aleutian' islands of North America. Both regions have windy winters.
10 Potapov, 1985. On Svalbard they winter several degrees of latitude north of the northernmost mainland wintering grounds on Taimyr at 75°N.
11 Semenov-Tyan-Shanskiy, 1960; Weeden, 1979; Pulliainen, 1980.
12 Salomonsen, 1939. Some hens in northeast Greenland have as much black on the head as cocks.
13 Gordon, 1951; Savile, 1951.
14 Steen & Unander, 1985.
15 Watson, 1987b.
16 Brockie, 1993.
17 Gordon, 1915.
18 Jacobsen et al., 1983.
19 MacDonald, 1970; Braun & Rogers, 1971.
20 Vaurie, 1985; Browning, 1979. On Svalbard, golden-brown summer feathers camouflage birds against the brownish background (Steen & Unander, 1985). This might be worth studying elsewhere.
21 See Brockie's (1993) painting of a Greenland cock, which in terms of colour is almost like a red grouse.
22 Holder et al., 1999.
23 Miltschew & Georgiewa, 1998.
24 Pfeffer, 1997.
25 Potapov et al., 2003; Potapov, 2004.
26 Salomonsen, 1950.
27 Pearson, 1907; Salomonsen, 1939; Potapov, 1985; Storch, 2000a.

28 Cramp & Simmons (1980) were too definite about the species. They were citing Williamson (1970), but his original detailed account makes it clear that it was not certain which species still occurred in the 1960s.
29 Watson, unpublished. High densities of sheep on the Faeroes have reduced the extent of Alpine heath plants such as blaeberry and heather, and their heavy grazing has lowered the height of the vegetation, thus removing physical cover.
30 MacPherson, 1893; Holloway, 1996.
31 Baxter & Rintoul, 1953.
32 Gordon, 1915.
33 Thom, 1986; Holloway, 1996. However, two were seen in the Southern Uplands in 1992 and one in 1994 (annual *Scottish Bird Report*).
34 Gordon (1944) reported an introduction there, but after a few years none was seen.
35 Witherby *et al.*, 1944.
36 Watson, 1965b.
37 Ibid.
38 Thom, 1986.
39 Annual *Scottish Bird Report*.
40 Watson, 1965b; Gibbons *et al.*, 1993; Kaye, 2007; and distribution maps therein.
41 Cook, 1992; Watson, unpublished.
42 Harvie-Brown & Buckley, 1895.
43 Buckland *et al.*, 1990.
44 Wynne-Edwards, 1954.
45 Cramp & Simmons, 1980.
46 Holder & Montgomerie, 1993a.
47 Storch, 2000a.
48 Ratcliffe, 1990; McGowan *et al.*, 2003.
49 Watson, 1965b. On 260km$^2$ of Alpine land.
50 Rae, 1994.
51 Braun & Rogers, 1971.
52 Watson, 1965a.
53 Ibid; Foggo, 1980; Rae, 1994.
54 McVean & Ratcliffe, 1962.
55 Study areas in order of decreasing latitude: Ny-Ålesund on Svalbard (Unander & Steen, 1985); Clavering Island in Greenland (Gelting, 1937); Lyngen and Lofoten in Norway (Watson, 1957a, unpublished); Baffin Island (Watson, 1957b, unpublished); north Iceland (Gardarsson & Bossert, 1997); Eagle Creek (800m) in Alaska (Weeden, 1965b, 1972); the five Scottish areas of Sgribhis Bheinn (180m, whose climate is 'very exposed with extremely mild winters' (Birse & Robertson, 1970)), Foinaven (370m), Applecross (550m), Cairngorms (610m) and Lochnagar (670m) (Watson, 1961, 1963a, 1965b); Amchitka in the Aleutian Islands (Jacobsen *et al.*, 1983); the Kurile Islands (100m; Potapov, 1985); Altay (1,300m) in China (Yue-Hua, 1995); Aletschgebiet (1,980m) in the Swiss Alps (Bossert, 1995); Lombardy (2,300m) in the Italian Alps (Scherini *et al.*, 2003); Haute-Savoie (1,800m) in the French Alps (Desmet, 1988a); the French west Pyrenees (2,260m; Boudarel, 1988); the Spanish east Pyrenees (1,900m; Novoa & Gonzales, 1988); and Honshu in Japan (Soichiro *et al.*, 1969).

These are lowest limits. The average is often higher, e.g. in Scotland, where it is 240m on Sgribhis Bheinn, 760m on the Cairngorms and 820m on Lochnagar (Watson, 1965b). Other data on altitudes are in Semenov-Tyan-Shanskiy (1960) and Potapov (1985).
56 Watson, 1963b.
57 Watson, 1965a, unpublished. In the warm summers of the Pyrenees and French Alps, birds favour cool aspects ranging from north by east to southeast (Boudarel, 1988; Desmet, 1988b).
58 Potapov & Flint, 1987.
59 Soper, 1928; Holder & Montgomerie, 1993a.
60 Soper, 1940; Olpinski, 1986.
61 Gardarsson & Bossert, 1997.
62 Gardarsson, 1988.
63 Bent, 1932; Soichiro *et al.*, 1969; Williamson & Emison, 1969; Bossert *et al.*, 1983; Jacobsen *et al.*, 1983; Marti & Bossert, 1985; Boudarel, 1988; Desmet, 1988b; Novoa & Gonzales, 1988; Scherini *et al.*, 2003; Favaron *et al.*, 2006. Photographs in the Aleutians show nests hidden in tall vegetation, and others were 'well hidden in the long grass'. Photographs of Amchitka show the main vegetation as crowberry-lichen heath, like a moor. Nearly

all nests on the Japanese area were at the border of pine scrub, one at the edge of juniper scrub, and one underneath alder branches. In the Swiss Alps, photographs in summer show a hen resting under a scrubby tree, and a hen on a nest partly concealed under woody branches, with surrounding dense plants above her. Wintering birds in the Pyrenees use rhododendron shrub-land. Hens and chicks in the French Alps favour vegetation taller than 20cm, with scrubby coniferous trees and bushes of rhododendron and juniper, and most Lombardy hens have nests that are completely concealed under rhododendron and juniper. Pennie (1957) noted that since the rock ptarmigan is the only gallinaceous bird in Iceland and south Greenland, it is found in summer in situations 'which would appear more appropriate for a Willow Grouse'. Icelandic nests in thick cover 'are not uncommon' and the bird 'occupies the niche filled in Britain by the Red Grouse'.

64 Moss, 1974.
65 Watson, 1965a.
66 Gelting, 1937; Salomonsen, 1939; Cramp & Simmons, 1980; Bernard-Laurent, 1987; Andreev, 1975.
67 Moss, 1968.
68 Watson, 1964.
69 Gelting, 1937; Gardarsson & Moss, 1970.
70 Elison, 1980; Emison & White, 1988.
71 Gelting, 1937.
72 Moss & Watson, 1984.
73 Gelting, 1937; Gardarsson & Moss, 1970.
74 Watson, unpublished.
75 Veghte & Herreid, 1965; Johnson, 1968; Braun *et al.*, 1993; Martin *et al.*, 1993.
76 Moss, unpublished.
77 Chapman, 1924; Mortensen *et al.*, 1983, 1985; Stokkan & Blix, 1986; Stokkan *et al.*, 1986. Chapman reported very fat birds in autumn, weighing 1kg each. Recent studies show that they feed continually in the dark winter months, so the weight of crop contents varies little. Captive birds that are fed pellets ad lib undergo the same seasonal changes in weight, fat deposition and depletion, and sometimes fast for several days even when food is available. In contrast, Norwegian rock ptarmigan have negligible body fat and are not adapted to withstand prolonged starvation.
78 Stokkan, 1992.
79 Gabrielsen & Unander, 1987. *See also* Chapter 3. The temperature of the eggs is a fairly steady 32°C before the incubating hen's feeding trip, drops 5–6° during the trip, but rises rapidly to 32°C after she returns. It takes 30–60 minutes before her heart rate and breathing rate fall to resting levels. Her rates rise each time she turns her eggs, when the eggs' cool sides touch her incubation patch.

Huber-Eicher (1995) studied Swiss nests at 2,000m. When hens returned after feeding, the eggs' temperature had very seldom fallen below 25°C and never below 22°C. Eggs can tolerate low ambient temperatures. Although low egg temperatures may not harm embryos, they lengthen the incubation period. Hens were off their nests a total of 40–90 minutes per day.
80 Anvik, 1969; Theberge & West, 1973; Pedersen & Steen, 1979.
81 Marti & Bossert, 1985.
82 Gardarsson, 1988.
83 Watson & Rae, 1993.
84 For example, Salomonsen, 1950. Birds are not in northeast Greenland during the three darkest months (Manniche, 1910). Hundreds have been seen crossing Hudson Strait between Baffin Island and Labrador, and often 'alight on ships and are easily caught' (Bent, 1932).
85 Soper, 1928.
86 Freuchen & Salomonsen, 1960. 'Multitudes of Ptarmigan then are crowded in winter quarters in the southernmost parts of the Arctic. In March the main migration toward the breeding places in the north takes place. The first flocks consist almost entirely of males; later in March new flocks leave the

wintering area, and these include many females. The percentage of females in the migrating flocks gradually increases, until in April they predominate. Sometimes in early March, when the landscape everywhere still has a winter-like aspect, the first flocks of Ptarmigan arrive; they may include hundreds if not thousands of birds. During the following days the number increases until they appear everywhere in vast numbers. Preferably, they settle in areas that the wind has swept clear of snow. Tens of thousands are shot or snared by the Eskimos in these March days, though in normal years when the Ptarmigan usually is scarce and local in the north, they are not particularly interested in catching this minor game. The Ptarmigan during such invasions are extremely fearless and even settle among the houses. They usually appear to be very thin and emaciated. Apart from the myriads killed by the inhabitants, a large number perish during migration or after arrival at the place of destination, and as a rule the density of birds on the breeding places after such mass movements is not essentially larger than in normal years. In April the migration appears to end, although it may sometimes continue into May. These Ptarmigan migrations, which are known in Baffin Island, Labrador, Greenland, Siberia and other areas, take place with tolerable regularity every tenth year. Particularly large numbers were encountered in 1889–1890, 1928–1930 and 1949–1950. Between these peak years there are periods in which Ptarmigan are very rare. Such a year was 1954 in Greenland, when you could walk for days without catching a glimpse of any Ptarmigan or find any sign of them. The difference between the situation in such years and that in peak years when Ptarmigan crowd everywhere is striking.'

87 Hantzsch, 1929.
88 Watson, 1957b.
89 Storch, 2000a.
90 Salomonsen, 1950.
91 Gudmundsson, 1972; Gardarsson & Bossert, 1997.
92 Preble, 1908; Bent, 1932.
93 Hannon et al., 1998.
94 Gudmundsson, 1960; Weeden, 1964.
95 Cotter et al., 1992; Cotter, 1999.
96 Bossert, 1980.
97 Unander & Steen, 1985; Olpinski, 1986; Holder & Montgomerie, 1993b.
98 Gudmundsson, 1960; Gardarsson & Bossert, 1997.
99 Gelting, 1937. 'In the old Eskimo settlements one is almost always certain to meet ptarmigan mothers with their broods. ... On July 4 the first female ptarmigan appeared with her young. Subsequently, several broods arrived, and until August 3 they were observed every day.'
100 Polunin, 1948. At Canadian Inuit settlements in the 1930s, Nicholas Polunin found bright green vegetation, including plant species that favour ground enriched by excrement.
101 Gardarsson & Bossert, 1997.
102 Gardarsson, 1988. They were found up to 900m near Akureyri in July 1949 (Watson, unpublished).
103 Gordon, 1915.
104 Watson, 1963b.
105 Millais, 1909. In September 1907, 'Two days of ordinary snow made no impression on these hardy birds, but a blizzard from the north on the third day made all the Ptarmigan, to the number of, I should say, 800 to 1000, leave the tops and north faces and come flying in coveys to a sheltered corner. They kept arriving for about two hours in a continuous stream. Next morning I passed through this sheltered hollow, and moved thousands of Ptarmigan, which only flew for a short distance.'
106 Boudarel, 1988. They winter at 1,980–2,260m, and summer at 2,260–2,540m.
107 Watson, unpublished.
108 Gardarsson, 1988.
109 Watson, 1965a, b, unpublished. He suggested that much Arctic heath may be a poor source of food. Chemical analyses show

that one of the main species, Arctic heather (*Cassiope tetragona*), is low in nutritional quality (Gelting, 1937).
110 Watson et al., 1998.
111 Cycles are interesting because they are evidence of unstable, as opposed to the more usual stable, population dynamics.
112 Nielsen & Pétursson, 1995; Zbinden & Salvioni, 1997; Cattadori & Hudson, 1999, 2000; Cattadori et al., 2000.
113 Weeden, 1965a, b; Weeden & Theberge, 1972; Cotter, 1991.
114 Watson et al., 1998.
115 Moss & Watson, 2001.
116 Watson, 1965a; Unander & Steen, 1985.
117 See Chapter 3. It is assumed that once an adult settles in summer, it will not be outside that area next summer. This is problematic where breeding ranges vary with snow-lie, as in Alaska. Even in the Cairngorms, some basins have no birds in snowy summers (Watson, 1965a).
118 Most studies are done in a short season during the summer, so 'summer' is short and winter comprises most of the year. Hence a 10 per cent summer loss (3–4 per cent per month), and a 40 per cent winter loss (about 5 per cent per month) differ little when expressed per month.
119 Weeden, 1965a; Watson et al., 1998. 'Summer' in the study at Eagle Creek ran from late May to early August, and on the Scottish areas from late April to early August.
120 Cotter et al., 1992.
121 Gardarsson, 1988.
122 Nielsen, 2003. Also, 27 per cent of radio-tagged cock ptarmigan were lost in May–June, all to gyrfalcons, but none in July–August.
123 Much of this difference would be down to the fact that 'winter' comprises most of the year in these studies, as explained in note 116.
124 Olpinski, 1986; Holder & Montgomerie, 1993a.
125 Parmelee & MacDonald, 1960; MacDonald, 1970; Holder & Montgomerie, 1993a, b. Three hens nested in a cock's territory on Bathurst Island, but he had been injected with testosterone.
126 Watson, 1965a; Watson et al., 1998. At Cairnwell and Meall Odhar this went the other way, with more cocks per hen during years of population increase. Unmated cocks there survived on very small territories in marginal habitat during years of high numbers towards and at the peak.
127 Watson, 1965a.
128 Weeden, 1963, 1965a; Soichiro et al., 1969; Unander & Steen, 1985; Desmet, 1988a; Cotter et al. 1992; Cotter, 1999; Scherini et al., 2003. Bossert (1995) recorded on average 1.4 territorial cocks per hen during years of population increase, and 2.9 during declines.
129 Gardarsson, 1988.
130 Olpinski, 1986.
131 Brodsky & Montgomerie, 1987; Holder & Montgomerie, 1993a. They did not state the numbers of unmated cocks.
132 Gardarsson, 1988.
133 Cotter et al., 1992.
134 Also, Gardarsson (1988) stated that Hrisey's predator situation was atypical because the island lacked Arctic foxes, which killed many ptarmigan on the mainland and 'may prey selectively on incubating and brooding hens'. The proportion of cocks among shot adults was 47 per cent on the mainland, but on Hrisey it was significantly lower at 41 per cent. The poorer survival of summering cocks was 'accounted for solely by the somewhat unusual predator situation on Hrisey'.
135 For example, Holder & Montgomerie, 1993b.
136 Emison & White, 1988.
137 Elison, 1980.
138 Watson & Parr, 1973; Watson et al., 1998.
139 Marti & Bossert, 1985.
140 Steen & Unander, 1985; Rae, 1994.
141 Watson, 1963b. Gordon (1932) also found a Scottish nest in tall heather.
142 Watson, unpublished.
143 Watson (1972) gave 1.5 per day, but this was a printer's error for 1.5 days per egg, as implied in later sentences.

144 Steen & Unander, 1985; Rae, 1994.
145 Watson, 1965a; Watson et al., 1998.
146 Watson, 1965a; Steen & Unander, 1985; Watson et al., 1998.
147 Watson, unpublished.
148 Moss & Watson, 1984.
149 Gardarsson & Moss, 1970; Watson, 1972, p. 20; Gardarsson, 1988.
150 Steen & Unander, 1985; Rae, 1994.
151 Bailey, 1993.
152 Marquiss et al., 1989.
153 Watson, 1965a; Gardarsson, 1988; Cotter et al., 1992; Holder & Montgomerie, 1993a; Watson et al., 1998.
154 Watson, 1996a; Watson & Moss, 2004.
155 Watson & Shaw, 1991.

## CHAPTER 5

1 For fuller details of the bird and its behaviour, see Cramp & Simmons (1980) and Lindström et al. (1998).
2 As in both sexes of all four species.
3 The verb 'lek' has also come to mean the display itself, and the place where the display is done (i.e. the display ground or arena).
4 Hovi et al., 1995.
5 Kokko et al., 1999.
6 Rintamäki et al., 1995.
7 Höglund et al., 1995.
8 Rintamäki et al., 1995.
9 Hovi et al., 1994; Alatolo et al., 1992.
10 Hovi et al., 1996.
11 Höglund et al., 1999.
12 Regnaut, 2004; Regnaut et al., 2006.
13 Höglund et al., 2002.
14 Alatolo et al., 1996. This applies to any one morning at a lek. Unless the hen re-lays, it probably also applies to each spring as a whole, but this is difficult to establish unequivocally.
15 Rintamäki et al., 1998.
16 Bowker & Bowker, 2003.
17 Zeitler, 2000.

18 We use *Lyrurus* in Chapter 1, where it is useful for distinguishing between the *Lyrurus* and *Tetrao* lineages.
19 In: Kirkman & Hutchinson, 1924.
20 Storch, 2000a.
21 Hancock et al., 1999. Of the displaying cocks, about 5,000 were in Scotland, 1,700 in northern England and 150 in Wales.
22 www.rspb.org.uk/scotland/action/blackgrouse.asp (as at 3 September 2006).
23 Tucker & Heath, 1994.
24 Whether the killing of predators (foxes and crows may legally be killed) is necessary to the long-term success of such management is a contentious issue.
25 *Rhododendron ferrugineum*.
26 Klaus, 1991. Increased temperatures, increased levels of carbon dioxide and input of atmospheric nitrogen seem also to have contributed to faster tree growth and more closed canopies. Furthermore, nitrogen pollution itself enriches soils and encourages grassy vegetation at the expense of dwarf shrubs.
27 Starling-Westerberg, 2001; Baines et al., 1996.
28 Lindley & Mellenchip (2005) provide some useful guidance from their experience in Wales.
29 www.gct.org.uk/blackgrouse/decline.html (as at 23 December 2003).
30 Thom, 1986. Baines et al. (2000) illustrated a typical sequence of events with counts from four Sitka spruce or lodgepole pine plantations in Perthshire. Counts were done with pointer dogs in August, one, four, six, eight, ten, 12 and 14 years after planting. Here, the density of greyhens in late summer increased from an average of about three per km$^2$ at one year after planting to some ten at four years after planting. It then fell back rapidly to six per km$^2$ at six years after planting and further declined to about one per km$^2$ by 12 years after planting. Cock densities followed a similar course but peaked at only four per km$^2$.

It is not clear how much of this increase was due to immigrants attracted from surrounding moorland or to young birds reared within plantations. Breeding success in the four plantations remained at about two chicks per hen throughout, and so breeding success did not decrease as hen densities declined with canopy closure.

It was also not clear whether breeding success in plantations differed from that on unplanted moorland, because there were no comparable counts from before planting or from surrounding moorland. The decline in density was apparently due to a decline in the area of open ground with dwarf shrubs, not to waning breeding success. The authors illustrated the likely role of open ground by contrasting two plantations. In one with less than 10 per cent open space, hen densities peaked at about four hens per km$^2$ some six years after planting, whereas in a plantation with more than 30 per cent open space they peaked at about 11 hens per km$^2$ at 13 years after planting and were still at four hens per km$^2$ 16 years after planting.

31 Pearce-Higgins et al., 2007.

32 Scarifying allows trees to root more deeply while leaving ground vegetation largely undisturbed. It also drains the ground more freely, especially on soils with iron pans, which are broken by the tine.

33 Geoff Shaw, pers. comm. 2004.

34 Grass is 'grazed', while woody plants such as heather are 'browsed'. This difference becomes clumsy when animals eat both grassy and woody vegetation, and so we often use 'grazing' to mean 'grazing or browsing'.

35 Baines, 1996.

36 Calladine et al., 2002.

37 The 128km$^2$ reserve includes about 20km$^2$ of semi-natural Scots pinewood and about 13km$^2$ of trees of planted origin, plus moorland and Arctic-Alpine ground up to the summit of Cairn Gorm.

38 Not all the open ground was suitable for woodland grouse, but the deer that were counted on open ground were likely to use the woodland and so affect the habitat of woodland grouse.

39 There was some canopy closure and loss of dwarf shrubs in planted parts of the pinewood, especially in the north, but this does not affect the argument.

40 This was practical conservation management and not a scientific experiment. Consequently it was not replicated and there were no comparable data from reference sites where sheep or deer were not reduced. Fences were removed in the early 1990s, and crows and foxes were killed in some years (1992–6 and 2001 onwards) but not in others, as part of a trial in predator management. These issues complicate the interpretation, but for present purposes we can regard capercaillie numbers as a control for factors such as predator abundance and deaths from flying into fences, which are likely to have affected the two woodland grouse species in similar ways.

41 Capercaillie lek counts (not shown) followed much the same course as numbers of capercaillie seen during deer counts, i.e. there was no boom and bust.

For analyses of population dynamics, counts of blackcocks at leks are a more useful measure of population trends than numbers seen during deer counts. This is because lek counts are of known precision, as they are based on two counts in the same season, and here we use the average count. Also, blackcocks at all leks in the reserve were counted, and so the number reflects the total breeding population of cocks in the reserve. Furthermore, blackcocks are more likely to be locally recruited than greyhens (see below), and hence any associations between local conditions and numbers are easier to interpret.

42 This ratio includes hens with no chicks.

43 Data from RSPB staff, and from Anneke Stolte, who collated them.

44 The 45 quadrats were laid out on a grid

covering the pinewood, with measurements in 1989, 1992, 1997 and 2003.
45 Some figures express densities or breeding success in natural logarithms, because this shows trends more clearly. Below is a chart for converting this logarithmic measure of breeding success to the number of chicks per hen:

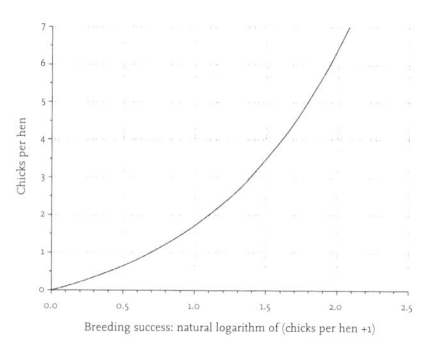

[Chart: x-axis "Breeding success: natural logarithm of (chicks per hen +1)" from 0.0 to 2.5; y-axis "Chicks per hen" from 0 to 7]

46 Population change was $\log_e N_t - \log_e N_{t-1}$ where $N_t$ was the number of displaying cocks in year $t$, breeding success was $\log_e$(chicks per hen in year $t$–1, plus one). Vegetation growth rate was as in Table 15, except that in 1992 it was estimated as $(1.81 + 3.13)/2 = 2.47$ and in 1997 as $(3.13 + 1.26)/2 = 2.20$. Simple correlations: between population change and breeding success $r = 0.66$, $P = 0.19$; between population change and vegetation growth rate $r = 0.86$, $P = 0.0003$. Partial correlations: $r = 0.40$, $P = 0.23$ and $r = 0.78$, $P = 0.004$, respectively.
47 Juvenile heather shoots (no flowers) contain more protein and phosphorus, and are more digestible, than mature (flowering) shoots. The greater nutritive value of juvenile heather shoots is thought to contribute to the well-documented increases in the density of red grouse that follow muirburn.
48 Cramp & Simmons, 1980.
49 In the north Pennines, Warren & Baines (2002) found that natal dispersal by eight radio-tagged first-year hens ranged from 5km to 19km, with an average of 9km. In the French Alps, Caizergues & Ellison (2002) radio-tagged 39 young black grouse. Most (81 per cent) young greyhens left the 836ha study area to nest 5–29km from their site of capture.
50 Autocorrelations are correlations between numbers in year $t$ and numbers in year $t-n$, where $n$ is the lag, here 1–6 years. A significant positive value (one above the 95% confidence limit) means that high (low) numbers in year $t$ went along with high (low) numbers in year $t-n$. The sudden decline in size of the Buccleuch autocorrelation coefficient at six years suggests a six-year 'moving average' process.
51 www.gct.org.uk/research/blackgrouse/index.html (as at 22 December 2003).
52 Baines, 1991.
53 Hughes et al., 1998.
54 Moss, unpublished data.
55 In 1985–93 the mean number of chicks per hen at Glen Tanar was 1.3 (standard error 0.3).
56 A comparison of annual variations in breeding success with weather records from Glen Tanar in 1975–2003, as done for capercaillie (Moss et al., 2001), revealed no obvious relationship.
57 The legend in question is 'The Brave Little Tailor', a fairy tale collected by the brothers Grimm.
58 Baines et al., 1996.
59 Picozzi et al., 1999.
60 In 1982–9, for example, the number of chicks reared per hen in the old pinewood of Glen Tanar was 1.8 (standard error 0.4) and on moorland edge at Birse some 6km away it was 1.1 (standard error 0.2), not significantly different (Moss & N. Picozzi, unpublished data).
61 Willebrand, 1992; Caizergues & Ellison, 1998a.
62 Caizergues & Ellison, 1998b.
63 A 'closed' population is one with no movement in or out.
64 Picozzi, 1986.
65 Warren & Baines, 2002.

66 Calladine et al., 2000.

## CHAPTER 6

1 Suter et al., 2002; Pakkala et al., 2003. This should not be taken to mean that capercaillie maintained by artificial means, such as killing predators, indicate a healthy forest.
2 Capercaillie were blamed, amongst other things, for biting off the leading shoots of growing Sitka spruce and leaving them lying on the ground – but these shoots are so tender that strong winds often blow them off. Bannerman (1963) has a good account of the havoc caused by capercaillie in nurseries and newly planted areas.
3 Others were slower to change. As late as 1979, in the agreement setting up Glen Tanar National Nature Reserve, the Nature Conservancy Council (a forerunner of Scottish Natural Heritage) classed capercaillie and black grouse as pests.
4 At closer range, both sexes reveal complex patterns. The cock is mainly dark grey with paler grey vermiculations, giving a slate-grey appearance. His lower head, chest, flanks, belly and tail are almost black, the chest with an iridescent green sheen, and the upper mantle and wing-coverts a warm dark brown. The dark plumage has white or pale grey markings on belly, flanks and tail. A white shoulder spot stands out when he displays, its message mysterious. White streaks and spots on the main tail-feathers make tail patterns as individual as fingerprints. Some authors claim that individual patterns recur moult after moult, although others dispute this.

Hens are rufous-brown on the back, paler below, with much individual variation. The brown back is densely barred with buff or blackish. The broader barring on the underparts includes buff, blackish and varying amounts of white. Barring is usually absent across the orange-buff breast, making the distinctive patch. The tail is barred rufous and dark brown, varying from mostly rufous to mostly brown.

Höglund (1956) distinguished newly hatched males and females by bill colour, but this has not been demonstrated in Scotland.
5 Desmond Dugan, pers. comm. 2003.
6 At small leks, mature cocks seem to occupy territories. In the 'piece of pie' model, each established cock has a spring territory that is shaped like a wedge of pie, the thin end containing his stance. In continuous habitat, leks are typically some 2–2.5km apart, the pie about 2km across.

There are many variations on the 'piece of pie', in accord with local topography, habitat distribution and disturbance. At several Scottish leks, cocks display among trees along each side of a track, so the lek takes a linear form. Larger leks can have more than one centre of activity and may cover up to 1km$^2$.

Studies of radio-tagged birds in Fennoscandia, central Europe and northern Russia (Storch, 2001) confirm that adult cocks have spring home ranges centred on the lek. In Fennoscandia, home ranges were more or less exclusive, whereas in central Europe and Russia they overlapped but cocks avoided each other. Overlapping was greater on bigger leks. Spring spacing behaviour does not seem to limit the number of cocks at a lek (Wegge et al., 2003). In short, it seems that cocks avoid each other around the lek, but do not have territories with defended boundaries, and so at high densities their ranges overlap.
7 The average number of cocks at seven leks in the Ilexa basin in 1981–6 and in 1988 was 24, with a range of 10–70 (Borchtchevski, 1993). In the Pinega nature reserve in 1986–2003, the average number of cocks at 5–13 leks varied from 3 to 12 (A. V. Sivkov, pers. comm. 2004).
8 The area of ground in which an animal lives.
9 Jones, 1982a.
10 James Oswald & Anneke Stolte, pers. comm. 2004.

11 Leks are often in the same place decade after decade, although some shift. Near Banchory in Deeside, an isolated lek of about four cocks moved a full kilometre between the late 1980s and the early 2000s, although individual cocks were occasionally heard singing at the old site up to spring 2004. Observations in Glen Tanar showed how this might happen. Over several years, a lek with about ten cocks and a single centre of activity developed a separate centre about 300m away, presumably comprising younger cocks. For a few years, both centres coexisted while the number of cocks declined at the original centre and increased at the new one. Cocks commuted between the two. Eventually, the original site became disused and the new site held all the activity.

12 Although Moss & Lockie (1979) reported that capercaillie song contained infrasound (noise below the threshold of human hearing), Lieser *et al.* (2005) were unable to detect this. Over the years, RM had three conversations with the late Ingemar Hjorth about infrasound in capercaillie song. In the first two, IH said that he could not find any infrasound. In the third, he said that he had been able to record it, but only at very close quarters, so this may be part of the answer. Moss & Lockie (1979) recorded only at close range (10cm), so contrary to their original suggestions, the sound may be audible only at close range. After the original paper was published, RM, like many other people, actually heard the upper reaches of the sound that we called infrasound. In the third phase of their song, cocks make a low grumbling noise at the lower reaches of human hearing, audible when the bird is very close to a hide. In captivity, we used to have a tenor cock that was particularly audible in this phase. Ivor Lockie also made some accelerometer measurements, which confirmed that this cock was vibrating at low frequency while producing these notes. An observer could put his hand on the bird's back while it was singing and feel the vibrations. In short, cocks certainly produce low-frequency sound that is not usually recorded in descriptions of the birds' song. It may not carry very far, hence its main function may be to impress other birds close by rather than attracting them from afar.

13 One cock attacked a golden eagle that had just killed the rival with which he was fighting; it killed him too. *See* www1.nrk.no/nett-tv/klipp/116233 (as at 18 November 2007).

14 On one occasion, a hen with chicks behaved like a great skua. Flushed by trained dogs during brood counts, she circled round and flew at head height directly towards RM, grunting threats as she approached. Just in front of her target, she jinked upwards, missing his head by a foot or two. She then repeated this unusual distraction display from the opposite direction.

15 Special Protection Areas are sites of international importance, designated according to EU directives.

16 In a constant, closed (i.e. no movement in or out) population with 30 per cent annual mortality of adult cocks, young cocks will comprise at least 30 per cent of the population, and sub-adults (cocks in their second year) at least 0.3 × 0.7 = 21 per cent of the population. For example, 45 cocks were counted at 22 known leks in the Vosges mountains in 1998–9 (Poirot & Preiss, 2002). These included adults and sub-adults, but not young cocks. The count was then increased by 20, based on the observation that one-third of cocks that attend leks were typically undetected by standard counts. Another 25 cocks lived solitarily away from any lek. In this case, lek counts accounted for half the adult and sub-adult cocks.

17 This will vary according to local conditions. *See,* for example, 'Snares' on p.170.

18 In other words, to assume that recorded counts had the same distribution as the counts that would have been noted had

similar ones been made at every lek in Scotland. In fact, most big leks were probably found, but more small ones might have been missed. If so, calculated proportions will be conservative, slightly underestimating true proportions.
19 Potapov & Flint, 1987.
20 Duriez et al., 2007.
21 Ibid.
22 Storch, 2000a.
23 Excluding open bog and water bodies. Vladimir Borchtchevski & Per Wegge (pers. comms 2004).
24 Storch, 2001.
25 Before agriculture, it is likely that they also used lowland forest bogs with sparse tree cover, and other natural forest opened up by events such as fire and wind-throw.
26 Pennie, 1950, 1951.
27 Anon., 1840; Pennie, 1950, 1951; Lever, 1977; Gilbert B. Stevenson, pers. comm. 2005. Thirteen Swedish cocks and 15 hens arrived at Taymouth Castle on the estate of the Marquis of Breadalbane in 1837 and a further 16 hens in 1838. Another five hens came from Atholl estate, survivors of a failed attempt to breed birds (of unknown provenance) in captivity (Stevenson). At Taymouth, 'A part of the birds [six cocks and four hens] were turned out in the autumn of 1837, and part were kept in a house. In the year 1838, a brace only was reared by the keeper, but two fine broods were seen in the woods… In the spring of 1839, instead of attempting to rear any capercaillies… [Lord Breadalbane's head keeper] placed the eggs laid by the birds in confinement in the nests of grey hens, who hatched them, and brought them up in a wild state.' In 1839 the head keeper estimated that 49 young were hatched by greyhens, and 60–70 poults reared by greyhens and capercaillie combined. In 1862 there were said to be 1,000–2,000 birds on this estate alone.

The Swedish birds were procured from local people by the Welsh-born naturalist Llewellyn Lloyd, then resident near Venusberg, on behalf of his cousin the great brewer Thomas Fowell Buxton (subsequently knighted), who had proposed the project to the Marquis of Breadalbane while shooting on his estate at Taymouth. Fowell Buxton continued to import birds in subsequent years, and to sell them in unknown numbers (but exceeding 30 because, in a letter to Lord Breadalbane dated 19 November 1842, he offered to sell 'some 14 or 15 brace of which I have still undisposed of') to unknown estates (Stevenson). Hence, the number of birds imported was well in excess of the approximately 50 brought to Taymouth in 1837–8.
28 Baines et al., 1991. So few were shot after the mid-1980s that bags became unreliable indicators of numbers.
29 Bigger bags, of up to 150 birds in a day, have been reported but are said to be erroneous (Gladstone, 1930, cited by Pennie, 1950, as Gladstone, 1922, but not in his reference list).
30 Based on data from Braemar village.
31 Based on constant repetition of an informed guess by an unknown source.
32 The 1992–4 estimate of 2,200 had 95 per cent confidence limits of 2,500–3,200 (Catt et al., 1998), the limits for the 1998–9 estimate of 1,100 were 500–2,000 (Wilkinson et al., 2002), and for the 2003–4 estimate of 2,000 they were 1,300–2,800 (unpublished result of Royal Society for the Protection of Birds survey, K. Kortland, pers. comm. 2004). Other evidence suggests that the real 2003–4 figure was closer to the lower confidence limit of 1,300 than to the central estimate of 2,000. We have rounded numbers to the nearest 100.
33 Birds from Finland were introduced to Dawyck near Peebles in 1930 (Pennie, 1950).
34 Climax forest is the last stage in an undisturbed forest's succession.
35 Canopy cover 50–60 per cent (Moss & Picozzi, 1994).
36 Kirikov, 1947, 1970.
37 In the managed forest of Varaldskogen in southeast Norway, cocks and hens avoided

forest with overstorey tree densities of less than 500 stems per ha, and cocks, though not hens, avoided densities of over 1,000 stems per ha (Gjerde, 1991a). But in Abernethy pinewood (Summers *et al.*, 2004), the cocks were found in trees with an average density of 195 per ha (interquartile range 130–350) and hens in trees with an average density of 350 (interquartile range 200–565). Abernethy trees had much broader canopies than Varaldskogen ones. Stem density alone is an ambiguous measure of habitat quality, but while canopy cover is more important it is less often measured.

38 Gjerde & Wegge, 1989.

39 These generalisations about habitat structure for broods in Scotland are based mostly on unpublished observations made during counts with dogs by RM.

40 But not so steep as to hinder birds walking back uphill after disturbance.

41 Baines *et al.*, 1994.

42 Although this seems obvious, there has been little formal study of the optimum structure of ground vegetation for capercaillie broods.

43 Bevanger (1995) estimated annual losses from flying into wires to be about 20,000 capercaillie in Norway alone, equivalent to some 90 per cent of the annual hunting harvest.

44 Moss *et al.*, 2000b.

45 Baines & Andrew (2003) found that marking fences reduced capercaillie strikes by roughly a half.

46 Seven leks occurred in 116km$^2$ in the Ilexa River basin, Russia (Borchtchevski, 1993), and 36 leks in 515km$^2$ in the Pinega nature reserve, Archangel Region, Russia (A. V. Sivkov, pers. comm. 2004).

47 Six leks occurred in 42km$^2$ (Per Wegge, pers. comm. 2004).

48 Moss *et al.* (2006) gave a median natal dispersal distance of 11km for 13 hens. Adding unpublished data for another two hens increases this to 12km.

49 Lodgepole pine proved a financial and silvicultural disaster, largely because British foresters did not recognise crucial differences between various strains of *Pinus contorta*, and planted vast areas of trees that fell over and grew twisted, unmarketable trunks. It is now being replaced by other species, although it still has a role as a nurse crop for Sitka spruce planted on heather moorland, where lodgepole pine is supposed to suppress heather and so prevent heather check in Sitka spruce. The FC, having subsidised the planting of this tree for decades, in the 1990s began to provide grants for removing it at the taxpayer's expense.

A fast-growing species, Sitka spruce can be established on ground where browsing of seedlings by deer or rabbits prevents other species from growing. It supplies much raw material for pulp, chipboard and paper, but its timber is of poor quality and is now undercut in price by better wood from the Baltic and other eastern European states.

50 The FC is beginning to recognise that its very future is threatened by the financial losses made by its own plantations and by private, grant-aided ones. It is therefore starting to mention forests as ecosystems, not as mere timber plantations, and aims to provide a range of benefits in return for public investment. In many places, this welcome change seems more rhetorical than practical, and old practices continue largely unchanged. In other places, conservation benefits are beginning to emerge. These include nature conservation, notably in the Highland Conservancy and parts of the Grampian Conservancy where Scots pine is still grown. (A conservancy is an administrative region headed by a conservator.) The FC has begun to manage some of its own woods with capercaillie in mind, and capercaillie management is now a recognised component of some grant schemes.

51 Picozzi *et al.*, 1996.

52 A counterargument is that wide spacing produces knotty timber of low value.
53 Moss et al., 2001.
54 For example, in Speyside on 15–16 January 1976, of nine crops from shot birds (seven cocks, two hens), six contained nothing but pine, but three cocks had heather (4, 10 and 30 per cent by volume), blaeberry shoots (1, 0 and 10 per cent, respectively) and bearberry leaves (0, 5 and 0 per cent). In general, cocks are seen on the ground in winter more often than hens.
55 In the Bavarian Alps, the birds seem to prefer silver fir to Norway spruce, and in Lapland they prefer juniper to spruce. Capercaillie in the west Carpathians, however, confound this generalisation by making Norway spruce their main winter food (Saniga, 1998), even though fir and beech are available.

The capercaillie that winter in deciduous forests at the southern extremity of the Ural ridge (Kirikov, 1970) must survive without conifers. Similarly, there are no indigenous conifers in the Cantabrian mountains of Spain, where the birds' winter diet comprises leaves of holly or beech buds, and herbs (Storch, 2001).
56 Moss & Picozzi, 1994; Picozzi et al., 1996.
57 In Scots pinewood, capercaillie seem to prefer feeding in particular trees, which are often said to be diseased, damaged or on unsuitable soils. Needles from such trees contain more protein and less of the resins that serve as plant defences (Spidsø & Korsmo, 1994). In Norway, feeding trees were removed experimentally and birds then spent more time in other parts of the forest (Gjerde, 1991b).

In Scottish plantations, droppings often lie thickly under the heavier branches of trees by rides or at compartment edges, presumably because birds prefer thicker branches for roosting or feeding.
58 Borchtchevski & Gubar, 2003.
59 Vladimir Borchtchevski, pers. comm. 2004.

60 Summers et al., 2004; Watson & Nethersole-Thompson, 2006.
61 Picozzi et al., 1999.
62 Summers et al., 2004.
63 Storch, 2001.
64 Picozzi et al., 1996.
65 Moss, unpublished observations.
66 Imprinted captive chicks allowed to forage under natural conditions, however, took few caterpillars, choosing instead spiders, springtails, grasshoppers, beetles and especially ants (Spidsø & Stuen, 1988). Perhaps the eye of a well-fed and naive captive is attracted more to rapidly moving prey than to sluggish and cryptic caterpillars. In Scotland, chicks took many caterpillars when these were available in early June, but turned more to other invertebrates (ants, beetles, spiders, harvestmen and flies) when caterpillars pupated and became scarce in late June (Picozzi et al., 1999). In the central European literature, anthills are often assumed to be an important part of brood habitat. This might be because chicks use ants, or because anthills tend to occur in the same places as blaeberry, or because ants favour sunny, open sites that chicks also prefer for drying out after rain and for dust-bathing.

In the Pyrenees, capercaillie broods are often in herb-rich, grassy subalpine meadows with no blaeberry (Ménoni, 1990), where their invertebrate prey comprises largely grasshoppers (Emmanuel Ménoni, pers. comm. 2004). In Scotland, one brood spent much time in an open ride in a plantation, where the bulk of the chicks' invertebrate food comprised click beetles and heather beetles (Picozzi et al., 1999). Their plant food, conventionally enough, was mostly heather and blaeberry. In a different plantation, another brood spent their first three weeks, to our astonishment, under closed-canopy Sitka spruce. In these dark conditions, there appeared to be hardly any growing vegetation to support the chicks or the invertebrates that they required. Tender new spruce shoots, however, lay in profusion on the ground, after unusually strong winds had broken them from the canopy. Subsequent analysis of the chicks' droppings showed that they had been eating spruce needles, supplemented by weevils that often live in leaf litter.

The success of these novel Scottish diets remains an open question. The hen of the brood that ate click and heather beetles was killed by a predator when her still dependent chicks were 19 days old. The other hen successfully nurtured her chicks under closed-canopy Sitka spruce for three weeks, but then lost them after the brood left the wood for more open ground. Even so, both hens had successfully reared chicks on the same ground in previous years.

67 The vagueness of this last category requires explanation. The traditional method of studying diet involves killing birds and examining the contents of their crops. Such methods are now less acceptable, especially for endangered species such as capercaillie, and workers must examine droppings for identifiable remains of food items. This works quite well for invertebrates with hard parts, and for plants with cell walls tough enough to retain recognisable characteristics after digestion. But it is not so good for identifying tender summer herbs, the well-digested remains of which are classified as 'miscellaneous' and can form a large part of the chicks' summer diet.

68 Black-billed capercaillie, the capercaillie species of northeast Asia, use Dahurian larch (*Larix gmelinii*, syn. *dahurica*) as a staple throughout the year. In winter, because larch are deciduous, the birds make do with twigs and buds. Our bird, the common or western capercaillie, also takes larch buds, flowers and needles as available in spring, summer or autumn. Larch is, however, often absent from their diet because it does not occur, for example, in large tracts of boreal forest with poor soils.

69 James Oswald, pers. comm. 1975.

70 Moss, 1980.
71 Moss & Oswald, 1985.
72 Moss, 1986.
73 James Oswald, pers. comm. 2004.
74 Moss *et al.*, 2000b.
75 Storaas *et al.*, 2000.
76 *See* Chapter 12 on how a hen's diet affects her condition and the quality of her eggs and chicks. The evidence for red grouse and ptarmigan is based on experiment, while that for capercaillie (Moss *et al.*, 2001) is correlative.
77 Picozzi *et al.*, 1999.
78 Caizergues & Ellison, 2002; Warren & Baines, 2002.
79 Schroeder, 1985; Hines, 1986; Small & Rusch, 1989.
80 If patches of summer and winter habitat are mixed on a small, fine-grained scale, seasonal movements are likely to be short. If patches are large and distinct, on a coarse-grained scale, movements will probably be longer.
81 Kirikov, 1947.
82 Storch, 2001.
83 R.W. Summers & R. Proctor, unpublished internal report to RSPB.
84 Wegge & Rolstad, 2000.
85 Storch, 1994. Broods were tracked until late August.
86 Picozzi *et al.*, 1999. Broods were tracked until late July.
87 Storch, 2001.
88 Moss *et al.*, 2006 – *see* note 48.
89 Pheasant-capercaillie hybrids also occurred, and there are several reports of lustful hen capercaillie offering themselves to humans during the mating season. *See* www.youtube.com/watch?v=jgSSpMu9CNA for a video of a hybrid (as at 9 November 2007).
90 Ménoni, 1991.
91 Borchtchevski & Gubar, 2003.
92 Cramp & Simmons, 1980.
93 Siivonen, 1948.
94 As shown by Moss & Oswald (1985).
95 Borchtchevski, 1993.

96 However, stoats are less abundant in the more agricultural south than in the more forested north (*see* Chapter 13).

97 In the Pinega nature reserve (421km$^2$), breeding success (about two young reared per hen) was no better within the reserve than in exploited forest outside (Borchtchevski *et al.*, 2003). The exploited forest still had some unlogged patches of old-growth spruce forest. Capercaillie densities in August (about six birds per km$^2$) were similar in old spruce forest within the reserve and on comparable unlogged patches outside. There was a greater density of capercaillie, however, in naturally regenerated young forest within the reserve than in young forest outside. Apparently, logging reduced capercaillie numbers because young forest after logging provided poorer habitat than natural regeneration after lightning fires and wind-throw.

At Pinega, signs of red fox were noted outside the reserve but not within it. Signs of pine marten and stoat showed a similar incidence inside and outside. More goshawks were seen inside, and more buzzards outside. The frequency of finding kills, and the proportion of kills attributed to mammals or to birds, was similar inside and outside. In a study at Pechora-Illych reserve, the densities of mammalian predators (red fox, pine marten, stoat) inside the reserve did not differ from those in logged forest outside (Beshkarev *et al.*, 1995). In short, the evidence goes against the idea that logged forest necessarily supports more predators and poorer breeding success of capercaillie than virgin forest.

Observations on the Pechora-Illych reserve raised another possibility. Capercaillie densities decreased between the mid-1960s and the mid-1970s, for reasons largely unconnected with logging. Intensive logging began in 1970 and left two reserves of virgin forest, a smaller one of 158km$^2$ surrounded by exploited forest, and, some 35km to the northeast, a large reserve of 7,055km$^2$. The smaller reserve had become an island of undisturbed habitat set in a vast sea of logged forest. Capercaillie numbers recovered from the natural decline on the large reserve but did not recover on the smaller one. The authors suggested that density-dependent dispersal drained birds from the smaller reserve into the surrounding logged areas, so preventing an increase in the reserve. Just how big a reserve must be to prevent such dispersal is not clear. The observation that densities in old-growth spruce forest were no higher inside than outside the Pinega reserve (*see* above) raises the alarming possibility that a virgin patch of 421km$^2$ was insufficient to maintain capercaillie densities when surrounded by degraded habitat.

98 The Onega-Pudoga massif in northern Russia comprises about 5,000km$^2$ of virgin forest surrounded by logged areas where the density of capercaillie is some three to four times lower. Data from a 650km$^2$ study area within the virgin massif suggested that many young birds left for the lower-density logged areas, and that some later returned as adults (Borchtchevski, 1993). Similar conclusions were reached, on the tiny Scottish scale, for the remnant Caledonian pinewood in Glen Tanar (Moss & Oswald, 1985), which covers about 12km$^2$ and lies adjacent to plantations. Here, the evidence suggested the occurrence of density-dependent emigration of young hens mostly in their first winter, and of young cocks mostly in their second year.

99 Segelbacher *et al.*, 2003.

100 The Scottish capercaillie population looks very much like a metapopulation, although, in hard scientific terms, there is not enough evidence to say that it has all the attributes of a theoretical metapopulation. Were we to wait for such evidence without taking action to safeguard them, the birds would probably become extinct. Our informed guess is that, by acting as if the birds do form a metapopulation, forest managers have the best chance of keeping them going.

101 S. B. Piertney, K. Kortland, F. Marshall, G. Segelbacher & R. Moss, unpublished manuscript.
102 An immediate problem, however, is that dispersing youngsters suffer heavy mortality by flying into fences. The removal and marking of fences have been done mostly on designated Special Protection Areas that are small relative to the distances moved by dispersing capercaillie. More youngsters would survive if more fences were removed, not only on Special Protection Areas but also in woods between them.
103 Grant, 1941.
104 Replanting of woodland on a large scale began in the mid-eighteenth century, too late to provide mature trees that would benefit capercaillie.
105 The greenhouse gases methane and carbon dioxide are released by agriculture and associated deforestation. It has been claimed that anthropogenic global warming, estimated after allowing for climatic fluctuations due to variations in the orbit of the earth around the sun, may have been occurring for 8,000 years (Ruddiman, 2003). During the last 2,000 years, warming has been briefly reversed by three periods of global cooling, which intriguingly followed the three biggest known periods of plague that have devastated human populations in various parts of the world. After each plague, much agricultural land reverted to forest, removing carbon dioxide from the atmosphere. The Little Ice Age was associated with bubonic plague in Europe and Russia (1499–1720), and the epidemic of smallpox and other diseases that reduced the population of the Americas from roughly 50 million to less than 10 million after Europeans arrived (1492–1680s). It is therefore just possible that the European invasion of the Americas contributed to the extinction of capercaillie in Scotland.
106 Declines during the Second World War, however, occurred also in black grouse, which do not depend upon mature forests, and in red grouse and ptarmigan, which do not live in forests at all. More generally, there was a widespread decline of grouse and other animals in much of northern Europe, from Scotland through Norway to the Ural mountains, including widespread declines of red grouse and willow ptarmigan, rock ptarmigan, capercaillie, black grouse and hazel grouse around 1939, and low numbers in the early 1940s (Siivonen, 1948; *see also* Chapter 3 for more on this). Hence sudden climatic change as well as habitat loss probably contributed to the large decline of capercaillie associated with the Second World War, not just in Scotland but in much of northwest Europe. Numbers in Scotland increased in the 1960s and early 1970s, but then there began the decline that lasted at least until the end of the century.
107 Moss *et al.* (2000b) give the wide confidence limits associated with these statements about breeding success.
108 The median is the middle item in an ordered list.
109 The general decline was not apparent at Glen Tanar at this time. Indeed, this core population seems to have been exporting birds during this period (Moss & Oswald, 1985), a likely example of density-dependent dispersal.
110 Moss *et al.*, 2000b; Moss, 2001.
111 Baines & Andrew, 2003.
112 *Deer and Fencing*, Forestry Commission Guidance Note 11, accessible at www.forestry.gov.uk/pdf/DeerFencingguidancenote11.pdf/$FILE/DeerFencingguidancenote11.pdf (as at 3 November 2006).
113 In the late 1990s, Scottish Natural Heritage (SNH) were making it plain that capercaillie conservation was a low priority with them. Following public outcry, a petition (PE16) to the Scottish Parliament organised by James Oswald, and a complaint (2000/4304) by RM to the European Commission (EC), the Scottish Executive and SNH, made about £750,000 available for removing and marking fences in

2000. Also, SNH together with the FC and the RSPB made successful application to the EC for LIFE funds totalling about £5 million for capercaillie conservation. This five-year programme began in 2002.
114 White et al., 2000. Snares are banned in all but five EU countries, the others being Ireland, Belgium, France and Spain. In all these four countries, regulations are more stringent than in the UK (Scottish Executive Consultation on Snaring, November 2006).
115 Cosgrove & Oswald, 2001.
116 A drive count involved a line of beaters walking noisily through a block of woodland and flushing birds towards a line of counters, who stood outside the block. The area covered changed slightly in 1990, from 4.1km$^2$ to 4.4 km$^2$, but this does not affect the conclusion that the sex ratio changed. There was no count in 2001.

## CHAPTER 7

1 Hjorth, 1970; Cramp & Simmons, 1980; Johnsgard, 1983; Lindström et al., 1998; Storch, 2001.
2 Nethersole-Thompson & Nethersole-Thompson, 1939; Watson & Jenkins, 1964.
3 Rusch & Keith, 1971; Jamieson & Zwickel, 1983.
4 MacDonald (1970) illustrated air sacs in a male rock ptarmigan's throat, including an inflatable walnut-sized membrane. All grouse species share with domestic fowls two inflatable air sacs, the walnut-sized one being extra. A loop in the cock capercaillie's windpipe makes the windpipe a third longer than the neck (Johnsgard, 1983). These features and drum-like membranes on the windpipe affect resonance (prolonging a sound by vibration) and frequency. Air spaces in the bones may help, for the whole body of a displaying cock grouse heaves with vibration. Grouse can call at much lower frequencies than those produced by organ-pipes of the same length, like blowing across the mouth of a laboratory flask (Helmholtz resonator).
5 Watson & Jenkins, 1964; Watson, 1972; Cramp & Simmons, 1980; Wike & Steen, 1987; Martin et al., 1995.
6 Pedersen et al., 1983.
7 AW noticed this at Lofoten in 1950, and in 1951 when Douglas Scott and Tom Weir agreed (Weir, 1953). Norwegian birds call in a higher key than red grouse (Chapman, 1897).
8 For example, Cramp & Simmons, 1980; Thaler, 1983.
9 International Phonetic Association, 1963.
10 Original transcriptions are in Watson & Jenkins (1964) and Watson (1972).
11 Watson, 1972; Cramp & Simmons, 1980; Thaler & Neyer, 1983.
12 Watson & Jenkins, 1964; Watson, 1972.
13 Watson, 1972.
14 Moss, 1972a; Watson, 1972, unpublished; Olpinski, 1986; Parr et al., 1993.
15 Watson & Jenkins, 1964; MacDonald, 1970; Watson, 1972.
16 Parker, 1981b. The average is 7.8 days, and the range 3–14 days.
17 Brockie, 1993, p.124.
18 Watson & Jenkins, 1964.
19 Nelson, 1887; Watson & Jenkins, 1964; Watson, 1972. The mean nearest-neighbour distance of willow ptarmigan in snow-burrows was 2.1m (Mossop, 1988).
20 MacDonald, 1970.
21 Moss et al., 1972; Savory, 1974.
22 Rae, 1994.
23 Gardarsson & Moss, 1970.
24 Watson, 1963b.
25 Gordon, 1915.
26 Holder & Montgomerie, 1993a; Pedersen et al., 2006; Watson, unpublished.
27 Savory, 1978.
28 Gelting, 1937.
29 Watson, 1966, unpublished.
30 Ellison, 1966; Pendergast & Boag, 1970.
31 The latent heat required to turn 1g of snow at 0°C to water at 0°C is 80 calories, which is

almost as much as the 100 calories needed to raise 1g of water from freezing point at 0°C to boiling point at 100°C.
32 Watson, 1972. Scottish ptarmigan snow-bathe at all seasons. *See* also photographs of captive Austrian birds in Thaler (1983).
33 Mercer & McGrath, 1963.
34 Storch, 2000a.
35 Savory, 1978.
36 Watson & Jenkins, 1964.
37 Robel, 1969.
38 Parr & Watson, 1988.
39 Storch, 2001.
40 A pack is a 'Number of hounds kept together for hunting, or of beasts (esp. wolves) or birds (esp. grouse) naturally associating' (*Concise Oxford Dictionary*, 3rd edn, 1953).
41 Bent, 1932; Kessel, 1989; Campbell *et al.*, 1990. AW counted 950 in a pack on Badalair at Glen Esk on 13 January 1959, and with his father and Tom Weir he counted 1,000 on Carn Aosda near the Cairnwell on 1 January 1965. Deep drifted snow covered low and high ground on both occasions.
42 Watson, 1963b.
43 Dementiev & Gladkov, 1952; Potapov & Flint, 1987.
44 Watson, 1972, unpublished.
45 Watson, 1972.
46 Millais, 1909.
47 Photograph in Steen, 1989, p.296, showing hatched eggshells around the nest. A greyhen with downy chicks died in a fire near Inverness (Bannerman, 1963).
48 Stuart Rae & Watson, unpublished. On Cairn Gorm above 1,140m, Rae found a hen lying dead on her eggs on 24 June, and AW found another the following day. Heavy snow fell on 6 and 7 June, and many drifts lasted until 11 June.
49 Sandercock, 1994.
50 Watson & Jenkins, 1964; Watson, 1972; Martin & Horn, 1993; Hannon *et al.*, 1998.
51 Macpherson & McLaren, 1959.
52 Marcström, 1986.
53 Sonerud, 1988.
54 Thaler, 1983. Included here are photographs of a hen ptarmigan standing while brooding.
55 Watson & Jenkins, 1964.
56 Watson, unpublished.
57 Watson, unpublished, recorded at Glen Esk. Most adults were back-tabbed, and the location, number and age of young were known for each brood before shooting. When families regrouped after shooting, he saw which had lost parents or young, and how many. Another observer noted tabbed birds shot in the bag.
58 Watson, unpublished.
59 Weeden, 1965b.
60 Gardarsson, 1988.
61 Watson, unpublished.
62 Watson unpublished, recorded at Glen Esk with red grouse, and at Beinn a' Bhuird and Glas Maol with ptarmigan.
63 Watson, 1972.
64 Martin, 1984; Holder & Montgomerie, 1993a; Hannon *et al.*, 1998.
65 Brodsky, 1988a.
66 Allen, 1977.
67 Watson & Jenkins, 1964.
68 Ibid.
69 Watson, 1972.
70 Moss, unpublished. Incubating hens flushed at a distance of several metres, without distraction display.
71 Jenkins *et al.*, 1963.
72 Hudson & Newborn, 1990.
73 Pedersen & Steen, 1985; Martin & Horn, 1993. At Churchill, Canada, hens in good condition before incubation took greater risks when defending nests.
74 Pedersen, 1989.
75 Hannon, 1984. Hens with a polygamous cock suffered a bigger rate of nest losses than hens in monogamous pairs, and a smaller percentage of them returned the following year.
76 Martin & Cooke, 1987.
77 Pedersen, 1993.
78 Martin, 1989. We wonder whether these cocks might have been related to the hens, and

though not fathers to the chicks, might perhaps have been uncles.
79 Unander & Steen, 1985.
80 MacDonald, 1952; Weeden, 1965b.
81 Freuchen & Salomonsen, 1960.

## CHAPTER 8

1 Large animals have small surface areas relative to their volume, and so lose less heat per unit of volume. This often applies to races within species, and is the basis of Bergmann's rule that big races live further north.
2 Sulkava, 1969; Zonov, 1983. Finnish redpolls dropped into snow and one penetrated 25–30cm within ten seconds.
3 Formozov, 1964; Johnsgard, 1983. For Britain see Pennant, 1771; Chapman, 1889, 1924; Bolam, 1912; Gordon, 1912 (photograph), 1915; Vesey-Fitzgerald, 1946; Watson, 1952, 1956, 1963b, 1972; Watson & Jenkins, 1964.
4 E. Pontoppidan, 1755, *Natural History of Norway*, cited by Chapman, 1924.
5 Pennant, 1771.
6 These species therefore do not fit Bergmann's rule.
7 Watson & Jenkins, 1964; Watson, 1972.
8 Watson & Moss, unpublished.
9 Gordon, 1915. 'Sometimes my old footprints were taken possession of by the ptarmigans as night-quarters' (Manniche, 1910).
10 For example, Nelson, 1887; Bent, 1932.
11 Roald Potapov, pers. comm. 2005.
12 Marjakangas, 1986.
13 Moss, in Watson, 1972, and unpublished.
14 James McIntosh, Dave Patterson and others, pers. comm. 2005.
15 Watson, unpublished, at Glen Esk, Kerloch and upper Deeside. Checks with dogs revealed birds underneath. Heather at roost sites showed freshly bitten shoots, so birds ate while underneath. Light penetrates up to 50cm in dry snow (McKay et al., 1970, citing G. D. Rikhter, 1963, *Problemy Severa* 7, 85–9).

Chapman (1889) noticed that red grouse vanish after snowfalls and are under the snow. Bolam (1912) wrote, 'shot seven grouse in rapid succession and without moving a yard…out of perhaps fifty "bolting" from their burrows around me'.
16 Moss, unpublished, at Kinveachy.
17 Butler, 1917. This was in 1912.
18 Watson, 1963b, 1965a. He never found Derry Cairngorm completely deserted of ptarmigan, as icy conditions affected only a band of altitude, with softer snow at higher or lower altitudes.
19 Koskimies, 1958; West, 1968, 1972; Korhonen, 1980.
20 Gates, 1962; Brander, 1965; Gullion, 1970.
21 Thompson & Fritzell, 1988; Swenson & Olsson, 1991. At air temperatures below –4°C, hazel grouse dig snow-burrows. On days of hard frost and insufficient snow, they roost 3.8m up in trees, favouring small spruces with a great depth of foliage above and around the roost site.
22 Mossop, 1988.
23 Gullion, 1970.
24 Pruitt, 1958.
25 Watson, unpublished. Also in northeast Greenland, rock ptarmigan roosting in open bowls were often 'frightened out of their holes' (Manniche, 1910) by Arctic foxes and ermines whose tracks were easily seen on newly fallen snow, but he saw no sign of any being caught. Birds disturbed from underneath powder snow fly in 'an explosion of snow-dust' (Semenov-Tyan-Shanskiy, 1960, Fig. 6), which probably distracts predators.
26 Formozov, 1964; Spidsø et al., 1997.
27 Gullion, 1970.
28 Andreev, 1978, 1980.
29 Watson, 1966.
30 Manniche, 1910; Watson, 1972.
31 Watson, 1972, Fig. 7.
32 Watson, 1972.
33 Watson & Jenkins, 1964.
34 Watson, unpublished.
35 Marjakangas, 1986, 1990. The 1986 paper is

the most detailed study of snow-roosts in grouse.
36 Semenov-Tyan-Shanskiy, 1960.
37 Höglund, 1980.
38 Manniche, 1910; Bent, 1932; Gelting, 1937; Freuchen & Salomonsen, 1960; Irving, 1960; Watson, 1972. Birds in northeast Greenland make open roosting bowls in frosts often down to −40°C, and sometimes at −45°C.
39 Marjakangas, 1986.
40 Marjakangas, 1990. At air temperatures of −3°C or above, snow-roosting 'may not be necessary' for saving energy.
41 Marjakangas, 1986.
42 Ibid.
43 Andreev, 1991.
44 Andreev, 1980.
45 Andreev, 1978, 1980.
46 Mossop, 1988.
47 Gelting, 1937.
48 Marjakangas, 1990.
49 Bent, 1932.
50 As described by Mossop (1988):

> *The fox's hunting method seemed most dependent on its ability to accurately locate a snow-roosting bird. In each instance the fox failed for essentially the same reason: the bird that was first flushed was not the bird being stalked. The fox's stalk or rush always took it past a bird it was apparently unaware of. The synchronous and contagious flushing of ptarmigan from snow-roosts may also startle foxes. During one observation a fox stepped on a snow-roosting bird. The bird bursting from underfoot and the flushing of the rest of the flock visibly shook the fox, which made no attempt to grab at any of the birds.*

51 Olaf Hjeljord, pers. comm. 2004.
52 Weeden, 1965a.
53 Freuchen, 1961.
54 Eric Pirie & John Pottie, pers. comm. 2006. Pirie is an instructor at the National Mountaineering Centre at Glenmore Lodge near Aviemore, while Pottie is an experienced cross-country skier. Two men take two-and-a-half hours to dig a hole in fairly compact snow in the Cairngorms (Pirie). Digging is faster in soft snow, but the hole must be made bigger to prevent the roof sagging, so the overall time needed differs little. Four people, including Pottie, took two to three hours at a snow bank to make a hole tall enough for standing inside, and he and another skier took one-and-a-half hours to dig sideways into a bank. Once when he found no bank during the evening of a lone ski tour, Pottie took 30 minutes to cut snow blocks on level snow with a ski and then dug a trench on their lee side. Drifting snow soon covered him, but his warm breath kept open a chimney above his head and he slept for eight hours.

## CHAPTER 9

1 Peterle, 1955; Watson & O'Hare, 1979b.
2 Watson & Jenkins, 1964; Martin *et al.*, 1990.
3 'Pairing' means staying together, not just being in brief contact.
4 Moss & Watson, 2001.
5 On Hrisey in Iceland, some hen rock ptarmigan maintained separate home ranges, each overlapping with a few male territories and involving inter-hen aggression (Gardarsson, 1988). This was associated with heavy losses of territorial cocks to gyrfalcons, and semi-promiscuous mating.
6 Hannon, 1983.
7 MacDonald, 1970; Olpinski, 1986; Holder & Montgomerie, 1993a.
8 MacDonald, 1970.
9 Watson, 1963b, 1972, unpublished.
10 Watson & O'Hare, 1979b; Pedersen *et al.*, 1983; Watson, unpublished.
11 Watson & Jenkins, 1964; Watson, 1972.
12 Eason & Hannon, 1994.
13 MacDonald, 1970.

14 Moss, 1972a.
15 Brodsky & Montgomerie, 1987.
16 Moss, 1972a; Watson, 1972. In one case in Alaska, after a long chase the subordinate was physically untouched but so petrified that he remained motionless as RM picked him up from the ground. When gently tossed into the air, he fell to the snow-covered ground, making no attempt to fly.
17 In Alaska, for instance, RM observed one such case with willow ptarmigan in spring. The hen of cock A walked into the territory of cock B, where she was courted by him. Cock A then followed his hen, whereupon cock B attacked cock A but was beaten in the ensuing dispute. After that, A's territory included the disputed ground that had formerly been cock B's. In Scotland, AW has often seen changes in territorial boundaries with red grouse and ptarmigan, especially in autumn when boundaries have only recently been established and are still fluid (Watson, unpublished). The autumn situation in Scotland is comparable with the Alaskan one observed by RM, both occurring at the start of the new territory establishment. In Scotland, AW observed another set of cases with both species during years of cyclic population decline, when many territorial cocks gave up their territories in spring and this again induced a temporarily fluid situation with regard territorial boundaries.
18 Other papers presented territory maps but not data on territory size (Watson et al., 1984a; Hudson, 1992; Moss et al., 1994).
19 Palmer & Bacon, 2000.
20 Watson & Miller, 1971.
21 Watson & Miller, 1971; Watson et al., 1984a; Moss et al., 1994; Palmer & Bacon, 2000; and published maps therein.
22 Jenkins et al., 1961, 1963; Watson & Jenkins, 1964; Watson & Miller, 1971. 'It was possible to measure territory size exactly, by plotting where neighbouring cocks paraded close together at the boundaries. Sufficient parades were seen to delimit the entire boundary on many territories and most of the boundary on others' (Watson, 1967b). On Dovrefjell, Pedersen (1984) mapped territories to the nearest 2m on ground with landmarks and to 10m on ground with few landmarks, even though territorial calling was confined to dawn and dusk (Pedersen et al., 1983).
23 Hannon, 1983; Unander & Steen, 1985; Gardarsson, 1988; Rae, 1994.
24 MacColl, 1998; MacColl et al., 2000.
25 Chapman (1924) wrote, 'ere daylight is fairly established we have half the grouse for a mile around exactly located; almost they advertise their addresses!'
26 Lance, 1977; Pedersen, 1984; Watson & Moss, unpublished.
27 Watson & O'Hare, 1979b. For example, two observers who hear a call at the same time can compare notes later and find the approximate location by extending the lines for the two directions until they meet.
28 Jenkins et al., 1963; Watson, 1965a; Watson & Miller, 1971.
29 AW lived 6km from the Glen Esk area, and at Kerloch 4km from the study area in the first year but later less effectively 11km away in a valley out of sight where weather often differed. Kerloch's bigger bogs, more numerous boulders and taller heather afforded worse access for vehicles, and the area was less concentrated, entailing more time driving between different sections and more effort to mark birds. Hans Pedersen and Johan Steen lived in a hut in the middle of their Dovrefjell area.
30 Watson, unpublished.
31 Jenkins et al. (1961) include examples of case histories at Glen Esk:

> One cock lived within another's territory for a week without being expelled; he was evidently a submissive bird because whenever the owner appeared he crouched low with his comb invisible and then looked very like a hen. When the owner was away, this intruder occasionally

threatened other intruders, and then he raised his comb and looked like a cock; but eventually he was expelled by the rightful owner.

Where the owner is replaced, prolonged conflict goes on for days or even for weeks until the situation becomes stabilised again. In one case the previous owner C had always had a hen, and cock D that replaced him had always been unmated in a territory a few hundred yards away, beyond another mated cock's territory. Within two days of C's disappearance, D had deserted his territory, occupied C's territory, and paired with C's hen… D's previous territory was now occupied by the three neighbouring cocks and also by a fourth cock E that had been trying to live within another cock's territory half a mile away. Within this other territory E had been silent, rarely showing his comb, and creeping away into cover as soon as the owner appeared. But as soon as E arrived in D's old territory his behaviour changed completely; he showed his comb and threatened vigorously as other cocks came near, and flew at the others and fought vigorously with them. He soon drove his neighbours back, defined new boundaries around a territory similar in size to that of D, and within a few days he had paired with the hen from one of his neighbours. On one day he had hens from two of his neighbours. It was remarkable to watch how the behaviour of this previously very submissive cock changed as soon as he found a vacant piece of ground.

In another case a vigorous cock F that had previously always had a hen became injured on one eye. He at once became quiet, spent much time resting in his territory, and the hen left him almost immediately. Within two days the three neighbouring cocks were advancing well into the territory, without being strongly threatened. On the third day the owner F was found unable to fly and looking ill. Later that afternoon two neighbours G and H had a fierce boundary dispute right in the middle of F's old territory, on his favourite sitting place. Meanwhile F was feeding only a few yards away, looking very subdued and hen-like. Next day G saw F and becked very loudly, landing only five yards away. Thereupon F crouched for 20 minutes, with his head touching the ground and moving not a feather, while G cackled loudly and strutted around apparently searching for F. F did not recover until long after G had flown away. The same day, F was seen panting and unable to fly, and looking very ill while being attacked by H. He then disappeared and has since been found dead on nearby communal ground. Long before this it was obvious that G and H had completely occupied F's territory, and that F now had the same status as a bird living within another's territory.

32 MacColl, 1998; Lock 2003. Watson & Moss (1971) distinguished birds such as E (see endnote 31) as Class 2 'non-territorial residents', which 'lived mainly on the moor, but were submissive to the territorial birds and were often chased by them out of the territories on fine mornings, when territorial behaviour was most vigorous', but 'were free to feed on the moor for most of the day' and 'on windy, snowy or heavily-overcast mornings'. Class 3 birds were 'non-territorial transients', which moved around more, 'suffered heavy mortality, and hardly any were left by January'. 'During fine calm weather, usually in January or February, there was a sudden change and territorial behaviour went on all day. Following this increase in territorial behaviour, Class 2 grouse were now forced off the moor to marginal habitats on scrub and fields where they were seldom attacked by

territory owners. The resident population on the moor suddenly decreased due to the departure of the Class 2 birds'.

33 Jenkins *et al.*, 1961, Fig. 6; Watson, 1967b. Watson (1970) says that in autumn one sees 'a psychosomatic effect after a territorial cock is ejected from its territory. It suddenly becomes much less aggressive, no longer courts hens, and spends prolonged periods resting and hiding. Such birds rapidly lose condition and may die within a week, even though other non-territorial birds are able to feed freely anywhere on the moor.'

34 Watson, unpublished.

35 Watson & O'Hare, 1979b; Pedersen *et al.*, 1983. The threshold is roughly 25 territorial cocks per km$^2$ (Watson, unpublished). An exception is that cock red grouse and Scottish ptarmigan at low density do beck when fog or falling snow restricts visibility. While burning heather in sunlight, we often heard cock red grouse becking in the smoke. Perhaps they felt safe to beck, because predators could not see them. White-tailed ptarmigan also confine calling to dawn and dusk, except in fog or falling snow (Schmidt, 1988).

36 Pedersen *et al.*, 1983.

37 Gordon, 1920.

38 Witherby *et al.*, 1944.

39 Watson & O'Hare, 1979b.

40 Unander & Steen, 1985. Perches were 'often ant-hill like hillocks, 0.2–1.0m high and with a base diameter of 0.2–1.0m. Dissection showed them to consist almost solely of old ptarmigan droppings, originally on a rock'. Droppings decompose very slowly on such excessively drained sites in high-Arctic climates (Watson, unpublished), and 'easily endure five years' (Wynne-Edwards, 1952).

41 Williamson & Emison, 1969.

42 Watson, 1965a.

43 Myrberget, 1983.

44 Watson & Moss, unpublished.

45 Watson, unpublished. Being naturally fragmented, hilltops have more peripheral areas than moorland.

46 Watson & Jenkins, 1968; Watson & Moss, 1971. The earliest that young cocks took daytime territories was on 3 August, after removal of most old territorial cocks in an experiment. In August and early September, young cock red grouse and Scottish ptarmigan took temporary territories at dawn before returning to their broods (Watson & O'Hare, 1979b; Watson, unpublished). Broods of red grouse finally broke up between August and November, usually in late September or early October.

47 Bossert, 1980.

48 Harper, 1953; Bergerud & Mercer, 1966; Mercer, 1967, 1968.

49 Gruys, 1993. Using data on marked birds, he inferred that many juvenile cocks also took part.

50 Haftorn, 1971.

51 Pedersen, *et al.*, 1983. Territorial calling began in the first week of September, when the oldest chicks reached 10–11 weeks. It peaked at about the start of November, before ceasing after mid-December when deep snow covered the area.

52 Johnsen (1953) found that during winter in northernmost Greenland the rock ptarmigan had tiny testes, much smaller than those in Scottish birds during winter (Watson, 1956, 1987b).

53 Gordon, 1912; Watson, 1965a.

54 An exception in Scotland can occur in late spring, when birds sometimes take temporary territories nearby on lower ground with less snow (*see* above in main text). If hens are already on nests when a deep snowfall occurs, however, the cocks do not leave their territories, as Gordon (1925) found in the Cairngorms on 29 May:

> *Each cock ptarmigan in spring marks out for himself and his mate a certain 'territory'. But this great May snowfall, ruthlessly wiping out such 'territories', had caused considerable confusion in the ptarmigan world, and no cock ptarmigan*

*were at the moment in possession of those undisputed areas, which, under normal conditions, they should have had at this season. This was the explanation of the restlessness and excitement that filled the ptarmigan community of Coire Beanaidh this day.*

He described many cocks in aerial becks, and also cocks displaying walking in line, sparring and chasing.

55 Moss, 1972a.
56 Ron Modafferi & Moss, unpublished.
57 For example, Watson, 1965a; Lance, 1978a; Erikstad, 1985a; Marti & Bossert, 1985; Unander & Steen, 1985; Gardarsson, 1988; Scherini *et al.*, 2003. Rock ptarmigan differ from *Lagopus lagopus* in that many cocks desert their hens before the eggs hatch, especially on Arctic and subarctic lands.
58 Unmated cocks tend to pack in summer, and cock Scottish ptarmigan that have been paired in spring will often join these packs Cocks in the summer packs give ground calls and occasional becks at dawn and dusk, but often stay in the packs while doing so, or show brief becks or walking-in-line encounters nearby within 20 m.
59 Watson & O'Hare, 1979b; and Watson, unpublished (in Scotland).
60 One had bred successfully on the main study area, but after all cocks on a nearby smaller section had been removed experimentally, he took a territory there and later paired with a hen that subsequently nested there. The other was the sole old cock that we recorded as moving just before the nesting season, after being territorial and paired on a different part of the study area in the previous winter and summer.
61 Watson, unpublished. For example, in the case of 14 hens at Glen Esk, only ten stayed on the same areas. Four shifted to nearby territories, including three that switched cocks, even though their cocks from the previous year still held territories.
62 Schieck & Hannon, 1989; Hannon & Martin, 1996. In hens, 31 per cent shifted territory.
63 MacColl, 1998; Lock, 2003; Moss *et al.*, unpublished manuscript.
64 Watson, unpublished. At Glen Esk in 1958–62, for example, there were 14 cases of marked hens being recorded in two successive years. Of these, ten were in the same area in the later year, eight of them paired with the same marked cocks as in the previous year, and two with new young cocks. Three hens had moved to adjacent territories that excluded ground used by them in the previous year, one being paired with a new young cock, and the other two shifting to adjacent old cocks even although their old partners were still present on territories. One young hen moved in the following year to a territory that lay immediately beyond the adjacent territory, and paired there with an old cock that had been there in the previous year, even though her first mate still had his territory, but was now unmated.
65 Hannon, 1983; Pedersen, 1984, 1988; Steen *et al.*, 1985.
66 For example, Lack, 1966; Wynne-Edwards, 1986; Newton, 1994.
67 Moss *et al.*, 1988.
68 Watson *et al.*, 1984a.
69 Moss & Watson, 1990, 2001.
70 Lance, 1978b.
71 Miller & Watson, 1978.
72 Watson, 1964b; Watson & Miller, 1971.
73 In all studies, e.g. Svalbard, cocks with large territories are more likely to pair with two hens, as in red grouse (Watson & Miller, 1971). On any area in one year, cocks in poor habitat have larger territories with fewer hens than cocks in good habitat. In habitat of similar quality, aggressive cocks have larger territories and more hens than less aggressive cocks. On Derry Cairngorm, vociferous aggressive cock ptarmigan had large territories and paired with one or sometimes two hens, while adjacent, less aggressive cocks

in the same habitat had small territories, seldom called, and were bachelors (Watson, 1965a).

In the study by Brodsky & Montgomerie (1987), 'bachelors' were smaller cocks with no mate or territory, and though resident neighbours had brief ritualised encounters, residents and bachelors had prolonged intense ones. Authors began observations in late spring (late May in this Arctic study) and described a bachelor as a cock usually on ground encompassing two or more paired cocks' territories, and not seen regularly with a lone hen. No other study has found that all unmated cocks lack territories. It seems likely that bachelors had territories earlier in spring, but after late May it was better to stay near paired cocks in the hope of mating with a hen than to continue territorial behaviour further away. Also, many encounters seen by us between neighbouring mated cocks in Scotland, Iceland, Baffin Island and Alaska were not brief and involved attacks, as MacDonald (1970) also found on Bathurst Island.

74 Watson & Parr, 1981; Moss et al., 1994.
75 This statement has its limits, for at Rickarton there was evidence that food quality declined at high densities of red grouse (Moss et al., 1996).
76 Watson & Miller, 1971; Pedersen, 1984; Hannon & Dobush, 1997.
77 Unander & Steen, 1985; Olpinski, 1986.
78 Bart & Earnst, 1999.
79 Territory size was estimated without mapping the boundaries. Large territories had fewer hens, but also contained unsuitable habitat.
80 Steen et al., 1985. None of the four main vegetation types that were classified on the study area occurred on all the territories, so the authors suggested that a territory signalled a cock's status more than what it offered in terms of food or shelter. In fact, however, what they showed was that none of the types was necessary for a territory, but they did not study what was offered by way of food or shelter.
81 Martin, 1991; Robb et al., 1992.
82 Hannon & Roland, 1984.
83 Miller & Watson, 1978.
84 Moss et al., 1988.
85 Watson & Parr, 1981.
86 Watson & O'Hare, 1979a; Watson et al., 1984a.
87 Miller & Watson, 1978.
88 Lance, 1978a.
89 For example, Lack, 1954, 1966; Wynne-Edwards, 1962; Watson & Moss, 1970; Newton, 1994. Wynne-Edwards (1986) argued that our work on red grouse backed his view on the importance of group selection in limiting numbers, but this was misinterpretation (Watson, 1987a).
90 Some authors recorded the presence of territorial birds, not their behaviour.
91 Watson, 1967a, 1985; Watson & Jenkins, 1968. Watson & Moss (1970) set out conditions necessary to show that territorial behaviour limits numbers. For autumn territorial behaviour to limit spring numbers, it is not necessary (Watson & Moss, 1990) that few or no territorial birds die or disappear over winter, although this did apply at Glen Esk, Kerloch (Watson & Moss, 1980; Watson, 1985), Rickarton (Watson & Moss, unpublished) and Glen Tanar (Moss et al., 1994). The necessary conditions are: the total number of birds in autumn exceeds that next spring; and the number of autumn territories is similar to that next spring. The owners' identity is irrelevant.
92 Moss et al., 1994.
93 MacColl, 1998.
94 Hudson & Renton (1988) and Hudson (1990, 1992) misconstrued removal experiments by Watson & Jenkins (1968), and Hudson (1992) ignored criticisms (Watson & Moss, 1990) of his (Hudson, 1990) experiments. Park et al. (2002) stated that territorial red grouse in Speyside survived in early winter no better than non-territorial

birds, and concluded, 'territorial behaviour did not determine breeding density'. This was fallacious, because it is the number of territories that determines breeding density, not the owners of them. In principle, territorial behaviour can limit density even when territorial birds have lower survival rates over the winter than birds that are non-territorial in autumn (Watson & Moss, 1990).

Evidence reviewed by Watson & Moss (1990) showed that many territorial birds gave up territories and then died or disappeared in late winter during a deep decline at Kerloch in the 1970s (Watson & Moss, 1980, 1990), and heavy overwinter losses of territorial birds occurred in some years of decline at Glenamoy (Lance, 1976). Territorial behaviour in autumn nevertheless limited spring numbers at Kerloch in all years, and at Glenamoy in two years although not in three others, in one of which there were no young cocks present in autumn.

Park et al. (2002) used radio-tagged birds caught on four moors over eight years, the location of birds being checked at least once a week. They gave no data to relate their findings to populations, and did not map territories. None the less, their data are interesting in another respect. Along with our findings from the declines at Kerloch and Glenamoy, their data indicate that good survival of territorial birds over winter does not apply on all areas. At Glas-choille, Andrew MacColl and others found much turnover among territorial birds between autumn and spring, some of them being killed by predators and then replaced, and some moving to take territories elsewhere (MacColl, 1998). Territorial behaviour in autumn limited spring numbers, though the identities of many participants changed.

Hudson (1992) presented territory maps of red grouse at low density on a Speyside moor. He stated that much heather-dominated ground remained unoccupied in two springs, and that some that was unoccupied in one spring was occupied in the next. To him, this implied that territorial behaviour did not limit spring numbers. However, he gave no data on numbers or territorial behaviour before the spring, so the fieldwork was insufficient. For territorial behaviour to be limiting, birds do not need to occupy all ground (see 'Territories on Poor or Peripheral Ground' in the main text).

Hudson (1992) stated that critical evidence for 'testing the importance of spacing behaviour' was that 'The population of grouse in spring should never exceed the number of territorial grouse in the previous autumn'. He counted grouse numbers in October on 20 study areas and again next spring, classifying pairs as territorial and also 'single cocks that showed territorial behaviour'. In 18 out of 20 cases, territorial hens in spring outnumbered those in autumn, and likewise for territorial cocks in 12 out of 20 cases, thus 'suggesting that spacing behaviour was not limiting their density'. Fieldwork was insufficient, however, because counts of grouse numbers cannot show reliably whether birds are territorial in October. Redpath & Thirgood (1997) counted calling cocks in October and the following April at Langholm, and the numbers of each sex. They studied overwinter survival of radio-tagged birds, whose status they judged as territorial if more than half the radio locations of a cock in October–December were within 25ha, and if a hen was paired with a cock on more than half the radio locations in October–December. Again, these methods were insufficient to judge status. The criterion of 25ha was an unsatisfactory surrogate of territory, because data confirming it were not presented. Calling cocks declined in number by 21 per cent between October and April, but there was no information about non-territorial birds.

95 Mougeot et al., 2003a, b, 2005c; Redpath et al., 2006a.

96 Lance, 1976.

97 Hannon, 1983; Mossop, 1988; Pedersen, 1988. Hannon did not know the origin of

replacements, but this does not affect whether territorial behaviour limits spring numbers on an area. It involves other topics, such as the status of replacement birds before removals. Mossop found that 46 per cent of removed birds were replaced, all by birds that had been non-territorial. Both authors noted that replacement birds might have moved to take territories elsewhere if removals had not created vacancies. This also is not relevant to the question of whether territorial behaviour limits numbers on a given area, and instead involves other topics such as habitat quality on core or marginal areas, and migration.
98 Moss, 1972a.
99 Watson, 1965a.
100 Unander & Steen, 1985.

## CHAPTER 10

1 Cramp & Simmons, 1980.
2 Humphrey & Parkes, 1959. Criticism by Howell et al., 2003, and in Condor since.
3 Jacobsen et al., 1983. We judge autumn plumage as Basic, winter plumage as Alternate, and summer plumage as Supplemental, and moults to them as Prebasic, Pre-alternate and Pre-supplemental.
4 Watson, 1972.
5 Watson et al., 1969.
6 Parr, 1975; Watson & Miller, 1976. Using the development of wing feathers and other plumage.
7 Flux, 1958; Semenov-Tyan-Shanskiy, 1960; Bergerud et al., 1963; Weeden & Watson, 1967; Braun & Rogers, 1971.
8 An after-shaft is a short feather that sprouts near the base of the main feather.
9 Höhn (1980) reviews the rosy flush. In willow ptarmigan, Bent (1932) reported a 'beautiful faint pink flush... fades quickly after death'.
10 Salomonsen (1939) emphasised temperature, but it and snow-lie often coincide.

11 Barth, 1855; Bent, 1932; Mikheev, 1939; Murie, 1946; Höhn, 1980; Hannon et al., 1998.
12 Johnsen, 1929.
13 Ibid.; Mikheev, 1939; Novikov, 1939.
14 A follicle is a feather's growth-point in the skin.
15 Parmelee et al., 1967.
16 Hewson, 1973; Watson, 1973; Stokkan & Steen, 1980.
17 Salomonsen, 1939.
18 Lorenz, 1904; Potapov, 1985, pers. comm. 2005. Coloured feathers grow in autumn, before the onset of cold weather.
19 Roald Potapov, pers. comm. 2005.
20 Salomonsen, 1939.
21 Watson, 1973; Jacobsen et al., 1983.
22 Elison, 1980; Jacobsen et al., 1983. Winters in Amchitka are almost as mild as at Braemar at 339m, below the Cairngorms. Amchitka's coldest month has a mean temperature only slightly below freezing.
23 Hewson, 1973.
24 Watson, 1973.
25 Bossert, 1980; Thaler & Neyer, 1983; Holder, 1994.
26 Watson, 1973.
27 Watson, 1965a.
28 Salomonsen, 1939; MacDonald, 1970.
29 Cott, 1940.
30 Wynne-Edwards, 1952; review by Pennie, 1957; Watson, 1957b; MacDonald, 1970; Steen & Unander, 1985.
31 Montgomerie et al., 2001.
32 Gardarsson, 1988.
33 Cotter et al., 1992; Cotter, 1999.
34 Poole, 1987.
35 Weeden, 1965a; MacDonald, 1970; Steen & Unander, 1985, Olpinski, 1986.
36 This perhaps shows (through a natural experiment) what might happen to cocks in Scotland were they to remain white in spring.
37 Watson, 1956, 1957b.
38 Salomonsen, 1939.
39 Hewson, 1973.
40 Wilson, 1911; Watson, 1963d.
41 Savory (1975) measured body-moult and

primary growth.
42 Wilson, 1911.
43 Ibid.; Witherby et al., 1944.
44 Gordon, 1944; Bannerman, 1963.
45 Leucism is partial loss of pigment in all colours, reducing their intensity (Campbell & Lack, 1985). Cream-coloured specimens of leucistic red grouse are on display in museums (see Bannerman, 1963).
46 Watson, 1963d.
47 Watson, 1956.
48 Hewson, 1973.
49 Cold and snow usually coincide. Authors have compared *Lagopus* whitening with temperature data, which are readily available. However, snow explains much of the variation in whitening of mountain hares and stoats (Jackes & Watson, 1975; Hewson & Watson, 1979).
50 Høst, 1942.
51 Novikov, 1939; Stokkan, 1979.
52 MacDonald, 1970. The injected cock's combs also remained large. He mated with three hens that nested on his territory, showed flight songs 'spectacular in height, frequently reaching an estimated 250 feet [75m], and he sang two, three, or even four times before alighting'. Other cocks skulked, and had small combs.
53 Höhn, 1980; Höhn & Braun, 1980. Experiments do not rule out that other endocrine glands are involved, such as the thyroid.
54 Höhn & Braun, 1980. Three hormones produced by the pituitary affect moult. One is melanophore-stimulating hormone (MSH), which induces melanin production as pigment granules inside cells. A second is luteinising hormone (LH), which stimulates the ovary to produce oestrogen and the testis to produce testosterone, and promotes final development of ovarian follicles and their end product of eggs. A third, follicle-stimulating hormone (FSH), stimulates growth of ovarian follicles and their eggs, and sperm formation in the testis.

55 Watson, 1986, 1987b. In the high Arctic, testes are still tiny even in mid-March, but by the end of May they are large, when they reach the same size as those of Scottish cocks in mid-March (Johnsen, 1953).
56 In the few studies that have been done involving counts of feathers, several bird species were found to have more feathers in winter than in summer (Campbell & Lack, 1985).
57 Salomonsen, 1939.
58 Mortensen et al., 1985.
59 Mortensen & Blix, 1986; West, 1972.
60 Also, birds have slightly more fat in winter; other explanations for the lower metabolic rate include the fact that birds puff out their winter plumage to trap more air, blood supply to the skin changes, and captives are less active in winter.
61 Each feather has a central shaft with many side-branches (barbs). On both sides of each barb are minute finer branches (barbules), with inbuilt hooks and grooves that interlock.
62 Chandler, 1916; Dyck, 1979.
63 Andreev, 1980.
64 Scholander et al., 1950; Veghte & Herreid, 1965. Snowy owls have extremely low heat conductance, which is equivalent to the pelts of Arctic foxes (Gessaman, 1976).
65 MacDonald, 1970.
66 Andreev, 1991.
67 Höhn, 1977.
68 Andreev, 1980.
69 Pruitt, 1960.
70 Watson & Miller, 1976. This also applies to other British grouse species.
71 Potapov et al., 2003.
72 In the non-erect state the comb of a blackcock and capercaillie is less flaccid than that of a *Lagopus* bird, and is less readily covered by feathers, so that the lowest part appears as a thin red streak, only partly under the feathers.
73 Tiny projections on the comb surface.
74 MacDonald, 1970.
75 Mougeot et al., 2005a. Comb size peaks in

October, coinciding with the main annual reorganisation of territories, and in April, when cocks show much territorial activity before the hens lay eggs.
76 Watson, 1987b.
77 MacDonald, 1970.
78 Sharp et al., 1975; Sharp & Moss, 1981.
79 Moss et al., 1979a.
80 Hannon, 1984; Brodsky, 1988b; Hannon & Eason, 1990; Holder & Montgomerie, 1993b; Hannon & Dobush, 1997.
81 Nethersole-Thompson & Watson, 1974. Of a cock red grouse in spring, they wrote: 'Look at his brilliant crimson combs raised far above his crown; on a fine day they catch the sun and glow with warm red light.'
82 Mougeot & Redpath, 2004; Mougeot et al., 2004, 2005d, in press; F. Mougeot et al., 2007 on carotenoid coloration and ultraviolet reflectance. Comb size in cock red grouse is related to the bird's 'immune function' (ability to show an immune response). Large combs indicate high-quality cocks with a good immune function and an ability to withstand threadworm parasites. The combs in all four British grouse species reflect ultraviolet light. Black grouse can see ultraviolet light (Siitari & Viitala, 2002), and it is probable that, unlike humans, diurnal birds in general can do so.

## CHAPTER 11

1 Joseph Grinnell's 1917 definition, quoted in Whittaker et al., 1973.
2 Höhn, 1980; Johnsgard, 1983; Holder & Montgomerie, 1993a; Hannon et al., 1998; Lindström et al., 1998; Storch, 2000a, 2001.
3 Pearsall, 1950; Ratcliffe & Thompson, 1988.
4 Johnstone & Mykura, 1989. It included most of North America and Greenland, and was named after Canada's Laurentian Shield. The motorway from Montreal to the Laurentian Mountains is the Autoroute des Laurentides.
5 Baltica comprised what is now Fennoscandia, north Russia and land around the Baltic Sea. Avalonia, named after the Avalon region of France, included what is now France, the Low Countries and most of central Europe, as well as the southern half of Ireland and all of Britain south of Scotland.
6 Stephenson & Gould, 1995; Gillen, 2003.
7 The texture of an igneous rock is determined by its rate of cooling. Granite is formed by the slow cooling of magma underground, for example, and so is composed of large, coarse crystals, whereas basalt cooled quickly at the surface and comprises small, fine crystals.
8 Watson, 1966; Jenkins et al., 1967; Moss, 1968, 1969; Watson & Hewson, 1973; Watson et al., 1973, 1998; Nethersole-Thompson & Watson, 1974; Moss et al., 1975.
9 Geikie, 1940; Johnstone, 1974; Watson & Miller, 1976.
10 The weight of ice-sheets presses land downwards. When they vanish, land rises slowly, but sea-level rises quickly owing to the melt-water.
11 Tipping, 1994; Edwards & Whittington, 2003.
12 McCormick & Buckland, 2003.
13 Stephenson & Gould, 1995.
14 Birks, 1988. In the Pennines it reached to the summit at 893m and in the Cairngorms to 793m (it is now at 610m).
15 Tipping, 2003a.
16 Darling, 1947, 1955. He wrote that man 'destroyed the ancient Highland forest', and that

> The Highlands... are unable to withstand deforestation and maintain productiveness and fertility. Their history has been one of steadily accelerating deforestation until the great mass of the forests was gone, and thereafter of forms of land usage which prevented regeneration of tree growth and reduced the land to the crude values and expressions of its solid geologic composition. In short, the Highlands are a devastated countryside and that is the plain, primary reason why there are now

*so few people... Devastation has not quite reached its uttermost lengths, but it is quite certain that present trends in land use will lead to it, and the country will then be rather less productive than Baffin Land.*

Black (1964) asserted that southern sheep farmers reduced the Highlands to 'its present semi-desert condition'. Some ideologists still proclaim Darling's views on infertility and people, e.g. Hunter (1994, 1995), who wrote, 'But if the ecological degradation of the Highlands began in the more or less distant past, there is equally no doubt – as Frank Fraser Darling so clearly discerned – that such degradation was enormously speeded up by developments which date from the century following the Battle of Culloden' (1746), notably the rise of sporting estates and human clearances for sheep farming. The Scottish Crofters Union & Royal Society for the Protection of Birds (1992) claimed that forced clearances caused most depopulation. In fact, non-enforced emigration was the key loss (Richards, 1985; Devine, 2004), and northeast Highland glens without clearances are now as empty as cleared ones (Watson & Allan, 1990).
17 Birks, 1988; Tipping, 2004.
18 Moore, 1975; Moore et al., 1975; Bennett, 1995, 1996. O'Connell (1990) was ambivalent, noting that prehistoric farming appeared to inhibit peat growth at one site and that peat developed in woodland at another. We infer that deforestation is not necessary for peat development. Cultivation of freely drained soil can prevent peat development (Davidson & Carter, 2003).
19 Tipping, 2003b, 2004. Woodland at west Glen Affric became established by 10,000 years ago, and was dominated by broadleaved trees. Blanket peat developed later, covering most ground by 7,000–6,000 years ago, but woodland continued for 2,000–3,000 years after that.
20 Nichols, 1969, 1976.

21 Andrews, 1920; Moreau, 1954; Holder & Montgomerie, 1993a; Stewart, 1999; Potapov et al., 2003.
22 Seiskari, 1962.
23 McCormick & Buckland, 2003.
24 White, 1987.
25 For more on soil profiles, see www.uwsp.edu/geo/faculty/ritter/geog101/textbook/soil_sy stems/soil_development_profiles.html (as at 23 November 2006).
26 Slopes tend to be fertile because movement prevents podzolisation. Hence the claim that 'Podsols and podsolised soils are common too, especially on steep slopes' (Averis et al., 2004, Introduction) is incorrect.
27 Tamm, 1950; White, 1987.
28 Birks, 1988.
29 Davidson & Simpson, 1984.
30 For example, Futty & Towers, 1982.
31 Hardened layers, such as an iron pan or a cement-like lower horizon.
32 Dimbleby, 1952.
33 Satchell, 1980. Some (e.g. Miles, 1988; Averis et al., 2004, Introduction) have since reasserted Dimbleby's idea, without mentioning Satchell's refutation.
34 Whittington (1993) on lake floors. Animals graze grass and browse woody plants, but this is hair-splitting when both are eaten in one mouthful, so we use 'grazing' for both.
35 Keatinge & Dickson, 1979.
36 Simmons, 2003.
37 Watson et al., 1995.
38 Caulfield, 1981.
39 This is also the case on mild west Norwegian islands, where sheep winter on deforested land with heather that farmers manage by burning (Kaland, 1986).
40 Whittington, 1978, 1993; Caulfield, 1983.
41 Whittington, 1993.
42 Ian Shepherd, pers. comm. 2007.
43 Parry, 1978.
44 Foster, 1992; Compton & Boone, 2000.
45 Dupouey et al., 2002, and references therein.
46 Briggs et al., 2006; Gillson & Willis, 2006.

47 McCullagh & Tipping, 1998; Davidson & Carter, 2003.
48 Botanists use the term 'heath' loosely. The heath family Ericaceae includes heather, bell heather, cross-leaved heath, blaeberry, crowberry and many other species. These are important food plants for grouse. Botanists use 'heath' for vegetation dominated by heath species, and for much vegetation with a heath component, even if this is minor. They use 'heathland' for land with heath, including all moorland, much Alpine vegetation and much understorey in woods. Moorland includes dry heath (e.g. heather moorland) and wet heath (e.g. blanket bogs).
Lowland heath has been defined as land below 250–300m in altitude with >10 per cent heather, and upland heath or moorland as land at higher altitudes with some heather (e.g. Thompson et al., 1995, Foreword). This is confusing, especially when the phrase 'heaths and moorland' is used. We avoid this.
49 Parr, 1992.
50 McVean & Ratcliffe, 1962; Rodwell, 1991; Averis et al., 2004. Some heather is a bonus for grouse for a reason other than food, in that it dries more quickly after rain than most plants of moorland, woodland, or Alpine land, and so chicks feed in it sooner and dry quickly (Watson, unpublished).
51 Thompson & Miles, 1995.
52 Hill grasses can survive heavier grazing than blaeberry, and blaeberry heavier grazing than heather. Hence overgrazing of heather moorland often leads to blaeberry-grass and then to grass alone.
53 Huntley, 1991.
54 Keatinge et al., 1995.
55 Pronounced 'ow' as in 'how', a flow is a wet bog, or a sea channel as in Scapa Flow. 'Flow country', a term coined by conservationists, is not used locally.
56 Tansley, 1939.
57 Vegetation climax is the relatively stable endpoint of plant succession, and in the case of moorland is forest.

58 Phillips & Watson, 1995; MacDonald, 1999.
59 Stevenson & Thompson, 1993.
60 Thompson & Miles, 1995.
61 Fenced wet heath on blanket bog remains devoid of scrub or trees, except on fertile flushes and freely drained stream edges, e.g. bogland fenced in the mid-1950s near the Peatland Experimental Station at Glenamoy (shown to AW by Director P. J. O'Hare in 1967–71).
62 Hunter, 1973.
63 Darling, 1955; Black, 1964. To Pearsall (1950), 'every animal carcase and its wool and hide represent... a considerable reduction in upland fertility'. For impartial reviews, see Mather (1978) and Smout (2000).
64 Cumming, 1994; Lister-Kaye, 1994. They asserted that burning and carcass removal exhaust moorland soils, and that woodland is needed to restore fertility, but adduced no evidence. Scottish Natural Heritage (1992) claimed, again without giving evidence, that many rural activities 'have been contributing to a draw-down of Scotland's natural capital... This degradation calls into question the capacity of the natural heritage to sustain the range of uses to which it is subjected.' In their Introduction, Averis et al. (2004) stated, 'nutrient extraction in timber, wool and meat has contributed to reducing the fertility and carrying capacity of upland soils', but gave no evidence to this effect.
65 Crisp, 1966.
66 On freely drained moorland, nitrogen is a limiting element, whereas phosphorus usually is not.
67 Lee et al., 1987; Grace & Unsworth, 1988.
68 Marrs et al., 1989.
69 Hobbs & Gimingham, 1987.
70 Mackenzie, 1924; Harrison, 1997.
71 Evans, 1998.
72 Some British authors use 'montane' loosely and confusingly for both subalpine and Alpine zones. 'Arctic-Alpine' is often used by scientists in Scotland, because of the Arctic affinities of the Alpine zone, but for brevity we use 'Alpine'.

73 Ratcliffe, 1990.
74 Baines *et al.*, 2000.
75 Parr & Watson, 1988; Watson, 2003.
76 Fremstad (1997) recognised six Norwegian types of pinewood, plus subtypes of most of them. Rodwell (1991) and Averis *et al.* (2004) recognised one British type with several subtypes.
77 Walker, 1988.
78 Lambert, 2001.

## CHAPTER 12

1 Savory, 1978.
2 Fresh weights are given, based on the assumption that heather contains 50 per cent moisture. The scaling from grouse to human is on the basis that food intake is proportional to (body weight)$^{0.75}$. The volume is of particles, from a grouse crop, loosely packed in a beaker, and includes the spaces between them (volume = 3.3 × fresh weight).
3 Moss & Picozzi, 1994; Picozzi *et al.*, 1996.
4 Singular caecum, plural caeca.
5 Also called the large intestine or colo-rectum.
6 Clench & Matthias, 1995.
7 Each caecal entrance has a ring of circular muscle, forming a sphincter that controls the flow of digesta into and out of the caeca, plus a mesh of long inter-digitating villi that acts as a sieve to keep out larger particles. The end of the small intestine protrudes slightly into the upper colon, and it too has a sphincter that, when contracted, prevents the reverse flow of digesta out of the colon from entering the small intestine, and directs it into the caeca.
8 Lignin is the generic class of complex polyphenols that gives wood its nature. Wood is essentially lignocellulose, i.e. lignin bound to cellulose.
9 Moss & Hanssen, 1980.
10 Moss, 1977.
11 Lignin digestion has been well studied in white-rot fungi. They oxidise lignin with enzymes called ligninases, which are peroxidases that use oxygen in the form of hydrogen peroxide to accept electrons from lignin. In theory, there are other possible electron acceptors, including carbon dioxide. 12 Braun & Duke (1989) made the general point that refluxed urine might contain electron acceptors that could facilitate lignin digestion.
13 Singer, 2003.
14 Proteins are long chains of amino acids. Essential amino acids cannot be synthesised in the animal and must come from the food or from the digestion of gut microbes. Non-essential amino acids can be synthesised by animals, and need not be derived from the food or from microbes.
15 In this respect, grouse are more like alligators than the textbook 'bird'.
16 Casotti & Braun, 2004.
17 Moss, 1983. Changes in response to a new diet typically occur over the course of a few weeks.
18 Moss, 1989.
19 Redig, 1989.
20 Moss, 1972c.
21 Weeden, 1968.
22 Moss, 1983.
23 Epigenetic inheritance comprises reversible heritable changes in gene function that occur without genetic change.
24 Or perhaps the ability to change gut size is epigenetic. Genes can be turned on or off. Epigenetic inheritance involves parents passing the state (on or off) of genes to offspring without altering the genotype.
25 Hence the domestic fowl is probably a poor model for digestion in wild gallinaceous birds.
26 Moss, 1989.
27 We use the unqualified term 'digestibility' to mean the proportion ([food eaten minus droppings excreted]/food eaten) on a dry-weight basis.
28 Moss & Hanssen, 1980.
29 Moss, 1974.
30 Moss, 1983.

31 Moss, 1997.
32 Data from Moss (1997).
33 If they were less costly, there would be less selective pressure to lose them and they would be retained for longer.
34 Ornithuric acid (a conjugate of ornithine with benzoic acid) and hippuric acid (a conjugate of glycine with benzoic acid) are plentiful in grouse urine. Moss & Hanssen (1980) summarised the evidence that red grouse excrete ornithuric acid. Remington & Hoffman (1997) showed that blue grouse excrete ornithuric acid and hippuric acid, and it is very likely that red grouse excrete hippuric acid too.
35 Remington & Hoffman, 1997.
36 Savory, 1983.
37 Ibid.
38 Andreev, 1991.
39 Moss & Hanssen, 1980.
40 Brittas, 1988.
41 Weeden, 1968; Moss, 1974.
42 Moss, 1972b; Moss & Hanssen 1980; Savory, 1983.
43 Andreev, 1991.
44 Borchtchevski & Gubar, 2003.
45 Moss et al., 1996.
46 McGowan, 1969.
47 Ibid.
48 www.scotland.gov.uk/library5/environment/hbois.pdf (as at 28 October 2006).
49 Savory, 1983.
50 Moss & Watson, 1984.
51 Moss, 1972b.
52 Moss et al., 1971.
53 Data from Moss & Watson (1984).
54 Brittas, 1988.
55 Compare Table 20 with Fig. 5 in Jenkins et al. (1963).
56 Moss et al., 1981.
57 On a dry-weight basis.
58 Based on dry weight in crops (Erikstad & Spidsø, 1982).
59 Savory, 1989.
60 Park et al., 2001.
61 Myrberget et al., 1977; Moss et al., 1993a.

62 Erikstad & Spidsø, 1982.
63 Picozzi et al., 1999.
64 Clutch size averages six to nine eggs, varying as much among studies within species as among species.
65 Hörnfeldt et al., 2001.
66 Unless the timing of peak insect abundance also advances.
67 The larvae of the favoured geometrid moths drop off the vegetation and pupate in the soil.
68 Moss et al., 1993a.
69 Paradoxically, roosting in snow-holes in cold weather might require less energy than roosting in the open in warmer but wetter and windier conditions. If so, an increase in winter temperature might make it harder for grouse to keep warm at night. This possibility has not been studied.

## CHAPTER 13

1 Unless predation affects numbers indirectly by altering the prey's spacing behaviour.
2 'Wholly additive' means that 100 deaths result in 100 fewer grouse. 'Partially additive' means that 100 deaths result in fewer grouse, but not 100 fewer. 'Fully compensatory' means that 100 deaths result in no fewer grouse. 'Partially compensatory' means the same as partially additive.
3 Watson & Moss, 2004. At Cairn Gorm, gulls and especially crows ate the eggs and chicks of ptarmigan, such that breeding ptarmigan were extirpated on the most heavily developed ground and reduced in density up to 4km from the main development. This happened even though golden eagles largely avoided the ski area after development. After 1996, increased killing of crows on lower ground led to fewer crows on Cairn Gorm, allowing ptarmigan to recolonise some of the heavily developed ground.
4 For grouse, exploiting the functional response of the predators in this way involves a delicate balance, because foxes, martens and

other predators opportunistically kill grouse. Hence, even when the proportion of grouse in the predators' diet is low, the proportion of grouse taken by predators can be high. In such conditions, good cover can be crucial to grouse survival.
5 Borchtchevski, 1993.
6 Another idea is that population cycles in prey species might function to reduce predator abundance in a brutal game of hide and seek, played out in space and time. Prey become scarce during cyclic troughs, and make predators' hunting more difficult by taking refuge in areas of good cover. Most predators then starve or disperse, whereupon prey rapidly increase again. This might be the result of a predator-prey cycle, or the cycle might be a behavioural adaptation that minimises predation upon cyclic genotypes (Moss & Watson, 1985, 2001; Hik, 1995).
7 Watson, 1997; Mick Marquiss, pers. comm. 2005.
8 Sergio et al., 2003.
9 Petty et al., 2003.
10 'Meso' means middle-sized. The idea of 'meso-predator release' is widely accepted because it explains much about observed patterns of predator abundance. There are, however, few well-documented examples.
11 A nice example of meso-predator suppression occurred when goshawks returned to Kielder Forest in northern England. Here they ate mostly pigeons and crows, but also kestrels, tawny owls, short-eared owls, long-eared owls, sparrowhawks, merlins, weasels and stoats. Predators made up some 5 per cent of their diet. About half of this comprised kestrels, which declined from 30 pairs in 1975 to five pairs in 1997 (Petty et al., 2003).
12 Nielsen, 1999.
13 Moss & Watson, 2001.
14 Holder & Montgomerie, 1993a.
15 Bailey, 1993.
16 Semenov-Tyan-Shanskiy, 1960. Rodents breed and die faster than grouse, thereby having a quicker turnover and forming an even bigger proportion of the potential prey than is indicated by their biomass.
17 Many studies show this, e.g. Semenov-Tyan-Shanskiy, 1960; Marcström et al., 1988; Saniga, 2002. The relationship between rodent densities and breeding success of grouse might also involve both being affected by blaeberry mast-years (Selas, 2000).
18 Borchtchevski, 1993.
19 Percentages do not include eggs and chicks.
20 Lake Ilmen is at 55°N, the same latitude as Newcastle, but has a continental climate.
21 The number of snares used in woods and on moors increased greatly in the 1990s (see Chapter 6). Wildcats are certainly killed in snares and there is much anecdotal evidence that they declined in the 1990s.
22 Moss et al., 1990b.
23 Ratcliffe, 1980.
24 Newton, 1993, 1994; Côté & Sutherland, 1995; Smedshaug et al., 1999.
25 Redpath & Thirgood, 1997. At its outset, the study was designed badly. A rigorous scientific approach was excluded for political reasons. As the editors admit in their foreword to the Langholm report, 'the most rigorous approach scientifically would have been experimental, comparing grouse numbers in the Langholm area where raptors were protected with grouse numbers in similar areas from which raptors were removed'. In the event, the study relied on 'measuring everything necessary to assess the impact of raptors' at Langholm, and using bags from 'two other moors in the same region, where raptors were much scarcer than at Langholm' to compare with those at Langholm. Ancillary studies were also carried out at five other Scottish moors where 'raptors were protected but the numbers of foxes and crows controlled by gamekeepers'.
26 The Langholm study led to greater hostility between the two camps. To game preservers it was obvious that raptors, especially hen

harriers, had been allowed to destroy a good grouse-moor. To conservationists such as the RSPB, the lesson was that excessive sheep grazing can cause heather loss and so damage grouse shooting. They argued that Langholm was atypical in that large sheep stocks had been allowed to destroy much heather, thereby leading indirectly to unusually many harriers. Most grouse-moors remain heather-dominated, and so there is no general case for changing the law to allow the legal killing of harriers.

27 Golden eagles kill adult and nestling hen harriers (Mick Marquiss, pers. comm. 2005). The idea that harriers avoid eagle hunting grounds is based on anecdotal observations that harriers are sparse where eagles hunt, but there is no experimental evidence to support this.

28 A golden eagle in Scotland eats about 230g per day (Brown & Watson, 1964). Surprisingly, the food intake of hen harriers has not, to our knowledge, been documented, and so we estimated it from their weight according to a graph relating food intake to body-weight in raptors (Fig. 26 in Borchtchevski, 1993), at 80g per day.

29 The Game Conservancy Trust (Fletcher, 2006) is carrying out an experiment at Otterburn in northern England, designed to find whether legal predator killing benefits upland birds, including grouse, waders and passerines. On two moors, crows, foxes, stoats and weasels are being killed by keepers, while on two other moors they are being left alone. In 2004, the treatment on the first two moors was reversed in a crossover design. An emerging result is that grouse and also waders may benefit from legal predator control.

30 Moss & Weir, 1987.

31 Keeper John Brownleigh's observations, noted at the time by RM.

32 In Glen Tanar, the first pine marten was seen in 1990 by head keeper James Oswald, accompanied by an Austrian guest who was familiar with the species. Noted at the time by RM.

33 Baines et al., 2004.

34 In 2006, brood counts showed 13 hens and 41 poults (over three poults per hen, as good as the best breeding at Glen Tanar in the 1970s) on Forestry Commission ground at Glenmore, where foxes and crows but not pine martens were killed (count done by Game Conservancy Trust for Scottish Natural Heritage). To judge from signs on the ground, martens were abundant. Hence capercaillie can breed well in the presence of pine martens.

35 Putman, 2000.

36 Zalewski et al., 1995; Kauhala et al., 2000; Saniga, 2002.

37 Calculations (Borchtchevski, 1993) suggest that they kill some 0.8 per cent of the spring (April–June) population of capercaillie, 0.1–0.2 per cent in August, 0.5 per cent in autumn (September–November) and 1.3 per cent in winter (December–March). Young were included from late July to early August, when they were first counted, while eggs and chicks were excluded.

38 Kokeš & Wolf, 1978.

39 Also, a general increase of capercaillie and black grouse in Bohemia during the second half of the nineteenth and the early twentieth centuries bore no relation to records of killed pine martens, and was attributed to an improvement in general conditions for woodland grouse.

40 Kurki et al., 1997. The authors measured breeding success as the proportion of hens with broods, and when assessing correlations they divided Finland into 32 blocks of 100 × 100km.

41 Marcström et al., 1988.

42 Small et al., 1993; Lindström et al., 1994; Smedshaug et al., 1999. Lindström et al. (1995a) calculated that foxes killed 13 per cent of radio-tagged martens each year.

43 Pine martens may have less impact than foxes upon grouse abundance, because foxes are usually commoner than pine martens or

because, individual for individual, foxes do more damage than pine martens.
44 Pulliainen & Ollinmäki, 1996.
45 Synonyms *Davainea* and *Raillietina*.
46 We know of only one case – a hen capercaillie from Morangie near Tain in March 2004. Alasdair Wood did the post-mortem and Justin Irvine identified the worms.
47 Other widespread parasites not mentioned further include caecal coccidia, gapeworms, tissue-dwelling threadworms and various blood parasites.
48 Watson & Shaw (1991) found 8 per cent of 83 ptarmigan from the Cairngorms and the Cairnwell hills to have *P. urogalli*.
49 Holstad *at al.*, 1994.
50 Two captive greyhens, experimentally dosed with *T. tenuis* larvae, subsequently produced no worm eggs in their droppings (Jennifer Shaw & Moss, unpublished results).
51 Newborn & Foster, 2002.
52 Possible side-effects of introducing powerful and long-lasting drugs into moorland ecosystems have not been studied.
53 Shaw, 1988b.
54 Wissler & Halvorsen, 1977.
55 Semenov-Tyan-Shanskiy, 1960.
56 Delahay, 1999.
57 Dick & Burt, 1971.
58 Thomas, 1985. The only effect detected was that the weight of the small intestine increased with the volume of tapeworms that it held.
59 Cobbold, 1873.
60 Leiper, 1910.
61 Committee of Inquiry on Grouse Disease, 1911.
62 In domestic ruminants, by contrast, *Trichostrongylus* species usually survive only three to four months.
63 Moss *et al.*, 1993b.
64 Once successfully ingested, an infective larva still has to establish itself in a caecum. The bird defends itself by engulfing larvae in mucus produced by specialised goblet cells in the walls of the caeca, or through antibodies produced by its immune system. About one ingested larva in three survives to become an adult worm. Having survived the bird's defences, the larva buries itself in the wall of a caecum, where it causes swelling and bleeding. Whitish scar tissue remains as a memento of serious damage caused by many larvae developing simultaneously.
65 Jenkins *et al.*, 1963.
66 Shaw, 1988a; Delahay *et al.*, 1995.
67 This has a practical consequence. It is common practice to count adult worms in grouse that are shot on grouse-moors in autumn, in order to assess the likelihood of disease the following spring and to decide on this basis whether to deploy anthelmintics. Such prognoses are most reliable if they are based on counts of adult worms from young birds, because these are most likely to reflect the numbers of arrested larvae. They would be yet more reliable if based on counts of arrested larvae, but counting these is time-consuming and expensive.
68 Moss *et al.*, 1990a.
69 Dougall, 1875, and many others since.
70 Hudson *et al.*, 1998.
71 Hudson *et al.*, 1998.
72 For each moor separately, the mean bag was subtracted from each year's bag and the result divided by the standard deviation.
73 To do this, we used data from another moor (not shown here), which confirmed that the number of birds on the ground was correlated with the bag. First, the number of birds on the ground was estimated as the intercept of a regression of birds on the ground versus the bag (excluding years with no shooting). Second, from a regression of bag versus the number of birds on the ground, the bag expected from the estimated number of birds on the ground was assessed. Third, the expected bag (680) was expressed as a proportion of the mean bag (1,576). This proportion was then multiplied by the mean bag for each moor separately.

74 Note that bags included young and old birds combined, so that any real differences between moors could have been solely due to differences in breeding success and not to differences in breeding density.

75 Lambin *et al.*, 1999.

76 Good experimental evidence (Redpath *et al.*, 2006a) confirms that anthelmintics improve breeding success and can moderate cyclic declines, but do not prevent cycles. The evidence suggests to us that drugs increased the birds' condition and hence the average density about which their numbers fluctuated. Densities of drugged populations at first increased relative to controls, but then declined as they began to cycle about the new average. This occurred on moors where caecal threadworm burdens were initially high or initially low. Evidently, caecal threadworms were not necessary for cyclic declines. Bird densities increased with the increased carrying capacity, but then declined as populations begin to cycle about the new carrying capacity. The authors give a woollier interpretation, apparently driven by a desire to placate proponents of the parasite hypothesis.

77 Mougeot & Redpath, 2004; Mougeot *et al.*, 2004, 2005c; Seivwright *et al.*, 2005.

78 This approach resolves a brief paradox that arises when considering the respective roles of parasites and aggressive behaviour in cyclic population declines. Increased parasite burdens reduce aggressiveness (Fox & Hudson, 2001; Mougeot *et al.*, 2005b) and contribute to some population declines. But population declines induced by social behaviour require increased aggressiveness. At first glance, it might seem that this contradicts the idea that behavioural declines can accompany higher parasite burdens. What seems to happen is that the increased testosterone that goes along with increased aggressiveness depresses the birds' immunity to parasites, allowing increased parasite burdens. More aggressiveness and more parasites together result in birds losing condition. Hence, during a cyclic decline, increased aggressiveness and more parasites can go together at the expense of reduced condition (Moss, Piertney, MacColl, Lock, Mougeot, Leckie, Bacon, Redpath, Dallas & Lambin, unpublished ms).

79 The virus is of the genus *Flavivirus*, family Flaviviridae.

80 Louping (Scots and north English) means 'leaping', and is pronounced 'lowping', with the 'ow' as in 'how'. Of infected sheep, 5–60 per cent develop clinical signs that vary from slight unsteadiness to sudden death.

81 Other strains of tick-borne encephalitis have a mortality rate of up to 10 per cent in humans, and half of the survivors suffer brain damage or epilepsy.

82 Reid, 1975.

83 McGuire *et al.*, 1998.

84 There is no evidence of virus transmission via eggs, so only larvae, nymphs and adult ticks act as vectors for the virus. Red grouse, like sheep, develop high concentrations of virus, but most die once infected, and so play a lesser role in sustaining the disease. Other known hosts do not develop virus concentrations consistently high enough to infect feeding ticks.

85 Jones *et al.*, 1997.

86 Reid *et al.*, 1980.

87 Gilbert *et al.*, 2000.

88 Laurenson *et al.*, 2000.

89 Reid & Moss, 1980.

90 This would seem especially likely if the little-studied willow ptarmigan that live at the edge of boreal-forest bogs are immune to tick-borne encephalitis. Tick-borne encephalitis is a disease of woodland and presumably infects woodland willow ptarmigan, which are not reported to show ill-effects. Hence, like black grouse and capercaillie, they are probably immune. The same argument applies to other woodland birds such as hazel grouse.

91 Laurenson *et al.*, 2003. The prevalence of louping-ill antibodies in shot young red

grouse also declined, lagging behind the tick decline by about two years. The number of young grouse reared per hen showed no change, but the number reared by hens on a control site declined somewhat, so allowing the authors to claim that breeding success had 'increased on the treatment site relative to the control'. Even so, there was no change in the total number of grouse on the treatment site relative to the control.

92 There were few red deer, but many roe deer were killed. This was a practical management trial with no control and little monitoring.

## CHAPTER 14

1 The NAO index used here (www.cgd.ucar.edu/cas/jhurrell/nao.stat.winter.html as at 10 September 2006) is a measure of the average difference in atmospheric pressure between Portugal and Iceland from December to March in the preceding winter. This reflects the strength and persistence of the Azores area of high pressure, which is associated with mild weather and westerly winds in western Europe. Although measured in winter, the index is associated with weather during the following summer.

2 Tetraonid is short for Tetraonidae, the family that includes all world grouse.

3 Past British shooting records give some indication of the density of birds on the ground, but vary more widely from year to year than the densities of birds present. They are least reliable at low densities, because shooting effort is then low or even nil. For black grouse and capercaillie, bags became increasingly unreliable indicators of density in the last few decades of the twentieth century, as densities and shooting effort declined. Indeed, capercaillie are now protected and black grouse are usually spared. There is no evidence that rock ptarmigan declined, but shooting effort on them did, as shooters became less willing to walk long distances on steep rocky hills in search of their quarry. Bags of red grouse still give a useful indication of density, but there are recent examples of bags declining owing to fewer shooting days, not fewer birds shot per day (François Mougeot, unpublished data).

4 We allowed for the autocorrelation structure of each series by means of an AR1 filter. This involved calculating the regression of bags in year $t$+1 upon bags in year $t$, and using the residuals in cross-correlations. A similar analysis using differenced data (the natural logarithm of the bag in year $t$+1, minus that in year $t$) gave comparable results. Similar results were obtained with unfiltered data (bottom left).

5 Moran, 1952.

6 Mackenzie (1952) collated bags of all four species throughout the UK and Moran (1952) analysed his data. It is not clear exactly which estates were included in the subset 'a number of Scottish estates' that Moran used for his correlation analysis. We use Mackenzie's manuscript data for 'east central Scotland', which include mostly the Atholl estates plus Cortachy and Ardvorlich, because these involved few changes in land ownership. After the Second World War, many changes in land management occurred, notably afforestation, and so we make no attempt to update the records.

Our measure of tetraonid abundance was a score based on the first component from a principal components analysis of the bag data. The weightings (eigenvectors) for the first component were 0.490, 0.427, 0.537 and 0.424 for red grouse, rock ptarmigan, capercaillie and black grouse, respectively. Its eigenvalue was 2.196, and it explained 55 per cent of the total variance.

The equation selected by Akaike's information criterion (AIC) from NAO data going back to year $t$–4 was:

$$PC1_t = 0.242(NAO_t) + 0.150(NAO_{t-1}) + 0.245(NAO_{t-2}) + 0.244(NAO_{t-3}) - 0.114$$

where $NAO_t$ is the value of the NAO in year $t$, and so on. ($R^2 = 0.26$; SE of parameter estimates and intercept respectively = 0.087, 0.086, 0.085, 0.087, 0.156; $P$ = 0.007, 0.08, 0.005, 0.007, 0.469).

When past values of PC1 were included in the selection, the equation now selected by AIC was:

$$PC1_t = 0.592(PC1_{t-1}) - 0.201(PC1_{t-3}) + 0.138(NAO_t) + 0.184(NAO_{t-2}) + 0.157(NAO_{t-3}) - 0.046$$

($R^2 = 0.50$; SE for parameter estimates and intercept respectively = 0.099, 0.101, 0.076, 0.074, 0.077, 0.129; $P$ = 0.0001, 0.050, 0.073, 0.015, 0.046, 0.723). The autoregressive part of this equation [$PC1 = 0.592(PC1_{t-1}) - 0.201(PC1_{t-3})$ ...] represents a strongly damped cycle. This is an empirical autoregressive equation with weather covariates. The analysis will be published in full elsewhere.

7 François Mougeot, unpublished.
8 Grouse might be influenced by weather aspects that are reflected in the NAO but not measured at meteorological stations. Hence this question might be more difficult to answer than it seems.
9 Williams et al. (2004) claimed that ten-year cycles in North American ruffed grouse, sharp-tailed grouse and greater prairie chicken 'collapsed' from north to south through 'period lengthening' in the south. Bizarrely, however, they gave no evidence of cycles with periods longer than ten years, and no evidence of any cycle collapsing. Haydon et al. (2002) analysed data on bags of red grouse from 289 moors. They found that 25 per cent of these showed evidence of cycle periods of more than 15 years. But, in essence, both papers redefine 'cycle' as fluctuations that differ from 'white noise' (random variations). Thus a 20-year segment from a sine curve with a 20-year period would qualify as 'cyclic'. Most previous workers have been more conservative, regarding cycles as regular fluctuations that recur at least three to four times. The 20-year fluctuation in Fig. 172 recurs three times, but we call it 'equivocal', partly because there were only three repetitions and partly because the regularity broke down after the third one. As data accumulate, there is increasing evidence of long-period fluctuations in grouse numbers – very possibly reflecting similar fluctuations in weather or perhaps socio-economic conditions. Whether these are called 'cycles' or not is partly a matter of semantics. But the causes of long-term fluctuations may well differ from those of short-term ones.
10 Unpublished data via P. J. O'Hare.
11 The trend was quadratic. Autocorrelations were of residuals after trend removal.
12 Note that bags declined just before the Second World War, and remained low during and after it, even though the Republic of Ireland was neutral during the conflict. Other equivocal evidence suggests cycles of about 30 years in Scotland.
13 Watson et al., 2000.
14 Watson et al., 1998.
15 Watson et al., 1998. 'Amplitude' can be measured as the ratio of the number at a peak to the number at a trough.
16 Watson et al., 2000. An 'omnibus' model uses a few early years' numbers to prime itself and then makes further predictions using predicted (not observed) numbers. To avoid delusions of foresight, we call 'pre'-dictions made after the event 'post'-dictions.
17 Watson et al., 2000. The original, empirical model was:

$$X_t = 0.74 X_{t-1} - 0.22 X_{t-4} + 0.094 J_{t-1} + 0.132 J_{t-2} + 0.091 J_{t-4} + k + \varepsilon_t$$

where $X_t$ is the natural logarithm of numbers in year $t$, and $J$ represents June temperature (°C). The constant $k$ merely establishes the average about which the population fluctuates, and $\varepsilon_t$ is random error. Just as good a representation (Watson & Moss, unpublished ms) is given by the simpler

$X_t = X_{t-1} - 0.4X_{t-2} + 0.1J_{t-1} + 0.1J_{t-2} + 0.1J_{t-4} + k + \varepsilon_t$

The autoregressive part of the equation ($X_t = X_{t-1} - 0.4X_{t-2}$) represents delayed density dependence, so that the resulting trajectory is a damped cycle modified by June temperatures. The postdictions shown in Fig. 174, from the original model, fluctuate less widely than observed numbers (compare axes). This can be remedied by substituting $J^a$ for $J$, where $1 < a \geq 2$. This implies that ptarmigan numbers responded disproportionately to extreme temperatures.

18 A 'damped' cycle diminishes in amplitude and eventually reaches constant numbers unless perturbed again, much like a swing that needs an occasional push to keep it going. The push in the case of models of damped population cycles can be given by weather. Density dependence means that numbers tend to go up following low numbers and down following high numbers. 'Delayed' density dependence means that there is a lag, or 'delay', in this effect, which can give rise to cycles.

19 Watson et al., 2000.

20 Watson et al., 1998.

21 The number of cock ptarmigan on the Cairnwell (the 40ha study area C in Watson et al., 1998) was:

$X_t = X_{t-1} - 0.4X_{t-2} - 0.025L_t + 0.023L_{t-1} + 0.016T_t - 0.25$

where $X_t$ is $\log_e$(ptarmigan) in spring $t$, $L$ is the number of days in May that snow was lying at both 750m and 1,300m, and $T$ is the mean daily temperature during 1–10 May. ($R^2$ = 0.59; SE for parameters and intercept 0.011, 0.011, 0.006 and 0.66, respectively; $P$ = 0.036, 0.043, 0.012 and 0.71). The autoregressive part of the equation ($X_t = X_{t-1} - 0.4X_{t-2}$) is the same as for the Cairngorms, but the weather covariates differ.

For cock grouse on an adjacent area (27ha), the number was:

$X_t = X_{t-1} - 0.4X_{t-2} - 0.038L_t + 0.028L_{t-1} + 0.012T_t - 0.47$

($R^2$ = 0.66; SE for parameters and intercept 0.011, 0.010, 0.010 and 0.63, respectively; $P$ = 0.002, 0.014, 0.049 and 0.46) (Watson & Moss, unpublished ms).

22 Burroughs, 1992.

23 An 'empirical' equation describes fluctuations in density without implying that the explanatory variables (e.g. density, weather) directly cause the observed fluctuations. A 'mechanistic' equation specifies the mechanism(s) involved (e.g. diet quality, breeding effort, territorial behaviour).

24 Lotka, 1925; Volterra, 1926.

25 Dougall, 1875.

26 Each mechanism comprises a two-part system in which one population consumes the other, thereby inducing a time lag in the way in which each affects the density of the other. Relevant 'trophic levels' include vegetation, herbivores and their predators. A vegetation-herbivore interaction is therefore a two-part 'trophic interaction', as is a herbivore-predator one. 'Extrinsic processes' is a broader category that includes trophic interactions, plus interactions with other processes that are external to the population, such as weather.

27 Chitty, 1967.

28 'Spacing behaviour' causes animals to space themselves out, for instance territorial behaviour or dispersal.

29 Doebeli & Hauert, 2005; Burtsev & Turchin, 2006. Models are usually based on game theory. Authors are typically interested in the conditions that enable cooperation to occur and hence in modelling the proportion of individuals cooperating or being selfish (called 'defecting' in the jargon of game theory). A side-effect of such models, which is of interest to population dynamics, is that total population size is often unstable. For our purposes, it is useful to note that selfishness often involves aggression.

30 Empedocles (of Akagras in Sicily, fifth century BC) broadly anticipated this mechanism in his formulation of the cosmic cycle. He posited two forces, personified as

Love (*Philia*, a force of attraction and combination) and Strife (*Neikos*, a force of repulsion and separation). These two forces engage in an eternal battle for domination, and each prevails in turn in an endless cycle. Biologists, however, while reprising Empedocles, have largely overlooked him. See www.utm.edu/research/iep/e/empedocl.htm (as at 18 December 2007).

31 Unstable dynamics can result in regular cycles, chaotic fluctuations and erratic fluctuations, in which, for example, periods of regular cycles are interspersed with irregular fluctuations. In an unstable grouse population, increases tend to follow increases, and declines to follow declines, more often than expected by chance. Hence an unstable population has alternating periods of increase and periods of decline. If successive fluctuations are regular, the population shows cycles.

32 This is true in principle. In practice, more complex procedures may be necessary if false conclusions are to be avoided (Royama, 1992). Indeed, all the tests used to detect density dependence in annual counts are flawed, and should be used cautiously.

33 Or, equivalently, the reproductive rate declining with increasing density. All mortality factors combined determine a closed population's annual growth rate and hence its annual fluctuations.

34 Formerly often called 'surplus', such birds are frequently now called 'floaters'. 'Non-territorial' is more objective but less evocative.

35 Unless the number of deaths exceeds the number of floaters (Watson & Moss, 1990).

36 Watson & Moss, 1980; Watson *et al.*, 1984b. *See also* Chapter 9. Spring dispersal of young birds occurs in all well-studied grouse species. In red grouse, cocks and hens that have been observed to disperse have left established territories. In 1975, RM watched a marked territorial pair preparing to disperse on Kerloch. During three successive evenings in April, they stopped feeding about half an hour before other pairs, stood together looking around for a few minutes, and then flew off together out of sight. They did not return on the fourth evening or later that spring. It seemed that they spent some days exploring a potential new home before finally moving from the old one.

37 Exceptions occur. For example, it is normal for peripheral parts of a moor to be unoccupied by territories when densities are low. This does not affect the argument, because some birds still fail to get territories on the main part of the moor (Watson & Moss, unpublished observations).

38 Also, resources and crowding interact, such that animals at a given density behave as if they are less crowded if they are on areas with better food or cover, and so they attain higher average densities.

39 Moss *et al.*, 1994.
40 Mougeot *et al.*, 2003b.
41 Watson *et al.*, 1994.
42 Lock, 2003.
43 MacColl *et al.*, 2000.
44 Lock, 2003.
45 Matthiopoulos *et al.*, 2003, 2005.
46 Crowding has two aspects. First is the obvious one of density. Second, successful kin selection during the increase phase of a cycle leads to cocks in the peak population being closely related to each other. Hence, close relatives (fathers, sons, siblings) gain less by cooperating with each other than was formerly the case, and so become less tolerant and more aggressive (Moss, Piertney, MacColl, Lock, Mougeot, Leckie, Bacon, Redpath, Dallas & Lambin, unpublished ms).
47 Although developed independently, the kinship hypothesis seems to be a special case of the general result (*see* above in main text) that unstable dynamics can stem from competition between individuals that are behaving either cooperatively or selfishly.
48 Matthiopoulos *et al.*, 2003.
49 A 'risky' experiment tests a crucial prediction that is not expected according to competing hypotheses.

50 Mougeot et al., 2003a, b, 2005c.
51 Breeding densities peaked at all areas in spring 2002. In England, 2002 was $t+2$; in Scotland, 2002 was $t+1$ at Glen Dye, and $t+2$ at Edinglassie. In Scotland, the implanted birds reared more young than the controls in summer $t+1$, although this was significant only at Glen Dye. Consequently, although density declined more on implanted areas between autumn $t+1$ and spring $t+2$, at Glen Dye it was not lower in spring $t+2$ than in spring $t+1$. Data from Mougeot et al., 2003b, 2005c.
52 Risky predictions based on the kinship hypothesis were made and confirmed. However, as is scientifically proper, the experiment was designed to refute the kinship hypothesis, and hence if the predictions had been 'falsified' (found to be incorrect), the hypothesis would have been disproved. The hypothesis survived this challenge, but the observed experimental results could in principle have been achieved through other, so far unspecified, biological mechanisms. Fortunately, it is not necessary to know the exact nature of the biological mechanism in order to make further deductions about the consequences of the experiment.
53 Matthiopoulos et al., 2003, 2005.
54 The mathematical form of the two-way interaction between recruitment and density does not specify the precise biological mechanism, and does encompass mechanisms other than the kinship hypothesis. The main result of the modelling makes sense. Imagine that a population at a constant 'equilibrium' density is then perturbed slightly, so causing density to change. (If a population is perturbed at equilibrium density it tends to return to that level.) The birds' territorial, aggressive behaviour will change in response to the perturbation in density. If the proportional change in aggressiveness is greater than the proportional change in density, then unstable population fluctuations, including cycles, can ensue.
55 Watson et al., 1994.
56 Moss & Watson, 2001.
57 Bergerud, 1970a; Bergerud & Gratson, 1988; Moss & Watson, 2001.
58 Watson et al., 1998. The 'fitness' of a parent is the number of its offspring that is recruited into the following year's breeding population. Similar speculation can explain why unmated, territorial, cock red grouse and ptarmigan form a higher proportion of the population during cyclic declines on poor soils. The speculation is that unmated cocks might invest fewer physiological resources into reproduction during declines, and more into the aggressiveness necessary for survival.
59 Watson et al., 1984a.
60 Watson et al., 1994.
61 Or, more precisely, to join that part of the population that will eventually breed.
62 Jenkins et al., 1964.
63 Moss et al., 2000a.
64 Redpath & Thirgood, 1997.
65 Watson & Moss, 2004. The ski development also became an all-year tourist attraction.
66 Watson & Moss, 2004.
67 Moss et al., 1996.
68 Ibid.
69 'Intrinsic' processes are defined under 'Population Dynamics and Behaviour' in the main text.
70 Burroughs, 1992.
71 Lindström et al., 1995b.
72 Kauhala & Helle, 2002.
73 Moss et al., 1996.
74 Siivonen, 1952.
75 From evidence to date, this is mainly loss of young grouse over winter.
76 Nielsen, 1999.
77 Dougall, 1875.
78 Jenkins et al., 1963.
79 Moss et al., 1996.
80 Moss & Watson, 2001.

## CHAPTER 15

1 For example, for red grouse, Lovat, 1911; Watson & Miller, 1976; Hudson & Newborn, 1995.
2 Storch, 2000a, b.
3 Watson & Moss, 1982. 'Game management is a synthesis of tradition, game biology, conservation and politics.'
4 Gordon, 1915; Andreev, 1988a.
5 Freuchen & Salomonsen, 1960.
6 Freuchen, 1936. 'I aimed at the breast, pulled the trigger, and the head and neck flew off! We could not have been happier had we shot a bear or a walrus...It was wonderful, and when we finished there were few feathers and no bones left over.'
7 Potapov & Flint, 1987; Holder & Montgomerie, 1993a.
8 Weeden, 1963.
9 Bags of blackgame and capercaillie have declined in several countries (Appendix in Lovel, 1979; Storch, 2000a; Observatoire des Galliformes de Montagne, 2002). Bags of these species and of rock ptarmigan have fallen in the Lombardy Alps, Italy (Luc Wauters, pers. comm. 2005, courtesy of Trento Province Wildlife Service), and Russian bags of all four species have decreased since 1935 (Flint, 1995; Gabuzov, 1995).
10 Jenkins et al., 1963; Hudson, 1992.
11 Mercer & McGrath, 1963.
12 Cattadori et al., 2003. These time-series analyses sought to extract general patterns from many bag records. On 60 independently managed hunting estates in England and Scotland, bags per $km^2$ were recorded, and grouse were counted in late summer on smaller sample sections so as to calculate density before hunting. That bags were a good proxy for density was applicable, because there were so many areas and years. The scatter of graphed data-points amongst areas and years was wide, and so, although bags could be used to extract general patterns, they were not such a good proxy for density on individual moors or study areas.
13 Watson & Miller, 1976; Hudson, 1992.
14 Jenkins et al., 1963. Numbers varied 2.8-fold, and bags 8.5-fold. In an English case, hen numbers in spring varied sixfold, and bags over 1,000-fold (Hudson et al., 1992, 1998; Lambin et al., 1999).
15 Hudson et al., 1998.
16 For example, Leslie, 1911.
17 At Bogeney, Forres.
18 Chapman, 1889; MacPherson, 1896.
19 Three Durham men who went becking before 1939 told this to AW in the 1960s at the Castle Howard game fair.
20 Hannon et al., 1998.
21 Bergerud & Huxter, 1969; Bergerud, 1970b, 1972.
22 Steen, 1989; Lindén, 1991; Hörnell-Willebrand, 2005.
23 Brøseth & Pedersen, 2000.
24 Hörnell-Willebrand, 2005. Arithmetic means on four areas were 10–38 per cent, and extremes within areas and years were almost zero and just over 50 per cent, respectively.
25 Gudmundsson, 1960; Nielsen & Pétursson, 1995. Up to 150,000 were taken annually in 1995–2000 (Holder et al., 2004).
26 Ellison et al., 1982, 1989.
27 Silliman & Gutsell, 1958.
28 Unlike birds, a given weight of fish can comprise a few whoppers, or many tiddlers of the same age.
29 Ellison, 1991; Hannon et al., 2003.
30 Bergerud & Huxter, 1969; McGowan, 1975.
31 Ellison et al., 1988.
32 Moss et al., 1979b.
33 Jones, 1982b.
34 Lande et al., 1995; Sæther et al., 1995; Steen & Erikstad, 1996; Hudson & Dobson, 2001; Willebrand & Hörnell, 2001; and Jonzén et al., 2003, all provide mathematical models.
    Smith & Willebrand (1999) believed that deaths of shot willow ptarmigan on a Swedish area were mostly if not totally additive. This seems dubious. They put radios on birds on

three areas, one of which was open to hunters. Aside from the small samples, a snag was that the main difference between the areas was a sharp fall in survival on the open area in the first ten days of hunting. Birds were radio-tagged from late July to mid-August, close to the opening of hunting on 25 August, and radios could have made their carriers more easily shot. Compensatory immigration of untagged birds could have occurred into the shot area. Also, birds on the shot area suffered heavier losses to predators in autumn and winter, and survived worse outside the hunting season, suggesting to us that the shot area had poorer habitat.

To avoid overhunting, Hörnell-Willebrand (2005) suggested limits to hunter effort, or the creation of sanctuaries where hunting is banned, but overhunting is not proven. Sanctuaries have been well known and publicised for centuries, e.g. in Scotland during the 1800s and 1900s to avoid overhunting of red deer.

35 Pedersen *et al.*, 2003. Hunting initially reduced autumn density. The main variation in winter survival occurred amongst areas. When this was excluded, inverse density dependence in winter survival became evident (i.e. better survival followed greater autumn density, the opposite of what is usually understood by density-dependent survival). Hence winter survival was low when density at the start of the winter was low, and so should fall following the initial reduction from shooting. In other words, the effect of hunting should have been neither compensatory nor additive, but multiplicative. In fact, however, winter survival did not fall following hunting, and instead there was weak compensation. When all study blocks were analysed over all years, only one-third of hunting deaths in autumn were found to be compensated, but this had a huge variance and was only just statistically significant. The authors stated that compensation disappeared when analysis was carried out by year or by block, but readers cannot assess this because the data on it were not presented. The authors regarded the apparent disappearance of compensation as probably due to long-distance juvenile dispersal that had not been affected by hunting, but this was speculation. It is as likely that compensation occurred in relation to equilibrium densities that varied from year to year.

36 Core areas have good habitat, and high density and breeding success. Sinks (often called marginal areas) have poor habitat, where populations suffer greater mortality and in most years are maintained by net immigration from core areas (*see* Chapter 14).

37 Conversion to grass has been unsubsidised for over 20 years, but some farmers still practise it with their own money. Most changes of use in farming and forestry are termed 'permitted development', and are not subject to planning approval. Grants to private owners for tree planting continue.

38 Less favoured areas (LFAs) include UK hill farms and 85 per cent of Scotland's land cover. Subsidies per ewe or cow in such areas were greater than in other areas for decades. These subsidies 'represent the annual disposable income of many LFA farms' (Mowle & Bell, 1988), so, without subsidies, farmers would have no money to live on. In 2001–2 the Scottish Executive gave over £61 million for LFA livestock (Scottish Executive, 2001, Annual Report), and in 2000–1 gave £56 million to Forest Enterprise, whose deficit was £49 million after timber sales. Under the EU's Common Agriculture Mid Term Review, payments per animal have been replaced in England by the Single Farm Payment, based on average annual subsidies to the farm in 2000–2. Scottish policy is a halfway house, with intentions to move to English regulations by 2010. As a result, British sheep numbers have fallen. In Scotland, June numbers dropped by nearly 2 per cent in 2006–7, and the Scottish ewe total fell from 2.9 million in

1995 to 2.3 million in 2007 (*The Scotsman*, 2007, farming notes).
39 Watson & Miller, 1976; Stewart & Lance, 1983, 1991; Hudson, 1986a, 1992.
40 Watson, unpublished. At Rottal, Glen Muick and Dinnet.
41 Lovat, 1911.
42 Phillips et al., 1992b; Straker-Smith & Phillips, 1994; Phillips & Watson, 1995.
43 Turner, 2004.
44 Watson, 1990.
45 The aim may be to destroy the habitat of ticks, which are the latest scapegoat for the woes of the grouse-shooting industry. There is no evidence that burning reduces tick burdens.
46 Stocks of hill cattle have also risen locally, but generally have fallen in recent decades.
47 Hardin, 1968.
48 Phillips, 1990a.
49 Watson, 1989.
50 Welch, 1984a, b. Heather declines if more than 30 per cent of annual production is eaten (Palmer et al., 2004).
51 Watson, unpublished.
52 Jenkins & Watson, 2001.
53 Watson & Miller, 1976; Phillips & Wilson, 1987; Scandrett & Gimingham, 1991; Hartley, 1993.
54 Harrison, 1997.
55 Chicks often fly into bracken as escape cover, and moulting adults also use it as cover. The birds occasionally eat it as well. The main costs are that it replaces much heath, provides no winter food and supports many ticks.
56 Marrs & Pakeman, 1995; Brown, 1997; Taylor, 1997.
57 Watson, unpublished. Disturbed by cultivation, machines, cattle or red deer.
58 Lovat, 1911; Lawton, 1990. Lovat wrote of 'the one great law of stock-management', to 'determine the number of birds that the moor will carry safely in March, and irrespective of all other considerations kill the birds down to that limit'.

59 Watson & Miller, 1976.
60 Despite shooting only moderate bags per day, it is possible to achieve a large bag for the season, even a record bag, by shooting day after day for weeks. This can lead to overshooting, not caring for tomorrow's stock, and should be avoided. On the other hand, traditional practices are often overcautious, with the result that peaks are reached and declines follow. There is a happy medium.
61 Wilson, 1990.
62 Moss et al., 1996.
63 Ogilvy & Bayer, 2003; Strutt & Parker, 2003.
64 Watson, 1978. 'Also, grouse shooting is part of the… tourist industry, brings in hard currency from abroad, and stands on its own feet economically, whereas hill sheep farming has to be subsidised by the taxpayer.' Some other kinds of tourism were unsubsidised, but unlike shooting they benefited from grants by state-funded tourist boards, sports councils and enterprise bodies.
65 Land-value taxation would be paid by landowners, based on valuation at current permitted uses. Without it, as is the case in Britain at the time of writing, a stony field that is earmarked for housing leaps in value because of society's past efforts in developing nearby land, developments that usually occurred without the owner paying for any improvements. Such leaps would end with land-value taxation, which would fix the sale price by law, based on the pre-development valuation. It would reduce or eliminate tax on income and investment, and is already in use across regions in several countries such as Denmark, Finland and the USA, and in Hong Kong and some towns such as in Virginia and other US states. Robin Harper MSP, Scottish Green Party, in 2003 tabled a motion that the Scottish Executive investigate 'the contribution that land value taxation could make to the cultural, economic, environmental and democratic renaissance of Scotland'. This was passed (Scottish

Parliament published proceedings, 30 January 2003, 17736).

66 Nethersole-Thompson & Watson, 1974; Watson & Hinge, 1989; Watson, 1990.

67 Watson, 2003.

68 There are signs that the FC is beginning to turn the corner, partly because east European timber is undercutting prices, but also partly because many of the new generation of forest managers are dedicated to wildlife.

69 Scottish Office, 1995. The EU Habitats Directive states that exploitation of mountain hares must be 'compatible with their being maintained at favourable conservation status', and prohibits 'indiscriminate means capable of causing local disappearance of, or serious disturbance to, populations'. Scotland's Moorland Forum (2003), produced by Scottish Natural Heritage states: 'We do not recommend the indiscriminate culling of hares... In certain circumstances, however, culling may be considered necessary.'

70 J. Watson, 1997; Ratcliffe, 1980; Etheridge et al., 1997; Raptor Round Up, 2000, 2001, 2002 (Supplements to *Scottish Birds*).

71 Watson et al., 1989.

72 Van Oss, 1987. Increased persecution followed frequent Game Conservancy overstatements about raptors keeping down grouse, in articles, annual reviews, broadcasts and talks to keepers. Its *Scottish Grouse Research Project Appeal* (1985) stated, 'It could be that predation is now holding numbers down... Firstly we must establish the facts; the implications and the recommendations which might follow are another matter... Some recommendations may imply changes in management practices; some could involve changes in legislation.'

73 Collins, 1988. This article contained an interview of Lord Mansfield, Scottish Office minister in 1979–83.

74 Ratcliffe, 1980, 1990.

75 Heather Trust, 1995.

76 As the Scottish Rural Property and Business Association was then called.

77 Gordon, 1996; Watson, 1996b.

78 Thomson, 1996.

79 Potts, 1998. Thirgood et al. (2000a) argued, 'Capping harrier densities in some areas while allowing them to breed in other areas where they are currently persecuted could enhance their conservation status and ensure the continued maintenance of heather moorland in private ownership.' This would be hard to monitor, and hence unrealistic. A 'policy paper' (British Association for Shooting and Conservation, Scotland, 2004) advocates arguments to 'support the contention that, in the first place, control of certain raptor species' eggs be licensed'.

80 Thirgood et al., 2000a.

81 Watson, 1998. The estate neglected muirburn and shepherding, resulting by 1969 in much old heather, vulnerable to heather beetles. By 1988 these pests had devastated much heather, grass took over, and grouse were few. The grass led to more voles and meadow pipits, the main food of hen harriers, and harriers increased. Study elsewhere had shown that harriers took a bigger percentage of a grouse population at low grouse density than at high. Hence, had heather been well managed, grouse would have been commoner, voles and pipits fewer, harriers fewer, and harrier predation on grouse lower.

82 Thirgood et al., 2000b; Redpath et al., 2001.

83 Phillips, 1990b. At the time of writing, dovecotes were being used on Glen Feshie grouse-moor.

84 Scottish Raptor Study Groups, 1997; Mackey et al., 2001; Whitfield et al., 2003; Scottish Agricultural Science Agency, 2004; Royal Society for the Protection of Birds, 2007 and earlier annual reports.

85 The Nature Conservation (Scotland) Act 2004.

86 Fairburn & Reynolds, 2004. A keeper who pleaded guilty to poisoning 22 buzzards and a goshawk (Royal Society for the Protection of Birds, 2005) could have been fined £5,000 per bird or jailed for six months; he was fined £5,500.

87 Scottish Gamekeepers Association, 2004. The Moorland Gamekeepers Association was established earlier and now covers mainly England and Wales.

88 Edwards, 2004. The RSPB filmed a keeper taking a peregrine from a nest, but a sheriff ruled the evidence inadmissible because the RSPB 'trespassed... It seems to me it is illegal to enter onto someone's land without permission.' Yet it was not, and is not, an offence to be on private land in Scotland. On delays, see Anonymous (2004).

89 MacMillan, et al., 2001; Price et al., 2002.

90 Galbraith et al. (2003) wish gamekeepers and conservationists to meet 'in a dialogue which is open and inclusive'. And 'Perhaps the conservation community could recognise more freely and openly the valuable role that land managers, gamekeepers and others play in the overall well-being of our countryside.' Reviewing the book, Rae (2004) wrote, 'surely the editors, as scientists, could have written in a tight scientific rather than fuzzy politically correct style'.

91 Redpath et al., 2004.

92 MacMillan, 2002; Hunt, 2003; Zonfrillo, 2005.

93 Scottish Raptor Study Groups, 1998. The Minister of Agriculture wrote, 'wildlife crime is a crime against us all... I regard it as a national disgrace that illegal persecution is still taking place on such a scale.'

94 Watson et al., 1995. This was a review about Ireland, but it applies equally to Britain.

95 Phillips & Watson, 1995.

96 Scottish Natural Heritage, 1994; Hunt, 2003.

97 Usher & Thompson, 1993. Heather moorland supports some globally uncommon plants and animals.

98 On UK moors in Environmentally Sensitive Areas or regional schemes, owners received £2.9 million in 2001. Many owners are exempt from inheritance tax, for allowing public access on their land and preserving the landscape. In 1993, 63 Scottish estates (not just grouse-moors) had been exempted of £20 million since 1983, and the total exemption for UK estates over the same period was £150 million (Cant, 1993). Exemptions for public access are anomalous in Scotland, where it is not an offence to be on private land. To cut predation on moorland birds, Scottish Natural Heritage (2004a) pays owners to kill crows and foxes on designated sites, at £40 per crow trap and £280 annually per keeper, and its consultation paper suggested extending the scheme. Scottish Raptor Study Groups (Patrick Stirling-Aird, *in litt.* to SNH, 2006) queried whether this produces public benefit and whether predators affect birds more than other management that might be grant-aided.

99 Ormiston, 1988.

100 A grouse-moor has a capital value, based on the gross average annual value of a brace of shot grouse, annual bags being totalled over the previous ten years and averaged. Grouse-moors in the 1950s sold at £40–50 per brace (Bates, 2002). In March 2005, the going rate for Scottish moors with driven grouse was £3,600 per brace, and for moors with red deer £25,000 per stag (David Strang Steel, pers. comm. 2006). Hence land with an average bag of 1,000 brace would fetch £3.6 million. This excludes houses for keepers and fenced woods without red deer. By August 2007, values had risen by about 40 per cent, and renting a moor was costing about £130 per brace of grouse shot.

101 National Audit Office, 1986.

102 Watson, 1990, 1997a; Beaumont et al., 1995; Ramsay, 1996.

103 For example, farmland that was abandoned during the early 1900s in the eastern USA was the site of classic research on plant succession, as trees colonised old fields. Magnificent woodland now occurs there.

104 Doyle, 1990.

105 Henderson, 1992.

106 Usher & Thompson, 1993.

107 Phillips & Watson, 1995.

108 Steven & Carlisle, 1959; Nethersole-Thompson & Watson, 1974.

109 Sannikov, 1983; Bonan & Shugart, 1989.

Forester Alexei Blagovidov told RM that Scots pinewood in Komi burns on average once per 80 years, in ground fires that move slowly because there is so little fuel in the lichen-dominated understorey. Hence on average an old pine survives four fires before dying. Apart from at rare lichen-dominated sites, such slow fires could not occur in Scottish pinewood because there is too much understorey fuel. Bakaeva & Galanin (1985) note lichen dominance in Komi. Sannikov (1985) describes 'low' fires that burn the understorey but leave old trees alive. Prolonged elimination of fire increases shade-tolerant dark conifers (spruce) and broadleaved trees, except on very freely drained or rocky soils and bogs.
110 Lack of fire in Swedish boreal forest reduces blaeberry, cowberry and pine regeneration (Nilsson & Wardle, 2005).
111 Mironov, 1984; Bonan & Shugart, 1989.
112 Watson, 1977a.
113 Mason et al., 2004, 'it would be wise to maintain fire protection measures at the highest practical level'.
114 For example, the decline in distribution of capercaillie (Catt et al., 1998).
115 Watson, 1997b.
116 Watson, unpublished, in Argyll (Sunart oaks) and Deeside (birch, aspen and hazel). FC staff told AW that this practice was widespread in the 1950s–70s.
117 Sluie Estate had mid-Deeside's biggest aspen wood and most juniper-rich birchwood.
118 Mason et al., 2004. 'Continuous cover' in this FC handbook excludes continuous mature or old trees, and after final thinning it leaves isolated scattered trees without old growth or deadwood. By continuous we mean a wood remaining as a woodland landscape and habitat.
119 Family Corvidae, e.g. crow, raven, rook, jackdaw, magpie and chough.
120 Watson & Moss, 2004. In Bavaria also, corvids have increased near mountain huts used by summer tourists (Storch & Leidenberger, 2003).
121 Meile, 1982; Delmas, 1986; Ellison, 1986; Miquet, 1990; Novoa et al., 1990; Magnani, 1995.
122 Zeitler, 2000.
123 e.g. Picozzi (1971) on grouse-moors.
124 Lee et al., 1992; Baddeley et al., 1994.
125 de Smidt, 1995.
126 Langan et al., 1995.
127 Porkert, 1979, 1991.
128 This pollution greatly exceeded that in Britain, because of poorly controlled heavy industry nearby.
129 AW sent unhatched ptarmigan eggs from Ben Macdui in May 1966. The Government Chemist found a trace of pp'-DDE, unmeasurable in parts per million, and no other toxic residues.
130 McSmith, 2006.
131 Hannon et al., 1998.
132 Langlois & Langis, 1995.
133 Pedersen & Myklebust, 1993; Wren et al., 1994.
134 Hulme & Jenkins, 1998.
135 Whittington & Edwards, 2003.
136 Hill et al., 1998; Ellis & Good, 2005; Royal Society for the Protection of Birds, 2005.
137 Harrison et al., 2001.
138 Kullman, 2005.

# Bibliography

The following reviews give many other references: Bent, 1932; Bergerud & Gratson, 1988; Cramp & Simmons, 1980˙; Hannon et al., 1998˙; Holder & Montgomerie, 1993a˙; Johnsgard, 1983˙; Lindström et al., 1998˙; Mikheev, 1948; Potapov, 1985˙; Semenov-Tyan-Shanskiy, 1960; Storch, 2000a˙, 2001˙. (˙Also contain distribution maps.)

Alamany, O. & de Juan Monzon, A. (1983). Le grand tétras (*Tetrao urogallus*) et le Lagopède (*Lagopus mutus*) dans les Pyrénées orientales iberiques. *Acta Biologica Montana* **2–3**, 363–81.

Alatolo, R. V., Höglund, J., Lundberg, A. & Sutherland, W. J. (1992). Evolution of black grouse leks – female preferences benefit males in larger leks. *Behavioral Ecology* **3**, 53–9.

Alatolo, R. V., Burke, T., Dann, J., Höglund, J., Lundberg, A., Moss, R. & Rintamäki, P. T. (1996). Paternity, copulation disturbance and female choice in lekking black grouse. *Animal Behaviour* **52**, 861–73.

Alexandrova, V. D. (1970). The vegetation of the tundra zones in the USSR and data about its productivity. In: *Productivity and Conservation in Northern Circumpolar Lands* (eds W. A. Fuller & P. G. Kevan), pp. 93–114. International Union for Conservation of Nature & Natural Resources, Morges, Switzerland.

Alexandrova, V. D. (1988). *Vegetation of the Soviet Polar Deserts*. Cambridge University Press, New York.

Allen, H. M. (1977). Abnormal parental behaviour of captive male willow grouse *Lagopus l. lagopus*. *Ibis* **119**, 199–200.

Andersen, J.-E. (1986). Habitat selection by willow grouse *Lagopus l. lagopus* in central Norway. *Fauna Norvegica Series C* **9**, 82–94.

Andersen, R., Steen, J. B. & Pedersen, H. C. (1984). Habitat selection in relation to age of willow grouse *Lagopus l. lagopus* broods in central Norway. *Fauna Norvegica Series C* **7**, 90–94.

Andersen, R., Pedersen, H. C. & Steen, J. B. (1986). Annual variation in movements of sub-alpine hatched willow ptarmigan *Lagopus l. lagopus* broods in Central Norway. *Ornis Scandinavica* **17**, 180–2.

Anderson, P. W. & Yalden, D. W. (1981). Increased sheep numbers and loss of heather moorland in the Peak District, England. *Biological Conservation* **20**, 195–213.

Andreev, A. V. (1975). Zimiyaia zeni i pitanie tundryanoy kuropatki (*Lagopus mutus*) na kraynem Severo-Vostoke SSSR. *Zoologicheskiy Zhurnal* **54**, 727–33.

Andreev, A. V. (1978). Temperature conditions

in snow cavities of the hazel grouse (*Tetrastes bonasia kolymensis* But.). *Soviet Journal of Ecology* **9**, 454–5 (translated by Plenum Publishing Corporation; Russian original in *Ékologiya* **5** (1977), 93–5).

Andreev, A. V. (1980). *Adaptatsiya Ptits k Zimnim Usloviyam Subarktiki*. Akademii Nauka SSR, Moscow; translation of contents, tables and figure legends into English by R. Visa, Helsinki, in *Tilfeldige Oversettelser fra DVF Viltforskningen* **1**. Direktoratet for Vilt og Ferskvannsfisk, Trondheim.

Andreev, A. V. (1982). Seasonal trends and some features of biology of willow grouse populations in north-east Asia. *Proceedings of the Second International Symposium on Grouse*, 96–105.

Andreev, A. V. (1988a). The ten year cycle of the willow grouse of Lower Kolyma. *Oecologia* **76**, 261–7.

Andreev, A. V. (1988b). Ecological energetics of Palearctic Tetraonidae in relation to chemical composition and digestibility of their winter diets. *Canadian Journal of Zoology* **66**, 1382–8.

Andreev, A. V. (1991). Winter adaptations in the willow ptarmigan. *Arctic* **44**, 106–14.

Andrews, C. W. (1920). Remains of the great auk and ptarmigan in the Channel Islands. *Annals & Magazine of Natural History* **9**, 166.

Anonymous (1840). The capercaillie. *Sporting Review* **3**, 274–7.

Anonymous (2004). Gamekeeper case dropped. *Press & Journal*, 11 October.

Anvik, J. O. (1969). The development and maintenance of homeothermy in the rock ptarmigan (*Lagopus mutus*). BSc thesis, University of British Columbia, Vancouver.

Aulie, A. (1976a). The pectoral muscles and the development of thermoregulation in chicks of willow ptarmigan. *Comparative Biochemistry & Physiology* **53A**, 343–6.

Aulie, A. (1976b). The shivering pattern in an arctic (willow ptarmigan) and a tropical bird (bantam hen). *Comparative Biochemistry & Physiology* **53A**, 347–50.

Aulie, A. & Moen, P. (1975). Metabolic thermoregulatory responses in eggs and chicks of willow ptarmigan (*Lagopus lagopus*). *Comparative Biochemistry & Physiology* **53A**, 605–9.

Averis, A., Averis, B., Birks, J., Horsfield, D., Thompson, D. & Yeo, M. (2004). *An Illustrated Guide to British Upland Vegetation*. Joint Nature Conservation Committee, Peterborough.

Baddeley, J. A., Thompson, D. B. A. & Lee, J. A. (1994). Regional and historical variation in the nitrogen content of *Racomitrium lanuginosum* in Britain in relation to atmospheric nitrogen deposition. *Biological Conservation* **84**, 189–96.

Bailey, E. P. (1993). Introduction of foxes to Alaskan islands: history, effects on avifauna, and eradication. *US Fish & Wildlife Service Resource Publication* **191**. US Fish & Wildlife Service.

Bain, C. (1987). *Native Pinewoods in Scotland. A Review 1957–87*. Royal Society for the Protection of Birds, Edinburgh.

Baines, D. (1991). Long term changes in the European black grouse population. *Game Conservancy Review* **17**, 157–8.

Baines, D. (1996). The implications of grazing and predator management on the habitats and breeding success of black grouse *Tetrao tetrix*. *Journal of Applied Ecology* **33**, 145–53.

Baines, D. & Andrew, M. (2003) An experiment to assess the value of fence markings in reducing the frequency of collisions with deer fences by woodland grouse. *Biological Conservation* **110**, 169–76.

Baines, D., Goddard, J. & Hudson, P. (1991). Capercaillie in Scotland. In: *The Game Conservancy Review of 1990*, pp. 153–6. The Game Conservancy, Fordingbridge.

Baines, D., Sage, R. B. & Baines, M. M. (1994). The implications of red deer grazing to ground vegetation and invertebrate communities of Scottish native pinewoods. *Journal of Applied Ecology* **31**, 776–83.

Baines, D., Wilson, I. A. & Beeley, G. (1996). Timing of breeding in black grouse and capercaillie *Tetrao urogallus* and distribution of insect food for the chicks. *Ibis* **138**, 181–7.

Baines, D., Blake, K. & Carradine, J. (2000). Reversing the decline: a review of some black grouse conservation projects in the United Kingdom. *Cahiers d'Ethologie* **20**, 217–34.

Baines, D., Moss, R. & Dugan, D. (2004). Capercaillie breeding success in relation to forest habitat and predator abundance. *Journal of Applied Ecology* **41**, 59–71.

Bakaeva, M. V. & Galanin, A. V. (1985). Ecological role of the lichen cover in white-moss pine forests. *Soviet Journal of Ecology* **16**, 69–75 (translated from the Russian original in *Ékologiya* **2** (1985), 25–30).

Bannerman, D. A. (1963). *The Birds of the British Isles. Vol. 12*. Oliver & Boyd, Edinburgh.

Barclay-Estrup, P. (1970). The description and interpretation of cyclical processes in a heath community. II. Changes in the biomass and shoot production during the *Calluna* cycle. *Journal of Ecology* **58**, 243–9.

Barnes, R. F. W. (1987). Long-term declines of red grouse in Scotland. *Journal of Applied Ecology* **24**, 735–41.

Bart, J. & Earnst, S. L. (1999). Relative importance of male and territory quality in pairing success of male rock ptarmigan (*Lagopus mutus*). *Behavioral Ecology & Sociobiology* **45**, 355–9.

Barth, G. B. (1855). Fortegnelse over de i Lofoten og Vesteraalen forekommende fuglearter. *Nytt Magasin for Naturvitenskap* **8**, 1–71.

Bates, R. (2002). No easy pickings in this sporting life. *Scotland on Sunday*, 27 October.

Baxter, E. V. & Rintoul, L. J. (1953). *The Birds of Scotland*. Oliver & Boyd, Edinburgh.

Beaumont, D., Dugan, D., Evans, G. & Taylor, S. (1995). Deer management and tree regeneration in the RSPB reserve at Abernethy Forest. In: *Our Pinewood Heritage* (ed. J. R. Aldhous), pp. 186–95. Forestry Commission, Royal Society for the Protection of Birds & Scottish Natural Heritage, Edinburgh.

Beeston, R., Baines, D. & Richardson, M. (2005). Seasonal and between-sex differences in the diet of black grouse *Tetrao tetrix*. *Bird Study* **52**, 276–81.

Bennett, K. D. (1995). Post-glacial dynamics of pine (*Pinus sylvestris* L.) and pinewoods on Scotland. In: *Our Pinewood Heritage* (ed. J. R. Aldhous), pp. 23–39. Forestry Commission, Edinburgh.

Bennett, K. D. (1996). Late-Quaternary vegetation dynamics of the Cairngorms. *Botanical Journal of Scotland* **48**, 51–63.

Bent, A. C. (1932). Life histories of North American gallinaceous birds. *Bulletin of the US National Museum* **162**; reprinted 1963, Dover Publications, New York.

Bergerud, A. T. (1970a). Population dynamics of the willow ptarmigan *Lagopus lagopus alleni* L. in Newfoundland 1955 to 1965. *Oikos* **21**, 299–325.

Bergerud, A. T. (1970b). Vulnerability of willow ptarmigan to hunting. *Journal of Wildlife Management* **34**, 282–5.

Bergerud, A. T. (1972). Changes in the vulnerability of ptarmigan to hunting in Newfoundland. *Journal of Wildlife Management* **36**, 104–9.

Bergerud, A. T. (1988). Population ecology of North American grouse. In: *Adaptive Strategies and Population Ecology of Northern Grouse* (eds A. T. Bergerud & M. W. Gratson), pp. 578–685. University of Minnesota Press, Minneapolis.

Bergerud, A. T. & Gratson, M. W. (eds) (1988). *Adaptive Strategies and Population Ecology of Northern Grouse*. University of Minnesota Press, Minneapolis.

Bergerud, A. T. & Huxter, D. S. (1969). Effects of hunting on willow ptarmigan in Newfoundland. *Journal of Wildlife Management* **33**, 866–70.

Bergerud, A. T. & Mercer, W. E. (1966). Census of the willow ptarmigan in

Newfoundland. *Journal of Wildlife Management* **30**, 101–13.

Bergerud, A. T. & Mossop, D. H. (1984). The pair bond in ptarmigan. *Canadian Journal of Zoology* **62**, 2129–41.

Bergerud, A. T., Peters, S. S. & McGrath, R. (1963). Determining sex and age of willow ptarmigan in Newfoundland. *Journal of Wildlife Management* **27**, 700–11.

Bernard-Laurent, A. (1987). Le régime alimentaire du lagopède alpin *Lagopus mutus* (Montin 1776): synthèse bibliographique. *Gibier Faune Sauvage* **4**, 321–47.

Beschel, R. A. (1970). The diversity of tundra vegetation. In: *Productivity and Conservation in Northern Circumpolar Lands* (eds W. A. Fuller & P. G. Kevan), pp. 85–92. International Union for Conservation of Nature & Natural Resources, Morges, Switzerland.

Beshkarev, A. B., Blagovidov, A., Sokolski, S. & Hjeljord, O. (1995). Populations of capercaillie and hazel grouse in large natural and logged forests in northern Russia, 1950–92. *Proceedings of International Symposia on Grouse* **6**, pp. 12–18. World Pheasant Association, Reading.

Bevanger, K. (1995) Estimates and population consequences of tetraonid mortality caused by collisions with high tension power lines in Norway. *Journal of Applied Ecology* **32**, 745–53.

Birks, H. J. B. (1988). Long-term ecological change in the British uplands. In: *Ecological Change in the Uplands* (eds M. B. Usher & D. B. A. Thompson), pp. 17–56. Blackwell, Oxford.

Birse, E. L. & Robertson, L. (1970). *Assessment of Climatic Conditions in Scotland. 2. Based on Exposure and Accumulated Frost*. Macaulay Institute for Soil Research, Aberdeen.

Black, J. M. (1964). The ecology of land use in Scotland. *Transactions of the Botanical Society of Edinburgh* **40**, 1–12.

Bliss, L. C. (1970). Primary production within arctic tundra ecosystems. In: *Productivity and Conservation in Northern Circumpolar Lands* (eds W. A. Fuller & P. G. Kevan), pp. 77–85. International Union for Conservation of Nature & Natural Resources, Morges, Switzerland.

Bliss, L. C., Svoboda, J. & Bliss, D. I. (1984). Polar deserts, their plant cover and plant production in the Canadian High Arctic. *Holarctic Ecology* **7**, 305–24.

Boggs, C., Norris, E. & Steen, J. B. (1977). Behavioural and physiological temperature regulation in young chicks of the willow grouse (*Lagopus lagopus*). *Comparative Biochemistry & Physiology* **58A**, 371–2.

Bolam, G. (1912). *The Birds of Northumberland and the Eastern Borders*. Blair, Alnwick.

Bonan, G. B. & Shugart, H. H. (1989). Environmental factors and ecological processes in boreal forests. *Annual Review of Ecology & Systematics* **20**, 1–28.

Borchtchevski, V.G. (1993). *Population Biology of the Capercaillie. Principles of the Structural Organization*. Izdatelstvo TSNIL Ochotnichjego chosjaistva zapovednikov, Moscow (in Russian with English summary).

Borchtchevski, V. G. & Gubar, J. P. (2003). The deficiency of main spring foods of capercaillie *Tetrao urogallus*. Is it possible? In: *Proceedings of the Third International Symposium on the Dynamics of Game Animals in Northern Europe (16–20 June 2002, Sortavala, Karelia, Russia)* (eds P. I. Danilov & V. B. Zimin), pp. 38–42. Petrozavodsk.

Borchtchevski, V. G., Hjeljord, O., Wegge, P. & Sivkov, A. V. (2003). Does fragmentation by logging reduce grouse reproductive success in boreal forests? *Wildlife Biology* **4**, 275–82.

Borisov, A. A. (1965). *Climates of the U.S.S.R.* Oliver & Boyd, Edinburgh & London.

Bossert, A. (1980). Winterökologie des Alpenschneehuhns (*Lagopus mutus*, Montin) im Aletschgebiet, Schweizer Alpen. *Der Ornithologische Beobachter* **77**, 121–66.

Bossert, A. (1995). Bestandsentwicklung und Habitatnutzung des Alpenschneehuhn

*Lagopus mutus* im Aletschgebiet (Schweizer Alpen). *Der Ornithologische Beobachter* **92**, 307–12.

Bossert, A., Marti, C. & Niederhauser, F. (1983). Zur Bestandsentwicklung des Alpenschneehuhns (*Lagopus mutus* Montin) im Aletschgebiet (Zentralalpen) von 1973–1983. *Bulletin Murithienne* **100**, 39–49.

Boudarel, P. (1988). Recherches sur l'habitat et le comportement spatial du lagopède alpin (*Lagopus mutus*) dans les Pyrénées-occidentales Françaises. *Gibier Faune Sauvage* **5**, 227–54.

Bowker, G. & Bowker, C. (2003). *Lake Vyrnwy Black Grouse Project*. Final report to Severn Trent Water, by Lagopus Services.

Brander, R. B. (1965). Factors affecting dispersion of ruffed grouse during late winter and spring on the Cloquet Forest Research Center, Minnesota. PhD thesis, University of Minnesota.

Braun, C. E. & Rogers, G. E. (1971). The white-tailed ptarmigan in Colorado. *Technical Publication* **27**. Division of Game, Fish & Parks, State of Colorado.

Braun, C. E., Martin, K. & Robb, L. A. (1993). White-tailed ptarmigan (*Lagopus leucurus*). *The Birds of North America* (eds A. Poole & F. Gill), **68**. Academy of Natural Sciences, Philadelphia, and American Ornithologists' Union, Washington DC.

Braun, E. J. & Duke, G. E. (1989). Conclusion to the First International Avian Cecal Symposium. *Journal of Experimental Zoology*, Supplement **3**, 127–8.

Brenot, J-F., Ellison, L., Rotelli, L., Novoa, C., Calenge, C., Léonard, P. & Ménoni, E. (2005). Geographic variation in body mass of rock ptarmigan *Lagopus mutus* in the Alps and Pyrenees. *Wildlife Biology* **11**, 281–5.

Briggs, J. M., Spielmann, K. A., Schaafsma, H., Kintigh, K. W., Kruse, M., Morehouse, K. & Schollmeyer, K. (2006). Why ecology needs archaeologists and archaeology needs ecologists. *Frontiers in Ecology & Environment* **4**, 180–8.

British Association for Shooting and Conservation (2004). *Raptor Policy Paper*. BASC Scotland, Dunkeld.

Brittas, R. (1988). Nutrition and reproduction of the willow grouse *Lagopus lagopus* in central Sweden. *Ornis Scandinavica* **19**, 49–57.

Brockie, K. (1993). *Mountain Reflections*. Mainstream Publishing, Edinburgh.

Brodsky, L. M. (1986) Correlates and consequences of the mating tactics of male rock ptarmigan (*Lagopus mutus*). PhD thesis, Queen's University, Kingston, Ontario.

Brodsky, L. M. (1988a). Mating tactics of male rock ptarmigan, *Lagopus mutus*: a conditional mating strategy. *Animal Behaviour* **36**, 335–42.

Brodsky, L. M. (1988b). Ornament size influences mating success in male rock ptarmigan. *Animal Behaviour* **36**, 662–7.

Brodsky, L. M. & Montgomerie, R. D. (1987). Asymmetrical contests in defence of rock ptarmigan territories. *Behavioral Ecology & Sociobiology* **21**, 267–72.

Brøseth, H. & Pedersen, H. C. (2000) Hunting effort and game vulnerability studies on a small scale: a new technique combining radio-telemetry, GPS and GIS. *Journal of Applied Ecology* **37**, 182–90.

Brown, L. (1993). *The New Shorter Oxford English Dictionary*. Clarendon Press, Oxford.

Brown, L. H. & Watson, A. (1964). The golden eagle in relation to its food supply. *Ibis* **106**, 78–100.

Brown, R. (1997). The biology and ecology of bracken. *The Heather Trust Annual Report* **1997**, 24–6.

Browning, M. R. (1979). Distribution, geographic variation, and taxonomy of *Lagopus mutus* in Greenland and northern Canada. *Dansk Ornithologisk Forenings Tidsskrift* **73**, 29–40.

Buckland, S. T., Bell, M. V. & Picozzi, N. (1990). *The Birds of North-east Scotland*. North-east Scotland Bird Club, Aberdeen.

Burroughs, W. J. (1992). *Weather Cycles: Real or Imaginary?* Cambridge University Press, Cambridge.

Burtsev, M. & Turchin, P. (2006). Evolution of cooperative strategies from first principles. *Nature* **440**, 1041–4.

Butler, F. H. (1917). *Through Lapland with Skis and Reindeer.* T. Fisher & Unwin, London.

Caizergues, A. & Ellison, L. N. (1998a). Age-specific reproductive performance of black grouse *Tetrao tetrix* females. *Bird Study* **47**, 344–51.

Caizergues, A. & Ellison, L. N. (1998b). Impact of radio-tracking on black grouse *Tetrao tetrix* reproductive success. *Wildlife Biology* **4**, 205–12.

Caizergues, A. & Ellison, L. (2002). Natal dispersal and its consequences in black grouse *Tetrao tetrix*. *Ibis* **144**, 478–87.

Calder, G. (1972). *A Gaelic Grammar.* Gairm, Glasgow.

Calladine, J., Baines, D. & Warren, P. (2000). Restoration of moorland habitat in northern England: A conservation initiative. *Cahiers d'Ethologie* **20**, 521–32.

Calladine, J., Baines, D. & Warren, P. (2002). Effects of reduced grazing on population density and breeding success of black grouse in northern England. *Journal of Applied Ecology* **39**, 772–80.

Campbell, B. & Lack, E. (1985). *A Dictionary of Birds.* Poyser, Calton.

Campbell, R. W., Dawe, N. K., McTaggart-Cowan, I., Cooper, J. M., Kaiser, G. W. & McNall, M. C. E. (1990). *The Birds of British Columbia. Vol. 2. Diurnal Birds of Prey through Woodpeckers.* Royal British Columbia Museum, Victoria.

Campbell, S., Smith, A., Redpath, S. & Thirgood, S. (2002). Nest site characteristics and nest success in red grouse *Lagopus lagopus scoticus*. *Wildlife Biology* **8**, 169–74.

Cant, A. (1993). Inheritance tax exemptions – is the public getting a fair return? *Wild Land News* **29**, 13.

Casotti, G. & Braun, E. (2004). Protein location and elemental composition of urine spheres in different avian species. *Journal of Experimental Zoology* **301A**, 579–87.

Catt, D. C., Baines, D., Picozzi, N., Moss, R. & Summers, R. W. (1998). Abundance and distribution of capercaillie in Scotland 1992–1994. *Biological Conservation* **85**, 257–67.

Cattadori, I. M. & Hudson, P. J. (1999). Temporal dynamics of grouse populations at the southern edge of their distribution. *Ecography* **22**, 374–83.

Cattadori, I. M. & Hudson, P. J. (2000). Are grouse populations unstable at the southern edge of their range? *Wildlife Biology* **6**, 213–18.

Cattadori, I. M., Merler, S. & Hudson, P. J. (2000). Searching for mechanisms of synchrony in spatially structured gamebird populations. *Journal of Animal Ecology* **69**, 620–38.

Cattadori, I. M., Haydon, D. T., Thirgood, S. J. & Hudson, P. J. (2003). Are indirect measures of abundance a useful index of population density? The case of red grouse harvesting. *Oikos* **100**, 439–46.

Caulfield, S. (1981). Forest clearance and land use in Mayo around 3000 B.C. *Irish Forestry* **38**, 92–100.

Caulfield, S. (1983). The Neolithic settlement of N. Connaught. In: *Landscape Archaeology in Ireland* (eds T. Reeves-Smyth & F. Hamond), pp. 195–215. BAR British Series **116**, Oxford.

Chandler, A. C. (1916). A study of the structure of feathers, with reference to their taxonomic significance. *University of California Publications in Zoology* **13**, 243–446.

Chapman, A. (1889). *Bird-life of the Borders.* Gurney & Jackson, London; reprinted (1990), Spredden Press, Northumberland.

Chapman, A. (1897). *Wild Norway.* Gurney & Jackson, London.

Chapman, A. (1924). *The Borders and Beyond.* Gurney & Jackson, London.

Chitty, D. (1967). The natural selection of self-regulatory behaviour in animal populations. *Proceedings of the Ecological Society of Australia* **2**, 51–78.

Clench, M. H. & Matthias, J. R. (1995). The avian cecum: a review. *Wilson Bulletin* **107**, 93–121.

Cobbold, T. S. (1873). Contributions to our knowledge of grouse disease. *The Veterinarian* **46**, 161–72.

Cobham Resource Consultants (1997). *Countryside Sports and their Economic, Social and Conservation Significance.* Standing Conference on Countryside Sports, Reading.

Collins, P. (1988). Return of the grouse. *Insight Spring* **38**–40.

Committee of Inquiry on Grouse Disease (1911). *The Grouse in Health and in Disease.* Vols 1 & 2. Smith, Elder & Co., London.

Compton, J. E. & Boone, R. D. (2000). Long-term impacts of agriculture on soil carbon pools and nitrogen dynamics in New England forests. *Ecology* **81**, 2314–30.

Cook, M. (1992). *The Birds of Moray and Nairn.* Mercat Press, Edinburgh.

Cosgrove, P. & Oswald, J. (2001). Western capercaillie captures in snares. *Scottish Birds* **22**, 28–30.

Côté, I. M. & Sutherland, W. J. (1995) The scientific basis for predator control for bird conservation. *English Nature Research Report* **144**. English Nature, Peterborough.

Cott, H. B. (1940). *Adaptive Coloration in Animals.* Methuen, London.

Cotter, R. C. (1991). Population attributes and reproductive biology of rock ptarmigan (*Lagopus mutus*) in the central Canadian Arctic. MSc thesis, University of Alberta, Edmonton.

Cotter, R. C. (1999). The reproductive biology of rock ptarmigan (*Lagopus mutus*) in the central Canadian Arctic. *Arctic* **52**, 23–32.

Cotter, R. C., Boag, D. A. & Shank, C. C. (1992). Raptor predation on rock ptarmigan (*Lagopus mutus*) in the central Canadian Arctic. *Journal of Raptor Research* **26**, 146–51.

Cramp, S. & Simmons, K. E. L. (eds) (1980). *Handbook of the Birds of Europe, the Middle East and North Africa: the Birds of the Western Palearctic.* Vol. 2. Oxford University Press, Oxford.

Crisp, D. T. (1966). Input and output of minerals for an area of Pennine moorland: the importance of precipitation, drainage, peat erosion and animals. *Journal of Applied Ecology* **3**, 327–48.

Cumming, W. G. (1994). Scotland's uplands – the future. *Scottish Forestry* **48**, 110–11.

Cymdeithas Edward Llwyd (1994). Cyfres Enwau Creaduriaid a Planhigion. 1. Creaduriaid Asgwrn-cefn Cymdeithas Edward Llwyd Wasg y Lolfa Tal y Bont. List of species names.

Darling F. F. (1947). *Natural History in the Highlands and Islands.* Collins, London.

Darling, F. F. (1955). *West Highland Survey.* Oxford University Press, Oxford.

Davidson, D. A. & Carter, S. P. (2003). Soils and their evolution. In: *Scotland after the Ice Age* (eds K. J. Edwards & I. B. M. Ralston), pp. 45–62. Edinburgh University Press, Edinburgh.

Davidson, D. A. & Simpson, I. A. (1984). The formation of deep topsoils in Orkney. *Earth Surface Processes and Landforms* **9**, 75–81.

de Smidt, J. T. (1995). The imminent destruction of north-west European heaths due to atmospheric nitrogen deposition. In: *Heaths and Moorland: Cultural Landscapes* (eds D. B. A. Thompson, A. J. Hester & M. B. Usher), pp. 206–17. Her Majesty's Stationery Office, Edinburgh.

Deer Commission for Scotland (2001). *Annual Report 2000–2001.* Deer Commission for Scotland, Inverness.

Delahay, R. J. (1999). Cestodiasis in the red grouse in Scotland. *Journal of Wildlife Diseases* **35**, 250–8.

Delahay, R. J., Speakman, J. R. & Moss, R. (1995). The energetic consequences of parasitism: effects of a developing infection of *Trichostrongylus tenuis* (Nematoda) on red grouse (*Lagopus lagopus scoticus*) energy balance, body weight and condition. *Parasitology* **110**, 473–82.

**Delmas, M.** (1986). I. Résultats de six années de dénombrements de Tétras-lyre au chant en Haute-Tarentaise (Savoie). In: *Journées d'Étude 'Tétras-lyre et ski'* (ed. H. Jaffeux), pp. 17–21. Parc National de la Vanoise, Chambéry.

**Dementiev, G. P. & Gladkov, N. A.** (1952). *Ptitsy Sovietskogo Soyuza*. Vol. 4. Nauka, Moscow.

**Desmet, J.-F.** (1988a). Densité de peuplement en période de reproduction, du Lagopède alpin (*Lagopus mutus helveticus*, Thieneman 1829) en haute vallée du Giffre (Haute-Savoie). *Gibier Faune Sauvage* **5**, 447–58.

**Desmet, J.-F.** (1988b). Le Lagopède alpin (*Lagopus mutus helveticus*, Thieneman 1829) dans Les Alpes Francaises Septentrionales descriptif de l'habitat en haute vallée du Giffre (Haute-Savoie, France). *Actes du Colloque Galliformes du Montagne, 14 et 15 décembre 1987, Grenoble, Isère*, 129–61.

**Devine, T. M.** (2004). *The Great Highland Famine*. Donald, Edinburgh.

**Dick, T. A. & Burt, M. D. B.** (1971). The life cycle and seasonal variation of *Davainea tetraoensis* Fuhrmann 1919, a cestode parasite of ruffed grouse, *Bonasa umbellus* (L.). *Journal of Experimental Zoology* **205**, 195–204.

**Dickie, I., Hughes, J. & Esteban, A.** (2006). *Watched Like Never Before. The Local Economic Benefits of Spectacular Bird Species.* Royal Society for the Protection of Birds, Sandy, Bedfordshire.

**Dimbleby, G. W.** (1952). Soil regeneration in the north-east Yorkshire moors. *Journal of Ecology* **40**, 331–41.

**Dimcheff, D. E., Drovetski, S. V. & Mindell, D. P.** (2002). Phylogeny of Tetraoninae and other galliform birds using mitochondrial 12S and ND2 genes. *Molecular Phylogenetics and Evolution* **22**, 203–15.

**Doebeli, M. & Hauert, C.** (2005). Models of cooperation based on the Prisoner's Dilemma and the Snowdrift game. *Ecology Letters* **8**, 748–66.

**Dougall, J. D.** (1875). *Shooting, its Appliances, Practice and Purpose*. Sampson Low, Marston Low & Searle, London.

**Doyle, G. J.** (ed.) (1990). *Ecology and Conservation of Irish Peatlands*. Royal Irish Academy, Dublin.

**Drovetski, S. V.** (1992). New data on functional significance of the toe corneous fringe of the tetraonid birds. *Zoologichesky Zhurnal* **71**, 100–9 (in Russian).

**Drovetski, S. V.** (2003). Plio-Pleistocene climatic oscilations [sic], Holarctic biogeography and speciation in an avian subfamily. *Journal of Biogeography* **30**, 1173–81.

**Dunaeva, T. N. & Kucheruk, V. V.** (1941). Materiali po ekologii nazemiikh pozvonotsnik tundri yuzhnogo Yamala. *Materiali pozn. Fauni i Flori SSSR, Izdanie Moskva, o-va isp. priroda* **4**, 1–80.

**Dupouey, J. C., Dambrine, E., Laffite, J. D. & Moares, C.** (2002). Irreversible impact of past land use on forest soils and biodiversity. *Ecology* **83**, 2978–84.

**Duriez, O., Sachet, J.-M., Ménoni, E., Pidancier, N., Miguel, C. & Taberlet, P.** (2007) Phylogeography of the capercaillie in Eurasia: what is the conservation status in the Pyrenees and Cantabrian Mounts? *Conservation Genetics* **8**, 513–26.

**Dwelly, E.** (1971). *The Illustrated Gaelic-English Dictionary*. 7th edn. Gairm, Glasgow.

**Dyck, J.** (1979). Winter plumage of the rock ptarmigan: structure of the air-filled barbules and function of the white colour. *Dansk Ornithologisk Forenings Tidsskrift* **73**, 41–58.

**Eason, P. & Hannon, S. J.** (1994). New birds on the block: new neighbors increase defensive costs for territorial male willow ptarmigan. *Behavioral Ecology & Sociobiology* **34**, 419–26.

**Edwards, K. J. & Whittington, G.** (2003). Vegetation change. In: *Scotland after the Ice Age* (eds K. J. Edwards & I. B. M. Ralston), pp. 63–82. Edinburgh University Press, Edinburgh.

**Edwards, R.** (2004). Gamekeepers move to block RSPB legal action. *Sunday Herald* 27 June.

**Elison, G. W.** (1980). Food habits study of rock ptarmigan (*Lagopus mutus*) on Amchitka Island, Alaska. MSc thesis, Washington State University.

**Ellis, N. E. & Good, J. E. G.** (2005). Climate change and effects on Scottish and Welsh mountain ecosystems: a conservation perspective. In: *Mountains of Northern Europe* (eds D. B. A. Thompson, M. F. Price & C. A. Galbraith), pp. 99–102. The Stationery Office, Edinburgh

**Ellison, L.** (1966). Seasonal foods and chemical analysis of winter diet of Alaskan spruce grouse. *Journal of Wildlife Management* 30, 729–35.

**Ellison, L.** (1986). Tétras-lyre et ski à Prorel (Hautes-Alpes). Résultats de 5 années de comptage au chant. In: *Journées d'Étude 'Tétras-lyre et ski'* (ed. H. Jaffeux), pp. 3–4. Parc National de la Vanoise, Chambéry.

**Ellison, L. N.** (1991). Shooting and compensatory mortality in tetraonids. *Ornis Scandinavica* 22, 229–40.

**Ellison, L. N., Magnani, Y. & Corti, R.** (1982). Comparison of a hunted and three protected black grouse populations in the French Alps. *Proceedings of the Second International Conference on Grouse*, 175–87.

**Ellison, L. N., Léonard, P. & Ménoni, E.** (1988). Effect of shooting on a black grouse population in France. In: *Atti del I Convegno Nazionale dei Biologi della Selvaggina. Supplemento Ricerchi Biolog. Selvaggina* (eds M. Spagnesi & S. Toso), 14, 117–28. Also in French in the more accessible *Gibier Faune Sauvage* 5, 309–20.

**Ellison, L. N., Ménoni, E. & Léonard, P.** (1989). Déplacements d'adultes de tétras lyre (*Tetrao tetrix*) en automne et en hiver. *Gibier Faune Sauvage* 6, 245–60.

**Emison, W. B. & White, C. M.** (1988). Foods and weights of the rock ptarmigan on Amchitka, Aleutian Islands, Alaska. *Great Basin Naturalist* 48, 533–40.

**Erikstad, K. E.** (1979). Effect of radio packages on reproductive success of willow grouse. *Journal of Wildlife Management* 43, 170–75.

**Erikstad, K. E.** (1985a). Territorial breakdown and brood movements in willow grouse *Lagopus l. lagopus*. *Ornis Scandinavica* 16, 95–8.

**Erikstad, K. E.** (1985b). Growth and survival of willow grouse chicks in relation to home range, brood movements and habitat selection. *Ornis Scandinavica* 16, 181–90.

**Erikstad, K. E. & Andersen, R.** (1983). The effect of weather on survival, growth rate and feeding time in different sized willow grouse broods. *Ornis Scandinavica* 14, 249–52.

**Erikstad, K. E. & Spidsø, T. K.** (1982). The influence of weather on food intake, insect prey selection and feeding behaviour in willow grouse chicks in northern Norway. *Ornis Scandinavica* 13, 176–82.

**Erikstad, K. E., Pedersen, H. C. & Steen, J. B.** (1985). Clutch size and egg size variation in willow grouse *Lagopus l. lagopus*. *Ornis Scandinavica* 16, 88–94.

**Etheridge, B., Summers, R. W. & Green, R. E.** (1997). The effects of human persecution on the population dynamics of hen harriers *Circus cyaneus* in Scotland. *Journal of Applied Ecology* 34, 1081–106.

**Evans, R.** (1998). The erosional impacts of grazing animals. *Progress in Physical Geography* 22, 251–68.

**Fairburn, R. & Reynolds, J.** (2004). Gamekeeper escapes prison term for 'worst case of wildlife crime'. *The Scotsman* 26 August.

**Fasel, M. & Zbinden, N.** (1983). Kausalanalyse zum Verlauf der südlichen Arealgrenze des Alpenschneehuhns (*Lagopus mutus*) im

Tessin. *Der Ornithologische Beobachter* **80**, 231–46.

**Favaron, M., Scherini, G., Preatoni, D., Tosi, G. & Wauters, L. A.** (2006). Spacing behaviour and habitat use of rock ptarmigan (*Lagopus mutus*) at low density in the Italian Alps. *Journal für Ornithologie* **147**, 618–28.

**Fletcher, K.** (2006). Predator control and ground-nesting waders. *Game Conservancy Trust Review of 2005*, 80–3.

**Flint, V. E.** (1995). Numbers of grouse and their conservation in Russia. *Proceedings of the International Grouse Symposium* **6**, 173.

**Flux, J. E. C.** (1958). Red grouse in autumn. Sex and age characteristics studied. *Scottish Landowner* **91**, 43–4.

**Foggo, M. N.** (1980). Vegetation analysis of the territorial boundary between red grouse (*Lagopus lagopus scoticus*) and ptarmigan (*Lagopus mutus*). *New Zealand Journal of Ecology* **3**, 44–9.

**Forestry Commission** (2001). *Guidance Note 11 – Deer and Fencing*, www.forestry.gov.uk/forestry/INFD5N6HHT.

**Formozov, A. N.** (1964). Snow cover as an integral factor of the environment and its importance in the ecology of mammals and birds. *Boreal Institute, University of Alberta, Occasional Paper* **1** (translated from the Russian original in *Materiali pozn. Fauni i Flori SSSR, Izdanie Moskva, o-va isp. priroda* **5(20)** (1946), 1–152).

**Foster, D. R.** (1992). Land-use history (1730–1990) and vegetation dynamics in central New England, USA. *Journal of Ecology* **80**, 753–72.

**Fox, A. & Hudson, P. J.** (2001). Parasites reduce territorial behaviour in red grouse (*Lagopus lagopus scoticus*). *Ecology Letters* **4**, 139–43.

**Framstad, E., Stenseth, N. C. & Østbye, E.** (1993). Time series analysis of population fluctuations of *Lemmus lemmus*. In: *The Biology of Lemmings* (eds N. C. Stenseth & R. A. Ims), pp. 97–116. Academic Press, London & New York.

**Fraser of Allander Institute for Research on the Scottish Economy** (2001). *An Economic Study of Scottish Grouse Moors: an Update (2001)*. Game Conservancy Ltd, Fordingbridge.

**Fremstad, E.** (1997). *Vegetationstyper i Norge.* Temahefte **12**. Norsk Institutt for Naturforskning, Trondheim.

**Freuchen, P.** (1936). *Arctic Adventure.* Heinemann, London.

**Freuchen, P.** (1961). *Book of the Eskimos.* Fawcett, New York.

**Freuchen, P. & Salomonsen, F.** (1960). *The Arctic Year.* Jonathan Cape, London.

**Fullard, H.** (ed.) (1976). *Philip's Universal Atlas.* George Philip & Son, London.

**Fuller, R. J. & Gough, S. J.** (1999). Changes in sheep numbers in Britain: implications for bird populations. *Biological Conservation* **91**, 73–89.

**Futty, D. W. & Towers, W.** (1982). *Northern Scotland.* Soil Survey of Scotland, Aberdeen.

**Gabrielsen, G. W. & Steen, J. B.** (1979). Tachycardia during egg hypothermia in incubating ptarmigan (*Lagopus lagopus*). *Acta Physiologica Scandinavica* **107**, 273–7.

**Gabrielsen, G. W. & Unander, S.** (1987). Energy costs during incubation in Svalbard and willow ptarmigan hens. *Polar Research, New Series* **5**, 59–69.

**Gabrielsen, G. W., Kanwisher, J. & Steen, J. B.** (1977). Emotional bradycardia: a telemetry study on incubating willow grouse (*Lagopus lagopus*). *Acta Physiologica Scandinavica* **100**, 255–7.

**Gabrielsen, G. W., Blix, A. S. & Ursin, S.** (1985). Orienting and freezing responses in incubating ptarmigan hens. *Physiology & Behaviour* **34**, 925–34.

**Gabuzov, O. S.** (1995). Grouse hunting statistics in Russia. *Proceedings of the International Grouse Symposium* **6**, 173.

**Galbraith, C. A., Stroud, D. A. & Thompson, D. B. A.** (2003). Towards resolving raptor-human conflicts. In: *Birds of Prey in a Changing Environment* (eds D. B. A. Thompson, S. M. Redpath, A. H. Fielding, M. Marquiss & C. A. Galbraith), pp. 527–35. The Stationery Office, Edinburgh.

**Game Conservancy** (1985). *The Scottish Grouse Research Appeal*. Fordingbridge, Hampshire.

**Gardarsson, A.** (1971). Food ecology and spacing behavior of rock ptarmigan in Iceland. PhD thesis, University of California, Berkeley.

**Gardarsson, A.** (1988). Cyclic population changes and some related events in rock ptarmigan in Iceland. In: *Adaptive Strategies and Population Ecology of Northern Grouse* (eds A. T. Bergerud & M. W. Gratson), pp. 300–29. University of Minnesota Press, Minneapolis.

**Gardarsson, A. & Bossert, A.** (1997). Ptarmigan. In: *The EBCC Atlas of European Breeding Birds* (eds W. J. M. Hagemeijer & M. J. Blair), pp. 198–9. Poyser, London.

**Gardarsson, A. & Moss, R.** (1970). Selection of food by Icelandic ptarmigan in relation to its availability and nutritive value. In: *Animal Populations in Relation to their Food Resources* (ed. A. Watson), pp. 47–71. Blackwell Scientific Publications, Oxford.

**Gates, D. M.** (1962). *Energy Exchange in the Biosphere*. Harper & Row, New York.

**Geikie, J.** (1940). *Structural and Field Geology*. 5th edn. Oliver & Boyd, Edinburgh.

**Gelting, P.** (1937). Studies on the food of the east Greenland ptarmigan. *Meddelelser om Grønland* **116**.

**Géroudet, P.** (1978). *Grands Échassiers, Gallinacés, Râles d'Europe*. Delachaux et Niestlé, Neuchâtel.

**Gessaman, J. A.** (1976). Bioenergetics of the snowy owl (*Nyctea scandiaca*). *Arctic & Alpine Research* **4**, 223–38.

**Gibbons, D. W., Reid, J. B. & Chapman, R. A.** (1993). *The New Atlas of Breeding Birds in Britain and Ireland: 1988–1991*. Poyser, London.

**Gilbert, L., Jones, L. D., Hudson, P. J., Gould, E. A. & Reid, H. W.** (2000). Role of small mammals in the persistence of Louping-ill virus: field survey and tick co-feeding studies. *Medical and Veterinary Entomology* **14**, 277–82.

**Gillen, C.** (2003). *Geology and Landscapes of Scotland*. Terra Publishing, Harpenden.

**Gillson, L. & Willis, K. J.** (2006). 'As Earth's testimonies tell': wilderness conservation in a changing world. *Ecology Letters* **7**, 990–8.

**Gjerde, I.** (1991a). Cues in winter habitat selection by capercaillie. I. Habitat characteristics. *Ornis Scandinavica* **22**, 197–204.

**Gjerde, I.** (1991b). Cues in winter habitat selection by capercaillie. 2. Experimental evidence. *Ornis Scandinavica* **22**, 205–12.

**Gjerde, I. & Wegge, P.** (1989). Spacing pattern, habitat use and survival of capercaillie in a fragmented winter habitat. *Ornis Scandinavica* **20**, 219–25.

**Gladstone, H. C.** (1930). *Record Bags and Shooting Records*. Witherby, London.

**Gordon, G.** (1996). The balance of wild life. *Landowning in Scotland* **240**, 12–13.

**Gordon, S.** (1912). *Birds of the Loch and Mountain*. Cassell, London.

**Gordon, S.** (1915). *Hill Birds of Scotland*. Arnold, London.

**Gordon, S.** (1920). *The Land of the Hills and the Glens*. Cassell, London.

**Gordon, S.** (1925). *The Cairngorm Hills of Scotland*. Cassell, London.

**Gordon, S.** (1932). Ptarmigan nest in long heather. *British Birds* **25**, 305–6.

**Gordon, S.** (1944). *A Highland Year*. Eyre & Spottiswoode, London.

**Gordon, S.** (1951). *Highlands of Scotland*. Richard Hale, London.

**Grace, J. & Unsworth, M. H.** (1988). Climate and microclimate of the uplands. In: *Ecological Change in the Uplands* (eds M. B. Usher & D. B. A. Thompson), pp. 137–50. Blackwell Scientific Publications, Oxford.

**Grammeltvedt, R. & Steen, J. B.** (1978). Fat deposition in Spitzbergen ptarmigan

(*Lagopus mutus hyperboreus*). *Arctic* **31**, 496–8.

Grant, W. (1941). *The Scottish National Dictionary.* SND Association, Edinburgh.

Grant, W. & Murison, D. D. (1956, 1965, 1974). *The Scottish National Dictionary.* SND Association, Edinburgh.

Griffiths, B. & Jones, D. G. (1995). *The Welsh Academy English Welsh Dictionary.* University of Wales Press, Cardiff.

Gruys, R. C. (1993). Autumn and winter movements and sexual segregation of willow ptarmigan. *Arctic* **46**, 228–39.

Gudmundsson, F. (1960). Some reflections on ptarmigan cycles in Iceland. *Proceedings XII International Ornithological Congress*, 259–65.

Gudmundsson, F. (1972). Grit as an indicator of the overseas origin of certain birds occurring in Iceland. *Ibis* **114**, 580.

Gullion, G. W. (1970). Factors affecting ruffed grouse populations in the boreal forests of northern Minnesota, USA. *Proceedings of the International Congress of Game Biologists* **8**, 103–17.

Gutiérrez, R. J., Barrowclough, G. F. & Groth, J. G. (2000). A classification of the grouse (Aves: Tetraoninae) based on mitochondrial DNA sequences. *Wildlife Biology* **6**, 205–11.

Haftorn, S. (1971). *Norges Fugler.* Universitetsforlaget, Oslo.

Hagemeijer, W. J. M. & Blair, M. J. (1997). *The EBCC Atlas of European Breeding Birds.* Poyser, London.

Hammond, R. F. (1979). *The Peatlands of Ireland.* An Foras Taluntais, Dublin.

Hancock, M., Baines, D., Gibbons, D., Etheridge, B. & Shepherd, M. (1999). Status of male black grouse *Tetrao tetrix* in Britain in 1995–96. *Bird Study* **46**, 1–15.

Hannon, S. J. (1983). Spacing and breeding density of willow ptarmigan in response to an experimental alteration of sex ratio. *Journal of Animal Ecology* **52**, 807–20.

Hannon, S. J. (1984). Factors limiting polygyny in the willow ptarmigan. *Animal Behaviour* **32**, 153–61.

Hannon, S. J. & Barry, T. W. (1986). Demography, breeding biology and predation of willow ptarmigan at Anderson River Delta, Northwest Territories. *Arctic* **39**, 300–3.

Hannon, S. J. & Dobush, G. (1997). Pairing status of male willow ptarmigan: is polygyny costly to males? *Animal Behaviour* **53**, 369–80.

Hannon, S. J. & Eason, P. (1990). Colour bands, combs and coverable badges in willow ptarmigan. *Animal Behaviour* **49**, 53–62.

Hannon, S. J. & Martin, K. (1996). Mate fidelity and divorce in ptarmigan: polygyny avoidance on the tundra. In: *Partnerships in Birds* (ed. J. M. Black), pp. 192–210. Oxford University Press, Oxford.

Hannon, S. J. & Roland, J. (1984). Morphology and territory acquisition in willow ptarmigan. *Canadian Journal of Zoology* **62**, 1502–6.

Hannon, S. J. & Smith, J. N. M. (1984). Factors influencing age-related reproductive success in the willow ptarmigan. *Auk* **101**, 848–54.

Hannon, S. J. & Wingfield, J. C. (1990). Endocrine correlates of territoriality, breeding stage, and body molt in free-living willow ptarmigan of both sexes. *Canadian Journal of Zoology* **68**, 2130–4.

Hannon, S. J., Eason, P. K. & Martin, K. (1998). Willow ptarmigan (*Lagopus lagopus*). *The Birds of North America* (eds A. Poole & F. Gill) **369**. Academy of Natural Sciences, Philadelphia, and American Ornithologists' Union, Washington DC.

Hannon, S. J., Gruys, R. C. & Schieck, J. O. (2003). Differential seasonal mortality of the sexes in willow ptarmigan *Lagopus lagopus* in northern British Columbia, Canada. *Wildlife Biology* **9**, 317–26.

Hanson, B. (1935). Kystrypenen i Møre og Trondelag. *Norsk Jaeger-og Fisker-Forenings Tidsskrift* **64**.

Hantzsch, B. (1914). Ornithologisches Tagebuch. Aufzeichnungen während einer

Reise in Baffinland. *Sitzungsberichte der Gesellschaft naturforschender Freunde zu Berlin* **4**, 129–65; translation by R. M. Anderson in 1927, Library of National Museum of Canada.

Hantzsch, B. (1929). Contribution to the knowledge of the avifauna of north-eastern Labrador. *Canadian Field-Naturalist* **43**, 11–18; translation from the original German by M. B. A. Anderson & R. M. Anderson.

Hardin, G. (1968). The tragedy of the commons. *Science* **162**, 1243–8.

Harper, F. (1953). Birds of the Nueltin Lake Expedition, Keewatin 1947. *American Midland Naturalist* **49**, 1–116.

Harrison, C. J. O. (1987). Pleistocene and prehistoric birds of south-west Britain. *Proceedings of the University of Bristol Spelaeological Society* **18**, 81–104.

Harrison, J. (1997). Changes in the Scottish climate. *Botanical Journal of Scotland* **49**, 287–300.

Harrison, J., Winterbottom, S. & Johnson, R. (2001). *Climate Change and Changing Snowfall in Scotland*. Research Findings **14**. Scottish Executive Research Unit, Edinburgh.

Hartley, S. (1993). Insect pests on heather moorland. *Annual Report of the Joseph Nickerson Reconciliation Project* **9**, 46–7.

Harvie-Brown, J. A. & Buckley, T. E. (1895). *A Vertebrate Fauna of the Moray Basin*. Vols 1 & 2. Douglas, Edinburgh.

Haydon, D. T., Shaw, D. J., Cattadori, I. M., Hudson, P. J. & Thirgood, S. J. (2002). Analysing noisy time-series: describing regional variation in the cyclic dynamics of red grouse. *Proceedings of the Royal Society of London, Series B – Biological Sciences* **269**, 1609–17.

Heather Trust (1995). Raptors on moorland – the Heather Trust's view. *Annual Report of the Heather Trust* **11**, 45.

Henderson, B. A. (1977). The genetics and demography of a high and low density of red grouse *Lagopus l. scoticus*. *Journal of Animal Ecology* **46**, 581–92.

Henderson, N. (1992). Wilderness and the nature conservation ideal: Britain, Canada and the United States contrasted. *Ambio* **21**, 394–9.

Hewson, R. (1973). The moults of captive Scottish ptarmigan (*Lagopus mutus*). *Journal of Zoology* **171**, 177–87.

Hewson, R. & Watson, A. (1979). Winter whitening of stoats (*Mustela erminea*) in Scotland and north-east England. *Journal of Zoology* **187**, 55–64.

Higgins, P., Wightman, A. & MacMillan, D. (2002). *Sporting Estates and Recreational Land Use in the Highlands and Islands of Scotland*. Report to the Economic & Social Research Council, Swindon.

Hik, D. (1995). Does risk of predation influence population dynamics? Evidence from the cyclic decline of snowshoe hares. *Wildlife Research* **22**, 115–29.

Hill, M. O., Coppins, B. J., Roy, D. B., Downing, T. E., Hammond, P. S., Telfer, M. G., Berry, P. M., Marquiss, M. & Welch, D. (1998). *Climate Changes and Scotland's Natural Heritage: an Environmental Audit*. Institute of Terrestrial Ecology, Huntingdon.

Hines, J. E. (1986). Survival and reproduction of dispersing blue grouse. *Condor* **88**, 43–9.

Hjeljord, O. & Kiær, A. (1991). Jaktjournalen fra 'Rypa'. *Villreinen* **5**, 57–9.

Hjorth, I. (1970). Reproductive behaviour in Tetraonidae. *Viltrevy* **7**, 181–596.

Hobbs, R. J. & Gimingham, C. H. (1987). Vegetation, fire and herbivore interactions in heathland. *Advances in Ecological Research* **16**, 87–173.

Höglund, J., Alatolo, R. V., Gibson, R. M. & Lundberg, A. (1995). Mate-choice copying in black grouse. *Animal Behaviour* **49**, 1627–33.

Höglund, J., Alatolo, R., Lundberg, A., Rintamäki, P. T. & Lindell, J. (1999). Microsatellite markers reveal the potential for kin selection on black grouse leks. *Proceedings of the Royal Society of London, Series B – Biological Sciences* **266**, 813–16.

Höglund, J., Piertney, S. B., Alatolo, R. V., Lindell, J., Lundberg, A. & Rintamäki, P. T. (2002). Inbreeding depression and male fitness in black grouse. *Proceedings of the Royal Society of London, Series B – Biological Sciences* **269**, 711–15.

Höglund, N. H. (1956). Om könsskiljande karaktärer hos småkycklingar av tjäder *Tetrao u. urogallus* Lin., *Viltrevy* **2**, 150–7.

Höglund, N. H. (1970). On the ecology of the willow grouse (*Lagopus lagopus*) in a mountainous area in Sweden. *Proceedings of the International Congress of Game Biologists* **8**, 118–20.

Höglund, N. H. (1980). Studies on the winter ecology of the willow grouse *Lagopus lagopus* L. *Viltrevy* **11**, 249–70.

Höhn, E. O. (1959). Birds of the mouth of the Anderson River and Liverpool Bay. *Canadian Field-Naturalist* **73**, 93–114.

Höhn, E. O. (1977). The 'snowshoe effect' of the feathering on ptarmigan feet. *Condor* **79**, 380–2.

Höhn, E. O. (1980). *Die Schneehühner*. A. Ziemsen Verlag, Wittenberg Lutherstadt.

Höhn, E. O. & Braun, C. E. (1980). Hormonal induction of feather pigmentation in ptarmigan. *Auk* **97**, 601–7.

Holder, K. (1990) Ornamental traits in rock ptarmigan: morphology, behaviour and mating success. MSc thesis, Queen's Universty, Kingston, Ontario.

Holder, K. (1994). Evolutionary divergence of rock ptarmigan: an Aleutian solution. *Information North* **20**(4), 1–4.

Holder, K. & Montgomerie, R. (1993a). Rock ptarmigan (*Lagopus mutus*). *The Birds of North America* (eds A. Poole & F. Gill) **51**. Academy of Natural Sciences, Philadelphia, and American Ornithologists' Union, Washington DC.

Holder, K. & Montgomerie, R. (1993b). Context and consequences of comb displays by male rock ptarmigan. *Animal Behaviour* **45**, 457–70.

Holder, K., Montgomerie, R. & Friesen, V. L. (1999). A test of the glacial refugium hypothesis using patterns of mitochondrial and nuclear sequence variation in rock ptarmigan (*Lagopus mutus*). *Evolution* **53**, 1936–50.

Holder, K., Montgomerie, T. & Friesen, V. L. (2004). Genetic diversity and management of Nearctic rock ptarmigan (*Lagopus mutus*). *Canadian Journal of Zoology* **12**, 564–75.

Holloway, S. (1996). *The Historical Atlas of Breeding Birds in Britain and Ireland: 1875–1900*. Poyser, London.

Holstad, Ø., Karbøl, G. & Skorping, A. (1994). *Trichostrongylus tenuis* from willow grouse (*Lagopus lagopus*) and ptarmigan (*Lagopus mutus*) in northern Norway. *Bulletin of the Scandinavian Society for Parasitology* **4**, 9–13.

Hörnell-Willebrand, M. (2005). Temporal and spatial dynamics in willow grouse *Lagopus lagopus*. PhD thesis, University of Agricultural Sciences, Umeå.

Hörnfeldt, B., Hipkiss, T. & Eklund, U. (2001). Juvenile sex ratio in relation to breeding success in capercaillie *Tetrao urogallus* and black grouse *T. tetrix*. *Ibis* **143**, 627–31.

Høst, P. (1942). Effect of light on the moults and sequences of plumage in the willow ptarmigan. *Auk* **59**, 388–403.

Hovi, M., Alatolo, R.V., Höglund, J., Lundberg, A. & Rintamäki, P. T. (1994). Lek centre attracts black grouse females. *Proceedings of the Royal Society of London, Series B – Biological Sciences* **258**, 303–5.

Hovi, M., Alatolo, R. V. & Siikamäki, P. (1995). Black grouse leks on ice – female mate sampling by incitation of male competition. *Behavioral Ecology and Sociobiology* **37**, 283–8.

Hovi, M., Alatolo, R. V., Höglund, J. & Lundberg, A. (1996). Traditionality of black grouse *Tetrao tetrix* leks. *Ornis Fennica* **73**, 119–23.

Howell, S. N. G., Corben, C., Pyle, P. & Rogers, D. I. (2003). The first basic problem: a review of molt and plumage homologies. *Condor* **105**, 635–53.

Huber, B. & Ingold, P. (1991). Bestand und Verteilung der Territorien des Alpenschneehuhns *Lagopus mutus* am Augstmatthorn BE. *Der Ornithologische Beobachter* **88**, 1–7.

Huber-Eicher, B. (1995). Energy costs of incubation in rock ptarmigan *Lagopus mutus* in Switzerland. *Proceedings of the International Grouse Symposium* **6**, 71–6.

Hudson, P. J. (1986a). *The Red Grouse: the Biology and Management of a Wild Gamebird.* Game Conservancy, Fordingbridge.

Hudson, P. J. (1986b). The effect of a parasitic nematode on the breeding production of red grouse. *Journal of Animal Ecology* **55**, 85–92.

Hudson, P. J. (1990). Territorial status and survival in a low density grouse population. In: *Red Grouse Population Processes* (eds A. N. Lance & J. H. Lawton), pp. 20–8. Royal Society for the Protection of Birds, Sandy, Bedfordshire.

Hudson P. J. (1992). *Grouse in Space and Time.* The Game Conservancy Ltd, Fordingbridge, Hampshire.

Hudson, P. J. (1993). The red grouse. In: *The New Atlas of Breeding Birds in Britain and Ireland* (eds D. W. Gibbons, J. B. Reid & R. A. Chapman), pp. 126–7. Poyser, London.

Hudson, P. J. & Dobson, A. P. (2001). Harvesting unstable populations: red grouse *Lagopus lagopus scoticus* (Lath.) in the United Kingdom. *Wildlife Biology* **7**, 189–95.

Hudson, P. J. & Newborn, D. (1990). Brood defence in a precocial species: variations in the distraction displays of red grouse *Lagopus lagopus scoticus*. *Animal Behaviour* **40**, 254–61.

Hudson, P. J. & Newborn, D. (1995). *A Manual of Red Grouse and Moorland Management.* Game Conservancy Trust, Fordingbridge.

Hudson, P. J. & Renton, J. (1988). What influences changes in grouse numbers? *Annual Review 1987*, 127–31. Game Conservancy, Fordingbridge.

Hudson, P. J., Renton, J. & Dalby, G. (1988). Red grouse homing for 35 kilometres. *Scottish Birds* **15**, 90–91.

Hudson, P. J., Newborn, D. & Dobson, A. P. (1992). Regulation and stability of a free-living host-parasite system, *Trichostrongylus tenuis* in red grouse. I. Monitoring and parasite reduction experiments. *Journal of Animal Ecology* **61**, 477–86.

Hudson, P. J., Dobson, A. P. & Newborn, D. (1998). Prevention of population cycles by parasite removal. *Science* **282**, 2256–8.

Hughes, J., Baines, D., Grant, M., Roberts, J., Williams, I. & Bayes, K. (1998). *RSPB Conservation Review* **12**, 18–28.

Hulme, M. & Jenkins, G. (1998). Climate change scenarios for the United Kingdom. Summary report. *UK Climate Impacts Programme, Technical Report* **1**.

Humphrey, P. S. & Parkes, K. C. (1959). An approach to the study of molts and plumages. *Auk* **76**, 1–31.

Hunt, J. F. (2003). *Impacts of Wild Deer in Scotland – How Fares the Public Interest?* Report for WWF Scotland & RSPB Scotland.

Hunter, J. (1973). Sheep and deer: Highland sheep farming 1850–1900. *Northern Scotland* **1**, 199–222.

Hunter, J. (1994). From West Highland Survey to Scottish Natural Heritage: the beginnings of a sustainable development strategy for the Highlands, the Islands and their surrounding seas. In: *The Islands of Scotland: a Living Marine Heritage* (eds J. M. Baxter & M. B. Usher), pp. 201–11. Her Majesty's Stationery Office, Edinburgh.

Hunter, J. (1995). *On the Other Side of Sorrow: Nature and People in the Scottish Highlands.* Mainstream Publishing, Edinburgh & London.

Huntley, B. (1991). Historical lessons for the future. In: *The Scientific Management of Temperate Communities for Conservation* (eds

I. F. Spellerberg, F. B. Goldsmith & M. G. Morris), pp. 473–503. Blackwell Scientific Publications, Oxford.

Ingold, P., Huber, B., Mainini, B., Marbacher, H., Neuhaus, P., Rawyter, A., Roth, M., Schnidig, R. & Zeller, R. (1992). Freizeitaktivitäten – ein gravierendes Problem für Tiere? *Ornithologische Beobachter* **89**, 205–16.

International Phonetic Association (1963). *The Principles of the International Phonetic Association*. University College, London.

Irving, L. (1960). Birds of Anaktuvuk Pass, Kobuk and Old Crow: a study in arctic adaptation. *Bulletin of the US National Museum* **217**.

Irving, L., West, G. C. & Peyton, L. J. (1967a). Winter feeding program of Alaska willow ptarmigan shown by crop contents. *Condor* **69**, 69–77.

Irving, L., West, G. C., Peyton, L. J. & Paneak, S. (1967b). Migration of willow ptarmigan in arctic Alaska. *Arctic* **20**, 77–85.

Jackes, A. D. & Watson, A. (1975). Winter whitening of Scottish mountain hares (*Lepus timidus scoticus*) in relation to daylength, temperature and snow-lie. *Journal of Zoology* **176**, 403–9.

Jacobsen, E. E., White, C. M. & Emison, W. B. (1983). Molting adaptations of rock ptarmigan on Amchitka Island, Alaska. *Condor* **85**, 420–6.

Jamieson, I. G. & Zwickel, F. C. (1983). Spatial patterns of yearling male blue grouse and their relationship to recruitment into the breeding population. *Auk* **100**, 653–7.

Jenkins, D. (1953). A study of habitat selection of birds in north-west Vesterålen. *Sterna* **9**, 1–51.

Jenkins, D. & Watson, A. (2001). Bird numbers in relation to grazing on a grouse moor from 1957–61 to 1988–98. *Bird Study* **48**, 18–22.

Jenkins, D., Watson, A. & Miller, G. R. (1961). *Seventh Progress Report*, Nature Conservancy Unit of Grouse & Moorland Ecology, University of Aberdeen.

Jenkins, D., Watson, A. & Miller, G. R. (1963). Population studies on red grouse *Lagopus lagopus scoticus* (Lath.) in north-east Scotland. *Journal of Animal Ecology* **32**, 317–76.

Jenkins, D., Watson, A. & Miller, G. R. (1964). Predation and red grouse populations. *Journal of Applied Ecology* **1**, 183–95.

Jenkins, D., Watson, A. & Miller, G. R. (1967). Population fluctuations in the red grouse *Lagopus lagopus scoticus*. *Journal of Animal Ecology* **36**, 97–122.

Johnsen, P. (1953). Birds and mammals of Peary Land in north Greenland. *Meddelelser om Grønland* **128(6)**.

Johnsen, R., Espmark, Y., Pedersen, H. C. & Steen, J. B. (1991). Characteristics of territorial and mating calls in willow ptarmigan *Lagopus l. lagopus*. *Bioacoustics* **3**, 17–30.

Johnsen, S. (1929). Draktskiftet hos lirypen (*Lagopus lagopus*) i Norge. *Bergens Museum Aarbok* **1**, 1–84.

Johnsgard, P. A. (1983). *The Grouse of the World*. Croom Helm, London.

Johnson, R. E. (1968). Temperature regulation in the white-tailed ptarmigan, *Lagopus leucurus*. *Comparative Biochemistry & Physiology* **24**, 1003–14.

Johnstone, G. S. (1974). Geology. In: *The Cairngorms*, by D. Nethersole-Thompson & A. Watson, pp. 200–9. Collins, London; 2nd edn 1981, Melven Press, Perth.

Johnstone, G. S. & Mykura, W. (1989). *The Northern Highlands*. Her Majesty's Stationery Office, London.

Jones, A. M. (1982a). Aspects of the ecology and behaviour of capercaillie in two Scottish plantations. PhD thesis, University of Aberdeen.

Jones, A. M. (1982b). Capercaillie in Scotland – towards a conservation strategy. *Proceedings of the Second International Conference on Grouse*, 60–73.

Jones Economics Ltd, Scotinform Ltd & Landwise Scotland (1995). *The Economic Impacts of Hillwalking, Mountaineering and*

Associated Activities. Highlands & Islands Enterprise, Inverness.

Jones, L. D., Gaunt, M., Hails, R. S., Laurenson, K., Hudson, P. J., Reid, H., Henbest, P. & Gould, E.A. (1997). Transmission of louping ill virus between infected and uninfected ticks co-feeding on mountain hares. *Medical and Veterinary Pathology* **11**, 172–6.

Jonzén, N., Ranta, E., Lundberg, P., Kaitala, V. & Lindén, H. (2003). Harvesting-induced population fluctuations? *Wildlife Biology* **9**, 59–65.

Jørgensen, E. & Blix, A. S. (1985). Effects of climate and nutrition on growth and survival of willow ptarmigan chicks. *Ornis Scandinavica* **16**, 99–107.

Jørgensen, E. & Blix, A. S. (1988). Energy conservation by restricted body cooling in cold-exposed willow ptarmigan chicks. *Ornis Scandinavica* **19**, 17–20.

Kaland, P. E. (1986). The origin and management of Norwegian coastal heaths as reflected by pollen analysis. In: *Anthropogenic Indicators in Pollen Diagrams* (ed. K.-E. Behre), pp. 19–36. Blakema, Rotterdam.

Kankaanpää, P. (ed.) (2002). *Arctic Flora and Fauna*. Edita, Helsinki.

Kastdalen, L., Pedersen, H. C., Fjone, G. & Andreassen, H. P. (2003). Combining resource selection functions and distance sampling: an example with willow ptarmigan. *Proceedings of 1st International Conference on Resource Selection by Animals.* 1–3 January 2003, 9 pp. Laramie, Wyoming.

Kauhala, K. & Helle, P. (2002) The impact of predator abundance on grouse populations in Finland – a study based on wildlife monitoring counts. *Ornis Fennica* **79**, 14–25.

Kauhala, K., Helle, P. & Helle, E. (2000). Predator control and reproductive success of grouse populations in Finland. *Ecography* **23**, 161–8.

Kaye, J. (2007). Project ptarmigan – tracing Scotland's montane specialist. *BTO Scotland News* **2007**, 1.

Keatinge, T. H. & Dickson, J. H. (1979). Mid-Flandrian changes in vegetation on mainland Orkney. *New Phytologist* **82**, 585–612.

Keatinge, T. H., Coupar, A. M. & Reid, E. (1995). Wet heaths in Caithness and Sutherland, Scotland. In: *Heaths and Moorland: Cultural Landscapes* (eds D. B. A. Thompson, A. J. Hester & M. B. Usher), pp. 20–7. Her Majesty's Stationery Office, Edinburgh.

Kessel, B. (1989) *Birds of the Seward Peninsula, Alaska*. University of Alaska Press, Anchorage.

Kirby, A. D. & Smith, A. A. (2005). Evidence of re-nesting after brood loss in red grouse *Lagopus lagopus scoticus. Ibis* **147**, 221.

Kirikov, S. V. (1947). Tokovanie i biologii razmiozheniya yuzhnouralskogo glukharya. *Zoologicheskii Zhurnal* **26**, 71–84 (English summary).

Kirikov, S. (1970). Ecological features of capercaillie populations in the southern parts of the area of its occurrence (the territory between the Volga and the Ural). *Proceedings of the International Union of Game Biologists* **8**, 164–8.

Kirkman, F. B. & Hutchinson, H. G. (eds) (1924). *British Sporting Birds*. T. C. & E. C. Jack, London.

Kitshinskiy, A. A. (1975). Novosibirskiy Ostrova. In: *Teterevinye Ptitsy* (ed. S. V. Kirikov), pp. 27–33. Nauka, Moscow.

Klaus, S. (1991). Effects of forestry on grouse populations – case studies from the Thuringian and Bohemian forests, central Europe. *Ornis Scandinavica* **22**, 218–23.

Kloster, R. (1928). Russiske ryper og norske ryper. *Bergens Jæger og Fisker Forening Rypeundersøkelser 1921–27* **10**.

Kokeš, O. & Wolf, R. (1978). Relation of capercaillie and pine marten in game management. *Folia Venatoria* (Polovnícky zborník, Myslivecký sborník) **8**, 237–51 (in Czech, with English summary).

Kokko, H., Rintamäki, P. T., Alatolo, R. V., Höglund, J., Karvonen, E. & Lundberg, A. (1999). Female choice selects for lifetime lekking performance in black grouse males. *Proceedings of the Royal Society of London, Series B – Biological Sciences* **266**, 2109–15.

Korhonen, K. (1980). Microclimate in the snow burrows of willow grouse (*Lagopus lagopus*). *Annales Zoologici Fennici* **17**, 5–9.

Koskimies, J. (1958). Lumipeitteen merkityksestä eläinten lämpösuojana. *Suomen Riista* **12**, 137–40.

Krebs, C. J., Keller, B. L. & Tamarin, R. H. (1969). *Microtus* population biology: demographic changes in fluctuating populations of *M. ochrogaster* and *M. pennsylvanicus* in southern Indiana. *Ecology* **50**, 587–607.

Kristoffersen, S. (1933). Tromsø Museums rypeundersøkelser i 1931. *Norsk Jæger-og Fisker-Forenings Tidsskrift* **62**, 1–17, 73–88, 153–61, 216–28.

Kullman, L. (2005). Wind-conditioned 20th century decline of birch treeline vegetation in the Swedish Scandes. *Arctic* **58**, 286–94.

Kurki, S., Helle, P., Linden, H. & Nikula, A. (1997). Breeding success of black grouse and capercaillie in relation to predator densities on two spatial scales. *Oikos* **79**, 301–10.

Lack, D. (1954). *The Natural Regulation of Animal Numbers*. Clarendon Press, Oxford.

Lack, D. (1966). *Population Studies of Birds*. Clarendon Press, Oxford.

Lack, P. (1986). *The Atlas of Wintering Birds in Britain and Ireland*. Poyser, Calton.

Lambert, R. A. (2001). *Contested Mountains*. White Horse Press, Cambridge.

Lambin, X., Krebs, C. J., Moss, R., Stenseth, N. C. & Yoccoz, N. G. (1999). Population cycles and parasitism. *Science* **286**, 2425a.

Lance, A. N. (1972). *Red Grouse in Ireland: a Summary of Research up to 1972*. Report to Forest & Wildlife Service, Department of Lands, Dublin.

Lance, A. N. (1975). Egg production and chick development in a marginal red grouse population. *Congress of the International Union of Game Biologists* **12**, Tema 3, 1–10. Lisbon.

Lance, A. N. (1976). *The Red Grouse Project at Glenamoy*. Progress report, An Foras Taluntais, Glenamoy.

Lance, A. N. (1977). *Red Grouse in Ireland: a Summary of Research up to 1972*. An Foras Taluntais, Glenamoy.

Lance, A. N. (1978a). Survival and recruitment success of individual young cock red grouse *Lagopus l. scoticus* tracked by radio-telemetry. *Ibis* **120**, 369–78.

Lance, A. N. (1978b). Territories and the food plant of individual red grouse. II. Territory size compared with an index of nutrient supply in heather. *Journal of Animal Ecology* **47**, 307–13.

Lance, A. N. (1983). Selection of feeding sites by hen red grouse *Lagopus lagopus scoticus* during breeding. *Ornis Scandinavica* **14**, 78–80.

Lance A. N. & Phillips J. (1975). Responses of red grouse to serial heather-burning in eastern Ireland. *Congress of the International Union of Game Biologists* **12**, Tema 3, 1–9. Lisbon.

Lande, R., Engen, S. & Sæther, B.-E. (1995). Optimal harvesting of fluctuating populations with a risk of extinction. *American Naturalist* **145**, 728–45.

Langan, S. J., Lilly, A. & Smith, B. F. L. (1995). The distribution of heather moorland and the sensitivity of associated soils to acidification. In: *Heaths and Moorland: Cultural Landscapes* (eds D. B. A. Thompson, A. J. Hester & M. B. Usher), pp. 218–23. Her Majesty's Stationery Office, Edinburgh.

Langlois, C. & Langis, R. (1995). Presence of airborne contaminants in the wildlife of northern Quebec. *Science of the Total Environment* **160**, 391–402.

Laurenson, M. K., Norman, R., Reid, H. W., Newborn, D. & Hudson, P. J. (2000). The role of lambs in louping-ill virus amplification. *Parasitology* **120**, 97–104.

Laurenson, M. K., Norman, R. A., Gilbert, L., Reid, H. W. & Hudson, P. J. (2003). Identifying disease reservoirs in complex systems: mountain hares as reservoirs of ticks and louping-ill virus, pathogens of red grouse. *Journal of Animal Ecology* 72, 177–85.

Lawton, J. H. (ed.) (1990). *Red Grouse Populations and Moorland Management.* Field Studies Council, Shrewsbury.

Lee, J. A., Press, M. C., Woodin, S. J. & Ferguson, P. (1987). Responses to acidic deposition in ombrotrophic mires in the UK. In: *Effects of Atmospheric Pollutants on Forests, Wetlands and Agricultural Ecosystems* (eds T. C. Hutchinson & K. M. Meema), pp. 549–60. Springer-Verlag, Berlin.

Lee, J. A., Caporn, S. J. M. & Read, D. J. (1992). Effects of increasing nitrogen deposition and acidification on heathlands. In: *Acidification Research. Evaluation and Policy Applications* (ed. T. Schneider), pp. 97–106. Elsevier, Colchester.

Leiper, R. T. (1910). Exhibition of the larval stage of *Trichostrongylus pergracilis* the causal factor of grouse disease. *Proceedings of the Zoological Society of London* 80, 387.

Leslie, A. S. (1911).The life history of the grouse. In: *The Grouse in Health and in Disease*, pp. 5–28. Smith, Elder & Co., London.

Lever, C. (1977). *The Naturalised Animals of the British Isles.* Hutchinson, London.

Lid, J. (1927). Om fjeldrypens næring. *Norsk Jæger-og Fisker-Forenings Tidsskrift* 56, 159–67.

Lieser, M., Berthold, P. & Manley, G. A. (2005). Infrasound in the capercaillie (*Tetrao urogallus*). *Journal für Ornithologie* 146, 395–8.

Lindén, H. (1991). Patterns of grouse shooting in Finland. *Ornis Scandinavica* 22, 241–4.

Lindén, W. G. & Pedersen, H. C. (1997). In: *The EBCC Atlas of European Breeding Birds* (eds W. J. M. Hagemeijer & M. J. Blair), pp. 196–7. Poyser, London.

Lindley, P. & Mellenchip, C. (2005). What is in the tool kit for black grouse recovery? In: *Proceedings of the 3rd International Black Grouse Conference*, pp. 65–78. Ruthin, North Wales.

Lindström, E. R., Andrén, H., Angelstam, P., Cederlund, G., Hörnfeldt, B., Jäderberg, L., Lemnell, P.-A., Martinsson, B., Sköld, K. & Swenson, J. E. (1994). Disease reveals the predator: sarcoptic mange, red fox predation, and prey populations. *Ecology* 75, 1042–9.

Lindström, E. R., Brainerd, S. M., Helldin, J. O. & Overskaug. K. (1995a). Pine marten red fox interactions – a case of intraguild predation. *Annales Zoologici Fennici* 32, 123–30.

Lindström, J., Ranta, E., Kaitala, V. & Lindén, H. (1995b). The clockwork of Finnish tetraonid population dynamics. *Oikos* 74, 185–94.

Lindström, J., Rintamäki, P. T. & Storch, I. (1998). Black grouse. *BWP Update* 2(3), 173–91.

Lister-Kaye, J. (1994). Ill fares the land. A sustainable land ethic for the sporting estates of the Highlands and Islands. *Occasional Paper* 3, 1–27. Scottish Natural Heritage, Edinburgh.

Lock, K. A. (2003). Kinship and red grouse: the dynamics and behaviour of a declining population. PhD thesis, University of Aberdeen.

Lockwood, W. B. (1976). Ptarmigan and other Gaelic names. *Scottish Gaelic Studies* 12, 271–8.

Longmuir, J. (1867). *Jamieson's Dictionary of the Scottish Language.* Nimmo, Edinburgh.

Longstaff, T. G. (1932). An ecological reconaissance in west Greenland. *Journal of Animal Ecology* 1, 119–42.

Lorenz, T. (1904). *Lagopus albus* (L.) nov. subsp. *maior. Ornithologisches Monatsberichte* 12, 177–8.

Lotka, A. (1925). *Elements of Physical Biology.* Williams and Wilkins, Baltimore.

Lovat, Lord (1911). Moor management (Chapter 17), Heather burning (Chapter 18), and Stock (Chapter 21). In: *The Grouse in Health and in Disease* (ed. A. S. Leslie), 372–413, 454–82. Smith, Elder & Co, London.

Lovel, T. W. T. (1979). *Woodland Grouse 1978.* World Pheasant Association, Lamarsh, Bures, Suffolk.

Lovel, T. (2005). Hunting grouse in Great Britain. *Grouse News* **29**, 11–12.

Lowe, V. P. W. (1961). A discussion of the history, present status and future conservation of red deer (*Cervus elaphus* L.) in Scotland. *Terre et Vie* **1**, 9–40.

Lucchini, V., Höglund, J., Klaus, S., Swenson, J. & Randi, E. (2001). Historical biogeography and a mitochondrial DNA phylogeny of grouse and ptarmigan. *Molecular Phylogenetics and Evolution* **20**, 149–62.

Luder, R. (1981). Die Avifauna der Gemeinde Lenk. *Der Ornithologische Beobachter* **78**, 193–208.

MacBain, A. (1982). *An Etymological Dictionary of the Gaelic Language.* Gairm Publications, Glasgow, reprinted from 1st edn, 1896.

MacColl, A. D. C. (1998). Factors affecting recruitment in red grouse. PhD thesis, University of Aberdeen.

MacColl, A. D. C., Piertney, S. B., Moss, R. & Lambin, X. (2000). Spatial arrangement of kin affects recruitment success in young male red grouse. *Oikos* **90**, 261–70.

McCormick, F. & Buckland, P. C. (2003). The vertebrate fauna. In: *Scotland after the Ice Age* (eds K. J. Edwards & I. B. M. Ralston), pp. 81–108. Edinburgh University Press, Edinburgh.

McCullagh, R. & Tipping, R. (1998). *The Lairg Project 1988–1996: the Evolution of an Archaeological Landscape in Northern Scotland.* Scottish Trust for Archaeological Research, Edinburgh.

MacDonald, A. (1999). Fire in the uplands: a historical perspective. *Information & Advisory Note* **108**, 1–4. Scottish Natural Heritage, Perth.

MacDonald, S. D. (1952). Report on biological investigations at Mould Bay, Prince Patrick Island, N.W.T. *Bulletin of the National Museum of Canada* **132**.

MacDonald, S. D. (1970). The breeding behavior of the rock ptarmigan. *Living Bird* **9**, 195–238.

MacEachainn, E. (1971). *Macaechen's Gaelic-English Dictionary.* Highland Printers, Inverness.

MacGillivray, W. (1837). *A History of British Birds. Vol. 1.* Scott, Webster & Geary, London.

MacGillivray, W. (1855). *The Natural History of Dee Side and Braemar.* Printers to the Queen, London.

McGilvray, J. (1996). *An Economic Study of Scottish Grouse Moors.* University of Strathclyde.

McGilvray, J. & Perman, R. (1991). *Grouse Shooting in Scotland: Analysis of its Importance to the Economy and Environment.* University of Strathclyde. Report to The Game Conservancy. Summarised version in: *Grouse in Space and Time*, by P. J. Hudson (1992), pp. 215–17. The Game Conservancy Ltd, Fordingbridge, Hampshire.

McGowan, J. D. (1969). Starvation of Alaskan ruffed and sharp-tailed grouse caused by icing. *Auk* **86**, 142–3.

McGowan, J. D. (1975). Effects of autumn and spring hunting on ptarmigan population trends. *Journal of Wildlife Management* **39**, 491–5.

McGowan, R. Y., Clugston, D. L. & Forrester, R. W. (2003). Scotland's endemic subspecies. *Scottish Birds* **24**, 18–35.

McGuire, K., Holmes, E. C., Gao, G. F., Reid, H. W. & Gould, E. A. (1998). Tracing the origins of louping ill virus by molecular phylogenetic analysis. *Journal of General Virology* **79**, 981–8

McKay, G. A., Findlay, B. F. & Thompson, H. A. (1970). A climatic perspective of tundra areas. In: *Productivity and Conservation in Northern Circumpolar Lands* (eds W. A. Fuller

& P. G. Kevan), pp. 10–33. International Union for Conservation of Nature & Natural Resources, Morges, Switzerland.

Mackenzie, J. M. D. (1952). Fluctuations in the numbers of British tetraonids. *Journal of Animal Ecology* **21**, 128–53.

Mackenzie, O. H. (1924). *A Hundred Years in the Highlands*. Arnold, London.

Mackey, E. C., Shewry, M. C. & Tudor, G. J. (1998). *Land Cover Change: Scotland from the 1940s to the 1980s*. The Stationery Office, Edinburgh.

Mackey, E. C., Shaw, P., Holbrook, J., Shewry, M. C., Saunders, G., Hall, J. & Ellis, N. E. (2001). *Natural Heritage Trends, Scotland 2001*. Scottish Natural Heritage, Perth.

MacLennan, M. (1979). *A Pronouncing and Etymological Dictionary of the Gaelic language*. Acair & Aberdeen University Press, Aberdeen.

MacMillan, D. (2002). The potential for producing a tradeable hunting obligation system as a mechanism for reducing deer numbers. SCOTECON report, University of Aberdeen.

MacMillan, D. C., Duff, E. I. & Elston, D. A. (2001). Modelling the non-market environmental costs and benefits of biodiversity projects using contingent valuation data. *Environmental and Resource Economics* **18**, 391–410.

Macpherson, A. H. & McLaren, I. A. (1959). Notes on the birds of southern Foxe Peninsula, Baffin Island, Northwest Territories. *Canadian Field-Naturalist* **71**, 63–81.

Macpherson, A. H. & Manning, T. H. (1959). The birds and mammals of Adelaide Peninsula, N.W.T. *Bulletin of the National Museum of Canada* **161**.

MacPherson, H. A. (1893). *Lagopus mutus* in Cumberland. *Zoologist* 1893, 97–9.

MacPherson, H. A. (1896). *The Grouse*. Fur & Feather Series, Longman's Green, London.

McSmith, A. (2006). Chernobyl: a poisonous legacy. *The Independent*, 14 March.

McVean, D. N. & Ratcliffe, D. A. (1962). *Plant Communities of the Scottish Highlands*. Nature Conservancy Monograph **1**. Her Majesty's Stationery Office, London.

Magnani, Y. (1995). Collisions oiseaux – câbles: un nouveau dispositif pour équiper les câbles de téléskis. *Supplement Bulletin Mensuel* **196**, Note technique 83. Office National de la Chasse, Paris.

Manniche, A. L. V. (1910). The terrestrial mammals and birds of north-east Greenland. Biological observations. *Meddelelser om Grønland* **45**.

Manning, A. H. (1948). Notes on the country, birds and mammals west of Hudson Bay between Reindeer and Baker Lakes. *Canadian Field-Naturalist* **62**, 1–28.

Manning, A. H. & Macpherson, A. H. (1961). A biological investigation of Prince of Wales Island, N.W.T. *Transactions of the Royal Canadian Institute* **33**, 116–239.

Manning, A. H., Höhn, E. O. & Macpherson, A. H. (1956). The birds of Banks Island. *Bulletin of the National Museum of Canada* **143**.

Marcström, V. (1986). Märkning av ripkycklingar – en utmanning för hunden. *Svensk Jakt* **124**, 508–10.

Marcström, V. & Höglund, N. H. (1980). Factors affecting reproduction of willow grouse (*Lagopus lagopus*) in two highland areas of Sweden. *Viltrevy* **11**, 285–314.

Marcström, V., Kenward, R. E. & Engren, E. (1988). The impact of predation on boreal tetraonids during vole cycles: an experimental study. *Journal of Animal Ecology* **57**, 859–72.

Marjakangas, A. (1986). On the winter ecology of the black grouse, *Tetrao tetrix*, in central Finland. *Acta Universitatis Ouluensis, Series A 183, Biology* **29**, 1–87.

Marjakangas, A. (1990). A suggested anti-predator function for snow-roosting behaviour in the black grouse *Tetrao tetrix*. *Ornis Scandinavica* **21**, 77–8.

Marjakangas, A., Rintamäki, H. & Hissa, R. (1984). Thermal responses in the capercaillie *Tetrao urogallus* and the black grouse *Lyrurus tetrix* roosting in the snow. *Physiological Zoology* **57**, 99–104.

Marquiss, M., Smith, R. & Galbraith, H. (1989). Diet of snowy owls on Cairn Gorm plateau in 1980 and 1987. *Scottish Birds* **15**, 180–1.

Marrs, R. H. & Pakeman, R. J. (1995). Bracken invasion – lessons from the past and prospects for the future. In: *Heaths and Moorland: Cultural Landscapes* (eds D. B. A. Thompson, A. J. Hester & M. B. Usher), pp. 180–93. Her Majesty's Stationery Office, Edinburgh.

Marrs, R. H., Rizand, A. & Harrison, A. F. (1989). The effect of removing sheep grazing on soil chemistry, above-ground nutrient distribution, and selected aspects of soil fertility in long-term experiments at Moor House National Nature Reserve. *Journal of Applied Ecology* **26**, 647–61.

Marti, C. & Bossert, A. (1985). Beobachtungen zur Sommeractivität und Brutbiologie des Alpenschneehuhns *Lagopus mutus* im Aletschgebiet (Wallis). *Ornithologische Beobachter* **82**, 153–68.

Martin, K. (1984). Reproductive defense priorities of male willow ptarmigan (*Lagopus lagopus*): enhancing mate survival or extending paternity options? *Behavioral Ecology & Sociobiology* **16**, 57–63.

Martin, K. (1989). Pairing and adoption of offspring by replacement male willow ptarmigan: behaviour, costs and consequences. *Animal Behaviour* **37**, 569–78.

Martin, K. (1991). Experimental evaluation of age, body size, and experience in determining territory ownership in willow ptarmigan. *Canadian Journal of Zoology* **69**, 1834–41.

Martin, K. & Cooke, F. (1987). Bi-parental care in willow ptarmigan – a luxury? *Animal Behaviour* **35**, 369–79.

Martin, K. & Hannon, S. J. (1987). Natal philopatry and recruitment of willow ptarmigan in north central and northwestern Canada. *Oecologia* **71**, 518–24.

Martin, K. & Horn, A. G. (1993). Clutch defense by male and female willow ptarmigan *Lagopus lagopus*. *Ornis Scandinavica* **24**, 261–6.

Martin, K. & Wiebe, K. L. (2004). Coping mechanisms of alpine and arctic breeding birds: extreme weather and limitations in reproductive resilience. *Integrative & Comparative Biology* **44**, 177–85.

Martin, K., Hannon, S. J. & Lord, S. (1990). Female–female aggression in white-tailed ptarmigan and willow ptarmigan during the pre-incubation period. *Wilson Bulletin* **102**, 532–6.

Martin, K., Holt, R. F. & Thomas, D. W. (1993). Getting by on high: ecological energetics of arctic and alpine grouse. In: *Life in the Cold: Ecological, Physiological, and Molecular Mechanisms* (eds C. Carey, G. L. Florant, B. A. Wunder & B. Horwitz), pp. 33–41. Westview Press, Boulder, Colorado.

Martin, K., Horn, A. G. & Hannon, S. J. (1995). The calls and associated behavior of breeding willow ptarmigan in Canada. *Wilson Bulletin* **107**, 496–509.

Mason, W. L., Hampson, A. & Edwards, C. (eds) (2004). *Managing the Pinewoods of Scotland*. Forestry Commission, Edinburgh.

Mather, A. S. (1978). The alleged deterioration of hill grazings in the Scottish Highlands. *Biological Conservation* **14**, 181–95.

Matthiopoulos, J., Moss, R., Mougeot, F., Lambin, X. & Redpath, S. M. (2003). Territorial behaviour and population dynamics in red grouse *Lagopus lagopus scoticus*. II. Population models. *Journal of Animal Ecology* **72**, 1083–90.

Matthiopoulos, J., Halley, J. M. & Moss, R. (2005). Socially induced red grouse population cycles need abrupt transitions between tolerance and aggression. *Ecology*, **86**, 1883–93.

Meile, P. (1982). Skiing facilities in alpine habitat of black grouse and capercaillie. *Proceedings of the International Grouse Symposium* **2**, 87–92.

**Ménoni, E.** (1990). Écologie et dynamique des populations du Grand Tétras dans les Pyrénées, avec des references speciales a la biologie de la réproduction chez les poules – quelques applications a sa conservation. PhD thesis, University of Toulouse.

**Ménoni, E.** (1991). Caquètements et territorialité des poules de grand tetras au printemps dans les Pyrénées. *Acta Biologica Montana* **10**, 63–82.

**Mercer, W. E.** (1967). Ecology of an island population of Newfoundland willow ptarmigan. *Technical Bulletin* **2**, Newfoundland & Labrador Wildlife Service, St John's.

**Mercer, W. E.** (1968). Ecology of an island population of Newfoundland willow ptarmigan. MSc thesis, University of Wisconsin, Madison.

**Mercer, E. & McGrath, R.** (1963). *A Study of a High Ptarmigan Population on Brunette Island, Newfoundland in 1962.* Department of Mines, Agriculture & Resources, St John's.

**Mikheev, A. V.** (1939). Linika i izmenyivosti beloyi kuropatki vostotsnoi Palearktiki. *Sb. Trudi Gosudarstvennogo Zoologicheskiy Muzeum Moskva* **5**, 65–108.

**Mikheev, A. V.** (1948). *Belaya Kuropatka.* Izdanie Glavni Upravleniye Zapovednika, Moscow.

**Miles, J.** (1988). Vegetation and soil change in the uplands. In: *Ecological Change in the Uplands* (eds M. B. Usher & D. B. A. Thompson), pp. 57–70. Blackwell Scientific Publications, Oxford.

**Millais, J. G.** (1909). *The Natural History of British Game Birds.* Longmans, London.

**Miller, G. R.** (1979). Quantity and quality of the annual production of shoots and flowers by *Calluna vulgaris* in north-east Scotland. *Journal of Ecology* **67**, 109–29.

**Miller, G. R. & Watson, A.** (1978). Heather productivity and its relevance to the regulation of red grouse populations. In: *Population Ecology of British Moors and Montane Grassland* (eds O. W. Heal & D. F. Perkins), pp. 277–85. Springer Verlag, Berlin.

**Miller, G. R., Jenkins, D. & Watson, A.** (1966). Heather performance and red grouse populations. I. Visual estimates of heather performance. *Journal of Applied Ecology* **3**, 313–26.

**Miller, G. R., Jenkins, D. & Watson, A.** (1970). Responses of red grouse populations to experimental improvement of their food. In: *Animal Populations in Relation to their Food Resources* (ed. A. Watson), pp. 323–5. Blackwell Scientific Publications, Oxford.

**Miltschew, B. & Georgiewa, U.** (1998). Erstbeobachtung des Alpenschneehuhns in Bulgarien. *Ornithologische Mitteilungen* **50**, 43–4.

**Miquet, A.** (1990). Mortality in black grouse *Tetrao tetrix* due to elevated cables. *Biological Conservation* **54**, 349–55.

**Mironov, K. A.** (1984). Recovery of bog bilberry and cranberry after ground fires. *Soviet Journal of Ecology* **15**, 199–204 (translated from the Russian original in *Ékologiya* **4** (1982), 18–24).

**Mitchell, A.** (ed.) (1906). *Geographical Collections relating to Scotland made by Walter Macfarlane.* Publications of the Scottish History Society **51**. Edinburgh University Press, Edinburgh.

**Montgomerie, R. D., Cartar, R., McLaughlin, R. L. & Lyon, B.** (1983). Birds of Sarcpa Lake, Melville Peninsula, Northwest Territories: breeding phenologies, densities and biogeography. *Arctic* **36**, 65–75.

**Montgomerie, R., Lyon, B. & Holder, K.** (2001). Dirty ptarmigan: behavioral modification of conspicuous male plumage. *Behavioral Ecology* **12**, 429–38.

**Moore, J. J., Dowding, P. & Healy, B.** (1975). Glenamoy, Ireland. In: *Structure & Function of Tundra Ecosystems* (eds T. Rosswall & O. W. Heal). *Ecological Bulletin* (Stockholm) **20**, 321–43.

**Moore, P. D.** (1975). The origin of blanket mires. *Nature* **256**, 267–9.

Moran, P. A. P. (1952). The statistical analysis of game-bird records. *Journal of Animal Ecology* **21**, 154–8.

Moran, P. A. P. (1954). The statistical analysis of game-bird records. II. *Journal of Animal Ecology* **23**, 35–7.

Moreau, R. (1954). The main vicissitudes of the European avifanua since the Pliocene. *Ibis* **96**, 411–31.

Mortensen, A. & Blix, A. S. (1986). Seasonal changes in resting metabolic rate and mass-specific conductance in Svalbard ptarmigan, Norwegian rock ptarmigan and willow ptarmigan. *Ornis Scandinavica* **17**, 8–13.

Mortensen, A., Unander, S., Kolstad, M. & Blix, A. S. (1983). Seasonal changes in body composition and crop content of Spitzbergen ptarmigan *Lagopus mutus hyperboreus*. *Ornis Scandinavica* **14**, 144–8.

Mortensen, A., Nordøy, E. S. & Blix, A. S. (1985). Seasonal changes in the body composition of the Norwegian rock ptarmigan *Lagopus mutus*. *Ornis Scandinavica* **16**, 25–8.

Moss, R. (1968). Food selection and nutrition in ptarmigan (*Lagopus mutus*). *Symposia of the Zoological Society of London* **21**, 207–16.

Moss R. (1969). A comparison of red grouse (*Lagopus lagopus scoticus*) stocks with the production and nutritive value of heather (*Calluna vulgaris*). *Journal of Animal Ecology* **38**, 103–12.

Moss, R. (1972a). Social organization of willow ptarmigan on their breeding grounds in interior Alaska. *Condor* **74**, 144–51.

Moss, R. (1972b). Food selection by red grouse (*Lagopus lagopus scoticus* Lath.) in relation to chemical composition. *Journal of Animal Ecology* **41**, 411–18.

Moss, R. (1972c). Effects of captivity on gut lengths in captive red grouse. *Journal of Wildlife Management* **36**, 99–104.

Moss, R. (1973). The digestion and intake of winter foods by wild ptarmigan in Alaska. *Condor* **75**, 293–300.

Moss, R. (1974). Winter diets, gut lengths and interspecific competition in Alaskan ptarmigan. *Auk* **91**, 737–46.

Moss, R. (1977). The digestion of heather by red grouse during the spring. *Condor* **79**, 471–7.

Moss, R. (1980). Why are capercaillie cocks so big? *British Birds* **73**, 440–7.

Moss, R. (1983). Gut size, body weight, and digestion of winter foods by grouse and ptarmigan. *Condor* **85**, 185–93.

Moss, R. (1986). Rain, breeding success and distribution of capercaillie *Tetrao urogallus* and black grouse *Tetrao tetrix* in Scotland. *Ibis* **128**, 65–72.

Moss, R. (1989). Gut size and the digestion of fibrous diets by tetraonid birds. *Journal of Experimental Zoology* Supplement **3**, 61–6.

Moss, R. (1997). Grouse and ptarmigan nutrition in the wild and in captivity. *Proceedings of the Nutrition Society* **5**, 1137–45.

Moss, R. (2001). Second extinction of capercaillie (*Tetrao urogallus*) in Scotland? *Biological Conservation* **101**, 255–7.

Moss, R. & Hanssen, I. (1980). Grouse nutrition. *Nutrition Abstracts Review – Series B* **50**, 555–67.

Moss, R. & Lockie, I. (1979). Infrasonic components in the song of the capercaillie *Tetrao urogallus*. *Ibis* **121**, 95–7.

Moss, R. & Oswald, J. (1985). Population dynamics of capercaillie in a North-east Scottish glen. *Ornis Scandinavica* **16**, 229–38.

Moss, R. & Picozzi, N. (1994). *Management of Forests for Capercaillie in Scotland*. Forestry Commission Bulletin **113**. Her Majesty's Stationery Office, London.

Moss, R. & Watson, A. (1982). Determination of clutch size in red grouse without implying the egg-'numerostat'. A reply to Steen and Parker.*Ornis Scandinavica* **13**, 249–50.

Moss, R. & Watson, A. (1984). Maternal nutrition, egg quality and breeding success of Scottish ptarmigan *Lagopus mutus*. *Ibis* **126**, 212–20.

Moss, R. & Watson, A. (1985). Adaptive value of spacing behaviour in population cycles of red grouse and other animals. *Symposia of the British Ecological Society* **25**, 275–94.

Moss, R. & Watson, A. (1987). Changes in the down colour of chicks during a population decline in red grouse. *Oecologia* **73**, 598–600.

Moss, R. & Watson, A. (1990). Red grouse numbers in relation to their resources. In: *Red Grouse Population Processes* (eds A. N. Lance & J. H. Lawton), pp. 53–61. Royal Society for the Protection of Birds, Sandy, Bedfordshire.

Moss, R. & Watson, A. (1991). Population cycles and kin selection in red grouse *Lagopus lagopus scoticus*. *Ibis* **133**, Supplement **1**, 113–20.

Moss, R. & Watson, A. (2001). Population cycles in birds of the grouse family (Tetraonidae). *Advances in Ecological Research* **32**, 53–111.

Moss, R. & Weir, D. (1987). Demography of capercaillie *Tetrao urogallus* in north-east Scotland. III. Production and recruitment of young. *Ornis Scandinavica* **18**, 141–5.

Moss, R., Watson, A., Parr, R. & Glennie, W. (1971). Effects of dietary supplements of newly-growing heather on the breeding of captive red grouse. *British Journal of Nutrition* **25**, 135–43.

Moss, R., Miller, G. R. & Allen, S. E. (1972). Selection of heather by captive red grouse in relation to the age of the plant. *Journal of Applied Ecology* **9**, 771–81.

Moss, R., Watson A. & Parr, R. (1975). Maternal nutrition and breeding success in red grouse (*Lagopus lagopus scoticus*). *Journal of Animal Ecology* **44**, 233–44.

Moss, R., Kolb, H. H., Marquiss, M., Watson, A., Treca, B., Watt, D. & Glennie, W. W. (1979a). Aggressiveness and dominance in captive cock red grouse. *Aggressive Behavior* **5**, 59–84.

Moss, R., Weir, D. & Jones, A. (1979b). Capercaillie management in Scotland. In: *Woodland Grouse 1978* (ed. T. W. I. Lovel), pp. 140–55. World Pheasant Association, Lamarsh, Bures, Suffolk.

Moss, R., Watson, A., Rothery, P. & Glennie, W. W. (1981). Clutch size, egg size, hatch weight and laying date in relation to early mortality in red grouse *Lagopus lagopus scoticus* chicks. *Ibis* **123**, 450–62.

Moss, R., Watson, A., Rothery, P. & Glennie, W. W. (1982). Inheritance of dominance and aggressiveness in captive red grouse *Lagopus lagopus scoticus*. *Aggressive Behavior* **8**, 1–18.

Moss, R., Watson, A. & Rothery, P. (1984). Inherent changes in the body size, viability and behaviour of a fluctuating red grouse (*Lagopus lagopus scoticus*) population. *Journal of Animal Ecology* **53**, 171–89.

Moss, R., Watson, A. & Parr, R. (1988). Mate choice by hen red grouse *Lagopus lagopus* with an excess of cocks – role of territory size and food quality. *Ibis* **130**, 545–52.

Moss, R., Shaw, J. L., Watson, A. & Trenholm, I. (1990a). Role of the caecal threadworm *Trichostrongylus tenuis* in the population dynamics of red grouse. In: *Red Grouse Population Processes* (eds A. N. Lance & J. H. Lawton), pp. 62–71. Royal Society for the Protection of Birds, Sandy.

Moss, R., Trenholm, I. B., Watson, A. & Parr, R. (1990b). Parasitism, predation and survival of hen red grouse *Lagopus lagopus scoticus* in spring. *Journal of Animal Ecology* **59**, 631–42.

Moss, R., Watson, A., Parr, R., Trenholm, I. B. & Marquiss, M. (1993a). Growth rate, condition and survival of red grouse *Lagopus lagopus scoticus* chicks. *Ornis Scandinavica* **24**, 303–10.

Moss, R., Watson, A., Trenholm, I. & Parr, R. (1993b). Caecal threadworms *Trichostrongylus tenuis* in red grouse *Lagopus lagopus scoticus*: effects of weather and host density upon estimated worm burdens. *Parasitology* **107**, 199–209.

Moss, R., Parr, R. & Lambin, X. (1994). Effects of testosterone on breeding density, breeding success and survival of red grouse. *Proceedings of the Royal Society of London B* **255**, 91–7.

Moss, R., Watson A. & Parr, R. (1996). Experimental prevention of a population cycle in red grouse. *Ecology* **77**, 1512–30.

Moss, R., Elston, D. A. & Watson, A. (2000a). Spatial asynchrony and demographic traveling waves during red grouse population cycles. *Ecology* **81**, 981–9.

Moss, R., Picozzi, N., Summers, R. W. & Baines, D. (2000b). Capercaillie *Tetrao urogallus* – demography of a declining population. *Ibis* **142**, 259–67.

Moss, R., Oswald, J. & Baines, D. (2001). Climate change and breeding success: decline of the capercaillie in Scotland. *Journal of Animal Ecology* **70**, 47–61.

Moss, R., Picozzi, N. & Catt, D. C. (2006). Natal dispersal of capercaillie *Tetrao urogallus* in northeast Scotland. *Wildlife Biology* **12**, 227–32.

Mossop, D. H. (1988). Winter survival and spring breeding strategies of willow ptarmigan. In: *Adaptive Strategies and Population Ecology of Northern Grouse* (eds A. T. Bergerud & M. W. Gratson), pp. 330–78. University of Minnesota Press, Minneapolis.

Mougeot, F. & Redpath, S. M. (2004). Sexual ornamentation relates to immune function in male red grouse *Lagopus lagopus scoticus*. *Journal of Avian Biology* **35**, 425–33.

Mougeot, F., Redpath, S. M., Leckie, F. & Hudson, P. J. (2003a). The effect of aggressiveness on the population dynamics of a territorial bird. *Nature* **421**, 737–9.

Mougeot, F., Redpath, S. M., Moss, R., Matthiopoulos, J. & Hudson, P. J. (2003b). Territorial behaviour and population dynamics in red grouse *Lagopus lagopus scoticus*. I. Population experiments. *Journal of Animal Ecology* **72**, 1073–82.

Mougeot, F., Irvine, J. R., Seivwright, L. J., Redpath, S. M. & Piertney, S. (2004). Testosterone, immunocompetence and honest sexual signaling in male red grouse. *Behavioral Ecology* **15**, 930–7.

Mougeot, F., Dawson, A., Redpath, S. M. & Leckie, F. (2005a). Testosterone and autumn territorial behavior in male red grouse *Lagopus lagopus scoticus*. *Hormones and Behavior* **47**, 576–84.

Mougeot, F., Evans, S. A. & Redpath, S. M. (2005b). Interactions between population processes in a cyclic species: parasites reduce autumn territorial behaviour of male red grouse. *Oecologia* **144**, 289–98.

Mougeot, F., Piertney, S. B., Leckie, F., Evans, S., Moss, R., Redpath, S. M. & Hudson, P. J. (2005c). Experimentally increased aggressiveness reduces population kin structure and subsequent recruitment in red grouse *Lagopus lagopus scoticus*. *Journal of Animal Ecology* **74**, 488–97.

Mougeot, F., Redpath, S. M. & Leckie, F. (2005d). Ultra-violet reflectance of male and female red grouse, *Lagopus lagopus scoticus*: sexual ornaments reflect nematode parasite intensity. *Journal of Avian Biology* **36**, 203–9.

Mougeot, F., Redpath, S. M. & Piertney, S. B. (2005e). Elevated spring testosterone increases parasite intensity in male red grouse. *Behavioral Ecology* **17**, 117–25.

Mougeot, F., Martinez-Padilla, J., Pérez-Rodríguez, L. & Bortolotti, G. R. (2007). Carotenoid-based colouration and ultraviolet reflectance of the sexual ornaments of grouse. *Behavioral Ecology & Sociobiology* **61**, 741–51.

Mountford, M. D., Watson, A., Moss, R., Parr, R. & Rothery, P. (1990). Land inheritance and population cycles of red grouse. In: *Red Grouse Population Processes* (eds A. N. Lance & J. H. Lawton), pp. 78–83. Royal Society for the Protection of Birds, Sandy, Bedfordshire.

Mowle, A. & Bell, M. (1988). Rural policy factors in land-use change. In: *Ecological Change in the Uplands* (eds M. B. Usher & D. B. A. Thompson), pp. 165–82. Blackwell, Oxford.

Munkebye, E., Pedersen, H. C., Steen, J. B. & Brøseth, H. (2003). Predation of eggs and incubating females in willow ptarmigan *Lagopus l. lagopus*. *Fauna Norvegica Series C* **23**, 1–8.

Murie, A. (1946). Observations on the birds of Mount McKinley National Park, Alaska. *Condor* **48**, 253–61.

Murray, M. & Simcox, H. (2003). *Use of Wild Living Resources in the United Kingdom – a Review*. UK Committee for IUCN, Cambridge.

Murray, R. D. (ed.) (1994). Scottish Bird Report 1992 **25**, 22.

Murray, R. D. (ed.) (1996). Scottish Bird Report 1994 **27**, 25.

Myrberget, S. (1975). Age determination of willow grouse chicks. *Norwegian Journal of Zoology* **23**, 165–71.

Myrberget, S. (1976). Hunting, mortality, migration and age composition of Norwegian willow grouse *Lagopus lagopus*. *Norwegian Journal of Zoology* **24**, 47–52.

Myrberget, S. (1983). Vacant habitats during a decline in a population of willow grouse *Lagopus lagopus*. *Fauna Norvegica Series C* **6**, 1–7.

Myrberget, S. (1984a). Årsvariasjoner i kroppsvekt hos lirype i Nord-Norge. *Fauna* **17**, 56–62.

Myrberget, S. (1984b). Population cycles of willow grouse *Lagopus lagopus* on an island in north Norway. *Fauna Norvegica Series C* **7**, 46–56.

Myrberget, S. (1984c). Population dynamics of willow grouse *Lagopus lagopus* on an island in north Norway. *Fauna Norvegica Series C* **7**, 95–105.

Myrberget, S. (1985). Egg predation in an island population of willow grouse *Lagopus lagopus*. *Fauna Norvegica Series C* **8**, 82–7.

Myrberget, S. (1986a). Annual variation in clutch sizes of a population of willow grouse *Lagopus lagopus*. *Fauna Norvegica Series C* **9**, 74–81.

Myrberget, S. (1986b). Age and breeding of willow grouse *Lagopus lagopus*. *Norwegian Journal of Zoology* **24**, 47–52.

Myrberget, S. (1987a). Effecter av sauebeiting i et rypeterreng. *Fauna* **40**, 144–9.

Myrberget, S. (1987b). Seasonal decline in clutch size of the willow grouse *Lagopus l. lagopus*. *Fauna Norvegica Series C* **10**, 11–20.

Myrberget, S. (1988). Demography of an island population of willow ptarmigan in northern Norway. In: *Adaptive Strategies and Population Ecology of Northern Grouse* (eds A. T. Bergerud & M. W. Gratson), pp. 379–442. University of Minnesota Press, Minneapolis.

Myrberget, S. (1989a). Philopatry in an island population of willow grouse *Lagopus lagopus*. *Fauna Norvegica Series C* **12**, 31–9.

Myrberget, S. (1989b). Norwegian research on willow grouse: implications for management. *Finnish Game Research* **46**, 17–25.

Myrberget, S., Aune, O. A. & Moksnes, A. (1969). Ytre kjønnsbestemmelse og vekter av ryper fra det nordlige Norge vinteren 1966/67. *Meddelelser fra Statens Viltundersøkelser* **2(31)**.

Myrberget, S., Erikstad, K. E. & Spidsø, T. K. (1977). Variations from year to year in growth rates of willow grouse chicks. *Astarte* **10**, 9–14.

National Audit Office (1986). *Review of Forestry Commission Objectives and Achievements*. Her Majesty's Stationery Office, London.

Nelson, E. W. (1887). Report upon the natural history collections made in Alaska between the years 1877 and 1881. *Signal Service US Army, Arctic Series, Part 1, Birds*, 19–226.

Nethersole-Thompson, C. & Nethersole-Thompson, D. (1939). Some observations on the sexual life, display and breeding of the red grouse. *British Birds* **32**, 247–54.

Nethersole-Thompson, D. & Watson, A. (1974). *The Cairngorms: their Natural History and Scenery*. Collins, London. (2nd edn 1981, Melven Press, Perth.)

Newborn, D. & Foster, R. (2002). Control of parasite burdens in wild red grouse *Lagopus lagopus scoticus* through the indirect application of anthelmintics. *Journal of Applied Ecology* **39**, 908–14.

Newton, I. (1993). Predation and limitation of bird numbers. *Current Ornithology* **11**, 143–98.

Newton, I. (1994). Experiments on the limitation of bird breeding densities – a review. *Ibis* **136**, 397–411.

Nichols, H. (1969). Chronology of peat growth in Canada. *Palaeogeography, Palaeoclimatology, Palaeoecology* **6**, 61–5.

Nichols, H. (1976). Historical aspects of the present northern Canadian tree-line. *Arctic* **29**, 38–47.

Nicolaisen, W. F. H. (1963). A short comparative list of Celtic bird names of the British Isles. In: *The Birds of the British Isles. Vol. 12*, by D. A. Bannerman, pp. 405–23. Oliver & Boyd, Edinburgh.

Nielsen, Ó. K. (1999). Gyrfalcon predation on ptarmigan: numerical and functional responses. *Journal of Animal Ecology* **68**, 1034–50.

Nielsen, Ó. K. (2003). The impact of food availability on gyrfalcon (*Falco rusticolus*) diet and timing of breeding. In: *Birds of Prey in a Changing Environment* (eds D. B. A. Thompson, S. M. Redpath, A. H. Fielding, M. Marquiss & C. A. Galbraith), pp. 283–302. The Stationery Office, Edinburgh.

Nielsen, Ó. K. & Pétursson, G. (1995). Population fluctuations of gyrfalcons and rock ptarmigan: analysis of export figures from Iceland. *Wildlife Biology* **1**, 65–71.

Nilsson, M.-C. & Wardle, D. A. (2005). Understorey vegetation as a forest ecosystem driver: evidence from the northern Swedish boreal forest. *Frontiers in Ecology & Environment* **3**, 421–8.

Novikov, B. G. (1939). Mechanismus der Saisonveränderungen am Federkleid bei *Lagopus lagopus* (L.). *Comptes Rendues Academy of Sciences of the USSR* **25**, 554–6.

Novoa, C. & Gonzales, G. (1988). Comparaison des biotopes sélectionnés par le lagopède alpin (*Lagopus mutus*) et la perdrix grise des Pyrénées (*Perdix perdix hispaniensis*) sur le massif du Carlit (Pyrénées-Orientales). *Gibier Faune Sauvage* **5**, 187–202.

Novoa, C., Hansen, E. & Ménoni, E. (1990). La mortalité de trois espèces de galliformes par collision dans les câbles: résultats d'une enquête pyrénéene. *Bulletin Mensuel* **151**, 17–22. Office National de la Chasse, Paris.

**Observatoire des Galliformes de Montagne** (2002). *Rapport Annuel 2002*. Office Nationale de la Chasse et de la Faune Sauvage, Sévrier.

O'Connell, M. (1990). Origins of Irish lowland blanket bog. In: *Ecology and Conservation of Irish Peatlands* (ed. G. J. Doyle), pp. 49–71. Royal Irish Academy, Dublin.

Ó Dónaill, N. (1977). *Foclóir Gaeilge-Béarla*. Oifig an tSoláthair, Baile Átha Cliath

O'Dwyer, R. (ed.) (1995). *Canada Life Irish Red Grouse Conference October 1993*. Irish Field Trials Grouse Ground Committee, Cappagh, Waterford.

Ogilvy, G. & Bayer, K. (2003). *Scotland on Sunday* 5 October.

O'Hare, P. J. (1973). Irish red grouse – position and prospects. In: *The Future of Irish Wildlife* (ed. F. O'Gorman & E. Wymes), pp. 39–44. An Foras Taluntais, Dublin.

Olpinski, S. C. (1986). Breeding ecology, habitat and morphometrics of rock ptarmigan *Lagopus mutus* L. in Nouveau-Québec. MSc thesis, McGill University, Montreal.

Ormiston, J. M. (1988). Economic implications of game on the Speyside estate. In: *Land Use in the River Spey Catchment* (ed. D. Jenkins), pp. 233–5. Aberdeen Centre for Land Use.

Pakkala, T., Pellika, J. & Lindén, H. (2003). Capercaillie *Tetrao urogallus* – a good candidate for an umbrella species in taiga forests. *Wildlife Biology* **9**, 309–16.

Palmer, S. C. F. & Bacon, P. J. (2000). A GIS approach to identifying territorial resource competition. *Ecography* **23**, 513–24.

Palmer, S. C. F. & Bacon, P. J. (2001). The utilization of heather moorland by territorial red grouse *Lagopus lagopus scoticus*. *Ibis* **143**, 222–32.

Palmer, S. C. F., Gordon, I. J., Hester, A. J. & Pakeman, R. J. (2004). Introducing spatial grazing impacts into the prediction of moorland vegetation dynamics. *Landscape Ecology* **19**, 817–27.

Park, K. J., Hurley, M. M. & Hudson, P. J. (2001). Territorial status and survival in red grouse *Lagopus lagopus scoticus*: hope for the doomed surplus? *Journal of Avian Biology* **33**, 56–62.

Park, K. J., Robertson, P. A., Campbell, S. T., Foster, R., Russell, Z. M., Newborn, D. & Hudson, P. J. (2002). The role of invertebrates in the diet, growth and survival of red grouse (*Lagopus lagopus scoticus*) chicks. *Journal of Zoology* **254**, 137–45.

Parker, H. (1981a). Renesting biology of Norwegian willow ptarmigan. *Journal of Wildlife Management* **45**, 858–64.

Parker, H. (1981b). Duration of fertility in willow ptarmigan hens after separation from the cock. *Ornis Scandinavica* **12**, 186–7.

Parker, H. (1984). Effect of corvid removal on reproduction of willow ptarmigan and black grouse. *Journal of Wildlife Management* **48**, 1197–205.

Parker, H. (1985). Compensatory reproduction through renesting in willow ptarmigan. *Journal of Wildlife Management* **49**, 599–604.

Parmelee, D. F. & MacDonald, S. D. (1960). The birds of west-central Ellesmere Island and adjacent areas. *Bulletin of the National Museum of Canada* **169**.

Parmelee, D. F., Stephens, H. A. & Schmidt, R. H. (1967). The birds of southeastern Victoria Island and adjacent small islands. *Bulletin of the National Museum of Canada* **78**.

Parr, R. (1975). Aging red grouse chicks by primary molt and development. *Journal of Wildlife Management* **39**, 188–90.

Parr, R. A. (1992). Moorland birds and their predators in relation to afforestation. PhD thesis, University of Aberdeen.

Parr, R. & Watson, A. (1988). Habitat preferences of black grouse on moorland-dominated ground in north-east Scotland. *Ardea* **76**, 175–80.

Parr, R., Watson, A. & Moss, R. (1993). Changes in the numbers and interspecific interactions of red grouse (*Lagopus lagopus scoticus*) and black grouse (*Tetrao tetrix*). *Avocetta* **17**, 55–9.

Parry, M. L. (1978). *Climate Change, Agriculture and Settlement*. Studies in Historical Geography. Dawson, Folkestone, & Archon Books, Hamden.

Pearce-Higgins, J. W., Grant, M. C., Robinson, M. C. & Haysom, S. L. (2007). The role of forest maturation in causing the decline of black grouse *Tetrao tetrix*. *Ibis* **149**, 143–55.

Pearsall, W. H. (1950). *Mountains and Moorlands*. Collins, London.

Pearson, H. J. (1907). On the ptarmigan of Franz Josef Land. *Ibis* **9**, 507–9.

Pedersen, Å. Ø., Lier, M., Routti, H., Christiansen, H. H. & Fuglei, E. (2006). Co-feeding between Svalbard rock ptarmigan (*Lagopus mutus hyperboreus*) and Svalbard reindeer (*Rangifer tarandus platyrhynchus*). *Arctic* **59**, 61–4.

Pedersen, H. C. (1984). Territory size, mating status, and individual survival of males in a fluctuating population of willow ptarmigan. *Ornis Scandinavica* **15**, 197–203.

Pedersen, H. C. (1988). Territorial behaviour and breeding numbers in Norwegian willow ptarmigan: a removal experiment. *Ornis Scandinavica* **19**, 81–7.

Pedersen, H. C. (1989). Effects of exogenous prolactin on parental behaviour in free-living female willow ptarmigan *Lagopus l. lagopus*. *Animal Behaviour* **38**, 926–34.

**Pedersen, H. C.** (1993). Reproductive success and survival of widowed willow ptarmigan hens. *Ornis Fennica* **70**, 17–21.

**Pedersen, H. C. & Myklebust, I.** (1993). Age-dependent accumulation of cadmium and zinc in the liver and kidneys of Norwegian willow ptarmigan. *Bulletin of Environmental Contamination & Toxicology* **51**, 381–8.

**Pedersen, H. C. & Steen, J. B.** (1979). Behavioural thermoregulation in willow ptarmigan chicks (*Lagopus lagopus*). *Ornis Scandinavica* **10**, 17–21.

**Pedersen, H. C. & Steen, J. B.** (1985). Parental care and chick production in a fluctuating population of willow ptarmigan. *Ornis Scandinavica* **16**, 270–6.

**Pedersen, H. C., Steen, J. B. & Andersen, R.** (1983). Social organization and territorial behaviour in a willow ptarmigan population. *Ornis Scandinavica* **14**, 263–72.

**Pedersen, H. C., Steen, H., Kastdalen, L., Brøseth, H., Ims, R., Svendsen, W. & Yoccoz, N. G.** (2003). Weak compensation of harvest despite strong density-dependent growth in willow ptarmigan. *Proceedings of the Royal Society of London* B, **271**, 381–5.

**Pendergast, B. A. & Boag, D. A.** (1970). Seasonal changes in diet of spruce grouse in central Alberta. *Journal of Wildlife Management* **34**, 605–11.

**Pennant, T.** (1771). *A Tour in Scotland 1769*. Monk, Chester; reprinted (2000), Birlinn, Edinburgh.

**Pennie, I. D.** (1950, 1951). The history and distribution of the capercaillie in Scotland. *Scottish Naturalist* **62**, 65–87, 157–78; **63**, 4–17, 135.

**Pennie, I. D.** (1957). Photographic studies of some less familiar birds. LXXIX. Ptarmigan. *British Birds* **1**, 102–5. (Photographs by D. G. Andrew, H. Auger, R. P. Bille, L. Portenko, J. H. Sears, P. O. Swanberg & A. Tewnion.)

**Pereira, S. L. & Baker, A. J.** (2006). A molecular timescale for galliform birds accounting for uncertainty in time estimates and heterogeneity of rates of DNA substitutions across lineages and sites. *Molecular Phylogenetics and Evolution* **38**, 499–509.

**Peterle, T. J.** (1955). Notes on the display of the red grouse. *Scottish Naturalist* **67**, 61–4.

**Petty, S. J., Anderson, D. I. K., Davison, M., Little, B., Sherratt, T. N., Thomas, C. J. & Lambin, X.** (2003). The decline of common kestrels *Falco tinnunculus* in a forested area of northern England: the role of predation by northern goshawks *Accipiter gentilis*. *Ibis* **145**, 472–83.

**Pfeffer, J.-J.** (1997). Découverte du lagopède alpin *Lagopus mutus* et observations ornithologiques au Tadjikistan. *Alauda* **65**, 379–80.

**Phillips, J.** (1990a). The problems of 'white' moorland. *Annual Report of the Joseph Nickerson Reconciliation Project* **6**, 40–1.

**Phillips, J.** (1990b). 'Buffer' feeding of raptors. *Annual Report of the Joseph Nickerson Reconciliation Project* **6**, 46.

**Phillips, J.** (1994). Study area reports: a summary of nine years field work. In: *The Heather Trust Annual Report 1994* (eds J. Phillips & A. Watson), pp. 7–19. Heather Trust, Kippen, Stirlingshire.

**Phillips, J.** (1999). Misty Law. In: *The Heather Trust Annual Report 1999* (eds J. Phillips, W. Gruellich & A. McCulloch), pp. 26–8. Heather Trust, Kippen, Stirlingshire.

**Phillips, J. & Watson, A.** (1995). Key requirements for management of heather moorland: now and for the future. In: *Heaths and Moorland: Cultural Landscapes* (eds D. B. A. Thompson, A. J. Hester & M. B. Usher), pp. 344–61. Her Majesty's Stationery Office, Edinburgh.

**Phillips, J. & Wilson, K.** (1987). The heather beetle (*Lochmaea suturalis*) and its effect on moorland. *Annual Report of the Reconciliation Project* **3**, 31–3.

**Phillips, J., Steen, J. B., Raen, S. G. & Aalerud, F.** (1992a). Effects of burning and cutting on vegetation and on a population of willow grouse *Lagopus lagopus* in Norway. *Fauna Norvegica Series C* **15**, 37–42.

Phillips, J., Watson, A. & MacDonald, A. (1992b). *A Muirburn Code*. Scottish Natural Heritage, Perth.

Picozzi, N. (1968). Grouse bags in relation to the management and geology of heather moors. *Journal of Applied Ecology* **5**, 483–8.

Picozzi, N. (1971). Breeding performance and shooting bags of red grouse in relation to public access in the Peak District National Park. *Biological Conservation* **3**, 211–15.

Picozzi, N. (1986). Black grouse research in north-east Scotland. Unpublished report, Institute of Terrestrial Ecology, Banchory, Kincardineshire.

Picozzi, N., Moss, R. & Catt, D.C. (1996). Capercaillie diet, habitat and management in a Sitka spruce plantation in central Scotland. *Forestry* **69**, 373–88.

Picozzi, N., Moss, R. & Kortland, K. (1999). Diet and survival of capercaillie *Tetrao urogallus* chicks in Scotland. *Wildlife Biology* **5**, 11–23.

Poirot, J. & Preiss, F. (2002). Update of number of capercaillie in the Vosges mountains. *Grouse News* **21**, 14–18.

Polunin, N. (1948). Botany of the Canadian eastern Arctic. Part III. Vegetation and ecology. *Bulletin of the National Museum of Canada* **104**.

Poole, K. G. (1987). Aspects of the ecology, food habits and foraging characteristics of gyrfalcons in the central Canadian Arctic. MSc thesis, University of Alberta, Edmonton.

Porkert, J. (1979). The influence of human factors on tetraonid populations in Czechoslovakia. In: *Woodland Grouse 1978* (ed. T. W. I. Lovel), pp. 74–82. World Pheasant Association, Lamarsh, Bures, Suffolk.

Porkert, J. (1991). Hoarfrost deposits as a factor contributing to the extinction of tetraonids in the eastern Sudetes. *Ornis Scandinavica* **22**, 292–3.

Potapov, R. L. (1974). Adaptations of the family Tetraonidae to the winter season. *Proceedings of the Zoological Institute of the Academy of Sciences of the USSR* **44**, 207–51 (in Russian).

Potapov, R. L. (1985). *Fauna SSSR Ptitsy. 3. 1. Galliformes. Tetraonidae*. Nauka, Leningrad.

Potapov, R. L. (2004). About 'Découverte du lagopède alpin *Lagopus mutus* et observations ornithologiques au Tadjikistan', *Alauda* (1997) **65**, 379–80. *Alauda* **72**, 338–9.

Potapov, R. L. & Flint, V. E. (1987). *Ptitsy SSR*. Akademii Nauka, Leningrad. (1989); reprinted as *Handbuch der Vögel der Sowjetunion. 4*. Ziemsen Verlag Wittenberg Lutherstadt, Germany.

Potapov, R. L., Potapova, O. R. & Pavlova, E. A. (2003). The genus *Lagopus* Brisson, 1760: taxonomy, paleontological dates, and evolution. *Proceedings of the Zoological Institute of the Russian Academy of Sciences* **299**, 101–20.

Potts, G. R. (1998). Global dispersion of nesting hen harriers: implications for grouse moors in the United Kingdom. *Ibis* **140**, 76–88.

Preble, E. A. (1908). A biological investigation of the Athabaska-Mackenzie region. *North American Fauna* **27**.

Price, M. F., Dixon, B. J., Warren, C. R. & Macpherson, A. R. (2002). *Scotland's Mountains: Key Issues for their Future Management*. Scottish Natural Heritage, Perth.

Pruitt, W. O. (1958). Observations on the bioclimate of some taiga mammals. *Arctic* **10**, 130–8.

Pruitt, W. O. (1960). Animals in the snow. *Scientific American* **202**, 61–8.

Pulliainen, E. (1976). Small intestine and caeca lengths in the willow grouse (*Lagopus lagopus*) in Finnish Lapland. *Annales Zoologici Fennici* **13**, 195–9.

Pulliainen, E. (1978). Behaviour of a willow grouse *Lagopus l. lagopus* at the nest. *Ornis Fennica* **55**, 141–8.

Pulliainen, E. (1980). Heart/body weight ratio in the willow grouse *Lagopus lagopus* and rock ptarmigan *Lagopus mutus* in Finnish Lapland. *Ornis Fennica* **57**, 88–90.

Pulliainen, E. & Ollinmäki, P. (1996). A long-term study of the winter food niche of the pine marten *Martes martes* in northern boreal Finland. *Acta Theriologica* **41**, 337–52.

Putman, R. J. (2000). Diet of pine martens *Martes martes* L. in west Scotland. *Journal of Natural History* **34**, 793–7.

Rae, S. (1994). Individual dispersion and productivity of ptarmigan in relation to their selection of food and cover. PhD thesis, University of Aberdeen.

Rae, S. (2004). Review of *Birds of Prey in a Changing Environment*. Ed. D. B. A. Thompson et al., 2003. *Bulletin of the British Ecological Society* **35**, 44.

Ramsay, P. (1996). *Revival of the Land – Creag Meagaidh National Nature Reserve*. Scottish Natural Heritage, Battleby, Redgorton, Perth.

Ratcliffe, D. A. (1980). *The Peregrine Falcon*. Poyser, Calton.

Ratcliffe, D. A. (1990). *Bird Life of Mountain and Upland*. Cambridge University Press, Cambridge.

Ratcliffe, D. A. & Thompson, D. B. A. (1988). The British uplands: their ecological character and international significance. In: *Ecological Change in the Uplands* (eds M. B. Usher & D. B. A. Thompson), pp. 9–36. Blackwell Scientific Publications, Oxford.

Redig, P.T. (1989). The avian ceca: obligate combustion chambers or facultative afterburners? – The conditioning influence of diet. *Journal of Experimental Zoology*, Supplement **3**, 66–9.

Redpath, S. M. & Thirgood, S. J. (1997). *Birds of Prey and Red Grouse*. The Stationery Office, London.

Redpath, S. M., Thirgood, S. J. & Leckie, F. M. (2001). Does supplementary feeding reduce predation of red grouse by hen harriers? *Journal of Applied Ecology* **38**, 1157–68.

Redpath, S. M., Arroyo, B. E., Leckie, F. M., Bacon, P., Bayfield, N., Gutiérrez, R. J. & Thirgood, S. J. (2004). Using decision modelling with stakeholders to reduce human-wildlife conflict: a raptor-grouse case study. *Conservation Biology* **18**, 350–9.

Redpath, S. M., Mougeot, F., Leckie, F. M., Elston, D. A. & Hudson, P. J. (2006a). Testing the role of parasites in driving the cyclic population dynamics of a gamebird. *Ecology Letters* **9**, 410–18.

Redpath, S. M., Mougeot, F., Leckie, F. M. & Evans, S. A. (2006b). The effects of autumn testosterone on survival and productivity in red grouse, *Lagopus lagopus scoticus*. *Animal Behaviour* **71**, 1297–1305.

Regnaut, S. (2004). Population genetics of capercaillie (*Tetrao urogallus*) in the Jura and the Pyrenees: a non-invasive approach to avian conservation genetics. PhD thesis, University of Lausanne.

Regnaut, S., Christe, P., Chapuisat, M. & Fumagilli, L. (2006). Genotyping faeces reveals facultative kin association in capercaillies' leks. *Conservation Genetics* **7(5)**, 665–74.

Reid, H. W. (1975). Experimental infection of red grouse with louping-ill virus (Flavivirus group). I. The viraemia and antibody response. *Journal of Comparative Pathology* **85**, 223–9.

Reid, H. W. & Moss, R. (1980). The response of four species of birds to louping-ill virus. In: *Arboviruses in the Mediterranean Countries, Zbl. Bakt.* Supplement **9** (eds J. Vesenjak-Hirjan et al.), pp. 219–23. Gustav Fischer Verlag, Stuttgart & New York.

Reid, H. W., Moss, R., Pow, I. & Buxton, D. (1980). The response of three grouse species (*Tetrao urogallus, Lagopus mutus, Lagopus lagopus*) to louping-ill virus. *Journal of Comparative Pathology* **90**, 257–63.

Remington, T. E. & Hoffman, R. W. (1997). Costs of detoxification of xenobiotics in conifer needles to blue grouse *Dendragapus obscurus*. *Wildlife Biology* **3**, 289.

Richards, E. (1985). *A History of the Highland Clearances*. Croom Helm, Beckenham; reprinted (2002), Birlinn, Edinburgh.

Rintamäki, P. T., Alatolo, R. V., Höglund, J. & Lundberg, A. (1995). Male territoriality and female mate choice on black grouse leks. *Animal Behaviour* **49**, 759–67.

Rintamäki, P. T., Lundberg, A., Alatolo, R. & Höglund, J. (1998). Assortative mating in black grouse. *Animal Behaviour* **56**, 1399–403.

Robb, L. A., Martin, K. & Hannon, S. J. (1992). Spring body condition, fecundity and survival in female willow ptarmigan. *Journal of Animal Ecology* **61**, 215–33.

Robel, R. J. (1969). Movements and flock stratification within a population of blackcocks in Scotland. *Journal of Animal Ecology* **38**, 755–63.

Robertson, C. M. (1898). The Prize Essay on 'The peculiarities of Gaelic as spoken in the writer's district'. Perthshire Gaelic. *Transactions of the Gaelic Society of Inverness* **22**, 4–42.

Robinson, M. (ed.) (1985). *The Concise Scots Dictionary*. Aberdeen University Press, Aberdeen.

Rodwell, J. S. (ed.) (1991). *British Plant Communities. Vol. 1. Woodlands and Scrub. Vol. 2. Mires and Heaths*. Cambridge University Press, Cambridge.

Rose, W. (1785). *Rules and Regulations Made in the Courts of the Lordship of Marr, Recommended by the Right Honourable the Earl of Fife to his Tenants*. Printed copy at Mar Estate Office, Braemar.

Rothwell, W. (1991). The missing link in English etymology: Anglo-French. *Medium Aevum* **60**, 173–96.

**Royal Society for the Protection of Birds** (2005). *The State of the UK's Birds 2004*. RSPB, Bedfordshire.

**Royal Society for the Protection of Birds** (2007). *Persecution: a Review of Bird of Prey Persecution in Scotland in 2006*. RSPB, Edinburgh.

Royama, T. (1992). *Analytical Population Dynamics*. Chapman and Hall, London.

Ruddiman, W. F. (2003). The anthropogenic greenhouse era began thousands of years ago. *Climatic Change* **61**, 261–93.

Rusch, D. H. & Keith, L. B. (1971). Ruffed grouse-vegetation relationships in central Alberta. *Journal of Wildlife Management* **35**, 417–29.

Ruwet, J. C. (1988). Lagopède d'Ecosse, *Lagopus lagopus scoticus*. In: *Atlas des Oiseaux Nicheurs de Belgique* (eds Devillers *et al.*), 96. Institut Royal des Sciences Naturelles de Belgique, Brussels.

Ryabitsev, V. K. (1989). Origin of male flocks and population reserve in the willow ptarmigan. *Soviet Journal of Ecology* **19**, 166–8 (translated from the Russian original in *Ékologiya* **3** (1988), 50–3).

Ryzhanovskiy, V. N., Ryabitsev, V. K. & Shutov, S. V. (1983). Nesting densities of birds in tundras of the Yamal Peninsula. *Soviet Journal of Ecology* **13**, 230–3 (translated from the Russian original in *Ékologiya* **4** (1983), 51–5).

Sæther, B.-E., Engen, S. & Lande, R. (1995). Density-dependence and optimal harvesting of fluctuating populations. *Oikos* **76**, 40–6.

Salomonsen, F. (1936). Notes on a new race of the willow grouse, *Lagopus lagopus variegatus* subsp. nov. *Bulletin of the British Ornithologists' Club* **56**, 99–100.

Salomonsen, F. (1939). Moults and sequence of plumages in the rock ptarmigan (*Lagopus mutus* (Montin)). *Videnskabelige Meddelelser fra Dansk Naturhistorisk Forening* **103**.

Salomonsen, F. (1950). *Grønlands Fugle*. Ejnar Munksgaard, Copenhagen.

Sandercock, B. K. (1993). Free-living willow ptarmigan are determinate egg-layers. *Condor* **95**, 554–8.

Sandercock, B. K. (1994). The effect of manipulated brood size on parental defence in a precocial bird, the willow ptarmigan. *Journal of Avian Biology* **25**, 281–6.

Sangster, G., Collinson, J. M., Helbig, A. J., Knox, A. G. & Parkin, D. T. (2004). Taxonomic recommendations for British birds: second report. *Ibis* **146**, 153–7.

Saniga, M. (1998). Diet of the capercaillie (*Tetrao urogallus*) in a Central-European mixed spruce-beech-fir and mountain spruce forest. *Folia Zoologica* **47**, 115–24.

Saniga, M. (2002). Nest loss and chick mortality in capercaillie (*Tetrao urogallus*) and hazel grouse (*Bonasa bonasia*) in West Carpathians. *Folia Zoologica* **51**, 205–14.

Sannikov, S. N. (1983). Cyclic erosional-pyrogenic theory of common-pine natural renewal. *Soviet Journal of Ecology* **14**, 7–16 (translated from the Russian original in *Ékologiya* **1** (1983), 10–20).

Sannikov, S. N. (1985). Hypothesis of pulsed pyrogenic stability of pine forests. *Soviet Journal of Ecology* **16**, 69–76 (translated from the Russian original in *Ékologiya* **2** (1985), 13–20).

Satchell, J. E. (1980). Soil and vegetation changes in experimental birch plots on a *Calluna* podzol. *Soil Biology and Biochemistry* **12**, 303–10.

Savile, D. B. O. (1951). Bird observations at Chesterfield Inlet, Keewatin, in 1950. *Canadian Field-Naturalist* **65**, 145–57.

Savile, D. B. O. (1961). Bird and mammal observations on Ellef Ringnes Island in 1960. *National Museum of Canada, Natural History Papers* **9**, 1–6.

Savile, D. B. O. & Oliver, D. R. (1964). Bird and mammal observations at Hazen Camp, northern Ellesmere Island, in 1962. *Canadian Field-Naturalist* **78**, 1–7.

Savory, C. J. (1974). The feeding ecology of red grouse in N.E. Scotland. PhD thesis, University of Aberdeen.

Savory, C. J. (1975). Seasonal variations in the food intake of captive red grouse. *British Poultry Science* **16**, 471–9.

Savory, C. J. (1977). The food of red grouse chicks *Lagopus l. scoticus*. *Ibis* **119**, 1–9.

Savory, C. J. (1978). Food consumption of red grouse in relation to the age and productivity of heather. *Journal of Animal Ecology* **47**, 269–82.

Savory, C. J. (1983). Selection of heather age and chemical composition by red grouse in relation to physiological state, season and time of day. *Ornis Scandinavica* **14**, 135–43.

Savory, C. J. (1986). Utilisation of different ages of heather on three Scottish moors by red grouse, mountain hares, sheep and red deer. *Holarctic Ecology* **9**, 65–71.

Savory, C. J. (1989). The importance of invertebrate food to chicks of gallinaceous species. *Proceedings of the Nutrition Society* **48**, 113–33.

Scandrett, E. & Gimingham, C. H. (1991). The effect of heather beetle *Lochmaea suturalis* on vegetation in a wet heath in NE Scotland. *Holarctic Ecology* **14**, 24–30.

Scherini, G., Tosi, G. & Wauters, L. A. (2003). Social behaviour, reproductive biology and breeding success of alpine rock ptarmigan *Lagopus mutus helveticus* in northern Italy. *Ardea* **91**, 11–23.

Schieck, J. O. & Hannon, S. J. (1989). Breeding site fidelity in willow ptarmigan: the influence of previous reproductive success and familiarity with partner and territory. *Oecologia* **81**, 465–72.

Schmidt, R. K. (1988). Behavior of white-tailed ptarmigan during the breeding season. In: *Adaptive Strategies and Population Ecology of Northern Grouse* (eds A. T. Bergerud & M. W. Gratson), pp. 270–99. University of Minnesota Press, Minneapolis.

Scholander, P. F., Walters, V., Hock, R. & Irving, L. (1950). Body insulation of some arctic and tropical mammals and birds. *Biological Bulletin* **99**, 225–36.

Schroeder, M. A. (1985). Behavioral differences of female grouse undertaking long and short migrations. *Condor* **87**, 281–6.

Schroeder, M. A. (2006). Blue grouse *Dendragapus obscurus* are now considered to be two species: dusky grouse *Dendragapus obscurus* and sooty grouse *Dendragapus fuliginosus*. *Grouse News* **9**, 4–6.

**Scotland's Moorland Forum** (2003). *Principles of Moorland Management*. Scottish Natural Heritage, Perth.

**Scottish Agricultural Science Agency** (2004). *Pesticide Poisoning of Animals 2003*. Scottish Executive Environment and Rural Affairs Department, Edinburgh.

**Scottish Crofters Union & Royal Society for the Protection of Birds** (1992). *Crofting and the Environment: a New Approach*. SCU & RSPB, Isle of Skye.

**Scottish Gamekeepers Association** (2004). *Scotland's Wildlife Managers*. SGA, Clunie Cottage, Braemar. Leaflet.

**Scottish Natural Heritage** (1992). *Agenda for Investment in Scotland's Natural Heritage*. SNH, Battleby, Redgorton, Perth. Policy Paper.

**Scottish Natural Heritage** (1994). *Red Deer and the Natural Heritage*. SNH, Battleby, Redgorton, Perth. Policy Paper.

**Scottish Natural Heritage** (2004a). *Consultation with The Moorland Forum over the Justification and Scope for Predator Control Payments in SNH Natural Care Scheme relating to Ground Nesting Birds*. SNH, Perth.

**Scottish Natural Heritage** (2004b). *The Role of the Natural Heritage in Generating and Supporting Employment Opportunities in Scotland*. SNH, Perth.

**Scottish Office** (1995). *Habitats and Birds Directives*. Circular 6/1995, Rural Affairs and Natural Heritage Division, Environment Department, Edinburgh.

**Scottish Raptor Study Groups** (1997). The illegal persecution of raptors in Scotland. *Scottish Birds* **19**, 65–85.

**Scottish Raptor Study Groups** (1998). *Counting the Cost: The Continuing Persecution of Birds of Prey in Scotland*. The Scottish Office, Edinburgh.

**Segelbacher, G., Storch, I. & Tomiuk, J.** (2003). Genetic evidence of capercaillie *Tetrao urogallus* dispersal sources and sinks in the Alps. *Wildlife Biology* **9**, 267–73.

**Seiskari, P.** (1962). On the winter ecology of the capercaillie, *Tetrao urogallus*, and the black grouse, *Lyrurus tetrix*, in Finland. *Papers on Game Research* **22**.

**Seivwright, L. J., Redpath, S. M., Mougeot, F., Leckie, F. & Hudson, P. J.** (2005). Interactions between intrinsic and extrinsic mechanisms in a cyclic species: testosterone increases parasite infection in red grouse. *Proceedings of the Royal Society B* **272**, 2299–2304.

**Selas, V.** (2000). Population dynamics of capercaillie *Tetrao urogallus* in relation to bilberry *Vaccinium myrtillus* production in southern Norway. *Wildlife Biology* **6**, 1–11.

**Semenov-Tyan-Shanskiy, O. I.** (1960). *Ekologiya Teterevinikh Ptits. Trudi Laplandskogo Gosudarstvennogo Zapovednika*. **5**. Glavnoe Upravleniye Okhotnichego i Zapovednikov pri Soviete Ministrov RCFSR, Moscow (English summary).

**Sergio F., Marchesi, L. & Pedrini, P.** (2003). Spatial refugia and the coexistence of a diurnal raptor with its intraguild owl predator. *Journal of Animal Ecology* **72**, 232–45.

**Sharp, P. J. & Moss, R.** (1981). A comparison of the responses of captive willow ptarmigan (*Lagopus lagopus lagopus*), red grouse (*Lagopus lagopus scoticus*), and hybrids to increasing daylengths with observations on the modifying effects of nutrition and crowding in red grouse. *General & Comparative Endocrinology* **45**, 181–8.

**Sharp, P. J., Moss, R. & Watson, A.** (1975). Seasonal variations in plasma luteinizing hormone in male red grouse (*Lagopus lagopus scoticus*). *Journal of Endocrinology* **64**, 44.

**Shaw, J. L.** (1988a). Arrested development of *Trichostrongylus tenuis* as third-stage larvae in red grouse. *Research in Veterinary Science* **45**, 256–8.

**Shaw, J. L.** (1988b). Epidemiology of the caecal threadworm *Trichostrongylus tenuis* in red grouse (*Lagopus lagopus scoticus* Lath.). PhD thesis, University of Aberdeen.

Shiel, A., Rayment, M. & Burton, G. (2000). *RSPB Reserves and Local Economies*. RSPB, Sandy, Bedfordshire.

Siitari, H. & Viitala, J. (2002). Behavioural evidence for ultraviolet vision in a tetraonid species: foraging experiment with black grouse *Tetrao tetrix*. *Journal of Avian Biology* **33**, 199–202.

Siivonen, L. (1948). Decline in numerous mammal and bird populations in north-western Europe during the 1940s. *Papers on Game Research* **2**.

Siivonen, L. (1952). On the reflection of short-term fluctuations in numbers in the reproduction of tetraonids. *Papers on Game Research* **9**.

Silliman, R. P. & Gutsell, J. S. (1958). Experimental exploitation of fish populations. *US Fish & Wildlife Service Fishery Bulletin* **58**, 215–52.

Simmons, I. G. (2003). *The Moorlands of England and Wales: an Environmental History 8000 BC–AD 2000*. Edinburgh University Press, Edinburgh.

Singer, M. A. (2003). Do mammals, birds, reptiles and fish have similar nitrogen conserving systems? *Comparative Biochemistry and Physiology Part B* **134**, 543–58.

Slagsvold, T. (1975). Production of young by the willow grouse (*Lagopus lagopus* (L.)) in Norway in relation to temperature. *Norwegian Journal of Zoology* **23**, 269–75.

Small, R. J., Marcström, V. & Willebrand, T. (1993). Synchronous and non-synchronous fluctuations of some predators and their prey in central Sweden. *Ecography* **16**, 360–4.

Small, R. J. & Rusch, D. H. (1989). The natal dispersal of ruffed grouse. *Auk* **106**, 72–9.

Smedshaug, C. A., Selås, V., Lund, S. E. & Geir, A. S. (1999). The effect of a natural reduction of red fox *Vulpes vulpes* on small game hunting bags in Norway. *Wildlife Biology* **5**, 157–66.

Smith, A. & Willebrand, T. (1999). Mortality causes and survival rates of hunted and unhunted willow grouse. *Journal of Wildlife Management* **63**, 722–30.

Smith, A. C., Virgl, J. A., Panayi, D. & Armstrong, A. R. (2005). Effects of a diamond mine on tundra-breeding birds. *Arctic* **58**, 295–304.

Smout, T. C. (2000). *Nature Contested*. Edinburgh University Press, Edinburgh.

Soichiro, T., Nobuo, S. & Chiba, S. (1969). On territory of Japanese ptarmigan (*Lagopus mutus japonicus* Clark) in the Murodô area, Tateyama, Japan Alps, in 1967 and 1968. *Miscellaneous Reports of the National Park for Nature Study* **1**, 13–18 (in Japanese with English summary).

Sonerud, G. (1988). To distract display or not: grouse hens and foxes. *Ornis Scandinavica* **51**, 233–7.

Soper, J. D. (1928). A faunal investigation of southern Baffin Island. *Bulletin of the National Museum of Canada* **53**.

Soper, J. D. (1940). Local distribution of eastern Canadian Arctic birds. *Auk* **57**, 13–21.

Spidsø, T. K. & Korsmo, H. (1994). Selection of feeding trees by capercaillie *Tetrao urogallus* in winter. *Scandinavian Journal of Forest Research* **9**, 180–4.

Spidsø, T. K. & Stuen, O. H. (1988). Food selection by capercaillie chicks in southern Norway. *Canadian Journal of Zoology* **66**, 279–83.

Spidsø, T. K., Hjeljord, O. & Dokk, J. G. (1997). Seasonal mortality of black grouse *Tetrao tetrix* during a year with little snow. *Wildlife Biology* **3**, 205–9.

Starling-Westerberg, A. (2001). The habitat use and diet of black grouse *Tetrao tetrix* in the Pennine Hills of northern England. *Bird Study* **48**, 76–89.

Steen, H. & Erikstad, K. E. (1996). Sensitivity of willow grouse *Lagopus lagopus* population dynamics to variations in demographic parameters. *Wildlife Biology* **2**, 27–35.

Steen, J. B. (1989). *Ryper. Rypeliv og Rypejakt*. Gyldendal Norsk Forlag, Oslo.

Steen, J. B. & Parker, H. (1981). The egg-'numerostat'. A new concept in the regulation of clutch-size. *Ornis Scandinavica* **12**, 109–10.

Steen, J. B. & Unander, S. (1985). Breeding biology of the Svalbard rock ptarmigan *Lagopus mutus hyperboreus*. *Ornis Scandinavica* **16**, 191–7.

Steen, J. B., Pedersen, H. C., Erikstad, K. E., Hansen, K. B., Høydal, K. & Størdal, A. (1985). The significance of cock territories in willow ptarmigan. *Ornis Scandinavica* **16**, 277–82.

Steen, J. B., Gabrielsen, G. W. & Kanwisher, J. W. (1988a). Physiological aspects of freezing behaviour in willow ptarmigan hens. *Acta Physiologica Scandinavica* **134**, 299–304.

Steen, J. B., Steen, H., Stenseth, N. C., Myrberget, S. & Marcström, V. (1988b). Microtine density and weather as predictors of chick production in willow ptarmigan, *Lagopus lagopus*. *Oikos* **51**, 367–73.

Steen, J. B., Erikstad, K. E. & Høidal, K. (1992). Cryptic behaviour in moulting hen willow ptarmigan *Lagopus l. lagopus* during snow melt. *Ornis Scandinavica* **23**, 101–4.

Stephenson, D. & Gould, D. (1995). *The Grampian Highlands*. British Regional Geology. Her Majesty's Stationery Office, London.

Steven, H. M. & Carlisle, A. (1959). *The Native Pinewoods of Scotland*. Oliver & Boyd, Edinburgh & London.

Stevenson, A. C. & Thompson, D. B. A. (1993). Long-term changes in the extent of heather moorland in upland Britain and Ireland: palaeoecological evidence for the importance of grazing. *The Holocene* **3**, 70–6.

Stewart, A. J. A. & Lance, A. N. (1983). Moor-draining: a review of impacts on land use. *Journal of Environmental Management* **17**, 81–99.

Stewart, A. J. A. & Lance, A. N. (1991). Effects of moor-drainage on the hydrology and vegetation of northern Pennine blanket bog. *Journal of Applied Ecology* **28**, 1105–17.

Stewart, J. (1999). Intraspecific variation in modern and quaternary *Lagopus*. *Smithsonian Contributions to Paleobiology* **89**, 159–68.

Stokkan, K.-A. (1979). Temperature and daylength dependent development of comb size and breeding plumage of male willow ptarmigan (*Lagopus lagopus lagopus*). *Auk* **96**, 106–15.

Stokkan, K. (1992). Energetics and adaptations to cold in ptarmigan in winter. *Ornis Scandinavica* **23**, 366–70.

Stokkan, K. & Blix, A. S. (1986). Survival strategies in the Svalbard rock ptarmigan. *Acta XIX Congressus Internationalis Ornithologici* **2**, 2500–6.

Stokkan, K. A. & Steen, J. B. (1980). Age determined feeding behaviour in willow ptarmigan chicks (*Lagopus lagopus lagopus*). *Ornis Scandinavica* **11**, 75–6.

Stokkan, K., Sharp, P. J. & Unander, S. (1986). The annual breeding cycle of the high-Arctic Svalbard ptarmigan (*Lagopus mutus hyperboreus*). *General & Comparative Endocrinology* **61**, 446–51.

Stone, B. H., Sears, J., Cranswick, P. A., Gregory, R. D., Gibbons, D. W., Rehfisch, M. M., Aebischer, N. J. & Reid, J. B. (1997). Population estimates of birds in Britain and in the United Kingdom. *British Birds* **90**, 1–22.

Storaas, T., Wegge, P. & Kastdalen, L. (2000). Weight-related renesting in capercaillie *Tetrao urogallus*. *Wildlife Biology* **6**, 299–303.

Storch, I. (1994). Habitat and survival of capercaillie nests and broods in the Bavarian Alps. *Biological Conservation* **70**, 237–43.

Storch, I. (compiler) (2000a). *Grouse Status Survey and Conservation Action Plan 2000–2004*. WPA/BirdLife/SSC Grouse Specialist Group. IUCN, Gland, Switzerland, and Cambridge, UK, and World Pheasant Association, Reading, UK.

Storch, I. (2000b). Conservation status and threats to grouse worldwide: an overview. *Wildlife Biology* **6**, 195–204.

Storch, I. (2001). Capercaillie. *BWP Update* **3**, 1–24.

Storch, I. & Leidenberger, C. (2003). Tourism, mountain huts and distribution of corvids in the Bavarian Alps. *Wildlife Biology* **9**, 301–8.

Straker-Smith, P. & Phillips, J. (1994). The logistics and arithmetic of heather burning. *The Heather Trust Annual Report 1994*, 7–19.

Strutt & Parker (2003). *Gannochy Land and Properties*. Brechin. Sales brochure.

Sulkava, S. (1969). On small birds spending the night in the snow. *Aquilo, Series Zoologica* **7**, 33–7.

Summers, C. F. (1978). Production in montane dwarf shrub communities. In: *Population Ecology of British Moors and Montane Grassland* (eds O. W. Heal & D. F. Perkins), pp. 263–76. Springer Verlag, Berlin.

Summers, R. W., Proctor, R., Thorton, M. & Avey, G. (2004). Habitat selection and diet of the capercaillie *Tetrao urogallus* in Abernethy Forest, Strathspey, Scotland. *Bird Study* **51**, 58–68.

Suter, W., Graf, R. F. & Hess, R. (2002). Capercaillie (*Tetrao urogallus*) and avian biodiversity: testing the umbrella-species concept. *Conservation Biology* **16**, 778–88.

Svoboda, J. (2002). The tundra and polar desert: dissimilarities between North America and Eurasia. In: *Arctic Flora and Fauna* (ed. P. Kankaanpää), p. 132. Edita, Helsinki.

Swenson, J. E. & Olsson, B. (1991). Hazel grouse night roost site preferences when snow-roosting is not possible in winter. *Ornis Scandinavica* **22**, 284–6.

Sydes, C. & Miller, G. R. (1988). Range management and nature conservation in the British uplands. In: *Ecological Change in the Uplands* (eds M. B. Usher & D. B. A. Thompson), pp. 323–37. Blackwell Scientific Publications, Oxford.

Tamm, O. (1950). *Northern Coniferous Forest Soils*. Scrivener Press, Oxford.

Tansley, A. G. (1939). *The British Islands and their Vegetation*. Cambridge University Press, Cambridge.

Taylor, J. (1997). Perceptions of bracken. *The Heather Trust Annual Report 1997*, 33–7.

Thaler, E. (1983). Beobachtungen zur Brutbiologie des Alpenschneehuhns (*Lagopus mutus*) im Alpenzoo Innsbruck. *Zoologischen Garten N.F., Jena* **53**, 101–23.

Thaler, E. & Neyer, S. (1983). Über die Mauser des Alpenschneehuhns (*Lagopus mutus helveticus*) – Beobachtungen aus dem Alpenzoo Innsbruck. *Bericht Nat-Med. Verein Innsbruck* **70**, 215–26.

Theberge, J. B. & West, G. C. (1973). Significance of brooding to the energy demands of Alaskan rock ptarmigan chicks. *Arctic* **26**, 138–48.

Thirgood, S., Redpath, S., Newton, I. & Hudson, P. (2000a). Raptors and red grouse: conservation conflicts and management solutions. *Conservation Biology* **14**, 95–104.

Thirgood, S. J., Redpath, S. M., Rothery, P. & Aebischer, N. J. (2000b). Raptor predation and population limitation in red grouse. *Journal of Animal Ecology* **69**, 504–16.

Thom, V. M. (1986). *Birds in Scotland*. Poyser, Calton.

Thomas, V. G. (1982). Energetic reserves of Hudson Bay willow ptarmigan during winter and spring. *Canadian Journal of Zoology* **60**, 1612–23.

Thomas, V. G. (1985). Body condition of willow ptarmigan parasitized by cestodes during winter. *Canadian Journal of Zoology* **64**, 251–4.

Thomas, V. G. & Popko, R. (1981). Fat and protein reserves of wintering and prebreeding rock ptarmigan from south Hudson Bay. *Canadian Journal of Zoology* **59**, 1205–11.

Thompson, D. B. A., MacDonald, A. J., Marsden, J. H. & Galbraith, C. A. (1995). Upland heather moorland: a review of international importance, vegetation change and some objectives for nature conservation. *Biological Conservation* **71**, 163–78.

Thompson, D. B. A. & Miles, J. (1995). Heaths and moorland: some conclusions and questions about environmental change. In: *Heaths and Moorland: Cultural Landscapes* (eds D. B. A. Thompson, A. J. Hester & M. B. Usher), pp. 362–87. Her Majesty's Stationery Office, Edinburgh.

Thompson III, F. R. & Fritzell, E. K. (1988). Ruffed grouse winter roost site preference and influence on energy demands. *Journal of Wildlife Management* **52**, 454–60.

Thomson, D. W. (1996). *Birds of Prey, Predation on Grouse and the Power to Grant Licences*. Paper RE-96-05 to Scottish Landowners' Federation.

Tickell, W. L. N. (2003). White plumage. *Waterbirds* **26**, 1–12.

Tipping, R. (1994). The form and fate of Scotland's woodlands. *Proceedings of the Society of Antiquaries of Scotland* **124**, 1–54.

Tipping, R. (2003a). Living in the past: woods and people in prehistory to 10000 BC. In: *People and Woods in Scotland. A History* (ed. T. C. Smout), pp. 14–54. Edinburgh University Press, Edinburgh.

Tipping, R. (ed.) (2003b). *The Quaternary of Glen Affric and Kintail*. Quaternary Research Association, London.

Tipping, R. (2004). Blanket peat in the Highlands: cause, spread and environmental determinism. In: *Terrestrial Environmental Change in the Highlands and Islands: from Summits to Coasts*. Conference proceedings. Inverness College.

Tucker, G. M. & Heath, M. F. (1994). *Birds in Europe – their Conservation Status*. BirdLife International, Cambridge.

Turner, G. (2004). The burning of uplands and its effect on wildlife. *British Wildlife* **April**, 251–7.

Ulianin, I. S. (1939). Biologii beloy kuropatki severnogo Kazakhstana. *Sbornik Trudy Gosudarstvennogo Zoologischeski Muzeum MGY Moskva* **5**, 109–26 (English summary).

Unander, S. & Steen, J. B. (1985). Behaviour and social structure in Svalbard rock ptarmigan *Lagopus mutus hyperboreus*. *Ornis Scandinavica* **16**, 198–204.

Usher, M. B. & Thompson, D. B. A. (1993). Variation in the upland heathlands of Great Britain: conservation importance. *Biological Conservation* **66**, 69–81.

Van Oss, R. (1987). The future for game? *Shooting Times & Country Magazine* **4457**, 14.

Vaurie, C. (1985). *The Birds of the Palearctic Fauna. Non-Passeriformes*. Witherby, London.

Veghte, J. H. & Herreid, C. F. (1965). Radiometric determination of feather insulation and metabolism of arctic birds. *Physiological Zoology* **38**, 267–75.

Vesey-Fitzgerald, B. (1946). *British Game*. Collins, London.

Volterra, V. (1926). Fluctuations in the abundance of species considered mathematically. *Nature* **118**, 558–60.

Voronin, R. N. (1978). *Belaya Kuropatka Bolshezemelskaya Tundra*. Nauka, Leningrad.

Voronin, R. N. (1991). Variation in clutch size in the willow ptarmigan in the Bol'shezemel'skaya tundra. *Soviet Journal of Ecology* **22**, 59–63 (translated from the Russian original in *Ékologiya* **1** (1991), 68–72).

Walker, A. D. (1988). Soils of the River Spey catchment. In: *Land Use in the River Spey Catchment* (ed. D. Jenkins), pp. 44–7. Aberdeen Centre for Land Use, University of Aberdeen.

Warren, P. K. & Baines, D. (2002). Dispersal, survival and causes of mortality in black grouse *Tetrao tetrix* in northern England. *Wildlife Biology* **8**, 91–7.

Watson, A. (1952). A contribution to knowledge of the life of ptarmigan. BSc thesis, University of Aberdeen.

Watson, A. (1956). The annual cycle of rock ptarmigan. PhD thesis, University of Aberdeen.

Watson, A. (1957a). Notes on birds in arctic Norway. *Sterna* **28**.

Watson, A. (1957b). Birds in Cumberland Peninsula, Baffin Island. *Canadian Field-Naturalist* **71**, 87–109.

Watson, A. (1961). Ptarmigan resident at low altitudes in Sutherland. *Scottish Naturalist* **70**, 81–2.

Watson, A. (1963a). Ptarmigan: distribution in the northern Scottish Highlands. In: *The Birds of the British Isles. Vol. 12*, by D. A. Bannerman, pp. 310–13. Oliver & Boyd, Edinburgh.

Watson, A. (1963b). A study of the ptarmigan in the northern Highlands. In: *The Birds of the British Isles. Vol. 12*, by D. A. Bannerman, pp. 321–31. Oliver & Boyd, Edinburgh.

Watson, A. (1963c). Bird numbers on tundra in Baffin Island. *Arctic* **16**, 101–8.

Watson, A. (1963d). Red grouse. Notes on moult and plumage. In: *The Birds of the British Isles. Vol. 12*, by D. A. Bannerman, pp. 293–5. Oliver & Boyd, Edinburgh.

Watson, A. (1964a). The food of ptarmigan (*Lagopus mutus*) in Scotland. *Scottish Naturalist* **71**, 60–66.

Watson, A. (1964b). Aggression and population regulation in red grouse. *Nature* **202**, 506–7.

Watson, A. (1965a). A population study of ptarmigan (*Lagopus mutus*) in Scotland. *Journal of Animal Ecology* **34**, 135–72.

Watson, A. (1965b). Research on Scottish ptarmigan. *Scottish Birds* **3**, 331–49.

Watson, A. (1965c). Scottish ptarmigan. *Bird Notes* **31**, 379–83.

Watson, A. (1966). Hill birds of the Cairngorms. *Scottish Birds* **4**, 179–203.

Watson, A. (1967a). Population control by territorial behaviour in red grouse. *Nature* **215**, 1274–5.

Watson, A. (1967b). Social status and population regulation in the red grouse (*Lagopus lagopus scoticus*). *Proceedings of the Royal Society Population Study Group* **2**, 22–30. The Royal Society, London.

Watson, A. (1967c). Red grouse in Scotland. *The Field*, 4 May, 1p.

Watson, A. (1970). Territorial and reproductive behaviour in red grouse. *Journal of Reproduction & Fertility* **11**, 3–14.

Watson, A. (1971). Key factor analysis and density dependence in red grouse populations. In: *Dynamics of Populations* (eds P. J. den Boer & G. R. Gradwell), pp. 548–9. Pudoc, Wageningen, the Netherlands.

Watson, A. (1972). The behaviour of the ptarmigan. *British Birds* **65**, 6–26, 93–117.

Watson, A. (1973). Moults of wild Scottish ptarmigan (*Lagopus mutus*), in relation to sex, climate and status. *Journal of Zoology* **171**, 207–23.

Watson, A. (1977a). Wildlife potential in the Cairngorms region. *Scottish Birds* **9**, 245–62.

Watson, A. (1977b). Exceptional red grouse nest made of straw. *Scottish Birds* **9**, 347.

Watson, A. (1978). Red grouse. *British Field Sports Society Annual Journal* **1**, 26–7.

Watson, A. (1979). Bird and mammal numbers in relation to human impact at ski lifts on Scottish hills. *Journal of Applied Ecology* **16**, 753–64.

Watson, A. (1983). Eighteenth century deer numbers and pine regeneration near Braemar, Scotland. *Biological Conservation* **25**, 289–305.

Watson, A. (1985). Social class, socially-induced loss, recruitment and breeding of red grouse. *Oecologia* **67**, 493–8.

Watson, A. (1986). Notes on the sexual cycle of some Baffin Island birds. *Canadian Field-Naturalist* **100**, 396–7.

Watson, A. (1987a). Review of V. C. Wynne-Edwards (1986). *Evolution through Group Selection. Journal of Animal Ecology* **56**, 1089–90.

Watson, A. (1987b). Weight and sexual cycle of Scottish rock ptarmigan. *Ornis Scandinavica* **18**, 231–2.

**Watson, A.** (1989). Recent influences on grouse habitat from increases in red deer. *Annual Report of the Joseph Nickerson Reconciliation Project* **5**, 45–6.

**Watson, A.** (1990). Land use, reduction of heather, and natural tree regeneration on open upland. *Annual Report of the Institute of Terrestrial Ecology for 1988–89*, 25–7.

**Watson, A.** (1993). Defects of fencing for native woodlands. *Native Woodlands Discussion Group Newsletter* **18**, 53–5.

**Watson, A.** (1996a). Human-induced increases of carrion crows and gulls on Cairngorms plateaux. *Scottish Birds* **18**, 17–19.

**Watson, A.** (1996b). Raptors and grouse. *Scottish Wildlife* **28**, 206–13.

**Watson, A.** (1997a). Disappearance and later colonisation of red deer on Cairn Gorm, Scotland. *Journal of Zoology, London* **242**, 387–9.

**Watson, A.** (1997b). Capercaillie and black grouse south of Banff in the 1940s. *Scottish Birds* **19**, 117–18.

**Watson, A.** (1998). A further response to Langholm. *Scottish Bird News* **51**, 2.

**Watson, A.** (2003). The main defects in treatment of woodland and scrub in the Cairngorms area. In: *Roots to the Summits. Report of a Conference reviewing the Future for Cairngorms Mountain Woodlands* (ed. N. Mackenzie), pp. 19–23. Cairngorms Campaign, Dunkeld.

**Watson, A. & Allan, E.** (1990). Depopulation by clearances and non-enforced emigration in the North East Highlands. *Northern Scotland* **10**, 31–46.

**Watson, A. & Hewson, R.** (1973). Population densities of mountain hares (*Lepus timidus*) on western Scottish and Irish moors and on Scottish hills. *Journal of Zoology* **170**, 151–9.

**Watson, A. & Hinge, M.** (1989). *Natural Tree Regeneration on Open Upland in Deeside and Donside*. Institute of Terrestrial Ecology, Banchory. Report to Nature Conservancy Council.

**Watson, A. & Jenkins, D.** (1964). Notes on the behaviour of the red grouse. *British Birds* **57**, 137–70.

**Watson, A. & Jenkins, D.** (1968). Experiments on population control by territorial behaviour in red grouse. *Journal of Animal Ecology* **37**, 595–614.

**Watson, A. & Miller, G. R.** (1971). Territory size and aggression in a fluctuating red grouse population. *Journal of Animal Ecology* **40**, 367–83.

**Watson, A. & Miller, G. R.** (1976). *Grouse Management*. The Game Conservancy, Fordingbridge.

**Watson, A. & Moss, R.** (1970). Dominance, spacing behaviour and aggression in relation to population limitation in vertebrates. In: *Animal Populations in relation to their Food Resources* (ed. A. Watson), pp. 167–220. Blackwell Scientific Publications, Oxford.

**Watson, A. & Moss, R.** (1971). Spacing as affected by territorial behavior, habitat and nutrition in red grouse (*Lagopus lagopus scoticus*). In: *Behavior and Environment* (ed. A. H. Esser), pp. 92–111. American Association for the Advancement of Science, Dallas Symposium. Plenum Press, New York.

**Watson, A. & Moss, R.** (1979). Population cycles in the Tetraonidae. *Ornis Fennica* **56**, 87–109.

**Watson, A. & Moss R.** (1980). Advances in our understanding of the population dynamics of red grouse from a recent fluctuation in numbers. *Ardea* **68**, 103–11.

**Watson, A. & Moss R.** (1982). Population biology, game biology and game management: is game biology a science? *Transactions of the International Congress of Game Biologists* **14**, 17–28.

**Watson, A. & Moss, R.** (1990). Spacing behaviour and winter loss in red grouse. In: *Red Grouse Population Processes* (eds A. N. Lance & J. H. Lawton), pp. 35–52. Royal Society for the Protection of Birds, Sandy, Bedfordshire.

Watson, A. & Moss R. (2004). Impacts of ski-development on ptarmigan (*Lagopus mutus*) at Cairn Gorm, Scotland. *Biological Conservation* **116**, 267–75.

Watson, A. & Nethersole-Thompson, D. (2006). Black grouse and western capercaillie on upper Speyside in 1934–42. *Scottish Birds* **26**, 55–9.

Watson, A. & O'Hare, P. J. (1979a). Red grouse populations on experimentally treated and untreated Irish bog. *Journal of Applied Ecology* **16**, 433–52.

Watson, A. & O'Hare, P. J. (1979b). Spacing behaviour of red grouse at low density on Irish bog. *Ornis Scandinavica* **10**, 252–61.

Watson, A. & O'Hare, P. J. (1980). Dead sheep and scavenging birds and mammals on Mayo bog. *Irish Birds* **1**, 487–91.

Watson, A. & Parr, R. (1973). Timing of reproduction in dotterel and ptarmigan. In: *The Dotterel*, by D. Nethersole-Thompson, pp. 78–88. Collins, London.

Watson, A. & Parr, R. (1981). Hormone implants affecting territory size and aggressive and sexual behaviour in red grouse. *Ornis Scandinavica* **12**, 55–61.

Watson, A. & Rae, S. (1993). Ptarmigan. In: *The New Atlas of Breeding Birds in Britain and Ireland: 1988–91* (eds D. W. Gibbons, J. B. Reid & R. A. Chapman), pp. 128–9. Poyser, London.

Watson, A. & Shaw, J. L. (1991). Parasites and Scottish ptarmigan numbers. *Oecologia* **88**, 359–61.

Watson, A., Miller, G. R. & Green, F. H. W. (1966). Winter browning in heather (*Calluna vulgaris*) and other moorland plants. *Transactions of the Botanical Society of Edinburgh* **40**, 195–203.

Watson, A., Parr, R. & Lumsden, H. G. (1969). Differences in the downy young of red and willow grouse and ptarmigan. *British Birds* **62**, 150–3.

Watson, A., Hewson, R., Jenkins, D. & Parr, R. (1973). Population densities of mountain hares compared with red grouse on Scottish moors. *Oikos* **24**, 225–30.

Watson, A., Moss, R., Phillips, J. & Parr, R. (1977). The effect of fertilizers on red grouse stocks on Scottish moors grazed by sheep, cattle and deer. In: *Écologie du petit Gibier et Aménagement des Chasses* (ed. P. Pesson), pp. 193–212. Gauthier-Villars, Paris.

Watson, A., Moss, R. & Parr, R. (1984a). Effects of food enrichment on numbers and spacing behaviour of red grouse. *Journal of Animal Ecology* **53**, 663–78.

Watson, A., Moss, R., Rothery, P. & Parr, R. (1984b). Demographic causes and predictive models of population fluctuations in red grouse. *Journal of Animal Ecology* **53**, 639–62.

Watson, A., Moss, R. & Parr, R. (1987). Grouse increase on Mull. *Landowning in Scotland* **207**, 6.

Watson, A., Payne, S. & Rae, R. (1989). Golden eagles *Aquila chrysaetos*: land use and food in northeast Scotland. *Ibis* **131**, 336–48.

Watson, A., Moss R., Parr, R., Mountford, M. D. & Rothery, P. (1994). Kin landownership, differential aggression between kin and non-kin, and population fluctuations in red grouse. *Journal of Animal Ecology* **63**, 39–50.

Watson, A., Phillips, J. & Moss, R. (1995). Moorland history and grouse declines in Ireland, with an outline policy for conservation and recovery. In: *Canada Life Irish Red Grouse Conference* (ed. R. O'Dwyer), pp. 26–100. Irish Field Trials Grouse Ground Committee, Cappagh, Waterford.

Watson, A., Moss, R. & Rae, S. (1998). Population dynamics of Scottish rock ptarmigan cycles. *Ecology* **79**, 1174–92.

Watson, A., Moss, R. & Rothery, P. (2000). Weather and synchrony in 10-year population cycles of rock ptarmigan and red grouse in Scotland. *Ecology* **81**, 2126–36.

Watson, J. (1997). *The Golden Eagle*. Poyser, London.

Weeden, R. B. (1963). Management of ptarmigan in North America. *Journal of Wildlife Management* **27**, 672–83.

Weeden, R. B. (1964). Spatial separation of sexes in rock and willow ptarmigan in winter. *Auk* **81**, 534–41.

Weeden, R. B. (1965a). Breeding density, reproductive success and mortality of rock ptarmigan at Eagle Creek, central Alaska, from 1960–64. *Transactions of the North American Wildlife Conference* **30**, 336–48.

Weeden, R. B. (1965b). *Grouse and Ptarmigan in Alaska. Their Ecology and Management.* Alaska Department of Fish & Game, Fairbanks, Alaska.

Weeden, R. B. (1968). Foods of rock and willow ptarmigan in central Alaska with comments on interspecific competition. *Auk* **86**, 271–81.

Weeden, R. B. (1972). Effects of hunting on rock ptarmigan along the Steese Highway. *Wildlife Technical Bulletin* **2**, Alaska Department of Fish & Game.

Weeden, R. B. (1979). Relative heart size in Alaskan Tetraonidae. *Auk* **96**, 306–18.

Weeden, R. B. & Ellison, L. N. (1968). *Upland Game Birds of Forest and Tundra.* Wildlife Booklet Series **3**. Alaska Department of Fish & Game.

Weeden, R. B. & Theberge, J. D. (1972). The dynamics of a fluctuating population of rock ptarmigan in Alaska. *Proceedings of XV International Ornithological Congress*, 91–106.

Weeden, R. B. & Watson, A. (1967). Determining the age of rock ptarmigan in Alaska and Scotland. *Journal of Wildlife Management* **31**, 825–6.

Wegge, P. & Rolstad, J. (2000). Lost hotspots and passive female preference: the dynamic process of lek formation in capercaillie *Tetrao urogallus*. *Wildlife Biology* **6**, 291–8.

Wegge, P., Kvålsgard, T., Hjeljord, O. & Sivkov, A. V. (2003). Spring spacing behaviour of capercaillie *Tetrao urogallus* males does not limit numbers at leks. *Wildlife Biology* **9**, 283–9.

Weir, T. (1953). *Camps and Climbs in Arctic Norway.* Cassell, London.

Welch, D. (1984a). Studies in the grazing of heather moorland in north-east Scotland. I. Site descriptions and patterns of utilization. *Journal of Applied Ecology* **21**, 179–95.

Welch, D. (1984b). Studies in the grazing of heather moorland in north-east Scotland. II. Responses of heather. *Journal of Applied Ecology* **21**, 197–207.

West, G. C. (1968). Bioenergetics of captive willow ptarmigan under natural conditions. *Ecology* **49**, 1035–45.

West, G. C. (1972). Seasonal differences in resting metabolic rate of Alaskan ptarmigan. *Comparative Biochemistry & Physiology* **42A**, 867–76.

West, G. C., Weeden, R. B., Irving, L. & Peyton, L. J. (1970). Geographic variation in body size and weight of willow ptarmigan. *Arctic* **23**, 240–53.

Westerskov, K. (1956). Age determination and dating events in the willow ptarmigan. *Journal of Wildlife Management* **20**, 274–9.

White, P., Baker, P., Cross, G. N., Smart, J., Moberly, R., McLaren, G., Ansell, R. & Harris, S. (2000). *Methods of Controlling Foxes, Deer, Hare and Mink.* Report to Lord Burns' Committee of Inquiry into Hunting with Dogs. Accessible at www.defra.gov.uk/rural/hunting/inquiry/mainsections/huntingframe.htm (as at 24 December 2007).

White, R. E. (1987). *Introduction to the Principles and Practice of Soil Science.* Blackwell Scientific Publications, Oxford.

Whitfield, D. P., McLeod, D. R. A., Watson, J., Fielding, A. H. & Haworth, P. F. (2003). The association of grouse moor in Scotland with the illegal use of poisons to control predators. *Biological Conservation* **114**, 157–63.

Whittaker, R. H., Levin, S. A. & Root, R. B. (1973). Niche, habitat, and ecotope. *American Naturalist* **107**, 321–38.

Whittington, G. (1978). A sub-peat dyke on Shurton Hill, Mainland, Shetland

Proceedings of the Society of Antiquaries of Scotland **109**, 30–5.

Whittington, G. (1993). Pollen analysis as a tool for environmental history. In: *Scotland since Prehistory* (ed. T. C. Smout), pp. 28–39. Scottish Cultural Press, Aberdeen.

Whittington, G. & Edwards, K. J. (2003). Climate change. In: *Scotland After the Ice Age* (eds K. J. Edwards & I. B. M. Ralston), pp. 11–22. Edinburgh University Press, Edinburgh.

Wike, R. & Steen, J. B. (1987). Intra-family communication in willow grouse *Lagopus lagopus*. *Fauna Norvegica Series C* **10**, 81–7.

Wilkinson, N. I., Langston, R. H. W., Gregory, R. D., Gibbons, D. W. & Marquiss, M. (2002). Capercaillie *Tetrao urogallus* abundance and habitat use in Scotland, in winter 1998–9. *Bird Study* **49**, 177–85.

Willebrand, T. (1992). Breeding and age in black grouse *Tetrao tetrix*. *Ornis Scandinavica* **23**, 29–32.

Willebrand, T. & Hörnell, M. (2001). Understanding the effects of harvesting willow ptarmigan *Lagopus lagopus* in Sweden. *Wildlife Biology* **7**, 205–12.

Williams, C. K., Ives, A. R., Applegate, R. D. & Ripa, J. (2004). The collapse of cycles in the dynamics of North American grouse populations. *Ecology Letters* **7**, 1135–42.

Williamson, F. S. L. & Emison, W. B. (1969). Studies of the avifauna on Amchitka Island, Alaska. *Annual Progress Report June, 1968–July, 1969*. Battelle Memorial Institute, Columbus Laboratories, Ohio.

Williamson, K. (1970). *The Atlantic Islands*. Collins, London.

Wilson, E. A. (1911). The changes of plumage in the red grouse. In: *The Grouse in Health and in Disease* (ed. A. S. Leslie), pp. 29–63. Smith, Elder & Co, London.

Wilson, K. (1990). A grouse counting system. *Annual Report of the Joseph Nickerson Reconciliation Project* **6**, 50–1.

Wilson, R. (1976). *The Land that never Melts. Auyuittuq National Park*. Ministry of Supply & Services, Canada.

Wissler, K. & Halvorsen, O. (1977). Helminths from willow grouse (*Lagopus lagopus*) in two localities in north Norway. *Journal of Wildlife Diseases* **13**, 409–13.

Witherby, H. F., Jourdain, F. C. R., Ticehurst, N. F. & Tucker, B. W. (1944). *The Handbook of British Birds*. Witherby, London.

Wren, C. D., Nygard, T. & Steinnes, E. (1994). Willow ptarmigan (*Lagopus lagopus*) as a biomonitor of environmental metal levels in Norway. *Environmental Pollution* **85**, 291–5.

Wynne-Edwards, V. C. (1952). Zoology of the Baird Expedition. I. The birds observed in central and south-east Baffin Island. *Auk* **69**, 353–91.

Wynne-Edwards, V. C. (1954). Ptarmigan on the Kincardineshire coast. *Scottish Naturalist* **66**, 42.

Wynne-Edwards, V. C. (1962). *Animal Dispersion in Relation to Social Behaviour*. Oliver & Boyd, Edinburgh.

Wynne-Edwards, V. C. (1986). *Evolution through Group Selection*. Blackwell Scientific Publications, Oxford.

Yue-Hua, S. (1995). Studies of grouse in China. *Proceedings of the International Grouse Symposium* **6**, 34–6.

Yurlov, K. T. (1960). Materiali po ekologii beloy kuropatki i tetireva v Barabinskoy i Kulundinskoy stepiach. *Trudy Biologicheskogo Instituta Sibirskogo Otdelenia Academii Nauk SSSR, Novosibirsk* **6**, 3–85.

Zalewski, A., Jedrzejewski, W. & Jedrzejewski, A. B. (1995). Pine marten home ranges and predation on vertebrates in a deciduous forest (Bialowieza National-Park, Poland). *Annales Zoologici Fennici* **32**, 131–44.

Zbinden, N. & Salvioni, M. (1997). La caccia al fagiano di monte in Ticino 1963–1995. *Der Ornithologische Beobachter* **94**, 331–46.

Zeitler, A. (2000). Human disturbance, behaviour and spatial distribution of black grouse in skiing areas in the Bavarian Alps. *Cahiers d'Ethologie* **20**, 381–400.

**Zimmerman, C. E., Hillgruber, N., Burril, S. E., St. Peters, M. A., & Wetzel, J. D.** (2005). Offshore marine observation of willow ptarmigan, including water landings, Kuskokwim Bay, Alaska. *Wilson Bulletin* **117**, 12–14.

**Zonfrillo, B.** (2005). Time to act. *Scottish Bird News* **77**, 7.

**Zonov, G. B.** (1983). Directions of ecological adaptations of birds and small mammals to winter conditions. *Soviet Journal of Ecology* **14**, 331–5 (translated from the Russian original in *Ékologiya* **5** (1982), 50–5).

**Zwickel, F.** (1992). *Dendragapus obscurus* blue grouse. *The Birds of North America* (eds A. Poole & F. Gill), **15**. Academy of Natural Sciences, Philadelphia, and American Ornithologists' Union, Washington DC.

# Index

Page numbers in **bold** refer to illustrations; page numbers in *italics* refer to information contained within tables.

Aberdeen, 58, 77–8
Aberdeenshire, 147
Abernethy, 119–22, 164, 288, 329, 406–7, 410
Aboyne, 138
afforestation, 113, 118–22, **391**, 400, 405–6
Alaska, 1, 31–3, 39, 43, 68–9, 76–82, 86–8, 174, 184, 197–9, 204, 206, 210, 215, 231, 250–1, 257, 300, 304–5, 365, 381
  Eagle Creek, 91–3, 95, 98, 194, 196, 209
  Porcupine Creek, **37**, 225, 233
alder, *Alnus glutinosa*, 113, 267, 270
Aleutian Islands, 32–3, 68, 76–7, 80, 82–3, 99, 222, 240–3, 320
Alps, 33, 67, 82, 109, 412
  Bavarian, 108, 163–4, 167
  French, 385–6
  Italian, 91
  Swiss, 87–9, 91, 95, 224
altitude, 39, 80–1, 90–1, 95
America, 31, 77, 79, 87–8, 134, 174, 260, 381
  North, 1, 4, 8–11, 56, 65, 78, 303, 373, 384, 407
Angus, 398
Argyll, 110, 131, 148
Argyllshire, 147
Arran, 77, 277
Asia, 146, 303, 305
aspen, *Populus tremula*, 157, 148, 270, 308, 409
Atholl estate, 124, **125**
Austria, 147
Avalonia, 259
avens, mountain, *Dryas octopetala*, 84
azalea, mountain, *Loiseleuria procumbens*, 81

Baffin Island, 33, 81, 87, 243, 266–7
Balkans, 146
Ballochbuie, 151, 407
Balmoral, 147
Baltica, 259
Baltic States, 32, 49
Banchory, 409
Bear Island, 77
beck, 20, 176, 212, 221–2, 384

bedrock, 260, 284–5, 288
    effect on soil fertility, 46–8, 91, 261, **262**,
        272, 350
bedstraw, heath, *Galium saxatile*, 309
beech, *Fagus sylvatica*, 113, 155
Belgium, 33
Ben Lomond, 77
Beringia, 1, 2, **4**, 8, 146
Bering Island, 76
bilberry, *see* blaeberry
bill, 253
Biodiversity Action Plan, 131
birch, *Betula*, 265–7, 276–7, 398, **399**, 406, **409**
    habitat, 38, 89, 148, 270
    in diet, 11, 83–4, 94, 113–4, 287, 291, 303–5,
        308
bistort, Alpine, *Polygonum viviparum*, 84, 88,
    94, 99, 183
blackcock, *see* grouse, black
blackgame, *see* grouse, black
blaeberry, *Vaccinium myrtillus*, 95, 110–13,
    116, 119, **149**, 151–4, 172, **304**, 413–14
    habitat, 81, 164, 270, 281, 288, 377–8, 410
    in diet, 10, 38–9, 83–4, 86, 113, 115, 148,
        155–6, 291, 300, 301–2, 305, 312
    influence of bedrock and soil on, 261, 277,
        284–6, 407
Blelack, 410
blueberry, *Vaccinium* (in North America),
    39–40
Bohemia, 333
bracken, *Pteridium aquilinum*, 156, 396, **397**,
    407, 414
Braemar, 350
Brecon, 109
Bristol Channel, 269
Buccleuch estate, 124, **125**

Buchan, 147
Bulgaria, 76
bursa of Fabricius, 237
buzzard, *Buteo buteo*, 66, 322, 324, 325, 332
Bylot Island, 87

Cabrach, 77
Cairn Gorm, 98, 100, 119, 201, 218, 318, 368,
    406, 412
Cairngorms, 33, 44, 52, 54, 78, 81, 87, 89, 91,
    95, 190, 203, 211, 240–1, 277, 311, 318, 320,
    345, 350, 353–4
    National Park, 154, 402
Cairnwell, 50, 52, 83–4, 87, **90**, 91–5, 98–9,
    205, 216, 221, 228, 240, 285, 311, 345,
    350–5, 372, 384, 411
Caithness, 77, 267, 270, 281
Caledonian mountains, 260
Caledonian pinewood, 148, **149**, 151, 168, 259,
    377, 406–7, **408**, 414
camouflage, 28, 74, 96, 100, 196, 238–40, 317
Canada, 32–3, 35, 50, 54, 62, 67, 78, 88–9, 91,
    93, 95, 98, 100, 184, 192, 194–5, 234, 238,
    247, 260, 277, 320, 337
    Baffin Island, 33, 81, 87, 243, 266–7
    Bathurst Island, 222
    British Columbia, 39, 76–7, 82, 257
        Chilkat Pass, 43, 49, 53, 57–8, 202, 208,
            213, 215, 224, 227–8, 231, 233
    Bylot Island, 87
    Churchill, 196
    Ellesmere Island, 86
    Hudson Bay, 269
    Labrador, 76–7, 87, 413
    Newfoundland, 31, 39, 57, 77, 187, 209, 224,
        239, 365–6, 384
        Brunette Island, 49–50, 53

Northwest Territories, 88, 93, 242, 413
Ungava Peninsula, 81, 87, 94, 213, 216, 242, 413
Cantabrian mountains, 146, 148
capercaillie, *Tetrao urogallus*, **6**, **16**, **134–7**, **290**
  behaviour, 137–8, **139–43**, 144–5, 314
    calls, 138, 175
    feeding, 182–4, 303
    parental care, 191–3
    preening, 184, 187
    resting, 187
    roosting, 188–9
      in snow, 198–9, 203–4, 207–8
    social, 189–90
    territorial, 173–4
  diet, 44, 155–7, 291, 307–10, 313, 315
  distribution, 147–8, 157
  enemies, 152, **153**, 168, **169–71**, 318–46, 400, 409, 413–14
  growth, 157
  habitat, **120**, 122, 148, **149–51**, 152, 154, 172, 287–8, 410
    fragmentation, 165–7, 376–7, 379
    improvement, 407
  metabolism, 157
  moult, 158
  movements, 162–5
  plumage, 136, 235–7
  population:
    decline, 134, 166–8, **169–1**, 331–2
    density, **120**, 122, 133–4, **145–6**, 147, 166–8, 319
    fluctuation, 52–4, 165, 372
    size, 147–8
  reproduction:
    breeding success, **163**, 168, 172, 313–5, **335**
  chicks, 144, 152, 154–7, 161, 163, 168, 180, **181**, 191–6
  eggs, **26**, 159, 161
  lek, 108, 137–8, **139–46**, 151–2
  nests, **153**, **159–60**
  shooting, 133–4, 333, 385–6
  size, 135–7, 157, 314
  survival, 157–8, 161, 314
  weight, 135
capercaillie, black-billed, *Tetrao parvirostris*, 2, 8, 10
caterpillar, 129, 156, 161, 164, 313, 315, 319, 396
Catterick, 363
cedar, *Cedrus*, 202
Channel Islands, 269
Chapman, Abel, 384
chickweed, *Stellaria*, 38, 84
China, 384
claws, 253–4
climate, 9, 12, 21, 91, 148, 167, 277–9, 289, 354
  change, 11, 55, 66, 100–1, 132, 154, 202, 283–4, 345–6, 413–14
  effect on egg development, 58, 95
  effect on habitat, 34, 46, 79, **80**, 263–5, **266–7**, 268–70, 276, 288
  effect on parasites, 336, 345–6
  effect on plumage, 238–9, 247, 258
Coilacriech, 164
combs, 255–8
compensation, 385–7
Corndavon, 53
Cornwall, 109
cotton-grass, *Eriophorum*, 281, **307**
  effect on breeding success, 60, 64, 94, 99, 155–6, 312
  hare's-tail, *E. vaginatum*, 38–9
  in diet, 34, 48, 57, 84, 114, 164, 183, 287, 308–9

courtship, 179–80, 232
Cowal Peninsula, 147
cowberry, *Vaccinium vitis-idaea*, 82–3
cranberry, *Vaccinium oxycoccus*, 407
crow (carrion, *Corvus corone*; hooded, *C. cornix*), 65, 100, 119, 324, **325**, 329, 368–9, 412
(Note: Taxonomists have long considered the carrion and hooded crow as varieties of one species, but recently decided that there were two. Because the two interbreed in much of Asia and Europe including Scotland, and produce many hybrids of varying colour from black birds typical of carrion crows to grey ones typical of hooded or grey crows, we refer in the text simply to crows.)
crowberry, *Empetrum*, 82–6, **85**, 115, 265–7, 281, 285–6, 291, 304–5, 312, 414
Cumbria, 283
Czechoslovakia, 412–13

Dartmoor, 33, 48
Deeside, 52, 127, 138, 167, 187, 240, 280, 287, 332, 407–10
deforestation, 34, 268–9, 277–9, 281–2, 284, 288, 344, 376
Denmark, 147
Derbyshire, 109
Derry Cairngorm, 78, 91–100, 223, 233, 240, 310
Deveronside, 409
Devon, 109, 265
diet, 154, 158–9, 300, 302, 304–5, 308–9, 312, 314, 316
digestion, 292–303, **293**, **295–6**, **301–2**, 316

disease:
  grouse, *see* threadworm, caecal
  louping ill, 342–6, 374–5, 379, 398, 400
dispersal, 4, 44–5, 88, 123, 152, 162–7, 227, 367
distraction display, 144, 191–2, 194–6
distribution, 8, 11–12
disturbance, 100, 108, 152, 193–4, 221, 315, 410
Donegal, 77
Donside, 167
Dorset, 109
dropping, 38, 187–8, 199, 221, **292**, 294, 296
  caecal, **292**, 294, 296
  clocker, 20, 60, 294, **297**
Dumfries and Galloway, 131
Dunkeld, 147
Durham, 336

eagle, golden, *Aquila chrysaëtos*, 99–100, 191, 322, 324, **326**, 330, 378,
  white-tailed, *Haliaeëtus albicilla*, 322
Easter Ross, 167
economics, 403, 404–5
Edinburgh, 265
Edinglassie, 363
Ellesmere Island, 86
elm, *Ulmus*, 266–7
Eurasia, 1, 4, 31, 36, 49–50, 61, 65, 109, 187
Europe, 133, 147, 152, 166, 260, 269, 277, 317, 333, 336, 348, 385, 412–13
evolution, 1, 2–3, **4**, 8, 9, 12, 315, 344
Exmoor, 33, 48
extinction, 11, 147, 172

Faeroes, 33, 77
falcon, peregrine, *Falco peregrinus*, 99, 322, 325, **328**, 402

feathers, **251**, 252–3, 258
felling, 133, 147, 154, 168
fences, 117–18, 152–3, 158, 168, **169**, 171, 407, 409
Fennoscandia, 32, 166, 305, 319, 333, 368, 373, 376, 385
Finland, 33, 49, 52–4, 76, 111, 147, 165, 190, 198, 204–9, 270, 333–5, 372–3, 376
fir, 10
   Douglas, *Pseudotsuga menziesii*, 155
Firth of Clyde, 265
flight, 28, 187
forest grouse, 2–3, **4**, 8, 10, 137, 372
forestry, 113, 148, 154, 409
Forestry Commission, 133, 409–10
Forvie, 53, 366
fox, Arctic, *Alopex lagopus*, 99, 320
   red, *Vulpes vulpes*, 41, 42, 59, 65, 99–100, 158, 170, 178, 192, 202, 209, 282, 318, 319, 320, 321, 324, 325, 329, 332–4, 378
France, 279, 381
Franz Josef Land, 77
Freuchen, Peter, 381

Galloway, 267–8, 282
Gannochy, 398
geological processes, 259, 260–1, **262**, 270–7, **271–3**, 274–5
Germany, 33
glaciation, 9, 265–6, 276
Glas-choille, 57, 218–20, 227, 233
Glen Affric, 269
Glenamoy, 29, 46, 60, 64, 175, 218, 222, 232–3, 278
Glen Clunie, 395
Glen Derry, 262
Glen Dye, 189, 363

Glen Esk, 39, 43, 56–62, 195, 217–19, 226–33, **229**, 279, 338–40, 374, 383, 390, 395–6
Glen Feshie, 278
Glen Gairn, 399
Glen Livet, 77
Glen More, 406, 410
Glen Tanar, 126–30, 157, 162–4, 171, 230, 233, 359, 407, 410
glutton (wolverine), *Gulo gulo*, 320, 321
Golspie, 147
Goshawk, *Accipiter gentilis*, 318, 322, 324, 329
Grampian, 110, 262
grazing, 388–9, 405
   effects on grouse populations, 66, 119, **120**
   effects on food availability, 60, 64, 78, 84, 94, 99, 152, 231, 307, 316
   effects on habitat, 50, 100, 112, 115, 121, 126, 132–3, **151**, 154, 277–8, 282–4, 286–8, 308, 330, 376–7, 393, 394, **395–6**, 404, 407, **408**, 414
   management, 116–17
Greenland, 25, 33, 43, 67, 76–8, 81–9, 183, 187, 196, 203–4, 208, 210, 243, 260
greyhen, *see* grouse, black
grit, 183–4, 292, **295**
grouse:
   black, *Lyrurus tetrix*, **7**, **114**, **165**, **254–5**, **310**
      behaviour, 314
      calls, 104, 175
      feeding, 182–4, 303
      parental care, 191–3
      preening, 184, 187
      resting, 187
      roosting, 188–9, 206
         in snow, 198–9, 202, 204, 207–8, 209

grouse: black, *continued*
  sexual, 141
  social, 189–90
  territorial, 173–4, 178, 211
  diet, 44, 113–15, 129, 155, 291, 307–9
  distribution, 109–10
  enemies, 126, 131, 318–46, 400, 413–14
  growth, 314
  habitat, 101, 110–13, **111–12**, **115–18**, **120**,
    **123**, 132, 259, 270, 286–8, 376–9, 387,
    409–10
  improvement, 115–8, 121, 122
  movements, 122–4, 162
  plumage, 101–3, 235–7, 248–9, 258
  population:
    decline, 124–27, **125**
    density, 52–4, 119–24, **120**, **123**, **126**,
      348–9, 381
    fluctuation, 124, **125**, 372
    size, 110
  reproduction:
    breeding success, 119, 122, **123**, **127**,
      128–9, 130, 314
    chicks, **102**, 114, 128, 129–31, 157, 287
    eggs, **26**, 129
    lek, **103–7**, 108–9, **120**, 123, 196
    nests, 128–9, **255**, 287
  shooting, 385–6
  size, 314
  survival, 129–31, 130, 157, 314
  weight, 101–2
blue, *Dendragapus obscurus*, 3, 8, 11, 162,
  174, 303
Caucasian black, *Lyrurus mlokosiewiczi*, 2,
  8, 9, 11–12, 109
Chinese, *Bonasa sewerzowi*, 2, 4, 8, 9, 12
dusky, *Dendragapus obscurus*, 3, 8

Gunnison sage, *Centrocercus minimus*, 3, 8,
  12
hazel, *Bonasa bonasia*, 52–3, 165, 187,
  207–8, 270, 321–4, 372, 385
red, *Lagopus lagopus scoticus*, **5**, **30**, **39**, **44**,
  **177**, **289**, **291**, **328**, **390**
  behaviour, 21, 28, 31, 41, 314
    calls, 174–9, *175*, 211–12, 218–22, 226
    feeding, 180–3, **184–5**
    parental care, 191–6
    predator avoidance, 190
    preening, 184, **186**
    resting, 187
    roosting, **181**, 188–9
      in snow, 197–210, **198**, **205**, 207–8
    sexual, 179–80
    social, 178, 180, 189–90
    territorial, 173–8, 211–16, **214**, 220–7,
      232–4, 244, 342
    effects on population density,
      358–9, **360**, **363**, 364–5
    kinship, 361, **362**, 364–6, 371, 373,
      375
  diet, 38–40, 44, 291, 300–3, **301–2**, 305,
    307–10, 313
  distribution, 32, 33
  enemies, **65**, 66, 190–1, 318–46, 368, 374,
    378, 400, 412–14
  growth, 27, **29**, 314
  habitat, **34**, 35–7, 36, 46–8, **47**, 52, 280–4,
    377, 379, 394–6, 403, 406
  metabolism, 40–2, *41*, 292
  movements, 43–6, 367
  plumage, 21, 23, 31, **59**, 235–7, 243–7,
    248–9, 250, **256**
  population:
    decline, 233, 339–41, 346

density, 36, 46–8, 51, 52–4, 55, 212–13,
    222–4, 226, 342, 346, 348, **349**, 381
  fluctuations, 339–41, 346, 350–3,
    **351–2**, **355**, 366, 367–74, **370**, 379,
    385–7
  size, 33
  reproduction:
    breeding success, 62–4, 63, 195,
      230–2, 336, 348, 366
    chicks, **27–8**, 42, 226
    eggs, **26**, 27, 58–60, 61, 309
      incubation, 41, 42, 58–9, 194–5, 226,
        244, 250
    nests, 58, **59**
  sex ratio in spring, 57
  shooting, **55**, 56, 62, 193, 329–30, 368,
    381–7, **382–3**, 397–8, 403, 414
  size, 23, 314
  survival, 56, 57, 340, 366, 387
  territory, 211–12, 216–17, 218, 220,
    223–4, 226–8, 230–2, 234, 367
  weight, 23
  ruffed, *Bonasa umbellus*, 2, 4, 8, 52, 137,
    162, 174, 202, 207, 308, 337, 385
  sage, *Centrocercus urophasianus*, 3, 8
  sharp-tailed, *Tympanuchus phasianellus*, 3, 8
  Siberian, *Falcipennis falcipennis*, 2, 8, 10, 12
  sooty, *Dendragapus fuliginosus*, 3, 8
  spruce, *Falcipennis canadensis*, 2, **4**, 8, 10,
    162, 184
  white, *see* ptarmigan, *Lagopus*
  willow, *see* willow ptarmigan, *Lagopus
    lagopus*
  wood, *see* capercaillie, *Tetrao*
growth, 29, 42, 236, 312, 315
gyrfalcon, *Falco rusticolus*, 93, 94, 242, 319,
  322, 373

habitat, 9–11, 276, 414
  effect of climate on, 263–5, **266–8**, 270
  effect on grouse, 261
  fragmentation, 10, 50, 66, 147, 319, 333,
    347, 368–9
  improvement, 168, 170
  management, 55, 387–400, 388–9, **390–2**,
    392–3, **394–7**, **399**, 403–10, 414
  man's effect on, 268–9, 277, **278–80**, 387,
    388–9, **390–2**, 398, 400, 409–14
Hampshire, 109
handicap principle, 241–2
hare, mountain, *Lepus timidus*, 66, 318, 400
hare, snowshoe, *Lepus americanus*, 54
harrier, hen, *Circus cyaneus*, 323, 324, 325,
  **327**, 329, 330, 368, 401
Harris, 77
hawthorn, *Crataegus monogyna*, 115
hazel, *Corylus avellana*, 267, 270, 277
heath, cross–leaved, *Erica tetralix*, 310
heather, *Calluna vulgaris*, **22**, 23, **39**, 276–7,
  **290**, 412–13
  beetle, 308, 330, 396, 414
  bell, *Erica cinerea*, 310
  browning, 38, 62, 228, 308, 339–40
  check, 154
  habitat, **82**, 119, 188–9, 285, 287, 318, 330, 358
  in diet, 10, 38–40, 83–4, 113–5, 156, 230–1,
    291, **289**, **294–5**, 297–8, 312
  moorland, 9–11, 21, 39–40, 48, 50, **51**, 64,
    66, 109–15, **229**, **280**, 281–2, 284,
    287–8, 359
  management, 34, 38, **47**, 118–19, 126,
    282, 377, 387–406, 388, **390–2**, 392–3,
    **394–7**, **399**
  nutritive value, 39, 184, 228, 230, 261, 289,
    300–3, **301–2**, 305, 310

heath hen, *Tympanuchus cupido cupido*, 11
Hebrides, Inner, 78, 110, 245
    Outer, 31, 54, 77–8, 110, 222, 245, 270
hedgehog, *Erinaceus europaeus*, 66
Herefordshire, 109
Highlands, Scottish, 78, 260, 262, 265, 267–8, 332, 336, 396, 403
holly, *Ilex aquifolium*, 10, 270
hormones:
    effect on behaviour, 230, 233
    effect on plumage, 247–50, 248–9, 257–8
horsetail, *Equisetum*, 83–4, 156
Hungary, 269
hybrid, 31, 58, 164, **165**

Iberia, 146
Ice Age, 8–9, **167**, 263, 269–70, 276, 279, 284, 288
Iceland, 33, 49–50, 69, 76, 78, 81, 83, 87–9, 91, 182, 187, 222, 250, 304, 319–20, 365, 373
    Hrisey, 49–50, 82, 84, 88, 93–4, 98–9, 196, 228, 242–3
    Husavik, 93
inbreeding, 44, 108, 152
Indian, American, 381
Inshriach, 150
insulation, 252
introductions, 33, 77, 99, 320, 331
Inuit, 253, 380
Invercauld, 52, 160–1
Inverness, 402
invertebrates, 88, 312–16
Italy, 97, 269

Japan, 37, 69, 76, 82, 92, 384
juniper, *Juniperus communis*, 113, **149**, 152, 182, 265–6, 278, 398, 407, 410

Jura, 77, 278

Kazakhstan, 23, 31–2, 38, 49–50, 61, 66, 77, 111, 239
Kent, 109
Kerloch, 27, 39, 43–6, 50–3, 56–60, 189, 195, 216–19, 222, 226–33, 364, 394–7
Kielder, 54
Kintyre, 277
Kinveachy, 332
kite, black, *Milvus migrans*, 322, 324
Kola, 76, 208
Kuriles, 80

Labrador, 76–7, 87, 413
Lake District, 77, 265
Lammermuirs, 279
Langholm, 329–30, 368, 378, 401
larch, *Larix*, 10, 114, 154–7, 183, 309, **310**, 377
Laurentia, 259
Leadhills, 397
Leicestershire, 109
lek, 20, 174, 237, 287, 385, 412
lime, *Tilia*, 266–7
Loch Laggan, 406
Loch Lomond, 167
Lochnagar, 33, 81, 221

Mala, 381
marten, pine, *Martes martes*, 318, 319, 320, 321, 324, **331**, **333**
    and capercaillie, 331–4
meadowsweet, *Filipendula ulmaria*, 38
Meall Odhar, 91, 94, 98–9
metapopulation, 167
Midlands, 277
migration, 42–6, 87–8, 164, 174, 225

Millden moor, 383
Minnesota, 33, 202
Misty Law, 64, 401
*Molophilus ater* (crane-fly), 313
Monaco, 269
Mongolia, 32, 77
Montgomery, 109
Moorhouse, 283, 363
Moran effect, 371
Moray, 77, 167, 384
moult, 158, 211, 235–49, 258
mouse-ear, *Cerastium*, 84, 309
movements, 42–6, 87–8, 122–4, 162–5, 367, 386
muirburn, **282**, 285
    effects on grouse densities, 46, 49, 64, 375
    effects on habitats, 282–3, 376, 389, **392**, **394**
Mull, 46, 77, 218, 221, 245, 396, 403
myrtle, bog, *Myrica gale*, 129, 274

names, origins of, 13–20, *18–19*
Nearctic (New World), 1–4, 2–3, 8, 12, 162
Netherlands, 412
North Atlantic Oscillation, 124, 147, 347–8, **349**, 353
North Pole, 77
North York Moors, 48
Norway, 31, 33, 38, 52, 54–5, 57–60, 69, 76, 82, 86, 89, 147, 163, 174, 182, 195, 224, 234, 238–9, 251, 257, 263, 278, 288, 313, 324, 334, 343–4, 365, 376, 378, 384, 387
    Dovrefjell, 49, 213, 221–2, 227–8, 231, 233
    Hitra, 238–9
    Karlsøy, 62, 336
    Tranøy, 49–50, 52–3, 57–8, 62, 64, 313
    Varaldskogen, 152, 164

Nottinghamshire, 109
nutrition, 289–316
    effect on breeding success, 308, **311**, 312–16

oak, *Quercus*, 157, 266–7, 277
oat, *Avena*, 157, 270
Orkney, 77–8, 277, 324
owl, short-eared, *Asio flammeus*, 66

Palearctic (Old World), 1–4, 2–3, 8, 162, 334
parasites, 330, **341**, 367
    effects on breeding success, 62, 64, 336, 340, 374–5
    roundworm, *Ascaridia compar*, 334
    tapeworms, *Hymenolepis microps* & *Paroniella urogalli*, 334, 336–7
    threadworm, caecal, *Trichostrongylus tenuis*, 42, 66, 195, 257, 336–9, **338**, **340**, 364, 373–5
    tick, sheep, *Ixodes ricinus*, 66, 100, 342–6, **343**, 400, 414
peat, 48, 60, 268–75, **273**, 278–81, 284, 288
pectinations, 254
Pennines, 48, 110, 113, 124, 131, 281
Perthshire, 118, 143–4, 147, 156, 167
pheasant, *Phasianus colchicus*, 8, 126, 188, 344
*Philaenus spumarius* (spittle bug), 313
philopatry, 45, 108
Pinega, 138
pine, *Pinus*, 10–11, 266–70, 276–7, 308, 377, 398, 407, 409
    Arolla, *P. cembra*, 155
    lodgepole, *P. contorta latifolia*, 118, 154, 377
    Scots, *P. sylvestris*, 187, 267
        habitat, 119, 148, **278**, 287–8, **399**, 407, 414
        in diet, 113, 155–6, 291, 303

plumage, 184–7, 252, 258
pollution, 65, 100, 412–14
*Polytrichum* (moss), 156
population, **349**, **355**, 358, **369**, 376, 386–7, 414
   decline, 11, 361–3, 374–5, 379, 384–5, 398
   density, 308, 382–7, 395–7
   fluctuations, 12, 347–79, **351–2**, **362**
      breeding success during, 365, 366
      causes of, 371–5
      effects of habitat on, 375–8
      effects of spatial organisation, 366–8
      effects of weather on, 350, **353**, 354, **355**, 378–9
Portugal, 32
prairie-chicken, Attwater's, *Tympanuchus cupido attwateri*, 11
   greater, *Tympanuchus cupido*, 3, 8
   lesser, *Tympanuchus pallidicinctus*, 3, 8
prairie grouse, 2, 3, **4**, 8, 10
predators, 308, 312, 321–3, 324–35, **333**, 346, 358, 367–9, 372–3, 378–9, 400, 412
   control of, 55, 64–5, 319, 324, 329–32, 346, 375–6, 378, **400**, 401–3, **402**
   effect on breeding success, 329, 333–4, **335**, 368
   pine marten, *Martes martes*, **331**, 332–6, **333**, **335**
   predator-prey relationships, 317–20, 372–3
   raptors, 318–24, 322–3, **326–8**, 332, 373, 403, 414
      gyrfalcon, *Falco rusticolus*, 93–4, 97, 242, 318–19, 373
      persecution, 329–30, 368, 378, 400, **401–2**
Priestlaw, 64

ptarmigan, *Lagopus*, 2, **4**, 8, 10, 13
   rock, *Lagopus mutus*, **6**, **15**, **293**, **326**, **327**, **411**
   behaviour, 68–9, 74, 91, 314
      calls, 174, **175**, 176–9, 218–22, 226
      feeding, 180–3, 304, 308, 310
      parental care, **191–2**, 193–4, 196
      predator avoidance, 190
      preening, 184
      resting, 187
      roosting, 188–9
         in snow, 197–210, **199**, **205**, 207–8
      sexual, **179**, 180
      social, 178, 180, 189–90
      territorial, 173–7, **178**, 213–16, **221**, 222–7, **223**, 232–4, 244
   diet, 83–6, **85**, 98, 291, 300, 304, 307, 309
   distribution, 33, 67, 76–80,
   enemies, 93–4, 99–100, 190–1, 318–46, 368–9, 373–4, 412
   growth, 314
   habitat, 36, **37**, **79–80**, 81, **82–3**, **90**, 259–61, 269, 284–8, **285**, 377–9
   metabolism, 86–7
   movements, 87–9
   plumage, 68–9, **70–3**, 235–44, 246–50, 248–9, **251**, 253, **254–5**, 258
   population:
      density, 36, 88–9, 91, 92, 212–5, 222–4, 242, 348–9, 355
      fluctuations, 91, 350–4, **352–3**, 365–9, 366, 372–3, 379
      size, 78
   reproduction:
      breeding success, 98–9, 230–2, **311**, 354, 365, 366, 368
      chicks, 74, **75**, **79**, 86–8, 99, **181**, 226, 284, **294**

eggs, **26**, 69, 74, 95–8, 97
   incubation, 86, 191, 194–6, 226, 242, 250, 257
   nests, **85**, **96**
sex ratio in spring, 93–5
shooting, 99, 233, 381, 384
size, 68–9, 314
survival, 91–3, 92, 311, 366, 387
territory, 93–4, 211–12, 216–17, 218, 220, 223–34
weight, **24–6**, 68–9, 86
white-tailed, *Lagopus leucurus*
   behaviour, 78, 86, 199, 203
   evolution, 2, 8, 9–10
   habitat, 78–9
   plumage, 237–8, 246, 254
   size, 69, 158
willow, *Lagopus lagopus*
   behaviour, 31, 40, 41
      calls, 174–9, *175*, 218–22, 226
      feeding, 180–3, 303–7, 312–13
      parental care, 191–6
      predator avoidance, 190
      preening, 184
      resting, 187
      roosting, 188–9
         in snow, 197–210, **198**, **205**, *207–8*
      sexual, 179–80
      social, 178, 180, 189–90
      territorial, 173–8, 211–16, 220–7, 232–4, 244
   diet, 38–40, 303–7, 312–13
   distribution, 31–3, *32*, 269
   enemies, 64–6, 190–1, 318–46, 374, 413
   growth, 27, **29**, 42
   habitat, 34–8, **35**, *36*, **37**, 67, 269–70, 287

metabolism, 40, *41*, 251
movements, 42–4
plumage, 21, **22**, 31, 235–9, 244, 246–58, *248–9*
population:
   decline, 54, **55**
   density, *36*, 49–50, 212–13
   fluctuations, 52–3, 365, 378
   size, 33
reproduction:
   breeding success, 63, 64, 195, 230–2, 365
   chicks, 27, 40, 42, 74, 226
   eggs, 27, 58–60, *61*
      incubation, *41*, 42, 59, 194–5, 226, 250
   nesting, 58–9, 62
sex ratio in spring, 57
shooting, **55**, *56*, 381, 384
size, 68
survival, 42, *56*, 57, 366, 387
territory, 57, 211–12, 216–17, 218–20, 223–4, 226–8, 230–2, 234
weight, 23, **24–6**, 62, 68
Pyrenees, 82, 89, 146, 163–4, 385, 412

Rannoch Moor, 265, 268
rape, *Brassica napus*, 157
recreation, 410–12
reintroduction, 9, 133, 147, 172, 324, 332
return rates, *56*, 91–3, *92*
rhododendron, *Rhododendron ponticum*, 110
Rickarton Moor, 52, 59, 195, 218–19, 222, 224, 227, 308, 366, 370, 372, 387, 398
rodents, 52–4, 318, 320, 330, 332–5, **333**, 368
roost, 188–9, 197–210, 303

Rothiemurchus, 288, 410
rowan, *Sorbus aucuparia*, 115, 398
Rum, 77, 277
Russia, 23, 27, 32–3, 43, 54, 58–60 67, 76, 78, 81, 87, 99, 147, 190, 201, 254, 286, 320, 337, 381, 384–5, 407
   Ilexa basin, 138, 307, 319, 324, 332–3
   Lake Ilmen, 324
   Pechora-Illych reserve, 163, 332
   Pinega, 138
   Timansk, 39–40
   Urals, 76, 113, 147–8, 163, 168

saxifrage, purple, *Saxifraga oppositifolia*, 84, **223**
Scandinavia, 57, 109, 146–7, 151, 260, 263, 286, 336, 413
Scarba, 77
sex ratio, 94–5, 314
Sgribhis Bheinn, 33
Shetland, 278
Shropshire, 109
Siberia, 1, 8, 23, 29–32, 40, 53, 67, 69, 76–7, 109, 147, 197, 203, 206, 208, 252
Sinkiang, 77
size, 68, 135–6, 157–8, 314
ski development, 100, 318, 320, 368, **369**, 410–12
Slovenia, 110
snares, 65, **170–1**, 384, 400
snow, **24**, 43, 59, 220, 224–6, 286, **355**
   effect on plumage, 239–40, 246
   feeding in, 10, 38, 182–4, 308
   roosts, 1, 40, 69, 197–210, **198–200**, **205**, 207–8, 252, 315
   shoes, 253
Snowdonia, 265

soil, 57, 94, 112, 270–81, **271**, 284–8, **311**, 377, 410
Somerset, 109
sorrel, sheep's, *Rumex acetosella*, 38, 309
Southern Uplands, 77–8, 110, 260
Spain, 146, 148
sparrowhawk, *Accipiter nisus*, 66, 190, 319, 322, 325, 332
Special Protection Area (SPA), 145–6
Speyside, 154, 167, 332, 345, 396
spruce, *Picea*, 10, 113
   Norway, *P. abies*, 148, 155, 187, 189, 303
   Sitka, *P. sitchensis*, 113, **114–5**, 118, 154–6, 159, 291, 377–8, **391**, **409**, 410
Spyhill, 59, 183, 188
Staffordshire, 109
status, 11–12
Stirling, 147
stoat (short–tailed weasel), *Mustela erminea*, 99, 131, 321, 325, 334
Strathavon, 164
Strathmore, 60
study areas, xi, xii
subspecies, 31, 76, 109, 146, 222
Surrey, 109
survival, 314–16
Sussex, 109
Sutherland, 77, 81, 147, 267, 281
Svalbard, 33, 41, 67–8, 76–7, 86, 88, 91–2, 95, 97–9, 196, 201, 228, 231–4, 242, 251, 260, 308
Sweden, 33, 49, 52–3, 63–4, 76, 78, 110, 113, 147, 165, 287, 312, 333–4, 373, 376, 384
systematics, 31, 76, 109, 146

Taymouth, 147
temperature, **162–3**, 207, **353**, 354, **355**

territory, 137, 164, 241, 339–40, 358–66, **360**, **370**, 374–5, 390
Thames, 269
toxins, plant, 300–4
Tweed Valley, 148

Uist, North, 270
    South, 277
Unimak, 32
Urals, 76, 113, 147–8, 163, 168

Virginia, 269

Wales, 23, 31, 33, 48, 78, 100, 108–10, 116, 131, 245, 260, 267, 281–2, 287–8, 324, 342–3, 377, 396

weasel, *Mustela nivalis*, 99, 131, 324, 325
whortleberry, bog, *Vaccinium uliginosum*, 312, 407
willow, *Salix*:
    effect of grazing, 94, 99
    habitat, 38, 82, 265, 267, 270, 398
    in diet, 38–40, 57, 83–4, 88–9, 113–14, 303–7, **306**
Wiltshire, 109
wires, **65**, 152, 410–12, **411**
woodland grouse, *Bonasa*, 2, 4, *8*, 154, 162, 174
Worcestershire, 109

Yakutia, 25
Yew, *Taxus baccata*, 270
Yorkshire, 277, 281

# The New Naturalist Library

1. *Butterflies* — E. B. Ford
2. *British Game* — B. Vesey-Fitzgerald
3. *London's Natural History* — R. S. R. Fitter
4. *Britain's Structure and Scenery* — L. Dudley Stamp
5. *Wild Flowers* — J. Gilmour & M. Walters
6. *The Highlands & Islands* — F. Fraser Darling & J. M. Boyd
7. *Mushrooms & Toadstools* — J. Ramsbottom
8. *Insect Natural History* — A. D. Imms
9. *A Country Parish* — A. W. Boyd
10. *British Plant Life* — W. B. Turrill
11. *Mountains & Moorlands* — W. H. Pearsall
12. *The Sea Shore* — C. M. Yonge
13. *Snowdonia* — F. J. North, B. Campbell & R. Scott
14. *The Art of Botanical Illustration* — W. Blunt
15. *Life in Lakes & Rivers* — T. T. Macan & E. B. Worthington
16. *Wild Flowers of Chalk & Limestone* — J. E. Lousley
17. *Birds & Men* — E. M. Nicholson
18. *A Natural History of Man in Britain* — H. J. Fleure & M. Davies
19. *Wild Orchids of Britain* — V. S. Summerhayes
20. *The British Amphibians & Reptiles* — M. Smith
21. *British Mammals* — L. Harrison Matthews
22. *Climate and the British Scene* — G. Manley
23. *An Angler's Entomology* — J. R. Harris
24. *Flowers of the Coast* — I. Hepburn
25. *The Sea Coast* — J. A. Steers
26. *The Weald* — S. W. Wooldridge & F. Goldring
27. *Dartmoor* — L. A. Harvey & D. St. Leger Gordon
28. *Sea Birds* — J. Fisher & R. M. Lockley
29. *The World of the Honeybee* — C. G. Butler
30. *Moths* — E. B. Ford
31. *Man and the Land* — L. Dudley Stamp
32. *Trees, Woods and Man* — H. L. Edlin
33. *Mountain Flowers* — J. Raven & M. Walters
34. *The Open Sea: I. The World of Plankton* — A. Hardy
35. *The World of the Soil* — E. J. Russell
36. *Insect Migration* — C. B. Williams
37. *The Open Sea: II. Fish & Fisheries* — A. Hardy
38. *The World of Spiders* — W. S. Bristowe
39. *The Folklore of Birds* — E. A. Armstrong
40. *Bumblebees* — J. B. Free & C. G. Butler
41. *Dragonflies* — P. S. Corbet, C. Longfield & N. W. Moore
42. *Fossils* — H. H. Swinnerton
43. *Weeds & Aliens* — E. Salisbury
44. *The Peak District* — K. C. Edwards
45. *The Common Lands of England & Wales* — L. Dudley Stamp & W. G. Hoskins
46. *The Broads* — E. A. Ellis
47. *The Snowdonia National Park* — W. M. Condry
48. *Grass and Grasslands* — I. Moore
49. *Nature Conservation in Britain* — L. Dudley Stamp
50. *Pesticides and Pollution* — K. Mellanby
51. *Man & Birds* — R. K. Murton
52. *Woodland Birds* — E. Simms
53. *The Lake District* — W. H. Pearsall & W. Pennington
54. *The Pollination of Flowers* — M. Proctor & P. Yeo
55. *Finches* — I. Newton
56. *Pedigree: Words from Nature* — S. Potter & L. Sargent
57. *British Seals* — H. R. Hewer
58. *Hedges* — E. Pollard, M. D. Hooper & N. W. Moore
59. *Ants* — M. V. Brian
60. *British Birds of Prey* — L. Brown
61. *Inheritance and Natural History* — R. J. Berry
62. *British Tits* — C. Perrins
63. *British Thrushes* — E. Simms
64. *The Natural History of Shetland* — R. J. Berry & J. L. Johnston
65. *Waders* — W. G. Hale
66. *The Natural History of Wales* — W. M. Condry
67. *Farming and Wildlife* — K. Mellanby
68. *Mammals in the British Isles* — L. Harrison Matthews
69. *Reptiles and Amphibians in Britain* — D. Frazer

70. *The Natural History of Orkney* — R. J. Berry
71. *British Warblers* — E. Simms
72. *Heathlands* — N. R. Webb
73. *The New Forest* — C. R. Tubbs
74. *Ferns* — C. N. Page
75. *Freshwater Fish* — P. S. Maitland & R. N. Campbell
76. *The Hebrides* — J. M. Boyd & I. L. Boyd
77. *The Soil* — B. Davis, N. Walker, D. Ball & A. Fitter
78. *British Larks, Pipits & Wagtails* — E. Simms
79. *Caves & Cave Life* — P. Chapman
80. *Wild & Garden Plants* — M. Walters
81. *Ladybirds* — M. E. N. Majerus
82. *The New Naturalists* — P. Marren
83. *The Natural History of Pollination* — M. Proctor, P. Yeo & A. Lack
84. *Ireland: A Natural History* — D. Cabot
85. *Plant Disease* — D. Ingram & N. Robertson
86. *Lichens* — Oliver Gilbert
87. *Amphibians and Reptiles* — T. Beebee & R. Griffiths
88. *Loch Lomondside* — J. Mitchell
89. *The Broads* — B. Moss
90. *Moths* — M. Majerus
91. *Nature Conservation* — P. Marren
92. *Lakeland* — D. Ratcliffe
93. *British Bats* — John Altringham
94. *Seashore* — Peter Hayward
95. *Northumberland* — Angus Lunn
96. *Fungi* — Brian Spooner & Peter Roberts
97. *Mosses & Liverworts* — Nick Hodgetts & Ron Porley
98. *Bumblebees* — Ted Benton
99. *Gower* — Jonathan Mullard
100. *Woodlands* — Oliver Rackham
101. *Galloway and the Borders* — Derek Ratcliffe
102. *Garden Natural History* — Stefan Buczacki
103. *The Isles of Scilly* — Rosemary Parslow
104. *A History of Ornithology* — Peter Bircham
105. *Wye Valley* — George Peterken
106. *Dragonflies* — Philip Corbet & Stephen Brooks

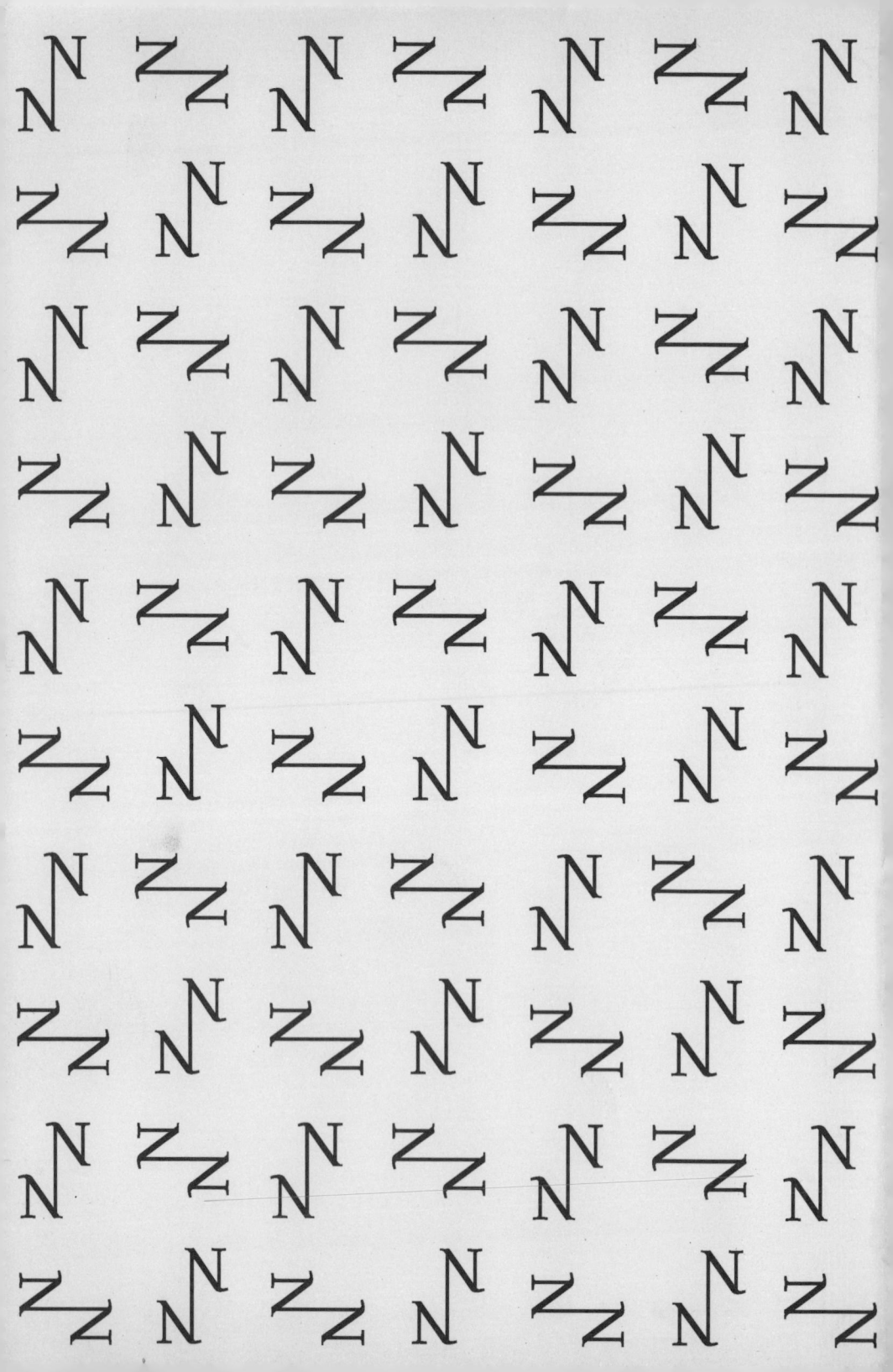